First, to my wonderful family and second, to my colleagues and students
who continue to be a source of inspiration.

BRIEF CONTENTS

CONTENTS

PART FOUR
Sampling and Statistical Theory

PREFACE

Never before has marketing research been more exciting or offered more and better career opportunities. Today's decision-makers are under more pressure than ever to act, and to act fast. To take effective actions, they need intelligence, and intelligence begins with information. That's where research steps in. Research provides insight that leads to better decision-making. Researchers have access to more data than ever before to help provide that insight. Tracking consumers is so easy today given that virtually every move we make leaves some type of data trail. Also, never before has communicating with consumers been easier in a world where so many consumers are connected all the time. Perhaps finding gems of insight amidst the colossal amounts of intelligence seems a lot like searching for a needle amidst a mountain of hay. But, the hay is not still; markets change quickly meaning that we search for the needle in a dynamic mountain of hay. Thus, "search" cannot be removed from "research."

Decision making in practically all industries, both for-profit and not-for-profit, depends on input from research. The research process described in this text helps provide that input. The process enables a company to identify its customers and design products that maximize the value they receive from a purchase. In return, the company receives value as the customers spend their hard-earned money. The result: customers win and businesses win! All are better off.

A lot has changed since the first edition of this text. One thing that has not changed though is that businesses succeed by coming together with customers to create value that addresses real consumer needs. Although addressing needs remains the *raison d'être* for business, the way consumer needs get addressed is ever changing. Value creation today involves all sorts of technologies. Today, value creation involves much more than computers and the Internet. Smartphones mean billions of consumers can access your business at their fingertips, GPS systems point consumers to market offerings, drones help provide information and may even make deliveries, social media means consumers spread their opinions about new products or service received almost instantly and widely, tap and pay systems involving iPay or Google Wallet make transactions faster and easier than ever. For the market researcher, the key advantage is that all of these systems leave behind a trail of information ready to mine for insight. That's where this text comes in: *Essentials of Marketing Research* equips students with the knowledge and skills involved in this basic research process. By mastering this process, students will know how to frame questions to get valuable answers, where to look for those answers, and know how to use tools that help convert raw data into intelligence.

Chapter 3 introduces this process, which includes six stages. Researchers must first work together with decision makers to decide why they are looking for that metaphorical needle in the haystack. The next two stages plot out the way to go about finding the needle. Next are two stages that focus on the actual search for the needle. The process concludes when the market researcher communicates the benefits of finding "pointed" information that can help mend problems or create something really new and special to the decision maker. Success in this process usually merits the researcher a reward that is a bit more valuable than that needle!

New to *Essentials of Marketing Research*

To ensure that students are able to conduct market research with an understanding of all the latest theories and techniques available to them, the seventh edition is substantially revised and updated. The first chapters describe the overall research process and emphasize the way that technologies affect the way marketing researchers go about their jobs. The middle chapters provide the basics of measurement and data quality. The latter chapters introduce the user to statistical analytics as a tool of turning information into intelligence.

Technological and social developments of the last few decades are revolutionizing information systems, sources of and ways of gathering secondary data, survey processes, sampling, question-naire design, qualitative analysis including focus group interviews, and communication of results. Practically every chapter includes significant coverage of technology-related topics. Most chapters also include review questions and activities that get students involved with the latest research tech-nologies in a hands-on way. New to this edition, the each chapter contains a Research in Action box that helps guide students through a marketing research project.

Key features of the seventh edition include:

- Project Outline—Chapter 16 includes an outline (downloadable in the student resources) suitable for use as a student project. The outline functions as a guide for the steps necessary to conduct a marketing research project like one suitable to serve as a term-long project in a mar-keting research course. The outline is geared to fit almost any type of comprehensive research project. By selecting only parts of the outline, a smaller project could be designed.
- Research in Action!—Instructors and students have asked for guidance in turning information from the chapters into a marketing research project. Each chapter now provides a feature box that helps frame the material for the chapter with respect to completing the research project. Combined with the outline for Chapter 16, *Essentials* provides *essential* direction in helping get the project done competently.
- Increased coverage of big data and analytics.
- Tips of the Trade—Each chapter contains a useful list of important tips that correspond to the particular stage of the research process discussed in the chapter. The tips provide information addressing practical questions such as interview length, question wording, interviewer involve-ment, sample size requirements, and guides for data reliability and validity, as well as useful tips for testing hypotheses using inferential statistics.
- Chapter Vignettes—All chapters open with a story relevant to the material featured in that particular chapter. Some of these vignettes involve famous brands and companies, so the reader may well be familiar with some of the topics. Other vignettes involve "slice of life" stories describing a businessperson's struggle to make smart decisions and demonstrate how research is intertwined with this struggle.
- More emphasis on "how to"—The boxed material, chapter objectives, and end-of-chapter materials seek to emphasize research in action or steps used to perform different approaches illustrated in the text. Boxed materials take the form of Research Snapshots that cover ethical angles of research, provide illustrations of research in practice, and offer relevant tips or detailed "how-to" examples. The chapter learning objectives provide coherence and structure to the chapters, each culminating with objective-directed end-of-chapter materials. In later chapters, the Research Snapshots provide step-by-step guides describing how to perform many of the marketing analytics approaches.
- Software Friendly—*Essential* recognizes that different students and instructors interact with multiple software platforms. Here, the illustrations do not focus on a single software platform. Rather, the how-to guides illustrate how to perform different analysis routines in multiple platforms. Most advanced analytical/statistical tools are illustrated in EXCEL, SPSS, SAS, and JMP (a fast growing analytical tool).
- Substantial Coverage on International Business Issues—The examples and illustrations make much greater use of international business. Readers of this book may end up working or deal-ing with issues anywhere in the world, so the increased international examples will increase awareness of research issues beyond North America and open up domestic students to global

market dynamics. This is a particularly important emphasis because cultural and language barriers often present challenges for the researcher.

■ Substantial Attention to Qualitative Research—Big data also creates a big demand for qualitative research tools. In response, several chapters provide insight into how to gather and use data not expressed in the form of quantities. Chapter 5 focuses exclusively on qualitative research. Phenomenology, grounded theory, ethnography, and case study approaches are all covered. Qualitative research is dramatically being changed by the Internet as consumers leave more and more artifactual data behind on social networking websites, company chat rooms, blogs, social networks, micro-blogs (such as tweets left on Twitter), and more. Just think about the potential gold mine of data available in all of the online consumer feedback, ratings, and recommendations.

Organization of the Book

The seventh edition of *Essentials of Marketing Research* follows the logic of the marketing research process. The book is organized into parts, and each part presents the basic research concepts for one of the stages in the research process; each part also discusses how these concepts relate to decisions about conducting specific projects.

Part 1: Introduction, emphasizes the interplay between research and business and how the importance and scope of research varies with the type of business orientation that characterizes a company. Included in this discussion is an overview of computerized data management and information systems, an overview of the entire marketing research process, and an explanation of how all of this is changing due to the Internet.

Without high ethical standards, no business is good. Thus, the introductory materials also include an emphasis on business ethics and the special ethical problems associated with marketing research.

Part 2: Designing Research Studies, covers the essentials involved in starting to study business problems. This part emphasizes decision-making, problem definition, and the process of how researchers translate business problems into research questions and perhaps even research hypotheses. The part includes coverage of research proposals in some detail, and the reader is encouraged to see these as the written agreement that helps put the decision maker and the researcher on the same page.

Chapter 5 emphasizes qualitative research applications. One role played by qualitative research is helping to separate business problem symptoms from true issues that researchers can attack with marketing research. However, qualitative research extends far beyond problem definition; it allows greater potential for discovery as well as deeper and potentially more meaningful explanations in marketing research. Chapter 5 now covers text exploring software in greater details to provide insight into how text data scraped from social media, review sites, and other communications can be mined for meaning.

Chapter 6 includes a detailed discussion of secondary data and emphasizes its increasing importance in an increasingly data-rich world. Other chapters include descriptions of survey designs (how to conduct, administer, and design survey instruments), observational studies (data on actual consumer behaviors), and causal designs involving marketing experiments.

Part 3: Measurement, gives readers working knowledge of building blocks absolutely critical to effective marketing research. This part describes the basics of measurement theory. Key topics include descriptions of the different levels of scale measurement and how this affects the interpretation of results. Basic ways to measure human attitudes and practical matters dealing with questionnaire design are also discussed. Measurement discussions emphasize the application of a sound psychometric approach. An increased emphasis is placed on the use of new media technologies. For instance, how does asking a question in an electronic medium change options for respondents and the researcher?

Part 4: Sampling and Sample Statistics, explains the difference between a population and a sample. Two chapters cover important issues that provide a basis for statistical inference. Another chapter provides useful guides for determining how large a sample is needed to make inferences with desired levels of confidence. Basic issues related to sampling distributions also are covered. All the coverage of sampling emphasizes generalizability, or external validity, and the properties needed to be able to make accurate inferences from a sample to a population.

Part 5: Basic Data Analytics (and Reporting), covers basic processes necessary in translating raw data into market intelligence. The part presents some of the most commonly used methods for analyzing data. For instance, basic descriptive statistics related to central tendency and dispersion are discussed in detail as a basis for understanding approaches that follow. The chapters also cover inferential statistics including often-used univariate and bivariate approaches such as the chi-square test, *t*-tests, and simple regression Elementary ANOVA applications are discussed in the context of analyzing experiments. Last, but certainly not least, the part concludes with a chapter on presenting research results. The chapter includes the outline useful in creating a student (individual or group) marketing research project. Also, basic guidelines for constructing research reports and presentations that are delivered orally or presented online are discussed.

Part 6: Comprehensive Cases with Computerized Databases makes up the last section of the book. These cases provide materials that challenge students to apply and integrate the concepts they have learned throughout the text. Instructors will find that these cases provide some flexibility either to expand or simplify the assignment to suit the demands of varying course assignments.

The cases provide more variety and include some that involve analysis of internal marketing problems as well as an opportunity to use qualitative research. When quantitative data are included, they can be easily analyzed with basic statistical tools like EXCEL, SPSS, or JMP. Excel files are also included with the same data. These files can be read directly by statistical programs like SAS, SPSS, R, JMP, or other programs. The seventh edition includes a new comprehensive particularly illustrating how useful data can be found online and turned into intelligence with basic data analytics.

Superior Pedagogy

More than other marketing research textbooks, the seventh edition of *Essentials of Marketing Research* addresses students' need to comprehend all aspects of the marketing research process. The following features facilitate learning throughout the book:

- **Learning Objectives.** Each chapter begins with a concise list of learning objectives that emphasize the major areas of competency the student should achieve before proceeding to the next chapter. The key is to avoid labeling everything a major learning objective and to provide the instructors with flexibility for emphasizing additional material from each chapter as they see fit.
- **Major Headings Keyed to Learning Objectives.** All first-level headings, with the exception of those labeled "Introduction," are keyed to learning objectives. This should be an aid in developing assessment rubrics and makes the book more user friendly in terms of identifying key material. Example assessment rubrics are available in the instructional resources.
- **Research Snapshots.** All of the box materials share a common title, Research Snapshots. Each chapter contains three Research Snapshots. The boxes explore marketing research processes in a variety of topical businesses situations, ranging from international considerations to research ethics. In later chapters in particular, boxes illustrate research techniques and step-by-step instructions for producing statistical results across multiple platforms.
- **Writing Style.** An accessible, interesting writing style continues as a hallmark of this book. With a careful balance between theory and practice and a sprinkling of interesting examples and anecdotes, the writing style clarifies and simplifies the market research process. In addition, the text offers a comprehensive treatment of important and current topics.
- **Statistical Approach.** Given the increased emphasis in industry on marketing analytics, the seventh edition provides balanced coverage of data analytics. *Essentials* takes a simple approach to give full coverage to basic tools like those used to test hypotheses involving differences between means or relationships among variables. Cross-tabulation, *t*-tests, ANOVA, and regression are covered in sufficient depth to allow a student to apply these techniques. The text includes screen shots to get students started running statistics using EXCEL, SAS, JMP, or SPSS, with easy-to-follow, click-through sequences.
- **Key Terms.** Learning the vocabulary of marketing research is essential to understanding the topic, and *Essentials of Marketing Research* facilitates this with key terms. First, key concepts are boldfaced and completely defined when they first appear in the textbook. Second, all key terms and concepts are listed at the end of each chapter, and many terms are highlighted in a marginal

glossary. Third, a glossary summarizing all key terms and definitions appears at the end of the book for handy reference. A glossary of frequently used symbols is also included.

■ **Research Activities.** The end-of-chapter materials include a few real-world research activities intended to provide actual research experience for the student. Most provide an opportunity for the student to gain experience with multiple content areas. Some involve ethical aspects of research, and some involve Internet usage.

■ **Cases.** Cases taken from real-life situations illustrate marketing research concepts and build knowledge and research skills. These cases offer students the opportunity to participate actively in the decision-making process, one of the most effective forms of learning.

Resources for Students

To promote learning and competency, it is also important to provide students with well-crafted resources. In addition to covering the latest information technology, the sixth edition includes the following student resources:

■ To access additional course materials and companion resources, please **visit** www.cengage.com. At the Cengage Brain home page, search for ISBN 9781337693974 using the search box at the top of the page. This will take you to the product page where free companion resources can be found.

MindTap: Empower Your Students

MindTap is a platform that propels students from memorization to mastery. It gives you complete control of your course, so you can provide engaging content, challenge every learner, and build student confidence. Customize interactive syllabi to emphasize priority topics, then add your own material or notes to the eBook as desired. This outcomes-driven application gives you the tools needed to empower students and boost both understanding and performance.

Access Everything You Need in One Place

Cut down on prep with the preloaded and organized MindTap course materials. Teach more efficiently with interactive multimedia, assignments, quizzes, and more. Give your students the power to read, listen, and study on their phones, so they can learn on their terms.

Empower Students to Reach Their Potential

Twelve distinct metrics give you actionable insights into student engagement. Identify topics troubling your entire class and instantly communicate with those struggling. Students can track their scores to stay motivated towards their goals. Together, you can be unstoppable.

Control Your Course—and Your Content

Get the flexibility to reorder textbook chapters, add your own notes, and embed a variety of content including Open Educational Resources (OER). Personalize course content to your students' needs. They can even read your notes, add their own, and highlight key text to aid their learning.

Get a Dedicated Team, Whenever You Need Them

MindTap isn't just a tool, it's backed by a personalized team eager to support you. We can help set up your course and tailor it to your specific objectives, so you'll be ready to make an impact from day one. Know we'll be standing by to help you and your students until the final day of the term.

Acknowledgments

Certainly, no list of acknowledgments will be complete. So many people have assisted in this project. Chief among these would be to the late Bill Zikmund for carrying the weight of this project for the first two editions. I enjoy carrying the project along into hopefully many more editions as the premier marketing research text. Also, thanks go to some of my team. My current and former graduate assistants including Christian Bushardt, Nina Krey, David Locander, Lauren Brewer, Kevin James, David Shows, Melanie Gardner, and Christina Chung have helped share some of the workload on other endeavors freeing up time for me to spend on this project. Nina has contributed significantly to some of the key chapters, including Chapter 16. I would be remiss not to also mention the support and patience of my family. Thanks especially to Laurie (Dr. Laurie Babin) for carefully proofreading chapters and providing suggested corrections. Also, thanks go to all the great faculty who mentored me during my days in the Ph.D. program at LSU. Most notable among these are Joseph F. Hair, Jr. and the late William R. Darden.

Special thanks go to all the good people at Cengage Learning who helped make this project possible. Thanks to Katherine Caudill, Julie Dierig, and Stacey Lutkoski, for motivating the whole team to stay on schedule. Also, a special thanks to Jenny Ziegler and the rest of the production team. They provided tremendous support through the writing and production process, including assistance with proofing, permissions, photos, and exhibits.

Many colleagues contributed ideas for this book. They made many suggestions that greatly enhanced this book. For their insightful reviews of the manuscript for this or previous editions of *Essentials of Marketing Research*, I would like to thank the following:

Karen Goncalves
Nichols College

Carol Bienstock
Radford University

Steven V. Cates
Averett University

Stephanie Noble
The University of Tennessee

Bob Lauman
Webster University

Natalie Wood
St. Joseph's University

Robert Jaross
Florida International University

Terry Paul
The Ohio State University

Mike Parent
Utah State University

Stephen Batory
Bloomsburg University

Michael R. Hyman
New Mexico State University

Rick Saucier
St. John's University

Xin Zhao
University of Utah

Gerald Albaum
University of New Mexico

William Bearden
University of South Carolina

Joseph A. Bellizzi
Arizona State University–West, Emeritus

James A. Brunner
University of Toledo

F. Anthony Bushman
San Francisco State University

Thomas Buzas
Eastern Michigan University

Roy F. Cabaniss
Huston-Tillotson College

Michael d'Amico
University of Akron

Ron Eggers
Barton College

H. Harry Friedman
City University of New York–Brooklyn

Ron Goldsmith
Florida State University

Larry Goldstein
Iona College

David Gourley
Arizona State University

Jim Grimm
Illinois State University

Christopher Groening
University of Missouri

Al Gross
Robert Morris College

Don Heinz
University of Wisconsin

Craig Hollingshead
Texas A&M University–Kingsville

Victor Howe
University of Kentucky

Roy Howell
Texas Tech University

Rhea Ingram
Columbus State University–Georgia

P. K. Kannan
University of Maryland

Susan Kleine
Arizona State University

David B. Klenosky
Purdue University

C. S. Kohli
California State University–Fullerton

Jerome L. Langer
Assumption College

James H. Leigh
Texas A&M University

Larry Lowe
Bryant College

Karl Mann
Tennessee Technological University

Charles R. Martin
Wichita State University

Marlys Mason
Oklahoma State University

Tom K. Massey
University of Missouri–Kansas City

Sanjay Mishra
University of Kansas

G. M. Naidu
University of Wisconsin–Whitewater

Charles Prohaska
Central Connecticut State University

Alan Sawyer
University of Florida

Robert Schaffer
California State University–Pomona

Leon G. Schiffman
City University of New York–Baruch

David Shows
Appalachian State University

K. Sivakumar
Lehigh University

Mark Speece
Central Washington University

Harlan Spotts
Western New England College

Wilbur W. Stanton
Old Dominion University

Bruce L. Stern
Portland State University

James L. Taylor
University of Alabama

Gail Tom
California State University–Sacramento

Deborah Utter
Boston College

David Wheeler
Suffolk University

Richard Wilcox
Carthage College

Margaret Wright
University of Colorado

Clifford E. Young
University of Colorado–Denver

William Lee Ziegler
Bethune-Cookman College

Weiling Zhuang
Eastern Kentucky University

Thanks also to all of the students who have inspired me and reinforced the fact that I made a great career decision over two decades ago. Thanks also to my close colleagues Mitch Griffin, Dave Ortinau, and Jim Boles for their continued support and insight.

Barry J. Babin
Max P. Watson, Jr. Professor of Business Research and Chair
Department of Marketing & Analytics
Louisiana Tech University
June 2018

In Remembrance

William G. Zikmund (1943–2002)

A native of the Chicago area, William G. Zikmund was a professor of marketing at Oklahoma State University and died shortly after completing the second edition. He received a Ph.D. in business administration with a concentration in marketing from the University of Colorado.

Before beginning his academic career, Professor Zikmund worked in marketing research for Conway/Millikin Company (a marketing research supplier) and Remington Arms Company (an extensive user of marketing research). Professor Zikmund also served as a marketing research consultant to several business and nonprofit organizations. During his academic career, Professor Zikmund published dozens of articles and papers in a diverse group of scholarly journals, ranging from the *Journal of Marketing* to the *Accounting Review* to the *Journal of Applied Psychology*. In addition to *Essentials of Marketing Research*, Professor Zikmund authored *Essentials of Marketing Research*, *Business Research Methods*, *Marketing*, *Effective Marketing*, and a work of fiction, *A Corporate Bestiary*.

Professor Zikmund was a member of several professional organizations, including the American Marketing Association, the Academy of Marketing Science, the Association for Consumer Research, the Society for Marketing Advances, the Marketing Educators' Association, and the Association of Collegiate Marketing Educators. He served on the editorial review boards of the *Journal of Marketing Education*, *Marketing Education Review*, *Journal of the Academy of Marketing Science*, and *Journal of Business Research*.

The Role of Marketing Research

iStock.com/Opidanus

LEARNING OUTCOMES

After studying this chapter, you should be able to:

1. Know what marketing research is and what it does for business
2. Understand the difference between basic and applied marketing research
3. Understand how the role of marketing research changes with the orientation of the firm
4. Be able to integrate marketing research results into the strategic planning process
5. Know when marketing research should and should not be conducted
6. Appreciate the way that technology and internationalization continue to change the way we do and use marketing research

Chapter Vignette:

Look Ma, No Hands!

What's the future of the automobile? In 1962, Hanna-Barbera created *The Jetsons*, a fictional family from 2062. And in 2062, the automobile had left the road behind, but George Jetson kept a hand on the stick to control the car. A decade ago, analysts widely predicted that by 2018, cars would be driving themselves. Well, we see that those predictions were a bit ambitious, but a host of companies including Uber, General Motors, Baidu, Didi, and others are betting on a future where autonomous vehicles (AVs) make hands-off driving a reality. In fact, an AV may not need a steering wheel or a joy stick. Waymo and GM continue to test AVs and many cars have some drive-itself features like automatic braking, parallel parking, and steering assist. The question for consumers may not be whether technological advances can produce a truly driverless car as it is whether consumers are ready for a driverless car experience.

For generations of Americans, a love affair with the automobile grew out of the sense of freedom that the car driving experience embodied. Driving the car meant going where you want to go, when you want to go, the way you want to go. The future of the AV will depend heavily on marketing research. Firms are investing in the technology because they see the potential for sales. Certainly, many consumers may be attracted initially by the added convenience of being able to go places while tending to other tasks like reading news or checking social media. But, look deeper and the questions are more complicated.

- Will consumers care to own a car that they don't drive? The implications for who buys cars, what amenities the car would have, and what the total market for cars would be are huge.
- Will consumer favorability be affected if they learn that AVs may well mean a loss of ability to determine what route a car takes or how fast the car can go? The onboard computers are not likely to allow even a little speeding.
- Will governments allow an environment where some cars drive themselves and others are controlled by humans, or will AVs be mandated?

EVERETT COLLECTION, INC.

- Will consumer attitudes be affected by the fact that a loss of satellite communication or an Internet disruption could bring all traffic to a halt?
- Will the U.S. lead or follow trends in AV adoption compared to other cultures that traditionally placed less value on driving and car ownership?

No doubt, questions like these and others will keep marketing researchers busy for years to come.*

Sources: Winton, N. (2018), "Autonomous Car Hype Is Way Ahead of Reality," *Forbes*, (Jan. 2), https://www.forbes.com/sites/neilwinton/2018/01/02/autonomous-car-hype-is-way-ahead-of-reality/#4461071f2d23, accessed January 3, 2018. Cooke, C. C. (2017), "Autonomous Vehicles Are About to Collide with the American Way," *National Review*, (Dec. 30), http://www.nationalreview.com/article/455018/autonomous-vehicles-will-spark-government-efforts-ban-driving, accessed January 3, 2018. Stuttaford, A. (2017), "Highway Robbery: Mandating Driverless Cars," *National Review*, (Nov. 18), http://www.nationalreview.com/corner/453877/highway-robbery-mandating-driverless-cars, accessed January 3, 2018. Abkowitz, A. (2017), "Ride-Sharing App Didi Attracts $4 Billion in New Funding," *Wall Street Journal*, (Dec. 22), A1.

Introduction

Given that we live in an era of big data, blockchain, the Internet of Things, etc., people like to say that the business world is changing faster now than ever before. Surprisingly, or perhaps not so surprisingly, businesspeople in other eras echoed the same refrain. Consider how radically the adoption of steam technology or the assembly line changed business. Indeed, only a few things in business are constant. One of those few things is change itself; another involves marketing. While the tools of marketing change over time, the overall role of marketing remains value creation and value creation comes about because marketing helps solve problems and create experiences. Both solving problems and creating experiences requires a firm to somehow be in touch. The firm needs to be in touch with the marketplace overall and with consumers, both its current and potential customers. Marketing research plays a vital role in firm success by keeping the firm in touch!

Staying in touch also means sifting through the profusion of data that exists today to identify actionable intelligence that assists the firm in making better decisions. Marketing decisions involve all of the 4 Ps: product, place, price, and promotion; but, in doing so, marketing research provides fuel for innovation and the development of mutually profitable firm–customer relationships. Marketing research also provides a way for firms to avoid the myopia that comes from focusing too much on controllable elements within the firm. Thus, marketing research is vitally important from a strategic view. More importantly though, marketing research becomes fascinating when one realizes that a lot of human behavior, which marketing research ultimately is tasked in predicting and understanding, is not so obvious or visible. As the opening vignette points out too, some issues with consumer adoption turn out a lot more complicated than they first appear. Here, we give a *taste* of marketing success and invite you to think about how marketing research fuels marketing decisions as you begin to explore the essentials of marketing research.

Tea or coffee? How do you take your caffeine? Is the market potential for coffee or tea better? United States consumers are neither the most prodigious coffee or tea drinkers in the world, but nonetheless, the average U.S. consumer 13 years and older takes in about 210 mg of caffeine each day, which amounts to more than a cup of coffee or more than 3 cups of tea per day. By late morning, 61 percent of all the caffeine taken in will have been consumed primarily because more than two-thirds of all the cups of coffee will have been consumed. The one segment that defies the morning caffeine intake trend is the adolescent segment.[1] Adolescents take caffeine in all day, but typically do so with drinks other than coffee or tea.

Both tea and coffee help consumers solve the problem of low energy, but is the pick-me-up the only reason for consumption. Are tea and coffee much the same product? Starbucks, more than any other company, brought the coffee experience to the U.S. less than 50 years ago. Prior to that, U.S. coffee was cheap and commoditized. Starbucks recognized that the coffee experience is more than coffee. They created modern, relaxing, accommodating environments where consumers could lounge over a coffee with a friend or with their device so that the

● ● ● ● ● ● ●

Unruly ad campaigns rely on research about the impact of viral videos.

Ionical/Shutterstock.com

If you are reading this book, there is a good chance that you'll be involved in a project involving marketing research. While you are only at the beginning of the book, chances are you already have some familiarity with some of the tools covered in this book. Each time you participate in a survey, provide an online review, or take part in a professor's experiment, you learned something about marketing research. Firms more and more rely on data to make decisions and the availability of data is more than ever before. But, the steps that one takes before analyzing the data are equally as important as data analysis. A mistake in any step of the research process can prohibit the project from turning data into marketing intelligence. In the very initial stages, the researcher must work with the decision-maker to express the problem in actionable terms and decide on the scope of the project. Sometimes, the researchers most critical decisions occur at this point. Should the research be done and if so, how can it best have a chance of creating intelligence? This chapter provides an introduction to help get you started on a path to a successful research project.

experience was not just a caffeine pick-me-up, but also an enjoyable time spent. Starbucks touches consumers away from the shop as well as through their successful app, and through content marketing. Their *Upstart* video series attempts to make consumers feel good about being Starbucks customers by showing the company's engagement with their employees' development, community issues, and wounded veterans' welfare. Based on the value they deliver, Starbucks enjoys greater flexibility in pricing than companies that only sell coffee. Consumers poked fun at the company by referring to them as "four-bucks." Today, Starbucks operates over 8,000 company-owned stores in the U.S. and over 24,000 worldwide.[2]

Why not then do the same thing for tea? After all, U.S. per-capita tea consumption has grown about 7 percent since 2010 and dollar sales about 10 percent. With that in mind, Starbucks purchased the Teavana brand in 2012 and opened up hundreds of stand-alone tea shops. Starbucks learned though that doing for tea what they did for coffee is not so easy. By 2019, Starbucks planned to be out of the Teavana tea shop business.[3] Why did they fail? Well, perhaps the same place strategies that work for coffee don't work for tea. Traffic patterns vary during the day and consumers' mood for tea is different than for coffee. The same pricing strategies likely won't work either. Tea is traditionally less expensive than coffee to purchase and while $4 is an expensive price for a coffee drink, consumers see $4 for hot water and a tea bag as outrageously expensive.[4] Perhaps Teavana promotions could have emphasized health more or altered the food offerings to better accommodate tea. Suffice it to say, while coffee and tea both caffeinate, the coffee and tea experiences are not the same.

Clearly, the role for information in making marketing decisions cannot be overstated. Marketing research can provide input to help predict the success of marketing efforts. Research can help predict how Starbucks' customers will react to a price change. Research can help explain why certain locations don't work out. Moreover, the data collected from customer apps can help make that customer happier by providing him or her with more value. This chapter provides an overview of marketing research and how it feeds into marketing strategy and marketing tactics. The opening vignette and the coffee versus tea examples provide useful contexts to help put everything into context.

What Is Marketing Research?

Part of business involves studying the different things that come together to create a business environment. Marketing research would not exist if business didn't exist. Thus, understanding marketing research requires at least a cursory understanding of business.

Business and Marketing Research

In its essence, business is very simple. Successful business enterprises offer value propositions to customers who are willing to buy. That means enough consumers view the propositions offered worth the price for the enterprise to survive. From this view, products are ultimately a bundle of value-producing benefits. The realized benefits amount to the way the firm applies resources in serving the customer. In return for the value received, the customer provides the firm with economic resources. Many factors affect consumer perceptions of value and successful companies are those that keenly understand the value equation. With this in mind, several key questions help provide understanding:

1. *What do we sell?* This includes not only the benefits that are easily seen, but also the more emotional benefits such as the comfort and relaxation of enjoying a cup of gourmet coffee in a pleasant atmosphere or the esteem that comes from having the latest electronic gadget. Companies offer value propositions that provide the potential for value beyond merely tangible product features.
2. *How do consumers view our company?* Companies often define themselves too narrowly based only on the physical good they sell and then fail to understand the meaning of the brand to consumers. For instance, how is Starbucks viewed relative to its competitors? Who are the competitors? Does Starbucks compete more directly with Maxwell House, Keurig, Nespresso, McDonald's, or something completely unassociated with coffee like a local lounge? Ultimately, companies ask themselves "Are we viewed more or less favorably relative to alternative brands?"
3. *What does our company/product mean?* What knowledge do people have of the company and its products? Do they know how to use them? Do they know all the different needs the company can address? solutions the company can assist with? What do our goods, services, promotions, and social media efforts communicate to consumers? Do they view our brand as ethical? Do we accurately communicate our total value proposition?
4. *What do consumers desire?* How can the company make the lives of its customers better, and how can it do this in a way that is not easily duplicated by another firm? Part of this lies in uncovering the things that customers truly desire, but which they can often not put into words.
5. How does our brand touch consumers? Does the company understand all the various touchpoints with its current customers and with potential customers? Beyond physical contact, digital marketing opens up less overt points of contact.

Answering these questions requires information. Marketing research's function is to supply information that helps provide these answers, thereby leading to more informed and more successful decision-making. Managers who use this information reduce the risk associated with decision-making.

All business problems require information for effective decision-making. Can researchers deliver the right information in a useful form and on time? Marketing research attempts to supply accurate information that reduces the uncertainty in decision-making. Very often, managers make decisions with little information for various reasons, including insufficient time to conduct research or management's belief that they already know enough. Relying on seat-of-the-pants decision-making—decision making without research—is like betting on a long shot at the racetrack because the horse's name is appealing. Occasionally the long shot pays off. More often, long-run uninformed decision-making is unwise. Marketing research helps decision-makers shift from intuitive guesswork to a more systematic, objective, and effective approach.

Marketing Research Defined

Marketing research is the application of the scientific method in searching for the truth about market and marketing phenomena. Research applications identify and define marketing opportunities and problems, generate and evaluate potentially innovative marketing ideas, monitor marketing performance, and describe the way consumers extract value from consumption. Marketing research includes idea generation and theory development, problem definition, information gathering, analyzing data, model building, and communicating the resulting implications clearly and concisely.

This definition suggests that the marketing research process is neither accidental nor haphazard. Literally, research (*re*-search) means "to search again." The term connotes patient study and scientific investigation wherein the researcher takes another, more careful look to try and successively know

marketing research

The application of the scientific method in searching for the truth about marketing phenomena.

Do Consumers Want the Real Joe?

Marketing creates value by providing solutions and creating experiences. Providing a solution is associated with utilitarian value while hedonic value results from rewarding experiences. Today, lots of experts espouse consumers' search for "authenticity," but sometimes authenticity butts heads with value creation.

A host of local and regional competitors promise an even more "authentic" coffee experience than Starbucks. Enter the pour-over. A barista serves a customer by lifting a kettle high into the air while pouring steamy water into a filtered vessel containing freshly ground coffee, making one cup at a time—a 4-to-5-minute process. All the while, the barista converses with the observant customer while constantly tending the process. In fact, this was the original non-cooked coffee-making technique that dates back over 200 years. The warm conversation, the anticipation, and the sensations of coffee aromas create an emotionally rewarding experience. The hedonic value brings the customer back!

But, this "authentic" experience has drawbacks. Baristas are not all equally skilled. The quality of an authentic pour-over varies from cup to cup. Also, it's time-consuming. Thus, lots of coffee shops adopt automated drip machines, which

Cultura Creative (RF)/Alamy Stock Photo

control temperature and coffee distribution closely, standardize the quality, and allow an individual customer to be served in seconds, not minutes. The customer's morning joe problem is solved with utilitarian value. As a compromise, some shops opt for fancy automated pour-over coffee machines that amount to a robotic barista. The robotic pour-over still takes about 4 minutes for an individual cup, but the employee can be taking payment and fetching a pastry during that time. In the era of artificial intelligence, we have some artificial authenticity! Marketing research can serve to strike the right balance between utilitarian and hedonic value for a market segment.

Sources: Jargon, J. (2018), "Is the 'Pour-Over' Over? Baristas Say Coffee Machines Have Their Perks," *Wall Street Journal*, (Jan. 2), https://www.wsj.com/articles/is-the-pour-over-over-baristas-say-coffee-machines-have-their-perks-1514913201, accessed January 8, 2018. Song, J. and H. Qu (2017), "The Mediating Role of Consumption Emotions," *International Journal of Hospitality Management*, 66, 66–76.

more. Ultimately, all findings tie back to previous knowledge and help develop theory and effective practice.

The definition also emphasizes, through reference to the scientific method, that any information generated should be accurate and objective. The researcher should be personally detached and free of bias attempting to find truth. Research isn't performed to support preconceived ideas but to discover and test them. If bias enters into the research process, the value of the research is considerably reduced. We will discuss this further in a subsequent chapter.

Clearly, marketing research is relevant to all aspects of the marketing mix. Research can facilitate managerial decision making about each of the four Ps: product, pricing, promotion, and place (distribution). By providing valuable input for marketing mix decisions, marketing research decreases the risk of making bad decisions in each area.

Finally, this definition of marketing research is limited by one's definition of *marketing*. Although one could hardly argue that research aimed at designing better products for a for-profit corporation like Coca-Cola is clearly marketing research, marketing research also includes efforts that assist nonprofit organizations such as the American Heart Association, the university alumni association, or a parochial elementary school. Every organization exists to satisfy social needs, and each requires marketing skills to produce and distribute their products and services. Governments also can use research in much the same way as managers at Samsung or Coke. For instance, the Food and Drug Administration (FDA) is an important user of marketing research, employing it to address the way people view and use various food and drugs. One such research study funded by the FDA addressed the question of how point of sale materials might influence consumers' perceptions, or better misperceptions, of the healthiness of fresh food offerings.[5] This book explores marketing research as it applies to all organizations and institutions engaging in marketing activities.

Digital Marketing

Change is a certainty and the tools of marketing research reflect technological evolution as much as any area of business. Later in the book, we will discuss state of the art research technologies, but here we introduce the notion of digital marketing and how it works with marketing research to help shape value. **Digital marketing** is a term used to capture all the various electronic, communicative technologies through which marketing enterprises (suppliers, manufacturers, retailers, etc.) work together with customers toward enhancing value from interaction, including exchange and relationships.[6]

In the early 20th century, the widespread adoption of telephones greatly facilitated communication. In the late 20th century, optical scanners made traditional mechanical cash registers obsolete, along with band-stampers (a device used to stamp the price, in purple ink, on cans, jars, boxes in stores) and label guns, and allowed the automatic recording of all sales to be fed into computers in real-time. Today, so-called smart technologies (phones, tablets, computers) are ubiquitous enabling not only online purchases to be recorded, but app usage, search behavior, and a consumer's whereabouts all become potentially useful data.

Exhibit 1.1 provides an overview of how marketing research fits into the business dynamic with a particular emphasis on digital technologies. Marketing research programs digital technologies to collect information and that information feeds back into marketing research as consumers use various devices and applications. When a consumer creates a product review and shares it on Facebook, that review has the potential to become data in a marketing research project. Marketing strategy helps shape research questions and the resulting research enables the design of the marketing mix. All of these activities feed directly or indirectly into consumption value. And, to the extent that marketing enables value creation, other stakeholders realize value as well. Marketing research serves as the nerve center for the socially engaged marketing firm.

digital marketing
A term used to capture all the various communicative technologies through which marketing enterprises (suppliers, manufacturers, retailers, etc.) work together with customers toward enhancing value from interaction, including exchange and relationships.

● ● ● ● ● ● ●

It's not your grandfather's marketing research anymore. Technological changes continue to provide more and more data, much of it automatically recorded and transmitted.

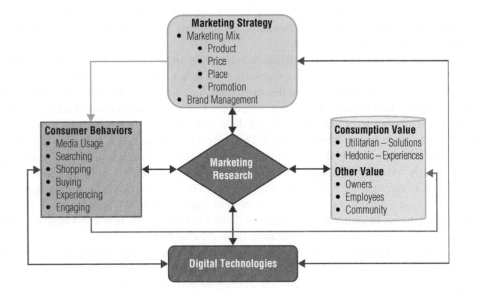

EXHIBIT **1.1**
Marketing Research is the Nerve Center for the Organization Always Receiving, Processing, and Distributing Information

Applied and Basic Marketing Research

One useful way to describe research is based on the specificity of its purpose. Is the research intended to address a very specific problem or is it meant to describe some overall marketing phenomenon?

Applied Marketing Research

applied marketing research

Research conducted to address a specific marketing decision for a specific firm or organization.

Applied marketing research is conducted to address a specific marketing decision for a specific firm or organization. If Costco needs to decide whether to open a warehouse store in Woodbury, NJ, applied marketing research can help provide answers. Similarly, the research that identifies the best market segments for its stores is applied. Applied research is relatively specific and aims to help a particular organization make better decisions regarding that issue.

Basic Marketing Research

basic marketing research

Research conducted without a specific decision in mind, which usually does not address the needs of a specific organization. It attempts to expand marketing knowledge in general and is not aimed at solving a particular business's problem.

Basic marketing research doesn't address the needs of a specific organization and doesn't typically address a specific business decision. Instead, basic research expands marketing knowledge in general and not at solving a particular business's problem. Basic research can test the validity of a general marketing theory (one that applies to all of marketing) or seek to learn more about some market phenomenon like social networking. A great deal of basic marketing research addresses the ways in which retail atmosphere influences consumers' emotions and behavior. From such research, we can learn how much the senses experienced in the time and space create value for consumers above and beyond any items purchased. This basic research does not examine the problem from any single retail or service provider's perspective. However, Starbucks' management may become aware of such research and apply the results in deciding how to design its stores. For instance, they may pay more attention to the control of in-store odors. Thus, these two types of research are not completely independent.

Researchers sometimes use different terms to represent the same distinction. Some reserve the term *marketing research* to refer to basic research. Then, the term *market research* is used to capture applied research addressing the needs of a firm within a particular market. Although the distinction provides useful terminology, very few aspects of research apply only to basic or only to applied research. Here, we will use the term *marketing research* more generally to refer to either type of research.

The Scientific Method

scientific method

The way researchers go about using knowledge and evidence to reach objective conclusions about the real world.

All marketing research, whether basic or applied, involves the scientific method. The **scientific method** is the way researchers go about using knowledge and evidence to reach objective conclusions about the real world. The scientific method is the same in social sciences, such as marketing, as in physical sciences, such as physics.

Exhibit 1.2 briefly illustrates the scientific method. Researchers usually begin with some understanding of theory in the problem area. Consumer researchers usually are familiar with consumer behavior theory and by elaborating on this theory and/or combining theoretical knowledge with pure discovery, research questions emerge. Discovery can involve any means of idea generation, including exploratory techniques that we will discover later or even eureka types of experiences like when the apple fell on Newton's head! The early stages of the research process in particular work better when creative thinking is applied. A host of creative thinking tools exist that managers and researchers can and should apply. The researcher then develops formal research hypotheses that play a key role through the remainder of the process. The next step involves testing hypotheses against empirical evidence (facts from observation or experimentation). Results either support a particular hypothesis or do not support that hypothesis. From the results, new knowledge is acquired that may lead to a new theory or modification of an existing theory.

Use of the scientific method in applied research ensures objectivity in gathering facts and testing creative ideas for alternative marketing strategies. In basic research, scientific research contributes to conclusions that over time contribute to the development of general laws about phenomena like

To the Point

"If you have knowledge, let others light their candle with it."

—WINSTON CHURCHILL

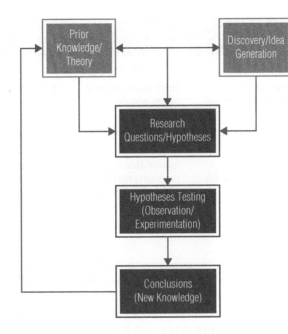

EXHIBIT **1.2**
The Scientific Method

price and value. The scientific method is the philosophy and way of doing *scientific* research, the results of which are the basis for knowledge growth and better decision making.

Marketing Research and Strategic Management Orientation

Organizations over time adopt a certain way of going about their business. These ways represent strategic management orientations and they provide a common theme for decision making. A firm can be **product oriented**. A product-oriented firm prioritizes decision making in a way that emphasizes technical superiority of their offerings. Thus, input from technicians and experts are very important in making critical decisions. The goal is to make what the firm sees as the best products possible. A firm can be **production oriented**. Production orientation means that the firm prioritizes efficiency and effectiveness of the production processes in making decisions. Here, input from engineers and accountants becomes important as the firm seeks to drive costs down. Production-oriented firms are usually very large firms manufacturing products in very large quantities resulting in good economies of scale. Marketing research may take a backseat with these orientations.

In contrast, marketing research is a primary tool enabling implementation of a marketing orientation.[7] The **marketing concept** is a central idea in modern marketing thinking that focuses more on how the firm provides value to customers than on the physical product or production process. The orientation has evolved over time as product- and production-oriented firms respond to changes in technology and competitive and economic environments. When a firm adapts the marketing concept, it develops a **marketing orientation**. A marketing-oriented firm must:

1. Be **customer oriented**—means that all firm decisions are made with a conscious awareness of their effect on the consumer
2. Emphasize long-run profitability rather than short-term profits or sales volume
3. Adopt a cross-functional perspective, meaning that marketing is integrated across other business functions

Going further, a **stakeholder orientation** recognizes that multiple parties are affected by firm decisions. When a company makes a decision to change a product line based on marketing research, that decision affects customers, employees, and their families; the owners of the company (shareholders in a public company); and even the community in general. Good decision making considers how all are affected when making decisions. Exhibit 1.3 provides an overview of business orientations.

product oriented

Describes a firm that prioritizes decision making in a way that emphasizes technical superiority in the product.

production oriented

Describes a firm that prioritizes efficiency and effectiveness of the production processes in making decisions.

marketing concept

A central idea in modern marketing thinking that focuses on how the firm provides value to customers more than on the physical product or production process.

marketing orientation

The corporate culture existing for firms adopting the marketing concept. It emphasizes customer orientation, long-term profitability over short-term profits, and a cross-functional perspective.

customer oriented

Describes a firm in which all decisions are made with a conscious awareness of their effect on the consumer.

stakeholder orientation

Recognizing that multiple parties are affected by firm decisions.

EXHIBIT **1.3**
Types of Business
Orientations

Product Orientation	Production Orientation	Marketing Orientation	Stakeholder Orientation
Internal focus	Internal focus	External focus	External focus
Emphasize product superiority	Emphasize efficiency and low costs	Emphasize customer tastes and desires	Emphasize a balance in satisfying all parties touched by organization
Product research is critical	Process research is important	Customer research is essential	Consumer research is important
Narrow or even niche markets served	Mass markets often required for success	Identifiable market segments matched with unique product	Select segments served balanced with great concern for public persona

To the Point

"Knowledge has to be increased, challenged and improved constantly, or it vanishes."

—PETER DRUCKER

● ● ● ● ● ● ●

Marketing research provides input that can make a traveler happy about the bag they tote through an airport

Customer Orientation

According to the marketing concept, the consumer should be the primary focus of attention, the pivot point about which the business moves to achieve the balanced best interests of all other stakeholders in the long run. According to this philosophy, the firm creates offers with consumers' needs in mind. The creation of value for consumers, after all, is the reason that a firm exists. Therefore, unlike the other two orientations, marketing research addressing consumer desires, beliefs, and attitudes becomes essential.

How could a good piece of luggage be designed without consumer research? Those who travel frequently, particularly by air, are very fussy about the bag they carry. When all is considered, research shows that price is hardly the most important criterion for the frequent traveler. These consumers are willing

Milles Studio/Shutterstock.com

to plunk down hundreds and sometimes even over $1,000 for the right bag. Well-known companies like Samsonite and lesser well-known companies, at least to the general public, like Mandarina Duck, use consumer input to design *perfect* bags. What factors do consumers consider more important than price and essential in a good bag? First, rollers. Not just any rollers, smooth and sturdy rollers and increasingly, four instead of two wheels. That enables the bag to stand up and provide an easy place to rest a computer or purse. Second, size. It has to hold at least a few days' attire but has to fit in the overhead bin of an airplane. Third, separate storage for items like shoes and toiletries and preferably, a garment compartment for more dressy attire. Fourth, sturdiness. The bag should stand abuse and last years, not months! Fifth, unique and fun appearance. When you

travel a lot, the bag should have personality that says something about the consumer. Thus, a bag that is a special khaki orange color with grey accents not only is fun, but unique enough to stand out in a crowd and much easier to pick out on a carousel should you have to check it. Mandarina Duck is a leader in style but does not take a backseat in function.[8] Consumer research plays a big role in this research.

Although technology firms are traditionally thought of as prototypically product oriented, that view is changing. In particular, social media has changed the technology firm by providing more avenues for users to provide feedback directly, like through chat-rooms, and indirectly through online reviews. Thus, if a new smartphone's microphone is aggravating, people will hear about it online. In fact, technology firms increasingly use their content marketing efforts as vehicles for consumer learning and consumer feedback.[9] Put another way, the organizations that continuously learn from their research and use that as input to their decision making also adopt a learning-orientation.

Long-Run Profitability

Customer orientation does not mean slavery to consumers' every fleeting whim. Implicit in the marketing concept is the assumption of the continuity of the firm. Thus, the firm must eventually experience profitability to survive although its orientation may be more toward building strong relationships with customers.

Lego works hard to build relationships with customers. Not only do they do research to try to predict how today's children would like to interact with the Lego brand, but they also study the market to integrate carefully their marketing efforts. Lego monitors social networks and general Internet communication constantly searching for positive and negative mentions of the brand. They refer to this as their **online sentiment analysis**.[10] Lego.com provides visitors with an interactive Lego experience from which Lego harvests more information about their customers and potential customers. This aggressive research approach allows them to build and maintain strong relationships with its customers.

The second aspect of the marketing concept argues against profitless volume or sales volume for the sake of volume alone. Sometimes, the best decision for a customer and the best decision in the end for the firm is the sale that is not made. For instance, a parts supplier might be able to mislead a customer about the relative quality of the parts he or she sells and make an immediate sale. However, when the parts begin to fail sooner than expected, the customer will almost certainly not do business with this firm again. If instead the salesperson had been honest and suggested another supplier, he or she may be able to find another opportunity to do business with that firm.

online sentiment analysis

Using data indicating the total positive or negative mentions of a brand on the Internet to assess and understand the strength of the brand.

A Cross-Functional Effort

The marketing concept requires the firm to provide marketing information to be used by all functional areas of a business. Production needs accurate forecasts to know how much should be produced; the design team needs input on consumer tastes, strategic management personnel need to understand the meaning of the brand, and so on. Problems are almost certain to arise from lack of an integrated, company-wide effort. The marketing concept stresses a crossfunctional perspective to achieve consumer orientation and long-term profitability.

When a firm lacks organizational procedures for communicating marketing information and coordinating marketing efforts, the effectiveness of its marketing programs will suffer. Marketing research findings produce some of the most crucial marketing information; thus, such research is management's key tool for finding out what customers want and how best to satisfy their needs. In a competitive marketplace, managers recognize the critical need for conducting marketing research. When conducted competently, the firm bases decisions on valid and reliable facts communicated effectively to decision-makers.

In a marketing-oriented firm, marketing researchers serve more than the external customers who buy the firm's offerings. Marketing research also serves internal customers with information. The internal customers include employees all along the value production chain from frontline service and sales employees, to production managers to the CEO. In fact, in a market-oriented organization, all employees are marketers in that they serve internal and external customers. An accountant who prepares a report for a sales manager should view the manager as a customer who uses the information to make decisions benefiting external customers. All employees share the common focus of providing value to customers; in such organizations, the focus on customers becomes tacit knowledge. Even, and perhaps especially, critical information becomes integrated.[11] Stakeholder-oriented companies also place a keen focus on processes that serve customers as well as others impacted by firm decisions.

Keeping Customers and Building Relationships

Marketers often talk about getting customers, but keeping customers is equally important. Effective marketers work to build long-term relationships with their customers. The term **relationship marketing** communicates the idea that a major goal of marketing is to build long-term relationships with the customers contributing to their success. Once an exchange is made, effective marketing stresses managing the relationships that will bring about additional exchanges. Effective marketers

relationship marketing

Communicates the idea that a major goal of marketing is to build long-term relationships with the customers contributing to their success.

RESEARCH
SNAPSHOT

Engaged to a Robot, I Do or I Don't?

Marketing research feeds artificial intelligence (AI) systems, which in turn, model consumers' behavior. All of those technologies that tell us what we want to buy, control our thermostat, and help drive our car add value. Right? Well, marketers are preparing for a backlash against automated technologies. Survey research suggests that consumers are skeptical. More than 2 of 3 respondents indicate they fear AI to some degree. Perhaps the rush to have machines take over for humans with things like chatbots is premature. Only 13 percent of respondents express a preference in communicating with a virtual service provider over an actual company representative. Indeed, a key to having consumers warm up to automated processes is to make sure they maintain a human touch. Otherwise, consumers will say "I don't" to an enagement with the robot.

Sources: Insights Team (2017), "4 Ways to Drive Customer Engagement with AI," *Forbes*, (Nov. 2), https://www.forbes.com/sites/insights-pega/2017/11/02/4-ways-to-drive-customer-engagement-with-ai/#435c23992cde, accessed January 7, 2018. Altman, I. (2017), "The Top 10 Business Trends that Will Drive Success in 2018," *Forbes*, (Dec. 5), https://www.forbes.com/sites/ianaltman/2017/12/05/the-top-business-trends-that-will-drive-success-in-2018/#1bb36189701a, accessed January 7, 2018.

view making a sale not as the end of a process but as the start of the organization's relationship with a customer. In fact, all touchpoints become an opportunity to invite the customer to engage with the firm. Nike's "JUST DO IT" serves as an invitation to engage with products. However, Nespresso takes every opportunity to engage with its customers as a way of building relationships. Nespresso coffee stores provide free guest Wi-Fi service that enables the Nespresso app, not just to be downloaded, but to provide useful information and promotional information as a way of enhancing the already enhanced in-store experience. Consequently, Nespresso customers are not just engaged, but committed.[12] At the same time, the connectivity allows data to be gathered about the customer's preferences and behaviors.

Marketing Research: A Means for Implementing the Marketing Concept

The real estate business has its ups and downs. Part of the reasons for these is that the things that appeal to consumers change over time. Companies like Camden Properties and Riverstone Residential manage apartment complexes all over the United States. In some markets, the apartment business is extremely competitive. These companies have learned several things about the modern apartment shopper. One big trend in their favor is that younger Americans tend to favor apartment complex living over stand-alone housing. Buying and owning a home is not as important a goal to younger generations as it was in the past. A second big trend is understanding how apartments ultimately are selected. It turns out that one of the biggest factors in judging the quality of a complex is its landscaping. Therefore, a lot of large apartment complexes invest heavily in sod, shrubs and even trees. Even a new complex can seem to be secluded in greenery. The landscaping gives the complex tremendous curb appeal that ultimately helps build sales. In addition, the landscaping may well keep the tenants happy longer, decreasing problems with turnover.

Analysis of data may also be a form of marketing research that can increase efficiency. Any consumer browsing the Internet sees how data fed into a marketing system attempts to make shopping efficient. A combination of browsing behavior and searches feeds a system that helps predict what the consumer wants to buy. Also, browse one item online and you will see suggestions of other purchases based on what other people have bought in combination.

Marketing Research and Strategic Marketing Management

Effective marketing management requires research. Think about the role that celebrity endorsers play for many companies. Given their importance, numerous firms monitor the favorability of different celebrities and firms seek this research information in making endorsement decisions.

Taylor Swift is considered among the most valuable celebrity endorsers overall. What makes a celebrity an effective endorser? Well, notoriety has a lot to do with it, but likability and fit with the brand matter a lot as well.

Opendorse provides a list of the leading professional athlete endorsers and also tracks their social media presence based on the number of Twitter followers. What athletes come first to your mind? Perhaps some NFL players? Well, the top three endorsers are from tennis, Roger Federor ($60M, 5.3 M Twitter followers); NBA, LeBron James ($54M, 32 M Twitter followers); and golf, Phil Mickelson ($50M, 0 Twitter followers).[13] No current NFL player makes the top 20. The twentieth spot is occupied by retired NFL player Peyton Manning, who remains well-liked and trusted. Data like these help firms know whether to invest in celebrity endorsers. The prime managerial value of marketing research comes from the reduced uncertainty that results from information and facilitates decision making about marketing strategies and tactics to achieve an organization's strategic goals.

Developing and implementing a marketing strategy involves four stages:

1. Identifying and evaluating market opportunities.
2. Analyzing market segments and selecting target markets.
3. Planning and implementing a marketing mix that will provide value to customers and meet organizational objectives.
4. Analyzing firm performance.

Exhibit 1.4 illustrates the integration of research and marketing strategy and the way they come together to create value in the marketplace.

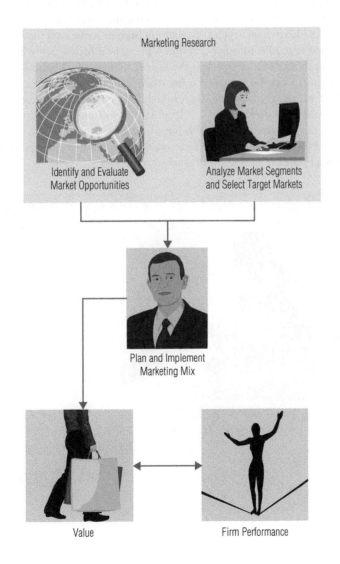

Marketing Research

Identify and Evaluate Market Opportunities

Analyze Market Segments and Select Target Markets

Plan and Implement Marketing Mix

Value

Firm Performance

EXHIBIT **1.4**
Marketing Research Cuts Decision Risk with Input That Leads to Value

Identifying and Evaluating Market Opportunities

One job that marketing research performs is monitoring the environment for signals indicating a business opportunity. A mere description of a social or economic activity, such as trends in consumer purchasing behavior, may help managers recognize problems and identify opportunities for enriching marketing efforts. In some cases, this research can motivate a firm to take action to address consumer desires in a way that is beneficial to both the customers and to the firm.

At times, evaluating opportunities may involve something as mundane as tracking weather trends. Consumers have a physical need to maintain some degree of physical comfort. Thus, changes in temperature patterns may create business opportunities for utility companies, appliance companies, and even beverage companies as more consumers will select a hot beverage like hot chocolate when the weather is cold and dreary. Companies can also adjust their logistic distribution patterns based on the weather. When hurricane weather companies forecast hurricanes for the Gulf or East Coasts, that information feeds into manufacturers' and retailers' distribution systems. Home Depot and Lowes redirect products like Honda generators, Poulan chainsaws, and Weyerhauser plywood intended for other places to try to satisfy the emergency-drive demand. As a result, the retailers can maintain inventory even when demand increases many times over normal. Thus, the misfortune of a hurricane created a business opportunity that also provides real value to consumers. In this case, the businesses and the consumers all benefited from the fact that firms scan the opportunity for trends.

Malls sometimes have research firms housed within them because the firm can interact with a steady stream of consumers. Some shopping centers in Texas near the United States–Mexican border spotted an opportunity when they realized that a significant number of the shoppers in their mall indicated their residency in Mexico. A survey project was launched to profile these consumers. The results revealed that these consumers were typically from somewhere near Monterrey, Mexico, typically households with children and typically relatively high in household income.[14] The results to that study can be used to market to other consumers living near Monterrey who match this profile and encourage them to take a day trip across the border to do some shopping.

Market opportunities may be evaluated using many performance criteria. Estimates of market sales potential allow managers to evaluate the profitability of various opportunities. Accurate sales forecasts are among the most useful pieces of planning information a marketing manager can have. Complete accuracy in forecasting the future is not possible because change is one of the few constants in marketing. Nevertheless, objective forecasts of demand or of changes in the environment can provide a strong foundation for a sound marketing strategy.

● ● ● ● ● ●

Fun in the snow depends on weather trends, equipment, and clothing—all subjects for a market researcher.

age fotostock/SuperStock

Analyzing and Selecting Target Markets

The second stage in developing a marketing strategy involves analyzing market segments and selecting target markets. Marketing research is a major source of information for determining which characteristics of market segments distinguish them from the overall market. Such research can help "locate" a market segment by describing it in terms of demographic characteristics. Geodemographics can be important to study and track in this effort. **Geodemographics** refers to information describing the demographic profile of consumers in a particular geographic region. The company may learn that consumers in a particular postal code within a region tend to be middle-aged, have multiple children over the age of twelve, and have college degrees and whitecollar jobs. Once the company knows the geodemographics of a market segment, the consumers within that segment can be reached by choosing media appealing to that particular profile. For example, *Architectural Digest* is a magazine that is read predominantly by consumers with very high social status in the most exclusive ZIP codes in the United States.

geodemographics
Refers to information describing the demographic profile of consumers in a particular geographic region.

Planning and Implementing a Marketing Mix

Using the information obtained in the two previous stages, marketing managers plan and execute a marketing-mix strategy. Marketing research may be needed to support specific decisions about any aspect of the marketing mix. For instance, the research can evaluate an alternative course of action. Perhaps an exercise products firm is trying to decide on whether or not they should pay a social media influencer like Jen Selter or Jake Paul to promote the brand in online video content. Certainly, the number of followers is an important piece of data for that decision, but the firm also needs to measure credibility among the relevant market segment. Jake has more followers, but perhaps for a segment of active, young women, Jen would hold more credibility.

An overall research plan involves all marketing strategy elements. Once research identifies a target market and media that can be used in promotion, the benefits required to create value for the customers must be known and communicated, the appropriate price to capture that value must be determined and not overlooked, and the best channel of distribution to reach the targeted consumers must be determined. Effective brand management requires integration of all the intelligence gathered from research.

Product Research

Product research takes many forms and includes studies designed to evaluate and develop new products and to learn how to adapt existing product lines. Concept testing exposes potential customers to a new product idea to judge the acceptance and feasibility of the concept. Product testing reveals a product prototype's strengths and weaknesses or determines whether a finished product performs better than competing brands or according to expectations. Brand-name evaluation studies investigate whether a name is appropriate for a product. Package testing assesses size, color, shape, ease of use, and other attributes of a package. Product research encompasses all applications of marketing research that seek to develop product attributes that will add value for consumers.

● ● ● ● ● ● ●
Product testing research provides valuable input to companies, customers, and policy makers.

The idea of a smokeless cigarette has been around for decades. Products like Reynolds's Premier, perhaps the most famous (or infamous) smokeless cigarette, typically failed because the experience was too different from traditional smoking. After all, one can hardly smoke if there is no smoke! E-cigarettes and vaping provide an alternative to traditional cigarette smoking. People smoke to get caffeine, flavor, and the sense of smoking. E-cigarettes provide all of this and are perceived as a safer alternative to cigarettes. Today, millions of people use one of hundreds of brands like blu eCigs, OM Vapors, or Green Smoke. Are they really safer? Research to date is inconclusive overall but does suggest that they are at least safer than traditional cigarettes.[15] Marketing research can help answer the question of whether consumer perceptions are in-line with the medical research findings.

Pricing Research

pricing

Involves finding the amount of monetary sacrifice that best represents the value customers perceive in a product after considering various market constraints.

Pricing research represents typical marketing research. Many test markets address the question of how consumers will respond to a new product offered at two different prices. **Pricing** strategy involves finding the amount of monetary sacrifice that best represents the value customers perceive in a product after considering various market constraints. Most organizations conduct pricing research. Starbucks may seem expensive now, but if the price doubled, would Starbucks lose half of its customers? How much extra are Toyota customers willing to pay for each extra mpg? How much is one willing to pay for same day delivery? Pricing research also investigates the way people respond to pricing tactics. How do consumers respond to price reductions? Do price gaps among national brands, regional brands, and private labels exist? Does an Amazon Dash Button reduce price sensitivity? Most importantly, research also addresses the way consumers determine perceived value at a given price.

Pricing research, by its nature, also involves consumer quality perceptions. Do groceries priced at 99 cents really sell a lot more than groceries priced at $1? A great deal of research explores the effects of "odd-ending" prices. For the most part, overall effects due to odd-ending prices seem subtle and have very little effect. However, when other variables are considered, the results become clearer. Research suggests that for premium brands, odd-ended pricing can lower sales whereas for discount brands, a 99-cent ending price can enhance sales.[16] Like other aspects of research, the story often is not as straightforward as some may think.

Distribution Research

marketing channel

A network of interdependent institutions that performs the logistics necessary for consumption to occur.

supply chain

Another term for a channel of distribution, meaning the link between suppliers and customers.

● ● ● ● ● ● ●

What types of marketing research would be useful to Redbox?

Distribution involves the marketing channels that will physically "distribute" products from a producer to a consumer. A **marketing channel** is a network of interdependent institutions that perform the logistics necessary for consumption to occur. Some channels are very short and involve only a producer and a consumer, and some are very long involving many transportation, wholesale, and retail firms. It may be somewhat obvious why the term **supply chain** is sometimes used to refer to a channel of distribution. Distribution is necessary to remove the separations between buyers and sellers.

Distribution research is typified by studies aimed at selecting retail sites or warehouse locations. A survey of retailers or wholesalers may be conducted because the actions of one channel member can greatly affect the performance of other channel members. Distribution research often is needed to gain knowledge about retailers' and wholesalers' operations and to learn their reactions to a manufacturer's marketing policies. It may also be used to examine the effect of just-in-time ordering systems or exclusive distribution on product quality. Research focused on developing and improving the efficiency of marketing channels is extremely important.

Consider today how the distribution channel for the entertainment industry is changing. Just a couple of decades ago, most Americans relied on the big three networks (CBS, NBC, ABC) for entertainment and even news. The customer typically watched programs on one of the networks when the network showed the program. Advertisers paid the networks to host shows. Today, the major three networks are just fractions of what they once were and consumers watch many network programs online from the network websites or from You Tube. Netflix, Amazon, and iTunes give other examples of new channel options for consumers looking for a little electronic entertainment. Redbox offers another novel channel option by making movies available in vending machines. So, when consumers visit Walgreens, they can also get a movie. Locations become critically important for Redbox. Location studies are indeed important for retailers and other members of the distribution channel.

Promotion Research

Promotion is the communication function of the firm responsible for informing and persuading buyers. **Promotion research** investigates the effectiveness of advertising, premiums, loyalty programs, coupons, sampling, discounts, public relations, and other sales promotions. However, among all of these, firms spend more time, money, and effort on advertising research, including a hefty chunk investigating the design and effectiveness of content marketing. One area of research deals with how long an ad should be. Research suggests the average human attention span has fallen below that of a goldfish, to less than 10 seconds.[17] As a consequence, ad agencies now purchase air time for less than 30 seconds. In fact, 10 second spots are common and spots as short as 6 seconds are sold.

Loyalty programs also involve considerable research. Amazon Prime provides one example, but others like Dunkin Donuts' (DD) Perk program have been successfully implemented within an overall branding strategy. Research on loyalty programs should consider the following:

1. Is the program earned through patronage like airline programs or purchased like Amazon Prime? If purchased, what should the membership price be?
2. At what rate do members accrue benefits and how substantial are those benefits?
3. Does the program create inertia only or true customer commitment?
4. Does the program entice current members to recruit other customers as loyalty members and what rewards should be associated with recruitment?

The latter point is more complicated than it may seem. For example, a significant amount of reward-scrounging, that is, the "recruitment" of members in a somewhat shady way. That could mean recruiting someone who was going to join anyway or recruiting someone who will not stay in the program just as a means of getting the benefits. Research suggests that reward scrounging decreases the overall profitability of a reward program.[18]

promotion

The communication function of the firm responsible for informing and persuading buyers.

promotion research

Investigates the effectiveness of advertising, premiums, coupons, sampling, discounts, public relations, and other sales promotions.

The Integrated Marketing Mix

Marketing today focuses increasingly on the fact that different promotional decisions should not be made in isolation. Instead, the concept of **integrated marketing communication** is adopted, meaning that all promotional efforts (advertising, digital/content marketing, public relations, personal selling, event marketing, social networking, and so forth) should be coordinated to communicate a consistent image. Likewise, more generally, marketing firms realize that the elements of the marketing mix itself must work together. For instance, a change in price can affect the quality of the product, which may also influence decisions about distribution. From a research standpoint, the **integrated marketing mix** means that research studies often investigate effects of various combinations of marketing mix elements on important outcomes like sales and image. Research suggests firms with a consumer orientation are particularly oriented toward integrating all aspects of their marketing into a single message.[19]

Integration means sending a consistent message. Part of Dunkin Donuts' (DD) transformation from a donut shop into a morning ritual experience involves replacing the visual image of donuts with coffee. Everywhere the consumer encounters the brand they see coffee and coffee beverages featured much more prominently than donuts. Southwest Airlines practices integrated communication. A constant message in their communications is transparency in fares. More specifically, Southwest refers to it as transfarency! Put transfarency.com into your browser address window and see where you end up.

integrated marketing communication

Means that all promotional efforts (advertising, public relations, personal selling, event marketing, and so forth) should be coordinated to communicate a consistent image.

integrated marketing mix

The effects of various combinations of marketing-mix elements on important outcomes.

● ● ● ● ● ● ●

An Integrated Marketing Mix sends a constant message, in this case, fairness in airfare.

Analyzing Marketing Performance

total value management

Trying to manage and monitor the entire process by which consumers receive benefits from a company.

After a marketing strategy has been implemented, marketing research may serve to inform managers whether planned activities were properly executed and are accomplishing what they were expected to achieve. In other words, marketing research may be conducted to obtain feedback for evaluation and control of marketing programs. This aspect of marketing research is especially important for successful **total value management**, which attempts to manage the entire process by which a consumer receives benefits from a company.

performance-monitoring research

Refers to research that regularly, sometimes routinely, provides feedback for evaluation and control of marketing activity.

Performance-monitoring research refers to research that regularly, sometimes routinely, provides feedback for evaluation and control of marketing activity. For example, most firms continuously monitor wholesale and retail activity to ensure early detection of sales declines and other anomalies. In the grocery and drug industries, sales research may use Universal Product Codes (UPCs) on packages read by optical scanners linked to computerized checkouts and inventory systems and providing real-time information on key variables such as store revenue, turnover, customer share, promotional effectiveness, and even market share. Marketshare analysis and sales analysis are the most common forms of performance-monitoring research. Almost every organization compares its current sales with previous sales and with competitors' sales. However, analyzing marketing performance is not limited to the investigation of sales figures.

marketing metrics

Quantitative ways of monitoring and measuring marketing performance.

Marketing metrics refer to quantitative ways of monitoring and measuring marketing performance. Research derives marketing metrics that allow a firm to know whether the resources invested in marketing activities have met their quantitative business goals. Marketing metrics allow the firm to assess the return on investment (ROI) associated with marketing activities. Recent research suggests that the more firms emphasize value creation in their marketing, the higher are these key performance metrics.[20] Thus, value appears to pay.

When Is Marketing Research Needed?

The need to make intelligent, informed decisions ultimately motivates marketing research. Not every decision requires marketing research. Thus, when confronting a key decision, a marketing manager must initially decide whether to conduct marketing research. The determination of the need for marketing research centers on (1) time constraints, (2) the availability of data, (3) the nature of the decision to be made, and (4) the value of the research information in relation to costs.

Time Constraints

Systematic research takes time. In many instances management believes that a decision must be made immediately, allowing no time for research. Managers often make decisions without adequate information or thorough understanding of market situations. Although making decisions without researching a situation is not ideal, sometimes the urgency of a situation precludes the use of research. The urgency with which managers often want to make decisions often conflicts with the marketing researchers' desire for rigor in following the scientific method.

Availability of Data

Often managers already possess enough information to make sound decisions without additional marketing research. When they lack adequate information, however, research must be considered. This means that data need to be collected from an appropriate source. If a potential source of data exists, managers will want to know how much it will cost to get the data.

If the data cannot be obtained or obtained in a timely fashion, this particular research project should not be conducted. For example, many nations do not have reliable population census data due to underdevelopment, corruption, ongoing conflicts, transient migration, etc. Organizations engaged in international business often find that data about business activity or population characteristics that are readily available in the United States are nonexistent or sparse in developing countries. Imagine the problems facing marketing researchers who wish to investigate market potential in places like Uzbekistan, Yugoslavian Macedonia, and Rwanda.

Nature of the Decision

The value of marketing research depends on the nature of the managerial decision to be made. A routine tactical decision that does not require a substantial investment may not seem to warrant a substantial expenditure for marketing research. For example, a computer company must update its operator's instruction manual when it makes minor product modifications. The research cost of determining the proper wording to use in the updated manual is likely too high for such a minor decision. The nature of the decision is not totally independent of the next issue to be considered: the benefits versus the costs of the research. In general, however, the more strategically or tactically important the decision, the more likely it is that research will be conducted.

Benefits versus Costs

Marketing research can be costly but it can also be of great benefit. Earlier we discussed some of the managerial benefits of marketing research. In any decision-making situation, managers must identify alternative courses of action and then weigh the value of each alternative against its cost. Marketing research can be thought of as an investment alternative. When deciding whether to make a decision without research or to postpone the decision to conduct research, managers should ask three questions:

1. Is the potential payoff worth the investment?
2. Will the information gained by marketing research improve the quality of the marketing decision enough to warrant the expenditure?
3. Is the proposed research expenditure the best use of available funds?

Consider a food company considering a change in packaging such as a move from Styrofoam to paper cups for coffee or from plastic to styrene for snacks. Firms often may make such decisions with little or no research input. Management may not appreciate the value of research into this issue because they believe the research costs exceed the potential benefits. Perhaps managers view a change in packaging as so inconsequential that extensive testing is unnecessary to make a quality decision. However, managers often end up regretting the decision not to do research. SunChips changed their packaging material to compostable paper and saw a tremendous drop in sales as customers ridiculed the packages publicly including on YouTube videos. One problem the brand overlooked was how incredibly noisy the new packages would be. In hindsight, perhaps more research was merited although a comparison of the loss in sales revenue with the costs of conducting further market tests would be needed to better address this question. Exhibit 1.5 outlines the criteria for determining when to conduct marketing research. If the any of the "Do Not Conduct Market Research" items is true, then the researcher should stop and not proceed with a new research project.

EXHIBIT **1.5**
Should We Conduct
Marketing Research?

Factor	Conduct Market Research	Do Not Conduct Market Research
Time	Sufficient time is available before decision will be made.	Time pressure requires a decision before adequate research can be completed.
Data Availability	Firm does not have access to data but data can be obtained.	Firm already has relevant data or data cannot be obtained.
Nature of Decision	Decision is of considerable strategic or tactical importance.	Decision is NOT of considerable strategic or tactical importance.
Benefits versus Costs	Potential value of research exceeds costs of conducting research.	Costs of research exceed potential value of project.
	GO!	STOP!

Marketing Research in the Twenty-First Century

Marketing research, like all business activity, continues to change. Changes in communication technologies and the trend toward an ever more global marketplace have played a large role in many of these changes.

Communication Technologies

Virtually everyone is "connected" today. Increasingly, many people are "connected" nearly all the time. The typical college student spends hours a day on YouTube, Facebook, and other social networking sites that connect him or her to content and to others. Each move provides access to information but also leaves a record of data that tells a great deal about that particular consumer. Walmart gathers and stores more data every hour (about 3 petabytes) than exists in the collections of the Library of Congress. The amount of data now is not discussed in terms of megabytes or terabytes, but zetabytes (1 sextillion bytes—1 and 21 zeros).

The speed with which people exchange information continues to increase. During the 1970s, exchanging information overnight from anywhere in the continental United States was heralded as a near miracle of modern technology. Today, we can exchange information from nearly anywhere in the world to nearly anywhere else in the world almost instantly. A researcher can get on Skype, WhatsApp, or FaceTime, and interview decision makers anywhere in the world as long as an Internet connection is present. Our smart devices enable us to converse, but they also serve as a means of communication that can even involve marketing research data. Marketing researchers arm trained interviewers with iPads and similar devices that can display graphic images to respondents and provide a structured guide to the interview. Thus, the expressions "time is collapsing" and "distance is disappearing" capture the tremendous revolution in the speed and reach of our communication technologies.

As recently as the 1970s, most computer applications required expensive mainframe computers found only in very large corporations, major universities, and large governmental/military institutions. Researchers could expect to wait hours or even longer to get results from a statistical program involving 200 respondents. Today, even the most basic laptop computers can solve complicated statistical problems involving hundreds of thousands of data points in practically a nanosecond. Small, inexpensive appliances like a smartphone access software and data existing on a cloud (large servers that supply information and software to large numbers of Internet users), reducing the need for specialized software and a conventional personal computers. More and more, all manner of appliances like refrigerators, air conditioners, and even lightbulbs deposit information in a database.

Global Marketing Research

Marketing research has become increasingly global as more and more firms take advantage of markets that have few, if any, geographic boundaries. Some companies have extensive international marketing research operations. Nielsen Holdings NV, founded in New York in 1923 and still based in the Big Apple, but now incorporated in the Netherlands, is the world's largest marketing research company. Less than half of its business comes from the United States these days. Nielsen researches all manner of topics internationally. It is probably best known as the television ratings company. However, their consumer watch business is heavily involved in research for clients in consumer goods markets.

A Nielsen report describes U.S. consumers food spending patterns. Spending on food away from home continues to increase. U.S. consumers spend a little more than $800 billion on food away from home and a little less than $800 billion on food to prepare at home. The portion of spending on food away from home varies demographically based on age and children at home. Those organizations

AP Images/Matthew Mead

When the Nudge Is Gone!

Lots of marketing managers today are excited by the idea of nudge marketing. Instead of trying to convince a consumer to use a product, just give them a nudge. Companies from Carl's Jr. to Accuweather employ tactics that nudge consumers into becoming customers! A nudge is a psychological push that encourages a certain type of behavior. For example, research might suggest that a certain musty type of odor at low levels could increase wine store sales because it gives the impression of a wine cellar. Put the same amount of food on a smaller plate and the consumer is nudged to eat less.

In the mid-2010s, investors jumped on the subscription "kit" service bandwagon. Blue Apron exemplifies the "meal-kit" subscription service where consumers subscribe to receive a box of pre-portioned, fresh food to prepare a meal. The nudge aspect is that the receipt of everything in a box evokes excitement like opening a gift. However, perhaps more marketing research would have exposed some limitations to the excitement of the nudge. The number of consumers renewing subscriptions to such services is no longer growing at a fast pace and the opportunity in the subscription box business seems far less promising. Why did this happen? Results from

interviews of Blue Apron customers suggest that the excitement wears off right away because of:

1. The stress associated with using the foods before they go bad. Fresh fish, for example, should be used within 48 hours.
2. The hassle with not being home for deliveries.
3. Boredom because they choose your food.
4. Frustration from opening all those vacuum-sealed packages!
5. Conventional retailers like Kroger began offering meal kits without the need for a subscription.

A nudge works better when backed up with a unified message.

Sources: Soat, M. (2018), "Just a Little Nudge," *Marketing News*, (January), 3. Haddon, H. (2018), "Meal-Kit Start-Ups Losing Sizzle," *Wall Street Journal*, (January 9), B2.

interested in nutrition or opportunities might find value in research comparing U.S. food spending with France. French consumers spend about 21 percent of their budget on food, spending about three times as much for food at home compared to food away from home. Although when U.S. consumers think of France, a French restaurant often comes to mind, French consumers eat fewer restaurant meals and they are much more picky about food quality. An international restaurant company finds such research critically valuable in decision making. However, public policy officials also find value in the data. Perhaps food spending habits are related to obesity. French consumers on average are far less likely to be obese than their U.S. counterparts. Global insights are very useful.

Companies that conduct business globally must understand the nature of those particular markets and judge whether they require customized marketing strategies. For example, although the fifteen nations of the European Union (EU) share a single formal market, marketing research shows that Europeans do not share identical tastes for many consumer products. Marketing researchers have found no such thing as a typical European consumer; language, religion, climate, and centuries of tradition divide the EU nations. Scantel Research, a British firm that advises companies on color preferences, found inexplicable differences in Europeans' preferences in medicines. The French prefer to pop purple pills, but the English and Dutch favor white ones. Consumers in all the three countries dislike bright red capsules, which are big sellers in the United States. Marketing practices that work in one place may not work the same way in another.

The internationalization of research places greater demands on marketing researchers and heightens the need for research tools that allow us to **culturally cross-validate** research results, meaning that the empirical findings from one culture also exist and behave similarly in another culture. The development and application of these international research tools are an important topic in basic marketing research.

culturally cross-validate

To verify that the empirical findings from one culture also exist and behave similarly in another culture.

TIPS OF THE TRADE

- Throughout this text, a Tips of the Trade section provides helpful hints for using and doing marketing research. The first tip is to pay attention to these sections as helpful references.
- Customers and employees are valuable sources for input that leads to innovation in the marketplace and in the workplace.
- Business problems ultimately boil down to information problems because with the right information, the business can take effective action.
- Research plays a role before, during, and after key marketing decisions.

- Research helps design marketing strategies and tactics before action is taken.
- Once a plan is implemented, research monitors performance with key metrics providing valuable feedback.
- After a plan is implemented, research assesses performance against benchmarks and seeks explanations for the failure or success of the action.
- Research that costs more than the right decision could return should not be conducted.
- Marketing researchers must stay in touch with changes in media technology and the way consumers contact companies with those devices.

:: SUMMARY

Six key learning objectives structure Chapter 1. After reading the chapter, the student should be competent in each area described by a learning outcome.

1. Know what marketing research is and what it does for business. Marketing research is the application of the scientific method in searching for the truth about market and marketing phenomena. Research applications identify and define marketing opportunities and problems, generate and evaluate potentially innovative marketing ideas, monitor marketing performance, and describe the way consumers extract value from consumption. Thus, it is the intelligence-gathering function in business. This intelligence assists in decisions ranging from long-range planning to near-term tactical decisions. Although many business decisions are made "by the seat of the pants" or based on a manager's intuition, this type of decision making carries with it a large amount of risk. By first researching an issue and gathering intelligence on customers, competitors, and the market, a company can make a more informed decision. The result is less risky decision making.

2. Understand the difference between basic and applied marketing research. Applied marketing research seeks to facilitate managerial decision making. Basic or pure research seeks to increase knowledge of theories and concepts. Both are important. Applied research examples are emphasized in this text although practically all of the tools and techniques that are discussed are appropriate to either type of research. Some use the term *market research* to refer to applied research and *marketing research* to refer to basic research.

3. Understand how the role of marketing research changes with the orientation of the firm. Every company has a particular operating orientation. Production-oriented companies emphasize producing outputs as efficiently as possible. Generally, this leads to an emphasis on low-cost production and low-cost positioning in the marketplace. Product-oriented companies emphasize producing a sophisticated product that is also technologically advanced. Firms that are oriented around the marketing concept become very consumer oriented. Market-oriented firms view all employees as customers who need marketing intelligence to make good decisions. Stakeholder oriented companies try to balance concerns of all internal and external constituencies, including consumers. Marketing-oriented and stakeholder oriented companies tend to do more marketing research and emphasize marketing research more than do other firms.

4. Be able to integrate marketing research results into the strategic planning process. Marketing research is a means of implementing the marketing concept, the most central idea in marketing. The marketing concept says that a firm must be oriented both toward consumer satisfaction and toward long-run profitability (rather than toward short-run sales volume). Marketing research can help implement the marketing concept by identifying consumers' problems and needs, improving efficiency, and evaluating the effectiveness of marketing strategies and tactics. The development and implementation of a marketing strategy consist of four stages: (1) identifying and evaluating opportunities, (2) analyzing market segments and selecting target markets, (3) planning and implementing a marketing mix that will provide value to customers and meet the objectives of the organization, and (4) analyzing firm performance. Marketing research helps in each stage by providing information for strategic decision making. In particular, marketing research aimed at the marketing mix seeks information useful in making better decisions about product design, promotion, distribution, and pricing.

5. Know when marketing research should and should not be conducted. Marketing managers determine whether marketing research should be conducted based on (1) time constraints, (2) availability of data, (3) the nature of the decision to be made, and (4) the benefit of the research information versus its cost. Research should only be conducted when time is available, relevant data can be found and does not already exist, the decision can be shaped by information, and the benefits outweigh the cost of doing the research.

6. Appreciate the way that technology and internationalization continue to change the way we do marketing research. Technology has changed almost every aspect of marketing research. Modern computing and media technologies including smart devices (phones, watches, tablets, etc.) and social networking media facilitate data collection, study design, data analysis, data reporting. Researchers do have to be aware of the multiple ways that companies interact with consumers. Digital marketing closely integrates marketing practice and marketing research. Furthermore, as more companies do business outside their own borders, companies are doing research in a global marketplace. This places a greater emphasis on research that can assess the degree to which research tools can be applied and interpreted the same way in different cultures. Thus, research techniques often must culturally cross-validate results.

:: KEY TERMS AND CONCEPTS

applied marketing research, *8*
basic marketing research, *8*
culturally cross-validate, *21*
customer oriented, *9*
digital marketing, *7*
geodemographics, *15*
integrated marketing communication, *17*
integrated marketing mix, *17*
marketing channel, *16*

marketing concept, *9*
marketing metrics, *18*
marketing orientation, *9*
marketing research, *5*
online sentiment analysis, *11*
performance-monitoring research, *18*
pricing, *16*
product oriented, *9*
production oriented, *9*

promotion, *17*
promotion research, *17*
relationship marketing, *11*
scientific method, *8*
stakeholder orientation, *9*
supply chain, *16*
total value management, *18*

:: QUESTIONS FOR REVIEW AND CRITICAL THINKING

1. What are the two key ways that marketing creates value? How can marketing research facilitate marketing's efforts at value creation?
2. Define digital marketing? How can marketing research be seen as "the nerve center" for the organization?
3. Define a marketing orientation and a product orientation. Under what strategic orientation(s) is there a greater need for marketing research?
4. What are the four key questions helpful in understanding the value equation for a given firm?
5. Define *marketing research* and describe its task. How is it different from research in the physical sciences?
6. In what stage of the scientific method is creativity and creative thinking most important? Briefly explain.
7. Which of the following organizations are likely to use marketing research? Why? How?
   a. Kelloggs
   b. Waygo
   c. Fastenol
   d. The Federal Trade Commission
   e. Mayo Clinic
   f. Cengage
   g. Google
8. An automobile manufacturer is conducting research in an attempt to predict consumer auto preferences in the year 2022. Is this basic or applied research? Explain.
9. Define online sentiment analysis. How can it be helpful in brand management?
10. What is the definition of an *integrated marketing mix*? How might this affect the research a firm conducts?
11. Comment on the following statements:
    a. Marketing managers are paid to take chances with decisions. Marketing researchers are paid to reduce the risk of making those decisions.
    b. A marketing strategy can be no better than the information on which it is formulated.
    c. The purpose of research is to solve marketing problems.
    d. Digital marketing makes marketing research less able to be used.
12. List the conditions that help a researcher decide when marketing research should or should not be conducted.
13. How have technological changes and globalization of the marketplace affected marketing research?
14. What types of tools does the marketing researcher use more given the ever-increasing internationalization of marketing?

:: RESEARCH ACTIVITIES

1. Consider the opening vignette. What are some of the questions that consumer research will need to address to assess U.S. consumers' willingness to support the move to AVs (self-driving technology)? Do a search of the Internet. Is there evidence that each of these questions is being addressed as of now? What, if any, evidence can you find? Would the research change if the focus shifted to India from the U.S.?
2. Find examples of news articles from the most recent week involving the use of marketing research in making decisions about each element of the marketing mix. The *Wall Street Journal* is a good source for such stories.
3. Find a list of the ten most popular smartphone apps at the current time. Is there anything in common among the apps? Do they indicate any trends about consumers in general or a particular segment of consumers? Describe any such trends. Which companies may benefit from such trends?

Harnessing Big Data into Better Decisions

iStock.com/Opidanus

LEARNING OUTCOMES

After studying this chapter, you should be able to:

1. Know why concepts like data, big data, information, and intelligence represent value
2. Understand the four characteristics that describe data
3. Know what a decision support system is and the technology tools that help make it work
4. Recognize some of the major databases and how they are accessed
5. Understand the basic concept of marketing analytics and its potential to enhance decision-making
6. Be sensitive to the potential ethical issues of tracking consumers' behavior electronically

Chapter Vignette:

Marketing Research Is Good for You!

Todd lives in Toronto and works a 40-hour week. When not at work, Todd likes being a couch potato. He spends a lot of time watching the Maple Leafs, Blue Jays, and other sports events. He subscribes to a premium television service to make sure he has access to what he wants to see when he wants to see it. He uses apps to order pizza regularly and often swipes his loyalty card at nearby fast-food restaurants. Todd doesn't like to cook! He receives a personalized invitation to participate in a clinical trial of a new obesity drug.

Across town, Jane stops for Asian food in a restaurant and is handed an electronic tablet for a menu. The home page says, "Hungry after your workout?"

Unbeknownst to Todd, all of this behavior is known to Blue-Chip Marketing, a company that combines consumer data with health facts to assist marketing efforts for companies, many in health-related fields. From his Internet behavior, social networking, the fact that his phone is often near the couch, and he subscribes to the premium television service, Todd becomes very interesting to Blue-Chip. A statistical model used by Blue-Chip puts these things together to predict that Todd is obese. With these models, they can more carefully identify candidates for trials without even having to ask any questions.

Also unbeknownst to Jane, the fact that she checked in at her gym 90 minutes before going through the turnstile at the restaurant is already known and the restaurant informed. An electronic turnstile system detects her presence (or at least her phone's presence) and the message is pushed to the restaurant. The hostess can then quickly choose the best opening page for the tablet before giving it to the customer.

gpointstudio/Shutterstock.com

This is marketing today. Decisions that used to require considerable time and judgment can now be nearly or completely automated and they can be applied at the individual customer level. The heart of this process is data, big data we might say. This chapter provides an overview of how marketing research today uses data, including big data, to help feed into decision systems that hopefully improve marketing performance.[1]

Introduction

data
Recorded facts or measures of certain phenomena (things).

Data have always been the fuel that marketing research uses to create knowledge. As long as research itself has been conducted, data provide the answer to research questions, allow exploration of ideas, and provide the testing mechanism for hypotheses. In its basic form, **data** are recorded facts or measures of certain phenomena. The phenomena could include objects or events. Objects might include the amount of sales attributed to a specific product in a specific country, the color of a package, or the price of a product. Data about events may include survey responses indicating how consumers feel during a service experience, the amount a consumer purchases during a sale, or the amount of time a consumer spends on an online game.

Today, a typical notebook computer has a memory capacity of over 250 GB (gigabytes). 1 GB = 1,024 MB (megabytes and 1 MB = about 1 million characters). Marketing research grew rapidly in the 1950s and 1960s. Part of the growth was fueled by the growth in computing power, which made analytical analysis using computationally complex statistics possible. In 1956, the most powerful IBM mainframe computer contained 50 disks (hard drives) that enabled a storage capacity of almost 5 MB. Not until 1980 did a mainframe computer have a 1 MB memory capacity.[2] Even a simple computer today has more than 1,000 times the capacity of the most powerful computer of three decades ago.

The ability to store and record data continues to grow. So today many of our everyday activities leave data traces behind. When we use our smartphone, browse the Web, use Facebook, make a purchase at a retail outlet, or drive a car with our GPS navigation system, we are leaving behind data. Through these simple types of activities, we leave behind 2.5 quintillion bytes of data each day.[3] Thus, everything about data has become bigger except the devices that enable us to record and store that data. The tremendous growth in data has led many to use the term "big data." While there is considerable disagreement about just what comprises **big data**,[4] we can think of it as large quantities of data taken from multiple, varied sources that were not intended to be used together, but can be analytically applied to provide input to organizational decision-making. Because these large data sets include data that have been previously collected for purposes other than the one at hand, this data can also be referred to as **archival data**.

big data
Large quantities of data taken from multiple, varied sources that were not intended to be used together, but can be analytically applied to provide input to organizational decision-making.

archival data
Data that have been previously collected for some purpose other than the one at hand. (see secondary data)

Like the growth of marketing research that occurred in the early days of sophisticated computational devices, the advances in big data technology are leading to another surge in the growth of the marketing research industry. As a result, marketing researchers with strong analytical skills are in high demand. That growth is expected to create 2,720,000 data jobs by 2020 according to IBM.[5] Thus, a career in marketing research is a real possibility for many readers of this book.

This chapter discusses big data, data systems, and the role decision support systems and predictive analytics play in helping firms make informed marketing decisions. The decision support systems can be complicated and extensive, extending beyond the internal organizational walls. Marketing research plays an important role in making sense out of the glut of data now available. Today, data technology allows businesses to more easily integrate research findings into marketing strategy and operations.

Data, Information, and Intelligence Equal Value

In everyday language, terms like *information* and *data* are often used interchangeably. Researchers use these terms in specific ways that emphasize how useful each can be. Marketing managers may not be as intimately involved in finding and analyzing data; however, the decisions that they

Now that you are familiar with marketing research in general and the notion of conducting a research project, it is time to start thinking about the different type of information you will need to provide input into a firm's decision-making process. While most projects rely on collecting new data, you can gain valuable information from existing data. Therefore, as a first step in your research project, it is essential to familiarize yourself with data and data sources you have at your disposal. To start understanding data better, begin to look into a research topic of interest and find valuable information that will contribute to your project. This information can later be used in the background and introduction section of your project report.

make based on the input received from research will make or break the firm. In this way, data, information, and intelligence all have the potential to create value to the firm through better decision-making.

Data by themselves do not provide valuable input to decision-making. For instance, raw data showing the amount of Wi-Fi usage in Starbucks stores means very little. That data has to be put into a usable form. **Information** is data formatted (structured) to support decision making or define the relationship between two or more data points. **Market intelligence** is the subset of information that actually has some explanatory power enabling effective decisions to be made. So, there is more data than information, and more information than intelligence. Most data are irrelevant to any specific decision-making situation and therefore not always valuable. When data become information, their relevance is examined more closely through some analytical procedure. Conclusions are drawn from the structured data (i.e., information) to actually shape marketing decisions. The result is market intelligence derived from data analysis, and this should enable better decision-making, better value provided to customers in that their desires are more closely met and thereby more value for the firm in the form of improved organizational performance.[6]

Think again about the millions of facts recorded by Amazon each day. Each time a product is sold, facts about that transaction are recorded and become data. The data include the selling price of purchased items, the amount of time a shopper spent on a given Web page, the number of consumers visiting a page without making a purchase, comments left by consumers, and much more. One way that Amazon tries to use big data is in improving customer service.[7] Each time a consumer interacts with Amazon.com, data are recorded. So, Amazon systems know a lot about the consumer, including things like phone numbers, address, credit card or other payment information, purchase history, and data on previous chats, e-mails, or phone calls. When a customer initiates a complaint online, all of this information is available to provide better service. Sometimes in under a minute, the consumer receives a call from an Amazon call center. The representative already knows the person's name and number and has pulled up information on common complaints about the recent purchase. As a result, the consumer's problem can often be addressed in less than 2 minutes.

information

Data formatted (structured) to support decision making or define the relationship between two or more data points.

market intelligence

The subset of information that actually has some explanatory power enabling effective decisions to be made.

The Characteristics of Valuable Information

Four important characteristics do much to determine the value of information. Exhibit 2.1 provides an overview of the characteristics discussed on the next page.

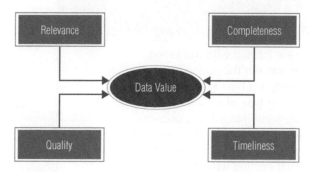

Relevance

relevance

The characteristic of data reflecting how pertinent these particular facts are to the situation at hand. When data are relevant, a change in that fact is associated with a change in an important outcome.

Relevance is the characteristic of data reflecting how pertinent these particular facts are to the situation at hand. Put another way, the facts are logically connected to the situation. Unfortunately, irrelevant data and information often creep into decision making. One particularly useful way to distinguish relevance from irrelevance is to think about how things change. Relevant data are facts about things that will materially alter the situation if they change. So, this simple question becomes important:

Will a change in the data coincide with a change in some important outcome?

American consumers' dietary trends are relevant to the restaurant industry. For instance, if Americans become more health-conscious, sales of doughnuts are likely to change. This may lead a restaurant like Dunkin' Donuts to rethink its product offering. However, information on the height of Mount Washington is irrelevant because it isn't going to change any time soon and even if it did, it would not affect U.S. doughnut preferences.

Completeness

information completeness

Having the right amount of information.

Information completeness refers to having the right amount of information. Marketing managers must have sufficient relevant information to develop explanations and predictions useful in decision-making. For example, managers trying to make a key decision about launching a technological innovation to their current software commission a quick research study in which consumers are asked to rate the perceived usefulness of the technological improvement. Based on the high usefulness scores, the managers launch the innovation only to find decreased sales and increased customer complaints. The complaints send a loud signal that the innovation made the product too complex. In their haste to act, the managers acted without input on this critical variable.

A follow-up study demonstrated that perceived complexity was equally as important in predicting adoption of new technologies and that as consumers see innovations as more complex, they find less value in the product. Theory can play a big role in helping to make information more complete and in this case a theory known as the technology acceptance model describes some key pieces of information in predicting the success of technological innovations.[8]

Quality

data quality

How accurately the data actually match reality.

Data quality reflects how accurately the gathered data actually match reality. High-quality data are valid and reliable—both concepts we'll turn to in detail later. In this chapter, we emphasize the vast quantity of data now available not in small part due to new technologies.

Not all data are equal in quality. Professional sales managers equip their salespeople with a plethora of technology to record information about sales calls. The data have numerous uses, not the least of which is allowing data systems to compute an expected value of the customer. In this way, the salesperson can know how much effort to put into winning each particular prospect. However, salespeople often are pinched for time and wait until the end of the day or even the end of the week to enter the required information. A pharmaceutical salesperson may wonder, "Did I spend 5 minutes or 12 minutes answering questions?" "Did the doctor make me wait 10 minutes or more?" "Did the doctor ask for samples or did I just leave them?" Each inaccurate answer lowers data quality and means the decision system's statistical models are less reliable. Managers can take advantage of technology by tracking their behavior through various location services tied to cellphones, tablets, and even product samples. The tracking devices record the time spent in each location automatically. However, sales managers might weigh the increased accuracy against the reality of management spying on its salespeople. The automated data collection also may need to be enhanced with salesperson input to explain nonroutine activities. Researchers offer this advice as a guide to enhanced data quality:[9]

1. Automate data collection and entry when feasible.
2. Inspect the data and cleanse for obvious errors.
3. Be mindful of the costs and benefits of efforts at improving data quality.

Timeliness

Timeliness means the data are not so old that they are irrelevant. Generally, timeliness requires highly current data. Imagine car companies currently trying to predict the types of cars that would interest consumers. Think of all the changes in the operating environment that have taken place since 2008. The economy went from boom to bust and consumer confidence dropped consequently. Fuel prices have fluctuated wildly ranging anywhere from a U.S. average for regular gas of $1.60 per gallon in late 2008 to nearly $4.10 per gallon in July of that same year only to briefly fall to nearly $1.60 by the first of 2009. By mid 2018, prices appeared reasonably stable at about $2.80 per gallon. Most auto executives believe gas prices are relevant to the automotive market and therefore desire input from such data. Car preference will change with these environmental factors, so data collected in one time period may not be entirely accurate. Similarly, imagine how the dramatic pace of technological change in the electronics industry hinders predicting consumer acceptance of new mobile phone models. The term **market dynamism** represents the rate of change in environmental and competitive factors.[10] Highly dynamic markets mean greater risk in relying on data, particularly on untimely data.

timeliness

Means the data are not so old that they are irrelevant.

market dynamism

Represents the rate of change in environmental and competitive factors.

Global Marketplace

By now, marketers around the world realize the potential marketplace is the entire world. A start-up company in Topeka, Kansas, only needs a website and the company's business isn't just in Kansas anymore. Large companies use a plethora of technology ranging from handheld tablets to satellites to gather and exchange data in an effort to keep track of business details globally.

Consider a simple example. At any moment, United Parcel Service (UPS) can track the status of any shipment around the world. UPS drivers use handheld electronic clipboards called delivery information acquisition devices (DIADs) to record appropriate data about each pickup or delivery. The data are then entered into the company's main computer for record-keeping and analysis. A satellite telecommunications system allows UPS to track any shipment for a customer. Consumers also can get near real-time information on the status of a delivery as information from the DIADs is available through www.ups.com.

To the Point

"Facts are stubborn things."

—RONALD REAGAN

Decision Support Systems

Marketing research serves four possible business functions. These functions align with purposes of marketing research:

1. Foundational—answers basic questions such as, "What consumers or consumer segments should the company serve and with what types of products?"
2. Testing—addresses things like new product concepts, product innovations, pricing, or promotional ideas. "How effective will they be?"
3. Issues—examine how specific, broad issues impact the firm. "How will a new competitor, a change in organizational structure, or increased investments in advertising influence the company?"
4. Performance—this type of research monitors specific metrics, including financial statistics like profitability and delivery times with questions such as, "How is variation in product lead-time affecting performance metrics?"

Bringing Home the Bacon!

Marketers employ big data because it helps them bring home the bacon. A McKinsey study found that companies that orient their marketing and sales decision making around results from the analysis of big data see a 15 to 20 percent improvement in return on investment (ROI). That's an attractive marginal return that likely will send more firms looking for marketing researchers who can make sense of big data.

Sometimes, bringing home the bacon becomes quite literal. A research project using data mining approaches analyzed consumer ratings of nearly 1,000,000 new menu items in an effort to reveal what ingredients most make food taste better. The results are clear. Nothing improves the flavor of food items like sandwiches more than bacon. Fast-food restaurants can use this data in their new product designs to help, well, bring home more bacon! Bacon has its limits, though. The project results showed that consumers did not

tend to rate dessert items that contained added bacon any better than the same items without the bacon. Is this the power of big data or big bacon?

Sources: McKinsey and Company (2013), "Big Data, Analytics and the Future of Marketing and Sales," *Forbes*, (7/22), http://www.forbes.com/sites/mckinsey/2013/07/22/big-data-analytics-and-the-future-of-marketing-sales/, accessed March 19, 2014. Thusco, A. (2014), "How Big Data Is Revolutionizing the Food Industry," Wired.com, (February), http://www.wired.com/insights/2014/02/bigdata-revolutionizing-food-industry/, accessed March 19, 2014.

The performance category is most relevant in decision support systems. Monitored metrics feed into automated decision-making systems and/or trigger reports for specific managers. These form the basis of a decision support system and best typify the way marketing research assists managers with day-to-day operational decisions.

A marketing **decision support system (DSS)** is a system that helps decision-makers confront problems through direct interaction with computerized databases and systems. A DSS stores and transforms data into organized information that is easily accessible to marketing managers and other specific internal customers of information. DSSs save managers countless hours by making decisions in minutes or even seconds that might otherwise take days or weeks.

Modern decision support systems greatly facilitate **customer relationship management (CRM)**. A CRM system is the part of the DSS that characterizes the interactions between firm and customer. It brings together information about customers, including sales data, market trends, marketing promotions, and the way consumers respond to them based on customer preferences. A CRM system describes customer relationships in sufficient detail so that managers, salespeople, customer service representatives, and perhaps the customers themselves can access information directly, match customer needs with satisfying product offerings, remind customers of service requirements, and know what other products a customer has purchased or might be interested in purchasing. CRM systems can compute the overall lifetime value of each customer. This data point often proves a key metric for triggering decisions.

The CRM systems are specifically responsible for promotions customized to individual customers. Casinos use loyalty or "player's" cards that the customer swipes with each activity. All this information gets stored and eventually the casino knows how to manage the customer by directing offers that the customer's previous behavior suggests a liking-for. Auto service centers can use information about a consumer's car to schedule routine maintenance and help diagnose problems before they occur.

Exhibit 2.2 illustrates how data systems work with a decision support system. Raw, unsummarized data are input to the DSS. Data collected in marketing research projects are a major source of this input, but the data may be purchased or collected by accountants, sales managers, production managers, or company employees other than marketing researchers. Effective marketers spend a great deal of time and effort collecting information for input into

decision support system (DSS)

A computer-based system that helps decision-makers confront problems through direct interaction with databases and systems.

customer relationship management (CRM)

Part of the DSS that characterizes interactions between firm and customer.

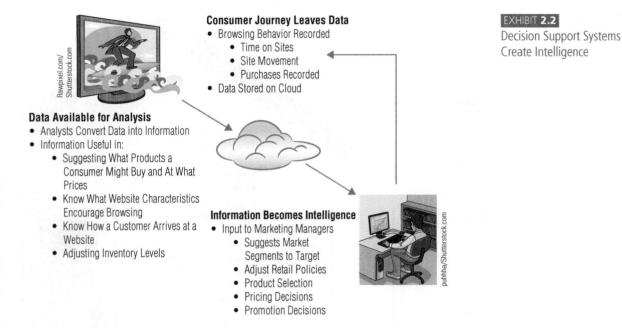

Rawpixel.com/
Shutterstock.com

Consumer Journey Leaves Data
- Browsing Behavior Recorded
  - Time on Sites
  - Site Movement
  - Purchases Recorded
- Data Stored on Cloud

Data Available for Analysis
- Analysts Convert Data into Information
- Information Useful in:
  - Suggesting What Products a Consumer Might Buy and At What Prices
  - Know What Website Characteristics Encourage Browsing
  - Know How a Customer Arrives at a Website
  - Adjusting Inventory Levels

Information Becomes Intelligence
- Input to Marketing Managers
  - Suggests Market Segments to Target
  - Adjust Retail Policies
  - Product Selection
  - Pricing Decisions
  - Promotion Decisions

puhhha/Shutterstock.com

EXHIBIT 2.2
Decision Support Systems Create Intelligence

the decision support system. Useful information is the output of a DSS. A decision support system requires both databases and software. For firms operating across national borders, the DSS becomes part of its global information system.

Databases and Data Warehousing

A **database** is a collection of raw data arranged logically and organized in a form that can be stored and processed by a computer. A customer mailing list is one type of database. Population characteristics may be recorded by state, county, and city in another database.

Data warehousing is the process allowing important day-to-day operational data to be stored and organized for simplified access. More specifically, a **data warehouse** is the multitiered computer storehouse of current and historical data. Data warehouse management requires that the detailed data from operational systems be extracted, transformed, placed into logical partitions (for example, daily data, weekly datas, etc.), and stored in a consistent and secure manner. Organizations with data warehouses may integrate databases from both inside and outside the company. Data warehousing allows for sophisticated analysis, such as data mining, discussed later in the book.

More and more, data storage exists in **cloud storage**, meaning data are stored on devices that make the files directly available via the Internet. This means that any authorized user from any computer, smartphone, or tablet with Internet accessibility. Salesforce.com is one of the largest providers of CRM systems.[11] They make the data gathered about customers easy to access by subscribers anywhere by utilizing cloud storage.

Input Management

How does data end up in a data warehouse? In other words, how is the input managed? Input includes all the numerical, text, voice, behavioral, and image data that enter the DSS. Systematic accumulation of pertinent, timely, and accurate data is essential to the success of a decision support system.

DSS managers, systems analysts, and programmers are responsible for the decision support system as a whole, but many functions within an organization provide input data. Marketing researchers, accountants, corporate librarians, sales personnel, production managers, and many others within the organization help collect data and provide input for the DSS. Input data can also come from external sources.

Exhibit 2.3 shows six major sources of data input: internal records, proprietary marketing research, salesperson input, behavioral tracking, Web tracking, and outside vendors and external distributors of data. Each source can provide valuable input.

database

A collection of raw data arranged logically and organized in a form that can be stored and processed by a computer.

data warehousing

The process allowing important day-to-day operational data to be stored and organized for simplified access.

data warehouse

The multitiered computer storehouse of current and historical data.

cloud storage

Data files stored on devices that make them directly accessible via the Internet.

Six Major Sources of
Marketing Input for Decision
Support Systems

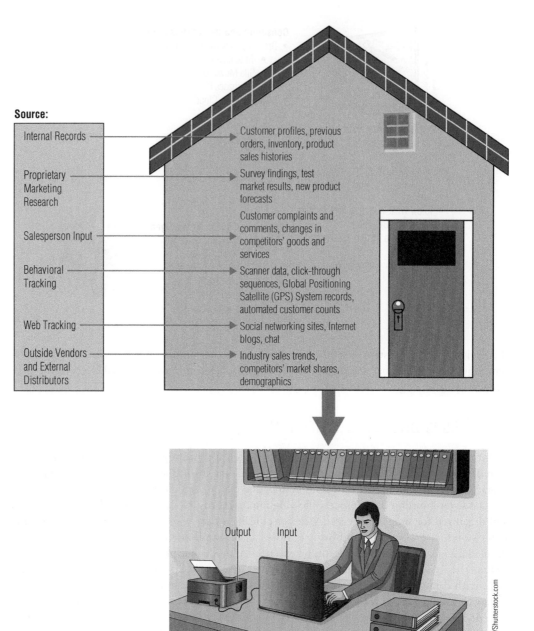

Internal Records

Internal records, such as accounting reports of sales and inventory figures, provide considerable data that may become useful information for marketing managers. An effective data collection system establishes orderly procedures to ensure that data about costs, shipments, inventory, sales, and other aspects of regular operations are routinely collected and entered into the computer.

Proprietary Marketing Research

proprietary marketing research

The gathering of new data to investigate specific company problems.

Research projects conducted to study specific company problems generate data; this is **proprietary marketing research**. Providing managers with nonroutine data that otherwise would not be available is a major function of proprietary marketing research. Earlier, we discussed four categories of research. Proprietary marketing research may involve either or both of the "testing" and "issues" types of research.

Salesperson Input

Salespeople work in firms' external environments, so they commonly provide essential marketing data. Sales representatives' reports frequently alert managers to changes in competitors' prices and new product offerings. Salespeople also hear customer complaints. As complaint trends become evident, this data may become marketing intelligence that leads to a change in service delivery.

Behavioral Tracking

Modern technology provides new ways of tracking human behavior. Global positioning satellite (GPS) systems allow management to track the whereabouts of delivery personnel at all times. This is the same system that provides directions through an automobile's navigation system. For example, if your delivery person takes a quick break for nine holes of golf or decides to stop at Neil's Bar for a couple of beers mid-afternoon, management can spot these as deviations from the appropriate delivery route. Smartphones generally have GPS capabilities that potentially allow systems to track customer whereabouts and maybe even driving patterns.

    Retailers also track purchase behavior at the point of sale. **Scanner data** refers to the accumulated records resulting from in-store point-of-sale data recordings. The **Universal product code**, or UPC, is the bar code on a product containing information on the category of goods, the manufacturer, and product identification based on size, flavor, color, and so on. This is what the optical scanner actually reads. Each time a reader scans a bar code, the information can be stored. Bar code readers are used in many places where data needs to be recorded and used, including in package delivery and on the bag check tickets at the airport.

scanner data

The accumulated records resulting from in-store point-of-sale data recordings.

universal product code

UPC is the bar-coded information that contains product information that can be read by optical scanners.

Web Tracking

The Internet greatly facilitates customer behavior tracking. For instance, Google tracks the "click-through" sequence of customers. Therefore, if a customer is searching for information on refrigerators and then goes to BestBuy.com, Google tracks this behavior and uses the information to calculate the value that a clickthrough provides as an advertising offer to Best Buy. For instance, if one out of every 500 users that go from a Google search buys a refrigerator at Best Buy, Google can tell them what the referral is worth. The tracking data also allows Google and other search engines to know how much to charge advertisers for premium listings in search results. Search for "used cars" and the results indicated by background shading (usually) are listings that Google sells as advertising. Companies listed on top of a list of search results pay more than do companies listed near the bottom of the list.

    Some marketing companies serve as search-engine optimizers. A **search-engine optimizer (SEO)** mines Internet data to provide consulting to firms who wish to move up the listing of hits for terms related to their product category. Given that so many purchases involve an Internet search early in the process, firms see it as critical that they appear somewhere near the top of the search results, and they are willing to pay to get to the top, one way or another.

GPS systems come in many forms on all sorts of devices. GPS allows management to track delivery personnel, the things being delivered, and even customer whereabouts.

search-engine optimizer (SEO)

Mines Internet data to provide consulting to firms who wish to move up the listing of hits for terms related to their product category.

Bruce Gifford/Moment Mobile/Getty Images

Marketing researchers also monitor postings and create vehicles such as contests that invite consumers to leave ideas and feedback about the brand. Other sources for information include Internet blogs and chat rooms, where consumers share information about their own experiences, including complaints that serve as a type of warning to other consumers. BlueKai, part of Oracle, and eXelate, part of the Nielsen Company, are companies that specialize in Web tracking.[12] BlueKai trades data on over 200 million U.S. consumers.

Some companies also supply real-time data on Web analytics. Do more consumers visit Amazon.com or walmart.com? Alexa (now part of Amazon Web Services – aws) provides access to this data. A visit to this website reveals the answer to that question and also provides a demographic breakdown of the visitors to each website. Are women more frequent visitors to Amazon relative to men? Is instagram really losing popularity worldwide? This information may be useful when choosing a possible Internet retail channel for goods.

Networks and Electronic Data Interchange

electronic data interchange (EDI)

Type of exchange that occurs when one company's computer system is integrated with another company's system.

Electronic data interchange (EDI) systems integrate one company's computer system directly with another company's system. Much of the input to a company's decision support system may come through networks from other companies' computers. Companies such as Computer Technology Corporation and Microelectronics market data services allow corporations to exchange business information with suppliers or customers. For example, every evening Walmart transmits millions of characters of data about the day's sales to its apparel suppliers. Wrangler, a supplier of blue jeans, receives the data and applies a model that sends orders to replenish Walmart stock. This DSS lets Wrangler's managers know when to send specific quantities of specific sizes and colors of jeans to specific stores from specific warehouses.

open source information

Structured data openly shared between companies.

Many firms share information in an effort to encourage more innovation. **Open source information** is a term that captures structured data openly shared between companies. Boeing builds innovative aircraft, including the Dreamliner 787 passenger jet and the Phantom Ray unmanned airborne system, with sophisticated stealth technology designed for military applications. Hundreds of suppliers manufacture components for these aircraft. Boeing came to a realization around the turn of the century that their core competency is more in systems integration than in manufacturing.[13] As a result, Boeing designs the electronic systems for nearly all of these components; but to do so, the suppliers need open access to Boeing data. Without this access, Boeing's pace of innovation would be slower.

Database Sources and Vendors

Some organizations specialize in recording certain marketing and consumer information. In some cases, these companies make that data available either for free or for a fee. Computer technology has changed the way many of these organizations supply data, favoring the development of computerized databases. Many organizations specialize in the collection and publication of high-quality information. One outside vendor for data is Nielsen. As mentioned earlier, Nielsen provides television program ratings, audience counts, and information about the demographic composition of television viewer groups.

Media sources like *Advertising Age*, the *Wall Street Journal*, *Sales and Marketing Management*, and other trade- and business-oriented publications are important sources of information. These publications keep managers up-to-date about the economy, competitors' activities, and other aspects of the marketing environment. In addition, they provide demographic and lifestyle statistics about their particular readers that can be very useful in advertisers' media planning.

Data Archives

Many government agencies around the world are important sources of data. The *Statistical Abstract of the United States* is a typical example of a data archive. The *Abstract* provides a comprehensive statistical summary of U.S. social, political, and economic organization. Users can access the *Abstract* as well as detailed data from the U.S. Census with projections through the current year via the Internet at http://www.census.gov.

Numerous computerized search and retrieval systems and electronic databases are available as subscription services or in libraries. Today, businesspeople access online information search and retrieval services, such as Dow Jones News Retrieval and Bloomberg Financial Markets, without leaving their offices. In fact, some information services can be accessed from remote locations via digital wireless devices.

Data wholesalers put together consortia of data sources into packages offered to municipal, corporate, and university libraries for a fee. Information consumers then access the data through these libraries. Some of the better-known *databases* include Wilson Business Center, Hoovers, ProQuest, INFOTRAC, LexisNexis, and Dow Jones News Retrieval Services. These databases provide all types of information, including recent news stories and data tables charting statistical trends. These companies sometimes become **data retailers** by selling data access directly to the end consumer. For instance, Hoovers data can either be purchased in a single transaction, through a subscription service, or by integrating the data access through cloud storage. A company may want to research the market potential for a new location in a certain area. For instance, a company that produces and sells devices for dental braces may wish to generate a database concerning all the orthodontists in a given metropolitan area. Data retailers can help with these kinds of data needs.

The DIALOG catalog is a useful source for finding databases. The DIALOG catalog can be searched through ProQuest, which is available through many university libraries. It identifies hundreds of databases in areas including business, science, the law, and humanities. A typical database may have a million or more records, each consisting of a one- or two-paragraph abstract summarizing the major points available in a given source.

data wholesalers
Companies that put together consortia of data sources into packages that are offered to municipal, corporate, and university libraries for a fee.

data retailers
Companies that provide access to data directly to the end consumer for a fee.

• • • • • • •

Example data available at alexa.com. This data compares Facebook, Twitter, YouTube, and Pinterest Internet Traffic Rankings.

Source: Alexa Internet, Inc.

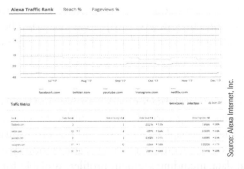

• • • • • • •

Hoovers offers retail access to data in three ways.

Source: www.hoovers.com

Is Your Smartphone Keeping Tabs on You?

Marie C Fields/Shutterstock.com

The notion that firms use data tools to watch and track online consumer behavior is not new. In fact, we are used to reappearing ads that follow us around from website to website as we complete our online shopping. But what if that happens outside of the Web retail environment? With the advancement of new Web tracking systems combined with GPS technology, firms now have the capability to track your physical location with the help of your smartphone. Unaware to the individual, ads embedded in apps identify a person's location and other personal information tied to the corresponding app. For example, the type of app reveals demographic information, daily habits, and consumption preferences in addition to location-specific details. Another way apps track your location is through photos stored in your camera roll on your phone. By enabling camera-roll sharing to post pictures on apps, location-identifiable details from these photos are accessible to the app itself. Firms use this information to identify likely routes to push location-specific advertisements or to learn more about your behavior. Yet, most consumers are not aware of being tracked by their own smartphone

device. So, next time you use an app or post a photo with your smartphone, think about how much information you are willing to share with the world.

Sources: Douglas, N. (2017), "How Apps Use Your Photos to Track Your Location," *Lifehacker*, (October 24), https://lifehacker.com/how-apps-use-your-photos-to-track-your-location-1819802266, accessed November 30, 2017. Dellinger, A. (2017), "Mobile Ads Invade Privacy: Advertisements Can Track Your Location," *International Business Times*, (October 18), http://www.ibtimes.com/mobile-ads-invade-privacy-advertisements-can-track-your-location-2603324, accessed April 2, 2018.

Several types of databases from outside vendors and external distributors are so fundamental to decision support systems that they deserve further explanation. The following sections discuss statistical databases, financial databases, and video databases in slightly more detail.

Statistical Databases

Statistical databases contain numerical data for market analysis and forecasting. Often, demographic, sales, and other relevant marketing variables are recorded by geographical area. Geographic information systems use these *geographical databases* and powerful software to prepare computer maps of relevant variables. Nielsen acquired a market segmentation system known as PRIZM and makes a host of statistical data, including segment profiles, available for free online. If a company needs more specific information on a segment, it can engage Nielsen for a fee. A host of other statistical sources are available, including government sources such as the U.S. Census, the FCC, and even the CIA, which maintains a database of country profiles known as the CIA *Factbook*. Other statistical databases include Datastream, part of Thomason-Reuters, Wharton Research Data Services (WRDS), and PolicyMap.

Financial Databases

Some statistical databases specialize in financial data. CompuStat publishes an extensive financial database on thousands of companies, broken down by industry and other criteria. To illustrate the depth of this pool of information, CompuStat's Global Advantage offers extensive data on about 100,000 securities in dozens of countries in Europe, the Pacific Rim, and North America. The database also contains statistics on hundreds of banking institutions in the United States.

Video Databases

Video databases and streaming media are having a major impact on the marketing of many goods and services. For example, movie studios provide clips of upcoming films, and advertising agencies put television commercials on the Internet (see http://ispot.tv or *Ad Age's* http://www.creativity-online.com, for example). YouTube.com is the world's largest video

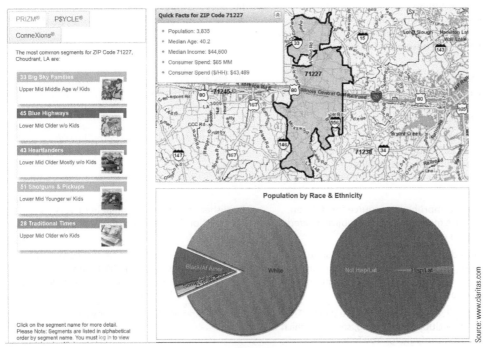

Example of statistical data available from Nielsen's PRIZM data.

(Source: http://www.claritas.com/MyBestSegments/Default.jsp?ID=20&pageName=ZIP%2BCode%2BLookup& menuOption=ziplookup#)

YouTube provides a digital archive that can be mined for data or used as a vehicle to test ideas and concepts.

EXHIBIT 2.4 Some Database Sources That Are Widely Available

Database	Description	Availability
ProQuest	A collection of databases that include published works such as academic articles, trade periodicals, newspapers, and some statistical databases.	Widely available through university libraries. The libraries pay for the services and grant access to patrons.
LexisNexis	A wide degree of business and media-related content, including business publications, newspapers, and other media sources from 1970. Also maintain a large consumer database (half a billion consumers) including business contacts.	Publication data often available through libraries via library subscription. Consumer data and big data services available for a fee.
U.S. Census	Tremendous amounts of historic and current data about the U.S. population and trends but also a lot of information about various U.S. industries and trends.	Access at www.census.gov. Access to data tables and site is free.
CIA Factbook	Contains statistical data on the countries of the world including demographic data, lifestyle data including religious affiliations, and basic data on commerce and the economy in the country.	Access at: https://www.cia.gov/library/publications/the-world-factbook/. Access is free.
Market Share Reporter	The most comprehensive source for data on the relative market share for publicly traded companies across many industries.	Published by Gale and available on a subscription fee basis. Available at some libraries.
Nielsen	Provides data on consumer media usage, including ratings for television programming and networks. Data from PRIZM segmentation also available among others.	Media data available on a fee for service or subscription basis. Basic PRIZM data on U.S. communities provided free with more detailed data available for a fee.
YouTube	Largest collection of videos in the world. The collection includes advertising, some of which is produced exclusively for YouTube.	YouTube.com (I think you know it). Free.
Alexa	Provides Web analytics for public websites. The data include visit information, United States and global rank, demographics of visitors, and more.	Alexa.com. Basic data available for free. More elaborate data and services available for a fee.

database, and companies routinely produce video commercials for release on YouTube. Each advertisement on YouTube will display how many times the ad has been "viewed" through that particular link. Such data serve as an indicator of the ad's reach and effectiveness. These days, most Super Bowl advertisements can be seen online even before the big game airs. Superbowl-commericals.org operates a site dedicated just to making Super Bowl ads and news about them available online.

The Internet and Research

The Internet in general provides tremendous access to data and information sources. An estimated 3,885,567,619 (3.88 billion) people use the Internet and about 50 percent of those live in Asia.[14] Even though half of all Asians have access to the Internet, as opposed to nearly three of four North Americans, the sheer size of the population means that most Internet users are in Asia. In contrast to the past, a computer is not required as increasingly consumers, particularly in lesser developed parts of the world, access the Internet through a smartphone or similar device. In fact, more people have smartphones than have access to a flush toilet! Web tracking means that there are billions, if not trillions, of traces of data left behind. Consumers are doing lots of surfing and leaving behind data with every site they visit.

Can Alexa Read My Mind?

How powerful are today's data tools? Some may say they are too powerful! What if a firm could accurately predict what you were going to buy before you actually placed an order? Would that be a good thing? To get an idea of how that might work, consider how often a consumer receives suggestions from a Web retail site shows what other customers "like you" purchased when they purchased the item being viewed. Data systems like these use previous consumer data to suggest what gets purchased together. Amazon combines data like this with personal information entered into their system, such as from an Amazon Prime account, as well as one's browsing history to build models of what a particular consumer is going to buy. Amazon believes they are so accurate with these predictions that they would like to ship things to consumers before they even buy them. Currently, the idea

is to ship something to a distribution center near a consumer's home to reduce the delivery time once an order is actually placed. However, the technology exists to actually have Amazon make the "purchase" without the consumer even making a selection. Technology like this, although convenient, is controversial. Amazon also has the capability of delivering those products with a fleet of GPS-directed drones that could take the item that was not purchased and drop it off right to your front lawn. No need to even ask Alexa! What do you think about that?

Sources: Bensinger, G. (2014), "Amazon Wants to Ship Your Package before You Buy It," *Wall Street Journal*, (1/21), B1. https://www.geekwire.com/2015/amazon-adds-automatic-ordering-capabilities-to-washing-machines-dog-bowls-printers-and-more/, accessed December 2, 2017. Manjoo, F. (2013), "Why Bezos's Drone Is More than a Joke," *Wall Street Journal*, (12/5), B1–B7.

Source: www.amazon.com

Navigating the Internet

Parties that furnish information on the World Wide Web are called **content providers**. Content providers maintain websites that contain information about the entity as well as links to other sites. Increasingly, users are able to add content to websites as well. In these cases, such as Wikipedia, the users manage the content. Most Web browsers also allow the user to enter a **Uniform Resource Locator (URL)** into the program. The URL is really just a website address that Web browsers recognize. Twenty years ago, a consumer often needed to know the URL of a site to find it on the Net. Today, modern search engines work so well that one or two key words will generally pull up the intended site or, if not the intended site, one very similar to it!

Most **keyword searches** are formed by simply entering a name or phrase. A student doing a term paper on Winston Churchill might simply put "Churchill" in the search window. A Boolean search is a search that combines relevant key words in very specific ways. The operators include words like *and*, *or*, and *not*. So, a search of Churchill will bring up thousands of hits, including Churchill Downs, the home of the Kentucky Derby, as well as a cigar store or two. However, enter "war" and "Churchill" and the search becomes quickly limited to sites that contain both words; enter "war and Churchill" and the search looks for content with that exact expression.

Modern data mining approaches can actually automate Web searches using Boolean operators. Researchers often are charged with monitoring negative information about a brand.[15] When researchers either manually or through an automated system detect negative information near the top of search results for a brand, the firm can take actions to counter the negative information by placing other content online that results in the negative information not appearing so close to

To the Point

> *"The Net is 10.5 on the Richter scale of economic change."*
>
> —NICHOLAS NEGROPONTE

content providers
Parties that furnish information on the World Wide Web.

Uniform Resource Locator (URL)
A website address that Web browsers recognize.

keyword search
Takes place as the search engine searches through millions of Web pages for documents containing the keywords.

the top of the results. In fact, the suppression of negative online associations, which many times includes false information about individuals or brands, has spawned an industry of its own as companies specialize in taking such counter measures.

Environmental Scanning

The Internet is an especially useful source for scanning many types of environmental changes. **Environmental scanning** entails all information gathering designed to detect changes in the external operating environment of the firm. Even things beyond the control of the firm can have a significant impact on firm performance.

Information Technology

The ability to use behavioral data that consumers generate when interacting with the Internet through any type of device has revolutionized the way some marketing functions are implemented. Today's information technology uses "smart agents" or "intelligent agents" to deliver customized content to a viewer's desktop. **Smart agent software** is capable of learning an Internet user's preferences and automatically searching out information and distributing the information to a user's computer. Numerous vendors offer smart agent software for sale or lease. Companies that purchase software hope to leverage the information consumers leave behind into more customized and therefore more effective sales appeals.

Push or Pull?

Data and information are delivered to consumers or other end users via either **pull technology** or **push technology**. Conventionally, consumers request information from a Web page and the browser then determines a response. Thus, the consumer is essentially asking for information through an e-mail, interactive chat, or automated response. In this case, it is said to be pulled through the channel. The opposite of pull is push. Push technology sends data to a user's device without a request being made. In other words, data analytics and systems that identify the consumer are used to guess what information might entice a consumer into engaging with the company. The goal is to turn a consumer into a customer!

Considering that there are more "smart" devices today than there are humans on Earth, the number of opportunities to push content to consumers is almost unlimited. Push technology delivers personalized information to consumers without any intentional effort on the consumers'

environmental scanning

Entails all information gathering designed to detect changes in the external operating environment of the firm.

smart agent software

Software capable of learning an Internet user's preferences and automatically searching out information in selected websites and then distributing it.

pull technology

Consumers request information from a Web page and the browser then determines a response; the consumer is essentially asking for the data.

push technology

Sends data to a user's computer without a request being made; software is used to guess what information might be interesting to consumers based on the pattern of previous responses.

● ● ● ● ● ● ●

Retailers like Michael Kors make good advantage of push technology.

part. Even if by happenstance you browse at a retail site like Michael Kors, for the next few days you may see banner ads for an item that was on a page you browsed previously. That is an example of push technology. However, that's the tip of the iceberg. One doesn't have to be browsing to receive push messages. Apple's iBeacon system allows an iPhone's location to be detected to a matter of inches. Retailers can place iBeacons in their store to detect other iPhones or other systems running Apple software.[16] If something in your browsing history indicates an interest in a product in the store, a text message or e-mail can be pushed to the phone once a consumer gets within its proximity. In essence, the iBeacon or similar technologies for other brands of smart agents function as a Near Field Communication Device.

Near Field Communication (NFC) Devices

RFID stands for radio frequency identification. A tiny chip, which can be woven onto a fabric, placed in packaging, attached to a card, including credit cards, or otherwise affixed to virtually any product, sends a radio signal that identifies that particular entity uniquely. When the tag comes into proximity of a reader, the reader records the programmed information allowing products and/or consumers to be tracked virtually anywhere. The U.S. military pioneered RFID technology as a logistical tool and Walmart was a leading proponent of the technology based on the improved ability to track goods and feed information into its global information system.[17] Wholesalers take advantage of data created through an RFID system that helps them rotate stock to make sure that the oldest stock goes out first.[18] Pharmaceutical companies also use RFID tags to track the whereabouts of medicines. RFID provides a major source of big data input.[19]

Retailers use RFID technology both to offer customers uniquely tailored promotions and to keep track of customers' shopping behavior. La Croissanterie, a fresh but fast-food chain based in Paris, replaced its traditional cardboard loyalty card with a plastic wallet-sized card that includes an RFID chip.[20] Once a customer enters the store, he or she can tap a smart poster that contains NFC (near field communication) technology. **NFC** works like a Wi-Fi system communicating with specific devices within a defined space like inside of a retail unit. The NFC essentially talks to

RFID

Abbreviation for radio-frequency-identification tags that use a small microchip to communicate with data systems.

NFC

Abbreviation for near-field-communication or Wi-Fi-like systems communicating with specific devices within a defined space like inside of a retail unit or near a poster billboard.

• • • • • •

Loyalty cards collect a wealth of data, but apps now do the job even more efficiently.

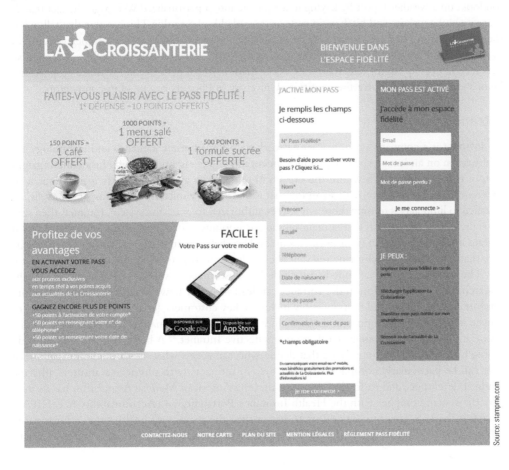

Source: stampme.com

the RFID chip. The smart poster identifies the customer's loyalty status, offers them a promotion based on this status, records all purchases, and updates the customer's status automatically (no hole punchers or stamps used here) but, most importantly from a research standpoint, records all the customer data no matter which of about 200 La Croissanterie units the customer visits. Some market researchers believe that soon, information from RFID chips will be integrated so that when a consumer enters a shopping list into a smartphone, lights may be able to direct the instore consumer to product options based on what is entered onto the list.[21]

As with the previous example, NFC push marketing no longer requires an RFID device as smartphones can function in much the same way. Smartphone technologies also allow consumers to download applications that allow their phones to be their loyalty card. Market researchers can use NFC data to track shoppers' movement through a store as well. By doing so, they can reveal how products can be placed in stores to increase the length of the path that a consumer takes through the store and, as a result, increase unplanned sales from that customer.[22] Once the consumer accepts such an app, data systems go to work recording information aimed at finding out just what makes customers like him/her receptive to offers. In fact, La Croissanterie offers its loyal customers the option of a loyalty app, which performs functions like the RFID card.

Increasingly, marketing efforts involve combinations of push and pull efforts. A pop-up generated by a smart agent may entice a consumer to click-through or begin a chat seeking further information. In addition, the more consumers come to accept mobile marketing efforts, the more marketers are likely to even further increase their efforts at employing information technology to enhance value.[23] Currently, in the United States, marketing efforts that actually function through the telephone such as calls or SMS require that consumers opt-in. This is not the case throughout the world, and thus the tools for marketing with push technology vary from place to place. In the end though, all of these tools leave data behind and that data feeds into research.

Cookies

cookies

Small data files that a content provider can save onto the computer of someone who visits its website.

Cookies, in computer terminology, are small data files that record a user's Web usage history. If a person looks up a weather report by keying in a zip code into a personalized Web page, the fact that the user visited the website and his/her zip code are recorded in the cookie. This is a clue that tells where the person lives (or maybe where he or she may be planning to visit). Websites can then direct information to that consumer based on information in the cookie. So, someone in College Station, Texas, may receive pop-up ads for restaurants in College Station. If that person visits graduate program sites, he or she may receive an advertisement from University of Phoenix or one of its competitors.

Intranets

intranet

A company's private data network that uses Internet standards and technology.

An **Intranet** is a company's private data network that uses Internet standards and technology. The information on an Intranet—data, graphics, video, and voice—is available only inside the organization or to those individuals whom the organization deems as appropriate participants. Thus, a key difference between the Internet and an Intranet is that security software programs, or "firewalls," are installed to limit access to only those employees authorized to enter the system. Intranets then serve as secure knowledge portals that contain substantial amounts of organizational memory and can integrate it with information from outside sources. The challenge in designing an Intranet is making sure that it is capable of delivering relevant data to decision-makers while still maintaining security.

The Intranet can be extended to include key customers or suppliers as sources of valuable research. Their participation in the Intranet can lead to better new product development efforts. An Intranet lets authorized users, possibly including key customers, look at product drawings, employee newsletters, sales figures, and other kinds of company information. The American Medical Association is widely recognized as having an effective Intranet.[24] A big part of the success is deciding how to draw the boundaries that define who can access what. For a medical organization, that can be particularly complicated as the system interacts with physicians, insurers, pharmaceutical developers, and so forth. On top of this, the American Medical Association has to make

HIPAA

Health Insurance Portability and Accountability Act.

sure the system complies with the Health Insurance Portability and Accountability Act (HIPAA). **HIPAA** is the U.S. government's effort to nationalize the privacy of health-related information while trying to still allow the transfer of information as it might better promote improved health.

Marketing Analytics

The terms *marketing analytics* and *predictive analytics* did not exist prior to the birth of the big data era. Both are extensions of traditional data analysis and we return to this in more detail later in the book. For now though, it's important to understand that marketing analytics is a part of marketing research that aids business decision-making. **Marketing analytics** is a general term that refers to efforts to measure relevant data and apply analytical tools in an effort to better understand how a firm can enhance marketing performance. Delta Airlines applies data from ticket sales and followup surveys to understand how sensitive its customers are to timing and service issues. Are customers willing to pay more for an 11 a.m. flight than a 5 a.m. flight and are they more satisfied if the flight includes breakfast? Statistical tools are heavily involved in marketing analytics and they can help explain the way the company should respond to consumer information.

Predictive analytics shares much in common with marketing analytics. Broadly speaking, **predictive analytics** refers to linking computerized data mined from multiple sources to statistical tools that can search for predictive relationships and trends. Here, the emphasis is very much on being able to create a pathway to a sale or improved profitability by guessing (with some success) what a consumer is going to do. As the term implies, predictive analytics is more about prediction than about explanation. Software companies like SPSS and SAS offer products that both look for data and then use statistical tools to reveal key predictive relationships. We'll learn more about SPSS and specific statistical tools later in the book.

Information taken from consumers' actual archived behavior along with preference data provided by direct input from the consumer is used to model sales levels that can be achieved with various amounts of discounts. Financial companies like Merrill Lynch use predictive analytics to find service innovations needed to enhance specific customers' satisfaction. In addition, financial firms also apply predictive analytics in fraud detection.[25] Previously, fraud detection was like finding a needle in a haystack. In the big picture, predictive analytics allows companies to better allocate resources. Beats finding a needle in a haystack!

Traditional marketing analytics was never meant to handle the enormous amount of data available in today's big data world.[26] Thus, researchers are working on ways to automate analytics as a way of making them more useful. By providing a ready way of converting data into intelligence, almost instantaneously, marketing analytics holds obvious potential to change, and hopefully enhance, the way many marketing decisions are made.

marketing analytics

A general term that refers to efforts to measure relevant data and apply analytical tools in an effort to better understand how a firm can enhance marketing performance.

predictive analytics

A system linking computerized data mined from multiple sources to statistical tools that can search for predictive relationships and trends.

Data Technology and Ethics

By this point in the chapter, one may feel a little like *big brother* could be watching. The news today is filled with stories about concerns for data privacy at the individual, national, and international levels. Advances in data technology have in a way made privacy seem like a thing of the past. The rapid advancement has outpaced society's ability to understand the ethical and moral implications of the high volumes of electronic communication, so much of which leaves an enduring and at least semipublic record. After all, text messages, device cameras, Web browsing, social media posts, not to mention e-mail, GPS systems, and mobile phone calls, all leave behind some type of record. Background checks now routinely involve mining records from social media sites. Some of these records can be used in market research and consumers experience some benefits from the intelligence produced.

Several companies today specialize in providing data through knowledge of consumers' whereabouts. **Geolocation technologies** allow your whereabouts and/or movement to be known through digital identification of some type, some of which we mentioned earlier when discussing near field communication. Location information is connected with other information on the individual to let users know potentially valuable information about the consumer. Several companies like Turnstyle Analytics and Viasense specialize in constructing a dossier on individual consumers based on where they go and spend time and putting this together with other information, including information from Facebook.[27] Now, without asking a consumer if they are a

geolocation technologies

Allow whereabouts and/or movement of a consumer or object to be known through digital identification of some kind.

golfer, the system knows the answer based on how often a person visits a golf course. With that knowledge, when the consumer enters a shopping center parking lot, they may receive an offer from the center's golf store. In some cases, a subscribing retailer may even be alerted that a good customer is in the area.

When consumers use Facebook or some other apps to check into bars, restaurants, stores, or theaters, it may be more than their friends who know his/her whereabouts. The behavioral tracking possible with this technology could be used by marketing research firms to feed data systems to push promotional offers to "friends," but the data could be used more strategically to understand the paths consumers take when they are out and about.

The marketing research industry and government agencies are interested in better understanding the ethical implications that come with improved technologies for "snooping." The convenience that a consumer gets from the technologies needs to be weighed against concerns for privacy. True anonymity becomes nearly impossible when data are extracted digitally. Data from social networks identify the user by name. Even if a device does not identify a consumer by name, the IP address of the devices being used allows an identifiable record. Thus, the wide availability of data put together with predictive analytics means that companies and agencies really have the capability to know us quite intimately. Many industry leaders believe that self-regulation is called for as an alternative to strict government intervention.[28] The EU's General Data Protection Regulation (GDPR) represents the most sweeping data privacy laws and any organization interacting with European citizens must comply or face serious penalties.

Here are four factors relevant for considering the ethics of data gathered through digital means.

1. Has the consumer implicitly or explicitly consented to being traced? When a consumer places information on Facebook, for instance, that consumer is making the information publicly available and therefore consenting to others seeing and using the information. However, phone conversations are generally considered to be private communications between two individuals. Thus, researchers tracking Facebook information are acting fairly by essentially only joining in on information users have agreed to make public to some extent. Conversely, researchers who might think about eavesdropping on conversations between two individuals are violating their privacy and acting in an unjust manner.

2. Does the tracking behavior violate any explicit or implicit contracts or agreements? As the legal issues involving electronic privacy develop, agreements for use of various technologies will increasingly include statements regarding the limits to which behavior can be traced. Researchers should be mindful of staying within these limits. For instance, if analytical devices predict one's medical condition, conveying that information could violate acts like HIPAA.

open data partnership

Researchers agree to make the information they collect from activities like Web tracking available to the consumers from whom they gather the information.

3. Can researchers enable users to know what information is available to data miners? Some companies, including a marketing data provider known as Turn, participate in an **open data partnership**. This partnership seeks to allow consumers access to the information collected from their digital interactions and even provides consumers an opportunity to edit the information.[29] The open data partnership potentially represents a fair way of handling data mining activities as at least consumers come to know what information researchers gather and can act to be more secretive if some of that information represents things they would rather keep private.

4. Do the benefits to consumers from tracking their behavior balance out any potential invasion of their privacy? Ethically, any imposition of consumers should be smaller than the benefit consumers obtain from the research activity. Greater convenience for consumers and being able to better communicate to them about desirable products are benefits enhanced from electronic data mining activities. If a company can predict what you would buy before you do, should it be able to complete the transaction without an actual transaction taking place?

history sniffing

Activities that covertly discover and record the websites that a consumer visits.

Concerned consumers can enhance security when using the Internet by using security settings that place limits on access to sites that collect data or prohibit the storage of cookies once the browser is closed. These settings can also delete one's browsing history at the same time. The consumer pays a price in convenience as the browser will no longer be able to fill in URLs, names and passwords, and so on automatically. Once again, however, technology creates workarounds to these security precautions. **History sniffing** is a term for activities that covertly discover and record the websites that a consumer visits without using cookies. Perhaps not totally surprisingly, the

Internet porn industry advanced the use of this technology—realizing that some of its customers would try to prevent their cookies from being traced. One history sniffing technique relies on the fact that hyperlinks change color from blue to purple when a user clicks through.[30] A browser code uses this technology to build profiles of users based on the sites they visit.

Going further, a consumer concerned that some institutions may know too much based on big data technologies may forgo owning a smartphone or other device that reveals their location. He or she may also stay away from social network sites where personal information may be revealed or even give up e-mail or Internet browsing. However, these steps seem drastic and few are willing to sacrifice these benefits out of concern for privacy. The advancement of technology has moved faster than our ability to understand when knowing too much really is too much.

TIPS OF THE TRADE

- Researchers should focus on relevance as the key characteristic of useful data.
- Do so by asking, "Will knowledge of some fact change some important outcome?"
- Automate data collection when possible to enhance data quality.
- Weigh the costs of technology investments against the benefits they will bring.
- Be mindful of ethical concerns and legal developments when using today's sophisticated data mining techniques.

:: SUMMARY

1. Know why concepts like data, big data, information, and intelligence represent value. From a research perspective, there is a difference between data, information, and intelligence. Data are simply facts or recorded measures of certain phenomena (things); information is data formatted (structured) to support decision making or define the relationship between two facts. Market intelligence is the subset of data and information that actually has some explanatory power enabling effective decisions to be made. Advancing communication technologies mean that consumers are constantly leaving behind data. Thus, researchers today use big data, taken from multiple sources not intended to be used together, to model what consumers are going to do. This data can be supplemented with data found or purchased from data providers. Marketing analytics are employed to try to make sense out of all of this and feed intelligence into the organization's decision systems. When used properly, and with good ethical practices in mind, employing data to make strategic and tactical decisions means greater value for the firm and its customers.

2. Understand the four characteristics that describe data. The usefulness of data to management can be described based on four characteristics: relevance, completeness, quality, and timeliness. Relevant data have the characteristic of pertinence to the situation at hand and when relevant facts change, the decision is affected. Completeness means having the right amount of information for decision making. Missing information can lead to erroneous conclusions. The quality of information is the degree to which data represent the true situation. High-quality data represent reality faithfully and present a good picture of reality. Timely means the data are not so old that they are irrelevant. Generally, timeliness requires highly current data.

3. Know what a decision support system is and the technology tools that help make it work. A marketing decision support system (DSS) is a system that helps decision-makers confront problems through direct interaction with computerized databases and systems. Decision systems systematically integrate marketing data. Marketing data come from six major sources: internal records, proprietary marketing research, salesperson input, behavioral tracking, web tracking, and outside vendors/external distributors. Data warehousing is the process allowing important day-to-day operational data to be stored and organized for simplified access. Data warehouse management requires that detailed data from operational systems be extracted, transformed, and stored (warehoused) so that the various database tables from both inside and outside the company are consistent. The DSS also is greatly aided by CRM systems and tools such as behavioral and Web tracking, among others.

4. Recognize some of the major databases and how they are accessed. A database is a collection of raw data arranged logically and organized in a useful form. Aside from internal databases, marketing researchers can access many publicly available databases, some of which are free and others which come with some sort of fee-based access. The U.S. Census Bureau contains a plethora of information about household demographics, population by region, and overall population trends; however, one can also access data about many industries through census.gov. The CIA Factbook provides a wealth of information about international markets. Nielsen provides data on media usage and even on lifestyles and demographics across the United States at the zip code level through PRIZM.

5. Understand the basic concept of marketing analytics and its potential to enhance decision making. *Marketing analytics* is a general term that refers to efforts to measure relevant data and apply analytical tools in an effort to better understand how a firm can enhance marketing performance. Predictive analytics involves mining computerized data sources with statistical tools that can search for predictive relationships and trends. Thus, it combines automated data mining with multivariate and other statistical tools to enhance prediction. The marketing researcher's job in predictive analytics is twofold. First, identify the key sources of information that may create predictive intelligence and second, use analytic tools to build predictive models.

6. Be sensitive to the potential ethical issues of tracking consumers' behavior electronically. Privacy is becoming a rare commodity as consumers enter a myriad of information into websites and pass information through their smart phones. The tracking of consumers can be made more ethical when (a) consumers have implicitly or explicitly consented to being tracked, (b) tracking activities do not violate any agreements with the consumer, (c) systems exist allowing consumers to know what information is gathered, and (d) the benefits to consumers in general outweigh any imposition from the data gathering process. Consumers can take steps to protect their own privacy, but they come at the price of the convenience that smart technologies give us.

∶∶ KEY TERMS AND CONCEPTS

archival data, *26*

big data, *26*

cloud storage, *31*

content providers, *39*

cookies, *42*

customer relationship management (CRM), *30*

data, *26*

database, *31*

data quality, *28*

data retailers, *35*

data warehouse, *31*

data warehousing, *31*

data wholesalers, *35*

decision support system (DSS), *30*

electronic data interchange (EDI), *34*

environmental scanning, *40*

geolocation technologies, *43*

HIPAA, *42*

history sniffing, *44*

information, *27*

information completeness, *28*

intranet, *42*

keyword search, *39*

market dynamism, *29*

market intelligence, *27*

marketing analytics, *43*

NFC, *41*

open data partnership, *44*

open source information, *34*

predictive analytics, *43*

proprietary marketing research, *32*

pull technology, *40*

push technology, *40*

relevance, *28*

RFID, *41*

scanner data, *33*

search-engine optimizer (SEO), *33*

smart agent software, *40*

timeliness, *29*

Uniform Resource Locator (URL), *39*

universal product code, *33*

::QUESTIONS FOR REVIEW AND CRITICAL THINKING

1. Define big data. How has big data created greater demand for people with research skills?
2. What is archival data? How does it relate to big data?
3. What is the difference between data, information, and intelligence?
4. What are the characteristics of useful information?
5. What is the key question distinguishing relevant data from irrelevant data?
6. How is CRM used as input to a DSS?
7. Define RFID. How can it provide input to a DSS?
8. What types of internal databases might one find in the following organizations?
   a. Hilton Hotels
   b. A major university athletic department
   c. AB Inbev
   d. Walmart
   e. iTunes
   f. Facebook
9. What type of operational questions could a delivery firm like UPS expect to automate with the company's decision support system?
10. What makes a decision support system successful?
11. What is data warehousing?
12. What is Web tracking? Visit http://www.kbb.com. While there, choose two cars that you might consider buying and compare them. Which do you like the best? What would you do now?

What are at least three pieces of data that should be stored in a data warehouse somewhere based on your interaction with Kelly Blue Book?
13. Give three examples of computerized databases that are available through your college or university library.
14. Describe what smart agent software is and how it may affect you as a typical consumer.
15. Describe the role of marketing analytics in assisting business decision-making.
16. What is predictive analytics? Think about your behavior in the last 48 hours. List at least 10 things that you've done which may have produced data that could be used as input into a predictive analytics system.
17. Suppose a retail firm is interested in studying the effect of lighting on customer purchase behavior. Which of the following pieces of information is the least relevant and why?
   a. Amount of natural light in the store
   b. The compensation system for store salespeople
   c. The color of the walls in the store
   d. The type of lighting: fluorescent or incandescent
18. How could New Balance, a maker of athletic shoes, use an NFC device like iBeacon (described in chapter)?
19. What are four questions researchers can ask in deciding whether their electronic data gathering systems violate good ethical principles?

::RESEARCH ACTIVITIES

1. Search the Internet and try to find the earliest use of the phrase "big data." Describe why the term has come to be used.
2. Use the Internet to see if you can find information to answer the following questions:
   a. What is the exchange rate between the U.S. dollar ($) and the Euro (€)?
   b. What are four traditional restaurants in the French Quarter in New Orleans?
   c. What are four musicals that currently play on Broadway in New York City?

   d. Do more people visit the foxnews.com or cnn.com website?
   e. What is the most popular TV show being watched by teenage girls aged 15–18? Does it differ for teenage boys aged 15–18?
3. Casually interview two consumers at least 20 years different in age. Describe to them a use of big data such as the restaurant consumer whose server knew she had worked out before coming to the restaurant just by data produced by her smartphone. How do they react? Is either concerned about the potential breach of privacy? Comment on your results.

Harvard Cooperative Society

Case 2.1

From his office window overlooking the main floor of the Harvard Cooperative Society, CEO Jerry Murphy can glance down and see customers shopping. They make their way through the narrow aisles of the crowded department store, picking up a sweatshirt here, trying on a baseball cap there, checking out the endless array of merchandise that bears the Harvard University insignia.

Ryan McVay/Getty Images

Watching Murphy, you can well imagine the Coop's founders, who started the store in 1882, peering through the tiny window-panes to keep an eye on the shop floor. Was the Harvard Square store attracting steady traffic? Were the college students buying enough books and supplies for the Co-op to make a profit? Back then, it was tough to answer those questions precisely. The owners had to watch and wait, relying only on their gut feelings to know how things were going from minute to minute.

Now, more than a hundred years later, Murphy can tell you, down to the last stock-keeping unit, how he's doing at any given moment. His window on the business is the notebook computer that sits on his desk. All day long it delivers up-to-the-minute, easy-to-read electronic reports on what's selling and what's not, which items are running low in inventory, and which have fallen short of forecast. In a matter of seconds, the computer can report gross margins for any product or supplier, and Murphy can decide whether the margins are fat enough to justify keeping the supplier or product on board. "We were in the 1800s, and we had to move ahead," he says of the $55 million business. Now, he considers investing in iBeacon and/or other NFC technology as a way of directing customers toward purchases as they browse through the store.

Questions

1. What is a decision support system? What advantages does a decision support system have for a business like the Harvard Cooperative Society?
2. How would the decision support system of a business like the Harvard Cooperative Society differ from that of a major corporation?
3. Briefly outline the components of the Harvard Cooperative Society's decision support system.
4. Look up some archival data on the development of department stores. How have department stores changed over the past 50 years regarding number of stores, store size, customer base, etc.?
5. How might the Harvard Cooperative Society use the iBeacon technology?

The Marketing Research Process

CHAPTER 3

LEARNING OUTCOMES

After studying this chapter, you should be able to:

1. Apply marketing research in making better marketing decisions
2. Classify marketing research as either exploratory research, descriptive research, or causal research
3. List the major stages of the marketing research process and the steps within each
4. Understand the concepts of theory, research hypothesis, and hypothesis and the critical role they play in research
5. Know the difference between a research project and a research program

iStock.com/Opidanus

Chapter Vignette:

Virtual Students

What are the largest higher education institutions in the USA? What schools come to mind? How did they get that way?

Some might say that college students always have been at least a little wired. In this high-tech world though, students don't even need a wire.[1] Changing educational technologies mean today's students increasingly participate in classes or entire programs virtually. While some universities specialize in delivering online education, traditional universities now are playing catch-up in an effort to attract virtual students who pay nonvirtual tuitions! Increasingly, new degree programs tailored specifically to these virtual students emerge and more traditional programs reach heretofore hard to reach segments.

Business schools now aggressively market MBAs delivered in a format tailored specifically to each student's situation. Although an MBA degree still provides an attractive line on the résumé, some question its value, in terms of salaries for MBA grads.[2] Over a quarter of a million U.S. students alone attend MBA classes of one form or another at any given time. For universities, the market for the MBA degree is particularly competitive and the fact is that those universities that offer a market-oriented program are most attractive to students. More and more universities see profit potential from online students who don't take up classroom space, require fewer student

services, and are sometimes taught by adjunct or part-time faculty who are cheaper than tenure track faculty.[3] Thus, universities are aggressively marketing online MBA programs. Marketing research helps answer important questions that feed into this marketing.

- How much does convenience drive consumer choice relative to quality or price perceptions?
- How much of a price premium, if any, is a student willing to pay for online convenience?
- How do employers view nontraditional vis-à-vis traditional MBA programs in terms of value, quality, and prestige?
- What is the demand? Are there enough potential students to make a particular program financially feasible? Where might the students come from?

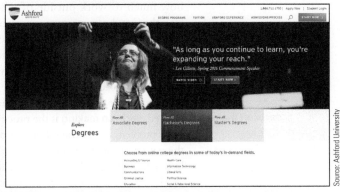

Source: Ashford University

- Do online MBA offerings cannibalize in-class MBA offerings?
- What kinds of consumer support should the MBA program create to increase the satisfaction of online MBA students?
- What is the impact of promoting online programs on the image of the college and university overall?
- Can a business school better accomplish its mission with an online-only MBA program?

The competitive MBA market typifies the landscape of many marketing firms. Clearly, universities could benefit from marketing research addressing some of these key questions. Each university maintains its own academic standards while still trying to attract enough students to make its MBA program feasible. Potential opportunities and potential problems fill this competitive landscape. Decisions made by university faculty and administrators will determine how successfully each school deals with the changing marketplace.

So, what U.S. university is the largest? Considering physical and virtual student enrollment, the University of Phoenix tops the list at about 150,000 students. Surprised? A private equity group purchased the university for $1 billion![4] More and more, state universities see the potential to expand into nontraditional markets. Arizona State University happens to be one of those schools and now often ranks as the largest state university in the United States. University of Central Florida, with about 60,000 students over several campuses, often tops the list based on traditional enrollment counts.

Introduction

This chapter focuses on the marketing research process. This process informs business decisions aiding in solving problems and seizing on opportunities. Quality decision making drives business success. Marketing researchers contribute to decision making in several key ways. These include:

To the Point
"There is no great trick to doing research … the trick is getting people to use it … [most people use research] as a drunkard uses a lamppost—for support, not for illumination."

—DAVID OGILVY

1. Helping to better define the organization's current situation
2. Identifying useful decision statements and related research questions
3. Defining the firm's meaning—how consumers, competitors, and employees view the firm
4. Providing ideas for product improvements or possible new product development
5. Testing ideas that will assist in implementing marketing strategy including innovations
6. Examining how well a marketing theory describes marketing reality

The chapter introduces the types of research that allow researchers to provide input to key marketing decisions. The chapter first discusses stages in the marketing research process and concludes by demonstrating the role that theory plays in better decision making.

Decision Making and Marketing Research

A college student makes many decisions that affect the future. These include important strategic decisions like whether to go to college or not. If the answer is yes, then a decision is faced about where to attend. Furthermore, the student must decide what subject to major in, what electives to take, which instructors to sign up for, whether to belong to a fraternity or sorority, how much to work outside of school, and so forth. The student may seek out data provided by other students, parents, or various media sources. These data may be critical in reaching decisions. Indeed, the answers to each of these questions shape a student's future, ultimately determine how successful he or she will be, and shape the way he or she is viewed by others.

Likewise, businesses face decisions that shape the future of the organization, its employees, and its customers. In each case, the decisions are brought about as the firm either seeks to capitalize on some opportunity or to lessen any potential negative impacts related to some market problem. Formally defined, **decision making** is the process of developing and deciding among alternative ways of resolving a problem or choosing from among alternative opportunities. A decision-maker must recognize the nature of the problem or opportunity, identify how much information is currently available and how reliable it is, and determine what information is needed to better deal with the situation.

Every decision-making situation can be classified based on whether it best represents a problem or an opportunity, and on whether it represents a situation characterized by complete certainty

decision making

the process of developing and deciding among alternative ways of resolving a problem or choosing from among alternative opportunities

Chapter 3 provides an overview of the research process. Many of you may be working on a market research project. Chapter 16, along with the online course resources, provides an outline of just such a project. Chapter 3 provides a way to get you used to the terminology of marketing research and get you prepared to make some of the key decisions about how the research should be designed and implemented. Not the least of those decisions, is should the project go forward at all?

Dmitriy Shironosov/Alamy Stock Photo

or absolute ambiguity. A **market opportunity** is a situation that makes some potential competitive advantage possible. Thus, the discovery of some underserved market segment presents such an opportunity. For example, many of the new consumer-to-consumer (or **sharing economy**) services capitalize by identifying underserved markets, such as the now numerous restaurant food delivery services epitomized by Ubereats, deliveroo, or WAITR. They provide technology that puts someone willing to use his/her own resources, such as car, bicycle, or scooter, to pick up and deliver app-ordered food to a stay-at-home consumer. As a consequence, many consumers who would go to those restaurants to dine in, now become customers. WAITR is experimenting with some app-only restaurant startups in response to the opportunity.[5]

A **market problem** is a business situation that makes some significant negative consequence more likely. The situation is because of some force acting in or on the firm's market. As more and more consumers take advantage of delivery services, are traditional dine-in restaurants facing potentially negative consequences? Traditionally, restaurant customers who linger at their table are most profitable, partly, because the margin for drinks is higher than for food. If the dine-in segment shrinks, might a potential market problem emerge for some restaurateurs? In fact, many restaurateurs today invest more into the physical design of their establishments in an effort to make the "dine-in" option a value-added experience. Companies should constantly monitor consumer trends to spot potential market problems.

Complicating matters, problems are usually not as obvious as they may seem. In fact, they usually are not easily observable. Instead, problems are inferred from **symptoms**, which are observable cues that serve as a signal of a problem because they are caused by that problem. A drop in market share is generally only a symptom of a market problem and not the problem itself. Research plays a role in identifying the causes of problems so decisions can shape cures and not just treat symptoms in a superficial way. Decision situations are also characterized by how much certainty or ambiguity exists.

market opportunity

A situation that makes some potential competitive advantage possible.

sharing economy

Term used to refer to services provided from one consumer (using his/her own resources) to another.

market problem

A business situation that makes some significant negative consequence more likely.

symptoms

Observable cues that serve as a signal of a problem.

Certainty

Complete certainty means that the decision-maker has all information needed to make an optimal decision. This includes the exact nature of the marketing problem or opportunity. For example, an advertising agency may need to know the demographic characteristics of subscribers to magazines in which it may place a client's advertisements. The agency knows exactly what information it needs and where to find the information. If a manager is completely certain about both the problem or opportunity and future outcomes, then research may not be needed at all. However, perfect certainty, especially about the future, is rare.

Uncertainty means that the manager grasps the general nature of desired objectives, but the information about alternatives is incomplete. Predictions about forces that shape future events are educated guesses. Under conditions of uncertainty, effective managers recognize that spending additional time to gather data that clarify the nature of a decision is needed. For instance, a university may understand that there is an objective of increasing the number of MBA students, but it may not know whether an online, weekend, or off-site MBA program is the best way to accomplish the objective. Marketing decisions generally involve uncertainty, particularly when a company is seeking different opportunities.

● ● ● ● ● ● ●
The sharing economy brings market opportunities to some, and perhaps market problems to others.

Ambiguity

Ambiguity means that the nature of the problem itself is unclear. Objectives are vague and decision alternatives are difficult to define. This is by far the most difficult decision situation, but perhaps the most common.

Marketing managers face a variety of problems and decisions. Complete certainty and predictable future outcomes may make marketing research a waste of time. However, under conditions of uncertainty or ambiguity, marketing research becomes more attractive to decision-makers. Decisions also vary in terms of importance, meaning that some may have great impact on the welfare of the firm and others may have negligible impact. The more important, ambiguous, or uncertain a situation, the more likely it is that additional time must be spent on marketing research.

Classifying Decision Situations

Exhibit 3.1 depicts decision situations characterized by the nature of the decision and the degree of ambiguity. Under problem-focused decision making and conditions of high ambiguity, symptoms may not clearly point to some problem. Indeed, they may be quite vague or subtle, indicating only small deviations from normal conditions. For instance, a fast-food restaurant may be experiencing small changes in the sales of its individual products, but no change in overall sales. Such a symptom may not easily point to a problem such as a change in consumer tastes. As ambiguity is lessened, the symptoms are clearer and are better indicators of a problem. A large and sudden drop in overall sales may suggest the problem that the restaurant's menu does not fare well compared to competitors' menus. Thus, a menu change may be in order to deal with the menu problem.

Similarly, in opportunity-oriented research, ambiguity is characterized by marketplace and environmental trends that do not suggest a clear direction. As the trends become larger and clearer, they are more diagnostic, meaning they point more clearly to a single opportunity. Trends showing how consumers may use social networking were not always so evident. Online gaming technologies have had to adapt quickly, though, as trends to games online at Facebook have shifted more toward smartphone–friendly alternatives. A problem for one industry often presents an opportunity for another.

Types of Marketing Research

Effective marketing research reduces uncertainty and helps focus marketing decision making. Sometimes marketing researchers know exactly what their marketing problems are and can design careful studies to test specific hypotheses. Universities, even not-for-profit universities, face

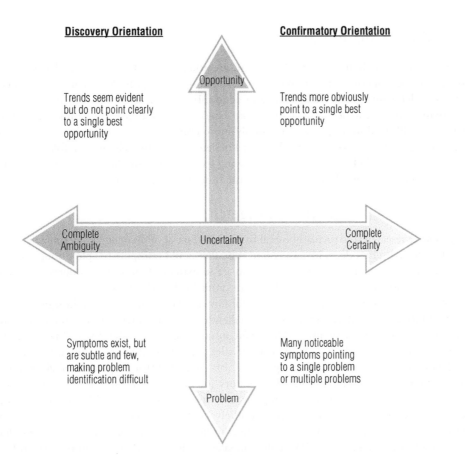

EXHIBIT **3.1**
Describing Decision-Making
Situations

Discovery Orientation

Confirmatory Orientation

Opportunity

Trends seem evident
but do not point clearly
to a single best
opportunity

Trends more obviously
point to a single best
opportunity

Complete
Ambiguity

Uncertainty

Complete
Certainty

Symptoms exist, but
are subtle and few,
making problem
identification difficult

Many noticeable
symptoms pointing
to a single problem
or multiple problems

Problem

marketing problems. For instance, input from employers, students, and alumni might suggest that
a school's curricula are outdated. The problem could even be contributing to low enrollment motivating university administration to address the problem. Thus, marketing researchers working for
the university may devise a careful test exploring which of three new, alternative curricula would
most improve the public's perception that the curriculum is of high quality. This type of research
is problem-oriented and seems relatively unambiguous. The marketing research may culminate
with researchers preparing a report suggesting the relative effect of each alternative curriculum on
enrollment. The decision should follow relatively directly from the research.

In more ambiguous circumstances, marketing managers may be totally unaware of a marketing problem. Alternatively, the company may be scanning the environment for opportunities. For
example, a small, private undergraduate university in a mid-sized Texas town may consider adding an online MBA program. University administrators may have little idea as to how this would
affect the image of their school among current students, employers, alumni, or faculty. They also
may not know exactly what programs would be most desired by its current or potential customer
bases. Some preliminary research may be necessary to gain insights into the nature of such a situation. Without it, the situation may remain too ambiguous to make more than a seat-of-the-pants
decision. The decision-makers almost certainly need input from marketing research.

The technique or purpose underlying marketing research provides a basis for classification.
Experiments, surveys, and observational studies are just a few common research techniques.
Classifying research by its purpose shows how the nature of a decision situation influences the
research methodology. The following section introduces the three basic research designs, each representing a different type of research, that help researchers create intelligence that leads to better
decision making:

1. Exploratory
2. Descriptive
3. Causal

Matching the particular decision situation with the right type of research is important in
obtaining useful research results.

Exploratory Research Design

exploratory research

Conducted to clarify ambiguous situations or discover ideas that may be potential business opportunities.

Exploratory research aims to clarify ambiguous situations or discover ideas that may amount to true business opportunities. Exploratory research does not provide conclusive evidence from which to determine a particular course of action. In this sense, exploratory research is not an end unto itself. Researchers usually undertake exploratory research with the full expectation that managers will need more research to supply more conclusive evidence. Using exploratory research can sometimes also make the difference in determining the relevance of follow-up research. Rushing into detailed research before knowing exactly what the key decisions should be will likely produce irrelevant data and thereby waste time, money, and effort.

Innovation and Exploratory Research

Exploratory research is particularly useful in new product development.[6] Sometimes, it may reveal insight into radical products like a vacuum tube that could transport people through it at speeds approaching that of a jet aircraft. Not all ideas are so extreme. Consumer products companies depend on a steady stream of new brand ideas or profitable brand extensions.

A brand like Kraft constantly explores consumer data for clues that might signal a successful product introduction. Kraft combined data taken from scanners with unstructured customer interviews to identify *superconsumers*.[7] The superconsumer epitomizes the Pareto Principle otherwise known as the 80/20 rule (i.e., 80 percent of sales come from 20 percent of customers). In fact, in the case of Kraft Velveeta, scanner purchase data suggested that 10 percent of all customers accounted for half of all brand profits. Exploratory interviews with some of these superconsumers suggested that they were always looking for new opportunities to use Velveeta. As a result, Kraft responded with new product extensions for Velveeta that included individual slices suitable for burgers or sandwiches and shredded Velveeta convenient for salads and tacos. Simple product extensions like these led to over $100 million in sales. Exploratory research can be very profitable.

The data explosion discussed previously also aids exploratory research. The Research Snapshot illustrates how companies are using technological innovations to gather exploratory research. Input gathered through these techniques helps fuel better decision making.

Exploratory Research and Problem Solving

Exploratory research can be useful in helping to better define a marketing problem or identify a market opportunity. An exploratory design may be implemented to try to reveal not just the symptoms observed in some situation, but potential underlying problems that are causing those symptoms. Usually, this process is not clear and yields numerous potential causes that require further research to pin down probable causes. Patients don't usually go to the doctor and point out their problem (like an ulcer). Instead, they point out symptoms (upset stomach). Similarly, decision-makers usually hear about symptoms and often need help from research to identify and attack problems. Whether facing an opportunity or a problem, businesses need quality information to deal effectively with these situations. The amount of certainty or ambiguity also characterizes all decision situations.

Descriptive Research

descriptive research

Describes characteristics of objects, people, groups, organizations, or environments; tries to "paint a picture" of a given situation.

Descriptive research, as the name implies, describes characteristics of objects, people, groups, organizations, or environments. Put more simply, descriptive research tries to "paint a picture" of a given situation. Marketing managers frequently need to determine who purchases a product, portray the size of the market, identify competitors' actions, and so on. Descriptive research addresses who, what, when, where, why, and how questions.

Descriptive research often helps describe market segments. What does the organic food market look like? Marketing researchers used simple descriptive surveys to describe consumers who are heavy consumers (buy a lot) of organic food products. One report shows that annual U.S.

Research Mission Possible

One would find it hard to understate the role of social media in marketing today. In particular, firms use social media to engage consumers for ideas and feedback. As a consequence, social media plays prominently in marketing research. General Electric (GE) epitomizes successful social media marketing efforts. Hundreds of thousands of Instagram users follow GE's account. GE uses Instagram to engage its customers in #Instawalks and content like Unimpossible Missions, a video series available through YouTube where GE scientists show how GE makes the impossible possible, such as showing a snowball does have a chance in Hell! The GE Twitter page also invites engagement by posting provocative images and tweets that invite reactions to new concepts and suggestions for product improvements. The Tweets also prove useful in exploring ideas for totally new product ideas. One thing though, too many people believe that a mere social media presence makes it meaningful. Particulary when it comes to marketing research, the user needs to know precisely what marketing research questions are to be addressed with the

resulting data. Clearly, we will see more and more bright success stories like GE's!

Sources: Davis, B. 2016 "10 Examples of Great GE Marketing Creative," *eConsultancy*, (September 13), https://econsultancy.com/blog/68268-10-examples-of-great-ge-marketing-creative/, accessed November 17, 2017; *iM* (2017), "The Dos and Don'ts of Social Media Market Research," http://www.insightsinmarketing.com/resources/blog/the-dos-and-donts-of-social-media-market-research, accessed November 17, 2017.

organic food sales are over $47 billion.[8] Fruits and vegetables (i.e., fresh produce) account for nearly 40 percent of those sales although organic meat, poultry, and fish sales are increasing rapidly. The organic beverage market is also growing with organic coffee and tea accounting for just over 35 percent of the global organic beverage market. These data provide a snapshot of the organic grocery market.

Whole Foods, a grocer known for its organic offerings, grew tremendously over the past decade or so and now operates nearly 500 stores across the United States and the United Kingdom. Whole Foods same store sales increased each year through 2017 except for 2009 and 2016, when sales dropped an average of 2.5 percent per store.[9] The average Whole Foods store captures weekly sales of about $750,000 and the average sales per square foot is just over $1,000. Thus, relative to other grocery stores, Whole Foods seems healthy. In 2017, Amazon purchased Whole Foods for more than $13 million, based partly on descriptive location, sales, and profitability data. Also, the diverse locations give Amazon more distribution outlets and the descriptive data gathered from Whole Foods customers provides valuable intelligence for adjusting product offerings. However, some risks appear in the form of other competitors offering more organic products and smaller stores offering high quality at low prices, like Trader Joes. In response, Whole Foods is opening 365 stores, which are smaller stores, with less emphasis on organics, and that sell a limited selection of private label products at prices lower than a traditional Whole Foods store. Descriptive statistics will continue to be analyzed critically as Whole Foods maneuvers through its challenges.

Similarly, the university considering the addition of an online MBA program might benefit from descriptive research profiling the market and the potential customers. Online students are not identical to the traditional MBA students. They tend to be older, averaging about 33 years of age. Another key statistic is that the dropout rate for online students is significantly higher than for traditional MBA students. Nearly 14 percent of online students drop before completing a course, compared to 7.2 percent for traditional in-class students.

Feel the Power...

In the end, businesses succeed or fail based on how consumers interact with the brand. If consumers stop buying, the business's days are numbered. With all the talk about big data today, one can form the opinion that research is all about quantities of data. However, some research firms specialize in getting deeply involved with consumers to describe better the motivations behind consumer behavior. The firms refer to such data as thick data. For instance, what does a television mean today? In a study for Samsung, researchers interviewed hundreds of consumers about the way they use their televisions and collected consumer videos of their interactions with TVs. One trend that emerged is that consumers often did not like the way their televisions looked when they were not on. The data described consumer desires to hide their TVs. Because of these descriptive studies, Samsung focused on redesigning TVs into a more sleek and elegant piece of furniture. The data

also revealed increasing frustration as the greater choice in channels comes at the price of making it more difficult to find specific programming. Samsung responded to these findings by making their televisions smarter by using patterns in program choices to aid users' ability to find the shows that they would most enjoy. Research provided the key to a more meaningful TV experience.

Sources: Madsbjerg, C. and M. B. Rasmussen (2014), "The Power of Thick Data," *Wall Street Journal*, (March 22–23), C3. http://www.samsung.com/us/news/20414, accessed November 14, 2017.

Accuracy is critically important in descriptive research. If a descriptive study misestimates a university's demand for its MBA offering by even a few students, it can mean the difference between the program sustaining itself or being a drain on already scarce resources. For instance, if a research predicts that twenty students will enroll in a cohort, but only fifteen students actually sign up, the program will likely not generate enough revenue to sustain itself. Therefore, descriptive research forecasting sales revenue and costs or describing consumer attitudes, satisfaction, and commitment must be accurate or decision-making quality will suffer.

Unlike exploratory research, researchers usually conduct descriptive studies with a considerable understanding of the marketing situation. This understanding, perhaps developed in part from

Exploratory research might suggest new ways to merchandise food products, descriptive research tells how much each item sells, and causal research suggests reasons why a customer makes a particular selection.

exploratory research, directs the study toward specific issues. Later, we will discuss the role of research questions and hypotheses. These statements help greatly in designing and implementing a descriptive study.

Survey research typifies a descriptive study. Many surveys try to answer questions such as "Why are store A's sales lower than store B's sales?" In other words, a **diagnostic analysis** seeks to detect reasons for market outcomes and focuses specifically on the beliefs, feelings, and reactions consumers have about and toward competing products. A research study trying to diagnose slumping French wine sales among casual consumers might ask a sample of consumers from this segment about the taste of French, Australian, and American wines. The results might indicate a deficiency in taste, suggesting that a reason why this segment is not buying as much French wine is that they do not believe French wines taste as fruity as do wines from Australia. Descriptive research can sometimes provide an explanation by diagnosing differences among competitors, but descriptive research does not provide direct evidence of causality.

diagnostic analysis

Seeks to detect reasons for market outcomes and focuses specifically on the beliefs, feelings, and reactions consumers have about and toward competing products.

Causal Research

If a decision maker knows what *causes* important outcomes like sales and employee satisfaction, then he or she can shape firm decisions in a positive way. Causal inferences are very powerful because they lead to greater control. **Causal research** allows decision-makers to make causal inferences. What brought some event about? That is, causal research seeks to identify cause-and-effect relationships to show that one event actually makes another happen. Heat causes ice to melt. Heat is the cause and melted ice (water) is the effect.

Exploratory and/or descriptive research usually precedes causal research. In causal studies, researchers typically have a substantial understanding of the decision-making situation. As a result, the researcher can make an educated prediction about cause-and-effect relationships that the research will test. The tests are usually quite focused, which is a good thing, but the trade-offs must be considered. Causal research designs can take a long time to implement. In addition, they often involve intricate designs that can be very expensive. Thus, even though managers may often want the assurance that causal inferences can bring, they are not always willing to spend that much time and money.

causal research

Allows causal inferences to be made—they identify cause-and-effect (x brought about y) relationships.

Causality

Ideally, managers want to know how a change in one event (say, using a new product logo) will change another event of interest, like sales. Causal research attempts to establish that when we do one thing, another thing will follow. A **causal inference** is just such a conclusion. Although we use the term *cause* all the time in everyday language, scientifically establishing something as a cause is not so easy and even researchers sometimes confuse causality with correlation. A researcher requires very specific evidence to draw a causal inference. Three critical pieces of causal evidence are

causal inference

A conclusion that when one thing happens, another specific thing will follow.

1. Temporal Sequence
2. Concomitant Variance
3. Nonspurious Association

Temporal Sequence
Temporal sequence deals with the time order of events. In other words, having an appropriate causal order, or temporal sequence, is a necessary criterion for causality. The cause must occur before the effect. How could a restaurant manager blame a decrease in sales on a new chef if the drop in sales occurred before the new chef arrived? If advertising causes sales, the advertising must appear before the change in sales.

temporal sequence

One of three criteria for causality; deals with the time order of events—the cause must occur before the effect.

Concomitant Variation
Concomitant variation occurs when two events "covary," meaning they vary systematically. In causal terms, concomitant variation means that when a change in the cause occurs, a change in the outcome also is observed. We often use the term correlation, discussed in a later chapter, to represent what concomitant variation means. Causality cannot possibly exist when there is no systematic variation between the variables. For example, if a retail store's competition has not

concomitant variation

One of three criteria for causality; occurs when two events "covary," meaning they vary systematically.

changed, then the competitors cannot possibly be responsible for changes in store sales. There is no *correlation* between the two events. On the other hand, if two events vary together, one event may be causing the other. If a university increases its number of online MBA course offerings and experiences a decrease in enrollment in its traditional in-class MBA offerings, the online course offerings may be *causing* the decrease.

One challenge in acting on results discovered by computer mining of big data is sorting out what is actionable. The data may identify patterns that suggest systematic variation, but at times the patterns don't seem practically actionable. More follow-ups on such patterns may be needed before taking action because systematic variation alone doesn't guarantee causality.

Nonspurious Association

nonspurious association

One of three criteria for causality; means any covariation between a cause and an effect is true and not simply because of some other variable.

Nonspurious association means any covariation between a cause and an effect is indeed because of the cause and not simply owing to some other variable. A spurious association is one that is not true. Often, a causal inference cannot be made even though the other two conditions exist because both the cause and effect have some common cause; that is, both may be influenced by a third variable. For instance, a city worker notices an alarming trend. On days when a large number of ice cream cones are sold at Virginia Beach, more people drown. So, when ice cream sales go up, so does drowning. Should the city decide to ban ice cream? This would be silly because the concomitant variation observed between ice cream consumption and drowning is spurious. On days when the beach is particularly crowded, more ice cream is sold *and* more people drown. So, the number of people at the beach, being associated with both outcomes, may cause both. Exhibit 3.2 illustrates the concept of spurious association.

Establishing evidence of nonspuriousness can be difficult. If a researcher finds a third variable that covaries with both the cause and effect, causing a significant drop in the correlation between the cause and effect, then a causal inference becomes difficult to support. Although the researcher would like to rule out the possibility of any alternative causes, it is impossible to observe the effect of all variables on the correlation between the cause and effect. Therefore, the researcher must use theory to identify the most likely "third" variables that would relate significantly to both the cause and effect. The research must control for these variables in some way, as we will see in a later chapter devoted to experimental methods. In addition, the researcher should use theory to make sure that the cause-and-effect relationship truly makes sense.

In summary, causal research should do all of the following:

1. Establish the appropriate causal order or sequence of events
2. Measure the concomitant variation (relationship) between the presumed cause and the presumed effect
3. Examine the possibility of spuriousness by considering the presence of alternative plausible causal factors

EXHIBIT 3.2

Ice Cream Is a Spurious Cause of Drowning

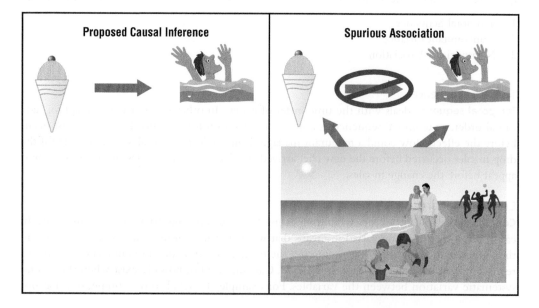

Degrees of Causality

In everyday language, we often use the word "cause" in an absolute sense. For example, a warning label used on cigarette packages claims "smoking causes cancer." Is this true in an absolute sense? **Absolute causality** means the cause is necessary and sufficient to bring about the effect. Thus, if we find only one smoker who does not eventually get cancer, the claim is false. Although this is a very strong inference, it is impractical to think that we can establish absolute causality in the behavioral sciences.

Why do we continue to do causal research then? Well, although managers may like to be able to draw absolute conclusions, they can often make very good decisions based on less powerful inferences. **Conditional causality** means that a cause is necessary but not sufficient to bring about an effect. This is a weaker causal inference. One way to think about conditional causality is that the cause can bring about the effect, but it cannot do so alone. If other conditions are right, the cause can bring about the effect. We know there are other medical factors that contribute to cancer. For instance, lifestyle and diet are also both plausible causes of cancer. Thus, if one smokes and has a diet and lifestyle that promote cancer, smoking could be a considered a conditional cause of cancer. However, if we can find someone who has contracted cancer and never smoked, the causal inference would be proven wrong.

Contributory causality may be the weakest form of causality, but it is still a useful concept. A cause need be neither necessary nor sufficient to bring about an effect. However, the three types of evidence shown on the previous page can establish causal evidence. For any outcome, there may be multiple causes. So, an event can be a contributory cause of something so long as the introduction of the other possible causes does not eliminate the correlation between it and the effect. This will become clearer when we discuss ways to test relationships later in the text. Smoking then can be a contributory cause of cancer so long as the introduction of other possible causes does not cause both smoking and cancer.

absolute causality

The cause is necessary and sufficient to bring about the effect.

conditional causality

Means that a cause is necessary but not sufficient to bring about the effect.

contributory causality

A cause need be neither necessary nor sufficient to bring about an effect; the weakest form of causality.

Experiments

Marketing experiments hold the greatest potential for establishing cause-and-effect relationships. An **experiment** is a carefully controlled study in which the researcher manipulates a proposed cause and observes any corresponding change in the proposed effect. An **experimental variable** represents the proposed cause and the researcher controls this variable by manipulating its value. **Manipulation** means that the researcher alters the level of the variable in specific increments. So, managers often want to make decisions about the price and distribution of a new product. Both price and the type of retail outlet in which a product is placed are considered potential causes of sales. A causal research design would manipulate both the price and distribution and assess the consequences on key outcome variables.

Suppose a company produces a new virtual reality headset called the MeSee. The company needs research to implement the best marketing mix for the product. The company may manipulate price in an experiment by offering it for $200 among some consumers and $500 among others. Likewise, they manipulate retail distribution by selling the MeSee at discount stores in some consumer markets and at specialty electronic stores in others. The retailer can examine whether price and distribution cause sales by comparing the sales results in each of the four conditions created. Exhibit 3.3 illustrates this study.

experiment

A carefully controlled study in which the researcher manipulates a proposed cause and observes any corresponding change in the proposed effect.

experimental variable

Represents the proposed cause that the researcher controls by manipulating its value.

manipulation

Means that the researcher alters the level of the variable in specific increments.

MeSee Sales by Condition		
	Low Price	**High Price**
Specialty Distribution	Peoria, IL Retail Price: $200 Retail Store: Best Buy	Des Moines, IA Retail Price: $500 Retail Store : Best Buy
General Distribution	St. Louis, MO Retail Price: $200 Retail Store: Big Cheap-Mart	Kansas City, MO Retail Price: $500 Retail Store: Big Cheap-Mart

EXHIBIT **3.3**
Testing for Causes with Experimental Manipulations

A marketing research experiment examined the effect of adding a higher-priced alternative to the set of products sold by a retailer. The researchers manipulated price by creating a scenario that either added a higher or lower priced alternative to a set of products reviewed by a consumer. The results show that for frequently purchased products, adding a higher-priced alternative causes consumers to believe that prices in general are lower.[10] We will say much more about manipulations and experimental designs later.

Uncertainty Influences the Type of Research

The amount of uncertainty surrounding a marketing situation does much to determine the most appropriate type and amount of research needed. Exhibit 3.4 contrasts the types of research, illustrates this idea, and shows how researchers conduct exploratory research during the early stages of decision-making. At this point, the decision situation is usually highly ambiguous and management is very uncertain about what actions to take. When management is aware of the problem but lacks some key knowledge, researchers conduct descriptive research. Causal research requires tightly defined problems.

Each type of research produces a different type of result. In many ways, exploratory research is the most productive because it produces many ideas. Exploratory research is discovery-oriented and relatively unstructured. Too much structure in this type of research may lead to more narrowly focused types of responses that could stifle creativity. At times, managers do take managerial action based only on exploratory research results because management may not be able to or may not care to invest the time and resources needed to conduct further research. Decisions made based only on exploratory research can be more risky because exploratory research does not test ideas.[11] For instance, a business school professor may ask a class of current, in-class, MBA students for ideas about online MBA programs. Although the students may provide many ideas that sound very good, that particular research design does not test any idea scientifically. An exploratory design is adequate for discovering ideas, but not for testing ideas.

The discovery process often culminates with research questions. These research questions can guide descriptive research designs. Research questions focus the research on specific variables, allowing for a more structured approach capable of producing managerially actionable results. For example, descriptive research might profile a market segment both demographically and psychographically. Results like this can greatly assist firms in taking action by deciding when and where to offer their service for sale.

Researchers who employ causal designs focus very specifically on a small number of research hypotheses. Experimental methods require tight control of research procedures. Thus, causal

EXHIBIT 3.4 Characteristics of Different Types of Marketing Research

	Exploratory Research	Descriptive Research	Descriptive Research
Amount of Uncertainty Characterizing Decision Situation	Highly ambiguous	Partially defined	Clearly defined
Key Research Statement	Research question	Research question	Research hypothesis
When Typically Conducted?	Early stage of decision making	Later stages of decision making	Later stages of decision making
Usual Research Approach	Unstructured	Structured	Highly structured
Examples	"Our sales are declining for no apparent reason" "How do members of our loyalty program engage in social media, particularly Instagram and Twitter?"	"What kind of people patronize our physical stores compared to those who buy from us online?" "What product features are most important to our customers?"	"Will consumers buy more products in a blue package?" "Which of two advertising campaigns will be more effective?"
Nature of Results	Discovery oriented, productive, but still speculative. Often in need of further research.	Can be confirmatory although more research is often still needed. Results can be managerially actionable.	Confirmatory oriented. Fairly conclusive with managerially actionable results often obtained.

research is highly structured to produce specific results. Causal research results are often managerially actionable because they suggest that if management changes the value of a "cause," some desirable effect will come about. So, by changing a package's color (i.e., the cause, from orange to blue), higher sales occur. The increased control associated with experiments reduces uncertainty in testing hypotheses.

Stages in the Research Process

Marketing research, like other forms of scientific inquiry, involves a sequence of highly interrelated activities. The stages of the research process overlap and not every research project follows exactly through each stage. These particular stages are relevant when the researcher realizes that data collection of some type is necessary. In those instances, marketing research generally follows a pattern represented by these stages:

1. Defining research objectives
2. Planning a research design
3. Planning a sample
4. Collecting data
5. Analyzing data
6. Formulating conclusions and preparing a report

Exhibit 3.5 portrays these six stages as a cyclical or circular-flow process. The circular-flow concept illustrates how one research project can generate new ideas and knowledge that lead to further investigation. Thus, the conclusions and reporting stage connects with the defining the research objectives stage with a dotted line. Notice also, that management is in the center of the process. The researcher cannot properly define research objectives without managerial input. After all, management must ultimately make a decision. Management also may ask for additional research once a report is given. This same general research process applies in basic marketing research and applied market research, whether for profit or nonprofit organizations.[12]

Alternatives in the Research Process

The researcher must choose among a number of alternatives during each stage of the research process. Like choosing a route on a map, no single path fits all journeys. The map analogy is useful because the marketing researcher faces multiple alternatives at each stage. When there are severe time constraints, these constraints override validity, resulting in choosing the fastest alternative. When money and human resources are more plentiful, the appropriate path differs and likely emphasizes validity over speed. Exhibit 3.6 shows the decisions that researchers must make in each stage.

● ● ● ● ● ● ●

One research question of interest to many retailers involves a comparison of virtual (online) versus in-store customers.

Stanisic Vladimir/Shutterstock.com

Teodor Lazarev/Shutterstock.com

EXHIBIT **3.5**
Stages of the Research
Process

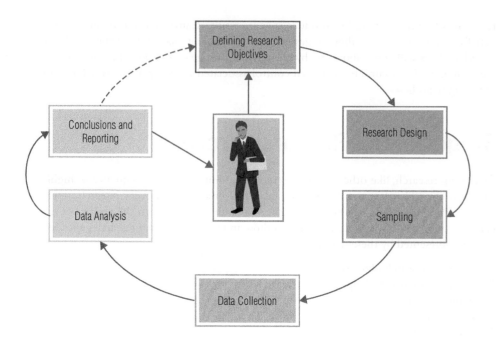

Defining the Research Objectives

research objectives

The goals to be achieved by
conducting research.

deliverables

The term used often in consulting to describe research objectives to a research client in
terms of how the research project will address the research
questions.

Exhibit 3.6 shows how the research process begins with defining research objectives. **Research objectives** are the goals that researchers intend to achieve through this particular effort. In consulting, researchers use the term **deliverables** to describe the objectives to a research client in terms of how the research project will address the research questions. The genesis of the research objectives lies in the type of decision situation faced. The objectives may involve exploring a new market's reaction to a new product offering. Alternatively, they may involve testing the effect of a policy change like self-service checkout on perceived service quality. A corresponding deliverable may be the results of a comparison of shoppers who use and who do not use self-checkout on key variables related to perceived service quality. Different types of objectives lead to different types of research designs.

In applied or market research, the researcher cannot list objectives until there is an understanding of the decision situation. The lead researcher and the chief decision-maker must share this understanding for effective research. We often describe this understanding as a *problem statement*. In general usage, the word *problem* suggests that something has gone wrong. This isn't always the case. Actually, the research objective may be to simply clarify a situation, define an opportunity, or monitor and evaluate current operations. Research objectives cannot be developed until managers and researchers have agreed on the actual business "problem" that will be addressed by the research. Thus, they set out to "discover" this problem through a series of interviews and through a document called a *research proposal*.

Managers and researchers alike may not have a clear-cut understanding of the situation at the outset of the research process. Managers may only be able to list symptoms that could indicate a problem. Sales may be declining, but management may not know the exact nature of the problem. Thus, the researcher in this case may only be able to state a research objective in general terms:

"Identify factors contributing to reduced sales."

The researcher needs this preliminary research to discover things that he/she should research more specifically.

Defining the Managerial Decision Situation

In marketing research, the adage "a problem well defined is a problem half solved" is worth remembering. This adage emphasizes that an orderly definition of the research problem lends a sense

EXHIBIT 3.6 Flowchart of the Marketing Research Process

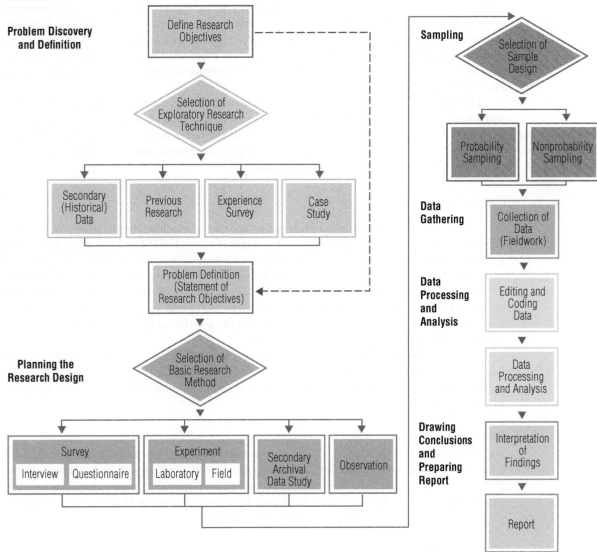

of direction to the investigation. Careful attention to problem definition allows the researcher to set the proper research objectives. If the purpose of the research is clear, the chances of collecting necessary and relevant information and not collecting surplus information will be much greater.

Albert Einstein noted that "the formulation of a problem is often more essential than its solution."[13] This is good advice for marketing managers but it is difficult to put into practice. Managers naturally concentrate on finding the right answer instead of asking the right question. They also want one solution quickly rather than having to spend time considering many possible solutions. Further, properly defining a problem often proves more difficult than solving a problem. As a result of the natural tendency to be done with issues, researchers sometimes end up collecting data before carefully thinking out the nature of the marketing problem. When this occurs, the data often do not lead to relevant results.

Marketing research must have clear objectives and definite designs. Unfortunately, little or no planning goes into the formulation of many research problems. Consider the slumping sales of Coca-Cola recently. If Coke sales are down, it's easy to conclude that some problem with the product must exist. Just as in the 1980s, Coke management may consider asking researchers to study the taste of the beverage in an effort to gain competitive positioning against Pepsi, its biggest rival. Right? Is Pepsi Coca-Cola's biggest rival and therefore a source of its problems? Well, Coca-Cola management, as happens so often, could easily make some false assumptions that would lead them to ignore relevant issues. A scan of consumer trends and perhaps a little exploratory research may lead Coke to some other possible reasons for slumping sales. In recent years, soft drink consumption has faced considerable negative publicity as an unhealthy beverage choice. Perhaps as a consequence, consumers more and more choose flavored waters, tea, filtered water, or a smaller sized soft-drink. Thus, chances are Pepsi and Coke face much the same research problem. Focusing on trying to improve taste relative to Pepsi is likely inappropriate on closer inspection.

research proposal

A written statement of the research design emphasizing what the research will accomplish.

The summary of the managerial decision situation, the research objectives and/or deliverables, and a basic description of the research process represent key elements of a research proposal. Put simply, a **research proposal** is a written statement of the research design emphasizing what the research will accomplish. A research proposal helps get management and the research team on the same page before a major research project begins.

Exploratory Research

Researchers use exploratory research to help discover and define the decisions themselves. Exploratory research progressively narrows the scope of research and helps transform ambiguous problem situations into a more focused project with specific research objectives. Exploration could involve interviews with experts, observation of consumers actually engaged with the product, or analysis of online content describing the product. Exploratory efforts help refine the decision statements and research questions and focus the overall project more toward relevant issues. Exhibit 3.5 indicates that researchers must decide whether to use one or more exploratory research techniques or bypass this stage altogether.

The marketing researcher can employ techniques from four basic categories to obtain insights and gain a clearer idea of the problem: previous research, pilot studies, case studies, and experience surveys. This section will briefly discuss previous research and pilot studies interviews, the most popular type of pilot study.

Previous Research

As a rule, researchers should first investigate previous research to see whether others may have addressed the same research problems previously. Researchers should search previous research reports within the company's archives. In addition, some firms specialize in providing various types of research reports, such as economic forecasts. The Survey of Current Business provides an example of previous research conducted by an outside source.[14]

Literature Review

literature review

A directed search of published works, including periodicals and books, that discuss theory and present empirical results that are relevant to the topic at hand.

Previous research may also exist in the public domain. A **literature review** is a directed search of published works, including periodicals, books, as well as publicly available government, industry, or company reports. The reports may discuss theory and/or present empirical results relevant to the research objectives. A literature survey is common in applied market research studies but it is a fundamental requirement of a basic (i.e., marketing) research report. Online searches using common library search tools or Internet search engines often yield many reports on a given subject. A major challenge for the researcher is to sort out the most relevant from among these. Search engines generally sort hits by either relevance or date. Relevance in this case is a function of keyword matches and can be misleading. A perusal of the abstracts of each article may prove more useful in spotting relevance.

Suppose a real estate developer is interested in developing a piece of commercial property. In particular, she has identified this property as a location for a lifestyle center containing places for people to shop, be entertained, dine, work and live—all in one location. Success will depend on attracting people to this place and creating the right feel. The decision to move forward with the project involves many dimensions, including the location, tenant mix, and the physical design or atmosphere of the place, which is affected by things like color, scents, and architecture. Obviously, prudence calls for more than a cursory study of the feasibility of this project and the implications for different types of designs. Before launching an exhaustive study, the researcher can first look

chuvipro/DigitalVision Vectors/Getty Images

Previous research results, published literature, and pilot studies all may come together to help form a theory of what design would be most successful.

through research journals and find hundreds of studies that address the different decision dimensions.[15] The review may give some idea on what type of architecture will work best to create the right atmosphere and enable the research to focus on a smaller set of possibilities.

Pilot Studies

Almost all consumers take a test drive before buying a car. A **pilot study** serves a similar purpose for the researcher. A pilot study is a small-scale research project that collects data from respondents like they are planned in the full study as sort of a dry run. Pilot studies are critical in refining measures and reducing the risk that the full study design contains a fatal flaw that will render its results useless. This is particularly true for experimental research, which depends critically on valid manipulations of experimental variables.[16] Pilot studies also often are useful in fine-tuning research objectives. Researchers sometimes refer to a pilot study as a *pretest*. A **pretest** is a very descriptive term indicating a small-scale study in which the results are only preliminary and intended only to assist in design of a subsequent study.

A pilot study sometimes includes a focus group interview. A **focus group** interview brings together six to twelve people in a loosely structured format. Today, a focus group interview can take place either in person or using online audio-visual capabilities. The technique assumes that individuals are more willing to talk about things when they are able to do so within a group discussion format. Focus group respondents sometimes feed on each other's comments to develop ideas that would be difficult to express in a different interview format. We discuss focus groups in much more detail in Chapter 5.

Imagine how important a pilot test is for a toy company. A pilot study likely would involve children actually interacting with new toy concepts in an effort to understand issues related to product longevity, durability, and safety, among other things. A separate pilot study may involve parents and explore how they select toys for their children and what price points might be appropriate for the toy. In some cases, toy designers end up being very surprised how children actually play with toys during pilot tests.

Exploratory research need not always follow a structured design. Because the purpose of exploratory research is to gain insights and discover new ideas, researchers may use considerable creativity and flexibility. Some companies perform exploratory research routinely as part of environmental scanning. If the conclusions made during this stage suggest marketing opportunities, the researcher is in a position to begin planning a formal, quantitative research project.

pilot study

A small-scale research project that collects data from respondents similar to those to be used in the full study.

pretest

A small-scale study in which the results are only preliminary and intended only to assist in the design of a subsequent study.

focus group

A small group discussion about some research topic led by a moderator who guides discussion among the participants.

Stating Research objectives

After identifying and clarifying the problem, with or without exploratory research, the researcher must formally state the research objectives. This statement delineates the type of research needed and what intelligence may result that would allow the decision-maker to make choices that are more informed. The statement of research objectives culminates the process of clarifying the managerial decision into something actionable.

A written decision statement expresses the business situation to the researcher. The research objectives try to address directly the decision statement or statements. As such, the research objectives represent a contract of sorts that commits the researcher to producing the needed research. This is why market researchers describe the research outcome in the form of deliverables in applied market research. Research objectives drive the rest of the research process. Indeed, before proceeding, the researcher and managers must agree that the objectives are appropriate and will produce relevant information.

What Is a Theory?

theory

A formal, logical explanation of some event(s) that includes predictions of how things relate to one another.

Ultimately, theory plays a role in determining the appropriate research objectives. A **theory** is a formal, logical explanation of some event(s) that includes descriptions of how things relate to one another. Researchers build theory through a process of reviewing previous findings of similar studies, simple logical deduction, and knowledge of applicable theoretical areas. For example, if a Web designer is trying to decide what color the background of the page should be, the researcher may first consult previous studies examining the effects of color on things like package design and retail store design. He or she may also find theories that deal with the wavelength of different colors or theories that explain retail atmospherics. This may lead to specific predictions that predict blue as a good background color.[17]

Although some may see theory as only relevant to academic or basic marketing research, theory plays a role in understanding practical market research as well. Before setting research objectives, the researcher must be able to describe the business situation in some coherent way. Without this type of explanation, the researcher would have little idea of where to start. Ultimately, the logical explanation helps the researcher know what variables need to be included in the study and how they may relate to one another. Businesspeople in all sorts of industries rely on theories for clues in how to deal with changes in business situations. The tourism industry relies on theories from many areas including consumer behavior, economics, marketing, and geography.[18]

What Is a hypothesis?

hypothesis

A formal statement, derived from theory, explaining some specific outcome.

A **hypothesis** is a formal statement explaining some specific outcome. The researcher derives hypotheses (pl.) from theory to point out what specific things the research will test. In other words, when one states a hypothesis, one makes a proposition. In its simplest form, a hypothesis is a scientific guess. Using our opening vignette as an example, the researcher may use theoretical reasoning to develop the following hypothesis:

> H1: *The more hours per week a prospective MBA student works, the more favorable his/her attitude toward online MBA class offerings.*

empirical testing

Means that some prediction has been examined against reality using data.

We often apply statistics to data to test hypotheses empirically. **Empirical testing** involves comparing a hypothetical proposition, such as a hypothesis, against reality using data. When the data are consistent with a hypothesis, we say, "The hypothesis is *supported*." When the data are inconsistent with a hypothesis, we say, "The hypothesis is *not supported*." We are often tempted to say that we prove a hypothesis when the data conform to the prediction; this isn't really true. Statistical results cannot prove anything because there is always the possibility that our inference is wrong. Now, at times we can be very, very confident in our conclusion, but from an absolute perspective, statistics cannot prove a hypothesis is true. Research reduces but does not eliminate uncertainty.

A Dash of Theory

James W Copeland/Shutterstock.com

Consumers have long faced many pricing options. For example, a consumer can pay for a phone up-front or pay monthly. Some marketers like "odd-pricing" like $7.99 instead of "even-pricing" like $8.00. Sometimes consumers pay for a bundle of items with one price, such as a Happy Meal, rather than paying for each item separately. Sometimes we know up-front what we pay, as used to be the case when every item in a supermarket was stamped with the price, other times we find out after the fact how much something cost, such as with many streaming services.

Marketing managers have a number of theories that come into play when deciding whether one method of pricing is preferable to another. Today's automatic (or near automatic) transaction technologies potentially put distance between a consumer and the price. Amazon continues to make purchasing easier and easier. One example is the Dash button. With Dash, which the consumer purchases for a modest fee, an Amazon customer merely taps the Dash button for Tide, or the Dash button for Doritos, etc., and voila, the purchase is made. No price is displayed so the customer would need to interact with an app or online to discover the price for the Tide, Doritos, etc., but, the products are on the way!

Many research questions may come to mind to assess the impact for the company and for the consumer. One relevant body of theory deals with psychological distance. If the price is somehow perceived as distant, because the consumer may only discover it on a statement, if ever, the theory would predict less reaction due to a higher price. This backdrop gives rise to a host of potential research questions with implications for retail managers and for retail consumers. Now Dash off and think of some of those questions!

Sources: Bushardt, C. (2018), "Is Ignorance (Price) Bliss?" Doctoral Dissertation, Louisiana Tech University. Isabella, G., J. A. Mazzon, and A. Dimoka (2017), "Impacts of Product Type and Representation Type on the Perception of Justice and Price Fairness," *Journal of Business Research*, 81 (Dec.), 203–211.

Exhibit 3.7 illustrates the connections between decision statements, research objectives, research hypotheses, and the deliverables. In this case, we illustrate the process with a single hypothesis. In reality, many research projects will involve more than one research objective, and each of these may often involve more than one hypothesis. Think about other decision statements related to the online MBA market and what a similar infographic may look like.

EXHIBIT 3.7 Illustrating How Decision Statements Determine Research Hypotheses

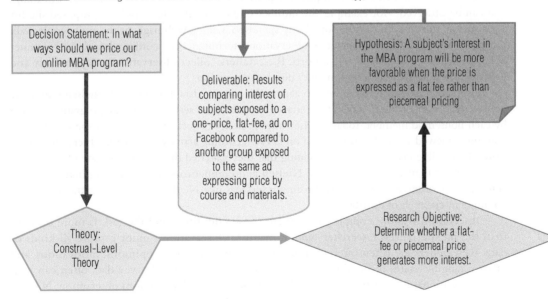

Planning the Research Design

research design

The methods and procedures for collecting and analyzing the needed information for a given type of research.

After the researcher has formulated the research problem, he or she must choose the research design. A **research design** is like a recipe that specifies the methods and procedures for collecting and analyzing the needed information. Each design type, exploratory, descriptive, and causal, provides a unique set of options in implementing the design. A research design provides a framework or plan of action for the research. The researcher also must determine the sources of information, the design technique (survey or experiment, for example), the sampling methodology, and the schedule and cost of the research.

Selection of the Basic Research Method

Here again, the researcher must make a decision. Exhibit 3.6 shows four approaches for implementing descriptive or causal research: surveys, experiments, secondary data, and observation. The objectives of the study, the available data sources, the urgency of the decision, and the cost of obtaining the data influence technique selection. Later, we describe how experiments typically are exclusive to causal designs.

survey

A research technique in which a sample is interviewed in some form or the behavior of respondents is observed and described in some way.

The most common method of generating primary data is the survey. Most people have seen the results of political surveys by Gallup or Harris Online, and some have been respondents (members of a sample who supply answers) to marketing research questionnaires. A **survey** is a research technique involving interviews of sample units in some form or recorded observations of some behavior. The term *surveyor* is most often reserved for civil engineers who describe a piece of property using a transit. Similarly, marketing researchers describe some market segment using a questionnaire. The task of writing a list of questions and designing the format of the printed or written questionnaire is an essential aspect of the development of a survey research design.

Research investigators may choose to contact respondents through social network pages, phone (home or mobile), mail (snail or e), via website invitations, sometimes text messages, or even in person. An advertiser spending more than $5 million for 30 seconds of commercial time during the Super Bowl reaches out through multiple media vehicles for feedback on its efforts. Some agencies even release Super Bowl ads on the Internet prior to the big game to monitor the number of views and comments the ads might generate. Anheuser Busch released the classic "Puppy Love" ad days before the Super Bowl. With its theme of familial attachment between a puppy and the famous Clydesdales, the ad went viral before Super Bowl Sunday. In addition, the ad agency will monitor social media, do telephone, text and Internet surveys beginning immediately after the game. Each of these survey methods has advantages and disadvantages. A researcher's task is to find the most appropriate way to collect the needed information.

The objective of many research projects, particularly descriptive research, is to record things that can be observed—for example, the number of automobiles that pass by a proposed site for a gas station, the amount of time somebody spends viewing a Web page, or the way people walk through a store. The main advantage of observational techniques is recording data about consumer behavior without relying on self-reports. Researchers collect observations unobtrusively and passively, meaning without a respondent's direct participation.

Automatic devices are often best to *observe* this type of data. For instance, Nielsen Company created the "People Meter," which they attached to television sets to record the programs watched by each household member. Today, Nielsen automatically collects not only real-time viewing but also shows viewed at another time based on DVR recording activity. Automatic observation eliminates the possible bias of respondents stating that they watched the president's State of the Union address rather than *Family Guy*. Today, Nielsen and competitors are developing better ways to automatically observe viewing from streaming services like Netflix and other nontraditional entertainment channels of distribution.

Observation is more complex than mere "nose counting," and the task is more difficult than the inexperienced researcher would imagine. Observation cannot capture all kinds of data. Researchers are often interested in things such as attitudes, opinions, motivations, and other intangible states of mind that they cannot directly observe. Survey data often can help provide additional information and complement intelligence derived from observation. Nielsen, for instance, uses the observational data from the People Meter together with survey data about viewing behavior to determine the ratings that networks use to decide which shows get canceled.

Research companies also hire people to record "observations" of behavior. Research personnel known as **mystery shoppers** act like customers while observing and recording data. Companies pay mystery shoppers to gather data about the way employees treat consumers, the cleanliness of the environment, price points, and other important marketing information. This data addresses questions like: How often are store policies followed? How often are customers treated courteously? Are employees prone to do unethical things? Mystery shoppers sometimes intentionally try to do something that would otherwise be unethical to see how an employee might respond. Even not-for-profit organizations use the mystery shopper approach as a way of trying to find out what is really happening during business hours. TSA employs mystery shoppers of a sort, known as the Red Team by U.S. Homeland Security, who test the accuracy of TSA airport screeners in finding items banned from planes as well as the general behavior of the screeners.[19] The Red Team's results identify problem personnel and problems with processes and bring greater scrutiny to the TSA.

mystery shoppers
Research personnel that pretend to be customers while observing and recording data describing their treatment by service employees.

The "Best" Research Approach

No single best research design fits all situations. Researchers often have several alternatives that can achieve a stated research objective. Consider a researcher who must forecast product sales for the upcoming year. Some commonly used forecasting methods are surveying executive opinion, collecting sales force composite opinions, surveying user expectations, projecting trends, and analyzing market factors. Any one of these may yield a reliable forecast.

The ability to select the most appropriate way to implement a research project develops with experience. Inexperienced researchers often jump to the conclusion that a survey methodology is usually the best design because they are most comfortable with this method. Chicago's Museum of Science and Industry wanted to determine the relative popularity of each exhibit. Museum personnel considered a survey approach. Instead, a creative researcher suggested a far less expensive alternative: an unobtrusive observation technique. The researcher suggested that the museum merely keep track of the frequency with which the floor tiles in front of the various exhibits needed replacing, indicating where the heaviest traffic occurred. The tile observation method showed that the chick-hatching exhibit was the most popular. This method provided the same results as a survey and at a much lower cost.

To the Point
"You cannot put the same shoe on every foot."
—PUBLILIUS SYRUS

Planning a Sample

If you take your first bite of a steak and conclude that the entire steak is cooked to the desired degree of wellness (rare, medium rare, etc.), you have just conducted a sample. **Sampling** involves any procedure that draws conclusions based on measurements of a portion of the entire population. In other words, a sample is a subset from a larger population. In the steak analogy, the first bite is the sample and the entire steak is the population. If certain statistical procedures are followed, a researcher need not select every item in a population because the results of a good sample should have the same characteristics as the population as a whole. Of course, when samples are erroneous, they do not give reliable estimates of the population. So, should the first bite come from the edge or the center of a steak?

A historic example of error due to sampling is the 1936 *Literary Digest* fiasco. The magazine conducted a survey and predicted that Alf Landon would win over Franklin D. Roosevelt by a landslide in that year's presidential election. This prediction was wrong and Roosevelt won the election. Poor sample selection led to this error. The postmortems showed that *Literary Digest* had sampled its readers as well as telephone subscribers. As has happened since 1936, the sample did not predict the outcome of the election because these people did not represent well the population of actual voters.

Sampling begins with the question, "Who is to be sampled?" The answer to this primary question requires the identification of a target population. Defining this population and determining the sampling units may not be so easy. If, for example, pinterest.com surveys Pinterest

sampling
Involves any procedure that draws conclusions based on measurements of a portion of the population.

users to determine its brand image, the answer may be in error because potential Pinterest users are not included in the sample. Specifying the target population is a crucial aspect of the sampling plan.

The next sampling issue concerns sample size. How big should the sample be? Although management may wish to examine every potential buyer of a product or service, doing so may be unnecessary as well as unrealistic. Typically, larger samples are more precise than smaller ones, but proper probability sampling can allow a small proportion of the total population to give a reliable measure of the whole. A later discussion will explain how large a sample must be to be truly representative of the universe or population.

The final sampling decision is how to select the sampling units. Simple random sampling may be the best-known type. In simple random sampling, every unit in the population has an equal and known chance of selection. However, this is only one type of sampling. For example, a cluster-sampling procedure may reduce costs and make data-gathering procedures more efficient. If members of the population are found in close geographical clusters, a sampling procedure that selects area clusters rather than individual units in the population will reduce costs. Rather than selecting 1,000 individuals throughout the United States, it may be more economical to first select twenty five counties and then sample within those counties. This will substantially reduce travel, hiring, and training costs. In determining the appropriate sampling plan, the researcher will have to select the most appropriate sampling procedure for meeting the established study objectives.

Collecting Data

The data-collection stage begins once the researcher has formalized the sampling plan. Data gathering is the process of gathering or collecting information. Human observers or interviewers may gather data, or machines like scanners or online stat counters may record data automatically.

Obviously, the many research techniques involve many methods of gathering data. Surveys require direct participation by research respondents. This may involve filling out a questionnaire or interacting with an interviewer. In this sense, they are obtrusive. **Unobtrusive methods** of data gathering are those in which the subjects do not have to be disturbed for data to be collected. They may even be unaware that research is going on at all. For instance, a simple count of motorists driving past a proposed franchising location is one kind of data gathering method. No matter how data are collected, it is important to minimize errors in the process. For example, the data gathering should be consistent in all geographical areas. If an interviewer phrases questions incorrectly or records a respondent's statements inaccurately (not verbatim), major data collection errors will result.

unobtrusive methods

Methods in which research respondents do not have to be disturbed for data to be gathered.

Editing and Coding

After a research team completes the fieldwork, someone must convert the data into a format that will answer the marketing manager's questions. This is part of the data processing and analysis stage. Here, the information content is mined from the raw data. Data processing generally begins with editing and coding the data. Editing involves checking the data collection forms for omissions, legibility, and consistency in classification. The editing process corrects problems such as interviewer errors (an answer recorded on the wrong portion of a questionnaire, for example) before the data are analyzed.

Data have to be coded to become useful. Computer-assisted data collection tools provide data downloads in multiple formats like Excel and Statistical Package for Social Sciences (SPSS), among others. Thus, much of the coding is automatic. When a respondent enters his/her age as 44 years when asked to enter his/her age, that 44 is entered directly into the file with practically the only possibility of error being something caused by the respondent (such as hitting the wrong keys or a dishonest response). However, researchers usually need to perform some additional coding. For instance, items requiring simple open-ended responses require coding in some type of categorical or numeric form.

Analyzing Data

Data analysis is the application of computation, summarizing, and reasoning to understand the gathered information. In its simplest form, analysis may involve determining consistent patterns and summarizing the relevant details revealed in the investigation. The nature of the data, the research design, and management's requirements help determine what type of data analysis is most appropriate. Statistical analyses may range from portraying a simple frequency distribution to more complex multivariate analyses approaches. Later chapters will discuss three general categories of statistical analysis: univariate analysis, bivariate analysis, and multivariate analysis. As with research in general, the appropriate data analysis approach depends on whether the research is exploratory or confirmatory.

data analysis

The application of computation, summarizing, and reasoning to understand the gathered information.

Drawing Conclusions

The research ends by drawing conclusions from the data analysis. These conclusions speak directly to the research questions developed in the early phases of the project and should fulfill the deliverables promised in the research proposal. Conclusions are what managers and other users of the research are interested in. As a result, the researcher highlights the main conclusions in both a written report and in any oral or electronic presentations resulting from the project.

Researchers prepare a formal report describing these conclusions and the research that leads to them. All too often, research reports are written without due consideration to the sophistication of the client. The researcher should write reports in as simple a manner as possible while still conveying the research adequately. Decision-makers end up ignoring overly complex sounding research reports and presentations. We return to this topic in detail Chapter 16 because the importance of effectively communicating results cannot be overstated.

The Research Program Strategy

Our discussion of the marketing research process began with the assumption that the researcher wished to collect data to achieve a specific marketing objective. When the researcher has only one or a small number of research objectives that can be addressed in a single study, that study is referred to as a **research project**. We emphasize the researcher's need to select specific techniques for solving one-dimensional problems, such as identifying market segments, selecting the best packaging design, or test-marketing a new product.

research project

A single study addressing one or a small number of research objectives.

However, if you think about a firm's marketing mix activity in a given period of time (such as a year), you'll realize that marketing research is not a one-shot activity—it is a continuous process. An exploratory research study may require follow-up in the form of a survey, or a researcher may conduct a specific research project for each aspect of the marketing mix. If a new product is being developed, the different types of research might include market potential studies to identify the size and characteristics of the market; product usage testing to record consumers' reactions to prototype products; brand name and packaging research to determine the product's symbolic connotations; and test-marketing the new product. Thus, when numerous related studies come together to address issues about a single company or phenomenon captured by multiple related research questions, we refer to this as a **research program**. Because research is a continuous process, management should view marketing research at a strategic planning level. The program strategy refers to a firm's overall plan to use marketing research. It is a planning activity that places a series of marketing research projects in the context of the company's marketing plan.

research program

Numerous research studies that come together to address multiple, related research questions.

Now that we have outlined the research process, note that the order of topics in this book follows the flowchart of the research process presented in Exhibit 3.4. Keep this flowchart in mind while reading later chapters.

TIPS OF THE TRADE

- Diagnostic analysis helps distinguish symptoms from problems.
- Use exploratory research tools in the interviews with managers to help establish research objectives.
- Ambiguous decision-making situations, particularly in opportunity seeking, usually call for exploratory research. With more certainty, very specific research questions will often call for a causal design. For example:

  - In what ways can Digitex leverage its brand name into new industries? Because this is a broad and relatively vague question, discovery-oriented exploratory research addressing the way consumers view Digitex is probably needed.
  - The use of an animated character in a Facebook ad leads consumers to click through more than does the use of a still image of the character. This hypothesis is very specific and suggests a causal research design.

- Don't overlook the first stage of the research process—defining research objectives.
- The deliverables can be the most important part of a research proposal.

  - Good deliverable: Provide a measure of consumer shopping value perceptions for Anthropologie consumers (both in-store and online shoppers) and a major competitor, Michael Kors.
  - Poor deliverable: Increase profitability at Anthropologie by luring customers from Michael Kors.

∷ SUMMARY

1. **Apply marketing research in making better marketing decisions.** Decision making means that businesses choose between numerous alternative courses of action. Each course of action likely leads to a different outcome. Marketing research can help identify symptoms, sort symptoms from problems, help identify reasonable objectives, and by providing an idea of what outcome will follow from different alternative courses of action, help managers make better decisions in response to both opportunities and problems.

2. **Classify marketing research as either exploratory research, descriptive research, or causal research.** Marketing research can be described as exploratory, descriptive or causal. Each type of research leads to a different research design. The clarity with which the team defines a decision situation determines whether exploratory, descriptive, or causal research is most appropriate. When the decision is very ambiguous, or the interest is on discovering ideas, exploratory research is most appropriate. Descriptive research attempts to paint a picture of the given situation by describing characteristics of objects, people, or organizations. Causal research identifies cause-and-effect relationships. Three types of evidence are needed to establish causality:

a) Temporal Sequentiality
b) Concomitant Variation
c) Nonspurious Association

3. **List the major stages of the marketing research process and the steps within each.** The six major stages of the research process are (1) defining research objectives, (2) planning the research design, (3) planning a sample, (4) collecting data, (5) analyzing data, and (6) drawing conclusions. Each stage involves a subsequent set of steps.

4. Understand the concepts of theory and hypothesis and the critical role they play in research. Theory offers a potential logical explanation for events in a given decision situation. Theory requires testing to know how true the explanations might be. Hypotheses are formal statements explaining some specific outcome in a way that is amenable to testing. Theory and hypotheses not only provide an idea of what might be expected in a given situation, but they guide the implementation of research by suggesting what things need to be measured.

5. Know the difference between a research project and a research program. A *research project* addresses one of a small number of research objectives that can be included in a single study. In contrast, a *research program* represents a series of studies addressing multiple research objectives. Many marketing activities require an ongoing research task of some type.

:: KEY TERMS AND CONCEPTS

absolute causality, *59*

causal inference, *57*

causal research, *57*

concomitant variation, *57*

conditional causality, *59*

contributory causality, *59*

data analysis, *71*

decision making, *50*

deliverables, *62*

descriptive research, *54*

diagnostic analysis, *57*

empirical testing, *66*

experiment, *59*

experimental variable, *59*

exploratory research, *54*

focus group, *65*

hypothesis, *66*

literature review, *64*

market opportunity, *51*

market problem, *51*

manipulation, *59*

mystery shoppers, *69*

nonspurious association, *58*

pilot study, *65*

pretest, *65*

research design, *68*

research objectives, *62*

research program, *71*

research project, *71*

research proposal, *64*

sampling, *69*

sharing economy, *51*

survey, *68*

symptoms, *51*

temporal sequence, *57*

theory, *66*

unobtrusive methods, *70*

:: QUESTIONS FOR REVIEW AND CRITICAL THINKING

1. List five ways that marketing research can contribute to effective business decision making.
2. Define *market opportunities*, *market problems*, and *market symptoms*. Give an example of each as it applies to a startup social networking company.
3. Consider the following list, and indicate and explain whether each best fits the definition of a problem, opportunity, or symptom:
   a. A 12.5 percent decrease in store traffic for a children's shoe store in a medium-sized city mall.
   b. The number of recent graduates joining the business school alumni club has dropped 50 percent from 8 years ago.
   c. A furniture manufacturer and retailer in North Carolina reads a research report indicating consumer trends toward Australian Jara and Kari wood. The export of these products is very limited and very expensive.
   d. The number of cigarette smokers in sub-Saharan Africa is expected to increase dramatically over the next decade.
   e. A local fine-dining establishment cannot find enough applicants with sufficient skills to learn how to deliver the quality of service its customers expect.
   f. Next winter is expected to bring record-setting cold to most of the United States.
4. What are the three types of marketing research? Indicate which type each item in the list below illustrates. Explain your answers.
   a. Establishing the relationship between digital marketing and sales in the beer industry

   b. Identifying target market demographics for a Juicy Snooze hotel/hostel (https://www.jucysnooze.co.nz/) considering a location in your town
   c. Estimating the 5-year sales potential for fMRI machines in the Ark-La-Tex (Arkansas, Louisiana, and Texas) region of the United States
   d. Testing the effect of the inside temperature of a clothing store on sales of outerwear
   e. Explain how making grocery orders available for online ordering and drive-through pickup would enhance business performance for Publix supermarkets
5. What is a diagnostic analysis?
6. Describe the type of research evidence that allows one to infer causality.
7. What is an experimental manipulation?
8. Describe how a literature search is useful in marketing research.
9. Do the stages in the research process seem to follow the scientific method?
10. Why is the "define research objectives" of the research process probably the most important stage?
11. Suppose Auchan (http://www.auchan.fr), a hypermarket chain based out of France, was considering opening three hypermarkets in the midwestern United States. What role would theory play in designing a research study to track how the shopping habits of consumers from the United States differ from those in France and from those in Japan? What kind of hypothesis might be examined in a study of this topic?

12. Referring to the question immediately above, what type of research design do you believe would be most useful to provide useful input to the Auchan decision-makers? What deliverable might go along with the research?

13. Describe ways that observation is used to create data for marketing research.

14. What type of research design would you recommend in the situations below? For each applied market research project, what might be an example of a "deliverable"? Which do you think would involve actually testing a research hypothesis?
    a. The manufacturer and marketer of flight simulators and other pilot training equipment wishes to forecast sales volume for the next five years.
    b. A local chapter of the American Lung Association wishes to identify the demographic characteristics of individuals who donate more than $500 per year.
    c. A major music producer wonders how buzz initiated through Facebook might affect the online revenue for new artists.
    d. A food company researcher wishes to know what types of food are carried in brown-bag lunches to learn if the company can capitalize on this phenomenon.
    e. A political campaign wants to know what resources would be required to make unflattering videos of political opponents go viral.
    f. The university wants to know how much of its marketing budget should go to digital marketing.

15. What is the difference between a research project and a research program? Talk to a graduate student or faculty member about a thesis or dissertation involving business research. Describe whether it best represents a research project or research program.

:: RESEARCH ACTIVITIES

1. Look up information about the online MBA programs at the University of Phoenix (http://www.phoenix.edu/MBA/Degree). Compare it to the traditional MBA program at your university. Suppose each was looking to expand the numbers of students in their programs. How might the research design differ for each?

2. Visit the Gallup Organization's home page (http://www.gallup.com). The Gallup home page changes regularly. However, it should provide an opportunity to read the results of a recent poll. For example, one recent poll projected Christmas season retail sales based on the relative optimism of consumers. Summarize your opinion of the poll that you found. Do you believe it is accurate? What companies or organizations might benefit from this data? Gallup provides a basic description of the way it conducts polls on the web site. Take a look at the information available. List the various stages of the research process and how they were (or were not) followed in Gallup's project.

3. Any significant business decision requires input from a research project. Write a brief essay (about 450 words) either defending this statement or refuting it.

4. What is Google Analytics? Look particularly at the component for digital analytics. What type of data does it provide (exploratory, descriptive, and/or causal)? What would be your position on the quality and usefulness of the data for questions about real estate marketing?

A New "Joe" on the Block

Case 3.1

Joe Brown is ready to start a new career. After spending 30 years as a market researcher and inspired by the success of Starbucks, he is ready to enter the coffee shop business. However, before opening his first shop, he realizes that a great deal of research is needed. He has some key questions in mind.

- What markets in the United States hold the most promise for a new coffee shop?
- What type of location is best for a coffee shop?
- What is it that makes a coffee shop popular?
- What coffee do Americans prefer?
- What type of app might give the shop a competitive advantage?
- How would consumers respond to coffee delivery?

A Google search reveals more previous research on coffee, markets, and related materials than he ever expected. Many studies address taste. For example, he finds several studies that in one way or another compare the taste of different coffee shop coffees. Most commonly, they compare the taste of coffee from Starbucks against coffee from McDonald's, Dunkin' Donuts, Burger King, and sometimes a local competitor. However, it becomes difficult to draw a conclusion as the results seem to be inconsistent.

- One study had a headline that poked fun at Starbucks' high-priced coffee. The author of this study personally purchased coffee at four places, took them to his office, tasted them, made notes, and then drew conclusions. All the coffee was tasted black with no sugar. Just cups of Joe. He reached the conclusion that McDonald's Premium Coffee (at about $1.50 a cup) did not taste quite as good as Starbucks House Blend (at about $2.00 a cup), both of which were much better than either Dunkin' Donuts (at about $1.20) or Burger King (less than $1). This study argued that McDonald's was best, all things considered.

- Another study was written up by a good critic who was simply interested in identifying the best-tasting coffee. Again, he tasted them all black with nothing added. Each cup of coffee was consumed in the urban location near the inner city center where he lived. He reached the conclusion that Starbucks' coffee had the best flavor although it showed room for improvement. McDonald's premium coffee was not as good, but better than the other two. Dunkin' Donuts coffee had reasonably unobjectionable taste but was very weak and watery. The Burger King coffee was simply not very good.

- Yet another study talked about Starbucks becoming a huge company and how it has lost touch with the common coffee shop coffee customer. The researchers stood outside a small organic specialty shop and interviewed 100 consumers as they exited the shop. They asked, "Which coffee do you prefer?" The results showed a preference for a local coffee, tea, and incense shop, and otherwise put Starbucks last behind McDonald's, Burger King, Panera Bread, and Dunkin' Donuts.

Ryan McVay/Getty Images

- Still another study compared the coffee-drinking experience. A sample of 50 consumers in St. Louis, Missouri, were interviewed and asked to list the coffee shop they frequented most. Starbucks was listed by more consumers than any other place. A small percentage listed Dunkin' Donuts but none listed McDonald's, despite their efforts at creating a premium coffee experience. The study did not ask consumers to compare the tastes of the coffee across the different places.

- Still another study about Dunkin' Donuts claims that more "hardworking" Americans prefer Dunkin' Donuts coffee to Starbucks.

Joe also wants to find data showing coffee consumption patterns and the number of coffee shops around the United States, so he spends time looking for data on the Internet. His searches don't reveal anything satisfying.

As Joe ponders how to go about starting "A Cup of Joe," he wonders about the relevance of this previous research. Is it useful at all? He even questions whether he is capable of doing any primary research himself and considers hiring someone to do a feasibility study for him. Maybe doing research is easier than using research.

Questions

1. What are the top three key decisions faced by Joe?
2. What are the key deliverables that an outside researcher should produce to help Joe with the key decisions?
3. How relevant are the coffee taste studies cited above? Explain.
4. What flaws in the coffee taste studies should Joe consider in trying to weigh the merits of their results?
5. Try to do a quick search to explore the question: "Are American consumer preferences the same all across the United States?"
6. If a consultant comes in to do the job, what are three key deliverables that would likely be important to Joe in making a decision to launch the Cup of Joe coffee shop?
7. In what ways might GPS technologies be used by Joe both for marketing and for data collection?

Sources: Cwalinski, K. (2015), "Starbucks, McDonalds, Dunkin... One Trader Makes His Pick," cnbc, https://www.cnbc.com/2015/07/26/starbucksmcdonalds-or-dunkin.html, accessed November 17, 2017; Associated Press, "McDonald's Coffee Beats Starbucks, Says Consumer Reports," *The Seattle Times*, (February 2, 2007), Seattle Times (2007), "McDonalds Coffee Beats Starbucks," https://www.seattletimes.com/business/mcdonalds-coffeebeats-starbucks-says-consumer-reports/,accessed November 17, 2017.

The Human Side of Marketing Research: Organizational and Ethical Issues

iStock.com/Opidanus

LEARNING OUTCOMES

After studying this chapter, you should be able to:

1. Know when research should be conducted externally and when it should be done internally

2. Understand career opportunities and career paths available within the marketing research industry

3. Become sensitive to the often conflicting relationship between marketing management and researchers

4. Understand marketing ethics and ways that researchers can face ethical dilemmas

5. Appreciate the rights and obligations of (a) research respondents—particularly children, (b) research clients or sponsors, (c) marketing researchers, and (d) society

6. Avoid situations involving a conflict of interest in performing marketing research

Chapter Vignette:

If It Feels Green Then It Is Green?

Consumers today are concerned about environmental sensitivities and as a result, companies are becoming *greener*. Marketing efforts communicate a company's environmental sensitivity through product packaging, labeling, advertising, and public relations. These efforts are complicated by the fact that knowing what truly is best for the environment is itself a complicated exercise. Do electric cars powered by high-powered batteries containing toxic chemicals really do less harm than would high-efficiency diesel-powered cars with matching power? Consider also that consumers may recharge the electric cars with electricity taken from an oil-burning or coal-burning power plant. These questions are difficult enough for scientists to answer much less for the average consumer. Research suggests that even environmentally "aware consumers" cannot discern the most green product alternative even half of the time and that consumers high in environmental involvement are susceptible to potential green washing.

Put yourself in the place of a young researcher asked to conduct research for a company that markets products from family-owned farms, including one that grows grapes. The family grows grapes the same way they have for almost 200 years. The practices were organic before anybody knew what

nito/Shutterstock.com

that meant. They ship grapes all over North America and to South Africa. Management asks the researcher for information useful in developing snack packaging that might help tap into consumers' green sensitivities. Management believes that sales will increase by placing the grapes in a green wrapper and putting the word sustainable on the packaging. In fact, management believes this so strongly that they have already invested in equipment and materials to produce the packaging. The researcher plans experiments comparing consumer beliefs about environmental friendliness, attitudes toward the brand, purchase intentions, and perceived tastiness using the green packaging versus using the traditional packaging (no plastic at all with crated grapes selected by the consumer stem by stem). In particular, the researcher examines whether or not consumers perceive this national brand as better than other national brands and the locally grown grapes that it competes with regionally. One thing seems clear, buying green makes consumers feel better and this means another reason why packaging decisions are meaningful to the company.[1]

Introduction

The vignette describes a situation emphasizing marketing research's human side. A company is looking for research to help sell a product, in this case produce. The researcher faces a number of dilemmas. Some of these introduce business ethics into the arena of marketing research. This chapter focuses on marketing research's human side by discussing the people who do, use, and participate in research.

Who Should Do the Research?

The vignette opening this chapter involves a situation in which a company is hiring an outside researcher to conduct a study critical to its marketing strategy. Although this is very typical, many companies have their own employees perform research projects and research programs. Thus, companies sometimes perform in-house research, meaning that employees of the company affected by the research project perform the research. In other cases, companies use an **outside agency** to perform the research, meaning that the company hires an independent, outside firm to perform a research project. In other words, the research is outsourced. Although it would seem that **in-house research** would usually be of higher quality because of the increased knowledge of the researchers conducting the studies, several reasons why employees of the firm may not always be the best people to do the job exist.

outside agency

An independent research firm contracted by the company that actually will benefit from the research.

in-house research

Research performed by employees of the company that will benefit from the research.

Do It Yourself or Let Your Fingers Do the Walking?

When the firm facing a decision encounters one of the following situations, they should consider having the research performed by an outside agency.

- An outside agency often can provide a fresh perspective. Too much knowledge potentially hinders creativity. When a firm desires new ideas, like those that come from discovery-oriented research, an outsider is not constrained by the groupthink that often affects a company employee. In other words, employees who spend so much time together in their day-to-day work activities begin to act and think alike to a large degree. History reveals many stories of products that remained unsuccessful commercially for years until someone from outside the company discovered a useful application. Most people think of the microwave oven as a marvel of the late twentieth century. A company called Raytheon invented microwave technology in the 1940s. Raytheon worked on radar systems for the Allied military in World War II. Not until Raytheon acquired an electronics company called Amana in 1965 did anybody realize that microwave technology could be a huge commercial success as a kitchen appliance. Today, a kitchen would be incomplete without a microwave oven.

To the Point

"To manage a business is to manage its future; and to manage the future is to manage information."

—MARION HARPER

Perhaps you are beginning to plan a research project. Professional marketing researchers must maintain a high degree of integrity or else they will lose credibility from stakeholders involved in their work. Last chapter, we provided an overview of the entire market research process. Realize that at every stage of the process, the chances that things could go ethically wrong exist. In the very beginning, the client and researcher must have an honest and frank discussion about what research is needed and what can be done. In implementing a research design, the researcher needs to give adequate protection to those who participate and provide data. In analyzing and interpreting the data, the researcher must avoid measures that would slant the results away from the truth, even if the results may be undesirable to the client or researcher. Finally, in reporting the results, the researcher must communicate honestly and completely. In this way, the researcher protects not only him/herself, but also the entire professional marketing research community.

Alliance/Shutterstock.com

- An outside agency often can be more objective. When a firm is facing a particularly sensitive situation that may even affect a large number of jobs within the company, researchers may have difficulty being objective. Alternatively, if a particular chief executive within the firm is in love with some new idea, researchers may feel a great deal of pressure to present results that are supportive of the concept. In these cases, outside researchers may be a good choice. Outsiders don't have to work for the company and interact with the players involved in the decision on a daily basis. Therefore, they are less concerned about presenting results that may not be truly welcome.

- An outside agency may have special expertise. When a firm needs research requiring a particular expertise that some outside agency specializes in, it may be a good idea to use that firm to conduct the research. For example, if a firm is searching for expertise in digital analytics to better extract data from consumer experiences, it may seek an outside agency like kissmetrics to assist in that effort. An outside agency may have greater competency in new and emerging research areas.

- An outside agency often has local expertise allowing it to specialize in research from its home area. When a company needs consumer research from a particular country or even from a particular part of a country, the outside agency becomes advantageous because of its knowledge of customs and values. The company probably also knows acceptable ways to get information from consumers in that particular area. For example, a research agency based here in the United States would probably not strongly consider a door-to-door survey for consumer research. However, in other parts of the world, particularly with a less developed communication infrastructure, door-to-door interviews may be a viable option.

Likewise, certain conditions make in-house research more attractive, as described below:

- If a research project needs completing very quickly, chances are that in-house researchers can get started more quickly and get quicker access to internal resources that can help get the project done in short order.

- If the research project requires close collaboration of many other employees from diverse areas of the organization, then in-house research may be preferable. The in-house research firms can usually gain cooperation and can more quickly ascertain just whom they need to interview and where to find those people.

- A third reason for doing a project in-house has to do with economy. Researchers nearly always save money by doing the research in-house relative to hiring an outside agency.

- If secrecy is a major concern, the company should conduct the research in-house. Even though an outside firm might be trusted, that same company may take slightly less care in disguising the research efforts. Thus, other companies may pick up signals in the marketplace that suggest the area of research for a firm.

Exhibit 4.1 summarizes the advantages of doing research internally (in-house) or outsourcing externally (out-house).

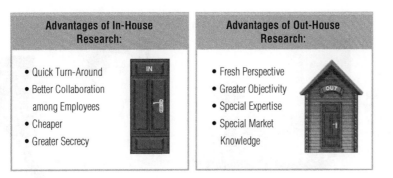

Advantages of In- and
Out-house Research.

Working in the Marketing Research Field

Perhaps never before have there been more career opportunities to work in the marketing research field.[2] The top 100 global market research firms account for about $4 billion in business annually. The explosion in data technologies means that firms are continuously in touch with and monitoring consumer behavior as consumers interact with apps, use GPS technologies, browse the Web, and use social media. Plus, the **Internet of Things**, where practically all manner of physical products, like cars, appliances, lightbulbs, etc., pass and record data electronically, means an ever-expanding base of data exists for research analysts to use to search for insight. Not surprisingly then, the number of jobs in marketing research grows faster than most other industries. This section provides an overview of the types of marketing research organizations that exist and the types of jobs that exist within those organizations.

internet of things

Term referring to the fact that common products like cars, appliances, etc., are connected to the Internet and provide large amounts of data.

In addition to market research firms, about three of four U.S. organizations have a department responsible for marketing research. Consumer product companies, manufacturers, service firms, health-care organizations, social media companies, hotels, and retailers are likely to have an in-house marketing research department. Marketing research clearly has a presence and this is particularly true for larger firms.

High tech firms rely heavily on research, much of it conducted during routine communications with consumers. Amazon's marketing research department consists of hundreds of people and illustrates how research gets integrated into decision-making. The marketing research team at Amazon particularly leverages communication into market research data by:[3]

- Tracking every e-mail communication
- Encouraging a subscription, Amazon Prime, which multiplies the amount of data obtained from the consumer
- Realization that e-mails are not merely transactional but data gathering opportunities
- Allow easy consumer review processes, again seeing each review as data.

The placement of marketing research within a firm's organizational structure and the structure of the research department itself vary substantially, depending on the firm's degree of market orientation and research sophistication. A marketing research department can easily become isolated with poor organizational placement. Researchers may lack a voice in executive committees when they have no continuous relationship with marketing management. Firms that place the research department at an inappropriately low level end up suffering this mishap. Given the critically important nature of the intelligence coming out of a research department, the organizational structure should place research high enough to ensure that senior management is well informed. Research departments also need to interact with a broad spectrum of other units within the organization. Thus, the position they occupy in the organizational hierarchy should allow them to provide credible information both upstream and downstream. MetLife's marketing research informs senior levels of the organization and seeks input from all levels of the organization.

"Your margin is my opportunity."
— JEFF BEZOS, AMAZON

Research departments that perform a staff function must wait for management to request assistance. Often the term "client" is used by the research department to refer to line management; the entity for whom services are being performed. The research department responds to clients' requests and is responsible for the design and execution of all research.

Source: The Nielsen Company

Research Suppliers and Contractors

research suppliers

Commercial providers of marketing research services.

As mentioned in the beginning of the chapter, sometimes obtaining marketing research from an outside organization makes good sense. In these cases, marketing managers must interact with **research suppliers**, who are commercial providers of marketing research services. Market research services are provided by organizations variously classified as marketing research consulting companies, such as Burke or Millward Brown, a division of Kantar; advertising agencies, such as Ipsos MediaCT, a division of Ipsos SA; suppliers of syndicated research services, such as Nielsen Holdings, N.V.; as well as thousands of smaller regional firms, business/management schools, and government agencies. The Nielsen Company alone employs over 40,000 people in more than 100 countries.[4] Research suppliers provide varied services that can be classified into several types.

Syndicated Service

syndicated service

A marketing research supplier that provides standardized information for many clients in return for a fee.

No matter how large a firm's marketing research department is, some projects are too expensive to perform in-house. A **syndicated service** is a marketing research supplier that provides standardized information for many clients in return for a fee. They are a sort of supermarket for standardized research results. For example, J.D. Power, which was acquired by the private XIO investment group of London in 2016,[5] sells research about customers' experiences with products they own and their reasons for satisfaction or dissatisfaction with those products. Consumers are perhaps most familiar with J.D. Power for their automobile ratings. For instance, the 2017 Power rankings list Lexus, Porsche, Toyota, Buick, and Mercedes-Benz as the most dependable brands. Looking for a dependable car or SUV? The Toyota Camry and Toyota Venza score highest based on ownership reports of problems and options in the first 90 days of ownership.[6] Most automobile manufacturers and their advertising agencies subscribe to this syndicated service because the company provides important industry-wide information gathered from a national sample of more than 35,000 consumers covering over 200 auto models. By specializing in customer ownership research, J.D. Power gains economies of scale by applying the same research techniques to a wide array of product categories.

Syndicated services provide information economically because the information is not specific to one client but interests many. In a way, the costs for producing the results spread among all subscribers. The cost would be prohibitive if a single firm had to conduct this research for its own use. Syndicated service companies offer standardized information measuring media audiences, wholesale and retail distribution data, social media usage, Internet statistics, customer satisfaction, and other forms of data.

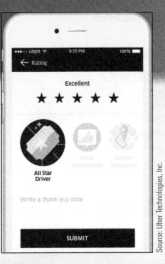

True Power of the Syndicate (Research Firm)

The customer's voice is as powerful as ever given all the ways to distribute opinions these days. A bad rating relative to competitors is a real cause for concern in competitive marketplaces. Ride share company Juno enjoyed competitive success in the NYC market by recruiting good drivers away from the mega-sized competitor, Uber. Clearly too, all their drivers know the importance of ratings and sometimes go to extremes like putting disco lights in their cars to coax a passenger into a high rating. Syndicated firms like J.D. Power and Yougov put large-scale, highly credible, consumer rating at the fingertips of marketing managers. Want to know where your company stands competitively? For example, the Houston Astros may have a World Series championship, but they come in second to the Houston Dynamos when it comes to consumer ratings of the fan experience in the Houston market. Sleep Number scores highest when it comes to the best mattress ranking far ahead of well-known brands like Sealy, who won't be sleeping too well based on these results!

Customer advocacy refers to how likely a customer would be to recommend a brand. Yougov provides customer advocacy data. The current top U.S. customer advocacy firm may not be so widely known. USAA, an insurance and financial services firm specializing in serving families of U.S. military veterans, edges out a very well-known brand, Band-Aid, as the firm most likely to get recommended by others. The results come from tracking data of over 500 consumers surveyed over a six-month period. Syndicated research firms are powerful because the information they provide is powerful.

Sources: http://www.brandindex.com/ranking/us/2017-advocacy, accessed November 23, 2017; http://www.jdpower.com/ratings-and-awards, accessed November 24, 2017.

Standardized Research Services

Standardized research service providers develop a unique methodology for investigating a business specialty area. Several research firms, such as Symphony Health Solutions, specialize in market research for the health-care industry. Standardized research suppliers conduct studies for multiple individual clients using the same methods.

Even when a firm could perform the research task in-house, research suppliers may be able to conduct the project at a lower cost, faster, and relatively more objectively. A company evaluating a new advertising strategy may find an ad agency's research department better able to provide technical expertise on copy development research than could be done within the company itself. Researchers also may wisely seek outside help with research when conducting research in a foreign country in which the necessary human resources and knowledge to collect data effectively are lacking.

standardized research service

Companies that develop a unique methodology for investigating a specific business specialty area.

• • • • • •

Doing research in a foreign country is often better done by an outside agency with resources in those places.

Limited Research Service Companies and Custom Research

Limited-service research suppliers specialize in particular research activities, such as field interviewing, data warehousing, or data processing. Full-service research suppliers sometimes contract these companies for ad hoc marketing research projects. The client usually controls these marketing research agencies or management consulting firms, but the research supplier handles most of the operating details of **custom research** projects. These are projects tailored specifically to a client's unique needs.

Exhibit 4.2[7] lists the top dozen suppliers of market research based on the number of U.S. employees. Over 20,000 U.S.-based research professionals work for just these 12 firms that account for almost $20 billion revenue. If we

EXHIBIT **4.2** Marketing Research Firms by Number of Employees

Rank	Organization	Headquarters	Web Site	U.S. Research Employees	Approximate Revenue ($ millions)
1	Nielsen Holdings NV	New York	nielsen.com	9,696	6,300
2	IQVIA	Danbury, CT	IQVIA.com	5,261	3,300
3	Kantar	London	kantar.com	3,300	3,900
4	Ipsos SA	Paris	ipsos.com	2,192	2,000
5	Westat Inc.	Rockville, MD	westat.com	1,922	512
6	GfK	Neuremberg	gfk.com	1,922	512
7	Information Resources Inc.	Chicago, IL	IRIworldwide.com	1,665	1,000
8	AbtSRBI	New York	abtassociates.com	1,198	147
9	NPD Group Inc.	Port Washington, NY	npd.com	1,035	340
10	ICF International Inc	Fairfax, VA	ICFI.com	1,016	224
11	Maritz	Lehi, UT	maritz.com	579	170
12	WoodMacKenzie	New York	woodmac.com	300	443
				30,086	$18,848

custom research

Research projects that are tailored specifically to a client's unique needs.

considered the top 50 firms, the number of employees and revenues would double. Most of the top firms provide multiple services ranging from fieldwork to research design.

The marketing research field is a massive, dynamic, and global industry. A few decades ago, large market research firms would've been almost exclusively U.S. based; today large global firms are based out of cities around the globe including London, Paris, Singapore, and Sao Paulo. The explosion in global data availability is only adding to growth in the research industry. Further, market research employees are productive with an average revenue per employee of nearly $300,000 across the top 50 U.S.-based firms. The market research industry presents an abundance of career opportunities for people with the right skills and desire.

Marketing Research Firm Size

Marketing research organizations themselves consist of multiple layers of employees. Each employee has certain specific functions to perform based on his or her area of expertise and experience. A look at these jobs describes the potential structure of a research organization and gives insight into the types of careers available in marketing research.

Small Firms

The precise boundary demarking small, mid-sized, and large firms is hardly precise. Government statistics usually consider firms with fewer than 100 employees to be small. Although the actual boundaries are blurry, it's still useful to talk about distinctions between sizes of firm because generally speaking, larger firms will have more official position titles than smaller firms. In small firms, a vice president of marketing likely is in charge of all significant market research. A sales manager collects and analyzes sales histories, trade association statistics, and other internal data. Small market research companies do not usually have the resources or special competencies to conduct large-scale, sophisticated research projects.

Small research firms often have fewer than five employees regularly involved in marketing research and often operate regionally. Small firms often operate as sole proprietorships, and it is not unusual for that to be literally true with a single research professional working alone without additional employees.

Small marketing research firms often have no major corporate clients. Instead, most business for small research firms comes from other small firms, especially start-up firms or even individuals wishing to do a feasibility study. In addition to feasibility studies, small marketing research firms typically conduct consumer attitude assessments and studies assessing the relationship between customer satisfaction and customer loyalty. A small firm can be a good place to start a career or to start your own business. Researchers working for a small firm generally perform all stages of research.

Mid-Sized Firms

Mid-sized firms range from just under 100 to about 500 employees. In a mid-sized firm, someone usually holds the position of **director of marketing research**. This person provides leadership in research efforts and integrates all staff-level research activities.

A **research analyst** is responsible for client contact, project design, preparation of proposals, selection of research suppliers, and supervision of data collection, analysis, and reporting activities. Normally, the research analyst is responsible for several projects simultaneously covering a wide spectrum of the firm's organizational activities. He or she works with product or division management and makes recommendations based on analysis of collected data.

Research assistants (or associates) provide technical assistance with questionnaire design, data analyses, and so forth. Another common name for this position is *junior analyst*. The **manager of decision support systems** supervises the collection and analysis of sales, inventory, and other periodic customer relationship management (CRM) data. Research assistants develop sales forecasts for product lines using analytical and quantitative techniques. They provide sales information to decision-makers to satisfy planning, analysis, and control needs. A **forecast analyst** who provides technical assistance, such as running computer programs and manipulating data to forecast sales, may assist the manager of decision support systems. **Digital market research specialists** specialize in examining the Internet and social networks to assist in target marketing identification, search-engine optimization (SEO), and related tasks.

Personnel within a planning department may perform the marketing research function in a mid-sized firm. At times, they may outsource some research functions. The planner may design research studies and then contract with outside firms that supply research services such as interviewing or data processing. They can combine the input from these outside agencies with their own work to write research reports.

Large Firms

As marketing research departments grow, they tend to specialize by product or strategic business unit. Major firms are those with over 500 employees. Marriott Corporation, for instance, has a director of marketing research for lodging (e.g., Marriott Hotels and Resorts, Courtyard by Marriott, and Fairfield Inn) and a director of marketing research for contract services (e.g., Senior Living Services). Each business unit's research director reports to the vice president of corporate marketing services. Many large organizations have managers of customer quality research who specialize in conducting surveys to measure consumers' satisfaction with product quality.

Exhibit 4.3 illustrates the organization of a major firm's marketing research department. Within this organization, the centralized marketing research department conducts research for all the division's product groups. This is typical of a large research department that conducts much of its own research, including fieldwork. The director of marketing research reports to the vice president of marketing.

The Director of Marketing Research as a Manager

A director of marketing research plans, executes, and controls the firm's marketing research function. This person typically serves on company executive committees that identify competitive opportunities and formulate marketing strategies. The various directors from each functional area

director of marketing research

This person provides leadership in research efforts and integrates all staff-level research activities into one effort. The director plans, executes, and controls the firm's marketing research function.

research analyst

A person responsible for client contact, project design, preparation of proposals, selection of research suppliers, and supervision of data collection, analysis, and reporting activities.

research assistants

Research employees who provide technical assistance with questionnaire design, data analyses, and similar activities.

manager of decision support systems

Employee who supervises the collection and analysis of sales, inventory, and other periodic customer relationship management (CRM) data.

forecast analyst

Employee who provides technical assistance such as running computer programs and manipulating data to generate a sales forecast.

digital market research specialist

Employee specializing in examining the Internet and social networks to assist in jobs like target marketing identification, search-engine optimization (SEO)

EXHIBIT 4.3 Example Large Market Research Firm's Organizational Chart

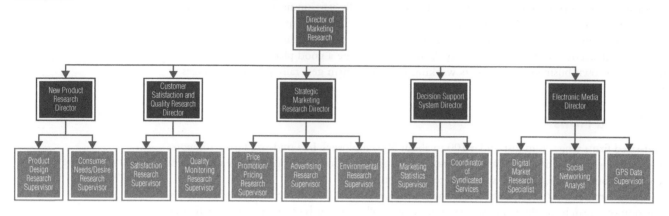

generally make up this committee (such as finance, sales, production, and so forth). The director of marketing research provides the research perspective during meetings. For instance, he or she can let the committee know what types of market intelligence might be obtained feasibly given the decision being discussed. Marketing research directors typically face on-the-job issues such as these:

- Skilled research professionals prefer doing research to managing people. However, a director spends more time in meetings and directing others than actually conducting his/her own research.
- Market research's role often is not recognized formally on par with financial management. The director must be an advocate for the function and its capabilities. In doing so, the director is an advocate for the market itself.
- Outstanding research professionals resist giving up responsibility for key decisions about significant research projects. As a result, they delegate only elementary or tedious tasks to subordinates who sometimes end up feeling underutilized and unhappy with their work.

Perhaps never before has the field of marketing research offered so much career potential. The growing demand for people with research skills means many job opportunities in the coming years. Additionally, the salary for many of these jobs is quite attractive. Being a global industry, opportunities exist on every continent and in practically every country. The Research Snapshot gives a rough idea of what marketing research salaries are like internationally.

Cross-Functional Teams

In a truly market-oriented organization, all employees are involved in the intelligence-gathering and dissemination process. Because of their involvement, employees from different areas of the organization are more likely to communicate and act on marketing information in market-oriented firms.

cross-functional teams

Employee teams composed of individuals from various functional areas such as engineering, production, finance, and marketing who share a common purpose.

Cross-functional teams are composed of individuals from various functional areas such as engineering, production, finance, and marketing who share a common purpose. Cross-functional teams help organizations focus on a core business process, such as customer service or new-product development. Working in teams reduces the tendency for employees to focus single-mindedly on an isolated functional activity. In market-oriented firms, cross-functional teams help employees increase customer value since communication about the customer and their specific desires and opinions spreads throughout the firm more naturally and fully.

New-product development often involves a cross-functional team of engineers, finance executives, production personnel, sales managers, and marketing researchers who take an integrated approach to leverage opportunities into success. In the old days, sales and marketing research seldom contributed to new product development until long after the company made key decisions regarding design, product specifications, and manufacturing. Now marketing researchers' input is part of an integrated team effort. Researchers act both as business consultants and as providers of technical services.

DR Travel Photo and Video/Shutterstock.com

Learning Marketing Research Can Pay!

Search career sites and you are likely to find jobs related to marketing research among the fastest growing and most attractive careers around today. Strategic thinking and business always has been interested in intelligence that could lead to better decision making. Today, that interest is as keen as ever, but the growth in data collection, data storage, and data analysis tools make the Big Data era a big opportunity era for students entering the marketing research field. Thus, jobs related to market research are among the top careers with statistical data analyst and market research professional coming in as among the very top non-medical professions according to *US News*.

The U.S. Bureau of Labor Statistics lists marketing research as a fast growing field. The market research analyst position alone accounts for nearly half a million jobs in the United States. Those individuals working as analysts with only a bachelor's degree average earning over $63,000 per year. Analysts with experience or a master's degree can earn a six-figure salary. The job is always interesting and requires someone who can understand consumer emotion while also having good quantitative skills. An analyst who gets promoted to marketing research director can expect an average salary around $125,000 per year. Marketing research requires people with other skills, too. Digital market research specialists earn $50,000–$60,000 per year to start. Also, most research jobs require good communication skills. The ability to translate technical information into easily understandable language is critically important.

Job opportunities in marketing research exist outside the United States as well. The salaries also can be very lucrative overseas. Salaries in Japan, for example, are considerably higher than in the United States. With the demand high and the salaries good, perhaps marketing research is worth getting into!

Sources: http://www.bls.gov/home.htm, accessed November 20, 2017. http://www.careers-in-marketing.com/mrfacts.htm, accessed November 20, 2017. https://money.usnews.com/careers/best-jobs/rankings/the-100-best-jobs, accessed November 20, 2017.

Conflict between Marketing Management and Marketing Research

In principle, the functions of marketing research should merge harmoniously with the objectives of marketing management for the benefit of both parties. In practice, the relationship between the marketing research department and the users of marketing research too often involves misunderstanding and conflict.

Top management seldom acknowledges marketing research as a factor when decisions are successful. At times, it's as if acknowledging intelligence developed by research demonstrates weakness by having to rely on marketing input like customer data. The late Steve Jobs epitomized this attitude by often boasting that Apple did no market research in developing their key product line offerings like the iPhone and iPad. However, the truth is that Apple was doing a substantial amount of survey research including descriptive studies providing insight into how people used their phones.[8] Apple reluctantly admitted this in court during its patent infringement case with Samsung while also acknowledging that market research at Apple remains top secret.

Research That Implies Criticism

A product manager who requests a survey of dealer loyalty will not be happy if the survey finds that the dealers are extremely critical. Similarly, a sales manager who informally projects a

5 percent increase in sales will not like hearing from the research department that the market potential indicates sales volume should be up by 20 percent. In each of these situations, marketing research presents information that implies criticism of management. Business is a part of life, and just as in personal relationships, people often do not take well to criticism, particularly if it indicates a lack of performance.

Money

Research budgets are a source of conflict between management and researchers. Financial managers often see research as a cost rather than as an investment or a way of lowering risk. Thus, as is often true in many areas of business, managers often want to spend as little as possible on research. In contrast, researchers often vigorously resist cutting corners in conducting research. For instance, they may feel the need for a large random sample to address a research question using descriptive research. This approach can be very expensive and sometimes time consuming. Inevitably, management's desire to save money and the researcher's desire to conduct rigorous research conflict. Successful research projects often involve compromise between researchers and managers. This may involve working within a budget that will produce meaningful results and sacrifice precision and rigor minimally.

Time

Researchers say, "Good research takes time!" Managers say, "Time is money!" Like oil and water, these two views do not go together easily. A look back at the research process in the last chapter makes it clear that it can take some time to complete a research project. Simply planning one can involve days, if not weeks, of study and preparation. For instance, conducting a literature review or a review of previous studies can take weeks. Without them, the researcher may not be able to develop specific research hypotheses that would direct the project very specifically toward the current issue. Other times, the researcher may wish to interview more people than time can allow or take the time to use a more sophisticated data analysis approach.

A quickly done research project almost certainly means cutting corners. This doesn't mean it can't provide valuable information. But, a study put together quickly and conducted quickly is not as certain to provide valuable answers as would a more deliberately planned project. When studies are rushed, the following problems become more likely:

- Conducting research that is not needed. Taking more time to perform a literature search, including through company and industry reports, may have provided the needed intelligence without new research.
- Addressing the wrong issue. Taking more time could help make sure the decision statement is well defined and that the research questions truly address issues relevant to addressing the true issues.
- Sampling difficulties. Correctly defining, identifying, and contacting a truly representative sample is a difficult and time-consuming task. However, in some types of research, the quality of results depends directly on the quality of the sample.
- Inadequate data analysis. The researcher may analyze the data quickly and without the rigor that would otherwise be taken. Therefore, certain assumptions may not be considered, and important information or problems within the data are not discovered.

Sometimes a marketing researcher must give in to time demands and do a quick- and- dirty study. A sudden event can make it necessary to acquire data quickly—but rush jobs can sometimes be avoided with proper planning of the research program. Researchers sometimes get backed into a corner where a study simply must be conducted under severe time limitations. When this happens, the researcher is obligated to disclose this limitation to management. The research report and presentation should include all the study limitations, including those that resulted from a shortage of time or money.

Intuitive Decision Making

Managers are decision-makers. They are action-oriented, and they often rely on gut reaction and intuition. Many times their intuition serves them well, so it isn't surprising that they sometimes do not believe a research project will help improve their decision making. Managers sometimes resist research because results may prove counter to managerial intuition or desires. Managers particularly dislike waiting for a research report. Sometimes, decision-makers learn the hard way that informed decisions are usually better.

When managers do use marketing research, they often want simple projects yielding concrete and certain results. Researchers tend to see problems as complex questions answerable only within probability ranges. One aspect of this conflict is the fact that a research report provides findings, but cannot make decisions. Decision-oriented executives may unrealistically expect research to make decisions for them or provide some type of guarantee that the action they take will be correct. Although research provides information for decision making, it does not remove all the uncertainties involved in complex decisions. Certain alternatives may be eliminated, but the research may reveal new aspects of a problem. Although research is a valuable decision-making tool, the executive is not freed from the decision-making task altogether but is simply able to perform the task in a more informed manner.

Presentation of the right facts can be extremely useful. However, decision-makers often believe that researchers collect the wrong facts. Many researchers view themselves as technicians who generate numbers using sophisticated mathematical and statistical techniques; they may spend more time on technical details than on satisfying managerial needs. Each person who has a narrow perspective of another's job is a partial cause of the problem of generating limited or useless information.

Intuition is not a replacement for informed market intelligence. The business news is replete with unforeseen consequences of business decisions that could have been avoided with a little research. Digital marketing, particularly using social media, comes with a strong urge to act fast. The urge to act fast often means launching ideas that are not well tested. Esurance's Super Bowl promotion experiences illustrate both the good and bad that can come with risky decisions. Esurance became the most mentioned brand on social media during a recent Super Bowl.[9] In a creative twist, they accomplished the feat without even purchasing any advertising time *during* the Super Bowl. They did, however, purchase the 30-second slot immediately *after* the Super Bowl, which sells for a fraction of the price of an advertisement during the game. Esurance put out a promotion on Twitter announcing a sweepstakes that could be entered by tweeting any message with the hashtag #EsuranceSave30. Two surprising results occurred. (1) Esurance became the most mentioned brand on Twitter during the Super Bowl with more than three times as many mentions as the second most tweeted brand—Doritos. (2) However, a large number of Tweets contained not only the hashtag but also obscenities, profanities, and ridiculously false statements. The result is that the company became electronically associated with undesirable characters and events, but their presence online was greatly increased. Just a little pretesting could have suggested the possibility that jokesters would play games with the campaign. As a consequence, the launch of the contest in effect became research that allowed the company to adjust the sweepstakes rules in subsequent years.[10]

Future Decisions Based on Past Evidence

Managers wish to predict the future, but researchers measure only current or past events. Back in 1957, Ford introduced the Edsel, one of the classic business failures of all time. One reason for the Edsel's failure was that the marketing research conducted several years before the car's introduction indicated a strong demand for a medium-priced car for the "man on his way up." Production facility and management delays followed and by the time the car hit the market, consumer preference had shifted favoring traditional cars or small imports for suburban wives. Not all research information is so dated, but all research describes what people have done in the past. In this sense, researchers use the past to predict the future.

Likewise, firms easily can get lulled into complacency about consumer behavior. Zynga, an online game company, made important capital decisions based on the idea that consumers would continue to use Facebook as an online gaming platform. Just after making these decisions, consumers abandoned Facebook in large numbers opting instead to use phone and tablet apps for online gaming.

Reducing Conflict between Management and Researchers

Given the conflicting goals of management and research, it is probably impossible to completely eliminate the conflict. However, when researchers and decision-makers work more closely together, there will be less conflict. The more closely they work together, the better the communication between decision-makers and researchers. In this way, business decision-makers will better understand the information needs and work requirements of researchers. It will allow for better planning of research projects and a greater appreciation for the role that research plays in minimizing the riskiness of business decision making. Exhibit 4.4 lists some common areas of avoidable conflict between research and management.

With closer cooperation, managers and researchers become more involved with projects from the beginning. Without cooperation, each party can have unclear role expectations. Research proposals and research job descriptions help make expectations clear. Management shouldn't ask for and researchers shouldn't state unrealistic objectives. Better planning and an annual statement of the research program for the upcoming year also help minimize emergency assignments, which usually waste resources and demoralize personnel.

Marketing researchers likewise will come to understand management's perspective better. Researchers enhance company profits by encouraging better decisions. The closer together managers and researchers work, the more researchers realize that managers sometimes need information urgently. Thus, they should try to develop cost-saving research alternatives and realize that sometimes a quick-and-dirty study is necessary, even though it may not be as scientifically rigorous as might be desired. Sometimes, quick-and-dirty studies still provide usable and timely information. In other words, they should focus practically on results.

Perhaps most important is more effective communication of the research findings and research designs. The researchers must understand the interests and needs of the users of the research. If the researchers are sensitive to the decision-making orientation of management and can translate research results into practical management language, conflict will diminish.

EXHIBIT 4.4 Improving Two-Way Communication to Reduce Conflict

Top Management	Conflict Area	Marketing Research
• Define Research Responsibilities Clearly	• Role Expectations	• Do Not Overstate Research Objectives
• Allow for Research in Planning	• Professional Consideration	• Sympathize with Management View
• Budget Responsibly	• Resources	• Know Resource Limits
• Be Objective (Open-Minded)	• Idea Generation	• Be Practically Decision-Oriented
• Avoid Compromising Research Standards	• Timeliness	• Recognize Time Constraints
• Emphasize High-Yield Projects	• Problem Definition	• Apply Rigor Appropriately
• Acknowledge Research Limitations	• Research Reporting	• Communicate Results Thoroughly but as Simply as Possible
• Minimize Management Filters	• Consideration of Work	• Presume Client (Management) Will Act on Research

Ethical Issues in Marketing Research

As in all human interactions, ethical issues exist in marketing research and in science in general. This book considers various ethical issues related to specific aspects of research throughout the text. The remainder of this chapter describes the makeup of ethical issues in research with an emphasis on societal and managerial concerns.

Ethical Questions Are Philosophical Questions

Ethical questions are philosophical questions. Several philosophical theories address how an individual develops a moral philosophy and how the resulting morals affect behavior. The theories include those addressing cognitive moral development, the bases for ethical behavioral intentions, and opposing moral values.[11] Although ethics remains a somewhat elusive concept, what is clear is that not everyone involved in business, or in fact involved in any human behavior, comes to the table with the same ethical standards or orientations.[12]

Marketing ethics is the application of morals to business behavior related to the exchange environment. Generally, good ethics conforms to the notion of "right," and a lack of ethics conforms to the notion of "wrong." Highly ethical behaviors are those that are fair, just, and do not cause one to feel shame.[13] Ethical values can be highly influenced by one's moral standards. **Moral standards** are principles reflecting one's beliefs about what is ethical and what is unethical. More simply, moral standards are rules distinguishing right from wrong. The Golden Rule, "Do unto others as you would have them do unto you," is one such ethical principle.

An **ethical dilemma** refers to a situation in which one chooses from alternative courses of actions, each with different ethical implications. Each individual develops a philosophy or way of thinking that guides decisions when facing moral dilemmas. Many people use moral standards to guide their actions when confronted with an ethical dilemma. Other people adapt an ethical orientation that rejects absolute principles. These individuals determine ethics based more on the social or cultural acceptability of behavior. To them, an act conforming to social or cultural norms is an ethical act. The sections below contrast these two ethical orientations.

marketing ethics

The application of morals to behavior related to the exchange environment.

moral standards

Principles that reflect beliefs about what is ethical and what is unethical.

ethical dilemma

Refers to a situation in which one chooses from alternative courses of actions, each with different ethical implications.

Relativism

Relativism is a term that reflects the degree to which one rejects moral standards in favor of the acceptability of some action. This way of thinking rejects absolute principles in favor of situation-based evaluations. Thus, an action is judged as ethical in one situation and unethical in another.

relativism

A term that reflects the degree to which one rejects moral standards in favor of the acceptability of some action. This way of thinking rejects absolute principles in favor of situation-based evaluations.

Idealism

In contrast, **idealism** is a term that reflects the degree to which one bases one's morality on moral standards. Someone who is an ethical idealist will try to apply ethical principles like the Golden Rule in all ethical dilemmas.

For example, a student may face an ethical dilemma when taking a test. Another student may arrange to exchange multiple-choice responses to a test via text messages. This represents an ethical dilemma because there are alternative courses of action each with differing moral implications. An ethical idealist may apply a rule that cheating is always wrong and therefore would not likely participate in the behavior. An ethical relativist may instead argue that the behavior is acceptable because many other students are doing the same thing. In other words, the consensus is that this sort of cheating is acceptable, so this student would be likely to go ahead and participate in the behavior. Marketing researchers, marketing managers, and even consumers face ethical dilemmas practically every day.

idealism

A term that reflects the degree to which one bases one's morality on moral standards.

General Rights and Obligations of Concerned Parties

Everyone involved in marketing research can face an ethical dilemma. Like other areas of marketing, marketing research involves multiple stakeholder groups.[14] For this discussion, we consider four groups of stakeholders:

1. The "doers" of research, or those actually involved in planning and implementing research.
2. The "users" of research, meaning research clients, management, or others who may access research products or reports.
3. The research participants, meaning those people who actually provide the data by being observed or responding in some way.
4. Society at large, including the populations that are affected by research and the governmental institutions that regulate research.

Each party has certain rights and obligations toward the other parties. Exhibit 4.5 shows these relationships. The research process works correctly and benefits stakeholders when all parties respect their respective rights and obligations. Like the rest of business, research works best when all parties act ethically.

Rights and Obligations of the Research Participant

In the past, most data collection took place with the research participant's active consent. Increasingly, marketing researchers use data gathered through participants' passive participation. Both active and passive participation present some potential vulnerability. Thus, marketing researchers need to examine the question, "What ethical duties and obligations are exchanged between the researcher and the research participant?"

Participant's Right to Privacy

Professional marketers long have been concerned with researchers acting as they morally *ought-to* act. In 1970, Don Robin expressed concern that modern marketing research tools may well impinge on the privacy of consumers beyond any benefit that consumer may receive in return.[15] Complicating the fact is that more and more research observations are passively collected without

EXHIBIT 4.5

The Rights and Obligations of Market/Marketing Research

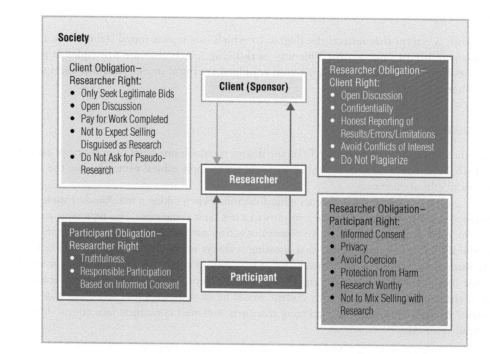

the explicit knowledge of consumers. Traditional survey research requires that a respondent volun-
tarily answer questions in one way or another. This may involve answering questions on a website,
using a phone (voice or text), through an e-mail request, face to face, or even sending a completed
questionnaire by snail mail. In these cases, **informed consent** means that the individual understands
what the researcher wants him or her to do and agrees to be a participant in the research study.
Before asking questions, the interviewer provides an opportunity for the participant to decline the
invitation. In other cases, research participants may not be aware that someone is monitoring them
in some way. Today's technology blurs the line between active and passive research, as behavioral
and sometimes personal information routinely becomes data via smartphones and other devices.
The ethical responsibilities vary depending on whether participation is active or passive.

informed consent

When an individual under-
stands what the researcher
wants him or her to do and
agrees to the research study.

Active Research

Do all Americans relish their privacy? The right to privacy is an important issue in marketing research.
If a research participant believes the researcher is being too nosy, he or she has the right to refuse
participation. However, critics argue that the very old, very young, the poorly educated, and other un-
derprivileged individuals are sometimes unaware of their right to provide informed consent or refuse.
Although the researcher should provide a clear indication of the nature of the questions, some surveys
initially ask questions that are relatively innocuous and then move to questions of a highly personal
nature. Respondents should know their right to refuse includes breaking off an interview at any time.

The privacy issue goes further into other ways that a research project could invade a person's privacy. Do the potential research activities below raise any privacy concerns for research participants?

- A telephone survey interrupts a consumer at dinnertime
- A follow-up phone call from information taken in an online chat
- Capturing consumer information from social media posts
- An e-mail requesting a response to a 30-minute survey on preferred furniture styles
- An interviewer requesting participation in a survey about airports to passengers awaiting a
  flight

Practically, people feel more more comfortable about the consent decision when they know
who is conducting the survey. In a face-to-face interview, interviewers should wear official name
tags and provide identification giving their name and the name of their company. Cover letters
and e-mail requests likewise should identify the reason for the research, the name of the institu-
tion conducting the research and in most cases, the name of the research sponsor. Requests in
Twitter or other social media likewise should identify the research agency and sponsor.

Generally, research firms deploying interactive interviews practice common courtesy by trying
not to do interviews at inconvenient times. Research companies should adhere to the principles
of the "do-not-call" policy and should respect consumers' "Internet privacy" even if the company
might be technically exempt from the legislation.[16] **Do-not-call legislation** restricts any telemarketing effort from calling consumers either who register with a national or statewide no-call list
or who ask the firm directly not to call. U.S. legislators aimed these laws at sales-related calls but
legislation in several states, including California, Louisiana, and Rhode Island, extends the laws to
apply to "those that seek marketing information." Research firms, particularly in these states, should
consider subscribing to the do-not-call registry to avoid breeching the law or ethical practice.

do-not-call legislation

Restricts any telemarketing
effort from calling consumers
who either register with a no-
call list or who request not to
be called.

Consumers often are confused about the difference between marketing efforts and true marketing research. Part of this is because unscrupulous telemarketing firms sometimes disguise their
sales efforts by opening conversations with "we are doing research." The resulting confusion contributes to both increased refusal rates and lower trust from the public. In the 1980s, about half of
people would respond to questions via an unexpected telephone interview. Today, response rates
have dropped to under 10 percent.[17] Part of the drop in participation is because consumers cannot
easily distinguish telemarketing from legitimate research.

Companies using the Internet to do marketing research also face legislative changes. For instance, legislatures around the United States are weighing whether or not any information taken
from password-protected social media without the consent of the user should be allowed.[18] Much
of this legislation aims at properly notifying respondents about the collection of data and informing them of to whom the results will be provided. Researchers should make sure to provide consumers a clear and easy way either to consent to participation in active research on the Internet

or to opt out easily. Research companies should be careful to protect research results from being used to contact respondents in sales attempts. Also, the researcher needs to clearly state the degree to which the information that they provide is private.

Passive Research

Passive research involves different types of privacy issues. Generally, researchers do not view unobtrusive observation of public behavior in places such as stores, airports, sidewalks and museums as an invasion of a person's privacy. Researchers justify this type of observation on the fact that the participants are willfully performing the actions publicly and they are indeed anonymous so long as they are not identified by name or there is not any attempt made to identify them. They are "faces in the crowd." As long as the behavior observed is typical of behavior commonly conducted in public, then there is no invasion of privacy; the public behaviors are tantamount to **implicit consent**. In contrast, recording behavior not typically conducted in public would be a violation of privacy. For example, recording people (without consent) taking showers at a health club using hidden cameras is inappropriate, even if the research addresses ways of improving the health-related aspects of the shower experience.

The line between public and private behavior is not always that clear. Technology pushes the limits of implied consent. Typically, we consider phone calls to be private. However, technology exists that allows our phone calls to be stored in massive databases. As discussed in Chapter 2, our smartphones allow our locations to be tracked and recorded. Companies employ GPS tracking, including the capabilities of employees' own smartphones to "spy" on their whereabouts. One company ended up firing one employee based on the GPS evidence that revealed he was having an affair during work hours.[19] The evidence came in the form of his phone ending up at the same address too often and for too long! Other companies place near-field communication devices in employee name badges to track their whereabouts inside the workplace. Interestingly, the research reveals low productivity both from those who spend too much and too little time at their desk.

One can make a better case for companies having the right to monitor employees than they can for consumers to be monitored without their consent, either explicit or implicit. For instance, does implied consent cover Web traffic and Web activity in general? When someone visits a real casino their behavior can be monitored by the sophisticated video system in the casino. Marketing researchers can use this data to help improve the casino design and casino experience in general. However, when one visits an online gaming site, does implicit consent exist for firms to use the data left behind or even to sell the data to other firms? Virtually all of our interactions online leave data behind and reveal quite a bit about our preferences for *virtually* everything.

Although people shown in a video walking through a casino or in an airport are considered anonymous, electronic tracking confuses the concept of anonymity. A guarantee of **anonymity** assures respondents that they cannot be identified or linked to their response in any way. When a respondent completes a survey using Qualtrics or similar online services, the survey data shows a map identifying the location of the person that responded. How is this possible? All the devices that connect to the Internet have Internet Protocol (IP) addresses. The IP address identifies the device and its location. Thus, to the extent that the owner is the user, true anonymity does not exist in the collection of this raw data. Already, consumers can even be pushed personalized appeals based on their Internet activity while they are inside a store.

The do-not-call legislation protects consumers from unwanted telemarketing. However, regulations and practices designed to sort out the limits of implied consent for electronic media are not yet developed largely. The U.S. Congress as well as governments in other countries are now debating such actions. More importantly, the marketing research industry is considering self-regulation that would provide ethical guidelines concerning how to treat such data.[20] Our lives are improved by the data. Legislation needs to balance the improvements against the loss of privacy that comes from the plethora of real-world tracking.

The Obligation to Be Truthful

When someone willingly consents to participate actively, the researcher assumes he or she will provide truthful answers. Honest cooperation is the primary obligation of the research participant. In return for being truthful, the subject has the right to expect confidentiality. **Confidentiality** means that researchers will not share any individual's information with others. Individuals who truly believe

implicit consent
Behaviors that are openly performed in public implies that one is willing to have others observe them.

anonymity
Assures respondents that they cannot be identified or linked to their response in any way.

confidentiality
The information involved in research will not be shared with others.

Even Giants Respect Rights; Right?

Today's Tech Giants are constantly in touch with millions of consumers as they exchange information through networks and interact behaviorally with smartphones, tablets, and other devices. It's easy to see how one may question whether the Giants prioritize consumer privacy over the ability to gain information that enables them to better sell advertising, manipulate search engines effectively, and improve technical hardware interfaces.

Apple and Alphabet, Google's parent company, depict two different positions on the issue. Google routinely collects information while Apple publically points to its intentional non-tracking of consumer activities to demonstrate a concern for protecting privacy. Consequently, Apple touts its use of differential privacy as a means of collecting information from consumers while keeping individual consumer activity private. The technology works by intentionally introducing erroneous information to the data it collects, meaning that only sophisticated algorithms can extract the real information from the erroneous. In this way, Apple claims to keep consumer information anonymous. The benefit, though, is that Apple then knows more about the way people use emojis, slang, expressions, and surf via Safari.

Apple is right to express concern about potential public backlash from consumer protection issues. Facebook was secretly conducting experiments with users involving manipulation of mood through newsfeeds for several years. As a consequence, Facebook set up a five-person panel to review research practices that operates much like an IRB (Institutional Review Board). Even Tech Giants know the threat from angry consumers!

Sources: Hernandez, D. and D. Seetharaman (2016), "Facebook Reveals Research Methods," *Wall Street Journal*, (June 15), B1. McMillan, R. (2016), "Apple Aims for Privacy as It Tracks User Data," *Wall Street Journal*, (June 17), B4. https://privacytools.seas.harvard.edu/differential-privacy, accessed November 24, 2017.

that the researcher maintains confidentiality are more likely to respond truthfully, even about potentially sensitive topics. Likewise, the researcher and research sponsor also may expect the respondent to maintain confidentiality. For instance, if the research involves a new food product from Nabisco, then they may not want the respondent to discuss the idea for fear that the idea may fall into the competition's hands. Thus, confidentiality helps ensure truthful responses and protects sensitive information.

Kid's Stuff Is Complicated

Researchers have a special obligation to ensure the safety of children. Children are involved in at least half of all spending in the United States. Thus, researchers need input from children to help create high-value products for children. Legislators rightly have special concern for privacy when business interacts with children in some way. The Children's Online Privacy Protection Act (COPPA) defines a child as anyone under the age of 13. Anyone engaging in contact with a child through the Internet is obligated to obtain parental consent before a child can provide any personal information or identification. Therefore, a researcher collecting a child's name, phone number, or e-mail address without parental consent is violating the law. Although the FTC levies substantial fines for violations, when the reach of the messages going to children is considered, the price per reach may be small and unscrupulous firms may not see the fine as a barrier.

In 2013, legislators modified COPPA to make clear that personal information included on-line activity records, GPS location data, audio recordings made by a child, or videos posted that include the child.[21] In addition, changes in COPPA implement procedures that help verify that parental consent really comes from a parent. Thus, some mechanism such as an official electronic signature is needed to provide consent. Officials also approved the kidSAFE seal program.[22] Companies that comply with COPPA and kidSAFE core safety rules, such as making sure a website has only age appropriate content and has specific and clear procedures for handling any parental safety constraints, can earn the seal. The seal intends to provide parents with some degree of comfort in allowing their children to use a website.

● ● ● ● ● ●

Firms that follow COPPA and take other safety precautions can earn this seal of approval – comes from http://www.kidsafeseal.com/aboutourseals.html

Policy makers consider children vulnerable because they may not be able to reasonably reach decisions that keep them safe in all cases. Should researchers allow a child to consent to participating in research without parental consent? Even something as innocuous as offering a child a cupcake for participating in research might not meet all parents' approval. Clearly, researchers should interview children under a certain age only in the presence of a parent. However, will the child respond the same way when a parent is present as when alone? Imagine asking a 14-year-old if he or she enjoys smoking cigarettes or consuming alcohol. How might a parent's presence change the response?[23] The age of consent for marketing research isn't clear even when research is within the guidelines of COPPA. To be safe, researchers should conduct most standard research with children under the age of 16 only with parental consent. When the research involves matters that are for "mature audiences," such as human sexuality or alcohol consumption, then the researchers should seek parental consent for anyone under the age of 18.

Doing research with children can yield extremely useful information. However, it is also more risky than doing research with adults. When in doubt, researchers should consider how they would like to see their own child treated and then go even further to make sure that there are no ethical problems with the use of children in research.

Deception and the Right to Be Informed

Experimental Designs

Experimental manipulations often involve some degree of deception. In fact, without some deception, a researcher would never know if a research subject was responding to the actual manipulation or to their perception of the experimental variable. This is why researchers sometimes use a placebo.

placebo

A false experimental effect used to create the perception that some effect has been administered.

A **placebo** is a false experimental effect used to create the perception of a true effect. Imagine two consumers, each participating in a study of the effect of a new herbal supplement on hypertension. One consumer receives a packet containing the citrus-flavored supplement, which is meant to be mixed in water and drunk with breakfast. The other also receives a packet, but in this case, the packet contains a mixture that will simply color the water and provide a citrus flavor. The second consumer also believes he or she is drinking the actual supplement. In this way, the psychological effect is the same on both consumers, and any actual difference in hypertension must be due to the actual herbs contained in the supplement. Interestingly, experimental subjects often display some placebo effect in which the mere belief that some treatment has been applied causes some effect.

This type of deception can be considered ethical. Primarily, researchers conducting an experiment must generally (1) gain the willful cooperation of the research subject and (2) fully explain the actual experimental variables applied following the experiment's completion. Every experiment should include a **debriefing** session. The debriefing session is the researcher's opportunity to fully inform subjects about the experiment's purpose and provide a chance for them to ask any questions that they may have about the experiment.

debriefing

Research subjects are fully informed and provided with a chance to ask any questions they may have about the experiment.

Protection from Harm

Researchers should do everything they can to make sure that participation in research does not endanger participants' safety in any respect. Most marketing research does not expose participants to any harm. However, the researcher should consider every possibility. For example, if the research involves tasting food or drink, the possibility exists that a research participant could have a severe allergic reaction. Similarly, researchers studying retail and workplace atmospherics often manipulate odors by injecting certain scents into the air.[24] The researcher is sometimes in a difficult situation. He or she has to find out somehow what things the subject is allergic to, without revealing the actual experimental conditions. One way a researcher can do this is by asking subjects to provide a list of potential allergies ostensibly as part of a separate research project.

Other times, research may involve some potential psychological harm. This may come in the form of stress or in the form of some experimental treatment, which questions some strongly held conviction. For instance, a researcher studying helping behavior may lead a subject to believe that another person is being harmed in some way. In this way, the researcher can see how much a subject can withstand before doing something to help another person. In reality, the other person is usually a research confederate simply pretending to be in pain. Three key questions that can determine whether the experimental procedures treat a research participant unethically are:

1. Has the research subject provided consent to participate in an experiment?
2. Is the research subject subjected to substantial physical or psychological trauma?
3. Can the research subject be easily returned to his or her initial state?

The issue of consent is tricky in experiments because the researcher cannot reveal exactly what the research is about ahead of time without threatening the validity of the experiment. In addition, the researcher generally provides experimental research subjects with some incentive to participate. We will have more on this later in the book, but ethically speaking, the incentives should always be noncoercive. In other words, a faculty member seeking volunteers should not withhold a student's grade if he or she does not participate in an experiment. Thus, the volunteer should provide consent without fear of harm for saying no and with some idea about any potential risk involved.

If the answer to the second question is yes, then the researcher should not go forward with the research design. If the answer to the second question is no and consent is obtained, then the manipulation does not present an ethical problem, and the researcher can proceed.

The third question is really helpful in understanding how far one can go in applying manipulations to a research subject. If the answer to the third question is no, then the research should not be conducted. Researchers sometimes show interest in reasons why and the implications of consumers wearing tattoos.[25] Consider an experiment that would investigate the effect of an altered mental state on tattoo selection. The research question is, "How does intoxication affect tattoo selection?" Subsequently, the experimental research design presents two potential risks for harm. First, the subject becomes intoxicated. Second, the subject may end up actually obtaining a visible tattoo. If the subject has a hangover, he or she will likely recover. However, tattoos are permanent barring drastic medical attention. Thus, the design is unethical because it presents the possibility of changing the subject in a way that would make returning him or her to normal practically impossible.

Many research companies and practically all universities and business schools maintain a **human subjects review committee**. This committee carefully reviews a proposed research design to try to make sure that no harm can come to any research participant. A side benefit of this committee is that it can also review the procedures to make sure that the research design does not create any legal problems. Sometimes, an organization may use the name **Institutional Review Board (IRB)** to refer to this committee. The harm can potentially even go beyond humans. Any research that involves animals, such as dogs trying food, deserves scrutiny from an IRB.

Rights and Obligations of the Client Sponsor (User)

Ethical Behavior between Buyer and Seller

The general business ethic expected between a purchasing agent and a sales representative should hold in a marketing research situation. For example, if a purchasing agent has already decided to purchase a product from a friend, the agent would be acting unethically by soliciting bids from others because those bids have no chance of being accepted. Similarly, a client seeking research should only seek bids from firms that have a legitimate chance of actually doing the work. In addition, any section on the ethical obligation of a research client would be remiss not to mention that the user is obligated to pay the provider the agreed-upon wage within the agreed-upon time.

An Open Relationship with Research Suppliers

The client/sponsor has an obligation to encourage the researcher to seek out the truth objectively. Managers and researchers must openly and honestly discuss the key issues and come to a consensus about what decision-statement(s), and thus what research question(s), best describes the need

human subjects review committee

Carefully reviews proposed research designs to try to make sure that no harm can come to any research participant. Otherwise known as an Institutional Review Board or IRB.

Institutional Review Board (IRB)

Another name for a human subjects review committee.

for the research. The more a decision-maker refuses to answer the researcher's questions, the less likely are the parties to come to a useful consensus about the research. Therefore, the researcher is better off not taking this particular job.

Once agreed upon, the research sponsor should support the research team in their effort to obtain information and perform analyses that will provide answers to the research questions. This means that the client needs to be open to actually using the research results. All too often, decision-makers want the research results only if they will support some preconceived answer—in other words the decision is already made and the research is needed for political cover. This is unethical. Time is simply too valuable to ask a researcher to perform a project when the sponsoring agent knows ahead of time that the results will not be used. Unfortunately, as a firm's performance suffers and as top management fails to show ethical leadership, that company tends to practice less ethical research practices as well.[26]

An Open Relationship with Interested Parties

Conclusions should be based on data—not conjecture. Users should not knowingly disseminate conclusions from a research project in a manner that twists them into some desirable interpretation. Twisting the results in a self-serving manner, or to support some political position, poses serious ethical questions. Such actions are morally inappropriate and the client-researcher relationship should be open enough to avoid encouraging anything but honest results.

Advocacy research—research undertaken to support a specific claim in a legal action or to represent some advocacy group—puts a client in a unique situation. Researchers often conduct advocacy research in their role as an expert witness. For instance, a law firm may ask a researcher to present evidence addressing how much a "knock-off" brand diminishes the value of a better-known name brand. In conventional research, the researcher weighs research attributes such as sample size, profiles of people actually interviewed, and number of questions asked, against cost. Trade-offs become appropriate if the research is too costly to conduct relative to the benefit. However, a court's opinion on whether research results are reliable might rely exclusively on any one specific research aspect. Thus, an opposing attorney may magnify the slightest variation from technically correct procedures attempting to demonstrate to the judge or jury that the project is flawed.

Advocacy research presents a number of serious issues that can lead to an ethical dilemma:

- Lawyers' first responsibility is to represent their clients. Therefore, they might be more interested in evidence that supports their client's position than anything else—including truthful results. Presenting accurate research results may harm the client.
- A researcher should be objective. However, he or she runs the risk of conducting research that does not support the desired position. In this case, an unethical lawyer may ask the researcher to present the results in a manner that obfuscates the truth.
- Should the lawyer (in this case a user of research) ask the researcher to take the stand and present an inaccurate picture of the results?

Ethically, the attorney should certainly not put the researcher on the stand and encourage an act of perjury. The attorney may hope to ask specific questions that are so limited that taken alone, they may appear to support the client. However, this is risky because the opposing attorney likely also has an expert witness that can suggest questions for cross-examination. Returning to our branding example, if the research does not support an infringement of the known brand's name, then the brand name's attorney should probably not ask the researcher to take the stand.

The question of advocacy research is one of objectivity: Can the researcher seek out the truth when the sponsoring client wishes to support its position at a trial? The ethical question stems from a conflict between legal ethics and research ethics. Although the courts have set judicial standards for marketing research methodology, perhaps only the client and individual researcher can resolve this question.

Privacy

Research participants deserve privacy, as discussed above, and this right means the researcher and sponsor are obliged to respect that right. Suppose a database marketing company is offering an e-mail list compiled by screening millions of households to obtain brand usage information. The

To the Point

"We are what we repeatedly do. Excellence then is not act but a habit."

—ARISTOTLE

advocacy research

Research undertaken to support a specific claim in a legal action or represent some advocacy group.

Honesty, the Only Policy?

Research provides the scientific mechanism through which disciplines grow the respective accumulated body of knowledge. Researchers who pursue motivations other than discovering and testing the validity of knowledge threaten the reputation of the research field and distort a truthful depiction of real-world phenomena.

Why might a researcher distort research results? The most typical motivation becomes when a researcher becomes more interested in being an advocate than identifying the truth. In other words, the researcher is promoting some position regardless of what the research may say because a certain position is more likely to keep him/her in the good graces of a supervisor, a client, governments, or a political society. Sometimes also, the motivation takes the form of self-promotion, where a researcher ends up distorting or even falsifying research reports to win a research grant and gain prestige within his/her discipline.

Unfortunately, the reality is that these pressures do affect what researchers report and publish. A large effort involving many psychology researchers aimed to replicate the experimental findings published in the top psychological research journals. The results were disappointing with only about 1/3 significant results being reproduced. Also, news about academic researchers who completely make up results and publish papers about research never conducted or who find ways to cheat publication systems by rigging the review process puts all of research in a bad light. This chapter discusses ways researchers should avoid allowing such influences to distort the research, not the least of which is to not do the research at all if the pressure for a certain result becomes stronger than the motivation to present the true results. When it comes to research, honesty should be the only policy!

Sources: Open Science Collaboration, (2015), "Estimating the Reproducibility of Psychological Science," *Science, 349*(6251), 943–952. Babin, B. J., M. Griffin, and J. F. Hair, Jr. (2016), "Heresies and Sacred Cows in Scholarly Marketing Publication," *Journal of Business Research*, 69, 3133–3138.

list would be extremely valuable to your firm, but you suspect the interviewers misled the individuals who filled out the information forms by telling them they were participating in an anonymous survey. Would it be ethical to purchase the mailing list? If respondents were deceived into providing their names, the practice is certainly unethical. The client and the research supplier have the obligation to maintain respondents' privacy, so selling it or buying it breeches good ethics.

Consider another example. Sales managers know that a marketing research survey of their business-to-business customers' buying intentions includes a means to attach a customer's name to each questionnaire. This confidential information could be of benefit to a sales representative calling on a specific customer. A client wishing to be ethical must resist the temptation to identify those accounts (i.e., those respondents) that are the hottest prospects.

Rights and Obligations of the Researcher

Marketing research firms and marketing research departments should practice good business ethics. Researchers are often the focus of discussions of business ethics because of the necessity that they interact with the public. Several professional organizations offer codes of ethics for marketing researchers, including the American Marketing Association, the European Society for Opinion and Market Research, and the Marketing Research Society. Many of these codes are lengthy and the full contents are available at the associations' websites. Key code components generally reflect the content of this chapter and prohibit:

- Representing a sales-pitch as marketing research
- Providing the name of respondents who were promised anonymity for some purpose other than the research
- Breaching the confidentiality of the research client or research participant

- Doing research for multiple firms competing in the same market
- Disseminating false or misleading results
- Plagiarizing the work of other researchers
- Violating the integrity of data gathered in the field

Unfortunately, researchers often succumb to pressures and violate the principles of ethical research. This even extends to academic researchers who feel pressure to publish research or who become zealous in supporting a social cause as the Research Snapshot illustrates. A well-regarded social psychologist published papers suggesting that people who eat meat are associated with selfishness. However, the pressure to publish and support this position proved too much and the researcher eventually admitted to fabricating data.[27] The discovery of the fabrication led to his resignation.

In addition, the researchers have rights. In particular, once a research consulting firm is hired to conduct some research, they have the right to cooperation from the sponsoring client. Also, the researchers have the right to be paid for the work they do as long as it is done professionally. Sometimes, the client may not like the results. But not liking the results is no basis for not paying. The client should pay the researcher for competent work in full and in a timely manner.

The Purpose of Research Is Research

Mixing Sales and Research
Consumers sometimes agree to participate in an interview that is purported to be pure research, but it eventually becomes obvious that the interview is really a sales pitch in disguise. This is unprofessional at best and fraudulent at worst. The Federal Trade Commission (FTC) has indicated that it is illegal to use any plan, scheme, or ruse that misrepresents the true status of a person seeking admission to a prospect's home, office, or other establishment. No research firm or basic marketing researcher should engage in any sales attempts. Applied market researchers working for the sponsoring company should also avoid overtly mixing research and sales. However, the line is becoming less clear with increasing technology.

Research That Isn't Research
Consider the following typical exchange between a product manager and a marketing researcher. The manager wants to hire the firm to do a test-market for a new product:

Researcher:	*What if the test results are favorable?*
Product manager:	*We'll launch the product nationally.*
Researcher:	*And if the results are unfavorable?*
Product manager:	*They won't be. I'm sure of that.*
Researcher:	*But just suppose they are.*
Product manager:	*I don't think we should throw out a good product just because of one little market test.*
Researcher:	*Then why test?*
Product manager:	*Listen, this is a major product introduction. It's got to have some research behind it!*

pseudo-research
Conducted not to gather information for marketing decisions but to bolster a point of view or satisfy other needs.

The product manager really wants research that will justify a decision he or she has already made. If the test-market's results contradict the decision, the product manager will almost certainly disregard the research. This type of study falls into the category of **pseudo-research** because the purpose is not to gather information for marketing decisions but to bolster a point of view and satisfy other needs.

In this situation, a researcher should walk away from the project if it appears that management strongly desires the research to support a predetermined opinion only. Although it is a fairly easy matter for an outside researcher to walk away from such a job, it is another matter for an in-house researcher to refuse such a job. Thus, avoiding pseudo-research is a right of the researcher but an obligation for the manager.

Occasionally, managers request marketing research simply to pass blame for failure to another area. A product manager may deliberately request a research study with no intention of paying attention to the findings and recommendations. The manager knows that the particular project is in trouble but plays the standard game to cover up for his or her mismanagement. If the project fails, marketing research will become the scapegoat. The ruse may involve a statement something like this: "well, research should have identified the problem earlier!"

Push Polls

Politicians concocted and specialize in a particular type of pseudo-research A **push poll** is telemarketing under the guise of research intended to "sell" a particular political position or point of view. The purpose of the poll is to push consumers into a predetermined response. For instance, a polling organization calls thousands of potential voters inviting each to participate in a survey. The interviewer then may ask loaded questions that put a certain spin on a candidate. "Do you think that candidate X, who is involved with people known to be linked to scandal and crime, can be trusted with the responsibility of office?" This is a push poll. An honest question may simply ask how much candidate X can be trusted.

Push polling doesn't always involve political candidates, but they usually involve political issues in some way. Residents do not always welcome new Walmart locations based on factors including the increase in traffic and congestion that the store can bring to an area. Chicago area residents received a polling call that went something like this:

> *The Mayor says that the proposed Walmart would bring over 400 jobs to this area and allow neighborhood residents access to fresh food. Do you support the new Walmart store's construction?*

The results indicated that over 70 percent of residents supported the new store.[28] However, the framing of the question by referencing the mayor and the mention of jobs without mentioning potential problems almost certainly swayed the results. Push polls may include only a single question like this whereas legitimate research almost always will ask more questions as researchers search for clues to understand a person's position on an issue.

Service Monitoring

Occasionally, the line between research and customer service is not completely clear. For instance, Toyota may survey all of its new car owners after the first year of ownership. Although the survey appears to be research, it may also provide information that could be used to correct some issue with the customer. For example, if the research shows that a customer is dissatisfied with the way the car handles, Toyota could follow up with the specific customer. The follow-up could result in changing the tires of the car, resulting in a smoother and quieter ride, as well as a more satisfied customer. Should a pattern develop showing other customers with the same opinion, Toyota may need to switch the original equipment tires used on this particular car.

push poll

Telemarketing under guise of research intended to "sell" a particular political position of point of view.

● ● ● ● ● ●

Push polling can be used to create a false impression of public opinion on controversial issues.

Sergey Yechikov/Shutterstock.com

Both research and customer service are involved and because the car is under warranty, no selling attempt exists. Researchers often design satisfaction surveys that include a means of opening a dialog between the company and the customer. Such practice is acceptable as long as the researcher makes the follow-up contact optional. The contact may provide a means of avoiding an experience that diminishes the value of a product.

To the Point

"He uses statistics as a drunken man uses a lamppost—for support rather than illumination. "

—ANDREW LANG

Misrepresentation of Research

Obviously, one sees that an ethical researcher does not misrepresent study results. This means, for instance, that the researcher states the statistical accuracy of a test precisely and does not overstate or understate the meaning of the findings. Both the researcher and client share this obligation. Consider a researcher reporting a positive relationship between advertising spending and sales. The researcher may also discover that this relationship disappears when the primary competitor's prices are taken into account. In other words, the competitor's prices account for at least part of the observed fluctuation in sales. Thus, it would be questionable, to say the least, to report a finding suggesting that sales could be increased by increasing ad spending without also mentioning the role that competitors' prices play in explaining sales.

Honesty in Presenting Results

Misrepresentation can also occur in the way a researcher presents results. For instance, charts can be created that make a very small difference appear very big. Likewise, they can be altered to make a meaningful difference seem small. Exhibit 4.6 illustrates this effect. Each chart presents exactly the same data. The data represent consumer responses to service quality ratings and satisfaction ratings. Both quality and satisfaction are collected on a 5-point strongly-disagree-to-strongly-agree scale. In frame A, the chart appears to show meaningful differences between men and women, particularly for the service-quality rating. However, notice that the scale range is shown as 4 to 5. In frame B, the researcher presents the same data but shows the full scale range (1 to 5). Now, the differences are reported as trivial.

All charts and figures should reflect fully the relevant range of values reported by respondents. If the scale range is from 1 to 5, then the chart should reflect a 1 to 5 range unless there is some value that is simply not used by respondents. If no or only a very few respondents had reported a 1 for their service quality or satisfaction rating, then it may be appropriate to show the range as 2 to 5. However, if there is any doubt, the researcher should show the full scale range.

The American Marketing Association's marketing Code of Ethics states that "a user of research shall not knowingly disseminate conclusions from a given research project or service that are inconsistent with or not warranted by the data." A dramatic example of a violation of this principle occurred in an advertisement of a cigarette smoker study. The advertisement compared two brands and stated that "of those expressing a preference, over 65 percent preferred" the advertised brand to a competing brand. The misleading portion of this reported result was that most of the respondents did *not* express a preference; they indicated that both brands tasted about the same. Thus, only a very small percentage of those studied actually revealed a preference, and the results were somewhat misleading. Such shading of results violates the obligation to report accurate findings.

Honesty in Reporting Errors and Limitations

Likewise, researchers should not keep any major error occurring during the course of the study a secret. Hiding errors or variations from the proper procedures can distort or shade the results. Similarly, every research design presents some limitations. For instance, the sample size may be smaller than ideal. The researcher should point out the key limitations in the research report and presentation. In this way, the users can understand any factors that qualify the findings. The decision-maker needs this information before deciding on any risky course of action.

Confidentiality

Confidentiality comes into play in several ways. The researcher must abide by any confidentiality agreement with research participants. For instance, a researcher conducting a descriptive research survey may have identified each participant's e-mail address in the course of conducting the

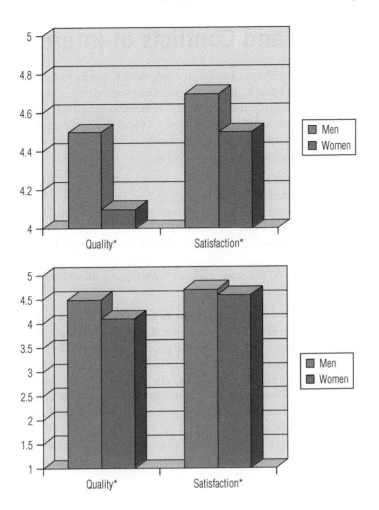

EXHIBIT **4.6**
How Results Can Be
Misrepresented in a Graphic

research. After seeing the results, the client may ask for the e-mail addresses as a logical prospect list. However, as long as the researcher assured each participant's confidentiality, he or she cannot provide the e-mail addresses to the firm. Indeed, a commitment of confidentiality also helps build trust among survey respondents.[29]

The marketing researcher often is obligated to protect the confidentiality of the research sponsor. In fact, business clients value marketing researchers' confidentiality more than any other attribute of a research firm.[30] Researchers must honor all implied and expressed promises of confidentiality, whether made to a research participant or research client.

The Role of Society at Large

Societies create and condone governments that oversee and regulate business and consumer activities. The do-not-call legislation provides an example of a way that governments restrict marketing research behavior. The Stop Online Piracy Act (SOPA) deals more with restrictions on consumers and Internet providers like Google with the intention of protecting the owners of intellectual and creative property. Society has an obligation to be fair and enact restrictions only when the benefits are justified in light of the difficulties those restrictions create. Furthermore, one point summarizes all the ethical obligations of marketing research in general. Marketing research offers benefits for individual members of and for society at large. However, research often involves some inconvenience in the form of intrusions like surveys. The potential benefits of the research should always outweigh the burdens placed on members of society. When this is true, the research is justified.

The role of society at large as a stakeholder also makes clear that ethics is not only for business. Business, society, and individuals all have ethical responsibilities. Marketing research value is diminished when any party breeches a responsibility.

The Researcher and Conflicts of Interest

Imagine a researcher conducting a test market for an Apple device that includes enhanced virtual reality (VR) capability among its benefits. Just after conducting the research, Samsung coincidentally contacts the same researcher. Samsung, who has yet to develop similar VR technology, wants research that addresses whether or not VR capability is something that will enhance the product's image. The researcher is now in a difficult position. Certainly, an ethical dilemma exists presenting multiple choices to the researcher, including the following.

- Agreeing to do the research for Samsung and using some results from the Apple study to prepare a report and recommendation for Samsung
- Agreeing to sell the new concept to Samsung without doing any additional research. In other words, provide Apple's company secrets to Samsung
- Conducting an entirely new project for Samsung without revealing any of the results or ideas from the Apple study
- Turning down the chance to do the study without revealing any information about Apple to Samsung

conflict of interest

Occurs when one researcher works for two competing companies and helping one could be detrimental to the other

Which is the best choice? Obviously, both of the first two options violate the principle of maintaining client confidentiality. Thus, both are unethical. The third choice, conducting an entirely new study, may be an option. However, it may prove nearly impossible to do the entire project as if the Apple study had never been done. Even with the best of intentions, the researcher may inadvertently violate confidentiality with Apple. The last choice is the best option from a moral standpoint. It avoids any potential **conflict of interest**. In other words, actions that would best serve one client, Samsung, would be detrimental to another client, Apple. Generally, it is best to avoid working for two direct competitors.

This would be a good time to revisit the opening chapter vignette. Does the situation present the researcher with any potential conflicts of interest? How can they be addressed?

TIPS OF THE TRADE

- Consider a career in research! A good way to get started in the marketing research industry is to target either a large marketing research firm or a small local research firm and offer to serve as an intern. An internship provides insight and experience that give one a leg up on others in getting a good research job.
- When a company faces a very emotional decision, it is usually better to have the research needed to address the related research questions done by an outside firm.
- One way to help ensure fair treatment of others involved in research is to consider whether you would like to be treated in this manner or whether you

would like someone to treat a close member of your family in such a manner.
- Research with particularly vulnerable segments such as children involves special care. When doing research with children under the age of 16, the researcher nearly always needs parental consent.
- Even the appearance of a conflict of interest can taint the research and the researcher. So, wise researchers stay away from such appearances.
- Remember that research is no longer research when its primary motivation is advocating a position or advocating the researcher's personal success or acclaim.

:: SUMMARY

1. **Know when research should be conducted externally and when it should be done internally.** The company that needs the research is not always the best company to perform the research. Sometimes, an outside supplier is more effective. An outside agency is better when the company desires a fresh perspective, when it would be difficult for inside researchers to be objective, and when the outside firm has some special expertise. In contrast, research in-house is better when the company needs it done very quickly, when the project requires close collaboration of many employees within the company, when the budget for the project is limited, and when secrecy is a major concern. The decision to go outside or stay inside for research depends on these particular issues.

2. **Understand the career opportunities and career paths available within the marketing research industry.** A marketing research career has never been more attractive. The demand for people with research skills continues to grow as the ability to record data unobtrusively expands with technology. Entry-level jobs may involve simple tasks such as searching social networks or performing survey research. A research analyst may be the next step on the career path. An experienced analyst typically earns a six-figure salary. Whereas there are several intermediate positions that differ depending on whether one works for a small or large firm, the director of marketing research is the chief information officer in charge of marketing information systems and research projects. The director plans, executes, and controls the marketing research function.

3. **Become sensitive to the often conflicting relationship between marketing management and researchers.** Researchers and managers often pursue conflicting goals. Some key sources of conflict include money, time, intuition, and experience. Managers want to spend the least amount of money on research as possible, have it done in the shortest time period conceivable, and believe that intuition and experience are good substitutes for research. Researchers will exchange greater expense for more precision in the research, would like to take more time to be more certain of results, and are hesitant to rely on intuition and experience. Better communication is a key to reducing this conflict. One tool that can be useful is the implementation of cross-functional teams.

4. **Understand marketing ethics and ways that researchers can face ethical dilemmas.** Marketing ethics is the application of morals to behavior related to the exchange environment. Generally, good ethic conforms to the notion of "right" and a lack of ethic conforms to the notion of "wrong." Those involved in marketing research face numerous ethical dilemmas. Researchers serve clients or, put another way, the doers of research serve the users. A doer may find himself or herself tempted to compromise professional standards in an effort to please the user. After all, the user pays the bills. Given the large number of ethical dilemmas involved in research, ethics is highly applicable to marketing research.

5. **Appreciate the rights and obligations of (a) research respondents—particularly children, (b) research clients or sponsors, (c) marketing researchers, and (d) society.** Each party involved in research has certain rights and obligations. These are generally interdependent in the sense that one party's right often leads to an obligation for another party. Although the rights and obligations of all parties are important, the obligation of the researcher to protect research participants is particularly important. Experimental manipulations can sometimes expose subjects to some form of harm or involve them in a ruse. The researcher must offer subjects the chance to be informed fully of the true purpose of the research during a debriefing. The researcher must also avoid subjecting participants to undue physical or psychological trauma. In the end, the total value of research should exceed the cost to society.

6. **Avoid situations involving a conflict of interest in performing marketing research.** A marketing research conflict of interest occurs when a researcher faces doing something to benefit one client at the expense of another client. One situation where this occurs is when a researcher could use results obtained in a study done for Brand A to prepare a report for its primary competitor Brand B. The researcher might consider recollecting the data anew for Brand B, but even this opens up the researcher to the appearance of a conflict of interest. The best way to avoid a conflict of interest is to avoid getting involved with multiple projects involving competing firms within some market.

:: KEY TERMS AND CONCEPTS

advocacy research, *96*
anonymity, *92*
confidentiality, *92*
conflict of interest, *102*
cross-functional teams, *84*
custom research, *82*
debriefing, *94*
digital market research specialist, *83*
director of marketing research, *83*
do-not-call legislation, *91*
ethical dilemma, *89*

forecast analyst, *83*
human subjects review committee, *95*
idealism, *89*
informed consent, *91*
implicit consent, *92*
in-house research, *77*
internet of things, *79*
Institutional Review Board (IRB), *95*
manager of decision support systems, *83*
marketing ethics, *89*
moral standards, *89*

outside agency, *77*
placebo, *94*
pseudo-research, *98*
push poll, *99*
relativism, *89*
research analyst, *83*
research assistants, *83*
research suppliers, *80*
standardized research service, *81*
syndicated service, *80*

:: QUESTIONS FOR REVIEW AND CRITICAL THINKING

1. What conditions make in-house research preferable? What conditions make outside research preferable? Would a family-owned agricultural company considering changing its name from the family name to Dynamic farming be better to research the idea in-house or out-house?

2. Explain what a syndicated service research firm does and contrast it with standardized research service. Provide examples of each.

3. Why is marketing research such an attractive career today?

4. What is a digital market research specialist?

5. What might the organizational structure of the research department be like for the following organizations?
   a. A large conglomerate like Alphabet
   b. An advertising agency like Wieden & Kennedy
   c. A family owned company specializing in drones for crop dusting. The company has 90 employees.
   d. A not-for-profit health-care organization like St. Jude Children's Hospital
   e. Your university

6. What problems do marketing research directors face in their roles as managers?

7. What are the managerial motivations that prove a source of conflict with marketing research?

8. What researcher motivations prove a source of conflict with management?

9. Search Internet job sites. Try to gather three to five want ads that are for marketing research positions of some type. Comment on the salary ranges and expected qualifications listed in these ads.

10. What is a cross-functional team? How is it relevant to marketing research?

11. What is the difference between research and pseudo-research? Cite several examples of each.

12. What is the definition of marketing ethics? How are marketing ethics relevant to research?

13. What is the difference between ethical relativism and ethical idealism? How might a person with an idealist ethical philosophy and a person with a relativist ethical philosophy differ with respect to including a sales pitch at the end of a research survey?

14. What is the difference between anonymity and confidentiality? What obligations does a researcher have with respect to confidentiality?

15. How should a marketing researcher help top management better understand the functions and limitations of research?

16. List at least one research obligation for research participants (respondents), marketing researchers, and research clients (sponsors).

17. What is a conflict of interest in a research context? How can such conflicts of interest be avoided?

18. What key questions help resolve the question of whether or not research participants serving as subjects in an experiment are treated ethically?

19. How do societal forces play a role in shaping research ethics?

20. Comment on the ethics of the following situations.
   a. A warehouse club advertises "savings up to 30 percent" after a researcher presented management with survey results suggesting store prices ranged from 5 percent above the competition to 30 percent below the average competitor prices.
   b. Hotel management ask a researcher to analyze data consisting of the names of guests attending a professional conference, the titles of any PPV movies (in-room) they purchased, a list of products consumed from the mini-bar, and a list of room service purchases.
   c. A researcher tells a potential respondent that an interview will last 10 minutes rather than the 30 minutes he or she actually anticipates.
   d. A respondent tells an interviewer that she wishes to cooperate with the survey, but her time is valuable and, therefore, she expects to be paid for her responses.
   e. An academic researcher performs basic research based on Facebook comments from guys talking about female acquaintances using salacious terms.
   f. An online dating company stores the GPS locations of users, tracks their whereabouts, and sells an app that offers users an alert when a lot of "daters" are within a 10-minute radius.

21. Go back and review the example of a researcher wishing to conduct research about consumers and tattoos discussed in the chapter. (a) What ethical concepts does the example illustrate? (b) Describe a way in which the research could be designed to avoid any ethical issues.

:: RESEARCH ACTIVITIES

1. Find the mission statement of three of the top research firms described earlier in the chapter (see Exhibit 4.2). What career opportunities exist at these firms (click on the careers tab)? Would you consider each firm a small, mid-sized, or large firm? How might working with one of these firms differ from working in your own market research business?
2. Imagine a study being conducted by a senior manager at Apple who is interested in driving more business through iTunes.

The manager's ideas require a huge capital investment and are predicated on Apple operating systems dominating the smartphone (and tablet) market. Do some research on the Internet to find statistics for the market shares of various operating systems. Prepare a chart that displays the relative market shares as if you were presenting to the manager. As a researcher, is there potential for conflict or even ethical consequences based on the results?

Global Eating

Case 4.1

Barton Boomer, director of marketing research for a large research firm, has a bachelor's degree in marketing from Kansas State University. He joined the firm nine years ago after a one-year stint as a marketing research trainee at the corporate headquarters of a western packing corporation. Barton has a wife and two children. He earns $70,000 a year and owns a home in the suburbs. He is typical of a marketing junior research analyst. He is asked to interview an executive with a local restaurant chain, Eats-R-Wee. Eats-R-Wee is expanding internationally. The logical two choices for expansion are either to expand first to other nations that have values similar to those in the market area of Eats-R-Wee or to expand to the nearest geographical neighbor. During the initial interviews, Mr. Big, Vice President of Operations for Eats-R-Wee, makes several points to Barton.

- "Barton, we are all set to move across the border to Ontario and begin our international expansion with our neighbor to the north, Canada. Can you provide some research that will support this position?"

- "Barton, we are in a hurry. We can't sit on our hands for weeks waiting to make this decision. We need a comprehensive research project completed by the end of the month."
- "We are interested in how our competitors will react. Have you ever done research for them?"
- "Don't worry about the fee; we'll pay you top money for a 'good' report."

Marla Madam, Barton's Director of Marketing Research, encourages Barton to get back in touch with Mr. Big and tell him that the project will get underway right away.

Questions
Critique this situation with respect to Barton's job. What recommendations would you have for him? Should the company get involved with the research? What might be conditions of the agreement presented to Mr. Big. Explain your answers.

Ryan McVay/Getty Images

Big *Brother* Is Watching?

Case 4.2

Technology is making our behavior more and more difficult to keep secret. Right at this very moment, there is probably some way that your location can be tracked in a way that researchers could use the information. Do you have a smartphone with you? Is there an RFID tag in your shirt, your backpack, credit card or some other personal item? Are you in your car, and does it have a GPS device? All of these are ways that your location and movements might be tracked.

For instance, rental cars can be tracked using GPS. Suppose a research firm contracts with an insurance firm to study the way people drive when using a rental car. A customer's every movement is then tracked. So, if the customer stops at a fast-food restaurant, the researcher knows. If the customer goes to the movie when he or she should be on a sales call, the researcher knows. If the customer is speeding, the researcher knows.

Clearly, modern technology is making confidentiality more and more difficult to maintain. Although legitimate uses of this type of

technology may assist in easing traffic patterns and providing better locations for service stations, shopping developments, and other retailers, at what point does the collection of such information become a concern? When would you become concerned about having your whereabouts constantly tracked?

Question

Suppose a Geographic Information Systems (GIS) research firm is approached by the state legislature and asked to provide data about vehicle movement within the state for all cars that can be tracked with direct GPS or through the owner's smartphone. Based on the movement of the cars (and phones) over a certain time, the police can decide when a car was speeding. They intend on using this data to send speeding tickets to those who moved too far, too fast. Also, if an underage driver spends too long parked by an adult only establishment, police will be notified to investigate. If you are the research firm, would you supply the data? Discuss the ethical implications of the decision.

:::::: Qualitative Research Tools

iStock.com/Opidianus

LEARNING OUTCOMES

After studying this chapter, you should be able to:

1. Contrast qualitative research with quantitative research
2. Know the role of qualitative research in exploratory research designs
3. Describe the basic orientations of qualitative research
4. Understand the strengths and weaknesses of common qualitative tools and how digital processes sometimes assist efforts
5. Prepare a focus group interview outline
6. Recognize ways social networking and the *blogosphere* provide opportunities for qualitative research
7. Appreciate the role of exploratory qualitative research in scientific decision making

Chapter Vignette:

Courtesy, Vans Classic Slip-On

The VF Corporation often doesn't register high top-of-mind awareness. However, consumers are very familiar with some of the many brands within its portfolio. While all the VF brands share a meaning related to an active lifestyle, brands like North Face, Timberland, Wrangler, Lee, and Vans each express this meaning in a slightly different way. VF continued to grow through the most recent economic malaise that began about 2009 and is only recently ending. A great deal of the growth comes from the brands that best match specific customer segments with lifestyle products capable of allowing consumers within those segments to express themselves meaningfully. VF is counting on Vans as a leader in their continued growth. To do this, Vans has to continue to understand exactly how the brand can create value and identify more customer segments eager for the same experience.

Qualitative research provides the focus of this chapter and provides tools that allow Vans to understand its value proposition. The Vans brand is long associated with shoes for skateboarding, although many of its shoes never see a skateboard these days. Vans' growth followed input from market research exploring the skateboard culture and the activities, interests, and opinions that appeal to this segment. So, what is in the mind and heart of a *boarder*? Researchers addressed the research question using an ethnographic approach and discovered that a carefree and detached attitude, a free spirit, and a rejection of

conventional society were characteristics defining the culture. Unlike mere shoes, Vans have to help the customer realize these feelings. Thus, Vans can't get by on comfort alone. Growth depends on creating hedonic value more than utilitarian value.

The research led to the adoption of an "off the wall" attitude, literally, as the slogan spun off product ideas, images, an Internet television series, and products that tapped into popular unpop culture! Vans embraces its heritage with old-school styles like the Slip-On, in various motifs, Era, and the Authentic. VF's research is now pointing them toward Europe, where they believe youth markets are eager to experience the "off the wall" lifestyle. Realizing Vans is very much an experience brand,

Source: ESQUIRE MAGAZINE

VF is spearheading this effort with the first and only **House of Vans**. Vans fans can experience the retail theater in London, England, where tourists from all around Europe can go off the wall. VF engineers a different meaning for its Timberland brand through an emphasis on direct to consumer marketing, with over 240 retail stores playing an important role in that effort, and outreach through community service often featured in social media images that highlight Timberland boots. A deep understanding of the brand becomes essential to market growth and success.[1]

Source: www.vfc.com

• • • • • • •

VF Corp, like other diversified marketers, must manage a portfolio of brands each offering a varied interpretation of the overall brand (from vfc.com).

Introduction: What Is Qualitative Research?

Chemists sometimes use the term *qualitative analysis* to refer to research that determines the makeup of some compound. In other words, the focus is on the inner meaning of specific chemicals—their *qualities*. As the word implies, qualitative research is interested more in *qualities* than quantities. In the same way, qualitative research aims to gain an understanding of phenomena, often extending beyond the obvious.

Describing Qualitative Research

Qualitative marketing research is research that addresses marketing objectives through techniques allowing the researcher to provide elaborate interpretations of market phenomena without depending on quantitative measurement. The focus is on discovering new insights and true inner meanings. Marketing researchers commonly perform and many research firms specialize in qualitative research.

Qualitative research designs employ less structure than most quantitative approaches. Participants in qualitative research do not choose numerical (or multiple choice) responses to a specific question. Instead, qualitative approaches are more **researcher-dependent** in that the researcher must extract meaning from open-ended responses, such as text from a recorded interview or a posting on a social media website like Facebook, or from a collage representing the meaning of some experience, such as skateboarding. The researcher interprets the data to extract its meaning, which informs marketing decision-makers or feeds into more research.

Uses of Qualitative Research

Mechanics can't use a hammer to fix everything that is broken. Instead, a mechanic chooses the tool from a toolbox that he/she believes matches best to a given problem. Marketing research is the same. The researcher has many tools available and the research design should try to match the

qualitative marketing research

Research that addresses marketing objectives through techniques that allow the researcher to provide elaborate interpretations of market phenomena without depending on quantitative measurement; its focus is on discovering new insights and true inner meanings.

researcher-dependent

Research in which the researcher must extract meaning from unstructured responses such as text from a recorded interview or a collage representing the meaning of some experience.

Most comprehensive research projects involve both qualitative and quantitative research. Oftentimes, qualitative research provides essential insight that is helpful in identifying relevant market or consumer phenomena and developing research questions, which provide structure for the remaining research. When researchers employ an exploratory research design, qualitative research may be the only type of research involved. Qualitative research also is facilitated by the ease of access to actual consumer communication left in online reviews, Tweets, and in Instagram and Facebook posts, among other outlets. Thus, when you get involved in research, quality does not take a back seat to quantity.

best tool to the research objective. Also, just as a mechanic is probably not an expert with every tool, each researcher usually has special expertise with a small number of tools. Not every researcher has expertise with tools that would comprise qualitative research.

Generally, the less specific the research objective, the more likely that qualitative research tools will be appropriate. Also, when the emphasis is on a deeper understanding of motivations or on discovering novel concepts, qualitative research is very appropriate. The following list represents common situations that often call for qualitative research.[2]

1. When a researcher faces difficulty developing specific and actionable decision statements or research objectives. For instance, if, after several interviews with a research client, a researcher still cannot determine what things he/she needs to measure, qualitative research approaches may help with problem definition and, as a result, identify research questions indicating what to measure.
2. When the research objective involves developing a very detailed and in-depth understanding of some phenomena. Qualitative research tools help reveal the primary themes indicating human motivations and the documentation of activities is usually very complete.
3. When the research objective is to learn how consumers use a product in its natural setting or to learn how to express some concept in colloquial terms. A survey can probably ask many useful questions, but watching how someone actually experiences a product will usually be more insightful. Qualitative research produces many product improvement ideas.
4. When some behavior the researcher is studying is particularly context-dependent—meaning the reasons something is liked or some behavior is performed depends very much on the particular situation surrounding the event. The skating environment frames the situation in which researchers understand the Vans brand best.
5. When the researcher needs a fresh approach. This is particularly the case when quantitative research results on some issue have been less than satisfying. Qualitative tools can yield unique insights, many of which may lead to new product ideas.

Each situation also describes a situation that may require an exploratory orientation. In Chapter 3, we indicated that researchers sometimes need exploratory research just to reach the appropriate decision statement and research objectives. Although equating qualitative research with exploratory research is an oversimplification, the application of qualitative tools can help clear up ambiguity and provide innovative ideas.

Qualitative "versus" Quantitative Research

In social science, one can find many debates about the superiority of qualitative research over quantitative research or vice versa.[3] We'll begin by saying that this is largely a superfluous argument in either direction. The truth is that qualitative research can accomplish research objectives that quantitative research cannot. Similarly truthful, but no more so, quantitative research can accomplish objectives that qualitative research cannot. The key to successfully using either is to match the right approach to the right research context.

Many good research projects combine both qualitative and quantitative research.[4] For instance, developing valid survey measures requires first a deep understanding of the concept measured and second a description of the way people express these perceptions in everyday language. Both of these are tasks best suited for qualitative research. However, validating the measure formally to make sure it can reliably capture the intended concept will likely require quantitative research.[5] Also, qualitative research may be needed to separate symptoms from problems and then quantitative research may follow to test relationships among relevant variables. The term **mixed-methods** now is commonly used to describe research employing both qualitative and quantitative research tools in a single project.

Quantitative marketing research addresses research objectives through empirical assessments that involve numerical measurement and analytical approaches. Quantitative research is more apt to stand on its own in the sense that it entails less interpretation and is quite appropriate when a research objective involves a managerial action standard. For example, a salad dressing company considered changing its recipe.[6] Researchers tested the new recipe using a sample of consumers who rated the product using 100-point numeric scales. Management established a rule requiring 90 percent confidence that a majority of consumers would rate the new product higher than the old product before replacing a recipe. The results require little interpretation beyond the computations. A project like this uses both quantitative measurement in the form of numeric rating scales and quantitative analysis in the form of applied statistical procedures.

Contrasting Qualitative with Quantitative Methods

Exhibit 5.1 illustrates some differences between qualitative and quantitative research. Certainly, these are generalities, and exceptions apply but it covers some of the key distinctions.

Quantitative researchers direct a considerable amount of activity toward measuring concepts with scales that directly or indirectly provide numeric values. The user inputs the resulting numeric

mixed-methods

Term frequently used to describe research employing both qualitative and quantitative research tools in a single project.

quantitative marketing research

Addresses research objectives through empirical assessments that involve numerical measurement and statistical and/or computational analysis.

EXHIBIT **5.1**

Comparing Qualitative and Quantitative Research

Qualitative Research	Research Aspect	Quantitative Research
Discover Ideas, Used in Exploratory Research with General Research Objects	Common Purpose	Test Hypotheses or Specific Research Questions
Observe and Interpret	Approach	Measure and Test
Unstructured, Free-Form	Data Collection Approach	Structured Response Categories Provided
Researcher Is Intimately Involved. Results Are Subjective.	Researcher Independence	Researcher Uninvolved Observer. Results Are Objective.
Small Samples—Often in Natural Settings	Samples	Large Samples to Produce Generalizable Results (Results That Apply to Other Situations)
Exploratory Research Designs	Most Often Used	Descriptive and Causal Research Designs

Source: William Zikmund and Barry Babin, *Essentials of Marketing Research*, 5th ed, Cengage Learning, 2012.

values into statistical computations and hypothesis testing. As will be described in detail later, this process involves comparing numbers in some way. In contrast, qualitative researchers are more interested in observing, listening, and interpreting. The qualitative researcher intimately involves him/herself in the research process and in constructing the results. For these reasons, qualitative research results are researcher-dependent, or **subjective**, meaning that different researchers may reach different conclusions based on the same data. In contrast, when a survey respondent provides a satisfaction score on a quantitative scale, the score is more objective because the number will be the same no matter what researcher is involved in the analysis.

subjective

Researcher-dependent results with the consequence that different researchers may reach different conclusions (meanings) based on the same interview.

Qualitative research usually involves smaller samples than the typical quantitative study. Instead of sampling hundreds of consumers, a handful of them are usually sufficient as a source of qualitative data. Small samples are perfectly acceptable in discovery-oriented research. All ideas discovered still need testing before companies put them into practice. Does a smaller sample mean that qualitative research is cheaper than quantitative? Perhaps not. Although researchers observe fewer respondents, the greater researcher involvement in both the data collection and analysis can drive up the costs of qualitative research.

Small samples, interpretive procedures that require subjective judgments and an unstructured interview format all make traditional hypotheses testing complicated with qualitative research. Thus, these procedures are not the best for drawing definitive conclusions. A causal design is better suited for testing. These disadvantages for drawing inferences, however, become advantages when the goal is to draw out potential explanations. The researcher spends more time with each respondent and is therefore able to explore much more ground due to the flexibility of the procedures.

Qualitative Research and Exploratory Research Designs

When researchers have limited experience or knowledge about an issue, exploratory research is useful. Exploratory research can be an essential first step to a more rigorous, conclusive, confirmatory study by reducing the chance of beginning with an inadequate, incorrect, or misleading set of research objectives.

Philosophically, we can classify research as either exploratory or confirmatory. Confirmatory research tests hypotheses. The test results help decision making by suggesting a specific course of action. Exploratory research, on the other hand, is different and plays a key role in developing ideas that lead to research hypotheses in the first place.

Most exploratory research designs produce **qualitative data**. Qualitative data are not characterized by numeric values and instead involve textual, visual, or oral information. The focus of qualitative research is not on numbers but on stories, visual portrayals, meaningful characterizations, interpretations, and other expressive descriptions. Exploratory designs do not rely so strongly on **quantitative data**, which represent phenomena by assigning numeric values in an ordered and meaningful way.

Researchers can sometimes conduct a qualitative study very quickly. Political researchers often are called on to address questions related to possible negative publicity due to some breaking news associated with a candidate. Within hours of the news breaking, researchers for the candidate, and likely those for the opposing candidate, conduct focus groups and interpret the results. Other types of qualitative research, as we will see, can take months to complete.

qualitative data

Data that are not characterized by numeric values and instead are textual, visual, or oral; focus is on stories, visual portrayals, meaningful characterizations, interpretations, and other expressive descriptions.

quantitative data

Represent phenomena by assigning numeric values in an ordered and meaningful way.

Idea Generation

Exploratory research plays a big role in new product development, including developing and screening new product ideas. It is particularly useful in idea generation and screening by producing multiple ideas and then narrowing the choices down to a small number of alternatives. In this process, exploratory research may indicate that some new product ideas are unworkable.

Qualitative research can generate ideas for new products, advertising copy, promotional ideas, and product improvements in numerous ways. Researchers using qualitative approaches can ask consumers to describe their product experiences in great detail. This data can reveal the consumer needs that a product can truly address. For example, a consumer may describe their dog food experiences. When asked what he/she wants in a dog food, the reply likely will be, "Something that is good for the dog." Once the consumer is encouraged to continue, however, we may learn that the dog food "smells bad in the refrigerator" and "is messy to clean up." Thus, the interview reveals that needs related to dog food are not entirely centered on the dog.

Idea generation proves difficult for students and for managers alike. Thus, researchers must keep an open mind when conducting qualitative research and interpreting data. No doubt, managers dismiss many good ideas because they sound crazy. But, just think of how many crazy products we use—at least products that would've seemed crazy at some point in time. Here is a quick and simple checklist to help create a creative mindset when looking for new ideas.

To the Point

"Innovation ... endows resources with a new capacity to create wealth."

—PETER DRUCKER

1. Quantity Leads to Quality—A breakthrough idea is more likely to exist in a list of 300 ideas than in a list of 3 ideas.
2. Wilder Is Better—In an exploratory mode, encourage respondents to think of wild ideas. Stretch beyond realistic boundaries to see what might be.
3. Do Not Judge—People are naturally judgmental. Premature judgment kills many great ideas. Idea generation is exploratory work and there is no room for judgment here.
4. Question Assumptions—When interpreting a respondent's comments, do not impose assumptions that may not exist. Follow up to examine important assumptions. The phrase "think outside of the box" is all about trying to break through false assumptions.

Concept Testing

Concept testing is a frequently performed type of exploratory research representing many similar research procedures all having the same purpose: to screen new, revised, or repositioned ideas. Despite the term *testing*, concept testing approaches aim to discover issues related to a potential product innovation. Typically, respondents see a description, picture, and/or model, or get to try out an actual sample, and then provide comments. The questions almost always include whether the idea is likable, whether it would be useful, and whether it seems new. Respondents then elaborate on the idea orally, in writing, or through some visual communication. Concept testing allows an initial

concept testing

A frequently performed type of exploratory research representing many similar research procedures all having the same purpose: to screen new, revised, or repositioned ideas.

EXHIBIT **5.2**

Testing New Product Concepts

Component	Concept	
	Havana's	Bekkah
Brand Image	Family oriented, Cuban themed, with generous portions of modestly priced food	Upscale hangout for on–the-go individuals looking for a change of pace
Atmosphere	Bright colors, Cuban music all day and every day with every restaurant built around a bar featuring genuine '57 Chevys	Muted colors and stone walls giving the appearance of an oasis in an arid climate
Product Assortment	Traditional Cuban slow-cooked meats with generous sides like black beans and fried plantains. Cuban sangria and a wide assortment of beer are featured.	Lebanese meats sliced very thin with traditional Middle Eastern seasonings, a variety of pita breads, feta cheese, and yogurt relishes. Lebanese wines are featured and supplement an otherwise domestic collection.
Price Points	Average ticket per customer is projected to be around $14.	Average ticket per customer is projected to be around $26.
Location	Suburban location around the top 10 largest metropolitan areas in the United States and Canada	Major SMSAs (standard metropolitan statistical areas) across the southern United States from San Diego, CA, to Jacksonville, FL

Source: William Zikmund and Barry Babin, *Essentials of Marketing Research*, 5th ed, *Cengage Learning*, 2012.

evaluation prior to the commitment of any additional research and development, manufacturing, or other company resources. Perhaps just as importantly, the researcher interprets respondent comments qualitatively searching for themes to potentially improve the product.

Concept testing processes work best when they not only identify ideas with the most potential but also lead to important refinements. Rite Aid drug stores first successfully concept-tested a new store layout. Dubbed the Wellness Store, the new design features lower shelves, wider aisles, and a more focused merchandise assortment emphasizing personal well-being. The redesign illustrates the brand's commitment to its customers' wellness. Through the concept testing, they learned that people are part of the design. Consequently, the Rite-Aid Wellness Store concept also includes a Wellness Ambassador.[7] The service associate adorned in a light-blue coat provides help communicating with the pharmacist and addressing questions that might otherwise require waiting for the pharmacist.

Likewise, if Vans introduces snowboarding and biking products as a way of increasing sales revenues, those products will have to undergo concept screening. Will consumers respond favorably to the ideas of a Vans Cushioned Snowboard or Vans Napoleon Dynamite line? Clearly, concept testing including probing interview techniques will be helpful in this effort.

Exhibit 5.2 shows excellent concept statements for two new alternative chain restaurant concepts. A national franchise operating various chain restaurants that compete with the likes of Hooters and Outback Steakhouse is interested in this concept. The statements portraying the intangibles (brand image, product appearance, name, and price) and a description of the product simulate reality. A researcher conveys the product idea clearly to the research participant, who then responds in some way. Their comments become the key information gleaned from the study.

Qualitative Research Orientations

Researchers perform qualitative research in many ways using many techniques. Each researcher's orientation toward qualitative research is influenced by the different fields of study. These orientations are each associated with a category of qualitative research. The major categories of qualitative research include:

1. Phenomenology—originating in philosophy and psychology
2. Ethnography—originating in anthropology

3. Grounded theory—originating in sociology
4. Case studies—originating in psychology and in business research

Precise lines among these approaches are difficult to draw, and a particular qualitative research study may involve elements of two or more approaches. However, each category does reflect a somewhat unique approach to human inquiry and approaches to discovering knowledge. Each will be described briefly, followed by a description of some of the more common qualitative techniques used to generate qualitative data.

Phenomenology

What Is a Phenomenological Approach to Research?

Phenomenology represents a philosophical approach to studying human experiences based on the idea that human experience itself is inherently subjective and determined by the contexts in which people live.[8] The phenomenological researcher focuses on how relationships between a person and the physical environment, objects, people, or situations shape a person's behavior. Phenomenological inquiry seeks to describe, reflect upon, and interpret experiences.

Researchers with a phenomenological orientation rely largely on conversational interview tools. The phenomenological interviewer is careful to avoid asking direct questions when at all possible. Instead, the interviewer asks respondents to tell a story about some experience. In addition, the researcher must do everything possible to make sure a respondent is comfortable telling his/her story. One way to accomplish this is to become a member of the group (e.g., becoming a skateboarder to understand skateboarding culture). Another way may be to avoid having the person use his/her real name. This might be particularly necessary in studying potentially sensitive topics, including smoking, shoplifting, or employee theft.

A phenomenological approach to studying the Vans brand may require considerable time. The researcher may first spend weeks or months fitting in with the person or group of interest to establish a comfort level. The researcher makes careful notes of conversations. If the interviewer seeks an actual interview, he/she would likely not begin by asking a skateboarder to describe his/her shoes. Rather, asking for favorite skateboard incidents or talking about what makes a skateboarder unique may generate productive conversation. Generally, the approach is very unstructured as a way of avoiding leading questions and to provide every opportunity for new insights.

What Is Hermeneutics?

The term *hermeneutics* is important in phenomenology. **Hermeneutics** is an approach to understanding phenomenology that relies on analysis of texts in which a person tells a story about him/herself.[9] The interpretive research extracts meaning by connecting text passages to one another or to themes expressed outside the story. The connections provide a way of coding the key meanings expressed in a story. Although a full understanding of hermeneutics is beyond the scope of this text, qualitative tools often employ some of the key terminology. For instance, a **hermeneutic unit** refers to a text passage from a respondent's story that is linked with a key theme from within this story or a theme provided by the researcher.[10] The qualitative researcher uses these passages to interpret the data.

Listening is a necessary skill for phenomenological researchers. A researcher with keen listening skills picks up on the meaningful themes. Researchers in New Zealand used a hermeneutic approach to explore how religion influences adoption of activities and services, particularly those with some multicultural meaning.[11] Hermeneutic units from conversations taking place in an environment where consumers are comfortable and candid reveal key themes about the ways products are used and can spur ideas for product improvement, advertising, or new products.

Software exists to assist in coding transcripts, texts, audio, video, or photographic evidence into meaningful units. ATLAS.ti is one such software package that adopts the term *hermeneutic unit* in referring to groups of phrases that are linked with meaning. The following Research Snapshot demonstrates the use of hermeneutics in interpreting a story about a consumer shopping for a car.

phenomenology

A philosophical approach to studying human experiences based on the idea that human experience itself is inherently subjective and determined by the context in which people live.

hermeneutics

An approach to understanding phenomenology that relies on analysis of texts through which a person tells a story about him/herself.

hermeneutic unit

Refers to a text passage from a respondent's story that is linked with a key theme from within this story or a theme provided by the researcher.

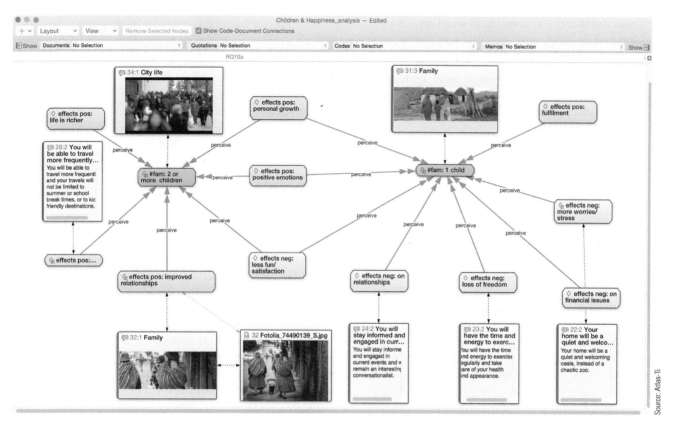

Source: Atlas-Ti

Qualitative research is facilitated by software like Atlas-Ti, which aids in interpretation by pulling data together into meaning units.

Ethnography

What Is Ethnography?

Ethnography represents ways of studying cultures through methods that involve becoming highly active within that culture. **Participant-observation** typifies an ethnographic research approach. Participant-observation means the researcher immerses him/herself within the culture that he/she is studying and draws data from the resulting observations. A *culture* can be either a broad culture, like American culture, or a narrow culture, like urban gangs or skateboarding enthusiasts. Increasingly, ethnographic approaches address the meaning of belonging to and participation in online communities. Often, the researcher participates as a member of the community in employing ethnographic procedures. The term **netnography** sometimes is used to refer to the application of ethnography to online phenomena.[12] A researcher may get involved in an online Vans social community to better understand the brand and the skateboarding lifestyle.

Indeed, issues like brand meaning and consumer-brand identity lend themselves very well to ethnographic study. Participants are typically more relaxed than in formal interview settings and thus more open. For instance, a research team used participant-observation while investigating the meaning of Nike.[13] Although "Just Do It" is easily recalled as associated with Nike, Nike also strongly evokes "fun" and "easy-going" in addition to a strong connection with famous athlete-endorsers. Nike's meaning stands in contrast to Vans' meaning, which associates more with anarchy.

Observation in Ethnography

Observation plays a key role in ethnography. Still and video photography prove useful in ethnographic research. With a home-owner's permission, small cameras can be placed in a person's home to see how certain products are used. For example, videos of the kitchen could lead to help interpretations leading to innovative appliance designs. Cameras can even be placed on pets to track their behavior!

Ethnographic study can be particularly useful when a certain culture is composed of individuals who cannot or will not verbalize their thoughts and feelings. For instance, ethnography has

ethnography

Represents ways of studying cultures through methods that involve becoming highly active within that culture.

participant-observation

Ethnographic research approach where the researcher becomes immersed within the culture that he/she is studying and draws data from his/her observations.

netnography

The application of ethnographic research procedures to online phenomena.

RESEARCH SNAPSHOT

AP Images/Lenny Ignelzi

"When Will I Ever Learn?"

A hermeneutic approach can be used to provide insight into car shopping experiences. The approach involves a small number of consumers providing relatively lengthy stories about recent car shopping experiences. The goal is trying to discover particular reasons why they eliminate certain car models from consideration. The consumer tells a story of comparing a Ford and a General Motors (GM) minivan. The researcher in this story goes on to interpret the plotline of the story as having to do with her responsibility for poor consumption outcomes. Consider the following passage.

"It has got GM defects and that is really frustrating. I mean the transmission had to be rebuilt after about 150 miles … and it had this horrible vibration problem. We took a long vacation where you couldn't go over sixty miles an hour because the thing started shaking so bad…. I told everybody, 'Don't buy one of these things.' We should have known because our Buick—the Buick that is in the shop right now—its transmission lasted about 3,000 miles. My husband's parents are GM people and they had one go bad. I keep thinking, When I am going to learn? I think this one has done it. I don't think I will ever go back to GM after this."

The research concludes that a hermeneutic link exists between the phrase "When I am going to learn?" and the plot of self-responsibility. The resulting behavior including no longer considering GM products and the negative word-of-mouth behavior are ways of restoring esteem given the events.

Sources: *Journal of Marketing Research* by Winer, Russ. Copyright 1997 by Am Marketing Assn (AMA) (CHIC). Reproduced with permission of Am Marketing Assn (AMA) (CHIC) in the format Textbook via Copyright Clearance Center. Thompson, Craig J., "Interpreting Consumers: A Hermeneutical Framework for Deriving Marketing Insights from the Tests of Consumers' Consumption Stories," *Journal of Marketing Research*, 34 (November 1997), 438–455 (see pp. 443–444).

© George Doyle & Ciaran Griffin

Alyson Aliano/The Image Bank/Getty Images

● ● ● ● ● ● ●

Ethnographic (participant-observation) approaches may be useful in understanding how children obtain value from their experiences with toys.

advantages for discovering insights among children because it does not rely largely on their answers to questions. Instead, the researcher can simply become part of the environment, allow the children to do what they do naturally, and record their behavior.[14]

● ● ●

The opening vignette describes a situation in which ethnographic research may be appropriate. A researcher might blend into a skateboard group. The artifacts shared by the group, including photos posted on the group's wall, may provide meaning. Also, researchers who act as customers can perform ethnography by becoming a natural part of the environment. Researchers posing as restaurant customers developed lists of the most critical service failures in restaurants and interpreted meanings for things such as slow service, inappropriate server behavior, and food waste.[15]

Grounded Theory

What Is Grounded Theory?

grounded theory

Represents an inductive investigation in which the researcher poses questions about information provided by respondents or taken from historical records; the researcher asks the questions to him/herself and repeatedly questions the responses to derive deeper explanations.

Grounded theory represents an inductive investigation in which the researcher poses questions about information provided by respondents or taken from historical records. The researcher asks the questions to him/herself and repeatedly questions the responses to derive deeper explanations. Grounded theory is particularly applicable in highly dynamic situations involving rapid and significant change. Two key questions asked by the grounded theory researcher are "What is happening here?" and "How is it different?"[16] The distinguishing characteristic of grounded theory is that it does not begin with a theory but instead extracts one from whatever emerges from an area of inquiry.

How Is Grounded Theory Used?

Consider a company that approaches a researcher to study whether or not the company sales force is losing its effectiveness. The researcher can use grounded theory to discover a potential explanation. A theory emerges based on text analysis of dozens of sales meeting transcripts recorded over the previous five years. By posing questions about events discussed in the sales meetings and scrutinizing differences in the situations that may have led to the discussion, the researcher develops a theory. The theory suggests that with an increasing reliance on e-mail and other technological devices for communication, the salespeople do not communicate with each other informally as much as they did previously. As a result, the salespeople had failed to bond into a close-knit "community."[17]

Computerized software also can be useful in developing grounded theory. Researchers input text from consumer interviews into a program called NVivo to develop a theory of things that interfere with consumers acting out ethical consumption intentions. The results suggested that consumers who lack deep motivation are unwilling to sacrifice other aspects of product quality only for the sake of appearing to act more responsibly as a consumer.

Case Studies

What Are Case Studies?

case studies

The documented history of a particular person, group, organization, or event.

Case studies refer to the documented history of a particular person, group, organization, or event. A case study may describe consumers' acceptance or rejection of a particular product or brand. Clinical interviews of individual consumers represent this type of case study. Alternatively, case studies may describe the events of a specific company introducing a new product. Sometimes, case studies document the way some company dealt with a crisis of some type. Case studies, for instance, proved useful in trying to explore ways firms dealt with the financial crisis occurring a few years ago.[18] Textbook cases typify this kind of case study.

themes

Identified by the frequency with which the same term (or a synonym) arises in the narrative description.

Themes are identified by the frequency with which the same term (or a synonym) arises in the narrative case description. The themes may be useful in discovering variables that are relevant to potential explanations. Thematic interpretation is a tool useful across all types of qualitative inquiry, not just in case studies.

How Are Case Studies Used?

Case studies are commonly applied in business. For instance, case studies of brands that sell "luxury" products helped provide insight into what makes up a prestigious brand. A marketing researcher carefully conducted case studies of higher-end wine labels (such as Penfolds Grange), including the methods of production and marketing. This analysis suggested that a key ingredient to a prestige brand may well be authenticity. When consumers know something is authentic, they attach more esteem to that product or brand.[19]

Case studies provide a primary advantage in that a researcher can study an entire organization or entity in depth with meticulous attention to detail. With this highly focused attention, the researcher is able to study the order of events carefully or to concentrate on identifying the relationships among functions, individuals, or entities. Conducting a case study often requires the cooperation of the party studied. This freedom to search for whatever data an investigator deems important makes the success of any case study highly dependent on the alertness, creativity, intelligence, and motivation of the individual performing the case analysis.

Common Techniques Used in Qualitative Research

Qualitative researchers apply a nearly endless number of techniques. These techniques overlap more than one of the categories previously discussed, although each category may display a preference for certain techniques. Exhibit 5.3 lists characteristics of some common qualitative research techniques. Each is then described.

PhotoCuisine RM/Alamy Stock Photo

● ● ● ● ● ● ●

Qualitative research reveals that products that are perceived as "authentic" offer more value for consumers.

Focus Group Interview

The focus group interview is so widely used that many advertising and research agencies do nothing but focus group interviews. A **focus group interview** is an unstructured, free-flowing interview with a small group of people, usually between six and ten. Focus groups are led by a trained moderator who follows a flexible format encouraging dialogue among respondents. Common focus group topics include employee programs, brand meanings, problems with products, advertising themes, or new-product concepts. Unfortunately, all people too often use the term loosely to refer to any

focus group interview

An unstructured, free-flowing interview with a small group of around six to ten people. Focus groups are led by a trained moderator who follows a flexible format encouraging dialogue among respondents.

EXHIBIT 5.3 Common Qualitative Research Tools

Tool	Description	Type of Approach (Category)	Key Advantages	Key Disadvantages
Focus Group Interviews	Small group discussions led by a trained moderator. Conducted in a focus group facility or using online technologies	Ethnography, case studies	• Can be done quickly • Gain multiple perspectives • Flexibility	• Results not intended to generalize to larger population • Difficult to use for sensitive topics • Expensive
Depth Interviews	One-on-one, probing interview between a trained researcher and a respondent	Ethnography, grounded theory, case studies	• Gain considerable insight from each individual • Good for understanding unusual behaviors	• Results not meant to generalize • Very expensive per each interview
Conversations	Unstructured dialogue recorded by a researcher	Phenomenology, grounded theory	• Gain unique insights from enthusiasts • Can cover sensitive topics • Less expensive than depth interviews or focus groups. Social media conversations can be used	• Easy to get off course • Interpretations are very researcher dependent
Semi-Structured Interviews	Open-ended questions, often in writing, that ask for short essay-type answers from respondents	Grounded theory, ethnography	• Can address more specific issues • Results can be easily interpreted • Cost advantages over focus groups and depth interviews	• Lack the flexibility that is likely to produce truly creative or novel explanations
Word Association/ Sentence Completion	Records the first thoughts that come to a consumer in response to some stimulus	Grounded theory, case studies	• Economical • Can be done quickly	• Lack the flexibility that is likely to produce truly creative or novel explanations
Observation	Recorded notes describing observed events	Ethnography, grounded theory, case studies	• Can be inobtrusive • Can yield actual behavior patterns	• Can be very expensive with participant observer series
Collages	Respondent assembles pictures that represent their thoughts/feelings	Phenomenology, grounded theory	• Flexible enough to allow novel insights	• Highly dependent on the researcher's interpretation of the collage
Thematic Apperception/ Cartoon Tests	Researcher provides an ambiguous picture and respondent tells about the story	Phenomenology, grounded theory	• Projective, allows to get at sensitive issues • Flexible	• Highly dependent on the researcher's interpretation

Source: William Zikmund and Barry Babin, *Essentials of Marketing Research*, 5th ed, Cengage Learning, 2012.

discussion among a small group of people. Without the appropriate structure and trained leader, a group discussion probably lacks the appropriate focus.

Focus group participants may range from consumers talking about hair coloring, petroleum engineers talking about problems in the "oil patch," children talking about toys, or employees talking about their jobs. A moderator begins by providing an opening statement intended to steer discussion in the intended direction. Ideally, discussion topics emerge at the group's initiative more than that of the moderator's. Consistent with phenomenological approaches, moderators should avoid direct questioning unless absolutely necessary.

Advantages of Focus Group Interviews

Focus groups allow people to discuss their true feelings, anxieties, and frustrations, as well as the depth of their convictions, in their own words. Although other approaches may also do much the same, focus groups offer several advantages:

1. Relatively fast
2. Easy to execute
3. Allow respondents to piggyback off each other's ideas
4. Provide multiple perspectives
5. Give flexibility to allow more detailed descriptions
6. Provide a high degree of scrutiny

Speed and Ease

In an emergency situation, a research company can conduct, analyze, and report on three or four group sessions within about a week. The large number of research firms that conduct focus group interviews makes it easy to find someone to conduct the research. Practically every state in the United States contains multiple research firms that have their own focus group facilities. The Green Book Directory (greenbook.org) provides a searchable directory of U.S. focus group facilities. Companies with large research departments likely have at least one qualified focus group moderator so that they need not outsource the focus group.

Piggybacking and Multiple Perspectives

Furthermore, the group approach may produce thoughts that would not be produced otherwise. The interplay between respondents allows them to **piggyback** off of each other's ideas. In other words, one respondent stimulates thought among the others and, as this process continues, increasingly creative insights are possible. A comment by one individual often triggers a chain of responses from the other participants. The social nature of the focus group also helps bring out multiple views as each person shares a particular perspective.

piggyback

A procedure in which one respondent stimulates thought among the others; as this process continues, increasingly creative insights are possible.

Flexibility

The flexibility of focus group interviews is advantageous, especially when compared with the more structured and rigid survey format. Numerous topics can be discussed and many insights can be gained, particularly with regard to the variations in consumer behavior in different situations. For

Traditional focus group facilities typically include a comfortable room for respondents, recording equipment, and a viewing room via a two-way mirror.

Marmaduke St. John/Alamy stockphoto

instance, a focus group was conducted on behalf of an athletic shoe brand interested in expanding into other areas, such as Vans into tennis or golf. After 15 minutes go by, the respondents bring up wearing the shoes in casual settings. Thus, the facilitator redirects the interview to explore issues related to brand introductions of casual shoes rather than athletic shoes.

Scrutiny

A focus group interview allows closer scrutiny in several ways. First, multiple people can observe the interview live because they are usually conducted in a room containing a two-way mirror. The respondents and moderator are on one side; an invited audience that may include both researchers and decision-makers is on the other. If the decision-makers are located in another city or country, they may watch through an Internet connection like Skype or through some other video media. No matter how agents from the decision-maker observe, the fact that they can look in provides a check on the eventual interpretations offered in the report. Second, the focus group organizers generally video the session. If video is not feasible, then they will produce an audio recording. Later, detailed examination of the recorded session can offer additional insight and help clear up disagreements about what happened.

Focus Group Illustration

Researchers often use focus group interviews for concept screening and concept refinement. Product development involves a continuous process of examining potential modifications, refinements, and idea generation. This process applies to existing and new products. Philip Morris and Lorillard are developing smokeless, electronic cigarette (e-cigarette) products for the U.K. market, where vaping is catching on. Focus groups with consumers in the United States, where vaping (smoking e-cigarettes) has a longer history, help them understand how U.K. consumers will react to the product and how it might be improved.[20] Voluntary focus group respondents used samples of the product and then discussed it among themselves. The interview results suggest that consumers like the key product features related to tidiness such as the fact that it produces no ashes, no side smoke, and very little odor. Focus group respondents show little concern about how the cigarette actually functions but hope that they will be able to use the product around nonsmokers without irritating them. Some respondents see e-cigarettes as a way of ending tobacco habits. This example illustrates how focus groups help develop and refine products and provide ideas for effectively marketing products once released.

● ● ● ● ● ● ●

Focus groups provide insight to companies by getting consumer reactions to novel new products.

PeopleImages/E+/Getty Images

Focus Group Respondents

What is a research supplier's responsibility when recruiting individuals to participate in a focus group? Practically every focus group interview requires that respondents be screened based on some relevant characteristic. For example, if the topic involves improving parochial school education, the group should probably not include couples without children or with no plans of having children. The respondents in this case should be parents who are likely to put or are currently putting a child through school.

Even after careful screening, some consumers that fit the desired profile make poor focus group participants. Respondents are inappropriate if they are either unwilling to express their views or they are overbearing. The group dynamics suffer when one or more respondents are too quiet or are a loudmouth. When a researcher finds good focus group participants, he/she may be tempted to use them over and over again. Is this appropriate? This is a dilemma a focus group planner may well face. Consider a research client viewing a series of six focus groups conducted about new kitchen appliance designs. The client realizes that four respondents appear in more than one of the six focus group interviews and that ten respondents appear in focus groups conducted by the same researcher on another topic six months previous. Whenever diversity of opinion is needed, relying on what essentially become professional focus group respondents is inappropriate. The researcher should take the extra effort to find new respondents rather than relying on conveniently available and appropriately talkative respondents.

Group Composition

A traditional focus group's ideal size is six to ten people. A very small group has less potential for good ideas and each person is very susceptible to influence from the others. In a very large group, some participants may have difficulty getting their ideas across.

Homogeneous groups allow researchers to concentrate on consumers with similar lifestyles, experiences, and communication skills. When every participant is more or less similar to the others, the discussion carries forward with less likelihood of becoming overly confrontational. Additionally, marketing campaigns generally communicate with specific market segments consisting of relatively homogenous consumers. Ethnographers like to deal with unique cultures. If an ethnographic researcher is looking to do a focus group about Vans, he/she may recruit participants from a local skate park or from members of an online social community.

Imagine how the opinions of the electronic cigarette would vary among a group of smokers and nonsmokers. Management would probably be nearsighted not to consider the input from nonsmokers because they ultimately will influence the acceptable places where these devices can be used. Although any one focus group consisting of both smokers and nonsmokers might be lively, it is very likely to be confrontational. If the researcher involves multiple interviews, the researcher may consider doing one with a mixed group, but researchers generally prefer separate interviews for disparate groups. The researcher obtains diversity in the sample by using different groups even though each group is homogeneous. For instance, in discussing smokeless cigarettes, four groups might be used:

1. Single current smokers
2. Married smokers whose spouses do not smoke
3. Former smokers
4. Nonsmokers

Although each group is homogenous, researchers obtain opinions from diverse respondents. Many research firms apply a rule of thumb that four different focus group sessions, each in a different city, can satisfy exploratory research needs dealing with common consumer product issues.

Environmental Conditions

A focus group session may typically take place at the research agency in a room specifically designed for this purpose. These agencies' facilities include the studio-like rooms where the focus groups are conducted, viewed, and recorded. Participants receive refreshments prior to the interview to help create a more relaxed atmosphere conducive to a free exchange of ideas. A relaxed atmosphere helps create a more open and intimate discussion of personal experiences and sentiments.

The Focus Group Moderator

During a focus group interview, a **moderator** ensures that everyone gets a chance to speak as he/she facilitates the discussion.

Several qualities characterize a good focus group moderator:

1. A moderator must develop rapport with the group and make all participants feel comfortable. Good moderators show genuine interest in people, establish rapport, gain participants' confidence, and make them feel eager to talk.
2. A moderator must be a good listener. Careful listening allows the researcher to separate productive discussion directed toward accomplishing the stated research objective from discussions that will take the group in an irrelevant direction.
3. A good moderator does not interject his/her personal opinion. Good moderators usually say less rather than more. They can stimulate productive discussion with generalized follow-ups such as, "Tell us more about that incident," or "How are your experiences similar or different from the one you just heard?" The moderator must be particularly careful not to ask leading questions such as "You do like Timberland, don't you?"
4. A moderator directs verbal traffic capably without turning off productive participants. The discussion needs to remain focused around the research objective. A moderator does not give the group total control of the discussion because it may well quickly lose focus. He/she normally has prepared questions on topics that aim to draw out ideas related to the research objective and therefore managerial issues. Normally, he/she starts out by encouraging a general discussion (i.e., "tell me what comes to mind when you think of boots") but usually *focuses* in on specific topics as the session progresses. Ideally, the group covers topics with little to no prompting.

Focus Groups as Diagnostic Tools

Focus groups typify exploratory research but they also can be helpful in later stages of a research project. Sometimes, the findings from surveys or other quantitative techniques raise more questions than they answer. Managers who are puzzled about survey research results may use focus groups as a way of better understanding what consumer surveys are actually saying. In such a situation, the focus group supplies diagnostic help as a follow up to other research.

Focus groups are also excellent diagnostic tools for spotting problems with ideas as an idea screening technique. The moderator presents a marketing concept to the group and then seeks elaborate comments on the idea. This usually leads to lengthy lists of potential product problems and some ideas for overcoming them. People are naturally inclined to offer reasons why things won't work so this approach can be effective.

Depth Interviews

An alternative to a focus group is a depth interview. A **depth interview** is a one-on-one interview between a professional researcher and a research respondent. Depth interviews are much the same as a clinical psychology interview, but with a different purpose. The researcher asks many questions and follows up each answer with probes for additional elaboration.

Like focus group moderators, the interviewer's role is critical in a depth interview. He/she must be a highly skilled individual who can encourage the respondent to talk freely without influencing the direction of the conversation. Probing questions are critical.

Probing

Probing is an interview technique that tries to draw deeper and more elaborate explanations from a respondent. Oftentimes, researchers may conduct interviews with key decision-makers in trying to separate symptoms from the relevant issues that should be the focus of the research. Probing techniques often are applied in such interviews. In addition, researchers apply probing techniques in interviews trying to reveal consumer values and motivations that drive specific consumer behaviors. For instance, why do some consumers avoid personal contact and try to communicate with companies only via Web electronic communication? Researchers will find probing useful for any of the following reasons:

1. Clarification—ask respondent to explain exactly what certain phrases or terms mean.
2. Free-form thinking—ask for top-of-mind associations by saying, "What does that make you think of?"
3. Pause—the researcher may simply wait in silence briefly. The silence can encourage the respondent to explain more deeply as a way of coping with the awkwardness that the silence brings.
4. Contrast—ask respondent to contrast events as similar or different from other events.
5. Meaning—ask respondent to "tell me something" or "tell me more" about some interesting point.
6. Change—ask respondent, "What has changed?" This is particularly useful in separating symptoms from issues when interviewing key decision-makers.

Laddering

Laddering is a term used for a particular approach to probing, asking respondents to compare differences between brands at different levels. A repertory grid interview is an approach developed in the mid-twentieth century to conduct interviews that drew out the way people distinguished concepts. Laddering evolved from the repertory grid interview and is very useful in identifying the potential meaning of brand names. What usually results with laddering is that respondents first distinguish things using attribute-level distinctions, second are benefit-level distinctions, and third are distinctions at the personal value or motivation level. Laddering, for example, can then distinguish two brands of skateboarding shoes based on (a) the materials they are made of, (b) the comfort they provide, and (c) the excitement they create.

laddering

A particular approach to probing asking respondents to compare differences between brands at different levels that produces distinctions at the attribute level, the benefit level, and the value or motivation level. Laddering is based on the classical repertory grid approach.

Depth Interview Procedure

Typical depth interviews last an hour or more. Not only does the researcher conduct the interview, with each interview producing about the same amount of text as does a focus group interview, but the resulting data must be analyzed and interpreted. Thus, depth interviews are time consuming. The interviewer also must be keenly aware of what is happening and record both surface reactions and subconscious motivations of the respondent. Analysis and interpretation of such data are highly subjective, and it is difficult to settle on a true interpretation.

Depth interviews provide more insight into a particular individual than do focus groups. In addition, since the setting isn't really social, respondents are more likely to discuss sensitive topics than are those in a focus group. Buick took depth interviews into respondents' homes. Here, respondents discussed their ideas about cars and car brands in great detail, sometimes going on for 2 hours or more.[21] The comfortable surroundings no doubt aided the discussion. Following the interviews, Buick researchers felt as though Buick customers desire premium items and special features but they aren't inclined to pay a premium price for a car. Also, they picked up on perceptions that consumers viewed Buick as a brand for older people.

Depth interviews are particularly advantageous when the focus is on some unique or unusual behavior. For instance, depth interviews revealed characteristics of consumer misbehavior, ranging from things like not honoring reservations, changing price tags, service belligerence, and even shoplifting.[22] Depth interviews are similar to focus groups in many ways. Focus groups and depth interviews cost about the same as long as only one or two respondents are interviewed in depth. However, if a dozen or more depth interviews are included in a report, the costs are higher than focus group interviews because of the increased interviewing and analysis time.

Conversations

Holding **conversations** in qualitative research is an informal data-gathering approach in which the researcher engages a respondent in a discussion of the relevant subject matter. This approach is almost completely unstructured and the researcher enters the conversation with few expectations. The goal is to have the respondent produce a dialogue about his/her lived experiences.

conversations

An informal qualitative data-gathering approach in which the researcher engages a respondent in a discussion of the relevant subject matter.

A conversational approach to qualitative research is particularly appropriate in phenomenologi-cal research and for developing grounded theory. In our Vans experience, the researcher may simply record a conversation about becoming a "skater." The resulting dialogue can then be analyzed for themes and plots. The result may be some interesting and novel insight into the consumption patterns of skaters, for example, if the respondent said,

"I knew I was a real skater when I just had to have Vans, not just for boarding, but for wearing."

This theme may connect to a rite-of-passage plot and show how Vans plays a role in this process.

A conversational approach is advantageous because conducting a single interview is usually inexpensive. Unlike depth interviews or focus groups, the researcher doesn't have to pay respondents because they are enthusiasts freely discussing their behavior. Often, the conversation takes place spontaneously, with little set up or with little need for any formal setting such as a focus group studio. They are relatively effective at getting at sensitive issues once the researcher establishes a rapport with them. Conversational approaches, however, are prone to produce a small portion of relevant information because they are not steered in the same way as a depth interview or focus group. Additionally, the data analysis is very much researcher-dependent.

Social Listening

social listening

Refers to marketing research using prompted or unprompted social media conversations to gather data.

Not all conversations take place face to face. **Social listening** refers to marketing research using prompted or unprompted social media conversations to gather data. Domino's Pizza initiated conversations about consumers' pizza preferences with its Pizza Turnaround campaign. The data collected helped improve their pizzas and as part of #newpizza, revealed a preference for the improved Domino's over competitors like Papa John's.[23] Other times, social media posts and online review comments can be scraped as data.

Semi-Structured Interviews

Semi-structured interviews usually ask respondents for short essay responses to specific open-ended questions. The interview design separates questions into sections typically and within each section, probing questions follow the opening question. In face-to-face, semi-structured, oral interviews, structured follow-ups are more difficult than with the written approach. Semi-structured interviews typically are part of a survey.

Advantages to semi-structured interviews include an ability to address very specific issues and the fact that responses are usually easier to interpret than with other qualitative approaches. In written form, the researcher prepares all questions ahead of time and thus the presence of an interviewer is not necessary. For this reason, among others, semi-structured interviews are relatively cost-effective.

Some researchers interested in studying car salesperson stereotypes used qualitative semistructured interviews to map consumers' cognitions (memory). The semi-structured interview began with a free-association task:

List the first five things that come into your mind when you think of a "car salesman."

A probing question followed:

Describe the way a typical "car salesman" looks.

Questions about how the car salesperson acts and how the respondent feels in the presence of a car salesperson followed this probe. The results led to research showing how the information that consumers process differs in the presence of a typical car salesperson as opposed to a less typical car salesperson.[24] One suggestion that followed addressed the way car salespeople dress. Perhaps something other than the prototypical attire would help create a less negative reaction.

Free-Association and Sentence-Completion Methods

free-association techniques

Record respondents' first (top-of-mind) cognitive reactions to some stimulus.

Free-association techniques simply record a respondent's first cognitive reactions (top-of-mind) to some stimulus. The Rorschach or inkblot test typifies the free-association method. Respondents view an ambiguous figure and say the first thing that comes to their mind. Free-association techniques allow researchers to map a respondent's thoughts or memory.

The sentence-completion method is based on free-association principles. Respondents simply are required to complete a few partial sentences with the first word or phrase that comes to mind. For example:

People who drink beer are _____
A man who drinks a dark beer is _____
Light beer is most liked by _____

Answers to sentence-completion questions tend to be more extensive than responses to word-association tests. Researchers often employ free-association and sentence-completion tasks in conjunction with other approaches. For instance, they provide effective icebreakers in focus group interviews.

Observation

Throughout this chapter, we describe how observation is an important qualitative tool. The participant-observer approach typifies how researchers use observation to explore various issues. The researcher's field notes play a large role in this process. **Field notes** are the researcher's descriptions of what he/she actually observes in the field. These notes then become the text from which he/she extracts meaning.

Observation may also take place in visual form. Researchers may observe consumers in their home, as mentioned earlier, or try to gain knowledge from photos observed there or pinned on Pinterest. Observation can either be very inexpensive, such as when a research associate sits at Starbucks and simply observes customer behavior, or it can be very expensive as is the case in most participant-observer studies. Observational research is keenly advantageous for gaining insight into things that respondents cannot or will not verbalize.

field notes

The researcher's descriptions of what he/she actually observes in the field; these notes then become the text from which meaning is extracted.

Collages

Marketing researchers sometimes have respondents prepare a collage to represent their experience with some good, service, or brand. Today, pinterest.com provides a good way to do qualitative research about brands. Multiple pages exist that depict in pictures the way people feel and use Harley-Davidson products and many, many other brands. Each page is a virtual collage providing data for interpretation.

On Instagram, Harley Davidson's #findyourfreedom contains tens of thousands of photos, some of which actually are collages, but together represent a pictorial conversation about all things Harley. Collages like these provide input leading Harley to reinforce freedom as a core meaning as seen in the tag line, "all for freedom, freedom for all."[25]

● ● ● ● ● ● ●

This Pinterest user has a deeply felt relationship with Harley-Davidson (photo found on **pinterest.com**).

Source: Pinterest.com

Thematic Apperception Test (TAT)

A **thematic apperception test (TAT)** presents subjects with an ambiguous picture(s) in which consumers and products are the center of attention. The investigator asks the subject to tell what is happening in the picture(s) now and what might happen next. Hence, the approach elicits themes (*thematic*) based on the perceptual-interpretive (*apperception*) use of the pictures. The researcher then analyzes the contents of the stories provided by respondents.

The picture or cartoon stimulus must be sufficiently interesting to encourage discussion but ambiguous enough not to disclose the nature of the research project. Clues should not be given

thematic apperception test (TAT)

A test that presents subjects with an ambiguous picture(s) in which consumers and products are the center of attention; the investigator asks the subject to tell what is happening in the picture(s) now and what might happen next.

to the character's positive or negative predisposition. Researchers contrasting the meaning of coffee brands may depict an ambiguous figure preparing coffee from a package of Folgers coffee to some subjects and to others, the same figures substituting Illy coffee (an Italian gourmet brand). The respondents could then be asked to describe the user. Surely, the Folgers and Illy users would be described differently. The differences might reveal ideas about the marketing of the two brands based on the meanings interpreted from the TAT. In much the same way, a TAT may be used to get a description of someone wearing Vans shoes.

picture frustration

A version of the TAT using a cartoon drawing in which the respondent suggests a dialogue in which the characters might engage.

A **picture frustration** version of the TAT uses a cartoon drawing in which the respondent suggests a dialogue in which the characters might engage. Exhibit 5.4 is a purposely ambiguous illustration of an everyday occurrence. The picture depicts two office workers and the respondent describes what the woman might be saying. This approach could be used for discussions about products, packaging, the display of merchandise, store personnel, and so on.

Projective Research Techniques

projective technique

An indirect means of questioning enabling respondents to project beliefs and feelings onto a third party, an inanimate object, or a task situation.

A TAT represents a projective research technique. A **projective technique** is an indirect means of questioning enabling respondents to project beliefs and feelings onto a third party, an inanimate object, or a task situation. Projective techniques usually encourage respondents to describe a situation in their own words with little prompting by the interviewer. The typical assumption is that respondents interpret the situation within the context of their own experiences, attitudes, and personalities. This allows respondents to express opinions and emotions otherwise hidden from others and possibly even themselves. All projective techniques are particularly useful in studying sensitive issues.

Researchers interested in the meaning of cigarette brand names and labels can employ projective techniques to avoid socially desirable responses. Instead of asking smokers their direct impression of a brand, the researcher could ask, "Tell me about a person like you (but not you) who smokes Dunhill Infinite White." Projective techniques are useful for socially sensitive topics, embarrassing behaviors, or any situation where self-reports may not be honest.

EXHIBIT 5.4

Picture Frustration Version of TAT Aimed to Get at Consumer Reactions to Salesperson Demeanor. The respondent fills in the customer's thoughts. What would they be?

Preparing a Focus Group Outline

Focus group researchers use a discussion guide to help control the interview and guide the discussion into product areas. A **discussion guide** includes written introductory comments informing the group about the focus group purpose and rules and then outlines topics or questions to be asked in the group session. Thus, the discussion guide serves as the focus group outline. Some discussion guides will have only a few phrases in the entire document. Others may be more detailed. The amount of content depends on the nature and experience of the researcher and the complexity of the topic.

A marketing researcher conducting a focus group interview for a cancer center had the following objectives in mind when preparing the guide for the interview and conducting the interview:

■ The first question was very general, asking that respondents describe their feelings about being out in the sun as an icebreaker. This opening question aimed to elicit the full range of views within in the group. Some individuals might view being out in the sun as a healthful practice, whereas others view the sun as deadly. The hope is that by exposing the full range of opinions, respondents would be motivated to explain fully their own position. This was the only question asked specifically of every respondent. Each respondent had to give an answer before free discussion began. In this way, individuals experience a nonthreatening environment encouraging their free and full opinion.

■ The second question asks whether participants could think of any reason one should warn them about sunlight exposure. This question intends only to introduce the idea of a warning label.

■ Subsequent questions became increasingly specific. They first asked about possible warning formats that might be effective. The moderator allows focus group participants to react to any formats suggested by another respondent. After this discussion, the moderator will introduce some specific formats the cancer center personnel have in mind.

■ Finally, the moderator presents the "bottom-line" question: "What format would be most likely to induce people to take protective measures?" There would be probing follow-ups of each opinion so that a respondent couldn't simply say something like "the second one." All focus groups finish up with a catchall question asking for any comments, including any thoughts they wanted passed along to the sponsor (which was only then revealed as the Houston-based cancer center).

Researchers who planned the outline established certain objectives for each part of the focus group. The initial effort was to break the ice and establish rapport within the group. The logical flow of the group session then moved from general discussion about sunbathing to more focused discussion of types of warnings about danger from sun exposure.

In general, the following steps allow for an effective focus group discussion guide:

1. Welcome and introductions should take place first. Respondents begin to feel more comfortable after introducing themselves.
2. Begin the interview with a broad icebreaker that does not reveal too many specifics about the interview. Sometimes, this may even involve respondents providing some written story or their reaction to some stimulus like a photograph, film, product, or advertisement.
3. Questions become increasingly more specific as the interview proceeds. However, the moderator will notice that a good interview will cover the specific question topics before they are asked. This is preferable as respondents do not feel forced to react to the specific issue; it just emerges naturally.
4. If there is a very specific question to ask, such as explaining why a respondent would either buy or not buy a product, the moderator should save that question for last.
5. A debriefing statement should provide respondents with the actual focus group objectives and answer any questions they may have. This is also a final shot to gain some insight from the group.

Disadvantages of Focus Groups

Focus groups offer many advantages. Like practically every other research technique, the focus group has some limitations and disadvantages, too. Problems with focus groups include those discussed as follows.

discussion guide

A focus group outline that includes written introductory comments informing the group about the focus group purpose and rules and then outlines topics or questions to be addressed in the group session.

First, focus groups require objective, sensitive, and effective moderators. Moderators may often find it difficult to remain completely objective. In large research firms, a lead researcher may provide the focus group moderator only enough information to conduct the interview effectively. The focus group moderator's opinion shouldn't influence the interview or its results. Although many people, even some with little or no background to do so, conduct focus groups, good moderators become effective through a combination of objectivity, good people skills (which cannot be taught), training (in qualitative research), and experience. Without them, the exercise could provide misleading results.

Second, researchers do not select focus group participants randomly and thus a focus group is not a representative, random sample. Participants do not represent the entire target market in any statistical sense. Consequently, focus group research provides no guarantee that the results hold in the relevant population.

Third, although not so much an issue with online formats where respondents can remain anonymous, traditional face-to-face focus groups may not be useful for discussing sensitive topics. Issues that people normally do not like to discuss in public may also prove difficult to discuss in a focus group.

Fourth, focus groups cost a considerable amount of money, particularly when not conducted by someone employed by the company desiring the focus group. Focus group prices vary regionally, but the following figures provide a rough guideline.

Renting Facilities and Equipment	$ 1,500
Paying Respondents ($100/person)	$ 1,000
Researcher Costs	
• Preparation	$ 800
• Moderating	$ 1,000
• Analysis and Report Preparation	$ 1,500
Miscellaneous Expenses	$ 500

Thus, a client can expect a professional focus group to cost more than $6,000. However, most marketing topics will call for multiple focus groups. A series of interviews does not increase the costs proportionately, however, because the only element repeated is the interview itself. Thus, a research firm's price for doing two or three interviews increases about $2,000 to $3,000 per interview.

Social Media and the Blogosphere

Technological advances have greatly improved researchers' ability to perform all aspects of marketing research, but perhaps they are changing qualitative marketing research more than any other area. This section focuses on ways that technological developments in communication and networking enable and facilitate modern qualitative research.

Facilitating Interviewing

Videoconferencing Technologies

The videoconferencing industry has grown dramatically in recent years. Most managers routinely conduct meetings using some Internet-based interface such as Skype, Adobe Connect, G+ Hangout, or Megameeting, just to name a few. Researchers can use these tools to conference with managers scattered in offices all around the world. However, researchers also apply the tools to conduct focus group interviews.

FocusVision Network (FV Video Insights) of New York provides specialized videoconferencing equipment and services and numerous technological platforms with which to conduct focus group interviews. A focus group via webcam allows advantages such as being able to push out images and information via the computer screen during the interview. Online focus groups also can involve a video game in some way.[27] The gamification of focus groups helps maintain respondent engagement through the interview.

Interactive Media and Online Focus Groups

Formally, the term **online focus group** refers to a qualitative research effort in which a group of individuals provides unstructured comments through some online medium. This could involve videoconferencing but commonly participants examine an Internet display and then use their keypad to make remarks either during a chat-room session or in the form of a blog. Because respondents enter their comments into the computer, transcripts of verbatim responses are available immediately after the group session. Online groups can be quick and cost-efficient. However, because there is less interaction among participants, group synergy and snowballing of ideas may be diminished.

Online focus groups allow access to groups that might be hard to tap otherwise. Sermo (sermo.com) is an online community of physicians that provides data to advertising agencies working for pharmaceutical firms and other institutions with a focus on health-care administration. At Sermo, on-demand focus groups comprised of physicians provide fast and efficient feedback on numerous issues related to product effectiveness, usage, and brand messaging.[28] Compared to the price of an in-person physician focus group, the $10,000–$20,000 price per interview is a bargain.

Facebook provides a less expensive alternative. Participants can be recruited for a group discussion about any element of the marketing mix. While a Facebook focus group does not have the flexibility of a traditional or online focus group, it does provide ability to integrate multimedia into the presentation to the respondents. YouTube, particularly with live-streaming capability, also offers potential for facilitating a focus-group interview.

Online versus Face-To-Face Focus Group Techniques

A research company can facilitate a formal online focus group by setting up a private, electronic chat room for that purpose. Participants in online focus groups feel that their anonymity is very secure. Often respondents will say things in this environment that they would never say otherwise. For example, a lingerie company was able to get insights into how it could design sexy products for larger women. Online, these women freely discussed what it would take "to feel better about being naked."[29] One can hardly imagine how difficult such a discussion might be face to face. Increased anonymity can be a major advantage for a company investigating sensitive or embarrassing issues.

Because participants do not have to be together in the same room at a research facility, the number of participants in online focus groups can be larger than in traditional focus groups. Twenty-five participants or more is not uncommon for the simultaneous chat-room format, where entries are typed and not spoken. Interviewers can even recruit participants using crowdsourcing on Facebook or a site like workersonboard.com. Online consumer participants are usually less expensive ($25–$50) than in a face-to-face interview. Participants can be at widely separated locations, even in different time zones, because the Internet does not have geographical restrictions. Of course, a major disadvantage is that often the researcher does not exercise as much control in precisely who participates. In other words, a person could very easily not match the desired profile or even answer screening questions in a misleading way simply to participate. A specialized firm like Sermo should be considered when it's critical to know the participants do indeed match the desired profile.

Another major drawback with online focus groups is that moderators cannot see body language and facial expressions (bewilderment, excitement, interest, etc.). Thus, they cannot fully interpret how people are reacting. Also, moderators' ability to probe and ask additional questions on the spot is reduced in online focus groups. Research that requires focus group members to actually touch something (such as a new easy-opening packaging design) or taste something is not generally suitable for an online format.

Social Networking

Social networking is one of the most impactful trends in recent times. Thus, as we've alluded to earlier, marketing research also takes advantage of social media channels. Social networking takes the place of large volumes of e-mail, phone calls, and even face-to-face communications. What is most relevant to marketing research is the large portion of this information that discusses marketing and consumer-related information.

Companies can assign research assistants to search these sites for information related to their particular brands. Branding and advertising researchers can Tweet out new commercials and other

online focus group

A qualitative research effort in which a group of individuals provides unstructured comments through some online medium.

To the Point

"Necessity, mother of invention."

—WILLIAM WYCHERLEY

Pearson Honda @Pearson_Honda · 46m
Evolution at its finest: the Honda Accord.

"Evolution" - 2018 Honda Accord :30

"Evolution" - 2018 Honda Accord :30
The Accord for this generation. The 2018 Accord. From Honda. Explore more at https://automobiles.honda.com/accord For more Honda Accord ...

Source: Honda

content and see whether it generates other Tweets, reTweets, likes, or comments. Each January, Superbowl ads show up on Twitter and other sites so that by the time the big media event comes, some really bad ads may not show up at all. The research analyst codes the information as either positive or negative. When too much negative information appears, the company can take steps to try and protect the brand. In a way, these social networking sites are a way that companies can eavesdrop on consumer conversations and discover key information about their products. Some of the most valuable consumer data found in social media, as with online conversations, is completely unsolicited.

Ethics

Marketing researchers should be aware of potential ethical issues that arise in conducting qualitative research involving social media or online posts. In netnography, a researcher may pose as a member of a brand-community under false pretense just to get access to the data. He or she also may interject some less-than-honest conversation as a way of getting reactions from other community members. Netnography illustrates ethical dilemmas that qualitative researchers face when dealing with online data. For instance, should the online researcher identify him/herself to the community as a researcher? If so, the community may not respond the same way. Alternatively, the researcher is extracting data without the informed consent of the participants otherwise. If a researcher takes the latter approach, he/she has a special duty to protect the identity of participants and to protect the brand community itself from harm. If this is the case, the netnography approach is similar to anonymously observing consumers moving about in a public environment. While the context is different and the impression of anonymity often exists, the ethical principles of marketing research should not change because of the online context.

Software Development

Interpretive Software

Computerized qualitative analysis is now commonly used. Two commonly used programs are ATLAS.ti (discussed earlier) and NVivo. These can save a lot of time by helping to identify themes and connections within text. In fact, today's programs can even assist in interpreting videotapes and photographs for meaning and they have some ability to extract data from social media sites like Twitter automatically. As you might imagine, the big qualitative data problem often is a problem of too much data rather than not enough. How is one to deal with so much data? Here is where software developments become practically useful.

Researchers extracted data from Adidas and Nike Facebook page comments using NVivo to address the question of what type of posts generate more consumer engagement. They concluded that videos, particularly those with inspirational performances by famous athletes, create the highest level of engagement.[30]

Some interpretative software is available as freeware. An SWR is available from the U.S. Centers for Disease Control and Prevention as is EZ-Text (https://www.cdc.gov/hiv/library/software/index.html). Transana will read video- and audiotape data and is available from the Wisconsin Center for Education Research (http://www.transana.org).

Text Exploring Tools

Generally, when managers think of data mining capabilities, they think of statistical analyses of large volumes of quantitative data. Large companies, including Sikorsky Aircraft, one of the largest helicopter companies in the world, and Cablecom, a Swiss telecommunications firm, employ text mining as a way of reducing customer churn. In addition to specialized qualitative software, leading

Fowl Language!

From Twitter:

"Got to the Chik-fil-a drive through and turns out it's @&*! Sunday!"

"&%@! all of that eat chik-fil-a sandwiches every day and be as skinny as &%@!"

"Chik-fil-a $%#! up my order and gave me 2 sandwiches instead of 1. Service is unmatched!"

Who could believe Chik-Fil-A could cause people to use such *fowl* language (pun intended)! Social media attracts all types and if bad language is offensive, you will be offended by social media! Sentiment analysis attempts to measure attitude toward brands using social media content. Qualitative research, though, is more interested in interpreting what the bad language might actually mean. Perhaps a lot of it can be dismissed as meaningless crassness. However, the bad language may also signal true conflict between a consumer and a brand, such as when service is poor, or even a consumer-to-consumer conflict (see the second Tweet above). Another interpretation might be that this particular consumer is unreasonable. Facebook also is filled with foul-language rants and that qualitative researcher must try to sort it all out.

Researchers also use focus group interviews to try to understand why people use and how they react to abusive language on social media. Perhaps not surprisingly, most respondents in face-to-face focus groups express disgust with the use of foul language and indicate that they would not do it. However, at the same time public sentiment falls short of calling for complete censorship of language. Rather, the focus groups think each social media site should establish rules for civil discourse and clearly disclose those rules. Would online focus groups reveal the same results? Would a ban of foul language decrease information available for brands?

Sources: Dineva, D. P., J. C. Breitsohl, and B. Garrod (2017), "Corporate Conflict Management on Social Media Brand Fan Pages," *Journal of Marketing Management*, 33, 679-698. *Science Daily* (2017), "Where's the Line?," https://www.sciencedaily.com/releases/2017/08/170829124502.htm, accessed January 14, 2018.

commercial software programs including SPSS and SAS, particularly with SAS JMP, offer advanced text-exploring capabilities. Although these programs can be expensive, they offer companies the ability to extract meaning from the tremendous amounts of verbal information generated by their customers, partners, and competitors.

Text-Exploring tools provide numerous functions. One useful function, sometimes called word-crunching, provides counts of how frequently a word appears in a text or dialog. Today's software can easily perform this function over thousands, even millions, of text passages. The software user must interact with the software and create stop words, meaning words that will not be counted including conjunctions, articles, and other not meaningful words in a given context, and word combinations that make phrases. The user also must make assumptions about words that are synonyms for each other. Is super the same as good? With emotional terms, is ashamed the same as embarrassed? Thus, the software does not remove the role of the researcher in qualitative research.

Word Clouds

Numerous software programs, including Atlas Ti, SAS JMP, and a number of online freeware sources, will generate a word cloud from text input. A **word cloud** is a graphical depiction of the frequency with which words or phrases occur. The more often a word or phrase occurs, the larger that word is depicted in the graphic. Others may use the term tag cloud to refer to the same thing. Word clouds will depict the word or terms that occur most frequently with large, bold typeface. Words or terms that are infrequently occurring are small and light. Word clouds are an easy way to portray the frequency with which terms occur in a given interview, story, or other text data unit. Clients easily understand the graphic.

Exhibit 5.5 depicts a word cloud generated using JMP's Text Explorer feature. The data come from hundreds of expert descriptions of the taste of wine posted on the Wine Searcher database (www.winesearcher.com). A research question related to whether certain words tend to be associated with wines that generate higher demand or prices can be addressed with such results. The large "finish" indicates how prominent a role the "finish" of a wine (how the taste lingers after swallowing a sip of wine) plays in establishing its quality. Perhaps in contrast to novices, experts fail to describe the wine with simple taste descriptors like "delicious" to any great degree.

However, a researcher should acknowledge that the frequency of occurrence does not necessarily mean importance. Sometimes, infrequently occurring themes can be very meaningful. Consider

word cloud

A graphical depiction of the frequency with which words occur; words occurring more frequently are shown in correspondingly large type face. Others may use the term *tag cloud* to refer to the same thing.

EXHIBIT 5.5
A Word Cloud of Expert Wine
Descriptions

the potential consequences of overlooking a pharmaceutical product's side effect like memory loss because consumers seldom mention it in open-ended interviews.

Technological changes make qualitative research easier in some ways compared to decades ago, but also bring some challenges. Exhibit 5.6 summarizes the way technological changes and the development of social media and the blogosphere interact with qualitative research.

Exploratory Research in Science and in Practice

Any research tool, qualitative or quantitative, can be misapplied. Qualitative research is no exception and researchers can apply these tools improperly and produce misleading results. Hopefully, the researcher has simply erred when this occurs. Intentionally misleading others with research results

EXHIBIT 5.6 Illustrating Some Ways Technological Developments Facilitate Qualitative Research

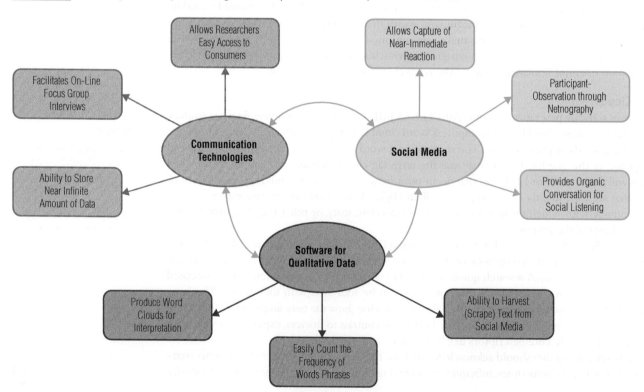

is blatantly unprofessional. A researcher needs to know what research tool to apply, how to apply it, and when to apply it to practice the craft professionally.

Misuses of Exploratory Qualitative Research

Exploratory research cannot take the place of conclusive, confirmatory research, and confirmatory research cannot take the place of discovery-oriented, exploratory tools. Qualitative tools generally offer the researcher a great deal of flexibility to cover a wide range of topics. As such, they are well suited to explore marketing issues. Subjectivity is a drawback of interpretive approaches, but that weakness predominantly limits testing—particularly hypothesis testing. The term *interpretive* research sometimes is nearly synonymous with qualitative research. When only one researcher interprets the meaning of what a single person said in a depth interview, one should be very cautious before making major marketing decisions on these results. Is the result **replicable**? Replicable means the same conclusion is intersubjectively certifiable—another researcher's interpretation would match (or they would get the same result by conducting the same research procedures). The temptation is to act on one interpretation because having other researchers interpret things like depth interviews takes resources that are not always readily available.

replicable

Something is intersubjectively certifiable meaning the same conclusion would be reached based on another researcher's interpretation of the research or by independently duplicating the research procedures.

Indeed, many researchers frowned on qualitative methodologies for years based on a few early and public misapplications during the so-called motivational research era. Although many of the ideas produced during this time had some merit, as can sometimes be the case, too few researchers did too much interpretation of too few respondents. Compounding this, marketers were quick to act on the results, believing that the results peaked inside one's subliminal consciousness and therefore held some type of extra power. Thus, often the research was flawed based on poor interpretation, as was the decision process when the deciders acted prematurely. Psychologists applied projective techniques and depth interviews to consumers frequently in the late 1950s and early 1960s, producing some interesting and occasionally bizarre reasons for consumers' purchasing behavior:

- A woman is very serious when she bakes a cake because unconsciously she is going through the symbolic act of giving birth.
- A man buys a convertible as a substitute mistress and a safer (and potentially cheaper) way of committing adultery.
- Men who wear suspenders are reacting to an unresolved castration complex.[31]

Decades later, researchers for McCann-Erickson and other advertising agencies interviewed women about roaches. Among other qualitative techniques, a form of TAT involving story completion about an encounter with an insect was applied in understanding the meanings of insects in consumers' lives. Research like this revealed themes including:

- The joy of victory over roaches (watching them die or seeing them dead).
- Using the roach as a metaphor through which women can take out their hostility toward men (women generally referred to roaches as "he" instead of "she" in their stories).
- A pervasive fear and hatred of roaches. When Orkin tested ads depicting roaches running on the television screen, viewers actually threw things at the screen before even thinking about whether the bugs were real. Although viewers felt real fear during the ads, Orkin decided to run the ads and even started a contest for people who could tell stories about damaging a television during the ad.[32]

Even today, we have the Pillsbury Doughboy as evidence that useful ideas originated from motivational research. However, many companies became frustrated when decisions based on motivational research approaches proved poor. Thus, marketing researchers moved away from qualitative tools during the late 1960s and 1970s. Today, however, qualitative tools have won acceptance once again as researchers realize they have greater power in discovering insights that would be difficult to capture in typical survey research.

Scientific Decision Processes

Objectivity and replicability are two characteristics of scientific inquiry. Are focus groups objective and replicable? Would three different researchers all interpret focus group data identically? How should a facial expression or nod of the head be interpreted? Have subjects fully grasped the idea or concept behind a nonexistent product? Have respondents overstated their interest because they tend to like all new products? A social listening comment, "man, my Vans are tight," might be interpreted as a very positive comment by one researcher while to another the interpretation is the shoes do not fit! Replicating exploratory conclusions is particularly problematic because they are not meant to be conclusive. Therefore, a focus group, or a depth interview, or TAT alone does not best represent a complete scientific inquiry.

However, if thoughts discovered through these techniques survive preliminary evaluations and are developed into conceptually sound research hypotheses, they can be further tested. These tests may involve survey research or an experiment testing an idea very specifically. Thus, exploratory research approaches using qualitative research tools are very much a *part* of *scientific* inquiry.

An exploratory research design is the most productive design, meaning the tools used produce more discoveries than do other research designs. A company cannot determine the most important product benefits until all benefits obtained from consuming the product are known.

Before making a *scientific* decision, a research project should include a confirmatory study using objective tools and an adequate sample in terms of both size and how well it represents a population. But, is a *scientific* decision approach always used or needed?

In practice, many marketing managers make decisions based solely on the results of focus group interviews or some other exploratory result. Given that some decisions involve relatively small risk, a scientific decision process is not always justified. However, as risk increases, the confidence that comes along with a rigorous research and decision process becomes well worth the investment. The primary barriers to scientific decisions are (1) time, (2) money, and (3) emotion.

Time

Sometimes, researchers simply lack sufficient time to follow up on exploratory research results. Marketing companies feel an increasingly urgent need to get new products to the market faster. Thus, a seemingly good idea generated in a focus group (like Diet Vanilla or Ginger Dr Pepper) is never tested. Managers may see the risk of delaying a decision as greater than the risk of proceeding without completing the scientific process. Thus, although the researcher may wish to protest, there may be logical reasons for deciding now. The decision-makers should be aware, though, that the conclusions drawn from exploratory research designs are just that—exploratory. Thus, there is less likelihood of good results from the decision than if the research process had involved further testing.

Money

Similarly, researchers sometimes do not follow up on exploratory research results because the cost is too high. The research team may already have spent thousands of dollars on qualitative research. Managers who are unfamiliar with research will be very tempted to wonder, "Why do I need yet another study?" and "What did I spend all that money for?" Thus, they choose to proceed based only on exploratory results. Again, the researcher has fulfilled the professional obligation as long as he/she makes the tentative nature of any ideas derived from exploratory research clear in the research report.

Again, this isn't always a bad approach. If a decision does not involve a great deal of risk or can be reversed easily, the best course of action may be to proceed to implementation without spending more time and money on confirmatory research. Remember, research should never cost more than the benefits that can come from an effective decision.

Emotion

Time, money, and emotion are all related. Decision-makers sometimes become so anxious to have something resolved, or they get so excited about some novel discovery resulting from a focus group interview, they may act rashly. Perhaps some of the ideas produced during the motivational research era sounded so enticing that decision-makers got caught up in the emotion of the moment and proceeded without the proper amount of testing. Thus, as in life, when we fall in love with something, we are prone to act irrationally. The chances of emotion interfering in this way can be lessened by making sure multiple decision-makers are involved in the decision process.

TIPS OF THE TRADE

- Qualitative research tools are most helpful when

  - The decision-makers don't know exactly what issues to take action on
  - Some specific behavior needs to be studied in depth
  - When the value of a product changes dramatically from situation to situation or consumer to consumer
  - When exploring a research area with the intent of studying it further
  - Concept testing

- Focus group questions should start with more general questions and work to the more specific.

- Don't be afraid to use props such as advertisements, photos, or actual products to get respondents talking.

- Apply qualitative tools to data already existing on social media like Twitter, Facebook, Instagram, corporate feedback listings, consumer review sites like Yelp or TripAdvisor, and blogs.

- Try using a text explorer to help make sense out of large volumes of text data.

∷ SUMMARY

1. **Contrast qualitative research with quantitative research.** The chapter emphasizes that any argument about the overall superiority of qualitative versus quantitative research is misplaced. Rather, each approach has advantages and disadvantages that make it appropriate in certain situations. The most noticeable difference is the relative absence of numbers in qualitative research. Qualitative research relies more on researchers' subjective interpretations of text or other visual material. In contrast, the numbers produced in quantitative research are objective in the sense that they don't change simply because someone else computed them. Qualitative research involves small samples. Quantitative research usually uses large samples. Qualitative procedures are generally more flexible and produce deeper and more elaborate explanations than quantitative research.

2. **Know the role of qualitative research in exploratory research designs.** The high degree of flexibility that goes along with most qualitative techniques makes it very useful in exploratory research designs. Therefore, exploratory research designs most often involve some qualitative research technique. Many of the things that some criticize qualitative research for, such as lack of structure, actually are advantageous in an exploratory design.

3. **Describe the basic orientations of qualitative research.** Phenomenology is a philosophical approach to studying human experiences based on the idea that human experience itself is inherently subjective and determined by the context within which a person experiences something. It lends itself well to conversational research. Ethnography represents ways of studying cultures through methods that include high involvement with that culture. Participant-observation is a common ethnographic approach. Netnography takes ethnographic techniques online and involves, among other things, immersion within brand communities in social networks. Grounded theory represents inductive qualitative investigation in which the researcher continually poses questions about a respondent's discourse in an effort to derive a deep explanation of their behavior. Case studies are documented histories of a particular person, group, organization, or event.

4. Understand the strengths and weaknesses of common qualitative tools and how digital processes sometimes assist efforts. Two of the most common qualitative research tools include the focus group interview and the depth interview. The focus group has some cost advantage per respondent because it would take ten times as long to conduct the interview portion(s) of a series of depth interviews compared to one focus group. However, the depth interview is more appropriate for discussing sensitive topics. Researchers today, though, have a wide variety of tools at their disposal aside from the focus group and depth interview. Many Online focus groups and social listening are helpful qualitative research tools.

5. Prepare a focus group interview outline. A focus group outline should begin with introductory comments followed by a very general opening question that does not lead the respondent. More specific questions should be listed until a blunt question directly pertaining to the study objective is included. It should conclude with debriefing comments and a chance for question-and-answers with respondents.

6. Recognize ways social networking and the *blogosphere* provide opportunities for qualitative research. Social media are replete with postings about brands, products, and consumer experiences. These natural conversations are fertile data for interpretative researchers. Some companies have even established pages intended for continuous commentary on a company. Consumer reviews on sites like tripadvisor.com provide another source of data online. A key strength of these approaches is cost-effectiveness, although virtually no control can be exercised over the respondents. Internet-based communication tools also greatly facilitate focus groups involving participants who need not travel to a focus group facility. This can be particularly useful when groups consist of professionals who would be unlikely to take the time to participate otherwise. Qualitative software, and in particular, text explorer tools, provide an effective way to summarize meaning and communicate results.

7. Appreciate the role of exploratory qualitative research in scientific decision-making. Qualitative research has a rightful place in scientific discovery, and the idea that qualitative research is somehow lacking in rigor because it is not quantitative is simply misplaced. Risks do come with using exploratory research procedures in general to make scientific decisions. Although not all decisions require a scientific decision process, companies sometimes do make major decisions using only exploratory research. A lack of time, money, and strong emotions to move on all represent barriers to a scientific decision process. Ultimately, the researcher's job is to make sure that decision makers understand the increased risk that comes along with basing a decision only on exploratory research results.

::KEY TERMS AND CONCEPTS

case studies, *118*
concept testing, *113*
conversations, *125*
depth interview, *124*
discussion guide, *129*
ethnography, *116*
field notes, *127*
focus group interview, *119*
free-association techniques, *126*
grounded theory, *118*
hermeneutics, *115*
hermeneutic unit, *115*

laddering, *125*
mixed methods, *111*
moderator, *124*
netnography, *116*
online focus group, *131*
participant-observation, *116*
phenomenology, *115*
picture frustration, *128*
piggyback, *121*
probing, *124*
projective technique, *128*
qualitative data, *113*

qualitative marketing research, *109*
quantitative data, *113*
quantitative marketing research, *111*
replicable, *135*
researcher-dependent, *109*
social listening, *126*
subjective, *112*
thematic apperception test (TAT), *127*
themes, *118*
word cloud, *133*

::QUESTIONS FOR REVIEW AND CRITICAL THINKING

1. Define *qualitative* and *quantitative* research. Compare and contrast the two approaches.
2. Describe the term *interpretive research*.
3. What types of situations call for qualitative research?
4. Consider the chapter vignette. Illustrate how researchers could apply at least four different qualitative tools to the business situation described in the opening vignette.
5. What does the term "mixed-methods" mean? Illustrate with an example.
6. What are the basic categories (orientations) of qualitative research?
7. Of the four basic categories of qualitative research, which do you think is most appropriate for a qualitative approach designed to better define a marketing situation prior to conducting confirmatory research?
8. How might ethnography be used in concept testing?
9. What type of qualitative research would you suggest in the following situations?
   a. A product manager suggests development of a non-tobacco cigarette blended from wheat, cocoa, and citrus.
   b. A research project has the purpose of evaluating potential brand names for a new insecticide.
   c. A manager must determine the best site for a drive-in convenience store in an urban area.
   d. An advertiser wishes to identify the symbolism associated with posting selfies online.
   e. Searching for ideas for new smartphone or tablet applications.
   f. Trying to identify motivations for inflammatory comments about a brand in social media.
10. What are the key differences between a focus group interview and a depth interview?
11. Visit some social media (Twitter, Facebook, or Instagram) sites for large companies like Honda, Qantas Airlines, Apple, Target, Auchan, and Marriott. Is there any evidence that they are using social media sites in some way to conduct social listening or some other form of qualitative data collection?
12. What is *laddering*? How might it be used in trying to understand which fast-food restaurant different segments of customers prefer? What is the relationship between probing and laddering?
13. How is a focus group outline used by a focus group moderator?
14. List at least five ways that technological advances have advanced the use of qualitative research. Explain your choices. Can you think of a way that SMS text messages or MMS messages might provide qualitative input?
15. Comment on the following remark by a marketing consultant: "Qualitative exploration is a tool of marketing research and a stimulant to thinking. In and by itself, however, it does not constitute market research."
16. A researcher tells a manager of a wine company that he has some "cool ethnography results from Facebook postings" suggesting that young consumers like the idea of a plastic individual serving size bottle that could be vended or offered at the cash register. Even before the decision-maker sees the report, the manager begins purchasing small plastic bottles and the new bottling equipment. Comment on this situation.
17. Define netnography. Provide an example. Comment on the potential ethical implications of the approach.
18. A packaged goods manufacturer receives many thousands of customer e-mails every year. Some are complaints, some are compliments. They cover a broad range of topics. Are these e-mails a possible source for interpretative research? Why or why not?

::RESEARCH ACTIVITIES

1. How might the following industries use an Internet social networking site for exploratory research? Search several well-known brand names on Facebook. Do you see any evidence that the brands in these industries are using the site to collect data useful in qualitative research?
   a. Ride sharing
   b. Vacation resorts
   c. Online game designers
   d. Insurance companies
2. Go back to the opening vignette. What if Vans approached you to do a focus group interview that explored the idea of offering casual attire (off-board) aimed at their primary segment (skateboarders) and offering casual attire for male retirees? How would you recommend the focus group(s) proceed? Would a face-to-face or online focus group provide richer data? Prepare a focus group outline(s) to accomplish this task.
3. Interview two people about their exercise behavior. In one interview, try to use a semi-structured approach by preparing questions ahead of time and trying to have the respondent complete answers for these questions. With the other, try a conversational approach. What are the main themes that emerge in each? Which approach do you think was more insightful? Do you think there were any "sensitive" topics that a respondent was not completely forthcoming about?
4. Search the Internet for some online posts from consumers describing Walmart shopping experiences. An experience that amounts to a complaint qualifies as relevant. Make sure the descriptions contain at least 200 words. Create a word cloud using freeware or other software and interpret it in an effort to explore ways to improve the Walmart experience.

Eating *Out*

Case 5.1

Bill Darden opened the Green Frog restaurant in his hometown of Waycross, GA, in the late 1930s. From that humble beginning, the Darden Restaurant Group grew and now consists of thousands of dine-in restaurants across the U.S. including The Olive Garden, Red Lobster, Cheddars, the Yard House, and many more. Two strategic issues face Darden and similar restaurant groups these days:

1. Trends toward "eating out."
2. International expansion.

Data suggests that Americans spend slightly more of their food dollar on food and drink outside of the home. However, grocers, meal kits, and other restaurants are capitalizing on a trend, to in one way or another, deliver restaurant quality food into the customer's kitchen. Some of these efforts are facilitated by ride-share efforts including Uber Eats. However, what constitutes "eating out" to the consumer? Is delivered food from Olive Garden considered eating out? The question of redoing or purchasing facilities to capitalize on any potential trends toward "eating out" at home could require major investment.

The same data indicate that Americans go to restaurants more than most other countries' citizens. French and other Europeans eat meals at restaurants about half as often as an American. Thus, an expansion into Europe with the Olive Garden or Red Lobster brand, among other potential brands, may not have as receptive an audience as greater expansion with new brands in the U.S.

Suppose you were asked to provide an opinion on the viability of the two strategic options, pursuing more food delivered to the home within the U.S. or international expansion with its top brands.

1. How might each orientation for qualitative research be used to do the exploratory research needed?
2. What qualitative tool seems most useful in trying to define what "eating out" constitutes in the U.S. and in continental Europe?
3. Check out social media sites for some of Darden's top brands. Do you think anything in the Tweets or posts might constitute qualitative data relevant to the decision issue?
4. Suppose you were going to do at least two focus groups, one on each issue. The U.S. focus group will be conducted in an Orlando, FL, focus facility. The European group will be conducted using crowd-sourced participants—all English speaking.
   a. Prepare a focus group outline for each interview
   b. Would the results for the two interviews be of equal validity?
5. Find some reviews of Olive Garden restaurant online. Post them into qualitative software. Generate a Word Cloud. Are the results meaningful? Explain using concepts from the Chapter.

Secondary Data Research in a Digital Age

LEARNING OUTCOMES

After studying this chapter, you should be able to:

1. Discuss pros and cons of secondary data and assess its reliability
2. Understand common objectives addressed by secondary data
3. Identify various internal and proprietary sources of secondary data
4. Give examples of various external sources of secondary data
5. Describe the impact of single-source data and globalization in the big data era

Chapter Vignette:

You Bet Your Life!

Suppose you or a loved one had to go into the hospital for heart surgery. Clearly, this is serious business! Research suggests that the majority of health-care customers do research before receiving critical services. In fact, nine of ten consumers say they would believe information about hospitals posted in social networks. Well, today consumers have abundant sources of data about doctors and hospitals at their fingertips. Numerous organizations including insurance companies, media sources, and government agencies publish health-care statistics online. Medicare.gov, for instance, puts hospital satisfaction data at a consumer's fingertips. Is the food good in the hospital? One controversial statistic available online is the hospital's mortality rate. If you are going in for heart surgery, perhaps you'd like to know what the odds of survival might be? Consumer ratings also can be found for hospital staff ratings, pain management, cleanliness, quietness, communication, among other attributes. Like many businesses, hospitals also show interest in getting recommended by their customer-patients. Many of the ratings include the average user recommendation scores. Some of the websites also summarize the rankings with the familiar star ratings.

The result is a wealth of data at the fingertips of researchers providing intelligence for health-care, insurance, and government administrators.

However, are these data all useful? How reliable are user ratings about a hospital? How reliable are the mortality rates posted on websites? Some argue that one must be very cautious about using this data. For example, some hospitals will not take certain high-risk patients. Those that do may report higher mortality rates but those rates are not because of a lack of skill of the doctors as much as it is the fact that the typical patient is more severely ill. Also, fraud in online posts is a reality of the Internet and makes postings online less than 100 percent reliable. Do the different data providers protect themselves from fraud? The fact that the data are easily available, meaning it just needs to be found, represents a huge advantage of secondary data. But, convenient data are not always good data. Unlike other data, the researcher had no control over the data collection. The data's validity still needs careful scrutiny just as if the researcher collected it him/herself.[1]

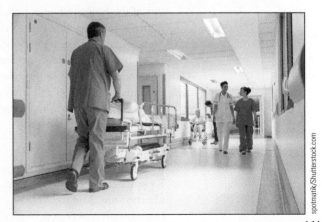

Introduction

Market researchers are always working under budget constraints. As a result, they are wise to ask if the data needed to examine the research questions already exist. If so, the analysis can proceed quickly and efficiently. If not, a much more laborious process lies ahead. This chapter focuses on instances where the data may indeed already exist. Preexisting data may be directly usable with a download or it may need to be transformed in some way to be useful. Given the big data explosion described in an earlier chapter, the chances are better than ever that some data relevant to a given marketing problem already exists.

Using Secondary Data in Marketing Research

secondary data

Data that have been previously collected for some purpose other than the one at hand.

Researchers often look for secondary data at some point in the research process. **Secondary data** are facts and information collected and recorded by someone else prior to and for purposes other than the current project. Secondary data usually are historical and already assembled. In Chapter 2, we introduced the concept of archival records as a major source of secondary data. They require no additional access to the entities that originally provided the data observations in some way. In fact, in almost all instances, the units that provided the original data could not possibly be identified or contacted again. For hospitals, the secondary data originates from sources including patient satisfaction surveys, observed waiting times, insurance company reports, and routine reporting required of hospitals. Before jumping into analyzing these data, though, the researcher must know their pros and cons.

Pros

To the Point

"If I have seen farther than others, it is because I have stood on the shoulders of giants."

—ISAAC NEWTON

The primary advantage of secondary data is that they are readily available. Obtaining secondary data generally is faster and less expensive than acquiring primary data. This is particularly true given that most secondary data is digitally stored and accessible electronically. In many situations, researchers can access secondary data nearly instantaneously.

Consider the money and time saved by researchers who obtain updated population estimates for U.S. towns from an external source. Instead of doing expensive fieldwork themselves, researchers can acquire population estimates online from the U.S. Census Bureau. The use of secondary data eliminates many of the activities normally associated with primary data collection, such as sampling, fieldwork, and data entry.

Access provides another secondary data advantage. Sometimes, companies cannot get the needed data using primary data collection procedures. For example, a manufacturer of farm implements could not duplicate the information in the *Census of Agriculture* because much of the information (e.g., amount of taxes paid) might not be accessible to a private firm. Banks like to know life-event data about customers such as when are children born, when are children moving out of the house, when is retirement, and so forth.[2] Collecting this data from customers proves difficult or impossible due to regulations limiting what a bank can ask customers. Health-care agencies face similar regulatory restrictions. In this case, researchers can apply analytical tools to secondary data showing the demographic profiles by neighborhood and data similarly profiling lifestyle information about those same neighborhoods. When the researcher takes secondary data from multiple sources and applies data analysis to guess when someone might be having a baby or retiring, big data is helping supply intelligence.

Cons

Researchers who use secondary data were completely uninvolved in collecting or recording the observations. The individuals or groups who originally gathered the data likely did so for an entirely different reason. Secondary data then do not usually fit the particular research question

Once a research team knows the research questions that must be addressed in a project, they probably quickly form ideas about what types of forms or tools might be needed to assess the relevant variables. Not so fast! Before spending a lot of time, effort, and potentially money recording new observations, the team should ask itself whether or not data might already exist that could address those questions well enough to give useful input to the decision-makers.

perfectly. The question is, Do they fit well enough to be useful? Researchers should consider the following in deciding whether to use the data:

- Do the data apply to the population of interest?
- Do the data apply to the time period of interest or are they too old to be relevant?
- Do the secondary data appear in usable form or can they be transformed to be usable?
- Do the data offer facts relevant to the research question?
- Do the data include enough variables to describe the phenomena of interest in adequate detail?
- Are the data reliable and valid?
- Can the data be merged with other secondary and/or primary data?

Researchers have to take care not to assume that secondary information is relevant, useful, and reliable simply because it is available. Consider the following typical situations:

- A researcher interested in forklift trucks finds 12-year-old secondary data on forklift trucks grouped together in a broader category also counting industrial trucks and tractors.
- An investigator who wishes to study consumers earning more than $300,000 per year finds secondary data in which household income is reported in levels with the highest indicating the number of households at $200,000 per year or more.
- A brewery that wishes to compare its per-barrel advertising expenditures with those of competitors finds that some companies' data report the cost of point-of-purchase promotional expenditures with advertising and others do not.
- Data from a Web analytics site supposedly show how many people entered a pet store's website directly from Facebook and from Twitter.

Secondary data often do not adequately satisfy research needs because:

1. the data are too old,
2. of variation in definitions of terms,
3. the use of different units of measurement, and
4. inadequate information to verify the data's validity or to allow any potential explanation for behavior.

In primary data collection, the researcher determines when data are collected and defines variables included in research question(s). Contrast this to a researcher investigating market potential for a new product within the Hispanic market in Chicago using secondary data reported as "percent white," "percent nonwhite," and "other." Researchers frequently encounter secondary data that report on a population of interest that is similar, but not directly comparable, to their population of interest.

Units of Measurement

Units of measurement may cause problems if they do not conform exactly to a researcher's needs. For example, consider a researcher comparing college students' grades across transcripts from different countries. In the United States, grades are typically on a 0 to 4 scale (F, D, C, B, or A). In

France, records indicate grades using a 20-point scale. Places like Turkey, China, and Indonesia use other scales. Can the researcher directly compare students' grades to assist university administrators in making graduate school admission decisions? In contrast, standardized tests like the GMAT (Graduate Management Admissions Test) or GRE (Graduate Record Exam) use the same scale no matter where a student takes the test. Thus, administrators may find it easier to compare students based on standardized test scores. Interestingly, though, the GMAT and GRE each use a different scale making comparisons across the two tests difficult.

data transformation

The process of changing the original form of the data to a format suitable to achieve the research objective; also called data transformation.

Sometimes, data using different scales can be mathematically transformed to a common metric. **Data transformation** is the process of changing the original form of data to a format more suitable for achieving a stated research objective. Researchers may find it easy to compare sales over the years by transforming all sales figures mathematically to some base year by using the inflation rate. For instance, $1 in 1980 = $2.09 in 2000, $2.65 in 2010, and $2.88 in 2015, and about $3.00 in 2018. Looked at from the other direction, $1 in 2018 represents only 1/3 of buying power in 1980. If a researcher wants to compute values in 1980 dollars, then each dollar in 2018 would be transformed to $0.33. Some data, such as U.S. Gross Domestic Product (GDP) estimates, are provided in constant (i.e., transformed) dollars.[3] Similarly, one can easily convert dollar values to euros or any other major currency using the exchange rate for that particular day. A quick Internet search will yield numerous websites that assist in this calculation, allowing for easy transformation of currency values. However, standardized tests assign points differently, so transforming a GRE score to a GMAT score, for instance, is not an exact process and can only be approximated. Indeed, valid transformations are not always possible.

Reliability and Validity

Researchers today might easily be more tempted than ever to use secondary data given the tremendous explosion of secondary data sources arising from increases in consumer tracking and data storage technologies. However, the usefulness of the results still depends on data quality. In some ways, having more data complicates the process of sorting out high from low quality data.

This brings us to another potential disadvantage of secondary data. That is, the user has no control over the data's reliability and validity—topics we will discuss in more detail later. But for now, think of these as representing data accuracy or trustworthiness. Although timely and pertinent secondary data may fit the researcher's requirements, the data could be inaccurate. The research methods used to collect the data may have somehow introduced bias to the data. For example, media often publish data from surveys to identify the characteristics of their subscribers or viewers. These data will sometimes exclude derogatory data from their reports. Some data releases are notorious for being "revised" later. Economic growth rates, the number of jobs created per quarter, and even the weather fall into this category. Initial weather data reported a May average temperature in Arkansas of 95.2°F, the hottest on record. Weeks later, the corrected report lowered that *slightly* to 85°F, just about normal.[4] Good researchers are suspicious of and avoid data with a high likelihood of bias or that have a history of substantial revision.

Many sites make Internet traffic data available. However, raw reports of Internet traffic are very dubious. Well over half of all Internet traffic is fake.[5] The increasing value of Internet advertising has spawned a host of unscrupulous efforts at boosting traffic counts including the introduction of computer viruses that spawn fake visits to websites. Advertisers pay for Web advertising based on traffic counts, and various intermediaries between the advertisers and the media selling advertising often participate in these unethical activities. The inaccurate traffic means marketers are paying unfair prices for online ads.

Thus, the researcher must work diligently to assess the reputation of the organization that gathers and reports data. Data published by political action committees (PAC) or by other organizations that have strong motivations not to be objective must be closely scrutinized. Also, they must critically assess the original research design. Unfortunately, such evaluation may be impossible because he/she cannot find or obtain full information explaining the original research's procedures in detail. At other times, such as in assessing Web traffic, determining a true hit on a page from a fraudulent hit based on automatic recording of data falls into the virtually impossible category.

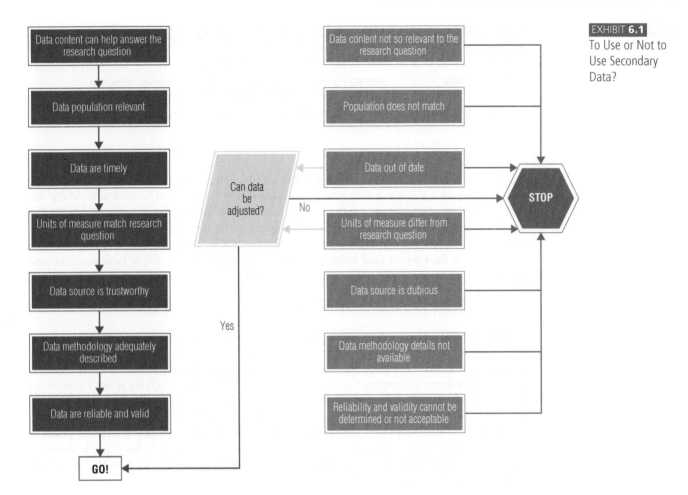

Researchers should verify data whenever possible. **Cross-checks** from multiple sources—that is, comparison of the data from one source with data from another—should be made to determine the similarity of independent projects. When the data are not consistent, researchers should attempt to identify reasons for the differences or to determine which data are most likely to be correct. When the researcher cannot verify the reliability and validity of the data, he/she must determine whether using the data is worth the risk. Exhibit 6.1 illustrates issues that are useful in deciding whether to rely on secondary data. At times, situations may dictate that a researcher move forward even when the researcher is uncertain about one of these issues. The researcher has a duty at that point to inform the decision-maker of the risks involved in relying on questionable secondary data.

cross-checks

The comparison of data from one source with data from another source to determine the similarity of independent projects.

Typical Objectives for Secondary-Data Research Designs

We could never list all possible purposes of secondary data in marketing research. However, secondary data plays a role in many commonly occurring marketing research questions. Exhibit 6.2 shows three general categories of research objectives: fact-finding, model building, and database marketing.

Fact-Finding

The simplest objective of secondary-data research is fact-finding. Considering opening a restaurant somewhere in the U.S.? You might want the researchers investigating locations to have a look at data suggesting how many people eat out. In fact, across the country, the amount of meals

EXHIBIT 6.2
Common Objectives of
Secondary Data Studies

Broad Objective	Specific Research Example
Fact-Finding	Identifying Web traffic, consumption patterns, tracking trends
Model Building	Forecasting market potential, sales in a time-period, selecting locations, determining relationships with sales
Database Marketing	Developing prospect lists, predicting future customer behavior, data mining

prepared and eaten in the home has dropped to less than 60 percent.[6] However, a relatively high number suggesting more at-home eating in a certain community could be misleading if the statistics do not take into account meals prepared in restaurants and either taken out or delivered to the home. In fact, some restaurants have taken advantage of apps like Waitr to sell a higher proportion of meals prepared to go. Other restaurant statistics are produced by NPD each year and show trends in the types of food being purchased in restaurants. These simple facts would interest a researcher who was investigating today's dining market.

Identification of Consumer Behavior for a Product Category

Another typical objective for a secondary research study might be to uncover all available information about consumption patterns for a particular product category or to identify demographic trends that affect an industry. For example, a company called Servigistics offers software that scans a company's own parts inventory data and compares it with marketing objectives and competitors' prices to suggest potential price adjustments. Kia Motors tried using this service in place of the usual method of marking up cost by a set fraction. By considering secondary data including internal inventory data and external data about competitors' prices, it was able to make service parts a more profitable segment of its business.[7] This example illustrates the wealth of factual information about consumption and behavior patterns available by carefully considering and analyzing secondary data.

Trend Analysis

market tracking

The observation and analysis of trends in industry volume and brand share over time.

Marketers watch for trends in the marketplace and the environment. **Market tracking** is the observation and analysis of trends in industry volume and brand share over time. Scanner research services and Internet analytics firms, as well as other organizations, provide facts about sales volume to support this work.

Almost every large consumer goods company routinely investigates brand and product category sales volume using secondary data. This type of analysis typically involves comparisons with competitors' sales or with the company's own sales in comparable time periods. It also involves industry comparisons among different geographic areas.

Environmental Scanning

In many instances, the fact-finding process simply seeks to identify trends. Environmental scanning entails information gathering and fact-finding designed to detect early indications of environmental changes. As mentioned in Chapter 2, the Internet and social media provide an easy tool facilitating environmental scanning. However, other means of environmental scanning include periodic reviews of contemporary publications and reports. Marketers today understand the importance of emerging markets. With golf growth slowing in the United States, companies like Callaway, Ping, and Titleist, as well as other companies involved in the resort business, may benefit from news reports showing that golf is booming in China. Mission Hills, in Shenzhen, boasts twenty-two golf courses and claims to be the world's largest golf resort. The reports also describe a noticeable number of young children on the practice grounds.[8] These trends may provide opportunities for many golf-related businesses.

Push technologies, which provide information to users that they did not specifically request, are everywhere today. Retailers push offers to you through apps that you download onto your

Magic 8 App?

In the 1950s, Mattel introduced the Magic 8-Ball. Ask the ball about your future, shake it, turn it over, and voila, you see the future! Well, now, you don't need a real Magic 8-Ball because the Magic 8-Ball app claims to predict your future. While the way the Magic 8-Ball *works* remains a mystery, the way researchers use secondary data created by our smartphone apps is not as mysterious. More and more, data gathered by the incidental use of consumers provides input to study marketing and other consumer-relevant problems. For example, asthma is a serious problem for many consumers. Researchers can use data on consumer usage of medically related apps to allow models to be built that tie the occurrence and intensity of asthma attacks to regions, weather, and environmental events like brush fires. Maybe closer to home, researchers also can model a college student's GPA based on his or her smartphone app usage patterns. Certain apps, usage times correlate with decreased academic performance as assessed by GPA. Why is that? The researchers claim that the apps

Keith Homan/Shutterstock.com

directly predict partying, which has been known to interfere with studying!

Sources: https://www.sciencedaily.com/releases/2015/05/150526100949.htm, accessed December 7, 2017. Hayden, E. C. (2016), "Mobile-Phone Health Apps Deliver Data Bounty," *Nature*, 531, 422–423.

VICTOR FRAILE/Alamy Stock Photo

phone. Check to see if you have a new offer from Starbucks, for example. The offers that one consumer gets may not be like those of another. Media outlets, including social media outlets, rely heavily on pushing accurate content to users as a means of creating valuable advertising space. Today's push technologies provide useful information to consumers, and in return, they allow data to be pushed back to the researchers. However, early push technologies proved bothersome because they provided too much irrelevant information. Today's technologies work together with search engine histories to direct users toward more relevant information faster. Smart agents and apps like Pinterest's Instapaper put the user more in control,[9] creating a combination of push and pull, and hopefully allowing the user to avoid information overload.

Model Building

model building

A mathematical representation of the relationship between two or more variables; shows how one thing responds to changes in another.

Model building, the second general objective for secondary research, is more complicated than simple fact-finding. **Model building** involves specifying relationships between two or more variables, perhaps extending to the development of descriptive, explanatory or predictive analytics. The models try to specify how one thing changes in coordination with another. Models need not include complicated mathematics, though. In fact, decision-makers often prefer simple models that everyone can readily understand to complex models that are difficult to comprehend. In particular, models should allow for a visual representation of how some important outcome, like market share or sales, can be changed. Mathematical model builders often use secondary data. A great deal of big data analysis involves scouring internal and external data sources for variables that help model sales or market share.

Estimating Market Potential for Geographic Areas

Marketers often estimate market potential using secondary data. In many cases, a trade association or another source publishes exact sales figures. However, when the desired information is unavailable, the researcher may estimate market potential by transforming secondary data from two or more sources. For example, managers may find secondary data about market potential for a country or other large geographic area, but this information may not be broken down into smaller geographical areas, such as by metropolitan area, or in terms unique to the company, such as sales territory. In this type of situation, researchers often need to make projections for the geographic area of interest.

Suppose a Belgian Abbey Ale (beer) company is looking for opportunities to expand sales by exporting or investing in other countries. Managers decide to begin by estimating market potential for several potential target markets. Secondary research uncovered data for per capita beer consumption in numerous sources, such as Data Monitor, a company that catalogs commercial statistics by country. Population estimates are available in several places, including the Census Bureau and through the CIA (see www.cia.gov to access the *World Factbook*). Exhibit 6.3 illustrates the main findings compiled two ways.

The per capita beer consumption for Czechia, formerly known as the Czech Republic, is found by dividing the country's overall beer consumption by the country's population estimate[10]:

1,930,000 kiloliters / 10,675,000 people = 0.181 kiloliters/person = 181 liters/person

That's over a bottle a day per person. To get a sense of the expected sales volume, the marketer would have to multiply this amount by the price per liter at which beer typically sells. Although Czechia may be an attractive market, greater overall volume might be offered by other markets with larger overall populations. As Exhibit 6.3 reveals, China, although with the lowest per capita consumption of the countries shown in the exhibit, offers the largest opportunity in terms of the total potential market for beer sales. Brazil and the United States also display relatively high total beer

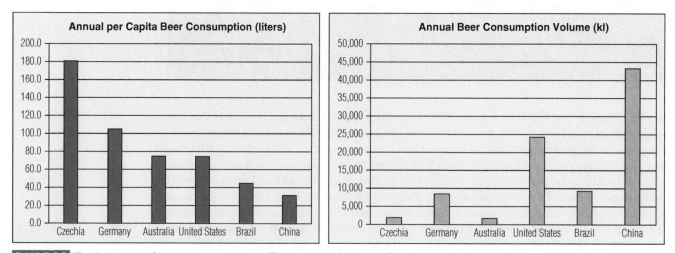

EXHIBIT 6.3 The Same Secondary Data Presented in Different Ways Addresses Different Research Objectives

consumption. Although China, Brazil, and the United States aren't known so much for beer consumption, as is Germany, the sheer size of the markets makes them attractive targets for the brewery.

Decision-makers should consider the calculated market potential for each country a rough estimate. Also, the marketer should consider whether each country is experiencing growth or decline in demand. For example, beer consumption is barely growing in Europe and Japan, but it is expanding in Latin America (at about 4 percent a year) and growing even faster in China (by at least 6 percent a year). Additionally, the researcher can probably find information on competitive intensity (how many competing beer companies) in each area and adjust projections for the competition.

Forecasting Sales

Sales forecasting is the process of predicting sales totals over a specific period. Accurate sales forecasts, especially for products in mature, stable markets, frequently come from secondary-data research that identifies trends and extrapolates past performance into the future. Marketing researchers often use internal company sales records to project sales. A rudimentary model would multiply past sales volume by an expected growth rate. A researcher might investigate a secondary source and find that industry sales normally grow about 10 percent per year; multiplying company sales volume by 10 percent would give a basic sales forecast.

Exhibit 6.4 illustrates trend projection using a moving average of growth rates. Average ticket prices for a Major League Baseball game are secondary data from Team Marketing Report (http://www.teammarketing.com). The moving average is the sum of growth rates for the past three years divided by three (number of years). The resulting number is a forecast of the percentage increase in ticket price for the coming year. Using the three-year average percentage change, or growth rate, of 12 percent over the 2015, 2016, and 2017 seasons, we can forecast the average ticket price for 2018:

$$\$41.74 + (41.74 \times 0.12) = \$46.75$$

Major League Baseball likely has great interest in financial metrics like projected revenue. Using the average listed ticket price for any season, one can compute average home ticket sales revenue for any upcoming season by multiplying the average Major League attendance projection times the number of home games (81) times the average ticket price. For the year 2018, the estimated attendance using the three-year moving average is 30,221. Thus, the estimated revenue for a typical team is:

$$30,221 \text{ tickets/game} \times \$46.75/\text{ticket} = \$1,412,832/\text{game}$$

$$\$1,412,832/\text{game} \times 81 \text{ games} = \$114,439,372$$

The moving average provides more weight to the most recent year. In this particular case, ticket prices show an increasing pattern of increases, with 2017 showing a double digit jump in prices. In part, the increased ticket prices helped contribute nearly $3.5 billion to the all-time record revenue for Major League Baseball of over $10 billion with the bulk coming from licensing and media contracts that include payments of the postseason.[12] Another factor justifying large ticket increases, with some teams increasing their prices by 20 percent, is the fact that other secondary data suggest that good tickets get resold in the secondary market for far more than the teams' asking prices.[13]

The moving average forecasting technique fits situations where more recent events carry greater influence. In situations with more consistent data, such as the attendance data in the Exhibit, a simple average may serve well. For overall attendance, the simple average and weighted average produce similar results. However, for even more dynamic situations, more advanced forecasting models exist. We will return to such techniques in later chapters.

Analysis of Trade Areas and Sites

Marketing managers examine trade areas using site analysis techniques that help management select the best locations for retail or wholesale operations. Secondary-data research helps managers make these site selection decisions. Some organizations, especially franchisers, have developed special computer software based on analytical models to select sites for retail outlets. The researcher must obtain the appropriate secondary data for analysis with the computer software.

Year	Average Ticket Price ($)	Observed Percentage Change from Previous Year	3-Year Moving Average % Change	Average Tickets Sold per Game	Average Revenue per Game
2005	21.17	6.8%	5.0%	30,957	$655,360
2006	22.21	4.9%	5.3%	31,438	$698,238
2007	22.70	2.2%	4.6%	32,785	$744,220
2008	25.43	12.0%	6.4%	32,528	$827,187
2009	26.64	4.5%	6.3%	30,350	$808,524
2010	26.74	0.4%	5.6%	30,141	$805,970
2011	26.92	0.7%	1.9%	30,352	$817,076
2012	26.98	0.2%	0.4%	30,895	$833,547
2013	27.73	2.7%	1.2%	30,514	$846,153
2014	27.93	0.7%	1.2%	30,437	$850,105
2015	28.94	3.5%	2.3%	30,477	$882,004
2016	31	6.6%	3.6%	30,163	$935,053
2017	41.74	25.7%	12.0%	30,023	$1,253,160
2018	*46.75*	*10.7%*	*6.0%*	*30,221*	*$1,412,231*

Notes: Numbers in italics are projections. 2005–2016 ticket prices taken from www.teammarketing.com, 2017 ticket price based on observed percentage increase over 2011 prices reported across all teams.

index of retail saturation

A calculation that describes
the relationship between retail
demand and supply as a ratio
of sales potential per unit area
of retail sales space.

The **index of retail saturation** offers one way to investigate retail locations and to describe the relationship between retail demand and supply.[14] The calculation gives an idea of how much revenue a market generates per a specific amount of retail space:

$$\text{Index of retail saturation} = \frac{\text{Local market potential (demand)}}{\text{Local market retailing space}}$$

For example, secondary data like that shown in Exhibit 6.5 would be relevant for a prospective retailer trying to identify market potential within a five-mile radius surrounding a Florida lifestyle center. Data like these are available from numerous vendors of market information such as Mapping Analytics. Presuming the prospective retailer is considering a retail shoe store, we first seek to estimate local market potential (demand), we multiply population by annual per capita shoe sales in the trade area. Then, we sum the selling floor size over all shoe stores in the trade area. These two figures make the numerator and denominator of the calculation, respectively:

$$\text{Index of retail saturation} = \frac{\$14,249,000}{94,000 \text{ sq.ft.}} = \$152/\text{sq.ft.}$$

Although the index is called saturation, a higher number actually indicates a less saturated area. An index value above 200 is considered to indicate exceptional opportunities. Trade area maps represent market potential using colors that indicate varying degrees of market potential. The result is a geographic information system (GIS) that pull secondary data together from multiple sources to provide useful information for better decision making. ATKearney Research generalizes this index into a Global Retail Development that identifies countries with high potential for retail growth based on retail demand potential by retail density. As the year 2020 approaches, they predict that India, China, and Malaysia offer the greatest opportunity for retailers.

Advertising Analytics and Metrics

A great deal of modeling in marketing research focuses on how advertising influences consumers and business performance including the way advertising intensity affects the rate at which a service is adopted or disadopted (meaning a consumer ends the service agreement). Particularly

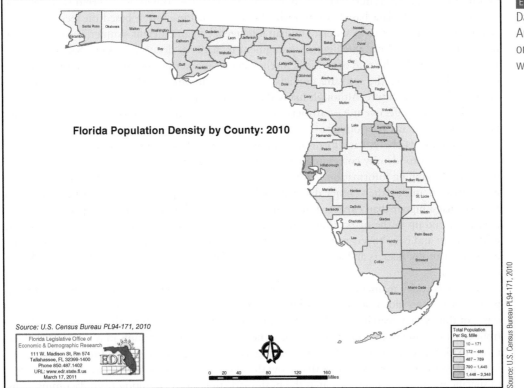

EXHIBIT **6.5**
Data Mining Tools May Analyze Population Densities or Traffic Patterns to Help with Location Decisions

Florida Population Density by County: 2010

Source: U.S. Census Bureau PL94-171, 2010

Florida Legislative Office of
Economic & Demographic Research
111 W. Madison St, Rm 574
Tallahassee, FL 32399-1400
Phone 850.487.1402
URL: www.edr.state.fl.us
March 17, 2011

Total Population
Per Sq. Mile
10 – 171
172 – 486
487 – 789
790 – 1,445
1,446 – 3,348

Source: U.S. Census Bureau PL94-171, 2010

in public services such as cable television, historic records on diffusion and firm advertising are readily available. The models include a relationship between the firm's own advertising and the primary competitor's advertising.[16] Additionally, other models show that although banner ad click through rates are very low, they do contribute to increased sales. With social media and the Internet, advertising effectiveness often is tied to quantities of exposures driven by websites with high traffic counts.

Google analytics is one of the most used advertising tracking services today. A user can find data about websites, apps, and other digital vehicles for managed sites.[17] Google offers both free and premium versions with varying capabilities. In particular, users can monitor the productivity of Google Adwords used in their media. Google Adwords uses user-provided key terms to tailor ads that appear at the top of search-list results. Google Adwords provides Google's biggest revenue source. Analytics tools like Google Analytics allow companies to know not only whether and how much consumers will engage their online efforts, but includes content marketing.

google analytics

Widely used analytics tool that allows a user to track traffic data about websites, apps, and other digital vehicles for managed sites.

Data Mining

Large corporations' decision support systems often contain millions or even hundreds of millions of records of data. In Chapter 2, we introduced the term *data mining* in discussing what happens after huge volumes of data become stored electronically and are accessible by a firm's research analysts. Data mining helps clarify the underlying meaning of the data.

The term **data mining** refers specifically to the use of powerful computer analytical routines to dig automatically through huge volumes of data searching for useful patterns of relationships. The analytics can take many forms from simple correlational routines to routines that involve artificial intelligence. For example, **neural networks** are a form of artificial intelligence in which a computer mimics the way human brains process information and make decisions. This type of data mining can help predict fast-food preference.[18] Neural networks simulate consumer decision making and work like human memory by relying on rules that have more often been shown to be true. For example, lemonade and Chick-fil-A become associated. If a consumer likes lemonade, he/she will more often go to Chick-fil-A. The program would use lemonade preference as one

data mining

The use of powerful computer analytical routines to dig automatically through huge volumes of data searching for useful patterns of relationships.

neural networks

A form of artificial intelligence in which a computer is programmed to mimic the way human brains process information.

artificial intelligence

data-based, computerized, decision making, often based on accessible secondary data.

of a host of predictive criteria. The term **artificial intelligence**, sometimes referred to as machine learning, represents data-based computerized decision making, often based on secondary data. Artificial intelligence aims to simulate human intelligence in an efficient manner. Today, marketing managers rely on artificial intelligence to augment managerial decision making. Salesforce.com's Einstein exemplifies the role of artificial intelligence in marketing research.[19] Using internal and external data mining, the software predicts consumer outcomes so the researcher has a type of crystal ball into the future. Although many digital innovations may work toward decreased customer loyalty, the effective use of artificial intelligence can help sales organizations maintain and build strong customer relationships.[20]

market-basket analysis

A form of data mining that analyzes anonymous point-of-sale transaction databases to identify coinciding purchases or relationships between products purchased and other retail shopping information.

Market-basket analysis is a form of data mining that analyzes anonymous point-of-sale transaction databases to identify coinciding purchases or relationships between products purchased and other retail shopping information.[21] Auchan, a large French hypermart firm, identified an interesting pattern among the scanner data gathered as customers pay for the things they buy. They noticed that a higher than expected number of customers who bought baby diapers also bought beer (they end up in the market basket together). A quick follow-up suggested further that most of the diaper and beer buyers were men. As a result, management decided to move some beer displays closer to the diapers and as a result, they raised the proportion of beer and customer buyers even higher.

Retailers today maintain extensive electronic records of practically every consumer touchpoint. They know not just purchases but what types of products consumers browse and what types of things they search for online. By using data mining to combine these records with data from other customers, the companies can generate suggested sales attempts in real time. More and more, marketers can mine text data for meaning. Data-mining routines mine Internet chatter and interpret words and phrases in ways that allow the development of models of customer satisfaction in specific industries.[22] Thus, although the push marketing efforts resulting from data mining discoveries sometimes make us feel creepy, evidence suggests they can produce value for customers.

Database Marketing and Customer Relationship Management

database marketing

The use of customer databases to promote one-to-one relationships with customers and create precisely targeted promotions.

A customer relationship management (CRM) system maintains customer databases containing customers' names, addresses, phone numbers, past purchases, responses to past promotional offers, and other relevant data such as demographic and financial data. **Database marketing** is the practice of using CRM databases to develop one-to-one relationships and precisely targeted promotional efforts with individual customers. Banks use database marketing to model not only a customer's lifetime value, but his/her lifetime potential value.[23] This allows managers to steer customers toward processes that enhance their value.

Effective database marketing requires vast amounts of secondary data to be integrated into a CRM system. Transaction records, which often list items purchased, prices, and customers' names and addresses, are the building blocks for many databases. Analysts supplement these records with data customers provide directly, such as data on a warranty card, surveys, or even other secondary data purchased from third parties. For example, credit services may sell databases about applications for loans, credit card payment history, and other financial data. Several companies, such as RRD Marketing and Nielsen (with PRIZM), collect primary data and then sell demographic data that can be related to small geographic areas, such as those with a certain zip code. (Remember that when the vendor collects the data, they are primary data, but when the database marketer incorporates the data into his/her database, they are secondary data.)

Sources of Internal Secondary Data

More and more, the exact distinction between internal and external secondary data becomes blurry with modern information technology. Some accounting documents are indisputably internal records of the organization. Researchers in another organization cannot have access to them. Clearly, a book published by Cengage and located in a university library is external to the company. However, in today's world of electronic data interchange, data gathered by an industry

The Data of Champions!

Sports and statistics have a long relationship with statistics like ERAs, home-field advantage, and quarterback ratings as part of the everyday vocabulary. The Elias Sports Bureau (**http://www.esb.com**) has tracked sports statistics since 1913. Today, every pitch that's thrown, every basket shot, and every snap of a football produces data that becomes archived in huge databases. In fact, NFL executives say they have so much data they don't know quite what to do with it.

On the field, data analytics has revolutionized baseball. Everything from the plane that hitters swing bats on to the velocity that outfielders run toward fly balls is analyzed. In recent years, home runs, strike outs, pitcher changes, and time between balls in play have increased as a result. The Houston Astros are well-known for their off-the-field analytics in evaluating talent. Thus, the Astros get a lot of wins per payroll dollar. On the field, managers used analytics to encourage hitters to be more aggressive by swinging at pitches early in the count rather than waiting until one or two strikes have gone by. In addition, every player's position in the field for every opposing batter is the result of data models.

However, analytics are not just about player performance. Sports marketing these days is sophisticated business and data

ZUMA Press, Inc./Alamy Stock Photo

analytics helps improve their business performance too. For example, analytics informs NCAA football programs of how much a hotshot football recruit is worth to a program. One study estimates that a 5-star recruit is indirectly worth nearly half a million dollars to a football program annually. A 4-star recruit generates about $181,000 annually and a 3-star only $60,000. The study concludes that programs without such players lose a lot of money.

Sources: Futterman, M. (2017), "NFL's Mountain of Unusable Data," *Wall Street Journal*, (February 5), A9. WSJ (2017), "How Much Are 5-Star Recruits Really Worth?" *Wall Street Journal*, (February 1), A14. Gay, J. (2017), "Hey Baseball, Let's Speed It Up!" *Wall Street Journal*, (October 6), A12.

organization may appear in a catalog and may be purchased. For example, international beverage consumption statistics broken down by category are available for purchase from an online information vendor and then made available to company analysts for instantaneous access within the DSS. The formerly external data is now available internally.

Internal data are data that originate in the organization and represent events recorded by or generated by the organization. **Proprietary data** is perhaps a more descriptive term and emphasizes the fact that company owns and controls the data.

Internal and Proprietary Data

Most organizations routinely gather, record, and store internal data to help them solve future problems. An organization's accounting system can usually provide a wealth of information. Routine documents such as sales invoices allow external financial reporting, which in turn can be a source of data for further analysis. If company employees properly code the data into a company database, the researcher may be able to conduct more detailed analysis using the decision support system. Companies organize sales information in several different ways including by account, by product, or by sales territory. The coding allows retrieval of information about orders delivered, back orders, and unfilled orders. Other useful sources of internal data include salespeoples' call reports, customer complaints, service records, warranty card returns, product returns, archived focus group recordings, and other records. As you can see, the data provide opportunities to forecast and potentially explain important outcomes to the firm including sales and return rates.

Researchers frequently aggregate or disaggregate internal data. A wine store compared its sales records to names registered on its e-mail mailing list. As a result, the store owner realized that the old 80/20 rule was no exaggeration. In fact, about 15 percent of customers accounted for

internal data

Data that originate in the organization and represent events recorded by or generated by the organization.

proprietary data

Secondary data owned and controlled by the organization.

80 percent of all sales. As a result, the store concentrated on extra incentives for the best customers to visit the store more often.

Internet technology is making it easier to research internal and proprietary data. Often, companies set up secure, internal networks allowing employees to store and share proprietary data within the organization. An **enterprise search**, which is like an Internet search but focuses on data within the enterprise's internal network, considers not only how many views a particular data page records, but also users' historical search patterns in determining what data might be useful.

Some firms like Boeing, Apple, and Honda use open-source software in an effort to develop innovations. The result is an **open-source innovation** effort that involves allowing other firms real-time access to otherwise proprietary data within the enterprise. The GENIVI Alliance represents a cooperative effort where firms from multiple automobile manufacturers share access to data with software and communications companies in an effort to create better automotive audio, communication, and entertainment systems.[24]

enterprise search

A search driven by an Internet type search engine that focuses on data within an organization's internal network.

open-source innovation

Effort that involves allowing other firms real-time access to otherwise proprietary data within the enterprise in an effort to expand the solution space developing innovations.

External Secondary Data Sources

external data

Facts observed, recorded, and stored by an entity outside of the researcher's organization.

External data are facts observed, recorded, and stored by an entity outside of the researcher's organization. The government, universities, newspapers and journals, trade associations, and other organizations perform these services either to serve industry or to offer for sale. Today, computerized access is the rule of the day making external data nearly as accessible as internal data. The Research Snapshot on the next page illustrates a company that specializes in data archives.

Information as a Product and Its Distribution Channels

Secondary data offers value, and thus, companies buy and sell data access regularly. Just as bottles of perfume or plumbers' wrenches go from production to consumer in different ways, secondary data also flow through various channels of distribution. Many users, such as Fortune 500 corporations, purchase documents and computerized lifestyle and population data from companies like Nielsen. However, smaller companies lacking the budget necessary to buy data from these companies can get a wealth of data free from sources like the U.S. Census Bureau (www.census.gov).

Libraries

Traditionally, libraries' vast storehouses of information have served as a bridge between users and producers of secondary data. The library staff deals directly with the creators of information, such as the federal government, and intermediate distributors of information, such as abstracting and indexing services. More and more, libraries access content through large consortiums that work with publishers to put together collections and make them available through search engines such as Ebscohost. The user need only locate the appropriate secondary data on the library *shelves* (physical or virtual). Large corporations also maintain libraries as do public institutions like the United Nations and the Library of Congress. As a result of the convenience of Internet access, university students don't actually visit the school library as much as in the past. Libraries are innovating to provide other reasons for people to actually visit the library.

The Internet

Today, vast amounts of secondary data are conveniently available over the Internet. Library Spot, at http://www.libraryspot.com, provides links to online libraries, including law, medical, academic, and government libraries. The virtual reference desk features links to calendars, dictionaries, encyclopedias, maps, and other sources typically found at a traditional library's reference desk. Remember, though, not all sources are equal as some are more credible than are others. Exhibit 6.6 lists some popular Internet addresses where one can find potentially useful data.

The opening vignette illustrates how health-care administrators might find useful data online. Consumers also use information posted here as a form of secondary data to aid in their own

EXHIBIT 6.6 Selected Internet Sources for Secondary Data

Source	Description	URL
U.S. Census Bureau	Demographic information about the United States overall and by state and county. Information about U.S. business and the economy.	www.census.gov
CIA *Factbook*	Profiles of over 250 countries providing descriptive statistics of population, commerce, geography, religion, history, and much more.	www.cia.gov
FedStats	A portal containing links to reports and data compiled by most federal agencies ranging from agriculture to education.	www.usa.gov/statistics
Datamonitor	Offers a very large collection of current business reports on industries, countries, markets, consumption statistics as well as tracking data for new product launches. Subscription required.	www.datamonitor.com
Advertising Age	Media source for advertising industry news and access to hundreds of research reports on specific issues within and affecting the industry (for a fee).	www.adage.com
YouTube	Online access to over 10 billion videos. User videos can reveal insights into product improvements. Huge source for television and video advertising.	www.youtube.com
Kantar Media	Source focusing on the integrated global media industry. Excellent source for statistics and reports on viewership, Internet usage, and basic consumer profiles such as the British teen market.	www.kantarmedia.com
European Union Commission	Comprehensive collection of statistics on Europe overall and the individual nations within the European Union. Statistics include detailed economic performance data, immigration, demographic data, and much more.	ec.europa.eu/eurostat
The Wall Street Journal Online	Provides a real-time view of business news and financial statistics including stock values, exchange rates, and more. Some content is free.	www.wsj.com
Harvard Business School	Not a database per se but like at most libraries, links to dozens of sources for data both public and private can be found here.	http://www.library.hbs .edu/all_databases.html
The ACSI	Customer satisfaction ratings for hundreds of large firms doing business in the U.S. Data are available by industry and free of charge.	http://theacsi.org/
Quandl.com	A venture launched by a Canadian technology company that aims to become a repository for quantitative data of all types, with a particular emphasis on economic data and data on international markets.	http://Quandl.com
Statista	Aggregate statistics on a wide array of consumer, industry, and production statistics from various global sources. Some data free to preview and others available for purchase.	www.statista.com

purchases. J.D. Power (jdpower.com) provides consumer ratings of many, many products. For instance, a consumer can look there and find what airlines customers score the highest and lowest. For 2017, Alaska Airlines and Delta Airlines top the list, whereas United Airlines and Air Canada score the lowest.[25] Consumers also leave behind comments and ratings and ask questions and get answers from other consumers who they may not even know. Consumers place more value on information provided by consumers who respond quickly to Internet queries for information, whose previous responses are positively evaluated by other consumers, and who seem to show knowledge in their responses.[26] Marketing researchers similarly weigh information posted by consumers based on some assessment of credibility.

Vendors

The information age offers many channels besides libraries through which to access data. Many external producers make secondary data available directly or through intermediaries, which are

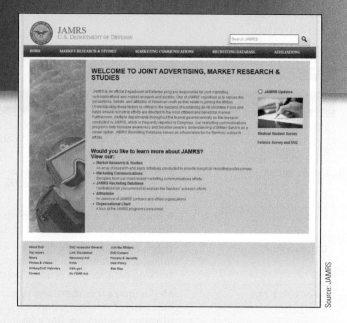

Source: JAMRS

Uncle Sam Finds You!

In a nation with an all-volunteer military, finding recruits is an ongoing need. The project is especially challenging in wartime, when more service members are necessary but the costs of serving are too daunting for many citizens. One way that the Department of Defense meets this challenge is by reviewing data that exist in a variety of sources. Its Joint Advertising, Market Research & Studies (JAMRS) project operates over a dozen research initiatives that make data available to military recruiters in all branches of the U.S. armed services. Some involve data collection, but many apply already-existing data (secondary data) to the task of recruitment.

JAMRS is partly a data warehouse storing all information gathered as potential recruits visit or contact recruiting stations. JAMRS also pays for data from third-party research firms. For example, it uses the PRIZM market segmentation data gathered and sold by Nielsen. Recruiters can use the data to identify the activities of potential recruits that live in their region—for example, to identify the magazines they read.

The U.S. Marines are learning more about applying secondary data in predicting individuals with a high probability of enlisting. Given privacy restrictions, Marine recruiters, and those for other branches, are limited in what information they

can keep about prospects. For example, Marine recruiters cannot use information from the cookies of someone who visits a recruiting website. So instead, they put together information about interests from secondary sources and try to match those to profiles of successful recruits. Recruiting is very much a marketing tool and leverages big data tools and artificial intelligence to help find the few and the proud.

Sources: "Market Research and Studies," *Joint Advertising, Market Research & Studies*, JAMRS website, http://jamrs.defense.gov/, accessed December 7, 2017. *Ad Age* (2013), "How the Marine Corps Enlists Big Data for Recruitment Efforts," http://adage.com/article/datadriven-marketing/marine-corps-enlists-big-data-recruitment/291009/, accessed December 7, 2017

often called *vendors*. D&B Hoovers (http://www.hoovers.com), typifies such vendors and specializes in providing information about thousands of companies' financial situations and operations.

Producers

Classifying external secondary data by the nature of the producer of information yields six basic sources: publishers of books and periodicals, government sources, media sources, trade association

A typical summary Statistica available at statists with more detailed reports available for sale.

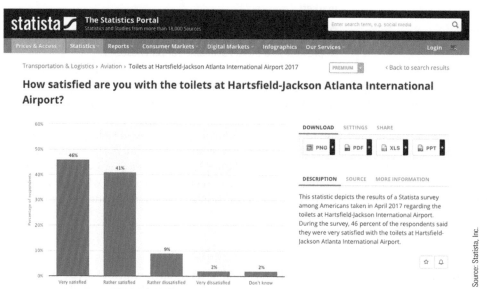

Source: Statista, Inc.

Source: https://www.statista.com/statistics/704877/us-air-travel-toilets-at-hartsfield-jackson-atlanta-international-airport/

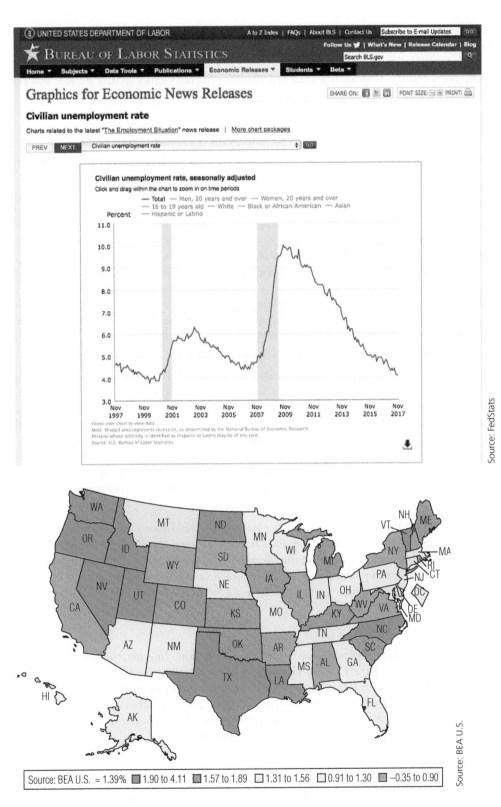

Fedstats (www.usa.gov/statistics) is a convenient portal to secondary data sources such as the Bureau of Labor Statistics (www.bls.gov).

Source: FedStats

Source: BEA U.S.

sources, commercial sources, and consumer sources. The following section discusses some secondary data sources briefly.

Periodicals

Professional journals such as the *Journal of the Academy of Marketing Science*, *Journal of Marketing*, *Journal of Marketing Research*, *The Journal of Business Research*, *Journal of Advertising Research*, *American Demographics*, and *The Public Opinion Quarterly*, as well as commercial business periodicals such as the *Wall Street Journal*, *Fortune*, and *Bloomberg Businessweek*, contain much useful material. *Sales and Marketing Management's Survey of Buying Power* is a particularly useful source of information about markets. To locate data in periodicals, indexing services such as the *ABI/INFORM and Business Periodicals Index* and the *Wall Street Journal Index* are very useful. Guides to data sources also are helpful. Most university libraries provide access to at least some of these databases.

Government Sources

Government agencies produce data prolifically. Most of the data published by the federal government can be counted on for accuracy and quality of investigation. Most students are familiar with the U.S. *Census of Population*, which provides a wealth of data.

The *Census of Population* is only one of many resources that the government provides. Banks and savings and loan companies rely heavily on the *Federal Reserve Bulletin* and *the Economic Report of the President* for volumes of data related to things like consumer credit and industrial productivity. Builders and contractors use the information in the *Current Housing Report and Annual Housing Survey* for their research. The ProQuest® *Statistical Abstract of the United States* is an extremely valuable source of information about the social, political, and economic organizations of the United States.

The federal government is a leader in making secondary data available on the Internet. Visit FedStats (**www.usa.gov/statistics**) for a central access point with links to many useful statistics. FedStats provides links to the sources mentioned above. Additionally, the following list provides illustrations of the types of facts easily found by exploring this portal:

■ Energy production statistics by state and for the country overall. The top four energy-producing states in the United States are West Virginia, Texas, Wyoming, and Louisiana.

■ Economic data series, current and historical, such as gross domestic product, retail sales data, and personal income by state. A map of personal income shows that states in the south tended to experience economic growth, whereas other areas, particularly in the west, showed economic declines during the end of the last decade.

■ Over a dozen reports documenting and providing statistics about what people eat across the United States broken down by state, in-home versus out-of-home, food category, and how much people pay.

State, county, and local government agencies can also be useful sources of information. Many state governments publish state economic models and forecasts, and many cities have metropolitan planning agencies that provide data about the population, economy and transportation systems in their town. Fortunately, many state and community statistics can be accessed from census.gov, but each state's economic development agency website is a good place to look for more on a particular state.

Media Sources

Information on a broad range of subjects is available from broadcast, Internet, and print media. The *Wall Street Journal* (wsj.com), the *Financial Times* (ft.com), and *Bloomberg Businessweek* (businessweek .com) are valuable sources for information on the economy and many markets. The latest stock values for publicly traded companies are available and may prove useful as a measuring stick to assess effectiveness of these companies' major strategic initiatives. Wsj.com is an excellent source for video updates on the latest business trends and news stories.

Trade Association Sources

Trade associations, such as the Food Marketing Institute or the American Petroleum Institute, serve the information needs of a particular industry. The trade association collects data on a number of topics of specific interest to firms, especially data on market size and market trends. Association members have a source of information that is particularly germane to their industry questions. For example, the Recording Industry Association of America (RIAA) provides reports tracking trends in the music industry that are useful to the artists, management companies, and the media in general. As one area of focus, the RIAA compiles a great deal of information related to protecting intellectual and creative property rights.

Commercial Sources

Numerous firms specialize in selling and/or publishing information. For example, the Polk Company specializes in information relevant to automobile marketing, such as the percentage of car buyers relying on the Internet in the search process and the relative health of dealerships by area. Datamonitor offers subscribers an impressive collection of reports, many of which are interactive, and they allow tracking of industry leaders globally, basic descriptions of markets, and statistics on new product introductions. *Fortune* rates the most admired companies annually in addition to providing the Fortune 500 list of the largest U.S. companies. Apple is the 2017 most admired company and Walmart tops the overall Fortune 500 Global list with net worth of about half a trillion dollars. Apple makes the top 10 on that list and Alphabet comes in at 65.[27] Here are a few sources of specialized data not mentioned earlier or in Exhibit 6.6.

Market-Share Data. A number of syndicated services supply either wholesale or retail sales volume data based on product movement. Information Resources, Inc. collects market-share data using Universal Product Codes (UPC) and optical scanning at retail store checkouts. Symphonies' InfoScan is a syndicated retail tracking service that collects scanner data from more than 90,000 retailers, including supermarkets, drug stores, and mass merchandisers. This data allows an estimate of market share for just about any consumer goods brand. InfoScan now tracks sales in other countries, including France, Germany, Italy, and the United Kingdom. The *Market Share Reporter* also is available through the reference desk in many university libraries and available online to subscribers. Gale Research publishes and markets the *Reporter* in a domestic and global version each year. The *Reporter* provides market share reports based on aggregated sales data.

Consumer Attitude and Public Opinion Research. Many research firms offer specialized syndicated services that report findings from attitude research and opinion polls. For example, Pew Research and the Gallup Organization track public opinion and consumer trends. In addition, marketing research firms such as Kantor provide public opinion tracking.

Harris Interactive is another public opinion research firm that provides syndicated and custom research for business. One of its services is the Harris survey. This survey, released three times per week, monitors the pulse of the American public on topics such as inflation, unemployment, energy, consumer products, politics, and so on. A recent poll gauges Americans' opinions about corporate responsibility. A Harris Poll of 23,000 American consumers asked each to rate the 100 most visible firms for "social responsibility."[28] According to the results, Wegmans, Public Supermarket, and Amazon ranked as the top three. However, the poll also reports generational differences with millennial consumers ranking Tesla at the top over Wegmans.

Consumption and Purchase Behavior Data. NPD's National Eating Trends (NET) is the most detailed database available on consumption patterns and trends for more than 4,000 food and beverage products. This is a syndicated source of data about the types of meals people eat and when and how they eat them. The data, called *diary panel data*, are based on records of meals and diaries kept by a group of households that have agreed to record their consumption behavior over an extended period of time.

National Family Opinion (NFO), Market Research of America (formerly MRCA), and many other syndicated sources sell diary panel data about consumption and purchase behavior. Since the advent of scanner data, diary panels are more commonly used to record purchases of apparel, hardware, home furnishings, jewelry, and other durable goods, rather than purchases of non-durable consumer packaged goods. More recently, services have been tracking consumer behavior online, collecting data about sites visited and purchases made over the Internet.

Advertising Research. Advertisers can purchase readership and audience data from a number of firms. Nielsen particularly specializes in supplying media usage data to advertising and brand managers. Nielsen's Arbitron is perhaps the best known tool for gathering data for radio. They also provide a great deal of data on television and streaming usage as well. By specializing in collecting and selling audience information on a continuing basis, these commercial sources provide a valuable service to their subscribers.

Consumer Data

Consumer data includes all information left behind online intentionally or unintentionally. This includes social network posts, consumer feedback on sites like Yelp, TripAdvisor, or Zomato, GIS data recording a person's whereabouts through the smartphone, YouTube videos, and everything deposited in cookies; all these leave behind data about consumers. Now, with the Internet of Things enabling many products including even things that we wear to produce data, companies will have even more potential knowledge about consumers. How do consumers feel about this? While consumers express some concerns about privacy, more and more say they fail to take measures to block such data as they also see the benefit.[29]

Single-Source and Global Research in the Big Data Era

As business has become more global, so has the secondary data industry. Any business with a website is a global company with potential to reach consumers anywhere in the world. As a result, many companies, large and small, need data on markets near and far. Single-source data firms help companies in that effort and provide ready access to data about global markets. This data has the potential to be productive input into marketing analytics routines.

Many private companies exist solely to provide secondary data and many marketing research firms provide this canned data as a big part of their business. Additionally, many government entities provide secondary information based on statistics that they must collect in administering programs in their own country. It's hard to think of a topic for which no secondary data would exist.

Single-Source Data-Integrated Information

Nielsen Company offers data from both its television meters and scanner operations. The integration of these two types of data helps marketers investigate the impact of television advertising on retail sales. In other ways as well, users of data find that merging two or more diverse types of data into a single database offers many advantages.

Nielsen's PRIZM, GfK Research's data services, and many other syndicated databases report product purchase behavior, media usage, demographic characteristics, lifestyle variables, and business activity by geographic area such as zip code. Although such data are sometimes called *geodemographic*, they cover such a broad range of phenomena that no one name is a good description. These data use small geographic areas as the unit of analysis.

single-source data

Diverse types of data offered by a single company; usually integrated on the basis of a common variable such as geographic area or store.

The marketing research industry uses the term **single-source data** for diverse types of data offered by a single company. Ideally, a firm could go to a single source and get any type of secondary data they may need. Quandl.com seeks to be a clearinghouse for all manner of quantitative statistical data, particularly economic and market data.

Government Agencies

Many countries include an office or have ties to a professional organization that is responsible for storing and making data about key market elements available. The Japan Management Association provides secondary research data to government and industry. One ongoing survey tracks Japanese executives' opinions on pressing business matters. The Institute's goal is to allow global firms access to its enormous store of data about Japan to develop and plan business in Japan.

Secondary data compiled outside the United States have the same limitations as domestic secondary data. However, international researchers should watch for certain pitfalls that frequently are associated with foreign data and cross-cultural research. First, data may simply be unavailable in certain countries. Second, researchers may question the accuracy of some data. This is especially likely with official statistics that may be adjusted for the political purposes of foreign governments. Finally, although economic terminology may be standardized, various countries use different definitions and accounting and recording practices for many economic concepts. For example, different countries may measure disposable personal income in radically different ways. International researchers should take extra care to investigate the comparability of data among countries.

The U.S. government and other organizations compile databases that may aid international marketers. The CIA's *World Factbook* and the National Trade Data Bank (NTDB) are especially useful for exploring potential markets overseas. The NTDB, the U.S. government's most comprehensive source of world trade data, illustrates what is available. The NTDB was established by the Omnibus Trade and Competitiveness Act. Its purpose was to provide "reasonable public access, including electronic access" to an expert promotion data system that was centralized, inexpensive, and easy to use. The CIA's *World Factbook* contains a tremendous amount of data useful in a preliminary assessment of foreign market potential. Exhibit 6.7 illustrates a small sample of the data available from the *Factbook*. Here, the Exhibit provides a quick overview of the consumers of New Zealand.

The U.S. Department of Commerce has the responsibility for operating and maintaining the NTDB and works with federal agencies that collect and distribute trade information to keep the NTDB up to date. Over 1,000 public and university libraries offer access to the NTDB through the Federal Depository Library system. By using the NTDB, small- and medium-sized companies get immediate access to information that until now only Fortune 500 companies could afford.

Topics in the NTDB include export opportunities by industry, country, and product; foreign companies or importers looking for specific products; how-to-market guides; demographic, political, and socioeconomic conditions in hundreds of countries; and much more. NTDB offers one-stop shopping for trade information from more than twenty federal sources. You do not need to know which federal agency produces the information: All you need to do is consult NTDB.

Characteristic	Data
Population	4.5 Million
Ethnic Background	71.2% European
Language	90% English
Religion	44.3% Christian (11.6% Catholic and 10.6% Anglican)
Birth Rate	13.2 births/1000 people annually
Healthcare Spending	11% of GDP

EXHIBIT 6.7
Familiar with New Zealand? Just a Quick Check at the CIA World Factbook Provides a Wealth of Relevant Consumer and Business Data

Familiar with New Zealand? Just a quick check at the CIA World *Factbook* provides a wealth of relevant consumer and business data.

TIPS OF THE TRADE

- Always consider the possibility that secondary data may exist which can address the research question at hand adequately.
- Check on the reliability and validity of secondary data. Most reputable sources provide details describing details of the research methods that allow the data quality to be assessed. Try to use multiple sources to corroborate data.
- Secondary data are particularly useful for trend analysis, environmental scanning, and estimating market potential for geographic areas. Secondary data are useful in a big data context.

- Government sites such as the Census Bureau (www.census .gov), the CIA *World Factbook* (www.cia .gov), and FedStats (www.usa.gov/statistics) are great sources for data about industries, businesses, and consumers, not only in the United States, but also around the world.

paffy/Shutterstock.com

:: SUMMARY

1. Discuss the pros and cons of using secondary data and assess its reliability. Someone other than the researcher typically gathers secondary data for some purpose other than the researcher's research question. The chief advantage of secondary data is availability, meaning they are almost always less expensive to obtain and faster to obtain than primary data. Often, researchers use secondary data when relevant primary data are impossible or impractical to obtain. The biggest disadvantage stems from the fact that secondary data were not collected with the researcher's needs in mind. In addition, the researcher may not know the quality of the data in terms of reliability and validity. One way to do this is to cross-check the data using a different source; of course, that isn't always possible.

2. Understand the typical objectives addressed by secondary data. Secondary research designs address many common marketing problems. Three general categories of research objectives often addressed with secondary data are fact-finding, model building, and database marketing. A typical fact-finding study might seek to uncover all available information about consumption patterns for a particular product category or to identify business trends that affect an industry. Model building is more complicated and involves specifying relationships between two or more variables to understand retail locations and advertising responses. More and more, consumers leave their purchase records and conversations about products and brands behind online and provide a great deal of valuable secondary data useful in data mining and even in database marketing efforts. Artificial intelligence results from the data providing prediction of consumers' behavior and augmenting managerial decisions.

3. Identify various internal and proprietary sources of secondary data. Managers often get data from internal proprietary sources such as accounting records. Data mining is the use of powerful computers to dig through volumes of data to discover patterns about an organization's customers and products. It is a broad term that applies to many different forms of analysis.

4. Give examples of various external sources of secondary data. External data are generated or recorded by another entity. Governments, trade organizations, media outlets, and syndicated data sources all record information and make it available for use by others. Sometimes, the data are available free, but other times a fee or subscription must be paid to use the data. The chapter provides an exhibit with some key sources of secondary data. usa.gov/statistics is nearly a one-stop source for any statistical information compiled by the U.S. federal government. Private sources like Datamonitor and Kantar Media are comprehensive sources of secondary data collected from various other sources and deal more specifically with marketing new products and monitoring brand perceptions.

5. Describe the impact of single-source data and globalization on secondary data research in the big data era. Single-source data firms help companies in that effort and provide ready access to data about global markets. Government resources also offer substantial amounts of data about international markets. As business has become more global, so has the secondary-data industry. International researchers should watch for pitfalls that can be associated with foreign data and cross-cultural research, such as problems with the availability and reliability of data. However, secondary data from single-source outlets and government portals can be synthesized and even combined with data from other sources to perform model building and, in doing so, typify the big data research era. The CIA *Factbook* provides a wealth of descriptive information about countries around the world.

∷ KEY TERMS AND CONCEPTS

artificial intelligence, *152*
cross-checks, *145*
data transformation, *144*
data mining, *151*
database marketing, *152*
enterprise search, *154*

external data, *154*
google analytics, *151*
index of retail saturation, *150*
internal data, *153*
market-basket analysis, *152*
market tracking, *146*

model building, *148*
neural networks, *151*
open source innovation, *154*
proprietary data, *153*
secondary data, *142*
single-source data, *160*

∷ QUESTIONS FOR REVIEW AND CRITICAL THINKING

1. Define secondary data. What is the primary advantage of using secondary data to a marketing researcher?
2. Thinking of secondary data as advantageous, how might a bank or health-care organization use a big data approach using secondary data to predict peak periods for loans or emergency care?
3. What questions should a researcher ask about secondary data in deciding whether or not the data are useful?
4. What factors might discourage a researcher from using a particular secondary data source?
5. In what ways might a researcher determine if a specific secondary data source is sufficiently reliable and valid to address a research question presuming the source does not describe the study methodology in detail?
6. Identify some typical research objectives for secondary-data studies.
7. What is model building? How does it use secondary data? What are some examples of different applications of model building in marketing research?
8. What would be a source for the following data?
   a. Population, average income, and employment rates for Oregon
   b. European trends in automobile ownership
   c. Divorce trends in the United States
   d. Use of Facebook, Instagram, and Twitter by age and region
   e. Annual sales of the top ten U.S. fast-food companies

   f. Top ten websites ranked by number of unique visitors
   g. Consumer spending on education in Canada, Zimbabwe, and China.
9. Suppose you are a marketing research consultant and a client comes to your office and says, "I must have the latest information on the supply of and demand for Idaho potatoes within the next 24 hours." What would you do?
10. What type of data source does the CIA *World Factbook* represent? What kind of data can one find there?
11. Report the following data:
    a. U.S. gross domestic product for the first quarter of 1965.
    b. U.S. exports of goods and services for the calendar year 2017
    c. U.K. imports of goods and services for the calendar year 2012
    d. U.S. gross domestic product for the first quarter of 2018
    e. Number of fast-food restaurants currently operating in North Dakota
    f. For any of a–e, are the data unavailable?
    g. For any of a–e, would you be uncomfortable relying on the number provided? Explain why or why not.
12. What is Google Analytics? What type of data can it provide to an entrepreneur just opening a new business?
13. Do you believe it is ethical for an employer to mine social networking sites for personal information about employees? Does it matter if the information refers to behavior solely away from

work or that is somehow tied to things done while at work? Address the same issue for a marketing research firm that distributes entertainment to mobile devices (movies, music, games). Is it ethical for them to search for relationships and market segments using information people post about themselves on the Internet?

∷ RESEARCH ACTIVITIES

1. Use secondary data to learn the size of the current U.S. golf market and to profile the typical golfer. Can secondary data address research questions related to changes and trends in the U.S. golf market?
2. Where could a researcher working for the U.S. Marine Corps (http://www.marines.com) find information that would identify the most productive areas of the United States in which to recruit? What would you recommend?
3. Compare population data from the CIA *World Factbook* for Uruguay, the United States, South Africa, Japan, and Italy with population data for those countries found through some other source (perhaps one originating in each country). Do the different data sources agree? Comment.
4. Try to find the U.S. market share for the following companies within 30 minutes:
   a. Home Depot
   b. Burger King
   c. Marlboro
   d. Google
   e. Was this a difficult task? If so, why do you think this information is so difficult to find?
5. Go to Statistics Norway at http://www.ssb.no. What data, if any, can you obtain in English? What languages can be used to search this website? What databases might be of interest to the business researcher?
6. Review the per capita beer consumption for Czechia provided in the chapter. Do your own search for the statistic directly. How close is the ranking and value that you found online? If the value differs, why do you think it does? Is the difference big enough to change your mind about the Czech beer market?

Easy Rider or Ease of Riding?

Case 6.1

Consumers have long had a love affair with driving. Driving a car represented freedom! A 1960s movie called *Easy Rider* particularly glorified motorbike riding. In 2017, Mercedes Benz resurrected *Easy Rider* for a Super Bowl spot where the star of the movie, Peter Fonda, drives off excitedly in his Mercedes AMG Convertible. Americans love to drive! Or do they?

A number of changes may potentially change things. One, Americans are getting older. As baby boomers move on and are replaced by millennials as the biggest consumer segment, some analysts suggest that they are less excited about owning automobiles. Two, ride-sharing is common and has come to represent the consumer sharing economy. Perhaps the idea of sharing rides may become more appealing to certain generations to free them from the responsibilities and hassles of car ownership. Three, self-driving technologies are fast evolving. Many autos are virtually capable of driving themselves and the idea of a driverless car seems inevitable.

In the face of all this, marketers continue to look for opportunities in the marketplace. One technology that exists in concept in the United States and as a reality in many parts of the world is the single-passenger automobile. Brand names like Elio and Solo have produced test cars, and international brands like India's Alibaba already offer single-passenger automobiles. In fact, the brand Cushman specialized in single-passenger utility vehicles in the United States in the mid-twentieth century.

Suppose you are asked to conduct a research project exploring the idea of a single-passenger sports car for the U.S. market. In particular, the entrepreneur launching the idea believes that younger, single consumers are the most attractive consumer market. The entrepreneur believes there is a sweet spot in the market willing to pay a bit of a premium for a sporty, fun to drive car, but unwilling to pay for self-driving technology. Most of the other single-passenger automobiles focus on utility and economy for their value propositions. Unfortunately, the entrepreneur has a limited budget and time for the project.

Questions

1. Using secondary data sources, what data might be available that suggests millennials, demand for automobiles? What conclusions can you draw from that data?
2. Using secondary data sources, what data exist that may shed light on consumer opinions about self-driving technologies?
3. What about generation Z? Is there data that suggests they may have different consumer preferences with respect to owning an automobile relative to millennials?
4. Based on your findings, what recommendations would you make to the entrepreneur? Do millennials or generation Z represent attractive market segments for the concept?

Ryan McVay/Getty Images

Survey Research

CHAPTER

7

LEARNING OUTCOMES

After studying this chapter, you should be able to:

1. Know what a survey is and how it can provide insight into explaining human behavior
2. Identify sources of error in survey research
3. Summarize the ways researchers gather information through personal interviews
4. Know the advantages and disadvantages of conducting surveys using self-administered questionnaires
5. Appreciate the importance of pretesting questionnaires
6. Describe ethical issues that arise in survey research

iStock.com/Opidanus

Chapter Vignette:

Survey Says!

With all the talk about Big Data and all the technologies that constantly track consumer and employee behavior, one could easily overlook the survey as an outdated research tool. Tracking data collect information on behavior and help address what, when, and where questions without respondent surveys. However, properly designed surveys remain integral to marketing research, particularly when it comes to answering why and how questions.

One prominent theory of human decision-making frames behavior as the result of either System 1 or System 2 thinking.[1] System 1 theories deal with behavioral reactions with little explanation as to why the behavior occurred. For example, we can know that 5,000 consumers responded to a Starbucks notification within 1 minute of its release with simple app analytics, but that data tells us nothing about why consumers responded. System 2 deals with non intuitive processes that require effortful thought. System 2 explanations go deeper than what occurred and try to explain how or why someone came to a certain decision. Surveys can be used in conjunction with observational data to try to come to a more complete explanation with actionable implications.

Complicating matters further, the average attention span for a U.S. consumer these days continues to drop. Estimates today suggest that a typical consumer will pay attention for 7 or 8

seconds before moving on to something else. Thus, effective survey designs call for shorter surveys with the use of varied and different scaling options to enhance engagement of the respondent.[2] Surveys must also accommodate mobile media as many consumers today primarily interact with the Internet via a phone or tablet. YouTube, Yelp, and practically all professional services rely heavily on survey input to diagnose potential problems with their business. Thus, what the *survey says* remains very important!

Andriy Popov/Alamy Stock Photo

Introduction

respondents

People who answer an interviewer's questions verbally or provide answers to written questions through any media delivery (paper or electronic).

sample survey

A more formal term for a survey emphasizing that respondents' expressed answers presumably represent a sample of the larger target population's opinion.

Marketing research focuses on human behavior. So, the marketing researcher needs input from or about people, and perhaps asking people questions is the simplest way to obtain input, particularly when the goal of research is explaining some behavior. We use the term **respondents** for people who answer questions during a survey. Researchers conduct interviews via e-mail, with display boards, through the Internet, text messaging, or even through an actual face-to-face question-and-answer discussion. A survey represents a way of describing human opinions, feelings, and intended or past behavior by collecting primary data through communicating directly with individual sampling units. Surveys provide a snapshot at a given point in time. More precisely, this is a **sample survey** because respondents' expressed answers presumably represent a sample of the larger target population's opinion. For consumer-oriented firms, sample surveys represent a primary tool for staying in touch with the population of consumers.

Practically every day, consumers receive requests for a survey response. Some of those appear as pop-ups while interacting with a website or app. Some invite feedback such as Yelp ratings of business establishments. Others arrive as an e-mail request, perhaps in response to a recent flight or hotel stay. More rarely these days, the survey may show up in the snail mail. Survey data continue to be useful on its own, but survey data used in conjunction with behavioral data can be extremely helpful in designing value propositions and managing brands.

The Types of Information Gathered Using Surveys

Information gathered in a survey varies considerably, depending on the objectives. Surveys often address multiple research questions relevant to the marketing mix. Typically, surveys describe what is happening, what people believe, what they are like, or reveal potential explanations for why one

● ● ● ● ● ● ●

A survey can provide input that would help advertisers know how consumers interpret an ad like this before going public.

Source: http://adsoftheworld.com/media/print/madcroc_old_man?size=_original, 4/12/2011, the company website is madcroc.com

ALMOST THIS MUCH ENERGY.

Using the face scale, please adjust the face until it matches the way you feel about your university experience.

Source: Qualtrics.com

Chances are, if you are involved in a research project involving consumer reactions to some business, be it for profit or not for profit, you likely will be using surveys at some point. This chapter provides a *survey*, pardon the pun, of survey research techniques. A survey provides a snapshot of some situation at a given point in time. When designing your survey, keep in mind that people today have short attention spans and need to be engaged. Thus, surveys that allow some graphical input serve to create interest and perhaps even turn the survey into a bit of gaming experience. Once your survey is designed, make sure to be aware of the common sources of error mentioned here.

participates in a particular marketing activity. Marketers can make decisions about what products to sell, what the prices should be, where to sell them, how to generate buzz and other things. Questions about product use, desirable features, and Web habits help with product development and advertising messages.

More specifically, surveys gather information to assess consumer knowledge and awareness of products, brands, or issues and to measure consumer attitudes, feelings, and behaviors. Additionally, surveys describe consumer characteristics, including purchasing patterns, brand usage, and descriptive characteristics including demographics and lifestyle. Thus, psychographic research involves surveys. Surveys are good tools for gathering demographic information and information on media exposure helpful in planning a market segmentation strategy.

A survey commissioned by eBay learned that almost 60 percent of people receive unwanted gifts, and 15 percent have sold an unwanted gift online. In addition, the survey indicated that selling unwanted gifts online was twice as common among the 25- to 34-year-old demographic. Another survey suggests that one in four Christmas gift shoppers shop all year long for good deals on yuletide gifts and nearly two of three believe they will overspend on gifts.[3] Other surveys indicate that consumers who receive gifts believe the giver will be more upset about regifting than do the actual givers. Further, givers voice a preference for regifting a gift than to have someone to whom they gave a gift throw it away.[4] Although consumer surveys are a common form of marketing research, not all survey research involves consumer opinion. Frequently, studies focus on other populations like wholesalers, retailers, or industrial buyers.

The term *survey* is most often associated with quantitative research. Most surveys seek to quantify certain factual information. However, aspects of surveys may also be qualitative. In new-product development, a survey often has a qualitative objective of refining product concepts. Surveys can reveal stylistic, aesthetic, or functional changes based on respondents' open-ended suggestions. Evaluating the qualitative nature of advertising may also be an objective of survey research.[5] An energy drink company created a viral ad depicting an elderly man moving along with the aid of a walker while trying to dodge a wrecking ball. The energy drink provides a boost to his step, enabling him to navigate the sidewalk without being smashed. Before going mainstream with the ad, the company applied a short survey following YouTube views, asking viewers what they thought of the ad. Based on the responses, the ad agency tried to judge whether the ad communicated product benefits and good feelings or whether the image offended respondents.

Advantages and Disadvantages of Survey Research

Survey research presents numerous advantages. Surveys provide a quick, often inexpensive, efficient, and accurate means of assessing information about a population. Researchers also can apply fairly straightforward statistical tools in analyzing sample survey results. Surveys are quite flexible and, when conducted properly, the results are extremely valuable to the manager.

One of the key disadvantages is that survey results are no better than the quality of the sample and answers obtained. A survey opens the door to errors in general and those errors contribute to misleading results. In addition to these general disadvantages, each individual survey tool introduces unique disadvantages. By understanding the nature of these errors, researchers can reduce the likelihood of producing misleading results by better matching a survey approach to a given situation.

Show Us Some Love

Lots of marketers like to survey past customers to assess their service quality and customer satisfaction. Did you ever have a service employee tell you that you might be invited to participate in a survey, and if you were to receive such an invitation, "Can you give us all 5s (a perfect score)?" The employee adds, "We aim always to exceed customer expectations!" Sure enough, a few days later the invitation to participate in the survey arrives via e-mail. The questionnaire contains several questions for which the respondent is to indicate whether or not the service quality was "much less than expected," "less than expected," "exactly what you expected," "slightly better than expected," or "exceeded expectations." The scores range from 1 to 5, respectively. The customer thinks about the service. Being very familiar with the company's service, she fully expected the service to be outstanding and the service was outstanding. She knows that the employee wants her to mark 5. But, honestly, answer

3, exactly as expected, is exactly correct. She puts 3. When a manager looks at the data, her response is flagged to represent a unhappy customer. If the goal of the company is truly to represent their customers' perceptions, have they introduced any sources of error illustrated in Exhibit 7.1 into the process?

Sources of Error in Surveys

A manager who is evaluating the quality of a survey must estimate its accuracy. The manager must consider all the possible sources of mistakes. Exhibit 7.1 outlines the various forms of survey errors.[6] From one perspective, total survey error contains two major sources, sampling error and systematic error due to some issue with the respondent or the survey administration.

In this chapter, we focus on errors that most directly distract from the representativeness of the survey results. In other words, a good survey should provide a snapshot of some larger population, such as all consumers in California or all consumers in the United States. Survey results from a sample should generalize to a larger population. Unfortunately, many factors can inhibit a survey's representativeness and a good researcher strives to understand the *total error* that can creep into survey results.[7] Later in the book, we'll focus more on topics related to scaling and measurement error.

Random versus Systematic Sampling Error

sampling error

Error arising because of inadequacies of the actual respondents to represent the population of interest.

systematic error

Error resulting from some imperfect aspect of the research design that causes respondent error or from a mistake in the execution of the research.

population parameter

Refers to some true value of a phenomenon within a population.

Successful surveys portray a representative cross-section of a particular population. Even with technically proper random probability samples, however, statistical errors occur because of chance variation in the elements selected for the sample. These statistical problems are unavoidable but become smaller as a sample grows in size. **Sampling error** refers to inadequacies of the actual respondents to represent the population of interest. Part of sampling error arises because of random fluctuation but part occurs because of a sampling frame's inappropriateness.

Conversely, **systematic error** results from some imperfect aspect of the research design or from a mistake in the execution of the research. Systematic errors include all sources of error other than those introduced directly by the sampling procedure. Therefore, systematic errors are *nonsampling errors*. Respondent and research administrator mistakes are primary sources for systematic errors.

The term **population parameter** refers to some true value of a phenomenon within a population. For instance, the number of Red Bulls consumed in 2018 by first-year university students in Indiana truly exists. Determining this number without error presents a formidable challenge. Given the difficulty in identifying the population parameter directly, researchers choose instead to

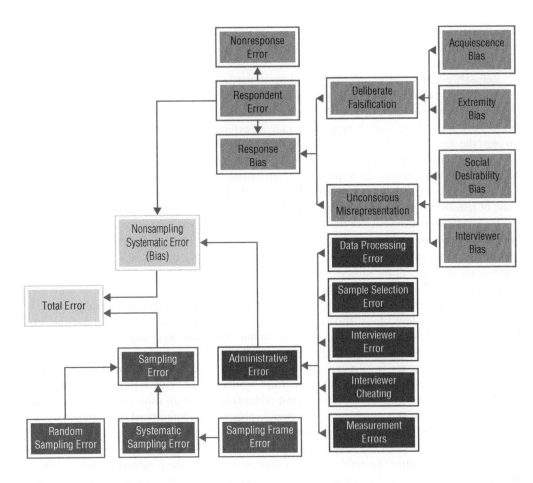

EXHIBIT **7.1**
Sources of Survey Error that Make the Results Miss the Target

estimate the number using a sample of these students. A **sample bias** exists when results of a particular sample deviate in one direction from the true value of the population parameter. For instance, if the researcher selects respondents during May of 2018, the Red Bull parameter estimate may be biased upward because the sample members were facing final exams. Systematic errors arise from two general categories: respondent error and administrative error.

Respondent Error

Surveys ask people for answers and hopefully people give truthful answers. Error exists otherwise and respondent error results. Response bias and nonresponse error bias are the two major categories of **respondent error**.

Nonresponse Error

Surveys rarely obtain 100 percent response rates, but a researcher employing a text message questionnaire about energy drink consumption may face a serious problem. The researcher must believe that sample members who respond to a text message questionnaire are not any different from sample members who did not respond. Sample members who refuse or cannot respond are **nonrespondents**. **Nonresponse error** is the statistical difference between a parameter value obtained using only actual survey respondents compared to the value obtained from a survey (hypothetical) including input also from those who did not respond (i.e., the nonrespondents). In other words, what would the value be if all potential sample members had responded? Of course, knowing precisely how big this error truly is becomes practically impossible because nonrespondents, by definition, did not provide information!

In a phone survey, nonresponse occurs when a call goes unanswered. The number of **no contacts** in survey research has been increasing for a host of reasons, including restrictions in who can be contacted and changes in technology. Increasingly, households do not have a home telephone. A traditional phone survey cannot reach these members of the sampling frame. Most people today screen

sample bias

A persistent tendency for the results of a sample to deviate in one direction from the true value of the population parameter.

respondent error

A category of sample bias resulting from some respondent action such as lying or inaction such as not responding.

nonrespondents

Sample members who are mistakenly not contacted or who refuse to provide input in the research.

nonresponse error

The statistical differences between a survey that includes only those who responded and a perfect survey that would also include those who failed to respond.

no contacts

Potential respondents in the sense that they are members of the sampling frame but who do not receive the request to participate in the research.

out unwanted communications or at the least just do not answer unrecognized numbers. An e-mail request sent to a potential respondent via an old unused e-mail address likewise creates nonresponse through no contact.

refusals

People who are unwilling to participate in a research project.

Refusals occur when people are unwilling to participate in the research. A research team reviewed fifty mail surveys of pediatricians conducted by the American Academy of Pediatrics (AAP) and found that response rates declined through the first decade of the twenty-first century. In the early years of the study period, an average 70 percent of pediatricians returned completed surveys; the response rate fell to an average 63 percent in the second half of the period.[8] No contacts and refusals can seriously bias survey data. In the case of the pediatricians, the researchers found little difference in the response rates attributable to differences in such easy-to-measure variables as age, sex, and type of membership in the AAP, leaving them to wonder whether the cause of refusals was some unknown but important difference among these doctors.

Researchers often investigate the causes of nonresponse. A primary reason deals with effort. Frankly, many people do not want to put in the effort to respond, even if the effort is small. People tend not to respond to questions that are difficult to answer. If a project requires that the same respondents answer multiple surveys, expect higher participation to the first series of surveys and participation to fall off as the series progresses.

How can a researcher assess nonresponse error? Comparing the sample demographics with the demographics of the target population provides one means of checking for potential response bias. For instance, if we know that 54 percent of freshmen university students in Indiana are female (based on state census counts), and our resulting sample in the Red Bull consumption survey turns out to be 75 percent male, we know females are underrepresented. Thus, the Red Bull consumption estimate would exhibit bias (error) to the extent that men and women do not drink as much Red Bull.

self-selection bias

A bias that occurs because people who feel strongly about a subject are more likely to respond to survey questions than people who feel indifferent about it.

Researchers know that those who are most enthusiastic about an issue are more likely to respond. **Self-selection bias** is a problem that frequently plagues self-administered questionnaires. Consumers decide where to shop, eat, and get their cars serviced and whether to answer a questionnaire. Thus, a researcher conducting a survey about consumer attitudes toward Abercrombie and Fitch (A&F) should expect more favorable responses than normal if he/she conducts the survey within an A&F store, invites a response through an A&F app, or if he/she uses a customer database for the sampling frame. In either case, the potential respondent has made a conscious selection to patronize A&F. Self-selection bias distorts survey results because favorable respondents are overrepresented. Oftentimes, self-selection bias can reflect more extreme attitudes than those that truly exist in a wider population.

Response Bias

response bias

A bias that occurs when respondents either consciously or unconsciously answer questions with a certain slant that misrepresents the truth.

A **response bias** occurs when respondents answer questions in a way that slants meanings away from true population values. As a result, willfully or not, the respondent contributes to misleading results. If a distortion of measurement occurs because respondents' answers are false or misrepresented, the resulting sample bias will be a response bias. When researchers identify response bias, they should include a corrective measure.

Deliberate Falsification. Occasionally people deliberately give false answers. A response bias occurs when people misrepresent answers. Consider a survey about grocery store prices. Rather than appear ignorant or unconcerned about prices, a respondent may provide their best estimate and not tell the truth—namely, that they cannot remember. Sometimes respondents become bored with the interview and provide answers just to finish the survey. Other times, respondents try to look smart by giving answers they think are expected. Similarly, respondents sometimes give answers simply to please the interviewer or to qualify as a respondent to obtain some incentive. Falsification comes in several forms.

Unconscious Misrepresentation. Even when a respondent is consciously trying to be truthful and cooperative, response bias can arise from the question format, the question content, or some other stimulus. For example, the administration technique can bias results. The results of two in-flight surveys concerning aircraft preference illustrate this point. Passengers flying on Boeing 747s preferred that plane over an Airbus A-380 (74 percent versus 19 percent), whereas passengers flying on an Airbus A-380 preferred it to the 747 (56 percent versus 38 percent). Obviously, presence in one company's aircraft biased the results.[9] Respondents could hardly make a fair comparison of planes when the awareness of one alternative was so much greater.

Respondents may not be able to give precise answers in some cases. Consider the following question:

When was the last time you went 36 hours without checking Facebook? _____days

Respondents may have to guess because they do not know the exact answer. In other cases, consumers cannot adequately express their feelings in words. The cause may be questions that are vague, ambiguous, or not specific enough. Researchers may ask someone to describe his/her frustration when using a computer. If the researcher has a specific interest in software usage, he/she will likely be disappointed with the answers. Language differences also may be a source of misunderstanding. A French researcher used an instrument developed in France to assess lunch habits. However, the French word for lunch, *dejeuner*, means "breakfast" in Quebec.

Many respondents will answer questions even though they have given them little thought. For example, in most investigations of consumers' buying intentions, the predictability of the intention scales depends on how close the subject is to making a purchase. The intentions of subjects who have little knowledge of the brand or the store alternatives or who have not yet made any purchase plans are relatively unlikely to predict purchase behavior accurately. Additionally, as more time passes since a purchase or a shopping event, the more people tend to underreport information about that event. Time lapse influences people's ability to communicate specific factors precisely.

Types of Response Bias

Response bias falls into four specific categories: acquiescence bias, extremity bias, interviewer bias, and social desirability bias. These categories overlap and are not mutually exclusive. A single biased answer may be distorted for many complex reasons, some distortions being deliberate and some being unintentional misrepresentations.

Acquiescence Bias. A tendency for a respondent to maintain a consistent response style often tending to try to go along and agree with the viewpoint of a survey is known as **acquiescence bias**. One good way to think about acquiescence bias is in the context of new-product research. Questions about a new-product idea generally elicit some acquiescence bias because respondents give positive connotations to most new ideas. For example, consumers responded favorably to survey questions about pump baseball gloves (the pump inserts air into the pocket of the glove, providing more cushioning). However, when these expensive gloves hit the market, they sat on shelves. When conducting new-product research, researchers should recognize the high likelihood of acquiescence bias.

A less common form of acquiescence comes in the form of respondents tending to disagree with all questions. A survey administered by a group protesting a new Walmart location in a residential area may show abnormally high disagreement with supporting the development. Other times, a respondent may be trying to respond with desirable responses because he believes the researcher will withhold a promised incentive for participation if the answers do not support the research purpose. Respondents from crowdsourced sites like Amazon's m-Turk sometimes answer a thousand or more surveys a month. Such *professional* respondents develop experience that allows them to pick up on clues on how they *should* respond as a way of making sure to receive payment. In essence, they acquiesce to what they believe the demand of the researcher might be. Other times, a respondent is just not putting much effort into responses, resulting in consistent responses. Thus, acquiescence bias occurs whenever a respondent

1. displays a tendency to concur with a particular position,
2. displays a tendency to please the researcher or answer consistent with the perceived research purpose by providing consistent responses, and
3. lazily gives consistent answers that result in deviations from true responses.

Extremity Bias. Some individuals tend to use extremes when responding to questions. In other words, they will tend to use the furthest left or right ends of a scale. Response styles vary from person to person, and extreme responses may cause an **extremity bias** in the data. Extremity bias is

acquiescence bias

Tendency of a respondent to maintain a consistent response style often tending to try to go along and agree with the viewpoint of a survey.

extremity bias

A category of response bias that results because some individuals tend to use extremes when responding to questions.

common in consumer satisfaction scales. The trick for the researcher in deciding if the data are valid is to sort out extremity bias from true responses like the kind that may result from self-selection.

Interviewer Bias. Response bias may arise from the interplay between interviewer and respondent. If the interviewer's presence influences respondents to give untrue or modified answers, **interviewer bias** results. Sometimes respondents may give answers they believe will please the interviewer rather than the truthful responses. Respondents may wish to appear intelligent and wealthy—of course they read *Architectural Digest* rather than the *National Enquirer*.

Interviewer characteristics, including age, sex, style of dress, tone of voice, facial expressions, or other nonverbal characteristics, may influence a respondent's answers. In a research study on sexual harassment against saleswomen, male interviewers might not obtain as candid responses from saleswomen as female interviewers would. Thus, interviewer techniques in which the interviewer remains unseen have an advantage of preventing this particular type of interviewer bias.

Many interviewers, contrary to instructions, shorten or rephrase questions to suit their needs. A researcher doing survey research for major U.S. newspapers asked a question about the Nazi holocaust in the following fashion:

> *"Do you believe it seems possible or does it seem impossible to you that the Nazi Extermination of the Jews never happened?"*[10]

Obviously, this question is confusing and yielded a result that should be meaningless. Instead, an unscrupulous blogger may use the results to state that 1 in 4 respondents believe the holocaust never occurred, or conversely that only 1 in 4 believe it did occur, when the survey results have no clear meaning.

This potential influence on responses can be avoided to some extent if interviewers receive training and supervision that emphasize the necessity of appearing neutral. Also, researchers with strong opinions may be steered toward other projects or be made aware that misleading results are unethical and likely do not further their cause in the long run.

Social Desirability Bias. **Social desirability bias** occurs because a respondent wishes to create a favorable impression or somehow save face during an interview. Respondents may inflate income, overstate education, or report heightened sensitivity to environmental issues. If the source for the research is known, imagine how it may bias answers to sensitive questions such as "Did you vote for the President in the last election?" "How often do you see a roach in your home?" "Do you color your hair?" or "How often do you go to church?"

The social desirability bias is especially significant in the case of research that addresses sensitive or personal topics, including respondents' sexual behavior. A researcher surveyed teens, asking the following question:

■ Have you ever *received* any nude pictures of a friend or peer via text message, Instagram, or Facebook?

Fifteen percent of teens reported "yes" to this question. The researcher also asked the following:

■ Have you ever *sent* nude pictures to your friends or posted them on Facebook or Instagram?

Only 4 percent indicated "yes" to this question.[11] Do you believe that the large difference in percentage is due to socially desirable responding? Do teens feel pressure to say they receive nude photos? Are teens unwilling to admit to sending or posting nude photos? An alternative explanation is that a few individuals send large numbers of photos of themselves or others in the nude to large numbers of teens. The social desirability makes it difficult to attribute any definitive meaning to this survey result.

Administrative Error

When a research employee improperly administers or executes his/her task, he/she creates **administrative error**. Administrative errors result from carelessness, confusion, neglect, omission, technical difficulties, or some other blunder. Four terms describe the different types of administrative error:

■ **Data processing error** results when data are improperly edited, coded, or entered into a computer. The accuracy of data processed by a computer depends on correct data entry and

Margin glossary

interviewer bias

A response bias that occurs because the presence of the interviewer influences respondents' answers.

social desirability bias

Bias in responses caused by respondents' desire, either conscious or unconscious, to gain prestige or appear in a different social role.

administrative error

An error caused by the improper administration or execution of the research task.

data processing error

A category of administrative error that occurs because of incorrect data entry, incorrect computer programming, or other procedural errors during data analysis.

programming. Data processing error is reduced by establishing careful procedures for verifying each step in the data processing stage.

■ **Sample selection error** results in an unrepresentative sample due to error in either sample design or execution of the sampling procedure. Executing a sampling plan free of procedural error is difficult. A firm that wants to represent a city's adult population and selects a sample from a telephone directory introduces systematic error in several ways, including:

- Many households have unlisted numbers and do not appear in the directory.
- Many households do not have a home (landline) phone.
- Cell phones are not listed in conventional directories.

sample selection error

An administrative error caused by improper sample design or sampling procedure execution.

Web responders also may be dishonest in some way as a means of being included as a respondent. For example, a respondent trying to earn a $1 incentive to answer a survey intended only for people living in Texas, Louisiana, or Mississippi answered the "in which state do you live?" with 25 different states before trying Texas. Obviously, this respondent cannot live in all of those places and further investigation suggested this respondent did not even live in the United States. Including this person would create sample selection bias.

■ **Interviewer error** occurs when interviewers record answers incorrectly, such as checking the wrong response or not writing fast enough to record respondents' statements verbatim. Also, selective perception may cause interviewers to misrepresent subtlety contrary opinions.

■ **Interviewer cheating** occurs when an interviewer falsifies entire questionnaires or fills in answers to questions that respondents skipped. Some interviewers cheat to finish an interview as quickly as possible or to avoid questions about sensitive topics. The term *curb-stoning* refers to interviewers filling in responses for respondents who do not really exist. Research firms can reduce interviewer cheating by recontacting a small number of respondents to verify previously recorded responses. In this way, curb-stoners might get revealed and face the consequences associated with this unethical behavior.

interviewer error

Mistakes made by interviewers failing to record survey responses correctly.

interviewer cheating

The practice of filling in fake answers or falsifying questionnaires while working as an interviewer.

What Can Be Done to Reduce Survey Error?

Knowing the many sources of error in surveys, you may have lost some of your optimism about survey research. Don't be discouraged! The discussion above emphasizes negativity because it is important for marketing managers to realize that surveys are not a panacea. Once one knows about the problems,

● ● ● ● ● ● ●

When is the researcher ever certain about who is really providing survey answers?

Twin Design/Shutterstock.com

michaeljung/Shutterstock.com

Electronic dating services have become a popular, successful, example of electronic interactive media.

steps can be applied to reduce survey errors. We'll discuss some ways to reduce error through effective questionnaire and sampling design in upcoming chapters. The good news lies ahead!

Ways Marketing Researchers Conduct Survey Interviews

When most people think of interviewing, they envision two people engaged in a face-to-face dialog or in a phone conversation. However, people don't always communicate in a two-way fashion. Sometimes, communication is one-way with little chance for spontaneous interaction. For example, traditional print advertisements employ one-way communication because they are noninteractive. The ad provides no mechanism in which the consumer talks back to the company. Likewise, we can summarize marketing communications with survey respondents into interactive and noninteractive media.

Interactive Survey Approaches

interactive survey approaches

Communication that allows spontaneous two-way interaction between the interviewer and the respondent.

Interactive survey approaches allow spontaneous two-way interaction between an interviewer and a respondent. Even when the communication is electronic, interactive approaches try to capture the dynamic exchange made possible through face-to-face interviews. Survey respondents, thus, need not be passive audience members. Today's interactive approaches allow respondents to be involved in two-way communication using electronic media such as smartphones, chat rooms, or other live Web interfaces. More detail on various electronic survey tools follows later in this chapter.

Noninteractive Media

noninteractive survey approaches

Communication approach by which respondents give answers to static questions that does not allow a two-way or dynamic dialog.

Noninteractive survey approaches do not facilitate two-way communications and are largely a vehicle by which respondents give answers to static questions. The traditional questionnaire received by mail, completed by a respondent, and mailed back to the researcher does not allow a real-time, dynamic exchange of information and is therefore noninteractive. Noninteractive questionnaires do have merit, but this type of survey is less flexible than surveys using interactive communication media. In fact, noninteractive media can be the best approach in some situations. Simple opinion polls, awareness studies, and even surveys assessing consumer attitudes can generally be collected adequately via one-way communication.

Conducting Personal Interviews

personal interview

Interactive face-to-face communication in which an interviewer asks a respondent to answer questions.

A **personal interview** is a form of direct, interactive communication in which an interviewer asks respondents questions face-to-face. This versatile and flexible method is a two-way conversation between interviewer and respondent. Personal interviews are truly interactive. Traditionally, researchers have recorded interview results using paper and pencil, by reading questions and recording answers. Today, computers are increasingly supporting survey research by automatically recording responses. In this section, we examine the general characteristics of face-to-face personal interviews, then compare and contrast door-to-door personal interviews with personal interviews conducted in shopping malls and those conducted on the phone.

Gathering information through face-to-face contact with individuals goes back many years. Military inscription and tax rates were set based on periodic censuses in ancient Egypt and Rome.

 RESEARCH
SNAPSHOT

Plus or Minus 3 Percent?

Surely, you've heard somebody give survey results predicting some outcome with the caution that the results are accurate to plus or minus 3 percent. Political polling typically reveals results with such a disclaimer. However, the history of such polling suggests they may not be that accurate! How can this be? Well, when the survey company provides the results to the media, the plus or minus 3 percent assumes that the only type of error is random sampling error. Looking back at Exhibit 7.1, obviously, a lot of other things can go wrong. Unconscious

misrepresentation and deliberate falsification, for example, could influence how someone responds to sensitive political issues. Thus, "Are you likely to vote? Who will you vote for?" Most respondents would not want to admit that they may not vote or that they may not even be registered to vote. Further, acquiescence may creep in as the respondent chooses the candidate he/she believes is most socially acceptable as a way of pleasing the polling agency or even public opinion. Thus, the expected error is nearly always plus or minus 3 percent.

During the Middle Ages, the merchant families of Fugger and Rothschild prospered in part because their far-flung organizations enabled them to get information before their competitors could.[12] Today, survey researchers present themselves in airports, shopping centers, and train stations and announce, "Good afternoon, my name is _____. I am with _____ Research Company, and we are conducting a survey on _____."

Advantages of Personal Interviews

Marketing researchers find that personal interviews offer many unique advantages.

Opportunity for Feedback

Personal interviews provide the opportunity for feedback and clarification. For example, if a consumer is reluctant to provide sensitive information, the interviewer may offer reassurance that his/her answers will be strictly confidential. Personal interviews offer the lowest chance that respondents will misinterpret questions, because an interviewer who senses confusion can clarify the instruction or questions. Circumstances may dictate that at the conclusion of the interview, the respondent be given additional information concerning the purpose of the study. This clarification is easily accomplished with a personal interview. If the feedback indicates that some question or set of questions is particularly confusing, the researcher can make changes that make the questionnaire easier to understand.

Probing Complex Answers

Another important characteristic of personal interviews is the opportunity to follow up by probing. If a respondent's answer is too brief or unclear, the researcher may request a more comprehensive or clearer explanation. The interviewer probes for clarification with standardized questions such as "Can you tell me more about what you had in mind?" (See Chapter 5 for an expanded discussion of probing.) Depending on the research purpose, personal interviews vary in the degree to which questions are structured and in the amount of probing required. The personal interview is especially useful for obtaining unstructured information. Skilled interviewers can handle complex questions that cannot easily be asked in telephone or mail surveys.

Survey Length

With the average attention time dropping to under 10 seconds, the general rule of thumb with respect to survey length is to keep it as short as possible to address the research questions. Sometimes, a very short survey can produce useful results. More and more, we see one-item surveys. For example, public restrooms may include a display board that allows users to answer one question as they leave the restroom. The question may be something like this:

■ How clean is our restroom today?
  ● Perfectly clean
  ● Acceptably clean
  ● Fairly clean
  ● Unacceptably dirty

The answer to this one-item survey contains very useful information, particularly when tied to data automatically recorded by the display board such as the time of day and the amount of use for the restroom.

However, more intensive self-administered surveys simply cannot be answered in 10 seconds or with a single question. Thus, when survey respondents are incentivized to participate in some way, a survey of a few minutes' length can produce good results. Typically, an engaging survey of 5 minutes or less can be used in such a situation. As surveys grow in length beyond 5 minutes, more error creeps into the responses. If the respondent is convinced his/her participation is very important and/or the respondent is being well-paid for his/her time, a survey of up to 10 minutes may be appropriate. Only in unusual situations can a researcher expect highly valid responses from questionnaires exceeding 10 minutes in length. In addition, however long the survey completion may take, the researcher needs to provide an honest assessment of the estimated time before the survey begins.[13] Clearly, a researcher acts unethically by inviting someone into a 30-second survey that ends up taking 5–10 minutes.

Completeness of Questionnaire

The social interaction between a well-trained interviewer and a respondent in a personal interview increases the likelihood that the respondent will answer all the items on the questionnaire. The respondent who grows bored with an online survey or telephone interview may terminate an interview at his/her discretion simply by shutting down the page or ending the call. Self-administered questionnaires require more effort from respondents and as such, they may just skip questions that require lengthy written answers. **Item nonresponse**—failure to provide an answer to a question—occurs less often when an experienced interviewer asks questions directly.

item nonresponse

Failure of a respondent to provide an answer to a survey question.

Props and Visual Aids

Interviewing respondents face-to-face allows the investigator to show them new-product samples, sketches of proposed advertising, or other visual aids. When Lego Group wanted to introduce new model train sets for its famous building bricks, the company targeted adults who build complex models with its product. The company invited adults who were swapping ideas at the Lego website to visit the New York office, where they viewed ideas and provided their opinions. The respondents wound up rejecting all the company's ideas, but they suggested something different: the Santa Fe Super Chief set, which sold out within two weeks of introduction due only to enthusiastic word of mouth.[14] Telephone interviews could not have yielded such rich results.

Marketing research that uses visual aids has become increasingly popular with researchers who investigate film concepts, advertising problems, and moviegoers' awareness of performers. Research for movies often begins by showing respondents videotapes of the prospective cast. Respondents see video clips and evaluate a movie's appeal based on the clips. This helps researchers know which scenes to use in trailers.

High Participation Rate

Although some people are reluctant to participate in a survey, the presence of an interviewer generally increases the percentage of people willing to complete the interview. People are often more hesitant to tell a person "no" face-to-face than they are over the phone, in an e-mail request, or

SOS Means Personal Interview

JEWEL SAMAD/Getty Images

SOS is an international symbol for a distress call. Although one could easily think that all the technological breakthroughs make face-to-face personal interviews obsolete, there are times when no other communication will work. Consider vulnerable populations. 2017 was an active hurricane season. Hurricanes Harvey, Irma, and Maria devastated areas in southeastern Texas, the Caribbean, and the Florida Keys, with Puerto Rico particularly hard hit. For some consumers hit by a storm, recovery comes slowly and they may not have access to telephones of any kind or access to the Internet for periods of weeks. Yet, marketers and public policy officials need research on what types of activities lead to the fastest recovery and what are such victims' greatest needs. Other vulnerable segments like young children and senior citizens are best reached with personal interviews. For example, personal interviews of assisted living residents examined the effect of losing or giving up a driver's license on transportation options. In both the case of natural disaster victims and the seniors giving up their licenses, elaborate responses evoked through personal interviews shined the light on the fact that psychological well-being, not just physical condition, is greatly affected by such events.

Sources: http://money.cnn.com/2017/09/28/news/economy/puerto-rico-hurricane-maria-damage-estimate/index.html, accessed November 28, 2017. Mullen, N. W., Parker, B., Wiersma, E., Stinchcombe, A., and Bédard, M. (2017). Looking Forward and Looking Back: Older Adults' Views of the Impacts of Stopping Driving. *Occupational Therapy in Health Care*, 31(3), 188–204.

through the snail mail. Respondents typically are required to do no reading or writing—all they have to do is talk. A personable interviewer can also do much to improve response rates. Many people enjoy sharing information and insights with friendly and sympathetic interviewers.

Disadvantages of Personal Interviews

Personal interviews also have disadvantages. Respondents are not anonymous and as a result may be reluctant to provide confidential information to another person. Suppose a survey asked top executives, "Do you see any major internal instabilities or threats to the achievement of your marketing objectives?" Many managers may be reluctant to tell the interviewer his/her thoughts about this sensitive question because complete anonymity is impossible.

Interviewer Influence

Imagine telling others about the past weekend. Would you have the same conversation with your mother as with your grandfather? Or, what about a roommate? In the same way, respondents act differently with different interviewers. One study's results suggest that male interviewers produced larger amounts of variance compared to female interviewers when 85 percent of respondents are female. Older interviewers who interviewed older respondents produced more variance than other age combinations, whereas younger interviewers who interviewed younger respondents produced the least variance.

Differential interviewer techniques may be a source of bias. The rephrasing of a question, the interviewer's tone of voice, and the interviewer's appearance may influence a respondent's answers. Consider the interviewer who has conducted 100 personal interviews. During the next one, he/she may lose concentration and either selectively perceive or anticipate the respondent's answer. The interpretation of the response may differ somewhat from what the respondent intended. Typically, the public thinks of a person who does marketing research as a dedicated scientist. Unfortunately, some interviewers do not fit that ideal. Considerable interviewer variability exists. Cheating is possible; interviewers cut corners to save time and energy or fake parts of their reports by dummying up part or all of a questionnaire. Control over interviewers is important to ensure that difficult, embarrassing, or time-consuming questions are handled properly.

Lack of Anonymity of Respondent

Because a respondent in a personal interview is not anonymous, he/she may be reluctant to provide confidential information to the interviewer. Researchers take care to phrase sensitive questions to avoid social desirability bias. For example, the interviewer may show the respondent a card that lists possible answers and ask the respondent to read a category number rather than be required to verbalize sensitive answers.

Cost

Personal interviews are expensive, generally substantially more costly than mail, e-mail, Internet, or phone surveys. The geographic proximity of respondents, the length and complexity of the questionnaire, and the number of people who are nonrespondents because they could not be contacted (not-at-homes) all influence the cost of personal interviews.

Mall Intercepts

mall-intercept interview
Personal interviews conducted in a shopping center or similar public area.

Interviewers conduct personal interviews in respondents' homes or offices or in many other places including shopping centers and airports. The phrase **mall-intercept interview** applies generally to a technique involving random approaches to passersby asking for participation in a survey. Interviewers intercept potential respondents in a public area, not necessarily a shopping mall, and invite him or her to complete the interview in a convenient place. Sometimes interviewees are asked to taste new food items or to view advertisements. Sometimes, the respondent may be escorted to a computer where an online survey is completed. The locale for the interview generally influences the participation rate, and thus the degree to which the sample represents the general population.

When the researchers need a sample representative of the U.S. consumer population, he/she needs to keep in mind that each shopping center has its own market characteristics. Larger bias follows to the extent that a particular shopping center likely has a unique demographic or psychographic profile. However, personal interviews in shopping centers are appropriate when the target group is a special market segment, such as households with school-aged children. A mall intercept approach may be particularly appropriate during the back to school sales period. The mall-intercept interview allows the researcher not only to interview, but to have respondents interact with physical objects, including backpacks, tablets, bicycles, and so on. Mall intercepts are great when demonstration is part of the research design. For example, electronics manufacturers often do not want to test new appliances in consumers' homes because of difficulty in moving and setting up appliances. Thus, bringing respondents to the appliances is a better option. The mall intercept approach also reduces response biases, including the types of acquiescence bias that come from low-response involvement and deliberative falsifications particularly in reporting observable demographic characteristics. Often, the researcher may be more interested in a population like the people who patronize the shopping center than they are in an exact match to the entire U.S. Thus, the mall intercept, even if not in a mall, remains an attractive interview technique.

Door-to-Door Interviews

The presence of an interviewer at the door generally increases the likelihood that a person will be willing to complete an interview, presuming someone answers the door. Because proper **door-to-door interviews** increase the participation rate and are conducted at a person's residence, they provide a more representative sample of the general population than other survey approaches such as e-mail. Today, door-to-door interviews seldom involve cold calling. An advance notice by e-mail or telephone notifying a household that interviews will be conducted and possibly arranging a convenient time increase cooperation. Otherwise, cold-call refusals mean that a representative sample of security-conscious consumers may prove difficult. For these reasons, door-to-door interviews are becoming a thing of the past as a widely employed survey approach.

door-to-door interviews
Personal interviews conducted at respondents' doorsteps in an effort to increase the participation rate in the survey.

Callbacks and Precalls

When an interviewer's first attempt to contact a potential respondent fails, a systematic procedure calling for more attempts should be in place. **Callbacks**, or attempts to try and contact those sample members missed in the initial attempt, can substantially reduce nonresponse error. Callbacks in door-to-door and the telephone interviews are important because not-at-home individuals (e.g., working parents) may systematically vary from those who *are* at home (nonworking parents, retired people, and the like). In non-personal modes, like e-mail surveys, callbacks can be automated. In computer-assisted telephone interviews (sometimes referred to by the acronym **CATI**), the computer automatically schedules initial calls and autodials a callback when a call to a specific number is unanswered. Many public opinion researchers believe CATI remains a good alternative for representativeness compared to other survey types.[15] A **precall** is another form of contacting respondents but is done before the interview to give the potential respondent notice that an interview request is on the way.

callbacks
Attempts to try and contact those sample members missed in the initial attempt.

CATI
Acronym for computer-assisted telephone interviews where a computer routine automatically selects numbers from a sampling frame and schedules calls and callbacks.

precall
A phone call notifying potential respondents that an interview request is on the way as a tool to increase participation rates.

Global Considerations

Marketing researchers recognize that the manner of conducting and the receptiveness to personal interview varies dramatically around the world. For example, in some Arab nations, a female mall-intercept interviewer may not be able to interview a male respondent. In many countries, the idea of discussing grooming behavior and personal-care products with a stranger would be highly offensive. Personal interviews on such topics would be a bad idea. Thus, cultural norms play a role in selecting a survey approach.

Researchers face both cultural and social norms when doing research that requires business-people to participate. For example, conducting business-to-business interviews in Japan during business hours is difficult because managers, strongly loyal to their firm, believe that they have an absolute responsibility to stick to the job! Managers also understandably feel uncomfortable answering too many questions about their decision making asked by a company researcher. In these instances, an outside research company might get better responses.

To the Point

"People have really odd opinions. They tell me I'm skinny as if that's supposed to make me happy—"

—ANGELINA JOLIE

Telephone Interviews

Remember when a telephone was a just telephone? Probably not. Phones come in many forms these days. The interviewer these days typically sits at a computer that lists the questions and provides a survey form on which the interviewer records the respondent's answers (another example of how CATI takes place). Researchers using phone interviews these days need to ponder this question: Are all types of phones equally prone to error?

● ● ● ● ● ● ●
Phone surveys were less
complicated back when phones
were phones.

Landline Phones

Landline telephone interviews have been a mainstay of commercial survey research since the 1940s. Traditionally, researchers consider data gathered in a phone interview comparable to that collected in a face-to-face interview. Phone interviews even possess advantages over face-to-face interviews as respondents are sometimes more forthcoming with information on a variety of personal topics while tucked away comfortably at home out of the sight of the interviewer.

Pollsters and many market researchers still consider an in-home phone interview survey capable of providing samples relatively representative of household populations in the United States and other developed nations. For instance, researchers used telephone interviews with over 1,600 households in Israel to assess the impact of regular drinking on social well-being among people who live daily with the realities of war and terrorism. The results point to the benefits of social drinking where people gather with family and friends as a tool in coping with trauma.[16] Several recent events including legislation making calls more difficult and decreasing landline phone ownership are challenging the assumption that phone interviews provide good representativeness.

No-Call Legislation

"No-call" legislation dates back to the mid-2000s. Marketers cannot call phone numbers listed on the do-not-call registry. The legislation exists at the federal and state levels and is not unique to the United States. The legislation originally targeted telemarketers, and although marketing research efforts do not always fall under the legislation, many commercial marketing research firms honor the do-not-call registry. Consumers who opt in to the system are unlikely to welcome survey research calls.

Marketers and marketing researchers can obtain the do-not-call lists of phone numbers from the FTC for $59 per area code. A subscriber can purchase the entire registry for just over $16,000. Although this may seem expensive, the FTC levies fines on the order of $10,000 per violation (per call), so obtaining the registry is a wise investment for those wishing to contact consumers via the telephone. The FTC's do-not-call website (http://donotcall.gov) provides access to detailed information for consumers and organizations.

robocalls

A phone call conducted by an autodialer and using a recorded voice message system.

The feds do take violations very seriously. One company found this out the hard way.[17] Versatile Marketing Solutions (VMS) purchased consumer phone numbers from companies that provide sales leads services without checking the do-not-call lists. In fact, the sales leads had been created when unsuspecting households responded to **robocalls** with a brief "survey" from "Tom

● ● ● ● ● ● ●
Information about do-not-call lists for each state can be found at the Direct Marketing Association's website at http://www.the-dma.org/government/donotcalllists.shtml.

Source: Federal Trade Commission

with Home Protection" about home security. A robocall is an autodialed phone call conducted by a recorded voice message system. VMS allegedly placed millions of calls to households who responded to the fake survey from Tom. Although VMS argued that the robocall respondents had opted in for calls about security, their arguments were not persuasive and in the end VMS agreed to a $3.4 million fine for the illegal calls. Using a survey to disguise selling is unethical.

The Canadian government instituted a nearly identical do-not-call program. The Canadian Radio-Television and Telecommunications Commission imposes steep fines for calls made to people on the Canadian do-not-call list. Other countries in Europe and elsewhere are also considering similar or even more aggressive legislation.

Ownership

We used to think that every household had a phone. Think again. Landline phone penetration is about 40 percent in the United States and even less in Europe.[18] That means that marketing researchers interested in representative samples in either place are starting out with a large piece of the population excluded from the list when landline phones are used. The percentage of cellphone-only households varies with demographics. Younger consumers are more likely to shun a landline phone as are consumers in the southern and western United States.[19] As a result, a sampling frame consisting of landline phone numbers creates the risk of increased error in the form of coverage bias. **Coverage bias** refers to misrepresentation of a population by survey results that disproportionately represent one group over another.

Even if the sampling frame is adequate to represent the population, the fact that different types of people are more or less likely to respond contributes to sample selection error as well. One in six households with landline phones reports not taking any incoming calls with their landline phone. Many other calls fail because of caller ID or due to hang-ups. To the extent that any of these issues are associated systematically with respondent characteristics, systematic error in the form of coverage bias becomes a strong possibility. Does one's personality relate to not answering, hanging up, or getting on a do-not-call list? Obviously, the chance of administrative error in

coverage bias

Misrepresentation of a population by survey results that disproportionately represent one group over another.

the form of sample selection bias seems highly plausible. Thus, landline phone interviews are still widely used, but researchers no longer automatically think of them as producing pristine data.

Researchers today supplement landline sampling frames with some other survey mode, potentially including a cell phone list as a way of reducing coverage error. Pollsters who correctly guess how much landline calls need to be supplemented with cell phone calls end up showing more accuracy in predicting election winners. More and more, though, even other modes are mixed into the sampling frame in an effort to gain adequate coverage of a population.

Mobile Phones

Mobile phone interviews differ from landline phones most obviously because they reach individuals rather than households. However, there are other less obvious distinctions.

■ In the United States, telemarketing toward mobile phone numbers is prohibited unless the user opts in.

■ The recipient of a mobile phone call is more likely to be distracted than are other respondents. The respondent may be driving a car, on the metro, or walking down a noisy street. Factors such as these are not conducive to a high-quality interview.

■ The area codes for mobile phones are not necessarily geographic. For instance, a person who moves from Georgia to Washington can choose to keep the old phone number. As a result, a researcher conducting a voice call survey may be unable to determine whether a respondent fits into the desired geographic sampling population.

Mobile phones are ubiquitous in most developed and even in some not so developed countries. Mobile phone penetration exceeds 100 percent in most developed nations. In some countries, such as the UAE, Bahrain, and Qatar, mobile phone ownership exceeds two phones for every person![20] In fact, out of 7 billion people worldwide, over 5 billion have access to a mobile phone, compared to 4.8 billion who have access to a flush toilet![21] Thus, mobile phones allow access to the masses. The consumer movement toward solely mobile phones may have less effect on research in Europe and other nations where researchers include mobile phone numbers alongside landline phone numbers in a sample frame listing. However, each sampling unit's chance of being contacted is multiplied by the number of phones he/she owns. Ideally, a sampling frame could be drawn that includes both a phone number and a name to identify a potential respondent. However, methods like random number dialing cannot identify people.

Phone Interview Characteristics

Phone interviews have several distinctive characteristics that set them apart from other survey techniques. These characteristics present significant advantages and disadvantages for the researcher.

Random Digit Dialing

random digit dialing
Use of telephone exchanges and random numbers to develop a sample of respondents in a landline phone survey.

Marketing researchers used to be tempted to use a telephone directory as a sampling frame. However, the typical telephone directory presents problems. Foremost, not every resident chooses to list his/her home phone number in the directory. Because people with unlisted phone numbers typically differ demographically and psychologically from those who list their numbers, unlisted phone numbers can introduce coverage bias. Researchers try to resolve the problem of unlisted phone numbers with random digit dialing. **Random digit dialing** in its simplest form takes telephone exchanges (area code + the first three numbers) for a geographic area and using computer-generated random numbers, adds the last four digits to obtain a phone number to call. The process excludes mobile phone numbers and if the firm complies, numbers on the do-not-call list. Random digit dialing also helps overcome the problem due to unlisted numbers, new listings, and recent changes in phone numbers. In the vast majority of random digit dialing, the computer actually selects the number from the list of potential respondents and places the call. Unfortunately, the refusal rate in commercial random digit dialing studies is higher than the refusal rate for telephone surveys that use only listed telephone numbers.

Landline versus Mobile Phone Results

Exhibit 7.2 provides a summary of potential differences in surveying by landline or mobile phones. Researchers should not be surprised to observe differences in the characteristics of heavy mobile phone users versus consumers who rely mostly on landline phone communications. For instance, compared to mobile phone users[22]:

■ Mobile phones are less likely to be shared than a landline phone.
■ Calls to mobile phone numbers are more likely than landline numbers to result in someone answering the phone—particularly during weekday working hours. About one in three calls to mobile phones are answered as opposed to about one in four calls to landline numbers.
■ Calls to mobile phone numbers are less likely to result in someone answering the phone on weekends than are landline numbers. Respondents answer less than one in three calls to mobile phones on the weekends as opposed to nearly four in ten calls to landline numbers.
■ Refusals are higher for calls to mobile phone numbers than for calls to landline numbers.
■ Mobile phone users should be duly compensated for their responses given the potential costs involved and the calls should be kept to a short duration given that a mobile phone user is more likely in a situation involving attention to some other activity.
■ Mobile phone users are different demographically than landline users. Mobile phone respondents tend to be younger, more likely college educated, and more affluent.
■ Mobile phone only users own different things than landline users. A survey suggests that mobile phone users are more likely to own durable goods like tablets, computers, and smart devices compared to landline users.[23]

These factors all affect the equivalence of data and samples obtained from landline and mobile phone sampling. Researchers should consider these factors before making a quick decision that any type of phone interviewing will satisfy the data needs at hand. In the end, a thorough understanding of the population of interest is essential in judging which type of interview is most appropriate.

EXHIBIT 7.2
Comparing and Contrasting Landline and Mobile Phones

	Landline Phone	Mobile Phone
Sampling units	Better for sampling household populations	Better for sampling populations of individual consumers/employees
Reaching respondents	Low probability of contact during working hours	Higher probability of getting an answer except on weekends
Cooperation	Once someone answers, slightly more willing to cooperate	Once someone answers, they often are preoccupied and less willing to talk particularly at any length
Restrictions	Do-not-call legislation restrictions may apply	Mobile phone numbers cannot be autodialed or conducted with computer voice assistance unless respondent gives written consent
Cost to respondent	Generally none	Charges may apply depending on plan, and respondent should receive compensation
Geography	Area codes and exchanges indicate location of household	Phone numbers are not good indicators of individuals' locations
Population	Tends to be older than median, married, own fewer electronic durable goods per person	Tend to be younger (not eligible to participate), single, college educated, likely to own more electronic durable goods per person
Technology	Relatively static	Changing rapidly with greater likelihood for visual presentation and text input
Ownership	About 40 percent in the United States and decreasing here and abroad	Over 90 percent in the United States with 70 percent being smartphones
Expense	Relatively economical	Relatively expensive due to added requirements of use

Speed

One advantage of telephone interviewing is the relative speed of data collection. Data collection with mail or personal interviews can take weeks. In contrast, interviewers can conduct hundreds of telephone interviews within a few hours. When an interviewer enters a respondent's answers directly into a computerized system, data processing speeds up even more relative to any other approach involving manual data coding and entry.

Cost

As the cost of personal interviews continues to increase, landline phone interviews appear relatively inexpensive. Estimates indicate that landline telephone interviews cost 25 percent of a comparable door-to-door personal interview. Mobile surveys are considerably more expensive than landline survey approaches because research personnel must dial and conduct them.

Absence of Face-to-Face Contact

Telephone interviews are more impersonal than face-to-face interviews. Respondents may answer embarrassing or confidential questions more willingly in a telephone interview than in a personal interview. However, mail and Internet surveys, although not perfect, are better media for gathering extremely sensitive information because they seem more anonymous. Some evidence suggests that people provide information on income and other financial matters only reluctantly, even in telephone interviews. Such questions may be personally threatening for a variety of reasons, and high refusal rates for this type of question occur with each form of survey research.

The inability of the interviewer to see respondents can cause problems. If a respondent pauses to think about an answer, the interviewer may simply interpret the pause as "no response" and go on to the next question. Hence, there is a greater tendency for interviewers to record no answers and incomplete answers in telephone interviews than in personal interviews.

Cooperation

One trend is very clear. In the last few decades, telephone response rates have fallen. Analysis of response rates for the long-running Survey of Consumer Attitudes conducted by the University of Michigan found that response rates fell from a high of 72 percent to 67 percent during the period from 1979 to 1996 and then even faster after 1996.[24] Lenny Murphy of the data collection firm Dialtek says survey response rates fell to below 20 percent by the mid-2000s.[25] Now, the response rate to telephone surveys is about 9 percent.[26] Fortunately, though, refusals do not seem to be strongly related to things like political affiliation, religious affiliation, or even demographics. However, certain socially sensitive activities like participating in elections or civic engagement are overstated in phone interviews.

Famous research companies like Pew or Nielsen usually identify themselves by name when calling as evidence suggests that respondents may be slightly more likely to answer if they recognize the firm to be a research firm and not a telemarketer or political call.[27] Even still, the response rate remains low. Callbacks and precalls provide one of the most successful approaches in increasing participation in phone interviews. In a study comparing response rates, the rates were highest among households that received an advance letter, somewhat lower when the notice came on a postcard, and lowest with no notice.[28]

Refusal to cooperate with interviews is directly related to interview length. Survey research finds that interviews of 5 minutes or less have refusal rates of about half of that of surveys that take between 6 and 12 minutes. A good rule of thumb is to keep telephone interviews under 10 minutes at the most, and preferably under 5 minutes.

Incentives to Respond

Respondents should receive some incentive to respond. Research addresses different types of incentives. For telephone interviews, tests of different types of survey introductions suggest that not all introductions are equally effective. A financial incentive or some significant chance to win a desirable prize will produce a higher telephone response rate than a simple assurance that the research is not a sales pitch, a more detailed description of the survey, or an assurance of confidentiality.[29]

Lack of Visual Medium

Visual aids cannot be used in traditional telephone interviews, meaning that they are not ideal for packaging/design research, copy testing of television and print advertising, and concept tests that require visual materials. Likewise, certain attitude scales and measuring instruments require the respondent to see a graphic scale, so they are difficult to use over the phone. Facetime or Skype video calls via a smartphone, tablet, or computer offer the possibility of presenting still or video images to respondents to accompany verbal dialog. Researchers may take greater advantage of this technology in the coming years. However, the phone is still inappropriate as a survey medium when respondents need to physically interact with a product.[30]

Central Location Interviewing

Research agencies or interviewing services typically conduct all telephone interviews from a central location. Such **central location interviewing** allows firms to hire a staff of professional interviewers and to supervise and control the quality of interviewing more effectively. When telephone interviews are centralized and computerized, an agency or business can benefit from additional cost economies. Research firms gain even better cost economies by outsourcing interviews to offshore call centers where labor costs are very low. However, a respondent will quickly become impatient with an interviewer who is difficult to understand. The cost savings that come from using interviewers who have difficulty communicating are soon outweighed by subsequent problems.

central location interviewing

Telephone interviews conducted from a central location, allowing firms to hire a staff of professional interviewers and to supervise and control the quality of interviewing more effectively.

Surveys Using Self-Administered Questionnaires

Marketing researchers distribute questionnaires to consumers in many ways (see Exhibit 7.3). They insert invitations to participate via pop-ups in websites and Facebook posts (or other social networking sites). They insert questionnaires in packages and magazines. They may place questionnaires at points of purchase, in high-traffic locations in stores or malls, or on tabletops in restaurants. Traditionally, survey researchers sent printed questionnaires via snail mail. Researchers

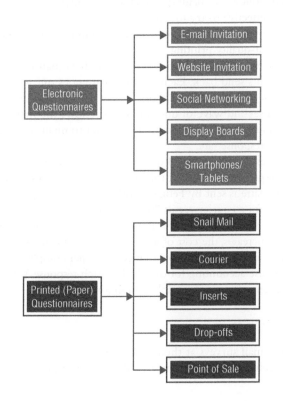

EXHIBIT **7.3**

Options for Self-Administered Questionnaires

self-administered questionnaires

Surveys in which the respondent takes the responsibility for reading and answering the questions without having them stated orally by an interviewer.

can administer surveys like these without the added expense of interview personnel. No matter how the **self-administered questionnaires** are distributed, they are different from interviews because the respondent takes responsibility for reading and answering the questions him/herself.

In mall intercepts, a research assistant usually stands by to answer any questions and provide basic instructions. The assistant does not typically read questions to respondents. More and more, the assistant hands the person an electronic tablet or takes them to a kiosk where each respondent completes the task electronically or on paper. In settings away from a research assistant completely, response quality becomes totally dependent on the questionnaire's ability to communicate the respondent task clearly and unambiguously. Below, we elaborate on a few of the more widely used survey techniques for self-administered questionnaires.

Mail Questionnaires

mail survey

A self-administered questionnaire sent to respondents through the mail.

A traditional **mail survey** is a self-administered questionnaire sent to respondents through a postal service. Most often, the general postal service, or snail mail, provides delivery. However, when fears of a low response rate, as typically occurs when the sample consists of professional workers like physicians or consultants, an express courier service like FedEx is a better but more expensive option. When researchers are concerned that the questionnaire actually gets delivered to the designated recipient, the courier (or postal agent) will obtain a certified return receipt.

Mail questionnaires have several advantages and disadvantages.

Geographic Flexibility

Mail questionnaires can reach a geographically dispersed sample simultaneously because interviewers are not required. Researchers can reach respondents who are located in isolated areas or those who are otherwise difficult to reach. For example, a pharmaceutical firm may find that doctors are not available for personal or telephone interviews. However, a mail or courier survey can reach both rural and urban doctors who practice in widely dispersed geographic areas.

Cost

Mail questionnaires are relatively inexpensive compared with personal interviews, though they are not cheap. Most include follow-up mailings, which require additional postage and printing costs. And it usually isn't cost-effective to try to cut costs on printing—questionnaires photocopied on low-grade paper have a greater likelihood of being thrown in the wastebasket than those prepared with more expensive, high-quality printing.

Low response rates contribute to high cost as researchers mail multiple questionnaires for every one that respondents send back. Each questionnaire goes out with a return postage-paid reply envelope, otherwise researchers should not expect respondents to return completed questionnaires. Very often, a second wave of questionnaires follows the first in an effort to increase responses. So, printing and postage costs add up quickly, not to mention the costs of any incentive provided to increase the response rate.

Exhibit 7.4 illustrates the cost of mail questionnaires per response. The goal is 400 completed responses. Nonrespondents represent the highest cost item. Response rates are substantially higher when a questionnaire is sent by FedEx or other courier company. This exhibit assumes a 50 percent response rate for a courier versus 20 percent for snail mail, meaning 2000 units mailed versus 800 units sent by courier, along with realistic assumptions for other cost items (cost of labor excluded). As that ratio increases, the cost of using a courier approaches that of snail mail. In fact, if the snail mail response rate were to fall to 12 percent, the per complete response cost would exceed $38 with nonresponse accounting for over $33 of each response. When a high response rate becomes critical, a courier can present a viable option for delivery.[31]

Respondent Convenience

Respondents complete mail surveys at their convenience so they are more likely to take time to think about their replies. Mail questionnaires allow the respondent to check records before

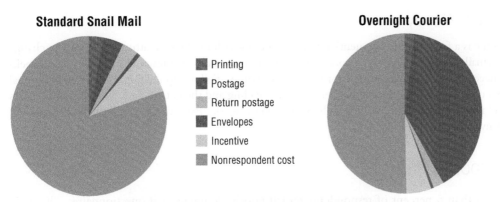

EXHIBIT **7.4**
Costs of Snail Mail versus
Courier Surveys

Standard Snail versus Overnight for 400 Complete Responses

Item	Standard Snail Mail (20% RR)		Overnight Courier (50% RR)	
	Per Unit	Total	Per Unit	Total
Printing	0.75	$1,500	0.75	$600
Postage	1.00	$2,000	15.00	$12,000
Return postage	0.80	$1,600	0.80	$640
Envelopes	0.20	$400	0.20	$160
Incentive	2.00	$4,000	2.00	$1,600
Nonrespondent cost	19.00	$7,600	18.75	$7,500
Respondent Cost (Total Cost/# of Responses)	**$23.75**	**$9,500**	**$37.50**	**$15,000**

responding. A manager replying to a survey about the number of workers hired in the last six months could easily check the records to get a more accurate answer than memory would provide. The added convenience helps minimize the annoyance factor of survey research.

Respondent Anonymity

In the cover letter that accompanies a mail or self-administered questionnaire, marketing researchers almost always state that the respondents' answers will be confidential. With this promise, the researcher cannot share information about any particular respondent by name. Respondents are even more likely to provide sensitive or embarrassing information when the researcher provides for anonymity, meaning responses cannot be traced to any individual. Researchers can guarantee confidentiality in practically any research. Electronic surveys, telephone responses, and personal interviews all make anonymity easier to promise than to guarantee because modern technology leaves traces that allow tracking. Mail surveys provide an alternative where the researcher can implement respondent anonymity with little difficulty.

A market researcher asked the following question through two approaches, "Have you borrowed money at a regular bank?" Researchers noted a 17 percent response rate for personal interviews and a 32 percent response rate for the mail survey. Although random sampling error may have accounted for part of this difference, the results suggest that for research on personal and sensitive financial issues, mail surveys provide a greater sense of confidentiality—the likely explanation being greater perceived anonymity. Although the absence of an interviewer can induce respondents to reveal sensitive or socially undesirable information, this lack of personal contact can also be a disadvantage. The respondent does not have the opportunity to question the interviewer. Problems that might be clarified in a personal or telephone interview can remain misunderstandings in a mail survey.

Standardized Questions

Self-response questionnaires typically are highly standardized, and the questions are quite structured. Questions and instructions must be complete but straightforward. Any ambiguity likely leads to response error. With mail and e-mail surveys, once the company sends the invitations, it is difficult to change the format or the questions.

Time Is Money

If time is a factor in management's interest in the research results, or if attitudes are rapidly changing, mail surveys may not be a good communication medium. A minimum of two or three weeks is necessary for receiving the majority of the responses. Follow-up mailings require an additional two or three weeks. The time between the first mailing and the cut-off date (when questionnaires will no longer be accepted) normally is six to eight weeks. Even personal interviews are faster in many cases.

Response Rates

response rate

The number of questionnaires returned and completed divided by the number of sample members provided a chance to participate in the survey.

Fewer than 5 percent of respondents return poorly designed mail questionnaires. The basic calculation for obtaining a **response rate** is to the number of legitimately completed questionnaires returned divided by the total number of sample members provided a chance to participate. Typically, the number in the denominator is adjusted for faulty addresses and similar problems that reduce the number of eligible participants.

Response rates represent a major issue of mail questionnaires. When response rates are extremely low, one wonders whether people who responded are unusual, meaning somehow not representative of the population. Nonresponse error might be high if so. If response rates are very high, respondents could be complying due to undue incentives that amount to coercion. The incentive may be more responsible for answers than honest cooperation. In any event, rarely will a mail survey exceed a 50 percent response rate, and those types of response rates usually require tremendous effort and expense.

Mail survey respondents are usually better educated and more likely to be a homeowner than nonrespondents. If they return the questionnaire at all, poorly educated respondents who cannot read and write well may skip open-ended questions to which they are required to write out their answers. Thus, systematic differences may correspond to differences between groups.

A researcher also has no assurance that the intended subject is the person who fills out the questionnaire. The wrong person answering the questions may be a problem when surveying corporate executives, physicians, and other professionals. Busy professionals may pass questionnaires on to subordinates to complete. This problem is not unique to mail surveys because electronic and telephone surveying also provide no guarantee that the actual response comes from a legitimate respondent. The problems here are not necessarily unique to mail surveys and would apply to electronic distribution surveys as well.

Increasing Response Rates for Mail Surveys

Who responds to mail surveys? Individuals who are interested in the general subject of the survey are more likely to respond than those with little interest. Wine enthusiasts are more likely than the average supermarket consumer to answer a survey addressing wine purchases. If the survey aims at measuring the typical supermarket attitudes and behaviors toward wine buying, the heavy responses by enthusiasts could represent error. People who hold extreme positions on an issue are more likely to respond than individuals who are largely indifferent to the topic. To minimize this bias, researchers have developed a number of techniques to increase the response rate to mail surveys. Designing and formatting attractive questionnaires and wording questions so that they are easily understood also help ensure a good response rate.

Cover Letter

cover letter

Letter that accompanies a questionnaire to induce the reader to complete and return the questionnaire.

A **cover letter** that accompanies a questionnaire is an important means of inducing a reader to complete and return the questionnaire. Exhibit 7.5 illustrates a cover letter and some of the points considered by a marketing research professional to be important in gaining respondents' attention and cooperation. The first paragraph of the letter explains why the study is important. The basic appeal alludes to the social usefulness of responding. Two other frequently used appeals are asking for help ("Will you do us a favor?") and the egotistical appeal ("Your opinions are important!").

EXHIBIT **7.5**
A Cover Letter Requesting
Participation in a Survey Is
Relevant for Snail Mail and
Electronic Survey Requests

MKTR Market Research Leaders

Component:	→	111 Eustice Square, Terroir, IL 39800-7600
Respondent's Address	→	Mr. Griff Mitchell 821 Shrewsbury Ave Hector Chase, LA 70809 Dear Mr. Mitchell:
Request/Time Involved	→	We'd like your input as part of a study of family media habits. This study is not involved in any attempt to sell anything. Rather, the results will help provide better media options for families. The survey typically takes about 12 minutes to complete.
Selection Method	→	You were selected based on a random sample of home owners living in the 70809 zip code.
Reason to Respond	→	We need your opinion about many important issues involving the way modern families interact with various media including print, television, radio, and Internet sources. Companies need input to create the most appealing and useful options for consumers; and local, state, and federal agencies need input to know what types of regulations, if any, are most appropriate. Without the opinions of people like you, many of these key issues will likely not be resolved.
Confidentiality/ IRB Approval	→	The information you provide, just as with all the information collected within the scope of this project, will be entirely confidential. It will only be used for the purpose of this research and no individual will be identified within the data. Additionally, this survey and the request for you to participate has been reviewed and approved by the Institutional Review Board of MKTR which monitors all research conducted and assures that procedures are consistent with ethical guidelines for federally funded research (although this particular project is not funded federally). If you have any questions, the MKTR IRB can be contacted at (888) 555–8888.
Incentive	→	Your response will improve the media choices that your family faces. In addition, a $10 check that you can cash at your personal bank is included as a token of our appreciation.
Willingness to Answer Questions	→	Additionally, you can direct any questions about this project directly to me. The contact information is available at the top of this letter. Additionally, we will be happy to provide you a summary of the results. Simply complete the enclosed self-addressed postcard and drop it in the mail or include it with the completed questionnaire. A self-addressed, postage-paid reply envelope is included for your return.
Thanks	→	Again, thank you so much for your time and for sharing your opinions.
Signature	→	*Laurie Thibodeaux*

Most cover letters promise confidentiality, invite the recipient to use an enclosed postage-paid reply envelope, describe any incentive or reward for participation, explain that answering the questionnaire will not be difficult and will take only a short time, and describe how the person was scientifically selected for participation.

A personalized letter addressed to a specific individual shows the respondent that he/she is important. Including an individually typed cover letter on letterhead rather than a printed form is an important element in increasing the response rate in mail surveys.[32]

Incentives Help

Researchers can increase a respondent's motivation for returning a questionnaire by offering monetary incentives or premiums. Although pens, lottery tickets, and a variety of premiums have been used, monetary incentives appear to be the most effective and least biasing incentive. Money attracts attention and creates a sense of obligation. Often, cover letters try to boost response rates with messages such as "We know that the attached dollar cannot compensate you for your time, but please accept it as a token of our appreciation." Response rates increase when a monetary incentive goes to a charity of the respondent's choice rather than directly to the respondent.

Advance Notification

Advance notification via a precall can increase response rates in some situations. Nielsen has used this technique to ensure a high cooperation rate in filling out diaries of television watching. Advance notices that go out closer to the questionnaire mailing time produce better results than those sent too far in advance. The optimal lead-time for advance notification is about three days before the mail survey is to arrive. Advanced notification can come in the form of a postcard, a phone call, or even an e-mail. A recent survey about respondent eating behavior employed a postcard prenotification for half of the sample and no reminder for the other half (control group).[32] The prenotification group obtained a response rate of 24 percent compared to 20 percent in the control group. This may not seem too impressive, but the authors conclude that the added costs of using the reminder were more than compensated for by the enhanced response rate.

Survey Sponsorship

Sometimes response quality is enhanced when the survey sponsor remains anonymous. Respondents who know who the research is for may, perhaps unintentionally, provide biased results. One business-to-business marketer wished to conduct a survey of its wholesalers to learn their stocking policies and their attitudes concerning competing manufacturers. A mail questionnaire sent on corporate letterhead very likely will yield a much lower response rate than a questionnaire using a commercial marketing research firm's letterhead.

Sponsorship by well-known and prestigious organizations such as universities or government agencies sometimes improves response rates. A mail survey sent to members of a consumer panel will receive an exceptionally high response rate because panel members have already agreed to cooperate as part of membership.

Keying Mail Questionnaires with Codes

A marketing researcher planning a follow-up letter, postcard, or e-mail would prefer not to disturb respondents who already have completed and returned a completed questionnaire. However, if the survey process is completely anonymous, the researcher has no way of knowing who has responded and who has not. Thus, the researcher has no choice but to send any second waves to everyone in the sample. One alternative is to clandestinely code questionnaires in a way that allows the researcher to know who has responded and remove them from the sample list. In this way, individual codes key questionnaires to individual members of the sampling frame. This code can appear on the questionnaire itself or on the envelope. For instance, blind keying might involve using a room number in the reply address as the code. Each envelope would contain a different room number and the sample list would include that number beside each person's name. The code might also appear somewhere on the questionnaire itself and in some cases a statement might indicate the number's purpose in identifying individual responses and not individual people. The researcher has to be cautious, as it would be unethical to promise anonymity if some type of identification coding is used.

Self-Administered Questionnaires Using Other Forms of Distribution

Other forms of self-administered printed questionnaires share many characteristics with mail questionnaires. When the research involves a long questionnaire, the drop-off method may be helpful. The **drop-off method** means that a research assistant physically drops the questionnaire off at a potential respondent's office or home. The assistant may arrange a time to come back and get the completed questionnaire. Clearly, this is an expensive method of distributing questionnaires but the response rate is generally improved. In the United States, researchers employ drop-offs when the sample involves businesspeople who are best reached at their place of work. Marketing researchers who study service provider behavior also may find this an effective means of administration. In this case, responding employees may deposit completed questionnaires into a collection box for later pickup. At times, the questionnaire may contain a postage-paid envelope for return via snail mail.

drop-off method

A survey method that requires the interviewer to travel to the respondent's location to drop off questionnaires that will be picked up later.

E-Mail Surveys

E-mail surveys involve making the questionnaire available to a potential respondent via e-mail. Today, respondents receive requests to participate in surveys more by e-mail than any other distribution method. E-mail surveys can put a respondent together with a questionnaire in one of three ways.

e-mail surveys

Survey requests distributed through electronic mail.

Using E-Mail

Three ways to contact respondents via e-mail include the following:

- A questionnaire can be included in the body of an e-mail. In this case, the questionnaire should be very short (no more than ten questions). These are likely to receive a relatively high response rate.
- Questionnaires can be included as attachments. To complete the questionnaire, a respondent must open the questionnaire, respond via radio boxes and areas to write short answers, save the questionnaire, and then reattach it to a reply e-mail. Researchers can use common software such as Microsoft Word or Adobe Acrobat to create these files. Alternatively, the respondent may have the option of marking the questionnaire with a pen or pencil and returning via fax or mail. As might be expected, response rates are low with this approach given all the effort and inconvenience of dealing with the attachment and, as a result, professional researchers typically avoid this approach.
- A third option, and by far the most common, is to include a hyperlink within the body of an e-mail that will direct the respondent to a Web-based questionnaire. The respondent then completes the response directly on that website. This approach is the most common way of soliciting responses via e-mail. In essence, the e-mail survey becomes a Web-based Internet survey.

Advantages and Disadvantages of E-Mail

The benefits of incorporating a questionnaire in an e-mail include the speed of distribution, lower distribution and processing costs, faster turnaround time, more flexibility, and less manual processing of paper questionnaires. The speed of e-mail distribution and the quick response time are major advantages when dealing with time-sensitive issues.

Some researchers also believe that respondents are more candid in electronically delivered surveys than in person or on the telephone. One caveat would exist when dealing with research directed at employers using company e-mail addresses. Employees often believe that their e-mails are not secure and "eavesdropping" by a supervisor could possibly occur. The belief that a response is not secure is particularly strong when the questionnaire is contained in the e-mail itself and a reply e-mail is needed to return a completed questionnaire. A link to an online survey will allay such concern to some degree.

In general, the guidelines for printed mail surveys apply to e-mail surveys. For example, delivering the material in the cover letter remains important despite the fact that people do not like e-mails that are more than two or three lines. For e-mail surveys, the researcher may include only personal information (if respondents are referred to by name), the request/time involved, and the selection method in the e-mail. The remaining sections can be included as the first page of the questionnaire providing an option for the recipient to opt in or out at the bottom.

Also, if the e-mail lists more than one address in the "to" or "CC" field, all recipients will see the entire list of names. This lack of anonymity has the potential to cause response bias and nonresponse error. E-mail requests should be addressed to a single person. Alternatively, the blind carbon copy, or BCC, field can be used if the same message must be sent to an entire sample. A drawback to this approach is that some spam filters will identify any message addressed to a large number of respondents as junk e-mail. Bulk-mailing programs exist that attempt to work around this problem by e-mailing potential respondents a few at a time. As can be seen, the problems associated with successful delivery to respondents remain a disadvantage of e-mail surveys.

Internet Surveys

Internet survey

A self-administered survey administered using a Web-based questionnaire.

An **Internet survey** is a self-administered questionnaire posted on a website. Typically, respondents know the questionnaire exists either by simply coming across it while browsing, through a pop-up notification, or via an e-mail containing a hyperlink, as described above. A consumer may randomly encounter the request while browsing a retailer's website. Many travel-related pages routinely provide survey invitations on their sites. Facebook pages also commonly include survey invitations. Today, a consumer might participate in an Internet survey as a way of earning some benefit. Pandora.com hosts short Internet surveys that allow consumers to listen for four hours uninterrupted after participating. The only distinction between an Internet survey and an e-mail survey hosted on a Web platform like Qualtrics is the way the researcher invites respondent participation.

Speed and Cost-Effectiveness

Internet surveys allow marketers to reach a large audience (possibly a global one), personalize individual messages, and secure confidential answers quickly and cost-effectively. The computer-based survey eliminates the costs of printing, postage, and data entry, as well as other administrative costs. Once the researcher develops the questionnaire and obtains a mailing list (e-mails of potential respondents in this case), the incremental cost of reaching additional respondents is minimal. The low incremental cost means that large samples are possible relative to other interview techniques. Speed isn't greatly affected either, as even surveys using large samples can be conducted in a week or less.

Visual Appeal and Interactivity

Internet survey designs allow more interactivity than paper-based surveys. For instance, questions can change based on the specific responses provided. A respondent might initially write in the name of the last retailer in which he/she spent more than $100: Walmart. Subsequent questions asking the respondent to rate the shopping experience can "pipe in," or fill in, the name Walmart

● ● ● ● ● ● ●

An invitation from a website allows respondents to earn benefits by participating in surveys like this one from Pandora

Andrey_Popov/Shutterstock.com

into questions. The Internet also is an excellent medium for the presentation of visual materials, such as photographs or drawings of product prototypes, advertisements, videos, or movie trailers. Additionally, Internet surveys offer the potential to add an element of gamification to a questionnaire as a way of maintaining respondent interest.

Respondent Participation and Cooperation

Internet survey respondents who intentionally click through a link they stumble across while browsing display high category involvement. For example, Ticketmaster quickly obtained more than 10,000 responses based on a survey invitation placed on their home page. The responses helped Ticketmaster better understand its customer purchase patterns and evaluate visitor satisfaction with the site. A response like this is possible only when consumers are involved and believe their cooperation will help make the experience better. Survey respondents can be crowdsourced using social networking and relevant Web pages. The idea behind **crowdsourcing** is that if many, many people are exposed to requests for participation, even a small percentage of completers can generate a large sample. Participants opt in, meaning they self-select to be part of the sample rather than being selected through some scientific sampling process. Caution is needed in such cases, though, as the sample is not likely to represent the population very well.

crowdsourcing

Inviting many, many people to participate (by opting in) in a project via the Internet and/or social networks so that even a small percentage of completers can generate a large sample.

Academic researchers sometimes crowdsource responses from Internet workers. For example, Amazon's Mechanical Turk allows workers with an account to opt in to survey requests in return for small financial payments, often less than $1 per survey. These types of responses can be useful in some specific research instances, particularly in pretesting portions of surveys. Results, however, should not be considered generalizable, and the researcher needs to be particularly wary of acquiescence bias as Internet workers learn through experience how to end up getting paid as a top priority (a requester can refuse to pay a worker if he/she is unhappy with the response). Thus, Internet workers are particularly eager to "please" the researcher. A more complete discussion of the pros and cons of using Internet workers in marketing research is beyond the scope of this chapter. However, researchers should remain skeptical about these responses, particularly when the research involves an experimental design or the true demographic profile (sex, age, occupation, etc.) is important.[33] The Research Snapshot illustrates some of the considerations concerning this type of crowdsourcing.

Today, many e-mail surveys employ members of consumer panels who have previously indicated a willingness to cooperate by completing questionnaires. Panel members click-through a hyperlink to a survey hosted on a server like the one maintained by Qualtrics. Different security settings can provide some confidence that the respondent who received the e-mail request is the one who actually responds. Panel members receive small incentives to respond. When professionally managed, panels give the researcher a good chance at deriving a sample that can adequately represent many populations such as consumers in Florida, consumers in the United States and Canada, salespeople in Germany, and so forth. The drawback to using panels is price. While prices vary considerably, a researcher can expect legitimate panel access prices to range from about $5 per complete response to over $50 per complete response. As a population becomes more difficult to access (such as CAT scan salespeople with less than 5 years of experience), or as quality of the response becomes more important, panel access becomes increasingly expensive. Also, not all panels are equal. The user is best not to rely only on price but also on the reputation of the panel provider with respect to its ability to maintain panels representative of key segments of the population.

Accurate Real-Time Data Capture

Internet surveys in effect allow respondents to record their own answers directly into a data file. Survey software also can prohibit improper data entry. For example, on a paper questionnaire a respondent might incorrectly check two responses even though the instructions call for a single answer. Online survey tools can make this type of mistake impossible by barring a second response and/or activating a warning message. Thus, the data capture is more accurate than when humans do the data entry. The researcher can watch the surveys come in and give input into when to stop the survey process.

Moving Around

A marketing researcher was pretesting marketing materials for application in a later survey targeting consumers in specific U.S. states. As a good measure, rather than asking are you from the state of Texas, for example, the researcher includes an initial screening question that asks, "In what state do you reside?" One frustrated mTurk worker left a message for the researcher (written exactly as the worker composed it): "i m from texas and I try to work on your task but it showing that you are not qualify to work on task and i put all the states (AL, FL, GA, LA, MS, NC, SC, TN, TX) it showing same for all states ... notify me so I can work.... I don't have much time now ... its near to expire." In other words, the worker first tried an ineligible state as a state of residence, then another state, then another, then another, all in a matter of minutes (actually the worker said 30 hours). However, once the worker tried one

michaeljung/Shutterstock.com

state, his/her device's IP address was recorded and entry into the survey was blocked no matter what state was selected. IP addresses in fact can help identify one's location, although a savvy worker can employ software to mask actual location.

E-Mail Callbacks

E-mail survey samples drawn from consumer panels allow for easy callbacks via e-mail. Computer software sends e-mail reminders automatically and like other survey forms, they can marginally increase responses.[34] Computer software can sometimes identify nonrespondents or respondents who started but did not complete a questionnaire and send those people customized messages. Sometimes follow-up e-mails offer additional incentives to those individuals who previously quit with only a few additional questions left to answer. When researchers assure respondents of complete anonymity, no individual computer tracking should take place, leaving the only callback option a reminder sent to the entire sample qualified by an "excuse me" message for those who may have already responded.

Personalized and Flexible Questioning

Survey software allows questioning to branch off into two or more different lines depending on a respondent's answer to a filtered question. In other words, the computer program asks questions in a sequence determined by the respondent's previous answers. This ability to sequence questions based on previous responses is a major advantage of computer-assisted surveys. The computer can be programmed to skip from question 6 to question 9 if the answer to question 6 is "no." Information can be piped in based on previous responses making questions less ambiguous and more relevant. Fewer, less ambiguous, and more relevant questions mean a survey that is easier to answer and thus increases response rates and response quality.

A related advantage of using a Web survey is that it can prompt respondents when they skip over a question. In a test comparing telephone and Internet versions of the same survey, the rate of item nonresponse was less for the Internet version, which issued a prompt for each unanswered item.[35] This was likely not a simple matter of motivation, because the rate of respondents who actually took the Web version was less than for the telephone version, even though the researchers offered a larger incentive to those asked to go online. Online survey software can force a respondent to answer questions by blocking them from moving further if they've left a forced response question blank. However, researchers may not always be comfortable with this choice as we will see below.

Respondent Anonymity

Respondents are more likely to provide sensitive or embarrassing information when they remain anonymous. In fact, Internet survey respondents may get the sense of anonymity that may come from the vastness of the Internet. However, a researcher using typical Internet survey approaches cannot guarantee anonymity. As mentioned in Chapter 2, the IP addresses for computers, smartphones, and tablets provide unique identifiers that reveal where the device was (by identifying the communication portal like a Wi-Fi device) when the response was recorded and includes, in essence, a signature for that particular device. Thus, researchers typically can go as far as promising confidentiality but without taking specific precautions to block the identification of the IP address (for instance, if combined with an intercept method many respondents are using the same device), complete anonymity does not come with Internet surveys.

Improving Response Rates

Methods for improving response rates for an Internet survey are similar to those for other kinds of survey research. A request delivered through Facebook may improve response likelihood. The subject line in any invitation should refer to a topic likely of interest to the audience, without being deceptive. Thus, the line might be worded in a way similar to the following: "Please give your opinion on [subject matter of interest]." Researchers should avoid gimmicks like dollar signs and the word *free*, either of which is likely to alert the spam filters installed on most computers.

Research suggests that the manner of invitation can enhance participation.[36] Invitations containing phrases like "shorter than the typical survey" or "participate and earn a chance to win cash prizes" increase participation. In contrast, "participate and earn frequent flyer miles" or "introducing a new credit card" lowers participation.

Unlike mail surveys, Internet surveys do not offer the opportunity to send a physical incentive, such as a dollar bill, to the respondent. Incentives to respond to a survey must be in the form of a coupon, gift card, or a promise of a future reward. A coupon can be included that contains a discount code which can be applied at a retail website or even in a store. For example, a respondent might receive a $10 Starbucks gift card. Otherwise, a promise can be offered: "As a token of appreciation for completing this survey, the sponsor of the survey will make a sizable contribution to a national charity. You can vote for your preferred charity at the end of the survey." Generally, promises are less effective than an incentive in hand.

Researchers also can use precalls for Web surveys. The research firm can send e-mail notices, phone messages, postcards, and/or letters informing potential respondents that an e-mail will be arriving containing a survey invitation. Researchers studying why students enroll in the universities that they attend might involve contacting recent college applicants. The applicants might first receive a letter indicating that a survey invitation will arrive via e-mail. With a study like this, one might expect about 20 percent of potential respondents to click through to the questionnaire, and all but a small percentage of these would respond, for an overall response rate of just under 20 percent and a **click-through response rate** of about 90 percent. Recall that highly engaged respondents are more likely to respond. Alternatively, they may receive only the e-mail invitation.

Mail notification has several potential advantages. Spammers do not send notifications via mail, so the survey may end up having a little more legitimacy. Additionally, the prenotification establishes the potential for a relationship and can even include a request to put the sender on the recipient's safe sender list. However, research provides no evidence of substantial response rate gains by using snail mail prenotification and any gains need to be weighed against the extra costs involved with physically mailing notices.[37] Telephone call prenotifications are slightly more effective but also add costs. Thus, nonautomatic prenotifications are used only when there are great concerns about responses.

Internet surveys, even those not associated with a panel, are often directed toward a finite population. For example, all members of the Atlanta area Sales and Marketing Executives Association might comprise a population of interest for researchers studying attitudes toward customer relationship management programs. Research shows that a combination of pop-up notification on a software user forum's home page plus a single e-mail notification (to all members of the forum) yields an overall response rate of about 14 percent.[38] Thus, respondent characteristics that indicate a stake in the issues studied are most responsible for increasing response rates.

click-through response rate

The portion of potential respondents exposed to a hyperlink to a survey who actually click through to view the questionnaire.

With Internet surveys, we can track both click-through rate, which assesses the portion of potential respondents who actually take a look at the questionnaire, and, if an e-mail request is sent, overall response rates based on the number of invitations. Generally, except for very long questionnaires, many respondents who click through to view a questionnaire also respond to it. Some researchers argue that the true response rate for an Internet survey initiated by an e-mail invitation should be the ratio of completed questionnaires to the number of click-throughs. This opinion argues that logically, the only respondents with a chance to respond are those that clicked through and many surveys close once a quota of completes is obtained. With this rationale, Internet survey response rates equal or exceed telephone and snail mail surveys. Like every other type of survey, Internet surveys have both advantages and disadvantages.

After reviewing hundreds of studies dealing with the use of incentives in increasing participation in surveys of all types, researchers reached the following conclusions[39]:

1. Incentives increase response rates across all survey modes.
2. Prepaid monetary incentives increase response rates better than promised incentives or lotteries.
3. The response rates increase with the size of incentive although published research does not consider large incentives. Very important surveys may consider substantial incentives such as $50.
4. The use of incentives can systematically influence what type of person responds to a survey across all modes.
5. Maximizing response rate does not guarantee sample representativeness. The use of incentives should be monitored for possibilities of increasing error while also increasing response rates.

When properly conducted, Internet surveys provide data equally accurate to traditional printed and phone survey approaches.[40]

Text-Message Surveys

Text-message surveys have all the advantages of mobile phone surveys, including increased reach, but share the disadvantages in terms of reaching only U.S. respondents who have opted in with expressed consent in some way. However, text-message surveys are catching on in other countries and are ideal for surveys involving only a few very short questions. Additionally, SMS messages can include graphic displays or even short videos. In particular, they can be useful in assessing a recent customer's satisfaction or liking of some product depicted in a photo or a video. They are not practical for comprehensive surveys.

Choosing an Appropriate Survey Approach

Each survey administration technique has advantages and disadvantages. A researcher who must ask highly confidential questions may use an anonymous mail survey, thus sacrificing follow-up possibilities to avoid interviewer bias. If a researcher must have considerable control over question phrasing (and potentially rephrasing), centralized location telephone interviewing may provide both control and a user-friendly format.

To determine the appropriate technique, the researcher must ask several questions:

- Is the assistance of an interviewer necessary?
- Are respondents interested in the issues being investigated?
- Will cooperation be easily attained?
- How quickly is the information needed?
- Will the study require a long and complex questionnaire?
- How large is the budget?

The criteria—cost, speed, anonymity, and so forth—may differ for each project.

Exhibit 7.6 summarizes some major advantages and disadvantages of different survey approaches. It emphasizes typical types of surveys. For example, a creative researcher might be able to design highly versatile and flexible mail questionnaires, but most researchers use standardized questions. An elaborate mail survey may be more expensive than a short personal interview, but generally this is

EXHIBIT **7.6** Advantages and Disadvantages of Typical Survey Methods

Characteristic:	Door-to-Door Personal Interview	Mall-Intercept Personal Interview	Telephone Interview	Snail Mail Survey	E-Mail/Internet Survey
Speed of data collection	Moderate	Fast	Very fast	Slow	Fastest
Geographic flexibility	Limited to moderate	Confined mostly to urban and suburban areas	High	High	High (worldwide)
Respondent cooperation	Moderate in getting an answer. Excellent once respondent agrees to participate	Good in agreement to respond. Moderate cooperation thereafter	Difficult to get an answer. Good cooperation thereafter. Varies landline versus cell	Moderate all the way around	Low from general population but high when hot button issue presented or sample is a computer panel
Versatility of questioning	Quite versatile	Extremely versatile	Limited versatility, particularly for cell calls	Not versatile; requires highly standardized format	Good versatility for logical branching and respondent assignment
Questionnaire length	Long	Moderate	Moderate for landline and short for cell	Moderate but varies depending on incentive	Moderate but varies depending on incentive
Item nonresponse rate	Low	Medium	Medium	High	Software can assure none
Possibility for respondent misunderstanding	Low	Low	Average	High	High
Degree of researcher or interviewer influence on responses	High	High	Moderate	Lowest	Low with exceptions depending on data source
Supervision of interviewers	Moderate	Moderate to high	High, especially with central location interviewing	Not applicable	Not applicable
Anonymity of respondent	Lowest	Moderate	Low	Highest	Moderate
Ease of callback or follow-up	Difficult	Most difficult	Easy	Easy, but takes time	Difficult if respondents are unknown. Easy if sample drawn from e-mail list
Cost	Highest	Moderate to high	Low to moderate	Low	Low to moderate depending on potential cost of access to sample
Special features	Visual materials may be shown or demonstrated; extended probing possible	Taste tests, product trials, viewing of marketing materials possible. Ideal for representing population of mall/shopping center shoppers	Fieldwork and supervision of data collection are simplified. Distinction must be made between landline and mobile/cell phone calls	Respondent may answer questions at own convenience; has time to reflect on answers	Streaming media software allows use of graphics and animation as well as random assignment to experimental conditions

not the case. One research team investigating consumer medical issues tested several different modes for generating results when the ability to generalize to a population was important.[41] In the end, once cost per valid response was considered, a generic snail mail survey proved most cost-effective based on a combination at $23 per response with a 7.5 percent response rate (compared to $25 for a personalized snail mail questionnaire with a 10.5 percent response rate—both proving cheaper than telephone and directed Internet surveys where response rates were less than 5 percent).

More and more, though, survey researchers employ **mixed-mode survey** approaches that employ more than one approach in a given survey. This means the sampling frame must be accessible from more than one survey mode. Polling organizations traditionally relied heavily on landline telephone surveys. However, the accuracy in representing populations of interest (such as voters or consumers) declined due to coverage error associated with declining incidence and the resulting nonresponse bias. Thus, polling organizations today supplement landline calling with cell phone calling and even some Internet surveys. Accurate polls come from sampling approaches that best match modes to subgroups within a population.

Pretesting Survey Instruments

A researcher spending $300,000 to survey a few thousand consumers does not want to find out after data collection that most respondents misunderstood some questions, all gave the same answer to a key variable, or misinterpreted the response instructions for an entire set of items. Researchers can minimize these possibilities by employing various screening procedures during *pretesting*. **Pretesting** involves trial runs using the survey instrument with a group of colleagues or actual respondents to iron out fundamental problems in instructions, items, or design of a questionnaire. Researchers benefit by spotting problems in the pretest and rightly inferring that a problem with this very small sample will likely be a problem in the full sample once data collection actually begins.

Broadly speaking, survey researchers choose from three basic ways of pretesting. The first two involve screening the questionnaire with other research colleagues, and the third—the one most often called pretesting—is a trial or pilot test with an actual group of respondents. First, when screening the questionnaire with other research professionals, the investigator asks them to look for such problems as difficulties with question wording, leading questions, and bias due to question order. An alternative type of screening might involve a client or the research manager who ordered the research. Often, managers ask researchers to collect information, but when they see the questionnaire, they feel that it does not really address their decision statements. The researchers then need to either explain things better to the client or make changes. Secondly, other research experts may sometimes be asked to judge the content of survey items as a way of trying to verify that the items are measuring what the researcher intended. Later, we return to this idea under the heading of validity.

The third form is basically a trial run of the entire research project. Once the researcher has decided on the final questionnaire, data are collected with a small number of respondents (perhaps as many as 100 but sometimes as few as three dozens) to determine whether the questionnaire needs refinement. The researcher is keen to spot problem items and analyzes these data for suspicious patterns indicating potential problems. For example, a researcher might find that all respondents indicate the same answer to a specific question. Such a result is highly unlikely when more than a handful of respondents are included. Thus, a response like this probably indicates a problem with item wording.

Unfortunately, although the value of a pretest is readily apparent, researchers often press forward without it due to time and budget concerns. The risk of collecting some items that end up not being very helpful increases without a pretest. Needless to say, pretests are highly recommended in almost all types of primary data collection efforts.

Ethical Issues in Survey Research

Chapter 4 mentioned that codes of ethics express researchers' obligation to protect the public from misrepresentation and exploitation under the guise of marketing research. Thou shall not disguise selling as research! Many ethical issues apply to survey research, such as respondents'

mixed-mode survey

Term used to refer to a survey approach that uses more than one survey medium to reach potential respondents.

pretesting

Screening procedure that involves a trial run with a group of respondents to iron out fundamental problems in the survey design.

To the Point

"Practice is the best of all instructors."

—PUBLILIUS SYRUS

CIRCA 42 BC

right to privacy, the use of deception, respondents' right to be informed about the purpose of the research, the need for confidentiality, the need for honesty in collecting data, and the need for objectivity in reporting data.

At this time, a few points are worth emphasizing. Researchers should not ask for information in a misleading way. Also, researchers must be careful to guard the resulting data carefully. For instance, a researcher may end up with data that identifies children's responses to several different new products. The data may also contain demographics and other material. Once that data becomes stored on a laptop or server, it is vulnerable to theft or misplacement. The researcher should follow good security procedures in protecting the data stored on various storage mediums.

Additionally, technology brings new issues to the forefront. Although e-mail is an extremely useful tool, researchers should avoid needlessly contributing to spam volume by sending unsolicited e-mails seeking survey respondents. At times, this may be the only way to reach a population, but whenever possible, e-mail requests for responses are better directed toward individuals who in some way may have indicated that the e-mail isn't so unwanted. For example, members of consumer response panels opt in and thus give their explicit approval to receive such e-mails. Additionally, consumers who query about certain information may end up being good research respondents. Consider someone who has sought information about hybrid cars from a website like Kelley Blue Book (www.kbb.com). A website like this may even include a place where a consumer can register and indicate whether they are open to further contact. If they appear open to responding to research that may be tied to new automobiles or environmentally sensitive products, sending a survey about attitudes toward new car features may not be an imposition. On the other hand, phoning someone during dinner or filling up a busy executive's inbox with requests to participate in irrelevant surveys pushes the boundaries of good ethics.

Technology brings other ethics challenges. Survey software can require someone to answer a question but this too could be seen as unethical by some—including some IRBs. A way around this and to maintain high ethical integrity is to include a "don't know" or "prefer not to answer" option. Certainly, as technology continues to evolve, even more ethics challenges may face survey researchers. Also, the researcher needs to be mindful about technology and the lack of complete anonymity that comes with many forms of electronic responses.

TIPS OF THE TRADE

- Even a perfectly written survey will produce erroneous results when the sample is incapable of adequately representing a population due to survey error.
- The longer the questionnaire, the lower the response rate. Anything longer than 10 minutes will get very low response rates unless special steps are taken, such as:
  - Look for respondents who are essentially a captive audience; like students in a class or people waiting for a plane.
  - Use a survey research panel.
  - Try to target the survey toward individuals who are highly involved in the topic.
  - Offer a nontrivial incentive to respond.

- Callbacks, and particularly precalls, can increase response rate significantly.
- Telephone surveys can still produce high-quality results. However, consider supplementing with a mixed-mode approach that involves a combination of landline calls, cell calls, and Internet surveys.
  - In the United States, cell calls cannot be automated unless a potential respondent has opted in.
- E-mail surveys and Internet surveys are good approaches for most types of surveys given an adequate sampling frame like those that come from professionally managed panels.
- Any pretest is better than no pretest.

∶∶ SUMMARY

1. Know what a survey is and how it can provide insight into explaining human behavior.
A survey represents a way of describing public opinion by collecting primary data through communicating directly with individual sampling units. Surveys provide a snapshot at a given point in time. More precisely, this is a sample survey because the respondents' opinions presumably represent a sample of the larger target population's opinion. Members of the sample are known as respondents. Surveys gather information to assess consumer knowledge and awareness of products, brands, or issues and to measure consumer attitudes, feelings, and behaviors. Additionally, surveys describe consumer characteristics, including purchasing patterns, brand usage, and descriptive characteristics including demographics and lifestyle. Surveys provide a quick, efficient, and accurate means of assessing information about a population. Students often confuse the term survey and questionnaire. A questionnaire is a tool that can be used in implementing a survey.

2. Identify sources of error in survey research. Two major forms of error are common in survey research. The first, sampling error is inadequacy of respondents to represent a population of interest even if other survey aspects are valid. Sampling error results from random sampling error, chance variation given that a sample is some fraction of the entire population, and systematic sampling error that results from a flawed sampling frame. The second major category of error, systematic error, takes several forms. Nonresponse error is caused by sampling units that fail to respond to a survey. This type of error can be detected by comparing the demographics of the sample population with those of the target population and making a special effort to contact underrepresented groups. In addition, response bias occurs when a response to a questionnaire is falsified or misrepresented, either intentionally or inadvertently. Administrative error also contributes to nonsampling, systematic error. Administrative error represents a flaw in the execution of the survey or sample plan. Exhibit 7.1 summarizes the sources of error.

3. Summarize the ways researchers gather information through personal interviews. An interactive survey approach facilitates two-way communication where the respondent and the interviewer truly have a personal dialog. A face-to-face personal interview typifies this approach, but other media, including mobile phones and landline phones, allow two-way communication. Face-to-face interviews can be conducted door-to-door, although this mode is used less and less these days. Mall intercepts provide another alternative for personal interviews. They give the advantage of allowing respondents to interact with actual products or marketing stimuli. Landline telephone interviews are still widely used when a representative sample becomes a priority. Mobile phone surveys have potential, but legal restrictions like the Telephone Consumer Protection Act (TCPA) make using them more difficult and expensive than landline surveys.

4. Know the advantages and disadvantages of conducting surveys using self-administered questionnaires. Self-administered questionnaires provide less interactivity than personal interviews but provide increased efficiency. Self-administered surveys can be administered through snail mail–delivered paper questionnaires or e-mail and Internet-based survey approaches. They typically are less expensive than personal interviews although gathering representative data generally is expensive through any means. Self-administered questionnaires also can provide for faster data collection. The structured response, though, provides little flexibility to stray beyond the questions written on the survey. Internet-based surveys display equal validity to standard mail or telephone interviews. Text-message surveys can be useful for very short questionnaires including only 2 or 3 items and few response points.

5. Appreciate the importance of pretesting questionnaires. Pretesting a questionnaire is a useful way to discover problems while they can still be corrected. Pretests may involve screening the questionnaire with other research professionals and/or conducting a trial run with a relatively small set of respondents. Despite their obvious value, researchers too often move forward without adequately pretesting survey instruments and sampling frames.

6. Describe ethical issues that arise in survey research. Researchers must protect the public from misrepresentation and exploitation. This obligation includes honesty about the purpose of a research project and protection of subjects' right to refuse to participate or to answer particular questions. Researchers also should protect the confidentiality of participants and record responses honestly. If a survey cannot be administered in a way that prohibits any unique identification of respondents, researchers should not promise anonymity. Lastly, as technology evolves, researchers should be mindful of ways that good ethics can be breeched in sometimes subtle ways, including adding volumes of spam and breeches of confidentiality.

:: KEY TERMS AND CONCEPTS

acquiescence bias, *171*
administrative error, *172*
callbacks, *179*
central location interviewing, *185*
click-through response rate, *195*
computer-assisted telephone interviewing
   (CATI), *179*
cover letter, *188*
coverage bias, *181*
crowdsourcing, *193*
data processing error, *172*
door-to-door interviews, *179*
drop-off method, *191*
e-mail surveys, *191*
extremity bias, *171*
interactive survey approaches, *174*

internet survey, *192*
interviewer bias, *172*
interviewer cheating, *173*
interviewer error, *173*
item nonresponse, *176*
mail survey, *186*
mall-intercept interview, *178*
mixed-mode survey, *198*
no contacts, *169*
noninteractive survey approaches, *174*
nonrespondents, *169*
nonresponse error, *169*
personal interview, *174*
population parameter, *168*
precall, *179*
pretesting, *198*

random digit dialing, *182*
refusals, *170*
respondent error, *169*
respondents, *166*
response bias, *170*
response rate, *188*
robocalls, *180*
sample bias, *169*
sample selection error, *173*
sample survey, *166*
sampling error, *168*
self-administered questionnaires, *186*
self-selection bias, *170*
social desirability bias, *172*
systematic error, *168*

:: QUESTIONS FOR REVIEW AND CRITICAL THINKING

1. What is a survey? Give an example of one that you've recently participated in. Find an example of survey results reported in the *Wall Street Journal*.
2. What is *self-selection bias?* Describe it as a source of total survey error.
3. Do surveys tend to gather qualitative or quantitative data? What types of information are commonly measured with surveys?
4. What potential sources of error listed in Exhibit 7.1 might be associated with the following situations?
   a. In an Internet survey of frequent fliers aged 50 and older, researchers conclude that price does not play a significant role in airline travel because only 25 percent of the respondents check off price as the most important consideration in determining where and how they travel, whereas 35 percent rate price as being unimportant. Management decides prices can be increased with little loss in business.
   b. A telephone survey of urban voters finds that most respondents express high dislike of negative political ads—that is, advertising by one political candidate that criticizes or exposes secrets about the opponent's "dirty laundry." Researchers conclude that negative advertising should not be used.
   c. A survey accessed through Instagram produces results ranking Apple iPads as far superior to MS Surface for business applications. A retailer decides to reduce inventory of tablets other than iPads.
   d. Researchers who must conduct a 45-minute personal interview offer $175 to each respondent because they believe that people who will sell their opinions are more typical than someone who will talk to a stranger for free for 45 minutes. Management uses the results to adjust their services offering.
   e. A company's sales representatives are asked what percentage of the time they spend traveling, on Facebook, on Instagram participating in meetings, in training, and filling out reports for management. The survey is conducted via the company's

e-mail network. Management concludes that sales reps are not spending enough time performing selling activities in the field.
   f. A health insurance company obtains a 75 percent response rate from a sample of college students contacted by mobile phone in a study of attitudes toward life insurance. Survey respondents received a code for a free meal from Raising Canes Chicken Restaurant. The company is concerned that consumers are less interested in life insurance these days.
5. A sample of 14-year-old schoolchildren is asked if they have ever smoked a cigarette in an SMS survey. What types of error might enter into this process?
6. Why is response rate a concern for survey researchers? Are there other issues that should be of greater concern?
7. A researcher sends out 2,000 questionnaires via e-mail and promises respondents anonymity. Fifty surveys are returned because the e-mail addresses are inaccurate. Of the 1,950 delivered questionnaires, 100 are completed and e-mailed back. However, 40 of these respondents wrote that they did not want to participate in the survey. The researcher indicates that the response rate was 5 percent. Is this the right thing to do? What concerns might you have about this approach?
8. Define interactive and noninteractive survey approaches. Why might a researcher choose an interactive survey approach over a noninteractive survey approach?
9. Suppose a firm wanted to conduct an interactive survey to predict whether to push marketing efforts aimed at families expecting their first child through Pinterest, Instagram, or Facebook efforts. The researcher is considering using a single-mode approach consisting of a telephone survey. Critique this decision and offer suggestions for improvement.
10. A publisher offers teenage boys (aged 14–17 years) one of four best-selling famous rock posters as an incentive for filling out a ten-page mail questionnaire about what makes a good guitar. What are the pros and cons of offering this incentive? Yes or no, should the incentive be offered (explain)?

11. What do you think should be the maximum length of a self-administered e-mail questionnaire using no financial incentive?

12. A survey researcher reports that "205 usable questionnaires out of 942 questionnaires delivered in our mail survey converts to a 21.7 percent response rate." What are the subtle implications of this statement?

13. What is do-not-call legislation? What effect has it had on survey research?

14. Agree or disagree with this statement: Landline and mobile phone surveys are essentially the same and can be used in the same situations with the same results.

15. What are the advantages and disadvantages of e-mail surveys? What are the situations when they may not be appropriate?

16. What is a click-through rate? How is it relevant to e-mail surveys?

17. What is the difference between an e-mail and an Internet survey?

18. Evaluate the following survey designs:
    a. A text-message survey asking the potential respondent to indicate with yes or no responses whether they are driving or not, whether they are alone, whether they believe the roads in their area can adequately handle traffic, whether more money should be devoted to better roadways, whether or not traffic is adequately policed, and whether or not automatic cameras should be used to issue speeding tickets. The sample is drawn from people who have agreed to be contacted via mobile phone regarding their new Subaru purchase.
    b. A shopping mall that wishes to evaluate its image places packets including a questionnaire, cover letter, and stamped return envelope in the mall where customers can pick them up if they wish.
    c. An e-mail message is sent asking respondents to complete a questionnaire on a website. Respondents answer the questions and then have the opportunity to play a slot-machine game on the website. Each respondent is guaranteed a monetary incentive but has the option to increase it by repeatedly playing the slot-machine game.
    d. A mall-intercept interviewing service is located in a regional shopping center. The facility contains a small room for television and movie presentations. Shoppers are used as sampling units to evaluate television commercials. However, mall-intercept interviewers recruit additional subjects for television commercial experiments by offering them several complimentary tickets for special sneak previews of movies. Individuals contacted at the mall are allowed to bring up to five guests. In some cases, respondents try to sell their complimentary tickets through Facebook and Craig's List posts.

19. Under what conditions might someone conducting a mail survey use an overnight courier to send questionnaires to sampling units?

20. What type of survey approach is most likely to yield the highest response rate? What approach(es) will yield the lowest response rate? What can be done to improve response rates in e-mail and Internet surveys?

21. Comment on the ethics of the following situations:
    a. A researcher plans to use invisible ink to code questionnaires to identify respondents in a mail survey designed to get honest opinions from people who have filed to run for political office. The code will allow their identities to be known by the researcher.
    b. A political action committee conducts a survey about its particular cause. At the end of the questionnaire, it includes a request for a donation.
    c. A telephone interviewer calls at 1 P.M. on Sunday and asks the person who answers the phone to take part in an interview.
    d. An industrial marketer wishes to survey its own distributors. It invents the name "Mountain States Marketing Research" and sends out an e-mail questionnaire under this name.

22. How might the marketing research industry take action to ensure that the public believes that landline phone surveys and door-to-door interviews are legitimate activities and that firms that misrepresent and deceive the public using marketing research as a sales ploy are not true marketing researchers?

23. Go to the Pew Internet and American Life page at http://www.pewinternet.org. Several reports based on survey research will be listed. Select one of the reports. What were the research objectives? What were the most important items on the survey?

:: RESEARCH ACTIVITY

1. Ask a small sample of students at your local university to report their ACT or SAT. Then, try to find the average ACT or SAT of students at your school. Does it seem that the student data are subject to error? Explain.

2. Look for opportunities to participate in surveys online. Is the sponsor identified and if so, how might it influence responses? Comment on the surveys with respect to their ability to deliver error-free data to the sponsor.

SAT and ACT Writing Tests

Case 7.1

The SAT and ACT college entrance exams once were completely multiple choice, but both tests recently began including an essay portion (which is optional for the ACT). Some researchers have investigated how the essay tests are used by one group they serve: the admissions offices of the colleges that look at test results during the selection process.[37]

Early survey research suggests that some admission officers harbor doubts about the essay tests. ACT, Inc., reported that among the schools it surveyed, only about one-fifth are requiring that applicants take the writing portion of the exam. Another one-fifth merely recommend (but don't require) the essay.

Kaplan, Inc., which markets test preparation services, conducted surveys as well. Kaplan asked 374 colleges whether they would be using the SAT writing test in screening candidates. Almost half (47 percent) said they would not use the essay at all.

Another 22 percent said they would use it but give it less weight than the math and verbal SAT scores.

Kaplan also surveys students who take the exams for which it provides training. On its website, the company says, "More than 25 percent of students ran out of time on the essay!"

Questions
1. What survey objectives would ACT have in asking colleges how they use its essay test? What objectives would Kaplan have for its survey research?
2. If you were a marketer for the College Board (the SAT's company) or ACT, Inc., what further information would you want to gather after receiving the results described here?
3. What sources of error or response bias might be present in the surveys described here?

National Do-Not-Call Registry

Case 7.2

Citizens' annoyance with phone calls from salespeople prompted Congress to pass a law setting up a National Do-Not-Call Registry. The registry was soon flooded with requests to have phone numbers removed from telemarketers' lists. By law, salespeople may not call numbers listed on this registry. The law makes exceptions for charities and researchers. However, a recent poll suggests that even though phone calls from researchers may be legal, they are not always well received.

In late 2005, Harris Interactive conducted an Internet survey in which almost 2,000 adults answered questions about the National Do-Not-Call Registry. About three-quarters of the respondents said they had signed up for the registry, and a majority (61 percent) said they had since received "far less" contact from telemarketers. In addition, 70 percent said that since registering, they had been contacted by

someone "who was doing a poll or survey" and wanted them to participate. But apparently respondents weren't sure whether this practice was acceptable. Only one-fourth (24 percent) of respondents said they knew that researchers "are allowed to call," and over half (63 percent) weren't sure about researchers' rights under the law.

Questions
1. Was an online survey the best medium for a poll on this subject? What were some pros and cons of conducting this poll online?
2. How might the results have differed if this poll had been conducted by telephone?
3. As a researcher, how would you address people's doubts about whether pollsters may contact households listed on the Do-Not-Call Registry?

Observation

iStock.com/Opidanus

LEARNING OUTCOMES

After studying this chapter, you should be able to:

1. Discuss the role of observational technologies as marketing research tools
2. Know the difference between direct and contrived observation
3. Identify ethical issues particular to research using observation
4. Explain the observation of physical objects and message content
5. Describe major types of mechanical observation
6. Summarize techniques for measuring physiological reactions

Chapter Vignette:

"I'll Be Watching You!"

Alexa, Siri, Home, Echo, they don't just hear us, but they watch us. They watch us by recording not only what we say, but what we do. The very business model for firms like Facebook, Waze, and Snap is based on observing what consumers do and using that information to make promotions more effective. With the Internet of Things, even our cars and appliances are watching us. Did you go to Starbucks before work or during work? How long did you stay there? Did you use your phone to pay? Did you search any terms on your smartphone's browser? Did you like anything on Facebook? Did you respond to a survey or visit a blog? Did you spend time looking at the new merchandise display? Did you get from point A to point B faster than the speed limit allows? Google depends on advertising revenue, and the more they know, the more they can carefully target content toward your behaviors. Apple considers how they may become a tool for conducting the bulk of consumer transactions by expanding iTunes technology to draw money right from your bank account. Once consumers find out about all of this peeking at their behavior, they are typically alarmed at the loss of privacy. Haier appliances offers a smart refrigerator that can deliver a beverage to the owner via remote control. Pretty cool, huh :-)! In return for conveniences like this, though, consumers give up privacy by allowing things to observe us. In fact, observational data reveals things we could never say. The legal debate over whether the products-turned robot learn about us can be used against us continues. Alexa, are you watching?[1]

Source: www.ibtimes.com

Introduction

Scientists rely heavily on observation. This was true yesterday, is true today, and certainly will be true tomorrow. Simple observation has played a key role in scientific discoveries for as long as people have pursued knowledge. Bernoulli developed the laws of buoyancy and fluid dynamics by *observing* what happened to his bathwater when he entered the tub; it went up in proportion to his mass. What a simple observation! According to legend, Newton developed the laws of gravitation by *observing* (and feeling) the way an apple fell onto his head while he rested under the tree. Observations play a key role in discovering ideas and developing theories. Inductive learning begins with collections of observations. Researchers also deductively develop logical theories that in turn test these ideas through the use of observation of the specific phenomena of interest. This chapter is all about observing marketing behavior directly.

Technology and Observation in Marketing Research

In marketing research, **observation** is a systematic process of recording actual behavioral patterns of people, objects, and events as they take place. No questioning or communicating with people is needed. Researchers who use observation method data collection either witness and record information while watching events take place or take advantage of a tracking system such as checkout scanners, information in cookies, or GPS tracking. These tracking systems can observe and provide data such as whether a specific consumer purchased more products on discount or at regular price, or how much time a consumer spent viewing a particular Web page before either exiting or clicking through to the next page. Advances in technology have given a bigger role for observational research tools in marketing research.

observation

The systematic process of recording the behavioral patterns of people, objects, and occurrences as they take place.

Observation can be a useful part of either qualitative or quantitative research. Additionally, actual observations of behavioral patterns can be part of an exploratory, descriptive, or even a causal design. For instance, researchers studying compliance with a diet program might manipulate different features of the program and then observe actual eating and exercise habits. These observations would play a key role as a dependent variable in a causal design. More often, however, observation is associated with qualitative research and with exploratory research designs. Observation is nearly synonymous with ethnographic research as researchers often try to blend into the environment and simply scrutinize the germane behavior. Callaway Golf may plant ethnographic researchers as caddies (who carry clubs for golfers) on nice golf courses to observe the actual behavior of golfers on the golf course. The caddies blend into the environment in a manner traditional to ethnographic research. Scientific observation is scarcely distinguished from simple observation. However, scientific observation addresses a research question aimed at discovering or testing market knowledge, whereas simple observation has no such motivation.

Technological Advances and Observation

We've covered numerous ways Internet, cellular, social networking and near-field technologies have fueled big data analytics. Because most of this data gathering involves no two-way communication (no survey or interview), these types of data qualify as behavioral observational. They leave behind a systematic recording of what people actually did and in that sense do not suffer from problems such as memory inaccuracy that may from time to time plague survey data. Plus, these technologies enable data collection to be automated.

The chapter vignette stresses observation of individual consumers using computers, appliances, and telecommunication technologies, but observation goes further than just peeking at individuals. Now, Apple can see how it feels to have their behavior tracked. Google's acquisition of Skybox satellite services gives Google the capability to track Apple's supply chain activity and predict company secrets in advance. For example, by tracking images around Apple production facilities,

● ● ● ● ● ● ●

Observational data predicting what other companies are doing could be useful to competitors' marketing decisions.

aPhoenixPhotographer/Shutterstock.com

Google may be able to know in advance when Apple is about to release a new iPhone or iPad version. Companies also now are concerned about competitors using drones to similarly observe activities that may feed predictive analytics and reveal company strategy or tactics. In the same way, our devices watch us, which may provide useful information to feed restaurant or other services locations. Evolving communication technologies clearly have changed the role of observation in marketing research.

What Can Be Observed?

Exhibit 8.1 summarizes primary types of phenomena that can end up recorded in observational research. These phenomena range from the pathway that one takes walking from store to store to the number of visits to political websites. Some observed behaviors are rather obvious, like the time it takes to get checked out at Wendy's. Others, though, can be much more inconspicuous. For instance, photos posted online contain codes that often reveal when and where the photo was taken. Facebook then stores this data, which can be useful in predicting user behavior.

The exhibit provides the impression that observational methods can cover a wide range of phenomena. Researchers use data to study phenomena related to these behaviors for numerous reasons. Not the least of the advantages of observational data is the fact that it is behavior. Observational data itself typically records behavior with little error because observational techniques are often simple and more and more occur automatically. Observational data collected automatically avoids expenses required with more labor-intensive processes. A Google Terra Bella satellite (formerly known as Skybox) may seem expensive to a small company, but for Google, it's a few million dollars that provides technology to take high-resolution images of the Earth twice daily. Consequently, the price for any particular observation is miniscule. If the observational data are already stored, they also have all the advantages of secondary data.

However, observational research is not perfect. While often one's behavior is observed easily, the reason for the behavior cannot be observed. Valuable explanations as to why someone behaves as they do may lie in phenomena that researchers cannot observe directly. Thus, the inability to tap into these latent variables represents a limitation to observational research tools.[2] This issue leads to another disadvantage of observational research. Analytical models using this data often provide better predictive power than they do explanatory power. Pharmaceutical companies use huge databases of medical observations to predict things like the potential side effects of their products.

RESEARCH IN
ACTION!

Observational data has advantages over self-report data in that it is not dependent on human memory or social pressures related to impression management. While you may not have access to data collected through the Internet of Things or smartphones, don't dismiss the possibility that hypotheses about human behavior could be addressed through simple observational techniques rather than relying on memory-dependent self-reports.

Cultura Creative (RF)/Alamy Stock Photo

EXHIBIT 8.1 Different Types of Observable Behaviors Tracked by Marketing Research

Observable Phenomenon	Illustration	Technologies Used to Observe
Physical Movements	The ways shoppers move through shopping centers and stores	Video, GPS, and NFC
Verbal Behavior	Statements recorded at the Walmart complaint line, posted on blogs, social networks, or sites like TripAdvisor	Voice recordings and Internet archives
Expressive Behavior and Physiological Reactions	Facial expressions of consumers in a restaurant, the body language of consumers waiting for service, or the amount of sweat produced under stress	Human observations, video or tools like GSR
Spatial Tensions and Locations	How close shoppers stand to a service provider while getting advice about what clothes look good	Human observations or video
Temporal Patterns	How long patients in a doctor's office will wait before going to the counter to complain	Human observations or timing devices
Physical Objects	What brands of shoes, clothing, and skateboards teens at a skate park own and use	Human observation
Verbal and Pictorial Records	Photographs or videos of early childhood Christmas experiences including photos posted on Instagram, Facebook, or other social network sites	Data archiving techniques, human observation
Neurological Activities	Brain activity in response to a consumer experiencing joy or disgust while reading advertising copy	Facial recognition or devices like fMRI
Internet Activities	Websites viewed, time spent viewing, social networking habits—what do consumers *like*? Search engine histories—what are consumers looking for?	Cookies and other tags that identify devices
Geographical Information	Where is someone physically located at any given time?	GPS tools, IP addresses, cell tower IDs
Physical Distribution	Movement of raw materials and finished products across the globe	NFC, satellite observation

While these studies are economical, the companies often are disappointed with the conclusions derived from them as they often end up conflicting with explanations derived from studies using other research designs.[3] Initial observational research associated one osteoporosis drug with increased risk of cancer of the esophagus. However, clinical data accumulated over time failed to display such an effect. Another limitation is that the observation period often is short. Observing behavior patterns that occur over a period of several days or weeks generally is too costly or even impossible. Big data technologies may change this, however, as various aspects of a person's everyday behavior can be captured through their phone.

The Research Snapshot illustrates a way that consumers are tracked with observations.

All That Jazz!

It's amazing how much the things we like to consume say about ourselves. For instance, how much do we know about somebody if we know what they like to drink or what music they like to listen to? Probably a lot!!

Researchers gather observational data on our Web behavior based on the assumption that we browse the things we like. For instance, consider two consumers, one who "likes" Smoking Loon and 2-Buck Chuck on Facebook and the other who "likes" Robert Mondavi and Sterling wines. The first two being edgy wine brands while the last two represent traditional California wine. Going further, the research can match these to political preferences evidence through online behavior in an effort to know how people vote. The study shows that the first wine lover leans heavily left in his or her politics while the latter leans heavily right.

Like music? In much the same way, Pandora is leveraging observational data suggesting a relationship between music preference and politics to sell advertising to political campaigns. Consider two consumers, one who creates a Bob Marley station with a touch of Daft Punk on Pandora and the other who creates a Yanni station with a touch of Frank Sinatra. How will these consumers vote? Probably no surprise but the Marley listener is going to vote democratic while the Yanni listener leans right. Knowing a consumer's preferences provides powerful information because knowing a few preferences allows one to predict many others.

Sources: Wilson, R. (2013), "What Your Favorite Drink Says about Your Politics, in One Chart," *Washington Post*, (12/31), http://www.washingtonpost.com/blogs/govbeat/wp/2013/12/31/what-your-favorite-drinksays-about-your-politics-in-onechart/, accessed February 22. Dwoskin, E. (2014), "Pandora Ads Tie Music to Politics," *Wall Street Journal*, February 14, B1–B2.

Keith Beaty/Getty Images

To the Point

"Where observation is concerned, chance favors only the prepared mind."

—LOUIS PASTEUR

unobtrusive

No communication with the person being observed is necessary so that he or she is unaware that he or she is an object of research.

visible observation

Observation in which the observer's presence or mechanical measurement device is obviously known to the subject.

hidden observation

Observation in which the subject is unaware that observation is taking place.

The Nature of Observation Studies

Marketing researchers can observe people, objects, events, or other phenomena using either human observers or machines designed for specific observation tasks. Human observation best suits a situation or behavior that is not easily predictable in advance of the research. In this sense, observational research fits best with a discovering orientation. Researchers employ a wide range of mechanical and electronic tools to capture consumer behavior. Mechanical observation, as performed by supermarket scanners or traffic counters, can very accurately record situations or types of behavior that are routine, repetitive, or programmatic. Cookies stored on computers record online browsing histories. Sophisticated machines that assess biological reactions such as a lie detector or neurological activities also make mechanical observations.

Human or mechanical observation is often **unobtrusive**, meaning no communication with a respondent takes place. For example, rather than asking customers how much time they spend shopping in the store, a supermarket manager might observe and record the time when a shopper enters and leaves the store. The unobtrusive nature of observational data collection often generates data without a subject's knowledge. A situation in which an observer's presence, or the mechanical device doing the recording, is easily known to the subject involves **visible observation**. A situation in which a subject is unaware that any observation is taking place is **hidden observation**. Hidden, unobtrusive observation minimizes respondent error. When respondents are unobtrusively recorded in a public area, an agreement to participate in research is not generally required. In such a situation, the respondent is in a public space and each person's identity is almost always unknown. On the other hand, a consumer who agrees to wash his or her hair in front of a video camera is visibly observed and should have provided formal consent to be involved in the research.

The data are recorded when and as the actual event takes place. Thus, they are free from nuisances like social desirability bias or memory problems.

Observation of Human Behavior

Whereas surveys emphasize verbal responses, observation studies emphasize and allow for the systematic recording of nonverbal behavior. Toy manufacturers such as Fisher Price use the observation technique because children often cannot express their reactions to products. By observing children at play with a proposed toy, doll, or game, marketing researchers may be able to identify the elements of a potentially successful product. Toy marketing researchers might observe play to answer the following questions:

- How long does the child's attention stay with the product?
- Does the child put the toy down after 2 minutes or 20 minutes?
- Are the child's peers equally interested in the toy?

Behavioral scientists have recognized that nonverbal behavior can be a communication process by which individuals exchange meanings. Head nods, smiles, raised eyebrows, winks, and other facial expressions or body movements serve as communication symbols. Observation of nonverbal communication may hold considerable promise for the marketing researcher. For example, a hypothesis about customer–salesperson interactions is that the salesperson would signal status based on the importance of each transaction. In low-importance transactions, in which potential customers are plentiful and easily replaced (say, a shoe store), the salesperson may show definite nonverbal signs of higher status than the customer. When customers are scarce, as in big-ticket purchase situations (real estate sales), the opposite should be true, with the salesperson showing many nonverbal indicators of deference. One way to test this hypothesis would be with an observation study using the nonverbal communication measures shown in Exhibit 8.2. Each row in the table indicates an aspect of nonverbal communication that one might observe in a common market situation.

Of course, researchers would not ignore verbal behavior. In fact, in certain observation studies, verbal expression is very important.

EXHIBIT 8.2 Observing and Interpreting Nonverbal Communication

Behavior		Description	Example
Facial Expressions		Expressions of emotion such as surprise (eyes wide open, mouth rounded and slightly open, brow furrowed)	A consumer reacts to the price quoted by a salesperson.
Body Language		Posture, placement of arms and legs	A consumer crosses arms as salesperson speaks, possibly indicating a lack of trust.
Eye Activity		Eye contact, staring, looking away, dilated pupils. In U.S. culture, not making eye contact is indicative of a deteriorating relationship. Dilated pupils can indicate emotion or degree of honesty.	A consumer avoids making eye contact with a salesperson knowing that he or she will not make a purchase.
Personal Space		Physical distance between individuals; in the United States, people like to be about eight feet apart to have a discussion.	A consumer may back away from a salesperson who is viewed to be violating one's personal space.
Gestures		Responses to certain events with specific body reactions or gestures	A consumer who wins something (maybe at the casino or a sports contest) lifts arms, stands tall, and sticks out chest.
Manners		Accepted protocol for given situations	A salesperson may shake a customer's hand, but should not touch a customer otherwise.

Direct and Contrived Observation

Researchers need always to take care of how much they interject themselves into a data collection situation. In a phenomenological approach, the researcher is often very much within the research situation. Consider the case where researchers ask restaurant employees to talk about working in a restaurant and how much emphasis restaurant management places on hygiene and customer safety. The researcher has to ask questions and may even provide some prop or stimulus to help get the respondent started. On the other hand, hidden cameras placed within the restaurants could record behavior and provide data without the need for a researcher's presence. Alternatively, an ethnographer may actually take a job in the restaurant and perform certain acts to see how other employees react. This brings us to the difference between direct and contrived observation.

Direct Observation

direct observation

A straightforward attempt to observe and record what naturally occurs; the investigator does not create an artificial situation.

Direct observation can produce detailed records of what people actually do during an event. The observer plays a passive role, making no attempt to control or manipulate a situation, instead merely recording what occurs. He or she must make every effort not to interject himor herself into the situation. For example, recording traffic counts and traffic flows within a supermarket can help managers design store layouts that maximize a typical customer's exposure to the merchandise offered while also facilitating search efforts. This data gathered through observation often are more accurate than what one would get by asking consumers about their movement through a store. A retailer can then better determine shelf locations, sales displays, the arrangement of departments and merchandise within those departments, the location of checkout facilities, and other characteristics that improve the shopping value consumers obtain from visiting a store.

For instance, if directly questioned in a survey, most shoppers would inaccurately portray the time they spent in each department. Likewise, many respondents would likely overstate the amount of effort they put into washing hands when directly questioned by a researcher. With the direct observation method, the data consist of records of events made as they occur. An observation form often helps keep researchers' observations consistent and ensures that they record all relevant information. A respondent is not required to recall—perhaps inaccurately—an event after it has occurred; instead, the observation is instantaneous. Direct observation such as described in the Research Snapshot dealing with hygiene may greatly reduce problems with perceptual distortion that lead to response error.

Why Use Direct Observation?

In many cases, direct observation is the most straightforward form of data collection—or the only form possible. The shaving business has become particularly competitive. Gillette is countering new competition from companies like Dollar Shave or Harry's by balancing continuous improvement in shaving technology with lines of low-priced shavers. How much can someone really say about the way they shave? Much better to watch the way people shave. Gillette researchers benefit from observing and videoing consumers as they actually shave. Thus, questions about how much shavers go with the grain or against it can be answered more accurately than they could with survey data. In another common type of observation study, a shopping center manager may observe the license plate (tag) numbers on cars in its parking lot. These data, along with automobile registration information, provide an inexpensive means of determining where customers live.

Researchers sometimes can obtain certain data more quickly or easily using direct observation than by other methods. If a research question involves what demographic characteristics are associated with spending time in a food court, a researcher can simply observe the gender, race, and other visible respondent characteristics rather than employing a survey. Researchers investigating a diet product may use observation when selecting respondents in a shopping mall. Overweight people may be prescreened by observing pedestrians, thus eliminating a number of screening interviews. Direct observation's advantages often make it the simplest, quickest, and most accurate way to gather data. On the other hand, direct observation has limited flexibility because not all phenomena are observable.

Errors Associated with Direct Observation

Although direct observation involves no interaction with the subject, the method is not error-free. When human observers record behaviors, the observer may record events subjectively. The same visual cues that may influence the interplay between interviewer and respondent (e.g., the subject's age or sex) may come into play in some direct observation settings, such as when the observer subjectively attributes a particular economic status or educational background to someone. A middle-aged person in a business suit will prime someone of high social class and the observer will frame expectations around that stereotype. We refer to a distortion of measurement resulting from the cognitive behavior or actions of the witnessing observer as **observer bias**. In a research project using observers to evaluate whether a retailer's salesclerks are rude or courteous, fieldworkers rely on their own interpretations of people or situations during the observation process. In these instances, nuisance situational factors such as the observer's own mood may bias their interpretations of others.

Also, accuracy may suffer if the observer does not record every detail that describes the persons, objects, and events in a given situation. Generally, the observer should record as much detail as possible. However, the pace of events, the observer's memory, the observer's writing speed, and other factors will limit the amount of detail that can be recorded.

Interpretation of observation data is another potential source of error. Facial expressions and other nonverbal communication may have several meanings. Does a smile always mean happiness? Does the fact that someone is standing or seated next to the president of a company necessarily indicate the person's status? Error creeps in the more pure observation moves into subjective judgment.

observer bias

A distortion of measurement resulting from the cognitive behavior or actions of a witnessing observer.

To the Point

"What we see depends mainly on what we look for."

— SIR JOHN LUBBOCK

Contrived Observation

Most observation takes place in a natural setting, but sometimes the investigator intervenes to create an artificial environment to test a hypothesis. This approach is called **contrived observation**. Contrived observation can increase the frequency of occurrence of certain behavior patterns, such as employee responses to complaints. An airline passenger complaining about a meal or service from the flight attendant may actually be a researcher recording the attendant's reactions. If situations were not contrived, the research time spent waiting and observing would expand considerably. A number of retailers use observers called *mystery shoppers* to visit a store and pretend to be interested in a particular product or service. After leaving the store, the "shopper" evaluates the salesperson's performance.

The Research Snapshot on the next page discusses direct observation of hand washing in public restrooms. Similarly, a study compared results from self-reported questionnaire data, focus group data, and observational data concerning hygiene among restaurant employees. The questionnaire responses suggested that 95 percent of employees washed their hands thoroughly after handling raw chicken, but that number averaged about 82 percent in the face-to-face interview condition, and when observation provides the data, 75 percent of the restaurant employees did not wash their hands adequately after handling raw chicken.[4] This direct observation could be turned into a contrived situation if a participant observer, pretending to be a new employee, asked another employee to assist in some way by handling raw chicken, and then observed the other employee's behavior. In the latter case, the researcher has interjected him- or herself into a situation, but perhaps for a very good reason. This may allow a hypothesis stating that interruptions will be associated with less hand washing compared to a no interruption condition.

contrived observation

Observation in which the investigator creates an artificial environment in order to test a hypothesis.

Complementary Evidence

Observational study results may amplify the results of other forms of research by providing *complementary evidence* concerning individuals' "true" feelings. Researchers typically conduct focus group

What We Say and What We Do

Michael Haegele/Getty Images

Most people know that hand washing is a fundamental way to stay healthy, not to mention simple good manners. So, when you ask them, most people say they faithfully wash their hands. But according to observational research, what people say about this behavior is not what they necessarily do.

Survey results based on a broad sample of American adults indicate that 96 percent of respondents say that "they always wash" their hands after using a public restroom. Do you think survey results on this topic may be subject to any response error? Many other studies examine hand washing using observational research designs. Typically, these studies employ research assistants who observe others' behavior in public restrooms while pretending to be just another public restroom user. Across dozens of studies of this type, results suggest that only 19 percent of people worldwide properly wash their hands with soap and water after using the bathroom. Researchers employed this observational research approach in a large-scale study of public restroom usage in a U.S. college town. Results from that study show that 78 percent of female users washed their hands with soap and water following use of the toilet while only 50 percent of male users did the same. Several factors influenced these percentages, including the presence of a sign stating the importance of hand washing in disease prevention. The sign increased hand washing among females but not males; in fact, the observed rate of hand washing among men actually went down when the sign was added. Time of day also influences results, with hand-washing frequency falling as

the day wears on. People who use their cell phone while in the toilet become less likely to wash hands. What do you make of the difference between survey and observational results? Realize too that with this method, no user was ever alone in the restroom. Might this influence results?

In the united States alone, nearly 50,000,000 people seek health care at clinics or emergency rooms each year because of food-borne illnesses. Estimates suggest that this number could be nearly cut in half if people just washed their hands after using the bathroom or otherwise coming into tactile contact with fecal matter, urine, mucus or other germ and bacterial carriers. Thus, hand washing is a legitimate cause of hand wringing among decision-makers in food and health-related industries.

Source: Freeman, M. C., M. E. Stocks, O. Cumming, A. Jeandron, J. T. Higgins, J. Wolf, and V. Curtis (2014), "Systematic review: Hygiene and Health: Systematic review of Hand Washing Practices Worldwide and update of Health Effects," *Tropical Medicine & International Health*, 19(8), 906–916. Borchgrevink, C. P., C. JaeMin, and K. SeungHyun (2013). Hand Washing Practices in a College town Environment. *Journal of Environmental Health*, 75(8), 18–24. https://www.thecut.com/2015/05/science-of-us-guide-to-bathroom-behavior.html, accessed December 13, 2017.

interviews behind two-way mirrors from which marketing executives observe as well as listen to what is occurring. This additional data source allows for interpretation of nonverbal behavior such as facial expressions or head nods to supplement information from interviews.

For example, in one focus group session concerning how women use hand lotion, researchers observed that all the women's hands were above the table while they were casually waiting for the session to begin. Seconds after the women were told that the topic was to be hand lotion, all their hands were placed out of sight. This observation, along with the group discussion, revealed the women's anger, guilt, and shame about the condition of their hands. Although they felt that people expected them to have soft, pretty hands, their household tasks include washing dishes, cleaning floors, and doing other chores, are hard on the hands.

Other research studies combine visible observation with personal interviews. During or after in-depth observations, researchers ask individuals to explain their actions.[5] Direct observation of women applying hand and body lotion identified two kinds of users. Some women slapped on the lotion, rubbing it briskly into their skin. Others caressed their skin as they applied the lotion. When the interviewer asked about their behavior, the researchers were able to interpret this finding. Women who slapped the lotion on were using the lotion as a remedy for dry skin. Those who caressed their skin were more interested in making their skin smell nice and feel soft.

Researchers also may follow up observations of customers in a shopping center with survey research. For example, if customers are observed looking into the window of a store (or web page) for more than 30 seconds but then moving on without going in, researchers may intercept them with a few questions potentially revealing reasons for this behavior.

Recording the decision time necessary to make a choice is a relatively simple, unobtrusive task easily accomplished through direct observation; it is also an example of complementary evidence. Survey responses combined with information on how long the respondent took to make a choice reveal more than either type of data alone. Recorded choice time is a measure of **response latency**. This measure is based on the hypothesis that the longer a decision-maker takes, the more difficult that decision was and the more thought the respondent put into the choice. A quick decision presumably indicates an easy or obvious choice. Computer-administered surveys can incorporate an automatic measure of response latency. The ability to combine behavioral observations with survey responses is a big advantage of Web-based surveys over paper-and-pencil approaches. Imagine how cumbersome a survey would become if respondents had to manually time themselves and enter the number of seconds it took to make responses.

response latency

The amount of time it takes to make a choice between two alternatives; used as a measure of the strength of preference.

Ethical Issues in the Observation of Humans

Observational researchers' tools are sometimes akin to snooping or spying.[6] Observation methods introduce a number of ethical issues, many raising the issue of the respondent's right to privacy. Suppose a research firm approaches a company interested in acquiring information about how women put on their bras by observing behavior in a spa dressing area. The researcher considers approaching spas in several key cities about placing small cameras inconspicuously to observe women getting dressed. Obviously, such a situation raises an ethical question. Even if the dressing room is an area where women often do dress where others can observe them, women do not expect to have their dressing behavior recorded and viewed. Therefore, unless the researcher can find a way to have women consent to such observation, this observational approach is unethical.

If the researcher obtains permission to observe someone, the subject may not act naturally. So, at times there is a strong temptation to observe without obtaining consent or gaining input from an Institutional Review Board (IRB). Many times, such as monitoring people walking through or waiting in an airport, obtaining consent from individual respondents is impractical, if not impossible. Further, asking for consent just before the actual observation will likely change the behavior.

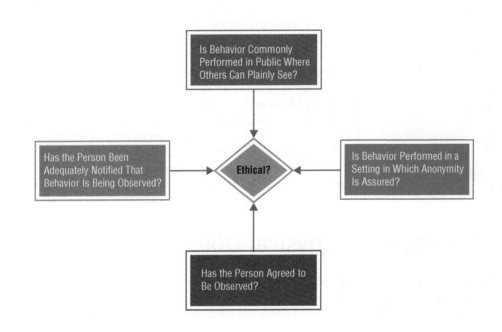

EXHIBIT **8.3**
Is the Observation Ethical?

New technologies afford opportunities to observe behaviors of interest to marketing managers. Deep-packet inspection refers to the ability of an Internet service provider to read data transmitted by users. The observation of this data might clue researchers in on how consumers search for marketing information. Observers may also snoop on Facebook and other social networking sites and both observe and provoke online comments all motivated by the need to discover information about consumers.

So, when should researchers feel comfortable collecting observational data? Although exceptions exist to every rule, here are four questions that can help address this question (depicted in Exhibit 8.3):

1. Is the behavior being observed commonly performed in public where it is expected that others can observe the behavior?
2. Is the behavior performed in a setting in which the anonymity of the person being observed is assured (meaning there is no practical way to identify individuals)?
3. Has the person agreed to be observed?
4. Has the person been adequately notified that their behavior (including data transfers) is being observed?

If the answer to the first two questions is "yes," then there is not likely a violation of privacy in collecting observational research data. If the answer to the third and/or fourth question is "yes," then gathering the data also is likely ethical. Otherwise, the researcher should carefully consider input from an IRB or other authority before proceeding with the research.

Also, some might see contrived observation as unethical based on the notion of entrapment. To *entrap* means to deceive or trick into difficulty, which clearly is an abusive action. For instance, in the handwashing example given, when the experimenter interrupts the real employee, he/she may entrap the employee into a lower probability of washing hands thoroughly. In this instance, if the employee was harmed or caused harm to others (by getting in trouble with a superior or making someone ill) then clearly the intrusion is unethical. However, if no possibility of harm exists, then the researcher can likely proceed, although, an IRB should be consulted whenever risk of harm is present.

Given that the Internet is not just a source that provides information but also a source of recorded information, many have concerns that any information (whether true or not) has potential to harm someone's reputation. A prank photo of a graduate student for example could surface in a background check and harm the student's chance at getting a job. These concerns underlie "Right to Be Forgotten" movements that include legislative efforts.[7] The initiatives are growing quickly in Europe following an EU court ruling supporting "a right to be forgotten." The ruling requires search providers like Google to respond to individuals' requests to remove information from search results. As a result, Google is hiring a staff to review individually the thousands and thousands of requests. However, Google thus far is reticent to remove information appearing in published sources. Given the complexity of dealing with Google on these matters, an industry of companies who assist individuals in these efforts has spawned with France's Reputation VIP leading the way. Relative to Europe, Americans appear a little less confident that a right to be forgotten movement will gain traction.

Even if fashion companies could learn a lot about the types of problems consumers typically have when purchasing and wearing clothes, would observation through two-way mirrors (a mirror that reflects on one side but can be seen through from the other) be appropriate?

pkline//iStock/Getty Images

Observation of Physical Objects

Physical phenomena may be the subject of observation study. Physical-trace evidence is a visible mark of some past event or occurrence. For example, the wear on library books indirectly indicates how many people actually handle and/or check out books and, therefore, wear represents a proxy for popularity based on the assumption that more wear means more readers. A classic example of physical-trace evidence in a nonprofit setting was erosion on the floor tiles around the hatching-chick exhibit at Chicago's Museum of Science and Industry. These tiles were replaced every six weeks; tiles in other parts of the museum did not need to be replaced for years. The selective erosion of tiles, indexed by the replacement rate, was a measure of the relative popularity of exhibits.

Artifacts

Clearly, a creative marketing researcher has many options for determining the solution to a problem. The story about Charles Coolidge Parlin, generally recognized as one of the founders of commercial marketing research, examining garbage cans at the turn of the twentieth century illustrates another study of physical traces. Physical traces often involve artifacts. **Artifacts** are things that people made and consumed within a culture that signal something meaningful about the behavior taking place at the time of consumption. Ethnographers are particularly interested in examining artifacts, and Parlin's garbage can escapades illustrate how a marketing researcher can apply an ethnographic approach involving observation of artifacts.

Parlin designed an observation study to persuade Campbell's Soup Company to advertise in the *Saturday Evening Post*. Campbell's was reluctant to advertise because it believed that the *Post* was read primarily by working people who would prefer to make soup from scratch, peeling the potatoes and scraping the carrots, rather than paying ten cents for a can of soup. To demonstrate that rich people weren't the target market, Parlin selected a sample of Philadelphia garbage routes. Garbage from each specific area of the city that was selected was dumped on the floor of a local National Guard Armory. Parlin had the number of Campbell's soup cans in each pile counted. The results indicated that the garbage from the rich people's homes didn't contain many cans of Campbell's soup. Although they may not have made soup from scratch themselves, their housekeepers may have. The garbage piles from the blue-collar area showed a larger number of Campbell's soup cans. This observation study was enough evidence for Campbell's. They advertised in the *Saturday Evening Post*.[8]

A scientific project conducted at the University of Arizona adopted this research approach in which aspiring archaeologists sifted through garbage for over thirty years. They examined soggy cigarette butts, empty milk cartons, and half-eaten Big Macs in an effort to understand modern life. Like other research involving observation, we can compare the observed garbage data with the results of surveys about food consumption. Garbage does not lie. This type of observation can correct for potential overreporting of healthful item consumption and underreporting consumption of, say, cigarettes or fast food.

To the Point

"What would you rather believe? What I say, or what you saw with your own eyes?"

— GROUCHO MARX

artifacts

The things that people made and consumed within a culture that signal something meaningful about the behavior taking place at the time of consumption.

● ● ● ● ● ●

Picking through the garbage on the side of the road can reveal behaviors of fast-food customers.

FRANK PERRY/AFP/Getty Images

Inventories

Another application of observing physical objects is to count and record physical inventories through retail or wholesale audits. This method allows researchers to investigate brand sales on regional and national levels, market shares, seasonal purchasing patterns, and so on. Marketing research suppliers offer audit data at both the retail and the wholesale levels.

An observer can record physical-trace data to discover information a respondent could not recall accurately. For example, measuring the number of ounces of liquid bleach used during a test provides precise physical-trace evidence without relying on the respondent's memory. The accuracy of respondents' memories is not a problem for the firm that conducts a pantry audit. The pantry audit requires an inventory of the brands, quantities, and package sizes in a consumer's home rather than responses from individuals. The problem of untruthfulness or some other form of response bias is avoided. For example, the pantry audit prevents the possible problem of respondents erroneously claiming to have purchased prestige brands. However, gaining permission to physically check consumers' pantries is not easy, and the fieldwork is expensive. In addition, the brand in the pantry may not reflect the brand purchased most often if consumers substituted it because they had a coupon, the usual brand was out of stock, or another reason.

Researchers studying hand washing employed an interesting observational approach involving inventories. They decided to measure hand washing by electronically monitoring the soap remaining in the restroom dispenser following each use.[9] In other words, the soap use unobtrusively assessed whether a user washed his or hands or not if one presumes that soap-use equates to hand washing (as hygiene experts presume). The study also explored the use of signs by displaying either a disgusting message or an informational message near the soap dispenser. Results show that:

1. just over 30 percent of men and 65 percent of women washed their hands,
2. that men were more likely to wash after exposure to a disgusting message,
3. while women were more likely to wash when exposed to the informational message.

Thus, the soap inventory served as an observational measurement tool.

Content Analysis

content analysis

The systematic observation and quantitative description of the manifest content of communication.

Besides observing people and physical objects, researchers sometimes use **content analysis**, which obtains data by observing and analyzing the contents or messages of advertisements, newspaper articles, television programs, letters, Web pages, blogs, Facebook photos, tweets, and the like. This method involves systematic analysis as well as observation to identify the specific information content and other characteristics of the messages. Content analysis studies the message itself and involves the design of a systematic observation and recording procedure for quantitative description of the manifest content of communication. This technique measures the extent of emphasis or omission of a given analytical category. For example, content analysis of advertisements might evaluate their use of words, themes, characters, or space and time relationships. Content analysis often counts the frequency of themes or occurrences within a given hermeneutic unit. For instance, the frequency with which women, African Americans, Hispanics, or Asians appear in advertising displayed on a television program represents a topic amenable to content analysis.

Content analysis might be used to investigate questions such as whether some marketers use certain themes, appeals, claims, or even deceptive practices more than others or whether recent consumer-oriented actions by the Federal Trade Commission have influenced the contents of advertising. For instance, content analysis of tweets from large companies aimed at consumers described the way companies seem to be using Twitter. The findings suggest that companies use tweets to share hyperlinks to other sites and hashtags more than they do to share photo or video content.[10] Content analysis also can explore the information content of television commercials directed at children, the company images portrayed in ads, and numerous other aspects of advertising.

Study of the content of communications sometimes involves more than simply counting the items. Researchers sometimes perform content analysis of YouTube and other social media content in an effort in understanding what types of videos might influence consumer behavior. For instance, a content analysis employed judges who watched sample retail advertisements placed on YouTube by companies and then judged the ads based on whether they were more emotional or informational in nature. Ideally, multiple judges (at least two or three coders) perform the coding task, allowing for an assessment of rater reliability or how replicable are the results. In this study, the retail ads that were deemed more effective tended to be judged as informational more than emotional.[11]

Mechanical Observation

In many situations, the primary—and sometimes the only—means of observation is mechanical rather than human. Video cameras, traffic counters, and other machines help observe and record behavior. Some unusual observation studies have used motion-picture cameras and time-lapse photography. An early application of this observation technique photographed train passengers and determined their levels of comfort by observing how they sat and moved in their seats. Another time-lapse study filmed traffic flows in an urban square and resulted in a redesign of the streets. Similar techniques may help managers design store layouts and resolve problems in moving people or objects through spaces over time. The soap inventory study of hand washing also illustrates a mechanical observation application.

Television, Radio, and Digital Monitoring

Perhaps the best-known marketing research project involving mechanical observation and computerized data collection is Nielsen's **television monitoring** system for estimating national television audiences. Nielsen Media Research uses a consumer panel and a monitoring device called a People Meter to obtain ratings for television programs nationwide.[12] We introduced this device in Chapter 3 to illustrate observation-based research. A company called Arbitron pioneered the technology and Nielsen acquired Arbitron in 2014. The Nielsen People Meter gathers data on what program is on a television and who is watching it at the time. The electronic devices capture information on program choices and the length of viewing time. This observational data is supplemented with consumer diaries that together provide valuable input on ratings, which helps price advertising time by program and lets advertisers know what programs reach the targeted audience.

Critics of the People Meter argue that subjects in Nielsen's panel grow bored over time and don't always record when they begin or stop watching television. More recently, innovations answer this objection with a new measuring system called the **Portable People Meter**.[13] PPM is a

television monitoring
Computerized mechanical observation used to obtain television ratings. Nielsen's People Meter technology best illustrates television (or more broadly, media) monitoring.

portable people meter
Device that looks and functions much like a small cell phone but automatically detects broadcast signals, satellite radio and tv transmissions, and most other digital signals.

• • • • • • •

Traffic cameras that monitor speeding on major highways are becoming commonplace in Europe, Australia, and even in some parts of the United States. Would car companies learn anything from the observed behavior?

AP Images/STEVE MITCHELL

device that looks and functions much like a small cell phone. The panel participant carries this with them and it automatically detects broadcast signals, satellite radio and television transmissions, and most other types of digital signals. Thus, the ratings are not based only on panel members interacting with traditional media like home-based television sets or AM/FM radios. Participants receive points that lead to modest compensation amounts whenever they turn the PPM on. Arbitron's meter simplifies the participants' role and collects data on exposure to radio and television programming outside the home.

Other devices monitor advertising on all types of digital media. For instance, Pretesting Group's PeopleReader™ unobtrusively measures the time a user spends on viewing printed advertising pages or pages displayed on a computer or other smart device such as a tablet. The company argues that they can assess consumer stopping power with the device or the degree to which an advertisement engages consumers and shifts their attention to the ad and away from the focal media. Moreover, observational data from Nielsen's various technologies suggests how consumers use one media form to complement another. In other words, radio usage encourages television usage, which together may relate to podcast and live-streaming usage.

Monitoring Web Traffic

Computer technology makes gathering detailed data about online behavior easy and inexpensive. The greater challenges are to identify which measures are meaningful and to interpret the data correctly. For instance, most organizations record the level of activity at their websites. They may count the number of *hits*—mouse clicks on a single page of a website. If the visitor clicks on many links, that page receives multiple hits. Similarly, they can track *page views*, or single, discrete clicks to load individual pages of a website. Page views more conservatively indicate how many users visit each individual page on the website and may also be used to track the path or sequence of pages that each visitor follows. Web traffic monitoring also allows a company to know how a potential customer came to their site and where they went afterward. Did someone make a reservation at Sofitel.com after visiting bing.com? This question can be answered. We also can monitor what type of device a consumer viewed a Web page on and where that device was located at the time of the viewing. Additionally, companies can track comments about their brands left on blogs and social networking sites. Thus, all the billions of clicks made on the Internet each day leave behind a trail that indicates our behavior.

Web Traffic and Buzz

click-through rate

The percentage of views of a page for which the user clicks on a target link that takes them to the desired website.

Marketers need to know if advertising is effective. For most advertising, that means it must be viewed. For companies placing ads online and on social media sites, knowing how many people even may have seen the ad becomes an important statistic. A **click-through rate (CTR)** for these ads can be computed in the same way as in assessing survey response rates to obtain the percentage of people exposed to a Web-based advertisement who actually click on the corresponding hyperlink that takes them to the company's website. If 10,000 people view a page and 100 click on the ad, the click-through rate is 1 percent. The CTR remains an important metric representing the portion of consumers exposed who engage with the brand through the ad. CTRs vary by category averaging less than 0.5 percent for professional employment ads and just over 1.5 percent for retail and legal services ads.

Counting hits or page views can suggest the amount of interest or attention a website is receiving, but these measures are flawed. First, hits do not differentiate between a lot of activity by a few visitors and a little activity by many visitors. In addition, the researcher lacks information about the meaning behind the numbers. If a user clicks on a site many times, is the person finding a lot of useful or enjoyable material, or is the user trying unsuccessfully to find something by looking in several places? Additionally, some hits are likely made by mistake. The consumers may have had no intention of clicking through the ad or may not have known what they were doing when they clicked on the ad.

A more specific count is the number of *unique visitors* to a website. This measurement counts the initial access to the site but not multiple hits on the site by the same visitor during the same day or week. Operators of websites can collect the data by attaching small files, called *cookies*, to the computers of visitors to their sites and then tracking those cookies to see whether the same visitors return. Google, Facebook, Twitter, and Apple rely heavily on research specialists who use analytical tools to gather data from consumers' cookies and other computer residuals to help forecast who may buy what and when. Google and Facebook dominate online advertising and hope to grow this revenue stream even more by linking ad spends with them to consumer spending in the store. Total spending on Twitter advertising is less than Facebook or Google, but Twitter ads typically have a higher CTR. However, other metrics provide data indicating the way consumers engage with online ads.

While the technology behind such tracking is complex and proprietary, you can get a sense for how this works each time you visit a website surrounded by banner ads for a retail site and even for a specific product that you recently viewed online. The technology allows consumers' personal data (including e-mail addresses, names) and data extracted from cookies and smart devices to be linked with in-store purchase histories. Personal identities are replaced with a numbering system in a process called hashing that purports to protect individuals' personal identities.

Research companies provide their clients with assessments of more than website effectiveness as the resulting data includes assessments of advertising effectiveness and social media buzz. Imagine how a company like Paramount might be interested in whether or not news about new products stirs up any activity online. **Conversation volume** represents a measure of the amount of Internet postings that involve a specific name or term. That name or term could be a brand name, a destination name, or the name of an event. Motion picture producers rely heavily on conversation volume to assess the success of motion pictures. Disney monitors conversation volume on release of new Star Wars films to assess how much of the conversation acknowledges Disney in some way.[14] Similarly, analysts monitor Twitter for positive or negative tweets. Researchers consider this observational data because they do not perform an interview of any type for its acquisition.

conversation volume
A measure of the amount of Internet postings that involve a specific name or term.

Extrapolating product success purely based on Web traffic or even online conversation volume can produce inaccurate projections. Mere counts of brand-name usage do not reveal whether the usages are in a positive or negative light. In addition, many brand names may have ambiguous meanings that can be confused.[15] Just imagine all the reasons why someone may search or use the word "kiss." Further, consumers employ differing levels of computer security systems limiting researchers' access to information. Difficulties such as these strongly point toward the need for observational data from the Internet to be professionally analyzed before relying on it for important decisions.

Crypto-currency generates considerable buzz, which investors try to interpret as a buy or sell sign.[16] Exhibit 8.4 lists some of the different metrics available as data from consumers' engagement with social media.

● ● ● ● ● ● ●
Kiss has many meanings.

Kristoffer Tripplaar/Alamy Stock Photo

Marketers use social media as a platform to engage with consumers in a way that allows data to describe that engagement.

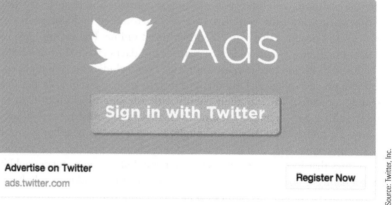

Twitter Ads Nordics ✓
@TwitterAdsNord

▲ Follow

Want to connect with potential customers? Use Twitter Ads. Start by setting up a campaign today!

Sign in with Twitter

Advertise on Twitter
ads.twitter.com

Register Now

EXHIBIT **8.4**

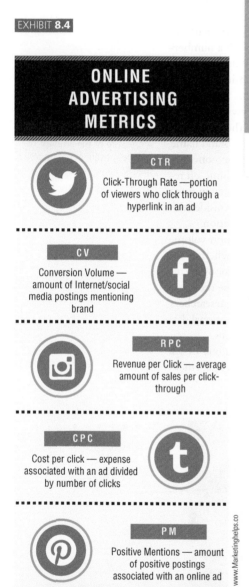

ONLINE ADVERTISING METRICS

CTR
Click-Through Rate —portion of viewers who click through a hyperlink in an ad

CV
Conversion Volume — amount of Internet/social media postings mentioning brand

RPC
Revenue per Click — average amount of sales per click-through

CPC
Cost per click — expense associated with an ad divided by number of clicks

PM
Positive Mentions — amount of positive postings associated with an online ad

www.marketinghelps.co

Source: www.Marketinghelps.co

scanner-based consumer panel

A type of consumer panel in which participants' purchasing habits are recorded with a laser scanner rather than a purchase diary.

CTR and Online Advertising

As online advertising has become more widespread, marketing research has refined methods for measuring the effectiveness of the advertisements. Applying the CTR to the amount spent on the advertisement gives the advertiser a *cost per click*. This presents a practical way to evaluate advertising effectiveness. However, marketers rarely see getting consumers to click on an ad as its primary objective. Companies more often expect advertising to help them meet sales goals.

Trivago has grown to one of the largest online travel agencies in the world. Part of their success lies in successful digital marketing driven by observed data usage patterns.[17] Recently, Trivago launched a dynamic Google Adwords campaign aimed at gaining more business for travel to less trafficked areas like South America. After employing the campaign, Trivago observed CTRs over twice as high as they were for their old online ads. Thus, the observations indicated a successful campaign.

Scanner-Based Research

Lasers performing optical character recognition and bar code technology like the universal product code (UPC, or "bar code") and RFID tags typify the use of mechanical observation in marketing research. A number of syndicated services offer secondary data about product category movement generated from retail stores using scanner technology.

This technology allows researchers to investigate questions that are demographically or promotionally specific. Scanner research has investigated the different ways consumers respond to price promotions and the effects of those differences on a promotion's profitability. One of the primary means of implementing this type of research is through the establishment of a **scanner-based consumer panel** to replace consumer purchase diaries. In a typical scanner panel, each household carries a shopper card, which members present at checkout. A scan of the card allows recording of a household's purchase information as data.

Aggregate data, such as actual store sales as measured by scanners, are available to clients and industry groups. For instance, data from Information Resources Inc. (IRI) have indicated a downward trend in sales of hair-coloring products. Demographic data suggest that an important reason is the aging of the population; many consumers who dye their hair reach an age at which they no longer wish to cover their gray hair. A smaller segment of the population is at an age where consumers typically begin using hair coloring.[18]

Data from scanner research parallel data provided by a standard mail diary panel, with some important improvements:

1. The data measure observed (actual) purchase behavior rather than reported behavior (recorded later in a diary).
2. Substituting mechanical for human record-keeping improves accuracy.
3. Measures are unobtrusive, eliminating interviewing and the possibility of social desirability or other bias on the part of respondents.
4. More extensive purchase data can be collected, because all UPC categories are measured. In a mail diary, respondents could not possibly reliably record all items they purchased.
5. The data collected from computerized checkout scanners can be combined with data about advertising, price changes, displays, and special sales promotions. Researchers can scrutinize them with powerful analytical software provided by the scanner data providers.

Scanner data is a mechanical observation form that requires no input from customers. From time to time, media express concerns about the accuracy of scanner pricing data. In an exhaustive study of scanner data from a single western state, researchers determined that overall scanner error is less than 5 percent, that undercharges were more common than overcharges, and that those errors often resulted from temporary price changes associated with short-term price promotions.[19] The key to this type of research was the sales data recorded by scanners.

Camera Surveillance

Modern society increasingly relies on cameras to keep tabs on all sorts of behaviors. Camera surveillance is practically everywhere in New York city including almost every private apartment building.[20] Cameras watch the entry doors and hallways as well as all other public spaces. Apartment managers say that the decrease in dealing with criminal incidences and lower insurance rates more than make up for the modest cost of camera surveillance systems. In particular, they note the decrease in illicit drug sales that used to occur commonly just out the front door of many apartment buildings.

Likewise, cameras planted inconspicuously in shopping centers, stores, and downtown streets can be useful in marketing research. Shopping center security video can help identify problems with merchandising and the types of things that attract consumers to come into and remain in an environment. This is only the tip of the iceberg as cameras have many more applications than these.

Researchers sometimes ask and get permission to place cameras inconspicuously in consumers' homes, offices, or even cars.[21] Microsoft commissioned research involving the observation of 50 homes via inconspicuous, in-home cameras. The research addressed problems encountered by consumers when using Windows products in their homes. Microsoft was able to study the consumer behavior involved and try to find a way to reduce the problems identified. Other companies, including Kimberly-Clark, Sony, and Old Spice, have also successfully applied observational research using cameras. The Old Spice research involved videos of guys taking showers in their homes (with permission and swimsuits), and the Kimberly-Clark research involved young parents wearing small hat cams while changing a baby's diaper. This type of observation allows close inspection of activities in places and at times when having an actual observer present would not work.

Other times, researchers may gather observational data without getting explicit permission. Imaging technologies today include facial recognition capabilities.[22] Thus, once a consumer is put together with a face, his/her behavior can be tracked and recorded as he/she moves around a store. In fact, on a broader scale, cameras can even track individuals via drones potentially providing some "high-level" data.

Smartphones

Modern people are increasingly dependent upon their smartphones and other devices such as tablet computers. Most people don't realize how much information is recorded through their everyday use of the phone. All text messages, browsing, and phone calls leave behind some kind of record. In this way, phones serve as a type of mechanical behavior recorder. As referenced earlier, smartphones also contain GPS devices capable of recording the phone's, and thus most likely the user's, whereabouts anytime the phone is connected. Observations from smartphones might reveal:[23]

- when people are happy based on their message content,
- their political opinions,
- when the customer may be unhappy with their smartphone service provider,
- where a person likes to party on the weekend, how fast he/she drives,
- what types of websites a person likes.

Like other areas, technology may outpace the ethics of using this type of data. The benefits of allowing researchers access to the data are being weighed against privacy concerns as policy makers ponder legal limits on what can be recorded and shared.

Measuring Physiological Reactions

Marketing researchers have used a number of other mechanical devices to evaluate consumers' physical and physiological reactions to advertising copy, packaging, and other stimuli. Five major categories of mechanical devices are used to measure physiological reactions: (1) eye-tracking monitors, (2) pupilometers, (3) psychogalvanometers, (4) voice-pitch analyzers, and (5) neurological activity.

● ● ● ● ● ● ●

Physiological responses to advertising can be recorded with a device like this one.

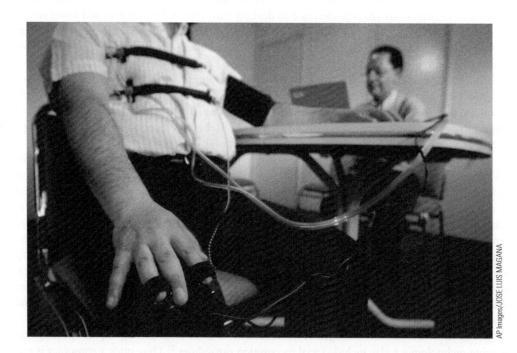

AP Images/JOSE LUIS MAGANA

Eye-Tracking Monitor

A newspaper or social media advertiser may wish to grab readers' attention with a visual scene and then direct attention toward a tagline, offer, or hyperlink. Or a consumer foods marketer wants to know how to get a new product noticed amongst the multitude of other items on a grocer's shelves. Eye-tracking equipment records how the subject reads a print ad or views a television commercial and how much time a respondent spends looking at various parts of a stimulus. In physiological terms, the gaze movement of a viewer's eye is measured with an **eye-tracking monitor**, which measures unconscious eye movements. Originally developed to measure astronauts' eye fatigue, modern eye-tracking systems need not keep a viewer's head in a stationary position. The devices track eye movements with invisible infrared light beams that lock onto a subject's eyes. The light reflects off the eye, and eye-movement data are recorded while another tiny video camera monitors which magazine page is being perused. The data are analyzed by computer to determine which components in an ad (or other stimuli) were seen and which were overlooked. Unilever, the parent company for brands such as Axe, Dove, Lipton, and Sunsilk, rely heavily on eye-tracking research performed in both research labs and actual retail stores to create effective package designs. In this case, an active research participant wears extremely unobtrusive glasses that record all gaze data. These data can then be transformed in numerous ways including into heat maps that suggest exactly where the shopper's eyes wander and become fixed. Even a fraction of a second translates into greater purchase probabilities. Similarly, companies use eye-tracking to monitor consumers' Internet viewing. In this case, eye tracking can be done without the need for any special glasses. Thus, eye-tracking is extremely unobtrusive and widely used.[24]

eye-tracking monitor

A mechanical device used to observe eye movements; some eye monitors use infrared light beams to measure unconscious eye movements.

Other physiological observation techniques are based on a common principle: that adrenaline is released when the body is aroused. This hormone causes the heart to enlarge and to beat harder and faster. These changes increase the flow of blood to the fingers and toes. The blood vessels dilate, and perspiration increases, affecting the skin's electrical conductivity. Other physical changes following the release of adrenaline include dilation of the pupils, more frequent brain wave activity, higher skin temperature, and faster breathing. Methods that measure these and other changes associated with arousal can apply to a variety of marketing questions, such as subjects' reactions to advertising messages or product concepts.

Marketing and Consumer Research

Source: Tobii Technology, Inc.

Pupilometer

A **pupilometer** observes and records changes in the diameter of a subject's pupils. A subject is instructed to look at a screen on which an advertisement or other stimulus is projected. When the brightness and distance of the stimulus from the subject's eyes are held constant, changes in pupil size may be interpreted as changes in cognitive activity that result from the stimulus, rather than from eye dilation and constriction in response to light intensity, distance from the object, or other physiological reactions to the conditions of observation. This method of research is based on the assumption that increased pupil size reflects positive attitudes toward and interest in advertisements. Eye-tracking software today sometimes includes the ability to measure eye dilation and thus also serve as a pupilometer.

pupilometer

A mechanical device used to observe and record changes in the diameter of a subject's pupils.

Psychogalvanometer

A **psychogalvanometer** measures galvanic skin response (GSR), a measure of involuntary changes in the electrical resistance of the skin. This device is based on the assumption that physiological changes, such as increased perspiration, accompany emotional reactions to advertisements, packages, and slogans. Excitement increases the body's perspiration rate, which increases the electrical resistance of the skin. The test is an indicator of emotional arousal or tension and can be used to help detect dishonest responses as a lie detector.

psychogalvanometer

A device that measures galvanic skin response, a measure of involuntary changes in the electrical resistance of the skin.

Voice-Pitch Analysis

voice-pitch analysis

A physiological measurement technique that records abnormal frequencies in the voice that are supposed to reflect emotional reactions to various stimuli.

Voice-pitch analysis is a relatively new physiological measurement technique that gauges emotional reactions as reflected in physiological changes in a person's voice. Abnormal frequencies in the voice caused by changes in the autonomic nervous system are measured with sophisticated, audio-adapted computer equipment. Computerized analysis compares the respondent's voice pitch during warm-up conversations (normal range) with verbal responses to questions about his or her evaluative reaction to television commercials or other stimuli. This technique, unlike other physiological devices, does not require the researcher to surround subjects with mazes of wires or equipment.

Neurological Devices

magnetic resonance imaging (MRI)

A machine that allows one to measure what portions of the brain are active at a given time.

What happens inside a consumer's brain during everyday activities like browsing advertisements online? More and more, we are able to observe what goes on in the consumer's mind. Neurological activity can reveal how much thought takes place and what types of feelings a person is probably experiencing. Similar processes involve things such as **magnetic resonance imaging (MRI)** or transcranial magnetic simulation.[25] If these things sound complicated, it's because they are. These tools allow actual direct observation of what is going on in the mind of a respondent by assessing and identifying where electromagnetic activity is taking place within the brain. Thus, these techniques may revolutionize research on information processing.

Marketing researchers employ the technology by having paid respondents view advertisements in an MRI machine.[26] The results help identify the patterns of cognitive and emotional reactions the ads may generate, at least when ads are viewed in an MRI machine. For instance, the brain activation patterns of consumers exposed to cigarette advertising versus anti-smoking ads are contrasted using MRI recordings. These tests are accomplished via the volunteer participation of consumers who must lie completely still inside the device for periods exceeding 30 minutes. Thus, the tools remain obtrusive and expensive, both factors limiting their application in practice. However, advancing technology provides smaller and more portable neurological measuring devices more amenable to studying consumer behavior somewhat more realistically. Researchers also should be concerned about the ethical implications of looking into someone's mind. As barriers such as these are overcome, observations of brain activity may become a mainstay of observational marketing research.

Companies like Tobii provide tools for research that tracks how the eye moves during an activity. Think about how useful this might be to companies considering product placements within video games or in designing more efficient instrument panels for airplanes.

Source: Tobii Technology, Inc.

Physiological measures have disadvantages and advantages. All of these devices assume that physiological reactions are associated with persuasiveness or predict a cognitive response. However, no strong theoretical evidence demonstrates exactly how physiological changes drive future sales. Another major problem with physiological research is the *calibration*, or sensitivity, of measuring devices. Identifying arousal is one thing, but precisely measuring *levels* of arousal is another. In addition, most of these devices are expensive and require an artificial setting for their use. However, as a prominent researcher points out, physiological measurement is coincidental: "Physiological measurement isn't an exit interview. It's not dependent on what was remembered later on. It's a live blood, sweat, and tears, moment-by-moment response, synchronous with the stimulus."[27]

TIPS OF THE TRADE

- Once someone knows that others are watching, the researcher cannot be sure how much that knowledge changes behavior.
- Researchers should strongly consider using measures of response latency when studying information processing. Computer-aided survey technology makes observing response latency easy and accurate.
- Complementary evidence combining observational and nonobservational approaches provide more complete explanations.

- The anonymity of people whose behavior is captured using observational data collection should be protected at all times unless consent has been obtained to identify the person.
- Eye-tracking software today provides an unobtrusive way to capture gaze observations that allow the researcher to analyze exactly where and for how long a consumer's eyes roam around a stimulus or environment.

∷ SUMMARY

1. Discuss the role of observation technologies as marketing research tools.   Scientific observation is the systematic process of recording the behavioral patterns of people, objects, and occurrences as they take place. Researchers use observation to record: (1) physical actions; (2) verbal behavior, such as sales conversations; (3) expressive behavior; (4) spatial relations and locations; (5) temporal patterns; (6) physical objects; (7) verbal and pictorial records; (8) neurological activity; (9) Internet activity; (10) geographic information; and (11) physical distribution in supply chains. Observational data is very advantageous in capturing behavior as it actually happens. Technology provides new ways of recording behavior automatically, and as a result, reliance on observation is increasing.

2. Know the difference between direct and contrived observation.   The most advantageous observational data techniques are unobtrusive, meaning the observation takes place without the knowledge of the observed person. Direct observation involves watching and recording what naturally occurs, without creating an artificial situation. For some data, observation is the most direct or the only method of collection. For example, researchers can measure response latency, the time it takes individuals to decide such as in choosing among alternatives. Contrived observation creates situations that prompt some reaction to be measured such as the case with mystery shoppers who pose as customers and complain about bad service (even if it isn't bad).

3. Identify ethical issues particular to research using observation. Contrived observation, hidden observation, and other observation research tools, including the use of electronic tracking via Web browsing or cell phone use, have the potential to involve deception or violate one's privacy. For this reason, these methods often raise ethical concerns about subjects' right to privacy and right to be informed. The chapter includes a short checklist that can be useful in determining the morality of an observational data gathering approach. An overriding concern when consent cannot or is not obtained is whether the person freely performs the observed behavior in public. Technological advances also create concern over individuals' "right to be forgotten."

4. Explain the observation of physical objects and message content. Physical-trace evidence serves as a visible record of past events. Researchers may examine whatever evidence provides such a record, including inventory levels, the contents of garbage cans, or the items in a consumer's pantry. Researchers can take advantage of artifacts that are left behind to try and explain the behavior associated with that particular object. Content analysis obtains data by observing and analyzing the contents of the messages in written or spoken communications.

5. Describe major types of mechanical observation. Mechanical observation uses a variety of devices to record behavior directly. It may be an efficient and accurate choice when the situation or behavior to be recorded is routine, repetitive, or programmatic. National television audience ratings are based on mechanical observation (e.g., People Meters) and computerized data collection. Website traffic and content are monitored easily through residuals left on computers. Barcode scanners automatically record purchase data and RFID tags can also track the movement of goods. Smartphones record many aspects of behavior including geographic location and movement.

6. Summarize techniques for measuring physiological reactions. Physiological reactions, such as arousal or eye movement patterns, may be observed using a number of mechanical devices. Eye-tracking monitors identify the direction of a person's gaze, and a pupilometer observes and records changes in the diameter of the pupils of subjects' eyes, based on the assumption that a larger pupil signifies a positive attitude. A psychogalvanometer measures galvanic skin response as a signal of a person's emotional reactions. Voice-pitch analysis measures changes in a person's voice and associates the changes with emotional response. MRIs and similar devices allow recording of neurological (i.e., brain) activity.

∷ KEY TERMS AND CONCEPTS

artifacts, *215*
click-through rate (CTR), *218*
content analysis, *216*
contrived observation, *211*
conversation volume, *219*
direct observation, *210*
eye-tracking monitor, *223*

hidden observation, *208*
observation, *205*
observer bias, *211*
magnetic resonance imagery (MRI), *224*
psychogalvanometer, *223*
portable people meter, *217*
pupilometer, *223*

response latency, *213*
scanner-based consumer panel, *220*
television monitoring, *217*
unobtrusive, *208*
visible observation, *208*
voice-pitch analysis, *224*

∷ QUESTIONS FOR REVIEW AND CRITICAL THINKING

1. Yogi Berra, the late baseball player and coach who was famous for mind-boggling sayings, said, "You can observe a lot just by watching." How does this fit in with the definition of scientific observation?

2. What are the major advantages of unobtrusive observation over other types of data collection?

3. What are the major limitations of observational data collection techniques?

4. What is the difference between direct and contrived observation?

5. What is conversation volume? What sources provide this type of data?

6. The chapter showed a photograph of a traffic-monitoring camera. Do you think the use of these cameras to issue speeding tickets is ethical? What types of behavior might cameras like these capture that would help automobile designers produce products that better match our needs as drivers?

7. What is "the right to be forgotten" movement?

8. A multinational fast-food corporation plans to locate a restaurant in La Paz, Bolivia. Secondary data for this city are sketchy and

outdated. How might you determine the best location using observational data collection? How might satellite imagery be useful?

9. What does it mean to use complementary evidence? Describe how observational data taken from users' smartphone browser history could be supplemented with complementary evidence to answer questions about some aspect of consumer behavior.

10. Click-through rates for advertisements placed in websites typically are usually very, very low (1 percent or less). What types of error might exist in using click-through rate data as a measure of an advertisement's success?

11. Outline a research design using observation for each of the following situations:
   a. A bank wishes to collect data on the number of customer services and the frequency of customer use of these services.
   b. A state government wishes to determine the driving public's use of seat belts.
   c. A fast-food franchise wishes to determine how long a customer entering a store has to wait for his or her order.
   d. University food services wonder if a smartphone app with which students can order food ahead of time will cut down on wait times and food waste.
   e. An overnight package delivery service wishes to observe delivery workers beginning at the moment when they stop the truck, continuing through the delivery of the package, and ending when they return to the truck.
   f. A political consulting agency would like to study consumers' reactions as they view national candidates' political commercials airing on cable and broadcast television.

12. What is an artifact to a marketing researcher? How might one use artifacts to study the types of things that fans at major sporting events might be willing to purchase when attending an event? Can artifacts also be used to study ergonomics in the office? If so, how?

13. What is a scanner-based consumer panel?

14. What are the major types of mechanical observation? What types of observations might Twitter potentially have access to that would be of interest to basic marketing researchers?

15. How can a marketing researcher determine if an observational data collection involving hidden cameras is ethical?

16. Comment on the ethics of the following situations:
   a. During the course of telephone calls to investors, a stockbroker records respondents' voices when they are answering sensitive investment questions and then conducts a voicepitch analysis. The respondents do not know that their voices are being recorded.
   b. A researcher plans to invite consumers to be test users in a simulated kitchen located in a shopping mall and then to videotape their reactions to a new microwave dinner from behind a two-way mirror (one that an observer behind the mirror can see through but the person looking into the mirror sees only the reflection).
   c. A marketing researcher arranges to purchase the trash from the headquarters of a major competitor. The purpose is to sift through discarded documents to determine the company's strategic plans.
   d. A political research firm considers technology that activates a consumer's tablet microphone to "observe dinner time conversations" in an effort to produce better political ads.

17. What is a psychogalvanometer?

18. Look back to the chapter on qualitative research and find the definition for ethnography. Why is observation such a big part of this important qualitative research approach?

19. What is an MRI device and how can it be used in research studying advertising effectiveness?

20. What does "gaze" mean, how can gaze data be observed, and how can it be used?

:: RESEARCH ACTIVITIES

1. William Rathje, a researcher at the University of Arizona, Department of Anthropology, has become well known for the "Garbage Project." The project involves observational research. Use the Internet to find information about the garbage project at the University of Arizona. What is the name of the book that describes some of the key findings of the Garbage Project? How do you think it involves observational research?

2. The Internet is filled with webcams. For example, Pebble Beach Golf Club has several webcams (http://www.pebblebeach.com). How could a researcher use webcams like these to collect behavioral data? In your short time viewing these webcams, are there any research questions that you think might be addressed based on behaviors that can be observed in these views? If so, what might one or two be?

3. Review the evidence presented regarding hand washing behaviors (or the lack thereof). Report results based on the way the data were obtained. What accounts for the differences in survey, observational, and mechanical-based studies? Do a little research of your own on hand washing and compare to the results reported here. Can you think of other ethical ways to "observe" this behavior that are not stated in this chapter?

Mazda and Syzygy

Case 8.1

When Mazda Motor Europe set out to improve its website, the company wanted details about how consumers were using the site and whether finding information was easy. Mazda hired a research firm called Syzygy to answer those questions with observational research.[26] Syzygy's methods include the use of an eye-tracking device that uses infrared light rays to record what areas of a computer screen a user is viewing. For instance, the device measured the process computer users followed in order to look for a local dealer or arrange a test drive. Whenever a process seemed confusing or difficult, the company looked for ways to make the website easier to navigate.

To conduct this observational study, Syzygy arranged for sixteen subjects in Germany and the United Kingdom to be observed as they used the website. The subjects in Germany were observed with the eye-tracking equipment. As the equipment measured each subject's gaze, software recorded the location on the screen and graphed the data. Syzygy's results included three-dimensional contour maps highlighting the "peak" areas where most of the computer users' attention was directed.

Questions

1. What could Mazda learn from eye-tracking software that would be difficult to learn from other observational methods?
2. What are the shortcomings of this method?
3. Along with the eye-tracking research, what other research methods could help Mazda assess the usability of its website? Summarize your advice for how Mazda could use complementary methods to obtain a complete understanding of its website usability.

Twitter Metrics

Case 8.2

Media companies rely greatly on observational data in an effort to convince advertisers to purchase advertising on their platform.[27] The media giants of Google, Facebook, Twitter, and so on report their observational research results often to send signals that advertising on that platform pays off. A standard measure is the number of monthly active users. Active users are defined as people who have an account and log-in during the month. That number can be divided into (1) the number of unique active users and (2) the number of total active users; the latter number counting each log-in and the former counting only the number of individuals who logged in at least one time during the month. These data are recorded automatically as users interact with the site. Thus, they are the result of observational data measurement. However, in 2014 Twitter's active user metrics stopped growing and actually showed some periods of declining usage. Growth dropped from near 20 percent in 2012 to nearly 0 at the beginning of 2014. Since 2015, the number of unique active users grew from 300 million to 330 million. As a result, Twitter considered whether these metrics really were the best to demonstrate how much consumers actually interact with Twitter, and as consequence, how good of an advertising platform Twitter actually is.

Twitter management examined observational data about how people ended up at its website (where did they link to Twitter) and how long they spent on the site. Based on the research, Twitter marketing managers argue that the old metrics do not accurately portray Twitter's value as an advertising tool. Many people actually interact with Twitter without logging in. For instance, if a Twitter feed is referenced in a news story, people often click through without logging in. In addition, other media often pick up images of Twitter artifacts (tweets and feeds) and place them in their own stories. Thus, indirect exposure results even if people do not actually visit Twitter. Management decided that one of the metrics used by researchers in the report, monthly unique visitors, as opposed to active users, is a better indicator of Twitter's value as an advertising medium. Through 2017, the monthly unique visitors number averaged about 195,000,000, with more than two times as many visitors as users. Thus, Twitter began to feed this number to potential advertisers in sales efforts.

Questions

1. Consider the pros and cons of observational data. Comment on the validity of the observational data used to form Twitter's metrics.
2. Do you agree that the number of unique visitors is a more accurate measure than the number of unique active users with respect to the value of Twitter as an advertising tool?
3. How might complementary evidence be added to this to improve Twitter's sales pitches to advertisers?
4. How does Twitter traffic compare to that of Facebook, Instagram, and YouTube?

Conducting Marketing Experiments

LEARNING OUTCOMES

After studying this chapter, you should be able to:

1. Know the basic characteristics of research experiments
2. Design an experiment using the basic issues of experimental design
3. Know tools for maximizing the validity of experiments with an emphasis on minimizing demand characteristics
4. Weigh the trade-off between internal and external validity
5. Recognize the appropriate uses of test-marketing
6. Avoid unethical experimental practices

iStock.com/Opidanus

Chapter Vignette:

Warning! This Product Causes . . .

What cigarette do you smoke, Doctor?" This was the question posed in a 1949 ad for Camel cigarettes. Not surprisingly, the result stated in the ad was that more doctors smoked Camels than any other cigarette. The intended inference here is obvious—if doctors choose Camels, then Camels must not cause as many harmful effects as do other cigarettes! Inevitably, debates about smoking then and now involve questions of *cause*.

- Does smoking *cause* cancer?
- Does smoking *cause* death?
- Does advertising *cause* people to smoke?
- Does smoking *cause* popularity?

In U.S. courts, plaintiffs' attorneys, and in some cases state governments, have successfully argued that cigarette companies are responsible for the health problems and even deaths associated with smoking even though the potential negative health consequences have long been known.[1] As a result, tobacco companies have paid huge settlements. However, a U.K.-based tobacco company, Imperial Tobacco, faced with a £500,000 lawsuit filed on behalf of a cancer patient who had smoked Player Cigarettes for 40 years, based a legal defense on the notion that a lack of certainty remains over whether or not cigarettes cause cancer. Defense attorneys claimed that the only evidence for causality is statistical association and that many

other factors are also statistically associated with the occurrence of cancer including a patient's socioeconomic status, childhood experiences (orientation toward healthy behaviors like exercise and diet), ethnicity, personality, and diet.

Further, they argued that advertising could not have caused the plaintiff to begin smoking. The Imperial defense was successful as the court ruled in their favor stating that the causal evidence was insufficient to hold the company responsible.

Nonetheless, many lawsuits in U.S. courts name the brand that a smoker first started smoking even if the person smoked many brands of cigarettes in the years and decades that followed. This tactic is based on the assumption that the branding

Source: www.youtube.com

and advertising efforts initially caused a person to smoke. The research evidence on this point is mixed, but researchers now are turning their attention toward experiments testing hypotheses related to the effectiveness of anti-smoking advertisements—particularly those aimed at adolescents.[2] Typically, these experiments involve multiple groups of individuals, each subjected to a different set of conditions, and then each measured on variables related to their actual smoking behavior or favorableness toward smoking. For instance, the procedures call for assignment to magazines with different types of ads to each of four groups:

- Group 1 views a magazine with several actual ads for cigarettes.
- Group 2 views a magazine with several anti-smoking ads that emphasize negative effects on health.
- Group 3 views a magazine with several anti-smoking ads that emphasize negative effects on one's social life.
- Group 4 views a magazine with no cigarette or anti-smoking ads.

The researchers analyze the differences across groups to examine the effectiveness of the ads. In this case, groups 2 and 3 should be less favorably inclined toward smoking than either group 1 or group 4 if anti-smoking ads are effective. Then, we can compare results from groups 2 and 3 to each other to see whether teens react with more fear at the thought of becoming ill or becoming less popular! The extent to which the researchers can truly establish causal evidence eventually will boil down to control.

Introduction

Most students are familiar with scientific experiments from studying physical sciences like physics and chemistry. The term *experiment* typically conjures up an image of a chemist surrounded by bubbling test tubes and Bunsen burners. Behavioral and physical scientists have used experimentation far longer than have marketing researchers. Nevertheless, both social scientists and physical scientists use experiments for much the same purpose.

Experiments are widely used in causal research designs. Experimental research allows a researcher to control the research situation to evaluate the potential for *causal* relationships among variables. The marketing experimenter manipulates one or more independent variables and holds constant all other possible independent variables while observing effects on dependent variables. A researcher can control variables in an experiment to a degree not possible in a survey.

A simple example would be thinking about how changes in drink prices might cause changes in drink sales. Price would be an independent variable and sales would be a dependent variable. The marketing researcher can experimentally control drink price by setting it at different levels and then study this problem by examining consumer reactions to each level in the form of drink sales.

A market researcher experimentally investigated the influence of price on consumer feelings and efficacy (ability on a task). The experimenter gave each subject in the experiment an energy drink. After consuming the energy drink, subjects took a cognitive test. In half the cases, the researcher told subjects that the energy drink cost $2. In the other half of the cases, the researcher told subjects that the energy drink cost $4. Each subject went through exactly the same process with the exception of the stated price of the energy drink. Does price cause performance? The results showed that the subjects in the $4 condition outperform those in the $2 condition. That is, they did better on the cognitive test. The explanation is that they felt more confident and that carried over into better performance.

The Characteristics of Experiments

Examples are probably the best way to illustrate marketing experiments. Here, we illustrate the characteristics of experiments by describing a study aimed at testing hypotheses inferring the potential causal effects of color. We will refer back to this example throughout this chapter and begin by describing the key characteristics of experiments in this section of the chapter.

Subjects

Let's take a look at an experiment investigating how color and lights might influence shoppers. This particular research is highly relevant for those involved in retail management and design. The key decisions facing managers is how to alter color and lighting to produce favorable consumer reactions. A corresponding research question is, "What is the effect of color and lighting on shopper patronage (patronage means how much someone would shop and buy in a store)?"[3]

Over two hundred female consumers participated in the experiment. Researchers refer to participants in experimental research as **subjects** rather than respondents—the term typically used for participants in survey research. This is because the researcher subjects research participants to some experimental treatment. In addressing the color and lighting research question, the experimental task involved asking subjects to provide responses to a "new fashion store" concept. The hypothetical new store would sell women's clothing and accessories to the fashion-minded professional woman.

subjects

The sampling units for an experiment, usually human participants in research who are subjected to some experimental manipulation.

Experimental Conditions

Perhaps the characteristic that most differentiates experimental research from survey research is the manner in which independent variables are created rather than simply measured. The illustration experiment involves two relevant independent variables. Researchers created fictitious store environments for the experiment. Four different hypothetical store environments were created corresponding to different combinations of the independent variable values. Thus, the only thing differing among the four is the particular combination of the predominant store color and the type of lighting.

The experimenter created the color independent variable by variously designing the new store as either predominantly blue or predominantly orange. Similarly, the experimenter created the lighting independent variable by designing the hypothetical store as either having bright or soft lights. Exhibit 9.1 illustrates the four different experimental conditions created by combining the two possible values for each independent variable. An **experimental condition** refers to one of the possible levels of an experimental variable manipulation.

The procedures assigned subjects randomly to one of these four conditions. As a result, each subject group experienced a store with one of the four color and lighting combinations as shown in the Exhibit. Thus, all participants within a group received the same description. Subjects in different groups received different descriptions. By analyzing differences among the groups, the researcher can see what effects occur due to the two experimentally controlled independent variables.

Independent variables that are not experimental conditions can also be included as a means of statistical control in the analysis of experiments. Researchers refer to these as either blocking variables or covariates. **Blocking variables** are categorical variables like a subject's gender or ethnicity.

experimental condition

One of the possible levels of an experimental variable manipulation.

blocking variables

Categorical variables included in the statistical analysis of experimental data as a way of statistically controlling or accounting for variance due to that variable.

● ● ● ● ● ● ●

Background color can be used as an experimental variable in this way. Which shirt do you prefer?

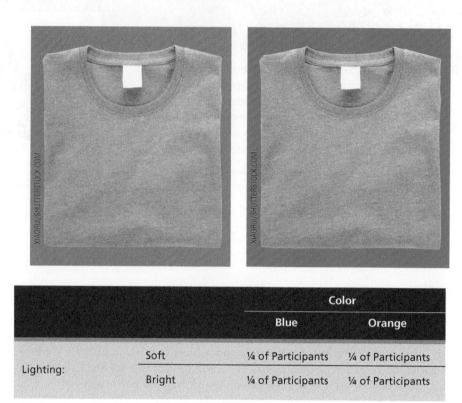

EXHIBIT **9.1**

Experimental Conditions in Color and Lighting Experiment

		Color	
		Blue	**Orange**
Lighting:	Soft	¼ of Participants	¼ of Participants
	Bright	¼ of Participants	¼ of Participants

For example, researchers may group results based on whether respondents are male or female. On the other hand, we refer to a continuous variable expected to show a statistical relationship with a dependent variables as a **covariate**. Once statistical analysis begins, researchers treat blocking variables in a similar way as experimental variables and covariates like a regression variable. We'll cover the statistical analysis of experiments later in the text.

covariate

A continuous variable included in the statistical analysis as a way of statistically controlling for variance due to that variable.

Effects

The key outcome, or dependent variable, in this example is a subject's perception of how much he or she would patronize the store. In this case, a rating scale asking how much each participant thought he/she would actually visit and buy things at the hypothetical store. The possible scores ranged from 0 (would not shop) to 300 (definitely would shop). A higher score means higher patronage. Effects are the characteristics of experiments that allow hypotheses to be tested. We can classify effects in several ways. Here, we will focus on the difference between main effects and interaction effects.

Main Effects

main effect

The experimental difference in dependent variable means between the different levels of any single experimental variable.

A **main effect** refers to the experimental difference in means between the different levels of any single experimental variable. In this case, there are two potential main effects, one for color and one for lighting.

Exhibit 9.2 shows the average patronage score for each experimental condition. The results show that among experimental subjects who rated a blue store, an average patronage score of 153.8 was reported, which is considerably higher than the average of 131.8 reported by subjects who rated an orange store. The lighting experimental variable, however, doesn't seem to make as much difference. Subjects in the soft lighting condition reported an average of 144.7 and subjects in the bright lighting condition reported only a slightly lower average of 140.4.

Thus, the conclusion at this point seems to be that changing a store's color can change consumer patronage. A blue store is better than an orange store! On the other hand, lighting doesn't seem to make much difference. Or does it?

		Color		
		Blue	Orange	
Lighting:	Soft	148.5	140.1	144.7
	Bright	159.1	122.6	140.4
		153.8	131.8	

EXHIBIT **9.2**
Consumer Average Patronage Scores in Each Condition

Interactions

An **interaction effect** is a change in a dependent variable due to a specific combination of independent variables. In this case, it's possible that the combination of color and lighting creates effects that are not clearly represented in the two main effects.

interaction effect

Differences in a dependent variable due to a specific combination of independent variables.

Researchers often depict experimental results with a line graph as shown in Exhibit 9.3. The lines drawn at different heights corresponding to the means for blue and orange depict a color main effect. If the lines were at the same height, no main effect due to color exists. However, the blue line is higher than the orange line. The midpoints of the lines correspond to the means of 153.8 and 131.8 for the blue and orange conditions, respectively. A lighting main effect is less obvious because the difference between the midpoint between the two soft points (144.7) is not too different than the corresponding height of the midpoint between the two bright points (140.4). When the lines have very different slopes, an interaction is likely present. In this case, the combination of lights and color is presenting an interaction leading to the following interpretation.

The best possible reaction occurs when the store has a blue color with bright lights and the worst combination occurs when the store is orange with bright lights. In contrast, the means are essentially the same for either color when the lights are soft. So, lights may indeed matter. When the lights are soft, there is little difference in patronage between a blue and orange store. But, when the lights are bright, there is quite a difference between blue and orange.

One can contrast the pattern of results depicted in Exhibit 9.3 with those from another experiment shown in Exhibit 9.4 on the next page. Here, researchers conducted an experiment to see how different promotions offered by a nightclub might affect the amount of drinks a college student would have during the promotion.[4] The researchers were also interested in potential differences between men and women—a blocking variable. Notice that the line for men is higher than the line for women, suggesting a main effect of sex; men have more drinks than women. Also, the mean number of drinks is higher for the 50-cent drink promotion than for either of the other two. But, in contrast to our illustration given, the lines are parallel to each other, suggesting that no interaction effect has occurred. In other words, men and women respond to the promotions in the same way.

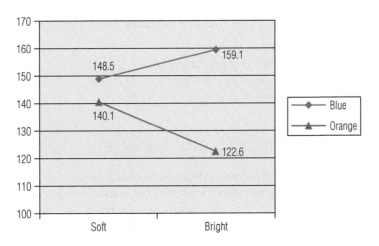

EXHIBIT **9.3**
Experimental Graph Showing Results within Each Condition

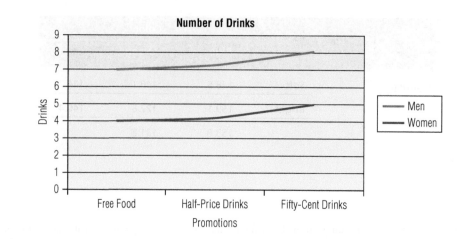

Summary of Experimental Characteristics

Experiments differ from ordinary survey research. The differences can be understood by identifying special characteristics of experiments. These characteristics include the following:

- Experiments use subjects instead of respondents. The experimental implementation exposes subjects to some treatment by manipulating an experimental variable. Survey respondents do not react to any experimental treatment or manipulation.
- Experimental variables become the key independent variables. The researcher creates the experimental variables rather than simply measuring them. Measured independent variables are called blocking variables or covariates in experiments.
- Experimental effects exist to the extent that treatment groups exhibit differences between means. Main effects are differences in the means based on a single experimental variable (treatment). Interaction effects are differences in means based on combinations of two or more variables.

To the Point

"Observation is a passive science, experimentation is an active science."

— CLUAD BERNARD

Basic Issues in Experimental Design

Experimental design is a major research topic and entire courses and books are devoted only to designing experiments. Here, we provide an introduction into experimental design. The terminology introduced in describing experimental characteristics will be helpful in learning how to implement a simple experimental design. Fortunately, most experimental designs in marketing are relatively simple and this introduction should provide a sufficient basis for implementing such designs.

Experimental designs involve no less than four important design elements:

1. Manipulation of the independent variable.
2. Selection and measurement of the dependent variable.
3. Selection and assignment of experimental subjects.
4. Control over extraneous variables.

Manipulation of the Independent Variable

Recall from Chapter 3, the thing that makes independent variables special in experimentation is that the researcher can actually create its values. This is how the researcher manipulates, and therefore controls, independent variables. In our color experiment, the researcher manipulated the values of the color independent variable by assigning it a value of either blue or orange. Experimental

Marketing research sometimes involves experiments that manipulate elements of the physical environments, price, promotion, or elements in the media such as newsfeeds.

independent variables represent hypothesized causal influences. Therefore, experiments are very appropriate in causal designs.

An **experimental treatment** is the term referring to the way an experimental variable is manipulated. For example, the illustration manipulates the store color experimental treatment by assigning subjects randomly to evaluate either a blue or orange store environment. Thus, there were two levels (or values) of the color variable. A medical researcher may manipulate an experimental variable by treating some subjects with one drug and the other subjects with a separate drug. Experimental variables often involve treatments with more than two levels. For instance, prices of $99, $149, and $219 might represent treatments in a pricing experiment examining how price causes sales for a new Samsung tablet. Treatments function experimentally as independent or predictor variables through manipulations.

> **experimental treatment**
> The term referring to the way an experimental variable is manipulated.

Experimental variables like these cannot only be described as independent variables, but they also can be described as a *categorical variable* because they take on a value to represent some classifiable or qualitative aspect. Color, for example, is either orange or blue. Advertising copy style is another example of a categorical or classificatory variable that a researcher could manipulate in an experiment. In other situations, an independent variable may truly exist as a *continuous variable*. When this is the case, the researcher must select appropriate levels of that variable as experimental treatments. For example, lighting can vary from dark to any level of brightness. Price can take on any value but the researcher will only include levels representing relevant distinctions in price in an experiment. Before conducting the experiment, the researcher decides on levels that would be relevant to study. The levels should be noticeably different and realistic.

Experimental and Control Groups

In perhaps the simplest experiment, the researcher manipulates an independent variable over two treatment levels resulting in two groups, an experimental group and a control group. An **experimental group** is one in which an experimental treatment is administered. A **control group** is one in which no experimental treatment is administered. For example, consider an experiment studying how advertising affects sales. In the experimental group, the advertising budget may be set at $200,000 more than the normal level. In the control condition, advertising remains unchanged at the normal level. All other conditions are controlled and thus are the same across the groups. The control group serves as a baseline for comparison. At the end of the experiment, the researcher compares sales (the dependent variable) in the two treatment groups to determine whether the level of advertising (the independent variable) had any effect. Note that this simple experiment can only produce a main effect. Multiple independent variables are necessary for an interaction to occur.

> **experimental group**
> A group of subjects to whom an experimental treatment is administered.
>
> **control group**
> A group of subjects to whom no experimental treatment is administered which serves as a baseline for comparison.

cell

Refers to a specific treatment combination associated with an experimental group.

Several Experimental Treatment Levels

The advertising/sales experiment with one experimental and one control group may not tell the advertiser everything he or she wishes to know. Suppose the advertiser wanted to know the effects of Facebook ad spending, and thus the frequency of ad placements, on click-through rates and on conversion volume. Currently, the advertiser has no Facebook ads. Thus, four levels of weekly spending might be considered: control ($0), low ($1,000), moderate ($5,000), and high ($15,000). The experiment might reveal more precise results than a simple two-level, control and experimental group experiment. However, such a design only produces a main effect of ad spending level. What happens though if a research question involves precise media source as well? Perhaps the question of Facebook versus Twitter arises as well. That brings us to the next section.

More Than One Independent Variable

An experiment can also be made more complicated by including the effect of another experimental variable. Going back to our extended example involving retail atmosphere would typify a still relatively simple two-variable experiment. Since there are two variables, each with two different levels, the experimental design creates four experimental groups. Often, the term **cell** refers to a treatment combination within an experiment. The formula described below shows how to compute the number of cells involved in any experiment:

$$K = (T_1)(T_2)..(T_m)$$

where K = the number of cells, T_1 = the number of treatment levels for experimental group number one, T_2 = the number of treatment levels for experimental group number two, and so forth through the mth experimental group (T_m). In the illustration experiment, there are two experimental variables each with two levels so the computation is quite simple:

$$K = 2 \text{ (color levels)} \times 2 \text{ (lighting levels)} = 4 \text{ } cells$$

Including multiple variables allows a comparison of experimental treatments on the dependent variable. Since there are multiple experimental variables, this design involves both main effects and interactions. Likewise, in the advertising example from the previous section, the experimenter may end up with:

$$K = 2 \text{ (media choices: Facebook and Twitter)} \times 3$$
$$\text{(ad spending levels: low, moderate, high)} = 6 \text{ cells}$$

plus a control condition for a total 7 cells.

Selection and Measurement of the Dependent Variable

Selecting dependent variables is crucial in experimental design. Unless the dependent variables are relevant and truly represent an outcome of interest, the experiment will not be useful. Sometimes, the logical dependent variable is fairly obvious. If researchers introduce a new cinnamon, pink grapefruit tea mix in a test-market, sales volume is most likely to be a key dependent variable. However, if researchers are experimenting with different forms of advertising copy appeals, defining the dependent variable may be more difficult. For example, measures of advertising awareness, recall, changes in brand preference, or sales might be possible dependent variables. In the retail atmosphere example, retail patronage was the key dependent variable. However, other potential dependent variables might include perceived product quality, excitement, or price perceptions.

Choosing the right dependent variable is part of the problem definition process. Like the problem definition process in general, researchers sometimes rush through this and don't devote the careful attention to the selection that is needed. The experimenter's choice of a dependent variable determines what type of answer a researcher can provide to assist managers in decision making.

The introduction of a product known as Crystal Pepsi, a clear cola, illustrates the need to think beyond consumers' initial reactions. When PepsiCo introduced Crystal Pepsi the initial trial rate was high, but only a small percentage of customers made repeat purchases. The brand never achieved high repeat sales within a sufficiently large market segment. Brand awareness, trial purchase, and repeat purchase are all possible dependent variables in an experiment. The dependent variable therefore should

Goldfishing or Bluefishing?

Food marketers are often claiming that their brand tastes better than the competitors. When a claim like this is made, it has to be supported somehow or else the company making the claim is liable and risks being sued for making a false or unsubstantiated claim. Thus, research is often needed to produce evidence supporting such claims. Marketers need to be very careful, however, that this type of research is conducted in a rigorous fashion.

Sea Snapper brand gourmet frozen fish products claimed in advertising that their fish sticks are preferred more than two to one over the most popular brand, Captain John's.[5] The advertisements all included a definitive statement indicating that research existed that substantiated this claim. Captain John's sued Sea Snapper over the claim and based the suit on the fact that the research was faulty. Sea Snapper managers conducted taste tests involving four hundred consumers who indicated that they regularly ate frozen food products. Two hundred tasted Sea Snapper premium fish sticks and the other two hundred tasted Captain John's premium fish sticks. Results showed a main effect with an average preference score for Sea Snapper of 78.2 compared to 39.0 for Captain

John's. Case closed? Not hardly. Captain John's attorney hired a marketing research firm to assist in the lawsuit.

The research firm was unable to duplicate the result. After intense questioning of subjects involved in the original research, it turned out that Sea Snapper fish sticks were always presented to consumers on a blue plate while Captain John's were always presented to consumers on a goldfish-colored (an orangish gold) plate. Therefore, the Sea Snapper results could be attributable to a variable other than taste and Captain John's came out as the winner of this legal action—with the help of marketing research.

Jo van den Berg/Getty Images

© George Doyle & Ciaran Griffin

be considered carefully and more than one can be included in an experiment. Thorough problem definition will help the researcher select the most important dependent variable(s).

Selection and Assignment of Test Units

Test units are the subjects or entities whose responses to the experimental treatment are measured. Individual consumers, employees, organizational units, sales territories, market segments, brands, stores, websites, or other entities may be the test units. People are the most common test units in most consumer behavior experiments. In our retail atmospherics example, individual consumers are the test units. In the book, we use the term subject to refer to test units given that individuals are most commonly observed in marketing research.

test units

The subjects or other entities whose responses to the experimental treatment are measured or observed.

Sample Selection and Random Sampling Errors

As in other forms of marketing research, random sampling errors and sample selection errors may occur in experimentation. For example, experiments sometimes go awry based on the geographic area chosen for a particular investigation. A case in point is an experiment testing a new lubricant for outboard boat motors by Dow Chemical Company. The research team tested the lubricant in Florida. They thought the hot, muggy climate would provide the most demanding test. In Florida the lubricant was a success. However, the story was quite different when consumers in Michigan bought and used the product. Although the lubricant sold well and worked well during the summer, the following spring Dow discovered the oil had congealed, allowing the outboard engines, idle all winter, to rust. The rusting problem never came to light in Florida, where the engines were in year-round use. Thus, sample selection error occurs because of flaws in procedures used to assign experimental test units. Testing units in Florida created error because the goal was understanding how the product worked in places other than Florida—like Michigan.

● ● ● ● ● ● ●

Although experiments are often administered in groups, if all groups are not the same, then systematic error is introduced.

systematic or nonsampling error

Occurs if the sampling units in an experimental cell are somehow different than the units in another cell, and this difference affects the dependent variable.

Systematic or nonsampling error may occur if the sampling units in an experimental cell are somehow different than the units in another cell, and this difference affects the dependent variable. For example, suppose some professors are interested in testing the effect of providing snacks during exams on students' scores. The experimental variable is snacks, manipulated over three levels: (1) fruit, (2) cookies, and (3) chocolate. The test units in this case are individual students.

When the professors conduct the experiment, for convenience, they decide to give all of the 8 a.m. classes chocolate for a snack, all of the 1 p.m. classes get fruit, and all of the 7 p.m. classes get cookies. While this type of procedure is often followed, if our tastes and digestive systems react differently to different foods at different times of the day, systematic error is introduced into the experiment. Furthermore, because the night classes contain students who are older on average, the professors may reach the conclusion that students perform better when they eat cookies, when it may really be due to the fact that students who are older perform better no matter what they are fed.

Randomization

randomization

The random assignment of subject and treatments to groups; it is one device for equally distributing the effects of extraneous variables to all conditions.

Randomization—the random assignment of subject and treatments to groups—is one device for equally distributing the effects of extraneous variables to all conditions. Randomizing assignments does not eliminate nuisance variables but controls for them because they likely exist to the same degree in every experimental cell. All cells should yield similar average scores on the dependent variables if it were not for the experimental treatments administered in a particular cell. In other words, the researcher would like to set up a situation where everything in every cell is the same except for the experimental treatment. Random assignment of subjects allows the researcher to make this assumption, thereby reducing the chance of systematic error. With proper randomization, the characteristics of each experimental group tend to be the same as the population characteristics.

Matching

Matching subjects on the basis of pertinent background information is another technique for controlling systematic error. Matching involves assigning subjects in a way that a particular characteristic is the same in each group. If a subject's sex is expected to influence dependent variable responses, as it may in a taste test, then the researcher may make sure that there are equal numbers of men and women in each experimental cell. In general, if a researcher believes that certain extraneous variables may affect the dependent variable, he or she can make sure that the subjects in each group are the same on these characteristics.

For example, in a taste test experiment for a dog food, it might be important to match the dogs in various experimental groups on the basis of age or breed. That way, the same number of Basset Hounds and Dobermans will test formulas A, B, and C. Although matching can be a useful approach, the researcher can never be sure that sampling units are matched on all characteristics. Here, for example, even though breeds can be matched, it is difficult to know if all dogs live in the same type of environment (indoors, outdoors, spacious, cramped, with table scraps or without, etc.).

Repeated Measures

Experiments that expose an individual subject to more than one level of an experimental treatment involve a **repeated measures** design. Although this approach has advantages, including being more economical since the same subject provides data on multiple conditions, the design has drawbacks that limit its usefulness. We will discuss these in more detail later.

repeated measures

Experiments in which an individual subject is exposed to more than one level of an experimental treatment.

Extraneous Variables

The fourth decision about the basic elements of an experiment concerns control over variables that may systematically influence the dependent variable(s). Earlier we classified total survey error into two basic categories: random sampling error and systematic error. The same dichotomy applies to all research designs, but the terms *random (sampling) error* and *systematic error* are used frequently when discussing experiments.

Experimental Confounds

We already discussed how systematic error can occur when extraneous variables, or the conditions of administering the experiment, influence the dependent variables. When this occurs, the results will be confounded because the design fails to control for or eliminate all extraneous variables. A **confound** in an experiment means that an alternative explanation exists beyond the experimental variables for any observed differences in the dependent variable. Once a potential confound is identified, the validity of the experiment is severely questioned.

confound

An experimental confound means that there is an alternative explanation beyond the experimental variables for any observed differences in the dependent variable.

Recall from the Research Snapshot on page 250 that the experimental procedures involved a taste test. The Research Snapshot illustrates how a confound can ruin an experiment. Sea Snapper fish sticks were always presented on a blue plate and Captain John's fish sticks were always presented on a goldfish-colored plate. The plate's color is confounding the explanation that the difference in brands is responsible for the difference in liking. Is the difference in liking due to the color or the product quality?

In a simple experimental group—control group experiment aimed at employee task efficiency, if subjects in the experimental group are always administered a treatment (an energy drink) in the morning and then have their efficiency measured also in the morning, and the control group always has their efficiency measured in the afternoon, a constant error has been introduced. In other words, the results will show a difference not only due to the treatment, but also due to the added efficiency that naturally occurs in the morning. In such a situation, time of day represents a confound. On the other hand, other types of error are random and not constant. For example, the natural fluctuations in efficiency that occur from day to day. Random errors are less of a problem for experiments than are constant errors because they do not cause systematic changes in outcomes.

Identifying Extraneous Variables

Most students of marketing realize that the marketing mix variables—price, product, promotion, and distribution—interact with uncontrollable forces in the market, such as competitors' activities and consumer trends. Thus, marketing experiments are subject to the effect of extraneous variables. Because extraneous variables can produce confounded results, researchers must make every attempt to identify them before the experiment.

The chapter vignette illustrates how important isolating causes can be in developing theoretical explanations. Does cigarette advertising cause young people to smoke? One of the primary reasons for the inconclusiveness of this debate is the failure for most of the research to control for extraneous variables.[6] For instance, consider a study in which two groups of U.S. high school students are studied over the course of a year. One is exposed to a greater percentage of foreign video media in which American cigarettes are more often shown in a flattering and glamorous light. In fact, the video programming includes cigarette commercials. The other group is a control group in which their exposure to media is not controlled. Subjects are left free to view whatever they may choose. At the end of the year, the experimental group reports a greater frequency and incidence of cigarette smoking. Did the increased media exposure involving cigarettes cause smoking behavior?

Although the result seems plausible at first, the careful researcher may ask the following questions:

■ Was the demographic makeup of the two groups the same? While it is clear that the ages of the two groups are likely the same, different ethnic groups have different smoking rates. Approximately 5 percent of high school students report smoking (smoking cigarettes every day), but the rate is higher among some demographic groups.[7] White teens, for instance, had a higher smoking rate in 2015 than did Hispanic teens. Therefore, if one group contained disproportionately more white teens than Hispanic teens, we might expect the study to report different smoking rates than if the sample were proportionately representative of the white to Hispanic population.

■ How did the control group fill the time consumed by the experimental group in being exposed to the experimental treatment? Could it be that it somehow dissuaded them from smoking? Perhaps they were exposed to media with more anti-smoking messages?

■ Were the two groups of the same general achievement profiles? Those who are high in the need for achievement may be less prone to smoke than are other students.

■ Although it is a difficult task to list all possible extraneous factors, some that even sound unusual can sometimes have an effect. For example, did the students have equally dispersed birthdays? Researchers have even shown that smoking rates correspond to one's birthday, meaning that different astrological groups have different smoking rates.[8]

Because an experimenter does not want extraneous variables to affect the results, he or she must control or eliminate such variables. It is always better to spend time thinking about how to control for possible extraneous variables before the experiment since often there is nothing that can be done to salvage results after a confounding effect is identified.

Demand Characteristics and Experimental Validity

demand characteristic

Experimental design element or procedure that unintentionally provides subjects with hints about the research hypothesis.

Most experiments involve some directed task performed by experimental subjects. Tasks like these are typically linked to the experimental hypotheses. The term **demand characteristic** refers to an experimental design element that unintentionally provides subjects with hints about the research hypothesis. Researchers cannot reveal the research hypotheses to subjects before the experiment or else they can create a confounding effect. Think about the retail atmospherics experiment. If the subjects were told before they participated that they were going to be involved in an experiment to see if they liked stores that were predominantly orange or predominantly blue, the researcher would never be sure if their responses to the dependent variable were really due to the differences in the experimental stimuli or due to the fact that the subjects were trying to provide a "correct" response, knowing that the experiment is about color. Once subjects believe they know the hypotheses, there is little hope that they will respond naturally.

demand effect

Occurs when demand characteristics actually affect the dependent variable.

So, knowledge of the experimental hypothesis creates a confound. This particular type of confound is known as a **demand effect**. Demand characteristics make demand effects very likely.

Experimenter Bias and Demand Effects

Demand characteristics are aspects of an experiment that *demand* (encourage) that the subjects respond in a particular way. Hence, they are a source of systematic error. If participants recognize the experimenter's expectation or demand, they are likely to act in a manner consistent with the experimental treatment. Even slight nonverbal cues may influence their reactions.

Radu Razvan/Shutterstock.com

● ● ● ● ● ● ●
The experimenter unintentionally can create a demand effect by smiling, nodding, or frowning at the wrong time.

The person administering experimental procedures often creates prominent demand characteristics. If an experimenter's presence, actions, or comments influence the subjects' behavior or sway the subjects to slant their answers to cooperate with the experimenter, the experiment has introduced *experimenter bias*. When subjects slant their answers to cooperate with the experimenter, they are exhibiting behaviors that might not represent their behavior in the marketplace. For example, if subjects in an advertising experiment understand that the experimenter is interested in whether they changed their attitudes in accord with a given advertisement, they may answer in the desired direction. When researchers pay subjects to participate in experiments, the subjects become particularly eager to please and are more likely to try to respond as they believe the researcher wants them to respond rather than answering questions in a natural way. Acting in a manner oriented toward pleasing the researcher reflects a demand effect rather than a true experimental treatment effect.

Reducing Demand Characteristics

Although it is practically impossible to eliminate demand characteristics completely from experiments, researchers can take several steps aimed at reducing them. Many of these steps make it difficult for subjects to know what the researcher is trying to find out. Some or all of these may be appropriate in a given experiment:

1. Use an experimental disguise.
2. Use a "blind" experimental administrator.
3. Administer only one experimental condition combination to each subject.
4. Avoid using subjects paid on task performance.
5. Avoid using professional subjects.

Experimental Disguise

The experimental administrator can tell subjects that the purpose of the experiment is somewhat different from the actual purpose. Most often, administrators simply tell less than the complete "truth" about what is going to happen. For instance, in the retail atmosphere study, the instructions informed subjects that the study sought their reaction to a new retail store concept. This really is true, but the instructions included nothing about color, lighting, or any other potential experimental effect.

In other cases, more deceit may be needed. Psychologists studying how much pain one person may be willing to inflict on another might use a ruse telling the subject that they are actually interested in the effect of pain on human performance. The researcher tells the actual subject to administer a series of questions to another person (who is actually a research assistant) and to provide the person with an increasingly strong electric shock each time an incorrect answer is given. In reality, the real dependent variable has something to do with how long the actual subject will continue to administer shocks before stopping.

placebo

A false experimental treatment disguising the fact that no real treatment is administered.

placebo effect

The effect in a dependent variable associated with the psychological impact that goes along with knowledge of some treatment being administered.

A **placebo** is an experimental deception involving a false treatment. A **placebo effect** refers to the corresponding effect in a dependent variable that is due to the psychological impact that goes along with knowledge that a treatment has been administered. A placebo is particularly important when the experimental variable involves physical consumption of some product. The placebo should not be different in any manner that is actually noticeable by the research subject. If someone is told that a special food additive will suppress appetite, and they are supposed to sprinkle it on their dinner before eating as part of an experiment, another group should receive a placebo that looks exactly like the actual food additive but actually is some type of inert compound. Both groups are likely to show some difference in consumption compared to someone undergoing no effect. The difference in the actual experimental group and the placebo group would represent the true effect of the additive.

Placebo effects exist in marketing research. For example, when subjects are told that an energy drink is sold at a discount price, they believe it is significantly less effective than when it is sold at the regular, non-discounted price.[9] Later, we will return to the ethical issues involved in experimental deception.

Isolate Experimental Subjects

Researchers should minimize the extent to which subjects are able to talk about the experimental procedures with each other. Although it may be unintentional, discussion among subjects may lead them to guess the experimental hypotheses. For instance, it could be that different subjects receive different treatments. The experimental integrity will be higher when each only knows enough to participate him/herself and the procedures prevent one subject from being concerned about other subjects.

Unfortunately, with social networking, experiments that take an extended time to complete allow subjects who ordinarily would have no way of contacting each other to communicate online. Pharmaceutical researchers worry that this social chatter online can damage the validity of their drug experiments.[10] For instance, social chatter in one experiment spread tips to subjects about when an inoculation would contain the placebo instead of the intended effect. If the subject knows the treatment is a placebo, it is no longer a placebo! Given the difficulty in completely isolating people in such a case, the researchers may seek pledges of confidentiality from the subjects promising not to discuss the experiment online.

Use a "Blind" Experimental Administrator

Many experiments today are administered automatically. However, when the experiment requires member of the research team to administer the procedure, it's best if that team member is blind. Here, we don't mean blind as in not being able to see. Rather, we mean blind in that the research assistant does not know the experimental hypotheses. Ignorance can be bliss in this case as the big advantage is that if the administrator does not know what exactly is being studied, he/she will not likely give off clues that result in demand effects. Like the subjects, administrators often do their job best when they know only enough to guide subjects through the task. A blind experimenter gives off few clues that would lead a subject to acquiesce to the desires of the researchers.

Administer Only One Experimental Condition Per Subject

When subjects observe more than one experimental treatment condition, they are much more likely to guess the experimental hypothesis. Despite the cost advantages, most researchers should avoid administering multiple treatments to an individual subject. In the retail atmospherics example, if subjects responded first to a blue retail store concept, and then saw the same store that was exactly the same except the walls had become orange, then they are very likely to know that the researcher is interested in color.

Paying for Performance

Researchers often pay an incentive for respondents' cooperation. However, when the incentive depends on the researcher approving the cooperation of individual respondents, and the subjects are aware of this condition, acquiescence bias creeps in as the subjects become increasingly interested in pleasing the researcher as the incentive grows larger. In other words, the subjects believe there is a way they are supposed to respond and think about that instead of or in addition to responding to the experimental stimuli. A pay for performance incentive creates a demand characteristic as subjects are more attentive to the reason for the experiment than they may be otherwise.

Avoid Professional Subjects

Although it may sound counterintuitive, experienced subjects can create problems for experimental validity. The wide availability of crowd-sourced pools for online surveys greatly increases concerns about **experience effects**. Experience effects occur when subjects participate in so many experiments that they are very susceptible to demand characteristics. In other words, they display a relatively high likelihood of being able to guess what the researchers are trying to do in their experiment. Thus, they also become very prone to acquiescence bias and subsequent demand effects. Amazon's Mechanical Turk typifies a way of crowd-sourcing subjects for experiments. Many of the "internet workers" spend hours each day responding to human interaction task requests for a small payment each. Thus, they may participate in hundreds of online experiments every month.[11] While researchers previously expressed concern that undergraduate psychology students were subject to experience effects as they seek extra credit for participating in faculty experiments, no student could possibly do even a fraction of the experiments that these online professional survey takers can do. Opt-in crowd sourced participants end up not being an ideal source to find experimental subjects.

Establishing Control

The major difference between experimental research and descriptive research is an experimenter's ability to control variables by either holding conditions constant or manipulating the experimental variable. If the color of beer causes preference, a brewery experimenting with a new clear beer must determine the possible extraneous variables other than color that may affect an experiment's results and attempt to eliminate or control those variables. Marketing theory tells us that brand image and packaging design are important factors in beer drinkers' reactions. Therefore, the researcher may wish to control the influence of these variables. He or she may eliminate these two extraneous variables by packaging the test beers in plain brown packages without any brand identification.

When extraneous variables cannot be eliminated, experimenters may strive for **constancy of conditions**. This means that subjects in all experimental groups participate in identical conditions except for the differing experimental treatments. The principle of matching discussed earlier helps make sure that constancy is achieved.

A digital marketing experiment picked up on the theme of color from environmental research and sought to investigate the impact of font color on consumer responsiveness. The experimenter designed four advertisements, each with the headline in a different font color (black, blue, red, green). One problem occurred because subjects viewed the stimuli on their own devices. Thus, some saw the experiment on a wide-screen display from a computer, some on notebooks, some tablets and still others on their cell phone. If for example, more subjects viewed the blue condition on a cell phone than in other conditions, the effects may not be due to color but due to type of device. The experiment would have more internal validity by holding the device type constant.

constancy of conditions

Means that subjects in all experimental groups are exposed to identical conditions except for the differing experimental treatments.

counterbalancing

Attempts to eliminate the confounding effects of order or other uncontrolled sources of variation by introducing randomization of assignment in some way.

If an experimental method requires that the same subjects be exposed to two or more experimental treatments, an error may occur due to the *order of presentation*. **Counterbalancing** attempts to eliminate the confounding effects of order of presentation, or other uncontrolled sources of variation, by randomizing assignment in some way. In a within-subjects experiment involving the effect of font color as described in the previous paragraph, counterbalancing can be implemented by randomly assigning one fourth of the subjects to treatment A first, one fourth to treatment B first, one fourth to treatment C first, and finally one fourth to treatment D first. Likewise, the other levels are counterbalanced so that the order of presentation is rotated among subjects.

Basic versus Factorial Experimental Designs

In *basic experimental designs* a single independent variable is manipulated to observe its effect on a single dependent variable. However, we know multiple factors influence complex marketing dependent variables such as recommendations, sales, product usage, and preference. The simultaneous change in independent variables such as price and advertising may have a greater influence on sales than if either variable is changed alone. *Factorial experimental design*s are more sophisticated than basic experimental designs and allow for an investigation of the interaction of two or more independent variables.

Laboratory Experiments

A marketing experiment can be conducted in a natural setting (a field experiment) or in an artificial or laboratory setting. In social sciences, the actual laboratory may be a behavioral lab, which is somewhat like a focus group facility. However, the experimental procedures may turn a classroom or an area in a shopping center into an experimental lab.

laboratory experiment

The researcher has more complete control over the research setting and extraneous variables.

In a **laboratory experiment** the researcher maximizes control over the research setting and extraneous variables. For example, some advertising researchers recruit subjects and bring them to the agency's office or perhaps a mobile unit designed for research purposes. Researchers then expose subjects to a television commercial within the context of a program that includes competitors' ads among the commercials shown. While viewing the ads, a lie detector type device measures the subjects' physiological arousal. The researcher measures trial purchase intentions for the focal product as well. In a short time span, the marketer is able to collect information on emotional responses and consumer decision making. Our retail atmospheric experiment also illustrates a laboratory experiment.

tachistoscope

Device that controls the amount of time a subject is exposed to a visual image.

Other laboratory experiments may be more controlled or artificial. For example, a **tachistoscope** allows a researcher to experiment with the visual impact of advertising, packaging, and so on by controlling the amount of time a subject sees a visual image. Each stimulus (for example, package design) is projected from a slide to the tachistoscope at varying exposure lengths (1/10 of a second, 2/10, 3/10, etc.). The tachistoscope simulates the split-second duration of a customer's attention to a package in a mass display.

Field Experiments

field experiments

Research projects involving experimental manipulations that are implemented in a natural environment.

Field experiments are research projects involving experimental manipulations implemented in a natural environment. They can be useful in fine-tuning marketing strategies and determining sales forecasts for different marketing mix designs.

Facebook routinely implements field experiments by subjecting subscribers to various manipulations. The experiments attracted considerable attention given that Facebook conducts these tests without the knowledge of the subjects.[12] One experiment involved almost 700,000 users who became subjects as Facebook manipulated newsfeeds to provide the users with relatively high amounts of either positive or negative news. The research questions that were being examined dealt with whether or not the nature of the news (positive or negative) influences social networking behavior. Thus, Facebook measured how many positive or negative posts followed exposure to this experimental treatment. In fact, they discovered that they could manipulate users as those with more bad news posted more critical posts and those exposed to good news posted more positive posts. The results have implications for decisions related to how they sell advertising.

Many companied perform food taste and nutrition tests in labs where people get paid to taste! Is a tasting lab the best setting for predicting the success of a food product?

Experiments vary in their degree of artificiality and control. Exhibit 9.5 shows that as experiments increase in naturalism, they begin to approach a pure field experiment. As they become more artificial, they approach a pure laboratory experiment. In contrast to applied market research, academic marketing research traditionally relies heavily on lab experiments. As a consequence, it's sometimes criticized for a lack of realism. More field experiments could help address that criticism.[13]

Generally, subjects know when they are participating in a laboratory experiment. Performance of certain tasks, responses to questions, or some other form of active involvement is characteristic of laboratory experiments. In field experiments, as in test-markets, subjects do not even know they have taken part in an experiment. Ethically, researchers should gain consent before having someone participate in an experiment. However, with field experiments consent is implied because subjects are not asked to do anything departing from their normal behavior nor do they typically know they are subjects in an experiment. The researchers should nonetheless maintain all precautions with respect to safety and confidentiality.

The naturally occurring noise that exists in the field can interfere with experimental manipulations.

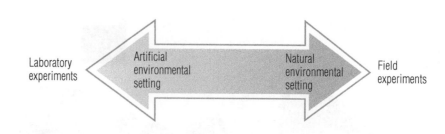

Advantages of Between-Subjects Designs

A basic question faced by the researchers involves how many treatments a subject should receive. For economic reasons, the researcher may wish to apply multiple treatments to the same subject. For instance, in the retail atmosphere experiment, each subject could rate each combination of colors and lighting. Thus, four observations on the dependent variable can be obtained from a single subject. Such a design is called a **within-subjects design**. Within-subjects designs involve repeated measures because with each treatment the same subject is measured.

within-subjects design

Involves repeated measures because with each treatment the same subject is measured.

In contrast, the researcher could decide that each person will receive only one treatment combination. This is referred to as a **between-subjects design**. Each dependent variable is measured only once for every subject.

between-subjects design

Each subject receives only one treatment combination.

Between-subjects designs are usually advantageous although they are usually more costly. The validity of between-subjects designs is higher because by applying only one treatment combination to one subject, the researcher reduces demand characteristics greatly. When a subject sees multiple conditions, he or she is more likely to be able to guess what the study's purpose might be. In addition, as we will see later, statistical analyses of between-subjects designs are simpler than within-subjects designs. This also means the results are easier to report and explain to management.

Internal versus External Validity

As mentioned earlier, researchers always face trade-offs. Experiments are no exception and many of the design decisions affect an experiment's validity—but not all validity is created equal.

Internal Validity

internal validity

Exists to the extent that an experimental variable is truly responsible for any variance in the dependent variable.

Internal validity exists to the extent that an experimental variable is truly responsible for any variance in the dependent variable. In other words, does the experimental manipulation truly cause changes in the specific outcome of interest? If the observed results were influenced or confounded by extraneous factors, the researcher will have problems making valid conclusions about the relationship between the experimental treatment and the dependent variable.

Thus, a lab experiment enhances internal validity because it maximizes control of outside forces. If we wish to know whether a certain odor causes increased productivity among service workers, we may set up a task in a room with a tightly controlled airflow so we can be sure that the specific odor exists in the air in the amount and intensity desired. We can also control temperature, lighting, density, sounds, and many other factors that would be difficult or impossible to control outside of a lab environment. If the only thing that varies from subject to subject is the odor, then we can safely say that any differences in performance must be attributable to human reactions to the scent.

Manipulation Checks

Internal validity depends in large part on successful manipulations. Manipulations should be carried out in such a way that it varies the experimental variable over meaningfully different levels. If the levels are too close together, the experiment may lack the power necessary to observe differences in the dependent variable. In a pricing experiment, it may be that manipulating the price of an automobile over two levels, $25,800 and $26,950, would not be successful in creating two truly different price categories.

The validity of manipulations is examined with a **manipulation check**. If a researcher administers a drug in different dosages that should affect blood sugar levels, the researcher could actually measure blood sugar level after administering the drug to make sure that the dosages were different enough to produce a change in blood sugar. In marketing, the manipulation check often consists of a survey question or two. In the pricing example, subjects may answer a question about how low they believe the price of the car to be. A valid manipulation would produce substantially different average responses to that question in a "high" and "low" price group. Manipulation checks should always be administered after dependent variables in self-response format experiments. This keeps the manipulation check item from becoming a troublesome demand characteristic.

Extraneous variables can jeopardize internal validity. The five major ones are history, maturation, testing, instrumentation, and mortality.

manipulation check

A validity test of an experimental manipulation to make sure that the manipulation does produce differences in the independent variable.

History

A **history effect** occurs when some change other than the experimental treatment occurs during the course of an experiment that affects the dependent variable. A common history effect occurs when competitors change their marketing strategies during a test-marketing experiment. History effects are particularly prevalent in repeated measures experiments that take place over an extended time. If we wanted to assess how much a change in recipe improves individual subjects' consumption of a food product, we would first measure their consumption and then compare it with consumption after the change. Since several weeks may pass between the first and second measurement, there are many things that could occur that would also influence subjects' diets.

Although it may sound extreme, examining the effect of some dietary supplement on various health-related outcomes may require that a subject be confined during the experiment's course. This may take several weeks. Without confining the subject in something like a hospital setting, there would be little way of controlling food and drink consumption, exercise activities, and other factors that may also affect the dependent variables.

A special case of the history effect is the **cohort effect**, which refers to a change in the dependent variable that occurs because members of one experimental group experienced different historical situations than members of other experimental groups. For example, two groups of managers used as subjects may be in different cohorts because one group encountered different experiences over the course of an experiment. If the experimental manipulation involves different levels of financial incentives and performance is the dependent variable, one group may be affected by an informative article appearing in a trade magazine during the experiment. Since the other group participated prior to this group, members of that group could not benefit from the article. Therefore, the possibility exists that the article rather than the change in incentive is truly causing differences in performance.

history effect

Occurs when some change other than the experimental treatment occurs during the course of an experiment that affects the dependent variable.

cohort effect

Refers to a change in the dependent variable that occurs because members of one experimental group experienced different historical situations than members of other experimental groups.

Maturation

A **maturation effect** is a function of time and the naturally occurring events that coincide with growth and experience. Experiments taking place over longer time spans may see lower internal validity as subjects simply grow older or more experienced. Suppose an experiment were designed to test the impact of a new compensation program on sales productivity. If this program were tested over a year's time, some of the salespeople probably would mature as a result of more selling experience or perhaps gain increased knowledge. Their sales productivity might improve because of their knowledge and experience rather than the compensation program.

maturation effect

A function of time and the naturally occurring events that coincide with growth and experience.

Testing

Testing effects are also called *pretesting effects* because the initial measurement or test alerts or primes subjects in a way that affects their response to the experimental treatments. Testing effects only occur in a before-and-after study. A before-and-after study is one requiring an initial baseline measure to be taken before an experimental treatment is administered. So, before-and-after experiments are a special case of a repeated measures design. For example, students taking standardized achievement and intelligence tests for the second time usually do better than those taking the tests for the first time. The effect of testing may increase awareness of socially approved answers, increase attention to experimental conditions (that is, the subject may watch more closely), or make the subject more conscious than usual of the dimensions of a problem.

testing effects

A nuisance effect occurring when the initial measurement or test alerts or primes subjects in a way that affects their response to the experimental treatments.

Instrumentation

instrumentation effect

A nuisance that occurs when a change in the wording of questions, a change in interviewers, or a change in other procedures causes a change in the dependent variable.

A change in the wording of questions, a change in interviewers, or a change in other procedures used to measure the dependent variable causes an **instrumentation effect**, which may jeopardize internal validity. If the experiment involves a personal interview with different interviewers asking questions after than before exposure to a treatment, the varying mannerisms of the interviewer may influence subject responses. Even when only a single interviewer is used for all subjects, problems may occur if he/she varies the wording, tone, or manner in which he/she asks the questions. There are numerous other sources of instrument decay or variation. Again, instrumentation effects are problematic with any type of repeated measures design.

Mortality

mortality effect (sample attrition)

Occurs when some subjects withdraw from the experiment before it is completed.

If an experiment takes place over a period of a few weeks or more, some sample bias may occur due to the **mortality effect (sample attrition)**. Sample attrition occurs when some subjects withdraw from the experiment before it is completed. Mortality effects may occur if subjects drop from one experimental treatment group disproportionately from other groups. Consider a sales training experiment investigating the effects of close supervision of salespeople (high pressure) versus low supervision (low pressure). The high-pressure condition may misleadingly appear superior if those subjects who completed the experiment did very well. If, however, the high-pressure condition caused more subjects to drop out than the other conditions, this apparent superiority may be due to the fact that only very determined and/or talented salespeople stuck with the program.

External Validity

external validity

Is the accuracy with which experimental results can be generalized beyond the experimental subjects.

External validity is the accuracy with which experimental results are generalizable beyond the experimental subjects. External validity increases as subjects comprising a sample truly represent some defined population meaning that the results extend to market segments or groups of people. The higher the external validity, the more researchers and managers can count on the fact that any results observed in an experiment will also be seen in the "real world" (marketplace, workplace, sales floor, etc.).

SUV safety continues to improve, but car companies including GM, Jeep, Toyota and Suzuki still face liability lawsuits based on claims that a design contributed to a high propensity of rollover.[14] The companies experiment with various types of suspensions and test the equipment in labs. Once the companies' design minimizes rollover problems in the lab, they move outside to a test track and see how a real vehicle handles. However, even this test leaves room for lawyers to argue that the tests lack external validity. After all, a track is not a highway and the test drivers are not typical SUV owners. Lab experiments are associated with low external validity because experimental procedures exact demanding control but do not adequately represent real-world intricacies. In other words, the experimental conditions may be too artificial. When a study lacks external validity, the researcher will have difficulty repeating the experiment with any change in subjects, settings, or time.

Convenient Subjects

Behavioral experiments conducted by basic marketing researchers such as academics often involve the use of convenient subjects rather than individuals randomly selected from some representative sampling frame (as we will discuss in Chapter 12). College students and crowdsourcing via social networks or Internet sites provide common approaches to finding convenient subjects, which results in a convenience sample. Convenience, time, money, and a host of other practical considerations often lead to using subjects from these easily accessible sources.

The issue of external validity represents a key concern in predicting how representative an experiment's results may be. Students are easily accessible, but they often are not representative of the total population. This is not always the case, however, and sometimes researchers focus on behaviors for which students have some particular expertise. Research directed at understanding how young adults react to Facebook promotions or how different studying techniques affect test performance can have a great deal of internal and external validity using students. This is because students fit within the population of interest. However, researchers wishing to conduct an experiment addressing a research question aimed at understanding how renovating church facilities affects clergy members' job satisfaction would probably not benefit much from using typical undergraduate business students as subjects. Why would anyone expect these students to behave like clergy? In the end, students provide higher internal than external validity in most research and in general, their use in marketing research experiments needs to be carefully considered within the context of the research.[15]

As an alternative to students without sacrificing convenience, basic researchers turn to samples crowd-sourced via Amazon's Mechanical Turk or other sources that serve as a conduit to Internet workers. Here, one can entice individual workers to serve as experimental subjects in return for small cash payments. The relatively low costs and speed with which researchers can obtain data in this manner are very enticing and often serve as justification for using "mechanical" subjects. As mentioned earlier, the researcher needs to be particularly concerned about problems due to experience effects and acquiescence bias with typical mTurk workers.[16]

In addition, because Internet workers are eager to please, screening questions are sometimes ineffective. Workers want to get paid. Thus, they often may answer screening questions in a manner that will get them included in the sample whether or not they actually fit the criteria. If a study is only about middle-aged males, workers of other types can still claim to fit this criterion to participate in the study. In one experiment seeking only female subjects, the researcher included an initial screening question that routed nonfemales out of the survey. However, at the end of the short survey that went along with the experiment, the researcher also asked subjects to report gender. Twelve percent reported being male. Thus, either their gender changed in the short time or they were being dishonest. Further, other "female" subjects may have remembered they were supposed to be male. Also, social networking sites exist where workers converse with one another. Topics include which worker requests are worth doing and advice on how a worker *should* respond. As we saw earlier in the chapter when discussing social network postings' effects on drug experiments, this chatter enhances the possibility that the results are confounded by knowledge and amount to demand artifacts rather than true effects.

Researchers are not likely to stop using this source because it is so convenient, but great caution needs to be taken. Workers with the greatest amount of experience should be avoided as candidates for experiments. Screening needs to be done in a manner that subjects cannot easily detect. This may include allowing subjects that don't match the desired profile to participate in some way so they can get paid and feel like they completed the task. Otherwise, the worker is likely to try to reenter fraudulently or spread word to others about the conditions. If such data sources are to be used, researchers are encouraged to use them for simple opinion surveys with no manipulations and where the respondent's actual characteristics are not important.

In both online surveys and experiments, researchers should consider using **attention filters**. Attention filters are items that have known and obvious answers included just to see if participants are playing along. A common attention filter item might be:

Have you ever had a fatal heart attack while watching television?

If someone answers yes, they would have to be in the afterlife to be telling the truth. Thus, their answers would be suspect. Research suggests that both students and Internet workers sometimes fail attention filters like this. In fact, a researcher using a convenience sample from these sources may expect 30 percent of subjects to be paying so little attention that they fail simple checks like these.[17]

attention filters

Items that have known and obvious answers included just to see if participants are playing along.

Trade-Offs between Internal and External Validity

Naturalistic field experiments tend to have greater external validity than artificial laboratory experiments. Marketing researchers often must trade internal validity for external validity. Retail researchers sometimes conduct field experiments concerning merchandising, traffic flow, and a host of other issues. Retailers invest a lot of resources into their store designs. One important decision involves when to remodel a store. A research team implemented a field experiment examining changes in customer perceptions of the atmosphere, service quality, and store sales due to a remodel.[18] They measured the key dependent variables before and at two points in time after the remodel. In particular, they were interested in how the remodel affects new and

Stop Nudging Me! I think?

Few people like to be nagged. But, do people like to be nudged? Nudge marketing refers to subtle manipulations that can influence consumer behavior. Sometimes, a nudge can be used for good. An experiment placing a salad in front of lasagna suggests that subjects would eat more of it, and thus more healthily, than if the lasagna is placed in front of the salad. The placement of the food nudges one into a healthier behavior. Nudging may not always be so benign.

In the era of big data and artificial intelligence, some researchers are concerned with the ethics of nudging or even hypernudging, referring to data-driven automated nudges encountered through smart technologies. In this light, one understands better the criticism of the field experiments in which Facebook manipulated users' newsfeeds to produce either good or bad moods. Some referred to them as anger experiments! Was Facebook studying how to nudge consumers into certain behaviors? For example, can the newsfeeds be manipulated to make advertising more effective and

improve Facebook revenues? Perhaps even more of a concern, can social media technology nudge consumers into certain political positions deemed acceptable to the respective media outlet? As nudge technology develops, researchers will have to address the ethical implications associated with potentially changing a nudge to a shove!

Sources: Kobie, M. (2015), "Nudge Theory: When Your Smart Gadgets Nag You," *The Guardian*, https://www.theguardian.com/technology/2015/aug/07/nudge-theory-smart-gadgets-silicon-valley, accessed December 17, 2017. Yeung, K. (2017), "Hypernudge: Big Data as a Model of Regulation by Design," *Information, Communication & Society*, 20, 118–136.

old customers. The researchers conclude that a remodel leads to significant increases in spending and improved perceptions following the remodel. This finding is particularly strong among new store customers who increase spending 16 percent after the remodel, with the increase falling only slightly to 14 percent after 12 months. Thus, a remodel seems to *cause* an increase in sales and improved perceptions of service quality and the store atmosphere.

Laboratory experiments with many controlled factors usually are high in internal validity, while field experiments like the remodel study generally have less internal validity, but greater external validity. While the store remodel study takes place in a real setting, giving some confidence that other remodels may produce similar outcomes, did the remodel really cause the change? Perhaps some road construction occurred simultaneously with the remodel and redirected traffic. Perhaps a competing store closed during the time of the remodel. The remodel may have coincided with a change in product assortment. Any of these factors may also drive a change in sales. Ideally, researchers could balance internal and external validity by using both experimental approaches. Results from lab experiments would be followed up with some type of field test.

Test-Marketing

The most common type of field marketing experiment is the test-market. Test-marketing has three broad primary uses in marketing research. Each use can be broken down more specifically to look at some issue in close detail. The three broad uses are as follows:

1. Forecasting the success of a newly developed product.
2. Testing hypotheses about different options for marketing mix elements.
3. Identifying weaknesses in product designs or marketing strategies.

Forecasting New Product Success

Test-markets frequently provide pilot tests for new products. The basic idea for a prototypical test-market is simple. A product is marketed on a small-scale under actual market conditions and the results allow a prediction of success or failure once the product is introduced on a large scale. Do people really want skinny beers? Heineken used a test-market to forecast the success of Heineken Premium Light (HPL) beer, which led Miller to test its own skinny beer (MGD 64) version, and now these beers have substantial market share.[19] Heineken also experiments with the type of can. Its light beer now comes in a skinny 8.5 ounce can as a result of positive tests.

Companies using test-markets should realize that a new product concept also involves issues like advertising, pricing, supply chains, and retail placement. These issues may also be manipulated within a test market. Estimates can then be made about the optimal advertising level, the need for product sampling, retail channel fit, or perhaps even advertising and retail channel selection interaction. Test-marketing permits evaluation of the entire new product concept, not just the physical good itself.

A researcher conducting a test-market may evaluate not only new products' sales as a dependent variable, but also existing products' sales as relevant dependent variables. This was a major concern in the introduction of HPL and MGD 64. Test-marketing allows a firm to determine whether a new offering will cannibalize sales from existing products, meaning that consumers are choosing the new offering as a replacement for another product offered by the same company. If Miller's MGD 64 sales in a test-market are impressive but sales of their other beers drop proportionately, then Miller would be less inclined to go through all the effort and expense of a full-scale new product launch.

Testing the Marketing Mix

Test-markets are equally useful as a field experiment manipulating different marketing plans for existing products. A manager can study any element of the marketing mix with a test-market.

Advertising researchers also can test the effectiveness of different media. Procter and Gamble (P&G) owns many brands. Are they better off trying to engage customers and potential customers on Facebook, Instagram, or Twitter? The company can test the relative effectiveness of each with one or two brands with the hope of generalizing results to many brands. One test

● ● ● ● ● ● ●

Test-marketing can be used to determine the impact of different promotional approaches on sales and brand image.

compared the engagement levels of the same brand video posted on the three social network media.[20] The conclusions were drawn by comparing engagement rates among brand followers across the three media. In the end, Facebook produced a miniscule engagement rate of 0.07 percent (that's 7 hundredths (1/100) of a percent) compared to an even lower rate 0.03 percent on Twitter. In contrast, Instagram produced an engagement rate of 4.2 percent. Thus, when engaging with videos, Instagram clearly produces the highest engagement.

Identifying Product Weaknesses

Test-market experimentation also allows identification of previously undetected product or marketing plan weaknesses. The company can deal with the weaknesses before committing to the actual sales launch. Although often this use of test-markets is accidental, in the sense that it isn't the reason for conducting the test-markets, companies save huge sums of resources by spotting problems before the full-scale marketing effort begins. Often, this use of test-marketing occurs when a product underperforms in at least one location. Researchers can then follow up with other research approaches to try and reveal the reason for the lack of performance. Once identified, product modifications address these faults specifically.

McDonald's test-marketed pizza periodically for years. The first test-market provided lower than expected sales results. The reasons for the underperformance included a failure to consider competitors' reactions and problems associated with the small, single portion pizza, which was the only way McPizza was sold. Additionally, McPizza didn't seem to bring any new customers to McDonald's. In the next round of test-marketing, the marketing strategy repositioned the pizza, shifting to a 14-inch pizza that was only sold from about 4 p.m. until closing. With still underwhelming results, McDonald's test-marketed "Pizza Shoppes" within the test McDonald's where employees could be seen assembling ingredients on ready-made pizza dough. As a result of the tests, McDonald's has shied away from pizza for the U.S. adult market. Pizza-like products, however, exist and succeed at many McDonald's locations in other nations.

When a product fails its market test, the test-market does not fail! In most cases, this represents an important *research success*. Encountering problems in a test-market either properly leads the company to introduce the new product or to make the planned change in marketing strategy. Thus, decision-makers avoid a huge mistake. In addition, test-market results may lead management to make adjustments that will turn the poor test-market results into a market success. The managerial experience gained in test-marketing can be extremely valuable, even when the performance results are disappointing.

Projecting Test-Market Results

Test-marketing is all about generalizing results. In other words, researchers do a trial test on a small-scale with the hope that the small-scale results will match those achieved in a full-scale product introduction. Therefore, external validity is a key consideration in designing a test-market. Test-markets are not appropriate for research questions that require very rigorous control of internal validity. However, the fundamental reason that test-markets are conducted is the hope that results can be accurately projected from the sample to the entire market or population of customers. Researchers take several steps to try to make these projections as accurate as they possibly can.

Most researchers support sales data with consumer survey data during test-markets. These help monitor consumer awareness and attitudes toward the test-marketed product as well as the repeat-purchase likelihood. Frequently this information is acquired via consumer panels.

Estimating Sales Volume: Some Problems

Test-marketing is all about estimating how well the product involved will do in the marketplace. Researchers project sales based on how well the product performs in the test-market. Numerous methodological factors cause problems in estimating national sales results based on regional tests. Often, these problems result from mistakes in the design or execution of the test-market itself.

Overattention

If managers give too much attention to a new product launch within a test-market, the product may be more successful than it would under more normal marketing conditions. In the test-market, the firm's advertising agency may make sure that the test-markets have excellent television coverage (which may or may not be representative of the national television coverage). If salespeople are aware of the test-market, they may spend unusual amounts of time making sure the new product is available or displayed better. This also means that managers should avoid any added incentives that would encourage extra sales efforts to sell the test-marketed product.

Unrealistic Conditions

The test-market should offer the product under the same conditions that would likely exist under real conditions. If greater effort leads to a relatively advantageous but unrealistic merchandising advantage, the results will not be valid. For example, extra shelf facings, eye-level stocking, and other conditions resulting from unrealistic distribution efforts would probably distort the test-market.

This situation may result from research design problems or overattention, as previously described. For example, if retailers know that someone is paying more attention to their efforts with a given product, they may give it artificially high distribution and extra retail support.

Reading the Competitive Environment Incorrectly

Another common mistake is to assume that the competitive environment will be the same nationally as in the test-market. If competitors are unaware of a test-market, the results will not measure competitors' reactions to company strategy. Competitors' responses after a national introduction may differ substantially from the way they reacted in the test-market. On the other hand, competitors may react to a test-market by attempting to undermine it. If they know that a firm is testing, they may attempt to disrupt test-market results with increased promotions and lower prices for their own products, among other potential acts of **test-market sabotage**.

test-market sabotage

Intentional attempts to disrupt the results of a test-market being conducted by another firm.

Time Lapse

One relatively uncontrolled problem results from the time lapse between the test-market experiment and the national introduction of the product. Often, the period between the test-market and national introduction is a year or more. Given the time needed to build production capacity, develop channels of distribution, and gain initial sales acceptance, this may be unavoidable. However, the longer the time between the test-market and the actual selling market, the less accurate one should expect the results to be.

Advantages of Test-Marketing

This discussion of test-marketing should make it clear that test-markets are advantageous in ways that are very difficult to match with other research approaches. The key advantage of test-marketing is the real-world setting in which the experiment is performed. Although focus groups and surveys also can be useful in describing what people may like in a new product, the actual behavior of consumers in a real test-market location is far more likely to lead to accurate projections.

A second advantage of test-marketing is that researchers can easily communicate results to management. Although the experiment itself can be difficult to implement for a host of reasons, most related to small-scale or temporary marketing, the data analysis is usually very simple. Very often, the same procedures used in any simple experiment provide a way of producing test-market results. As we will see, this relies heavily on comparing means in some way. Researchers find marketing managers much more receptive to these types of results than they may be to results drawn from complicated mathematical models or qualitative approaches relying on deep subjective interpretation. Many consumer industries depend heavily on test-market results for help in decision making. The Research Snapshot on page 255 illustrates a typical test-market application and some problems that can occur.

Disadvantages of Test-Marketing

Test-markets also have disadvantages. Although the power of test-markets in providing accurate predictions are apparently such that companies would use test-markets for all major marketing changes, this is hardly the case. The disadvantages are such that test-markets are used less frequently than one might think.

Cost

Test-marketing is very expensive. Consider that for most new products, companies have to actually create production facilities on a small-scale, develop distribution within selected test-market cities, arrange media coverage specific to those locations, and then have systems and people in place to carefully monitor market results. All of this leads to high cost overall and very high unit costs. Heineken faced all these issues in test-marketing HPL. As a result, each six-pack could cost several times over the actual selling price. However, when HPL was introduced throughout the United States, the economies of scale that come with full-scale marketing left unit costs below the selling price.

Test-marketing a packaged-goods product typically costs millions. As with other forms of marketing research, decision-makers must weigh the value of the information against the research costs. The expense of test-marketing certainly is a primary reason why marketing managers refuse to use the approach. Although they do reduce error in decision making, they are not perfect and certainly some risk remains in basing decisions on test-market results. If they were risk-free, managers would use them far more frequently. Because they are not risk-free and are very expensive, managers may decide to make go or no-go decisions based on less expensive techniques that are often less accurate.

Time

Test-markets cost more than just money. Test-markets cannot be put together overnight. Simply planning a test-market usually takes months. Actually implementing one takes much longer. On top of the time for planning and implementation, researchers also must decide how long is long enough. In other words, when is the amount of data collected sufficient to have confidence in drawing valid conclusions?

The appropriate time period for a test-market varies depending on the research objectives. Sometimes, as in Procter & Gamble's testing of its unique new products Febreze, Dryel, and Fit Fruit & Vegetable Wash, the research takes several years. In other situations, as in P&G's testing of Encaprin pain reliever (a product that ultimately failed in national distribution), the time period may be shorter. HPL's test-markets lasted less than a year, relatively short by most standards.

Thus, even a quickly planned and implemented test-market can cost the firm a year or more in time. During this time, competitors are also trying to gain competitive advantage. The fear that competitors may make a big move first puts added pressure on marketing managers to move quickly. For this reason, the time costs associated with test-markets are a primary reason for forgoing them.

How long should a test-market be? Test-markets should be long enough for consumers to become aware of the product, have a chance to purchase it, consume it, and repurchase it at least one more time. Thus, it must be longer than the average purchase cycle for that particular product. A test-market that is too short may overestimate sales, because typically the early adopters are heavy users of the product. Thus, projections are based on consumers who are far from average.

Loss of Secrecy

As pointed out in the Research Snapshot on the next page, one drawback to actual field experimentation is that the marketplace is a public forum. Therefore, secrets no longer exist. In the case of a new product, not only does the competition know about the new product, but a competitor can sometimes benefit from the test-market by monitoring the same dependent variables as is the sponsoring firm. This may cause them to launch a competing product. In some cases, the competitor can even beat the originating company to the national marketplace.

The Hidden in Hidden Valley Ranch

A few years ago, Hidden Valley Ranch (HVR) conducted a field market experiment to examine how effective three new flavors of salad dressings would be in the marketplace. Thus, there were three levels of the experimental variable, each representing a different flavor. HVR had to produce small batches of each flavor, get them bottled, and ship them to their sales representatives, who then had to stock the dressings in the participating retail stores. All of this was very expensive and the costs to produce each bottle used in a test-market were almost $20.

So, the first day of the test was consumed with sales reps placing the products in the salad dressing sections of retail stores. The second day, each rep went back to each store to record the number of sales for each flavor. By the third day, all of the bottles of all flavors had sold!! Amazing! Was every flavor a huge success?? Actually, one of HVR's competitors had sent their sales reps around beginning on the second day of the test to buy every bottle of the new HVR dressings in every store it had been placed in. Thus, HVR was unable to produce any sales data (the dependent variable) and the competitor

was able to break down the dressing in their labs and determine the recipe.

This illustrates one risk that comes along with field tests. Once a product is available for sale, there are no secrets. Also, you risk espionage of this type that can render the experiment invalid.

© George Doyle & Ciaran Griffin

Selecting test-markets is, for the most part, a sampling problem. The researcher seeks a sample of test-market cities that is representative of the population comprised of all consumers in the relevant market area. If a new product is being launched throughout Australia, for example, the researcher must choose cities that are typical of all Australians.

Thus, test-market cities should represent the entire competitive marketplace. For companies wishing to market a product through the United States, there is no single ideal test-market city. Nevertheless, the researcher must usually avoid cities that are not representative of the nation. Regional or urban differences, atypical climates, unusual ethnic compositions, or different lifestyles may dramatically affect a marketing program. Sometimes, although the researchers may wish to sell a product throughout the entire region of the United States, they may have a certain benefit segment in mind. Food companies may consider introducing a product for segments that enjoy spicy food, for example. In this case, they may choose cities known to favor spicier, more flavor-filled foods, such as New Orleans and San Antonio. In this case, those test-market city populations fit the benefit segment and in this way represent the relevant population better than more typical cities.

Certain cities are used repeatedly for test-market operations because researchers see them as typical of U.S. consumers overall. Whereas some larger cities like Tampa, Peoria, and San Antonio provide potential test-markets, test-markets often take place in smaller cities. Exhibit 9.6 lists several popular U.S. test-markets. Their popularity lies in how close they come to duplicating the average U.S. demographic profile.

A look at the table suggests Grand Junction as an apparently representative location. However, marketers may sometimes adjust the test-market to match the marketing strategy for a product. If a product is geared toward a certain consumer segment, for example, the Hispanic market, then Midland, Texas, may make more sense.

Metropolitan Area	Population	Median Age	Percent of Family HHS	Hispanic Population
Cedar Rapids, IA	262,421	35.2	58.0%	3.5%
Eau Claire, WI	164,570	33.2	59.6%	1.9%
Grand Junction, CO	147,554	37.3	58.5%	13.9%
Columbus, OH	1,967,066	31.5	53.0%	5.4%
Wichita Falls, TX	151,201	32.5	62.3%	18.9%
Birmingham (Hoover), AL	1,140,300	35.5	55.0%	3.2%
Midland, TX	156,780	33.3	71.0%	38.0%
Entire U.S.A.	316,128,839	37.6	55.0%	16.0%

Americans and Canadians are similar in many respects. However, one shouldn't assume that a product that is successful in the United States will be successful in Canada. Thus, even after a successful American launch, a company may wish to conduct a test-market in Canada. In addition, even if Canadians like a new product, a unique marketing approach may be in order. Generally, Calgary, Alberta, represents a prime test-market location for the Canadian market. When Italy's Podere Castorani Winery wished to expand to Canada, Calgary provided the test-market location. Likewise, when Shell introduced a fast-pay charge system, Calgary again proved a suitable test-market. Edmonton also is frequently used to test-market products. Imperial Tobacco selected Edmonton for a test-market of SNUS, a smokeless, spitless tobacco product, positioned as a safe alternative relative to smoking cigarettes.[21]

Like the United States, Canada is comprised of many different ethnic segments. Companies should also be aware that French Canada is quite different from the rest of the country. Edmonton may represent Canadians well enough but not French Canadians. Thus, companies may consider a test-market in Quebec City, Quebec, to see how French Canadian consumers will react.

Test-marketing in Europe can be particularly difficult. Although companies can test their products country by country, the sheer costs involved with test-marketing motivate firms to look for cities more representative of large parts of Europe. Copenhagen, Denmark, is one such city. While the population is somewhat homogenous demographically, the Danes tend to be multilingual and open to product innovation. Copenhagen is particularly representative of northern Europe. Other cities to be considered include Frankfurt, Germany; Birmingham, England; and Madrid, Spain.

Ethical Issues in Experimentation

Ethical issues with experimentation were discussed in Chapter 4 so we touch on them lightly here. The question of deception is a key ethical dilemma in experimentation. Although deception is necessary in most experiments, when debriefing procedures return subjects to their prior condition, then the experiment is probably consistent with good moral standards. When subjects have been injured significantly or truly psychologically harmed, debriefing will not return them to their formal condition and the experiment should not proceed. Therefore, we offer additional commentary on debriefing.

Researchers should debrief experimental subjects following an experimental procedure. In fact, many academic researchers, such as those conducting basic marketing research, are required to debrief subjects by their university IRB procedures. Debriefing experimental subjects by communicating the purpose of the experiment and the researcher's hypotheses about the nature of consumer behavior is expected to counteract negative effects of deception, relieve stress, and provide an educational experience for the subject.

Proper debriefing allows the subject to save face by uncovering the truth for himself. The experimenter should begin by asking the subject if he has any questions or if he found any part of the experiment odd, confusing, or disturbing. This question provides a check on the subject's suspiciousness and effectiveness of manipulations. The experimenter continues to provide the subject cues to the deception until the subject states that he believes there was more to the experiment than met the eye. At this time, the purpose and procedure of the experiment [are] revealed.[22]

Debriefing therefore is critical because it allows us to return subjects to normal. If this cannot be done through a simple procedure like debriefing, the experiment is likely to be unethical. If an experimenter, for example, took 100 nonsmokers, divided them into 4 groups of 25, and had them smoke 20 or 50 cigarettes a day for 5 years (manipulation 1) that were either called Nicky's or BeFrees (manipulation 2), no debriefing could restore them to normal and therefore, this experiment should never be conducted.

In addition to the Facebook experiments feeding disproportionately negative news as part of an experimental treatment embedded in newsfeeds, Facebook conducted experiments involving a treatment that locked users out of their Facebook accounts for potentially fraudulent behavior.[23] The manipulation involved creating the impression among users in the experimental condition that they are suspect of creating a false identity. Facebook gathered the data as an effort to better understand their own anti-fraud measures. However, some subjects became alarmed about the e-mails and compounding the matter, they were never debriefed. After facing public scrutiny, Facebook now claims to have implemented review procedures that amount to an IRB to approve research.

Additionally, there is the issue of test-markets and efforts extended toward interfering with a competitor's test-market. When a company puts a product out for public consumption, they should be aware that competitors may also now freely consume the product. If a competitor buys a lot of the product, the test-market results will be misleading. Further, any design secret is probably no longer secret as competitors dissect the new product. When a company actively attempts to sabotage or invalidate another company's test-market or they aim to infringe on some patent/copyright protection, those acts are ethically questionable. Finally, all of the cautions listed in Chapter 4 concerning the integrity of the data including the avoidance of any steps that tend to "massage" the data to be consistent with hypotheses apply stringently.

Peoria is considered more representative of the general U.S. population than is Miami.

TIPS OF THE TRADE

- Experiments test for causal evidence and thus represent the primary tool for causal research designs.
- Experimental manipulations in marketing research should possess the following characteristics:
  - Comprise distinct categories or magnitudes.
  - Two, three or, at the most, four treatment levels per experimental variable—particularly when multiple experimental variables are used in a single study.
  - Administered randomly across subjects.
- Experimental graphs are useful in displaying results, particularly when interactions are involved.
- Laboratory experiments provide greater internal validity at the cost of lower external validity.
  - That's a primary way that basic researchers justify student subjects as legitimate.

- Great care needs to be taken in using Internet crowdsourcing to find subjects to participate in causal designs involving experiments.
- Response error is often very high in the form of maturation, acquiescence, and dishonesty.
- Field experiments, including test-markets, increase external validity at the cost of internal validity.
  - Traditional test-markets remain expensive and technology offers some virtual alternatives. Test-markets also take a lot of time and involve a loss of secrecy.
  - When a product can easily be duplicated by competitors who obtain an actual product, then a test-market may not be wise.

:: SUMMARY

1. **Know the basic characteristics of research experiments.** Independent variables are created through manipulation in experiments rather than through measurement. The researcher creates unique experimental conditions, each representing a unique level of an independent variable. Researchers refer to human sampling units as subjects in an experiment rather than respondents. This is because researchers subject them to experimental manipulations. Experimental manipulations are examined for the extent to which they affect outcomes. Main effects are due to differences in observed outcomes based on any single experimental variable. Interaction effects are due to combinations of independent variables.

2. **Design an experiment using the basic issues of experimental design.** Systematic experimental error occurs because sampling units (research subjects) in one experimental cell are different from those in another cell in a way that affects the dependent variable. In an experiment involving how people respond to color, the researcher would not want to have all males in one color group and all females in another. Randomization is an important way of minimizing systematic experimental error. If research subjects are randomly assigned to different treatment combinations, then the differences among people that exist naturally within a population should also exist within each experimental cell. Additionally, the researcher must try to control for all possible extraneous variables. Extraneous variables can render any causal inference as spurious. Control is necessary to reduce the possibility of confounding explanations.

3. **Know tools for maximizing the validity of experiments with an emphasis on minimizing demand characteristics.** Demand characteristics are experimental procedures that somehow inform the subject about the actual research purpose. Demand effects can result from demand characteristics. When this happens, the results are confounded. Demand characteristics can be minimized by following these simple rules: using an experimental disguise, isolating experimental subjects, using a "blind" experimental administrator, administering only one experimental treatment

combination to each subject, and avoid using subjects who believe they are paid based on their performance. The more experiments someone participates in, the more likely they are to succumb to demand characteristics through something known as the experience effect. A between-subjects design means that every subject receives only one experimental treatment combination. The main advantages of between-subjects designs are the reduced likelihood of demand effects and simpler analysis and presentation, all of which can improve validity.

4. Weigh the trade-off between internal and external validity. Lab experiments offer higher internal validity because they maximize control of extraneous variables. High internal validity is a good thing because we can be more certain that the experimental variable is truly the cause of any variance in the dependent variable. Field experiments maximize external validity because they take place in a more natural setting, meaning that the results are more likely to generalize to the actual business situation. The increased external validity comes typically at the expense of internal validity and vice-versa.

5. Recognize the appropriate uses of test-marketing. Major uses of test-marketing include forecasting the success of a newly developed product, testing hypotheses about different options for marketing mix elements, and identifying weaknesses in product designs or marketing strategies. The two major advantages of test-markets discussed in the chapter are the real-world setting and the ease in interpretation and communication of results. These advantages have to be weighed against several key disadvantages. These include the great amount of money that it costs to conduct a test-market, the length of time it takes to design, implement, and analyze a test-market, and the loss of secrecy that comes when the product is marketed publicly.

6. Avoid unethical experimental practices. Experiments involve deception. Additionally, research procedures sometimes expose subjects to stressful or possibly dangerous manipulations. Every precaution should be made to ensure that subjects are not harmed. Debriefing subjects about the true purpose of a lab experiment following its conclusion is important for the ethical treatment of subjects. If debriefing can restore subjects to their pre-experimental condition, the experimental procedures are likely consistent with ethical practice. If the procedures change subjects in some way that makes it difficult to return them to their prior condition or subjects them to undue distress, then the experimental procedures probably go beyond what ethical researchers consider appropriate.

:: KEY TERMS AND CONCEPTS

attention filters, *249*
between-subjects design, *246*
blocking variables, *231*
cell, *236*
cohort effect, *247*
confound, *239*
constancy of conditions, *243*
control group, *235*
counterbalancing, *244*
covariate, *232*
demand characteristic, *240*
demand effect, *240*
experience effect, *243*

experimental condition, *231*
experimental group, *235*
experimental treatment, *235*
external validity, *248*
field experiments, *244*
history effect, *247*
instrumentation effect, *248*
interaction effect, *233*
internal validity, *246*
laboratory experiment, *244*
main effect, *232*
manipulation check, *247*
maturation effect, *247*

mortality effect (sample attrition), *248*
placebo, *242*
placebo effect, *242*
randomization, *238*
repeated measures, *239*
subjects, *231*
systematic or nonsampling error, *238*
tachistoscope, *244*
test-market sabotage, *253*
test units, *237*
testing effects, *247*
within-subjects design, *246*

:: QUESTIONS FOR REVIEW AND CRITICAL THINKING

1. Define *experimental condition, experimental treatment, and experimental group.* How are these related to the implementation of a valid manipulation?

2. A tissue manufacturer that has the fourth-largest market share plans to experiment with a 50¢ off coupon during November and a buy one, get one free coupon during December. The experiment will take place at Target stores in St. Louis and Kansas City. In addition, coupons will be issued either through the Internet or in the local newspaper. Sales will be recorded by scanners from which mean tissue sales for each store for each month can be computed and interpreted.

   a. What are the experimental variable and the dependent variable?

   b. Prepare a mock experimental graph that shows hypothetical results (simply guess at what the mean values for each experimental condition would be).

   c. What types of people would make good subjects for this experiment?

3. What is the difference between a *main effect* and an *interaction* in an experiment? In question 2, what will create a main effect? Is an interaction possible?

4. How can experimental graphs be used to show main effects and interactions?

5. What purpose does the random assignment of subjects serve?

6. Why is an experimental confound so damaging to the conclusions drawn from an experiment?

7. What are demand characteristics? How can they be minimized?

8. Suppose researchers were experimenting with how much more satisfied consumers are with a "new and improved" version of some existing product. How might the researchers design a placebo within an experiment testing this research question? Is using such a placebo ethical or not?

9. If a company wanted to know whether to implement a new management training program based on how much it would improve return on investment in its southwest division, would you recommend a field or lab experiment?

10. Suppose you wanted to test the effect of three different e-mail requests inviting people to participate in a survey posted on the Internet. One simply contained a hyperlink with no explanation, the other said if someone participated $10 would be donated to charity, and the other said if someone participated he or she would have a chance to win $1,000. How would this experiment be conducted differently based on whether it was a between-subjects or within-subjects design? What are the advantages of a between-subjects design?

11. What is a manipulation check? How does it relate to internal validity?

12. When conducting an experiment, should a researcher seek participants to serve as subjects who participate in experiments an average of 4 hours a day or more? Take a yes or no stance and justify your answer.

13. Define internal validity and external validity. It's been said that external validity decreases when internal validity is high. Do you believe that is so? List some major threats to internal and external validity. Explain your choices.

14. The idea of nonspurious association was introduced in Chapter 3. How does a confounding variable affect whether an association is spurious or nonspurious?

15. Why is a test-market usually considered an experiment?

16. When is test-marketing likely to be conducted? When is it not as appropriate? Which type of validity is most relevant to test-marketing?

17. What are the advantages and disadvantages of test-marketing?

18. What role does debriefing play in ensuring that experimental procedures are consistent with good ethical practice?

19. A university researcher asks students to participate in an experiment that takes 4 hours to complete in the last week of a semester. Each student receives 5 points extra credit. Another researcher conducts the same experiment using Internet crowd-sourced subjects paid $0.50 to participate. The subjects know they will be paid after the researcher checks the quality of each subject's response. Contrast these two approaches including a discussion of any ethical issues that might be involved.

:: RESEARCH ACTIVITIES

1. Consider the situation of a researcher approached by Captain John's in the Research Snapshot on page 32.
   a. Provide a critique of the procedures used to support the claim that Sea Snapper's product is superior. Prepare it in a way that it could be presented as evidence in court.
   b. Design an experiment that would provide a more valid test of the research question, "Do consumers prefer Sea Snapper fish sticks compared to Captain John's fish sticks?"

2. Conduct a taste test involving some soft drinks with a group of friends. Pour them several ounces of three popular soft drinks and simply label the cups A, B, and C. Make sure they are blind to the actual brands. Then, let them drink as much as they want and record how much of each they drink. You may also ask them some questions about the drinks. Then, allow other subjects to participate in the same test, but this time, let them know what the three brands are. Record the same data and draw conclusions. Does brand knowledge affect behavior and attitudes about soft drinks?

3. Consider the information in the chapter describing Facebook's experiments with their own users. Do you see any evidence of such experiments going on today at Facebook, Instagram, or Twitter? Would you consider Facebook's experimentation lab or field experiments? Do you share concerns that experiments are taking place through social media in an effort to learn how to "nudge" consumers toward specific behaviors? Given the backlash Facebook experienced from conducting the experiments, what advice would you have for them to improve the way they go about conducting experiments through their platform?

Examining Product Failure at No-Charge Electronics

Case 9.1

No-Charge Electronics owner Buzz Auphf needs to know how much product failure affects customer loyalty. Buzz contacts David Handy, a local market researcher, and they ultimately decide on examining a research question asking, "How do current customers react to different levels of product failure?" David designs the following experiment to examine the causal effect of product failure on customer purchase intentions, satisfaction, and loyalty.

The experiment is implemented via e-mail using a sample of current and prospective customers. Three free Netflix movies are provided as an incentive to participate. Subjects are asked to click through to an Internet site to download a product that will enhance their computer's graphics capability. In the low-failure condition, after the subjects click to the site, there is no change in the graphics

of their computers. In the high-failure condition, once they click through to the site, the subjects' computers go into an infinite loop of obscene graphical images until a message arrives indicating that a severe virus has infected their computer and some files may be permanently damaged. This goes on for 45 minutes with no remedy. At that time, a debriefing message pops up telling subjects that it was all part of an experiment and that their computer should now function properly. Prepare a position statement either agreeing or disagreeing that the experiment is consistent with good ethical practice.

Tooheys

Case 9.2

Sixty-six willing Australian drinkers helped a Federal Court judge decide that Tooheys didn't engage in misleading or deceptive advertising for its 2.2 beer. The beer contains 2.2 percent alcohol, compared to 6 percent for other beers, leading to a claim that could be interpreted as implying it was non-alcoholic.

Volunteers were invited to a marathon drinking session after the Aboriginal Legal Service claimed Tooheys' advertising implied beer drinkers could imbibe as much 2.2 beer as they wanted without becoming legally intoxicated. Drunken driving laws prohibit anyone with a blood-alcohol level above 0.05 from getting behind the wheel in Australia.

So, an experiment was conducted to see what happens when a lot of 2.2 is consumed. But the task wasn't easy or that much fun. Some subjects couldn't manage to drink the required 10 "middies," an Aussie term for a beer glass of 10 fluid ounces, over the course of an hour.

Thirty-six participants could manage only nine glasses. Four threw up and were excluded. Two more couldn't manage the "minimum" nine glasses and had to be replaced.

Justice J. Beaumont observed that consuming enough 2.2 in an hour to reach the 0.05 level was "uncomfortable and therefore an unlikely process." Because none of the ads mentioned such extreme quantities, he ruled they couldn't be found misleading or deceptive.[24]

Questions

1. Would a lab experiment or a field experiment be more "valid" in determining whether Tooheys could cause a normal beer consumer to become intoxicated? Explain.
2. Describe an alternate research design that would have higher validity.
3. Is the experiment described in this story consistent with good ethical practice?
4. Is validity or ethics more important?

PART THREE
Measurement

Measurement and Attitude Scaling

iStock.com/Opidanus

LEARNING OUTCOMES

After studying this chapter, you should be able to:

1. Determine what things need to be measured to address a research question
2. Distinguish levels of scale measurement
3. Create an index or composite measure
4. Assess scale reliability and validity
5. Understand why the concept of attitude is so important in marketing research
6. Design a scale that measures an attitudinal concept
7. Implement a multi-attribute model

Chapter Vignette:

Do You Know How to Score?

*I*n sports, one can always know who won a match by looking at the final score. Although sports statisticians keep track of countless statistics, in the end, the final score is all that is needed to judge the outcome. For a long time, marketers gauged performance by their customer satisfaction score. Over time though, the relationship between satisfaction and overall performance proved weaker than first thought. Some analysts believe they now know what that single score might be. Indeed, the **net promoter score (NPS)** proposes to be the single indicator that tells how well a business has performed. Researchers can easily apply the NPS by asking them a single survey item scored on a 0 to 10 scale, as such:

Consumers' responses equal their scores. A score of 6 or below is associated with a label of detractor, a score of 7 or 8

Robert Llewellyn/Photolibrary/Getty Images

On the 0 to 10 point scale shown below, how likely is it that you would recommend Spirit Airlines to a friend or colleague?										
0	1	2	3	4	5	6	7	8	9	10

is labeled passively satisfied, and a score of 9 or 10 signifies a promoter. Companies with a high proportion of promoters tend to outperform competitors significantly. A primary reason is that these loyal, promoter customers help perform the sales and promotion functions for the firm. In fact, promoters tend to spread more positive word of mouth, including online reviews, comments, and social network posts.

Obviously, the simplicity of this approach is attractive to many businesses. However, the method is not without controversy. Questions about the usefulness and the validity of the NPS approach have surfaced. Some question exactly what the NPS item measures. The NPS best represents intent to spread positive word of mouth. Some researchers question the one-size-fits-all approach or suggest that although the item may predict, the prediction accuracy is far from perfect and leaves room for other concepts to explain variance in performance. Models that predict do not always offer useful explanations. Some researchers claim that without controlling for other factors, any correlation between the NPS and things like profitability could be misleading. Factors such as the length of the relationship between a firm and a customer and the type of industry may change the nature of the relationship between the NPS and performance. Despite such skepticism, the NPS is widely used as about 2 of 3 Fortune 500 firms rely on the NPS to benchmark performance. Most also rely on a few additional items providing insight into reasons for the score. No doubt though, like the scoreboard in sports, the NPS lets managers know the score![1]

Introduction

net promoter score (NPS)

A single survey item upon which a consumer indicates how likely he/she would be to recommend a business on a 9-point scale. The NPS is widely used as a marketing performance metric.

Anyone who has ever followed a recipe knows the importance of good measurement. Following a recipe may seem easy, but understanding the quantities represented and the units of measure can be critical. Confuse salt with sugar or tablespoons for teaspoons and the dish is ruined. Just as in the culinary arts, researchers can measure business and marketing in more than one way. Also, researchers often may have to use imperfect measurement devices. Measure a concept poorly and the "recipe" is a likely disaster. Only in this case, the "recipe" is usually an important business decision poorly made instead of a ruined dish.

What Needs to Be Measured?

Managers can't know if their strategies are creating value and the firm is performing well without valid measurement. However, decision-makers often express problems in terms of things that are complex and abstract. Managers want to "out-perform" their competitors but knowing exactly what good performance means is not so simple. A measure cannot be any better than the concepts' definitions. Measurement, then, begins with a definition.

measurement

The process of describing some property of a phenomenon of interest, usually by assigning numbers in a systematic way.

Measurement is the process of describing some property of a phenomenon, usually by assigning numbers in some systematic way. Good measurement results when the assignment produces both reliable and valid measures. The decision statement, corresponding research questions, and any subsequent research hypotheses determine what concepts researchers need to measure. The numbers convey information about the phenomenon. When numbers are used, the researcher must have a rule for assigning a number to an observation in a way that provides an accurate description.

We can illustrate measurement by thinking about the way instructors assign students' grades. Instructors try systematically to represent students' varying levels of performance; how well a student has mastered the course material. A grade represents student performance. Students with higher performance should receive a different grade than do students with lower performance. Even the concept of student performance defies a universally applied measurement approach. Consider the following options:

1. A student can be assigned a letter corresponding to his/her performance as is typical of U.S.-based grading systems.

   a. A—Represents excellent performance
   b. B—Represents good performance
   c. C—Represents average performance
   d. D—Represents poor performance
   e. F—Represents failing performance

2. A student can be assigned a number from 1 to 20, which is the system more typically used in France.

   a. 20—Represents outstanding performance
   b. 11–20—Represent differing degrees of passing performance
   c. Below 11—Represents failing performance

It's hard to imagine a research project that does not involve measurement. If your research project involves a survey, then certainly you are measuring something of relevance to the research questions. Individual items may measure some concepts directly or it may take multiple items to form a scale of some type. A researcher must be aware of several important characteristics in preparing a research report:

1. What is the level of scale measurement? Nominal, ordinal, interval, or ratio? The answer determines what statistics should be used.
2. How well does the content of an item correspond to the concept it is intended to represent? The answer determines how much face validity exists.
3. When multiple items come together to represent a construct, what are the indicators of the scale's validity? The answer to this question provides an indication of how much confidence the user can have in the results.

© George Doyle & Ciaran Griffin

3. A student can be assigned a number corresponding to a percentage performance scale.

   a. 100 percent—Represents a perfect score indicating the best performance.
   b. 60–99 percent—Represents differing degrees of passing performance, each number representing the proportion of correct work.
   c. 0–59 percent—Represents failing performance but still captures proportion of correct work.

4. A student can be assigned one of two letters corresponding to performance.

   a. P—Represents a passing mark
   b. F—Represents a failing mark

Each measurement scale has the potential of producing error or some lack of validity. Exhibit 10.1 illustrates a common student performance measurement application.

EXHIBIT **10.1**

Are There Any Validity Issues with This Measurement?

Student	Percentage Grade	Difference from Next Highest Grade	Letter Grade
1	79.4%	0.5%	C
2	70.0%	9.4%	C
3	69.0%	1.0%	D
4	79.9%	NA	B

Often, instructors may use a percentage scale all semester long and then at the end, have to assign a letter grade for a student's overall performance. Does this produce any potential measurement problems? Consider two students who have percentage scores of 79.4 and 70.0, respectively. The most likely outcome when these scores are translated using a conventional ten-point spread into "letter grades" is that each receives a C (70–80 percent range for a C). Consider a third student who finishes with a 69.0 percent average and a fourth student who finishes with a 79.9 percent average.

Which students are happiest with this arrangement? The first two students receive the same grade, even though their scores are over 9 percentage points apart. The third student gets a grade lower (D) performance than the second student does, even though their percentage scores are only 1.0 percentage point different. The fourth student, who has a score only 0.5 percentage points higher than the first student, would receive a B. Thus, the measuring system (final grade) suggests that the fourth student outperformed the first (assuming that 79.9 is rounded up to 80) student (B versus C), but the first student did not outperform the second (each gets a C), even though the first and second students have the greatest difference in percentage scores.

One can make a case that error exists in this measurement system. In fact, all measurement systems present the potential for error. Researchers, if we are to represent concepts truthfully, must make sure that the measures used are accurate enough to yield useful conclusions. Making use of measures requires that the researcher at least somewhat understands the flaws in the particular measurement tools used. When this is the case, researchers can sometimes account for the error statistically. Ultimately, scientific research would be impossible without measurement.

Concepts

A researcher has to know what to measure before knowing how to measure something. The research questions should emphasize the relevant concepts involved in the decision facing the firm. A **concept** can be thought of as a generalized idea that represents something of identifiable and distinct meaning. Demographic concepts such as *age*, *sex*, and *number of children* are relatively concrete concepts having relatively unambiguous meanings. They present few problems in either definition or measurement. Other concepts are more abstract. Concepts such as *loyalty*, *personality*, *performance*, *channel power*, *trust*, *corporate culture*, *guilt*, *customer satisfaction*, *value*, and so on are more difficult to both define and measure. Consumer involvement may seem like a simple idea until the researcher tries to unambiguously define it and measure it. Recently, marketing managers use the term engagement to represent how much a consumer is interested in and interacts with a brand. Engagement and involvement seem very similar. If, however, engagement and involvement are different concepts, marketing researchers must develop distinct scales for each concept.[2]

concept
A generalized idea that represents something of identifiable and distinct meaning.

Operational Definitions

Researchers measure concepts through a process known as **operationalization**. This process involves identifying scales that correspond to properties of the concept. **Scales**, just as a scale you may use to check your weight, are measurement devices that provide a range of values that correspond to different characteristics or amounts of a characteristic in a concept. In other words, scales provide **correspondence rules**, which indicate that a certain value on a scale corresponds to some true value of a concept. Hopefully, they do this in a truthful way. A student receiving an A should be among the best performers in a class.

Here is an example of a correspondence rule: "Assign numerals 1 through 9 according to how much you would be willing to recommend this business to other consumers. If a customer feels completely confident in recommending the firm, a 9 is selected to match the opinion. If the customer feels that in no way would he/she recommend the firm to others, assign the numeral 1. Numbers between 1 and 9 represent varying degrees of willingness to recommend." The chapter vignette describes the NPS concept in more detail but the idea is that the numbers correspond to different levels of consumer affinity with the business.

operationalization
The process of identifying scale devices that correspond to properties of a concept involved in a research process.

scales
A device providing a range of values that correspond to different characteristics or amounts of a characteristic exhibited in observing a concept.

correspondence rules
Indicate the way that a certain value on a scale corresponds to some true value of a concept.

Variables

Researchers use the variance in concepts to make meaningful diagnoses. Therefore, when we defined *variables*, we really were suggesting that variables capture different values of a concept. Scales capture a concept's variance and, as such, the scales provide the researcher's variables. Consider the following hypothesis:

> H1: *Salesperson experience* is related positively *to salesperson job performance.*

The hypothesis implies a relationship between two variables, experience and job performance. The variables capture variance in the experience and performance concepts. One employee may have fifteen years of experience and be a top performer. A second may have ten years' experience and be a good performer. The scale used to measure experience is quite simple in this case and would involve providing the number of years an employee has been with the company. Job performance, not quite so simple a concept, might involve a correspondence rule with which a supervisor places an employee into one of several performance categories.

Constructs

Sometimes, a single variable cannot capture a concept alone. Using multiple variables to measure one concept often provides a more complete account of some concept than could any single variable. Even in the physical sciences, scientists apply multiple measurements to obtain representations that are more accurate. As concepts become more abstract, multiple items become necessary for good measurement.

A **construct** is a term used for latent concepts measured using multiple variables. By latent, we mean the concept is not directly observable and instead we infer a value by using multiple indicators such as individual scale items. For instance, a salesperson's customer orientation is inferred by using responses to scale items like these (each captured on a 1–5 scale of some type):[3]

1. I offer the product that is best suited to a customer's problem.
2. A good employee has to have the customer's best interests in mind.
3. I try only to sell my customers things that will provide him/her value.
4. I put my customer's best interests before the profitability of my company.
5. I try to find out what kind of products will be most helpful to a customer.

Marketing researchers deal with many latent constructs that represent concepts such as personality, lifestyle, consumer traits like price consciousness, representations of experiences including consumer emotions, and consumption outcomes such as value perceptions.

Operational definitions translate conceptual definitions into measurement scales. An operational definition is like a manual of instructions or a recipe. Even the truth of a statement like "Gaston makes good seafood gumbo" depends on the definition of gumbo and the ingredients used in the gumbo. If salesperson customer orientation is defined as a salesperson placing relatively high priority on the customer's best interests, then applying the five items stated previously provides an operational definition.

To the Point

"Not everything that can be counted counts, and not everything that counts can be counted."

—ALBERT EINSTEIN

construct

A term used to refer to latent concepts measured with multiple variables.

● ● ● ● ● ● ●

Athletes wear nominal numbers on their jerseys.

AP Images/Rusty Kennedy

Levels of Scale Measurement

Marketing researchers use many scales. Not all scales capture the same richness in a measure and not all concepts require a rich measure. But, a researcher can classify all measures based on the way they represent distinctions between observations of a variable. The four levels or types of scale measurement are *nominal, ordinal, interval,* and *ratio level scales.* Traditionally, the level of scale measurement is important because it determines the mathematical comparisons that are allowable. Each of the four scale levels offers the researcher progressively more power in testing the validity of a scale and analyzing the way it corresponds to other concepts. The largest line of demarcation in this respect lies between the ordinal and interval levels. We begin though by taking a look at the most basic type of measurement system.

Nominal Scale

Nominal scales represent the most elementary level of measurement. A nominal scale assigns a value to an object for identification or classification purposes. The value can be a number, but does not have to be a number, because nominal scales do not represent quantities. In this sense, a nominal scale is a qualitative scale. Nominal scales are extremely useful even though some may consider them elementary.

Marketing researchers use nominal scales quite often. For instance, suppose Barq's Root Beer experimented with three different types of sweeteners (cane sugar, corn syrup, or fruit extract) in an effort to decide which created the best tasting soft drink. Basically, Barq's researchers designed a taste test experiment. Experimental subjects taste one of the three recipes and then rate how much they like it and how likely they would be to buy that particular drink. The researchers would like the experiment to be blind so that he/she does not bias subjects' perceptions. Thus, when subjects actually taste one of the three root beers, the cups containing the drinks say X, Y, or Z, not cane sugar, corn syrup, or fruit extract. The X, Y and Z become the measuring system that represents the variance in sweeteners.

Nominal scaling is arbitrary in the sense that each label can be assigned to any of the categories without introducing error; for instance, in the root beer example, the researcher can assign the letter Z to any of the three options without damaging scale validity. Cane sugar could just as properly be labeled Z as X, or Y, or even A, or B. The researcher might use numbers instead of letters without any change in the validity of the measuring system. If so, cane sugar, corn syrup, and fruit extract might be identified with the numbers 1, 2, and 3, respectively, or even 543, -26, and 8080, respectively. Either set of numbers is equally valid since the numbers are not representing different quantities. They are simply identifying the type of sweetener.

We encounter nominal numbering systems all the time. Uniform numbers are nominal numbers. Tom Brady is identified on the football field by his jersey number. What is his number? Airport terminals are identified with a nominal numbering system. In the Atlanta airport, a departing traveler can go through terminals T, A, B, C, D, and E before reaching a departure gate at terminal F. School bus numbers are nominal in that they simply identify a bus. Elementary school buses sometimes use both a number and an animal designation to help small children get on the right bus. So, bus number "8" may also be the "tiger" bus.

The first drawing in Exhibit 10.2 depicts the number 7 on a horse's colors. This is merely a label to allow bettors and racing enthusiasts to identify the horse. The assignment of a 7 to this horse does not mean that it is the seventh fastest horse or that it is the seventh biggest or anything else meaningful. But, the 7 does let you know when you have won or lost your bet!

Exhibit 10.3 lists some nominal scales commonly used by marketing researchers. Nominal scale properties mean the numbering system simply identifies things.

Ordinal Scale

Ordinal scales have nominal properties, but they also allow for categorization based on how much a characteristic exists relative to others. In other words, an ordinal scale is a ranking scale. When a professor assigns an A, B, C, D, or F to a student at the end of the semester, he or she is using an ordinal scale. An A represents relatively greater performance than B, which is relatively greater performance than C, and so forth.

Surveys often ask research participants to *rank order* things based on preference. So, preference is the concept, and the ordinal scale lists the options from most to least preferred, or vice versa. Five objects can be ranked from 1–5 (least preferred to most preferred) or 1–5 (most preferred to least preferred) with no loss of meaning. In this sense, ordinal scales are somewhat arbitrary, but not nearly as arbitrary as a nominal scale.

nominal scales

Represent the most elementary level of measurement in which values are assigned to an object for identification or classification purposes only.

ordinal scales

Ranking scales allowing things to be arranged based on how much of some concept they possess.

EXHIBIT **10.2**

Nominal, Ordinal, Interval, and Ratio Scales Provide Different Information

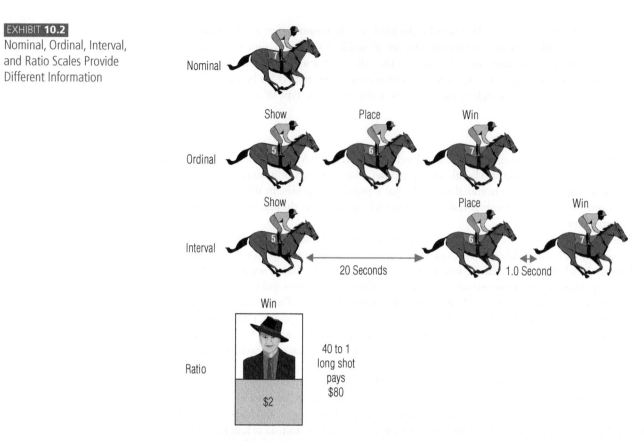

EXHIBIT **10.3**

Facts about the Four Levels of Scales

Level	Examples	Numerical Operations	
Nominal	Yes – No Female – Male Buy – Did Not Buy Postal Code: _____	Counting	• Frequencies • Mode
Ordinal	Rankings Choose from the Following: • Dissatisfied • Satisfied • Very Satisfied • Delighted Indicate Your Level of Education: • HS Diploma • Some College • Bachelor's Degree • Graduate Degree	Counting and Ordering	• Frequencies • Mode • Median • Range
Interval	10-Point Job Performance Ratings Assigned by Supervisors: 1 = Worst Performers 10 = Best Performers Temperature-Type Attitude Scales: Low Temperature = Bad Attitude High Temperature = Good Attitude	Common Arithmetic Operations	• Mean • Median • Variance • Standard Deviation
Ratio	Amount Purchased Salesperson Sales Volume Likelihood of performing some act: • 0% = No Likelihood to • 100% = Certainty Number of stores visited Time spent viewing a particular Web page Number of Web pages viewed	All Arithmetic Operations	• Mean • Median • Variance • Standard Deviation

Dan Kitwood/Getty Images News/Getty Images

● ● ● ● ● ● ●

Olympic medals represent an ordinal measurement system. Gold is better than silver, and silver is better than bronze. But, the system says nothing about how much better the gold medal winner is from silver or silver from bronze.

When marketing professors take some time off, they sometimes like to place a wager. They may place a wager on a horse race online or even go to the racetrack itself. The race results are described with an ordinal scale consisting of three categories: win, place and show. A horse finishing in the "show" position has finished after the "win" and "place" horses (see the second drawing in Exhibit 10.2). This ordinal scale captures the order of finish accurately, to which one can apply an ordered number rule:

■ Assign 1 to the "win" position
■ Assign 2 to the "place" position
■ Assign 3 to the "show" position

Sometimes, the winning horse defeats the place horse by only a fraction (wins by a "nose"). The place horse defeats the show horse by 20 seconds or more. Yet, they still finish 1, 2, and 3. An ordinal scale does not tell by how much a horse won. But, the scale is good enough to separate winning bets from losing bets. Typical ordinal scales in marketing research ask respondents to rate brands, companies, and the like as excellent, good, fair, or poor. Researchers know excellent is higher than good, but they do not know by how much.

Interval Scale

Interval scales have both nominal and ordinal properties, but they also capture information about differences in quantities of a concept. So, not only would a sales manager know that a particular salesperson outperformed a colleague, but the manager would know by how much. If a professor assigns grades to term papers using a numbering system ranging from 1.0–20.0 points, not only does the scale represent the fact that a student with a 16.0 outperformed a student with a 12.0, but the scale would show by how much (4.0 points).

The third drawing in Exhibit 10.2 depicts a horse race in which the win horse is one second ahead of the place horse, which is 20 seconds ahead of the show horse. Not only are the horses identified by the order of finish, but the difference between each horse's performance is known. So, using an interval scale we know horse number 7 and horse number 6 performed similarly, but horse number 5 performed not nearly as well.

A classic example of an interval scale is a Fahrenheit temperature scale. Consider the following weather:

■ June 6 was 80° F
■ December 7 was 40° F

interval scales

Scales that have both nominal and ordinal properties, but that also capture information about differences in quantities of a concept from one observation to the next.

The interval Fahrenheit scale lets us know that December 7 was 40°F colder than June 6. But, we cannot conclude that June 6 was twice as hot as December 7. Although the actual numeral 80 is indeed twice as great as 40, remember that this is a scaling system. In this case, the scale is not iconic, meaning that it does not exactly represent some phenomenon. In fact, these temperatures can be converted to the more common Celsius scale. Then, the following would result:

- June 6 was 26.7°C
- December 7 was 4.4°C

Obviously, now we can see that June 6 was not twice as hot as December 7. June 6 was 40°F or 22.3°C warmer, depending upon your thermometer. Interval scales are very useful because they capture relative quantities in the form of distances between observations. No matter what thermometer is used, December 7 was not as hot as June 6.

Ratio Scale

ratio scales

Represent the highest form of measurement in that they have all the properties of interval scales with the additional attribute of representing absolute quantities; characterized by a meaningful absolute zero.

Ratio scales are scales represent the highest form of measurement because they have all the properties of interval scales with the additional attribute of representing absolute quantities. Interval scales represent only relative meaning whereas ratio scales represent absolute meaning. In other words, ratio scales provide iconic measurement. Zero, therefore, has meaning in that it represents an absence of some concept.

An absolute zero is a defining characteristic in determining between ratio and interval scales. For example, money is a way to measure economic value. Consider the following items offered for sale in an online auction:

- Antique railroad pocket watch circa 1910—sold for $50
- Authentic Black Forest cuckoo clock—sold for $75
- Antique gold-filled Elgin wristwatch circa 1950—sold for $100
- "Antique" 1970s digital watch—did not sell and there were no takers for free

We can make the ordinal conclusions that the cuckoo clock was worth more than the pocket watch and that the wristwatch was worth more than the cuckoo clock, all of which were worth more than the 1970s digital watch. We can make interval conclusions such as that the cuckoo was worth $25 more than the pocket watch. We can also conclude that the wristwatch was worth twice as much as the pocket watch and that the 1970s digital watch was worthless (selling price = $0.00). The latter two conclusions are possible because money price represents a ratio scale.

Temperature can also be captured by a ratio scale. The Kelvin scale begins at 0 K, corresponding to −273.2° on the Celsius scale (an interval scale). This temperature is known as absolute zero. Zero K is the point at which the kinetic energy of atoms in a water molecule approaches 0, meaning the molecules are moving as slowly as possible. This is as cold as water can get since there is no way of slowing the molecules further (they never completely stop). Thus, 0 K indeed has absolute meaning.

To the Point

"When you can measure what you are talking about and express it in numbers, you know something about it."

—WILLIAM THOMPSON, LORD KELVIN

Mathematical and Statistical Analysis of Scales

Although it is true that one can perform mathematical operations with numbers from nominal scales, the result may not have a great deal of meaning. For instance, a school district may perform mathematical operations on school bus numbers. With this, they may find that the average school bus number is 77.7 with a standard deviation of 20.5. Will this help them use the buses more efficiently or better assign bus routes? Probably not. Thus, although you can put nominal numbers into formulas and perform calculations with almost any numbers, the researcher has to know the meaning behind the numbers before drawing useful conclusions.[4]

Discrete Measures

discrete measures

Measures that take on only one of a finite number of values.

Discrete measures are those that take on only one of a finite number of values. A discrete scale is most often used to represent a classificatory variable. Therefore, discrete scales, possessing nominal properties, do not represent intensity of measures, they represent only membership. Common discrete scales include any yes-or-no response, matching, color choices, or practically any scale that involves selecting from among a small number of categories. Thus, when someone selects from the following responses the result is a discrete value that can be coded 1, 2, or 3, respectively. When discrete scales represent an ordered arrangement of agreement, as in this case, they can possess ordinal properties and nominal properties.

■ Disagree
■ Neutral
■ Agree

Certain statistics are most appropriate for discrete measures. Exhibit 10.3 shows statistics for each scale level. The central tendency of a discrete measure, whether nominal or ordinal, is best captured by the mode. When a student wants to know what the most likely grade is for MKTG 4311, the mode will be very useful. Observe the results below from the previous semester:

A	5 Students	D	6 Students
B	20 Students	F	6 Students
C	12 Students		

The mode is a "B" since more students obtained that value than any other value. Therefore, the "average" student would expect a B in MKTG 4311.

Continuous Measures

Statistical terminology sometimes draws the distinction between statistics used for *discrete* versus *continuous* measures. **Continuous measures** are those assigning values anywhere along some scale range in a place that corresponds to the intensity of some concept. Ratio measures are continuous measures. Thus, when we measure sales for each salesperson using the dollar amount sold, we are assigning continuous measures. We could construct a number line ranging from the least to the most amount sold and a spot on the line would correspond exactly to a salesperson's performance.

Strictly speaking, interval scales are not necessarily continuous. Consider the following common type of survey question:

continuous measures

Measures that reflect the intensity of a concept by assigning values that can take on any value along some scale range. Continuous measures require at least interval level measurement.

	Strongly Disagree	Disagree	Neutral	Agree	Strongly Agree
I enjoy providing ratings of businesses in Yelp	1	2	3	4	5

This is a discrete scale because only the values 1, 2, 3, 4, or 5 can be assigned. Furthermore, it is an ordinal scale because it only orders based on agreement. We really have no way of knowing that the difference in agreement somebody marking a 5 and somebody marking a 4 is the same as the difference in agreement between somebody marking a 2 and somebody marking 1. The scale difference is 1 in either case, but is the difference in true agreement the same? There is no way to know. Therefore, the mean is not an appropriate way of stating central tendency, and we really shouldn't use many common statistics on these responses.

However, as a scaled response of this type takes on more values, the error introduced by assuming that the differences between the discrete points are equal becomes smaller. Imagine a *Likert scale* with a thousand levels of agreement rather than three or four. The differences between the different levels become so small with a thousand levels that only tiny errors are possible by assuming each interval is the same. Therefore, marketing researchers generally treat interval scales containing five or more categories of response as interval. When fewer than five categories are used, this assumption is inappropriate. Consequently, marketing researchers treat interval scales as continuous when five or more categories are used.

The researcher should keep in mind, however, the distinction between ratio and interval measures. Errors in judgment are possible when one treats interval measures as ratio. For example, the concept of attitude is usually measured with an interval scale. An attitude of zero means nothing— literally. In fact, attitude only has meaning in a relative sense. Therefore, attitude takes on meaning when a researcher compares one person's response to another person's response. Zero on an interval scale is arbitrary.

Means and standard deviations provide acceptable statistics for continuous data. Using the actual quantities for arithmetic operations is permissible with ratio scales. Thus, the ratios of scale values are meaningful. A ratio scale has all the properties of nominal, ordinal, and interval scales. However, the same cannot be said in reverse. An ordinal scale, for example, has nominal properties, but it does not have interval or ratio properties.

Reliable and Valid Measures

Earlier, we distinguished constructs as concepts that require multiple variables to measure them adequately. Looking back to the chapter vignette, could it be that multiple items will be required to adequately represent the concept of customer promotion? Likewise, a consumer's commitment toward some brand or store is usually represented by multiple items.

attribute

A single characteristic or fundamental feature of an object, person, situation, or issue.

An **attribute** is a single characteristic or fundamental feature of an object, person, situation, or issue. Attribute assessment is common in marketing research. The measures of attributes are often combined to represent some less concrete concept.

Indexes and Composites

index measure

Assigns a value based on a mathematical formula separating low scores from high scores. Index formulas often put several variables together.

Multi-item instruments for measuring a construct are either called *index measures* or *composite measures*. An **index measure** assigns a value based on a mathematical formula separating low scores from high scores. Index formulas often put several variables together. For example, researchers often form a social class index using three weighted variables: income, occupation, and education. Sociologists see occupation as the single best indicator and it gets the highest weight. A person with a highly prestigious occupation and a graduate degree but lacking a very high income would be more characteristic of high social class than one with a very high income but lacking formal education and a prestigious occupation.

Indexes do not require that the different attribute measures used in the formula strongly correlated with each other. A person's income does not always relate strongly to their education, yet the two sometimes represent an index of a person's social class. The American Consumer Satisfaction Index (ACSI) provides a level of American consumers' general satisfaction with businesses based on scores across diverse and unrelated industries and competitors within those industries. Users can compare scores across brands and across industries.[5] In 2018, consumers rate Costco highest in satisfaction amongst all "Department and Discount Stores." Overall, American consumers report higher satisfaction with beer and soft drinks than they do with wireless service providers.

composite scales

Assign a value to an observation based on a mathematical derivation of multiple variables to create an operational measure of a construct.

Composite scales also assign a value based on a mathematical derivation of multiple variables but do so to represent a latent construct. For example, a restaurant satisfaction scale might result from combining respondent scores from the following questions assessed with 10-point scales:

- How satisfied are you with your restaurant experience today?
- How pleased are you with your visit to our restaurant today?
- How content are you with the overall restaurant experience today?
- How satisfied are you with the overall service quality provided today?

For most practical applications, one computes composite measures and indexes in the same way.[6] However, researchers distinguish composite representations of constructs from index measures in that a composite representation of a construct is valid only when its indicators relate to each other both theoretically and statistically. In the customer satisfaction items listed above, one can hardly imagine that respondents would say they were highly satisfied and then provide a low score for how pleased they felt. That would seem very unusual. The item responses therefore should display positive correlations.

Computing Scale Values

summated scale

A scale created by simply summing (adding together) the response to each item making up the composite measure. The scores can be but do not have to be averaged by the number of items making up the composite scale.

Exhibit 10.4 demonstrates how a researcher creates a composite measure from individual rating scales. This particular scale assesses how much a consumer trusts a website.[7] This particular composite represents a **summated scale**. One creates a summated scale by summing the response to each item making up the composite measure. In this case, the consumer would have a trust score of 13 based on responses to five items. A researcher may sometimes choose to average the scores rather than summing them. The advantage to this is that the composite measure is expressed on the same scale as are the items that make it up. So, instead of a 13, the consumer would have a score of 2.6. The information content is the same.

Recoding Made Easy

Most survey-related software makes scale recoding easy. The screenshot shown here is from SPSS, perhaps the most widely used statistical software for survey-related marketing research. All that needs to be done to reverse-code a scale is to go through this click-through sequence:

1. Click on transform.
2. Click on recode.
3. Choose to recode into the same variable.
4. Select the variable(s) to be recoded.
5. Click on old and new values.
6. Use the menu that appears to enter the old values and the matching new values. Click add after entering each pair.
7. Click continue.

This would successfully recode variable X13 in this case. Other software, including Qualtrics, provide easy

Courtesy of spss statistics 17.0.

procedures like these for recoding variables. A recoding routine can be employed in Excel as well by employing the appropriate formula in a new column. Survey implementation software like Qualtrics also provides a recode feature that automatically performs the recoding prior to the data being downloaded from the Internet.

Item	Strongly Disagree (SD) → Strongly Agree (SA)				
This site appears to be more trustworthy than other sites I have visited.	SD	(D)	N	A	SA
My overall trust in this site is very high.	SD	D	(N)	A	SA
My overall impression of the believability of the information on this site is very high.	SD	(D)	N	A	SA
My overall confidence in the recommendations on this site is very high.	SD	(D)	N	A	SA
The company represented in this site delivers on its promises.	SD	D	N	(A)	SA
Computation: Scale Values: SD=1, D=2, N=3, A=4, SA=5					
Thus, the Trust score for this consumer is $2 + 3 + 2 + 2 + 4 = 3$					

EXHIBIT **10.4**
Computing a Composite Scale

Sometimes, a response may need to be reverse-coded before computing a summated or averaged scale value. **Reverse coding** is a specific type of recoding in which the value assigned for a response takes on a value opposite to that normally assigned to the scale labels. If a sixth item was included on the trust scale that said, "I do not trust this website," reverse coding would be necessary to make sure a composite made sense. The content of this item is the reverse of trust (distrust), so the item score is reversed for consistency yielding a trust scale and not a distrust scale. Thus, on a 5-point scale, the values are:

reverse coding

Means that the value assigned for a response is treated oppositely from the other items.

- 5 becomes 1
- 4 becomes 2
- 3 stays 3
- 2 becomes 4
- 1 becomes 5

The Research Snapshot above shows how a recode can be carried out using SPSS. SAS JMP contains a very similar recode option. Sometimes, one can come up with a simple mathematical

● ● ● ● ● ●

Reverse coding in SPSS is straightforward.

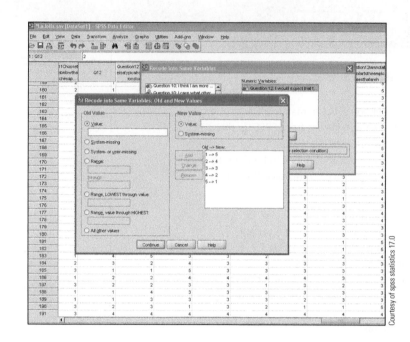

Courtesy of spss statistics 17.0

expression to recode a measure. For instance, if the variable above was named T1, the following mathematical expression would perform the recoding:

$$T1 = 6 - T1$$

Survey software also accommodates automatic recoding. Qualtrics, for example, provides an option to automatically recode flagged variables. After choosing the recode option, a window opens that allows the user to assign values manually to each response category. In these cases, the software will automatically perform the recoding for the user. Caution should be taken in using such shortcuts for several reasons. First, the user must be very certain that survey takers will see the item as opposite of other items making up a scale. A more conservative approach would be to analyze the data prior to any recoding. In fact, some advanced analytical methods do not require recoding. Second, occassionally the user may not realize that the items are recoded. In such cases, the meaning of the scale could be affected dramatically. If the items are recoded after downloading, they can be given a new name that clearly indicates that they are recoded from the original form. Thus, although the shortcuts can be handy, they also can contribute to user error. Use them with caution.

Reliability

reliability

An indicator of a measure's internal consistency.

internal consistency

Represents a measure's homogeneity or the extent to which each indicator of a construct converges on some common meaning.

split-half method

A method for assessing internal consistency by checking the results of one-half of a set of scaled items against the results from the other half.

Reliability is an indicator of a measure's internal consistency. Consistency is the key to understanding reliability. A measure is consistent when multiple attempts at measuring something converge on a common result. If a professor's marketing research tests are reliable, a student should tend toward consistent scores on all tests. In other words, a student that makes an 80 on the first test should make scores close to 80 on all subsequent tests. If it is difficult to predict what students would make on a test by examining their previous test scores, the tests probably lack reliability.

Internal Consistency

Internal consistency is a term used by researchers to represent a composite measure's homogeneity. An attempt to measure trust may require asking several similar but not identical questions. An overall measure often comprises a *battery* of scale items. *Internal consistency* of a multiple-item composite measure can be assessed by correlating scores on subsets of items making up a scale. Internal consistency is not a concern for index measures that do not represent latent constructs.

The **split-half method** of checking reliability takes half the items from a scale (for example, odd-numbered items) and checks them against the results from the other half (even-numbered items). The two scale *halves* should correlate highly (approaching an absolute value of 1.0) if the measure is internally consistent. They should also produce similar scores. Multiple techniques exist for estimating scale reliability, all based on this basic principle of correspondence.

Coefficient alpha (α) is the most commonly applied estimate of a composite scale's reliability.[8] Coefficient α estimates internal consistency by computing the average of all possible split-half reliabilities for a multiple-item scale. The coefficient demonstrates whether the different items converge on some single point. Many researchers use coefficient α as the sole indicator of a scale's quality largely because statistical programs like SPSS and SAS's JMP readily provide the result. Coefficient α can only take on values ranging from 0, meaning no consistency among items (they are all statistically independent), to 1, meaning complete consistency (all items correlate perfectly with each other).

Generally speaking, researchers consider scales exhibiting a coefficient α between 0.80 and 0.96 as possessing very good reliability. Scales with a coefficient α between 0.70 and 0.80 are considered to have good reliability, and an α value between 0.60 and 0.70 indicates fair reliability. When the coefficient α is below 0.60, the scale has poor reliability.[9] Researchers generally report coefficient a for each

Reliability
Scale: Positive Feelings

Case Processing Summary

		N	%
Cases	Valid	457	100.0
	Excluded[a]	0	.0
	Total	457	100.0

[a]Listwise deletion based on all variables in the procedure.

Reliability Statistics

Cronbach's Alpha	N of Items
.960	5

Item-Total Statistics

	Scale Mean if Item Deleted	Scale Variance if Item Deleted	Corrected Item-Total Correlation	Cronbach's Alpha if Item Deleted
Excited	14.58	51.459	.859	.955
Happy	14.16	51.611	.886	.950
Interested	14.04	50.138	.891	.949
Pleased	14.29	51.352	.910	.946
Satisfied	14.30	51.603	.886	.950

composite measure involved in a study. A full accounting of measurement quality, though, should also include other indicators aimed at a more thorough assessment of validity as shown below.

Test-Retest Reliability

The **test-retest method** of determining reliability involves administering the same scale or measure to the same respondents at two separate times to test for stability. If the measure is stable over time, the test, administered under the same conditions each time, should obtain similar results. Test-retest reliability represents a measure's repeatability.

Suppose a researcher at one time attempts to measure buying intentions and finds that 12 percent of a population is willing to purchase a product. A few weeks later under similar conditions, the researcher assesses intentions in the population again and finds the result to be 12 percent. The measure, thus, appears reliable. High stability correlation or consistency between two measures at time 1 and time 2 indicates high reliability.

Assume that a person does not change his or her mind about dark beer with time. A scale item like the one shown below:

I prefer dark beer to all other types of beer

should produce the same score in November 2019 as it did in April 2019 or December 2018. When a measuring instrument produces unpredictable results from one testing to the next, the results lack consistency and suggest an unreliable measure. Research based on unreliable measures is itself unreliable because of measurement error.

Reliability is a necessary but insufficient condition for validity. A scale can display high reliability but still lack validity. For example, a composite scale assessing purchase intention may consistently indicate that respondents are 40 percent likely to purchase a new product. The measure is valid to the extent that 40 percent of the population actually does purchase the product. In reality, 10 percent of consumers end up purchasing the product. Thus, the scale would be consistent but not valid. A reliable but invalid instrument will yield consistently inaccurate results. Perhaps you've come across results from polls or other research in the media that appear reliable but inaccurate in this manner?

coefficient alpha (α)

The most commonly applied estimate of a multiple item scale's reliability. It represents the average of all possible split-half reliabilities for a construct.

test-retest method

Administering the same scale or measure to the same respondents at two separate points in time to test for stability.

Here are some results from using a software package to estimate coefficient α for a 5-item scale measuring the positive feelings shoppers had during a shopping trip. The results show a value of 0.96 for the scale. Also, the item-total statistics indicate that all the items correlate highly with the scale. Overall, these are positive results.

● ● ● ● ● ● ●

A golfer may hit reliable but not valid putts and thus tend to miss them in some repeated fashion. This golfer's putts tend to converge to the left of—rather than in—the hole!

PhotoTalk/E+/Getty Images

Validity

validity

The accuracy of a measure or the extent to which a score truthfully represents a concept.

Good measures should be both precise and accurate. Reliability represents how precise a measure is in that the different attempts at measuring the same thing converge on the same point. Accuracy deals more with how a measure assesses the intended concept. **Validity** is the accuracy of a measure or the extent to which a score truthfully represents a concept.

Achieving validity is not a simple matter. Researchers who study job performance often resort to asking employees to self-rate their own performance. A multiple item self-rated performance scale is usually reliable, but does one's opinion reflect his/her actual job performance? Perhaps some bias creeps in causing the scale to represent something besides true job performance.

Researchers need to know if their measures are valid. The question of validity expresses the researcher's concern with accurate measurement. Validity addresses the problem of whether a measure indeed measures what it is supposed to measure. When a measure lacks validity, any conclusions based on that measure are also likely to be faulty.

Students should be able to empathize with the following validity problem. Consider the controversy about highway patrol officers using radar guns to clock speeders. An officer clocks a driver at 75 mph in a 55 mph zone. However, the same radar gun registered 28 mph when aimed at a house. The error occurred because the radar gun had picked up impulses from the electrical system of the squad car's idling engine. The house was probably not speeding—and the radar gun was probably not completely valid.

Establishing Validity

Researchers attempt to assess validity in many ways. The following questions represent some of these approaches:

- Is there a consensus among experts that the scale items actually correspond to the definition of the concept being measured?
- Does the latent construct (factor) fully capture all systematic variation among a scale's items?
- Does any particular measure of the concept correlate with other measures of the same concept?
- Can the behavior associated with the concept be accurately predicted using the specific measurement scale?

The three basic aspects of validity are *face* or *content validity*, *criterion validity*, and *construct validity*.

Face (content) validity refers to the extent to which individual measures' content match the intended concept's definition. One way to check this involves using a few experts to judge how well each item in a scale represents the concept definition. This test provides evidence of face validity when the judges tend to agree that the items' content matches the concept. If expert judges cannot be used, the researcher him/herself must carefully inspect each item's content.

Criterion validity addresses the question, "Does my measure correlate with measures of similar concepts or known quantities?" Criterion validity may be classified as either *concurrent validity* or *predictive validity* depending on the time sequence in which the new measurement scale and the criterion measure are correlated. If the researcher applies the new measure at the same time as the criterion measure, then concurrent validity is relevant. Predictive validity is established when a new measure predicts a future event. The two measures differ only on the basis of a time dimension.

A practical example of predictive validity is illustrated by a commercial research firm's test of the relationship between a rough content marketing video's effectiveness (as determined, for example, by recall scores) and a finished content marketng video's effectiveness (also by recall scores). Ad agencies test animatic, photomatic, or live-action scenes before developing actual finished content. One marketing research consulting firm suggests that this testing has high predictive validity. Rough commercial recall scores provide correct estimates of the final finished content recall scores more than 80 percent of the time.[10]

Construct Validity

Construct validity exists when each measure involved in a project reliably and truthfully represents a unique concept. Construct validity is multifaceted and exists to the extent that a scale exhibits the following characteristics:

1. Face validity
2. Criterion validity
3. Convergent validity
4. Discriminant validity
5. Fit validity

Criterion validity and face validity were discussed in the preceding paragraphs. **Convergent validity** depends on internal consistency meaning that multiple measures converge on a consistent meaning. Highly reliable scales contain convergent validity. One indicator of convergent validity is that each scale item should display high correlation with the actual construct (or latent factor) being measured. **Discriminant validity** represents how unique or distinct is a measure. A scale should not correlate too highly with a measure of a different construct. For example, a customer satisfaction measure should not correlate too highly with a cognitive dissonance scale if the two concepts are truly different. As a rough rule of thumb, when two scales are correlated above 0.75, discriminant validity may be an issue. In addition, each individual scale item should correlate more highly with the construct.

Fit validity is a little more complex to understand but can be thought of as the extent to which a researcher's proposed measurement approach (how all the constructs in a study will be measured) fully explains the covariation (the way each item corresponds with all other items measured) among all the items involved in the research. High fit validity suggests the absence of influence of unmeasured concepts on the scale items employed. Multivariate statistical procedures like confirmatory factor analysis can be useful in establishing construct validity. We return to this topic in the marketing analytics chapters.

Reliability versus Validity

The differences between reliability and validity can be illustrated by picturing target shooting as illustrated in Exhibit 10.5. Using an analogy, consider someone practicing target shooting. Suppose the person fires an equal number of rounds with a century-old rifle and a modern rifle.[11] The shots from the older gun end up considerably scattered, but those from the newer gun cluster closely together. The inconsistency of the old rifle compared with that of the new one indicates lower reliability.

face (content) validity

Extent to which individual measures' content match the intended concept's definition.

criterion validity

The ability of a measure to correlate with other standard measures of similar constructs or established criteria.

construct validity

Exists when a measure reliably measures and truthfully represents a unique concept; consists of several components including face validity, convergent validity, criterion validity, discriminant validity, and fit validity.

convergent validity

Depends on internal consistency so that multiple measures converge on a consistent meaning.

discriminant validity

Represents how unique or distinct is a measure; a scale should not correlate too highly with a measure of a different construct.

fit validity

Represents the extent to which a researcher's proposed measurement approach it represents than with other constructs.

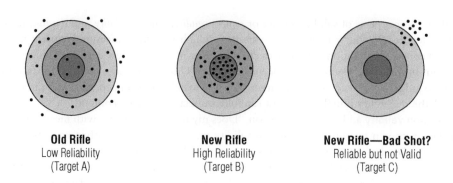

Old Rifle
Low Reliability
(Target A)

New Rifle
High Reliability
(Target B)

New Rifle—Bad Shot?
Reliable but not Valid
(Target C)

The target on the right of the Exhibit shows results from a new, low priced air gun. All the shots cluster tightly but on the edge of the target. The shots fired with the new gun indicate a reliable tool because they are consistent with each other. The shots are reliable, but not valid because they miss the target by a substantial margin. If you've tried to target shoot at a carnival, you may have used a gun like this.

What Is an Attitude?

attitude

An enduring predisposition to consistently respond in a given manner to various aspects of the world; composed of affective, cognitive, and behavioral components.

What does one mean when they accuse someone of having a "bad attitude"? The idea is that one's disposition about the relevant matter is not positive and the result is less than productive behavior. Formally, an **attitude** is a social-psychological concept defined as a relatively enduring predisposition to respond consistently to various things including people, activities, events, and objects. Attitudes are predispositions toward behavior and as such represent rules that inform a person of the appropriate reaction in a given situation. If someone has a negative attitude toward broccoli, then that person is likely to avoid eating, smelling, or even approaching any dish with the obvious presence of broccoli. If a fan "loves the Bulldogs," he or she is more likely to buy tickets and attend their games. Additionally, attitudes are latent constructs, and because of this, they are not directly observable.

Social psychologists believe that attitudes have three identifiable components:

1. An affective component that expresses how much affinity someone has toward the relevant matter. More simply, this is the feeling of liking or not liking something. For example, a consumer might say "I love Chick-fil-A." This expresses strong affinity.
2. A cognitive component that represents a person's awareness and knowledge of the relevant matter. In other words, what a person believes about the subject matter. When someone says, "Chick-fil-A has a wide selection," they are expressing a belief about this particular consumer alternative. Together with other relevant beliefs about Chick-fil-A, the beliefs comprise knowledge—which need not be correct to shape attitude.
3. A behavioral component representing the action undertaken as a result of the affective and cognitive components. If the attitude is positive, the person will display approach responses. If the attitude is negative, the person will display avoidance reactions. "I'll never eat at Chick-fil-A again" expresses a behavioral component of a negative attitude. Researchers often capture the behavioral component using intentions toward future behavior.

Sometimes researchers need to study overall attitude. Other times, they may focus on one of these components more than others. Whenever overall attitude or any of these components are measured through survey research, the researcher is conducting attitudinal research.

Research results generally show that attitudes do predict behavior with at least some accuracy. Consequently, marketing managers place a great deal of importance on attitudes. If a marketing approach changes consumers' aggregate attitude about some product, sales volume changes consequently. If employees' aggregate attitude about their job improves, their work output is likely to increase proportionately. Further, if knowledge about a product can be changed, the product can be repositioned to capture some new market.

After years of riding high in terms of fan favorability, many fans' attitudes toward the NFL and watching NFL games took a turn for the worse. Fans disappointed with player protests that seem unpatriotic and the inconveniences and high prices of NFL game attendance have contributed to

● ● ● ● ● ● ●

Marketing Researchers measure attitudes and behavioral intentions about all manner of things, including eating "mor chikin" at Chick-fil-A.

make NFL among the least favorable professional sports in 2017.[12] Fan attendance and television ratings both have fallen. In response, the new NFL stadium in Atlanta has improved Wi-Fi capability, wider, more comfortable seats, and lower concession prices. The hope is the moves will improve fans' attitudes and, subsequently, create more attendance and viewership.

Attitude Measures and Scaling

Researchers face a wide variety of choices in measuring attitudinal concepts. One reason for the variety is that no complete consensus exists over just what constitutes an attitude or an attitudinal variable. Researchers generally agree however that the affective, cognitive, and behavioral components of an attitude can each be measured effectively. However, attitudes may also be interpreted using qualitative techniques like those discussed in Chapter 5. Even if no agreement exists over the precise boundaries delineating attitudinal variables from others, researchers widely apply approaches used to measure attitude components in measuring many attitude-like variables.

Physiological Measures

Research may assess the affective (emotional) components of attitudes through physiological measures like galvanic skin response (GSR), blood pressure, magnetic resonance imaging (MRI), and pupil dilation. These measures provide a means of assessing affect without verbally questioning the respondent. In general, they can provide a gross measure of likes or dislikes, but they are not extremely sensitive to the different gradients of an attitude. Researchers studying attitudes toward music used a physiological approach in studying what types of music tend to become popular.[13] MRI recordings for instance, showing brain activity consistent with increased liking, correlate positively with purchases of music. A phenomenon known as an ear-worm tends to drive the perceptions that a song is "stuck in my head." Over time, this feeling can erode attitudes toward the song as typified by Disney's "It's a Small World."

Self-Report Scales

In contrast to physiological measures, an entire class of psychological measures involve gaining a respondent's structured response to some specific query or stimulus. Researchers can ask respondents to rank, rate, sort, or choose one of multiple responses as a way of indicating a response. A **ranking task** requires the respondent to rank order a small number of stores, brands, feelings, or objects based on overall preference or of some characteristic of the stimulus. Rankings provide ordinal measurement. **Rating** requires the respondent to estimate the magnitude or the extent to which some characteristic exists or some choice is preferred. Researchers typically treat most rating scales as yielding better than ordinal measurement.

ranking task

A measurement task that requires respondents to rank order a small number of stores, brands, or objects on the basis of overall preference or some characteristic of the stimulus.

rating

A measurement task that requires respondents to estimate the magnitude of a characteristic or quality that a brand, store, or object possesses.

sorting

A measurement task that presents a respondent with several objects or product concepts and requires the respondent to arrange the objects into piles or classify the product concepts.

choice

A measurement task that identifies preferences by requiring respondents to choose between two or more alternatives.

The rating task involves marking a response indicating one's position using one or more attitudinal or cognitive scales. A **sorting** task might present the respondent with several product concepts on cards and require the respondent to classify the concepts by placing the cards into stacks, each representing a different meaning. Another type of attitude measurement requires respondents to make a **choice** between two or more alternatives. If a respondent chooses one object over another, the researcher assumes that the respondent prefers the chosen object, at least in this setting.

Marketing researchers commonly use rating scales to measure attitudes. This section discusses many rating scales designed to enable respondents to report the intensity of their attitudes. In its most basic form, attitude scaling requires that an individual agree or disagree with a statement or indicate how much some term describes his or her feeling. For example, respondents in a political poll may be asked whether they either agree or disagree with a statement like, "Politicians are likable." Or, an individual might indicate whether he or she likes or dislikes jalapeño bean dip. This type of self-rating scale merely classifies respondents into one of two categories, thus having only the properties of a nominal scale, and the types of mathematical analysis that may be used with this basic scale are limited.

Simple attitude scaling can be a practical way of implementing a survey when questionnaires are extremely long, when respondents have little education, or for other specific reasons. In fact, a number of simplified scales are merely checklists where a respondent indicates past experience, preference, or likes and dislikes simply by checking an item. Common checklist questions may ask respondents to place checks besides products or brands that they use or are familiar with as illustrated below:

Which of the fast-food restaurants below have you purchased food from in the last 30 days? Place a check by each that qualifies.

- Chick-fil-A
- Raising Canes
- McDonald's
- Taco Bell
- Wendys
- KFC
- Have not purchased food at any of these in last 30 days

Which of the celebrities listed below are you familiar with?

- Celion Dion
- Shay Mitchell
- Lucy Hale
- Rachel Parcell
- Lisa Mantier
- Not familiar of any of these

Simple approaches like these produce results that are easy to convey to management.[14] In addition, they sometimes overcome problems common to rating scale approaches that we will touch on later. Marketers might even consider a Facebook "like" as an indicator of a favorable attitude. The question of whether a Facebook "like" turns into consumer behavior that supports the brand though remains uncertain. Some research on the question suggests that likes translate into favorable behavior when brands use their Facebook sites as a platform to boost their content.[15] Thus, organic "likes" may not be so indicative of attitude.

Scales with better than ordinal measurement quality are needed to discern small differences between attitudes or to scale different brands along a continuum. The following sections describe some popular techniques for measuring attitudes quantitatively.

Measuring the Affect Component

Not all rating approaches are the same. Exhibit 10.6 displays an interesting approach to get respondents to rate their affect toward some object or activity. Respondents are asked to choose a "manikin" from each row to show not only their general affective state (like or dislike), but the degree to which they get emotionally aroused (the middle row), and how much the thing being rated makes them feel small (unimportant) or important. This approach is useful in all manner of measures involving emotion.

EXHIBIT **10.6**
Novel Approach to Rating Affect using "Manikins"
Sources: Morris, J. D. (1995), "Observations: SAM: The Self-Assessment Manikin: An Efficient Cross-Cultural Measurement of Emotional Response," *Journal of Advertising Research*, 35, 63–68. Morris, J. D., C. Woo, and A. J. Singh (2005), "Elaboration Likelihood Model: A Missing Intrinsic Emotional Implication," *Journal of Targeting, Measurement and Analysis for Marketing*, 14 (October), 79–98.

● ● ● ● ● ●

Generally, consumers act in a way consistent with their attitudes. Therefore, attitudes are a popular marketing research topic.

michaeljung/Shutterstock.com

Category Scales

I like the idea of attending Cool State University.

    ○ *Yes*   ○ *No*

Expanding the response categories provides the respondent with more flexibility in the rating task. Even more information is provided if the categories are ordered according to a particular descriptive or evaluative dimension. Consider the following question:

How often do you think favorably about attending Cool State University?

    ○ *Never*   ○ *Rarely*   ○ *Sometimes*   ○ *Often*   ○ *Very often*

This **category scale** measures attitude with greater sensitivity than a two-point response scale. By having more choices, the potential exists to provide more information. However, a researcher will create measurement error if he/she uses a category scale for something that is truly bipolar (yes/no, member/non-member, and so on).

Response category wording is an extremely important factor. Exhibit 10.7 shows some common wordings used in category scales measuring common marketing research variables. As you can see, the more categories, the more difficulty a researcher has in coming up with precise and readily understandable category labels. Survey software often automatically inserts category headings into

category scale

A rating scale that consists of several response categories, often providing respondents with alternatives to indicate positions on a continuum.

EXHIBIT 10.7

Commonly Applied Category Scale Descriptions

Quality				
Poor	Fair	Good	Excellent	
Very bad	Bad	Neither good nor bad	Fairly good	Very good
Importance				
Not at all important	Not so important	Neither important nor unimportant	Fairly Important	Very Important
Interest				
Very interested		Somewhat interested		Not at all interested
Satisfaction				
Completely dissatisfied	Somewhat dissatisfied	Neither satisfied nor dissatisfied	Somewhat satisfied	Completely satisfied
Very satisfied	Quite satisfied	Somewhat satisfied	Not at all satisfied	
Frequency				
Never	Sometimes	About half the time	Most of the time	Always
Never	Once a Year	Once a Month	Weekly	Daily

questionnaire items based on the number of categories selected. The user should pay attention to what the software does to avoid unintended category labels.

The Likert Scale

likert scale

A measure of attitudes designed to allow respondents to rate how strongly they disagree or agree with carefully constructed statements, ranging from very positive to very negative attitudes toward some object.

The Likert scale may well be the most commonly applied scale format in marketing research. Likert scales are simple to administer and understand. Likert scales were developed by and named after Rensis Likert, a 20th century social scientist. With a **Likert scale**, respondents indicate their attitudes by checking how strongly they disagree or agree with carefully constructed statements. The scale results reveal the respondent's attitude ranging from very positive to very negative. Individuals generally choose from multiple response alternatives such as strongly agree, agree, neutral, disagree, and strongly disagree. Researchers commonly employ five choices, although they also often use six, seven or even more response points. In the following example, from a study of food- shopping behavior, there are five alternatives:

I like to go to Walmart when buying food for my family.				
Strongly Disagree	**Disagree**	**Neutral**	**Agree**	**Strongly Agree**
O	O	O	O	O
(1)	*(2)*	*(3)*	*(4)*	*(5)*

The researcher (or survey software) assigns scores to each possible response. In this example, numericals scores of 1, 2, 3, 4, and 5 are assigned to each level of agreement, respectively. Here, strong agreement indicates the most favorable attitude on the statement and receives a score of 5.

Realize that if the statement were worded in a way that indicated dislike for shopping for food at Walmart, a 5 would mean a less favorable attitude about this activity. For example, responses to the item above could even be combined with those from an item like this:

Walmart is a bad place to shop for fresh foods.				
Strongly Disagree	**Disagree**	**Neutral**	**Agree**	**Strongly Agree**
O	O	O	O	O
(1)	*(2)*	*(3)*	*(4)*	*(5)*

Before one could form a composite scale with these items, the responses to this last item would have to be reverse coded as shown previously.

Remember too, an attitude score is arbitrary and has little cardinal meaning—in other words, attitude scores are at best interval and clearly not ratio. They could also just easily be scored so that a higher score indicated less favorable attitudes. However, the convention is to score attitude scales so that a higher score means a more favorable attitude. In this way, researchers can compare consumer attitudes for competing brands with higher scores indicating relatively more favorable predispositions.

Selecting Items for a Likert Scale

Typically, a researcher will use multiple items to represent a single attitudinal concept. The researcher may generate a large number of statements before putting together the final questionnaire. A pre-test may be conducted using these items allowing for an *item analysis* to be performed. The item analysis helps select items that evoke a wide response (meaning all respondents are not selecting the same response point such as all strongly agree), allowing the item to discriminate among those with positive and negative attitudes. Items are also analyzed for clarity or unusual response patterns. Thus, the final Likert items should be clearly understood and elicit an accurate range of responses corresponding to respondents' true attitudes.

Semantic Differential

A **semantic differential** is a scale type on which respondents describe their attitude using a series of bipolar rating scales. Bipolar rating scales involve respondents choosing between opposing adjectives—such as "good" and "bad," "modern" and "old-fashioned," or "clean" and "dirty." One adjective anchors the beginning and the other the end (or poles) of the scale. The subject makes repeated judgments about the concept under investigation on each of the scale. Exhibit 10.8 shows an example semantic differential approach for assessing consumer attitudes toward a branded video displayed on Instagram.

The scoring of the semantic differential can be illustrated using the scale bounded by the anchors "complex" and "simple." Respondents are instructed to check the place that indicates the nearest appropriate adjective. From left to right, the scale intervals represent the belief that the stimulus is somewhere between extremely complex. One advantage provided by using scale labels over each category is the ability to influence the distribution of responses.

semantic differential

A measure of attitudes that consists of a series of bipolar rating scales with opposite terms on either end.

How complex is streaming video with Apple TV?

Extremely Simple	Very Simple	Simple	Neither Simple nor Complex	Complex	Very Complex	Extremely Complex
○	○	○	○	○	○	○
(-3)	(-2)	(-1)	(0)	(1)	(2)	(3)

Semantic Differentials And Meaning

The semantic differential technique originally was developed as a method for measuring the meanings of objects or the "semantic space" of interpersonal experience.[16] Researchers see the semantic differential as versatile and useful in a wide variety of business situations.

When opposites are available, the semantic differential is a good scale choice. In typical attitude or image studies, simple anchors such as very unfavorable and very favourable work well. However, the validity of the semantic differential depends on finding scale anchors that are semantic opposites and this can sometimes prove difficult. For example, consider the following scale in which the respondent is asked to place a check on the space closest to the way they feel about the phrase:

Shopping at the H&M makes me:
Sad __ __ __ __ __ __ __ Happy

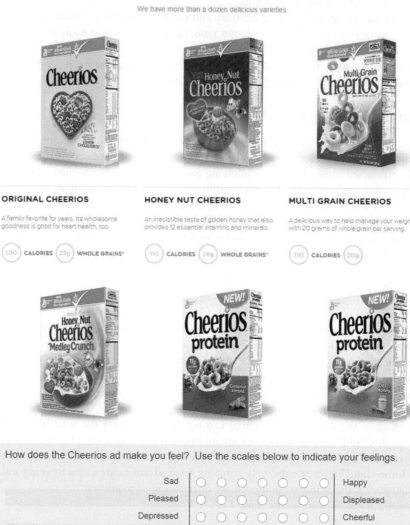

What's your favorite flavor of Cheerios cereal?

We have more than a dozen delicious varieties.

ORIGINAL CHEERIOS

A family favorite for years. Its wholesome goodness is good for heart health, too.

⟨100⟩ CALORIES ⟨25g⟩ WHOLE GRAINS*

HONEY NUT CHEERIOS

An irresistible taste of golden honey that also provides 12 essential vitamins and minerals.

⟨110⟩ CALORIES ⟨14g⟩ WHOLE GRAINS*

MULTI GRAIN CHEERIOS

A delicious way to help manage your weight with 20 grams of whole grain per serving.

⟨110⟩ CALORIES ⟨20g⟩

Source: www.Cheerios.com

How does the Cheerios ad make you feel? Use the scales below to indicate your feelings.

Sad	○	○	○	○	○	○	○	Happy
Pleased	○	○	○	○	○	○	○	Displeased
Depressed	○	○	○	○	○	○	○	Cheerful
Good	○	○	○	○	○	○	○	Bad

Few would question that sad is the opposite of happy. However, what if this were to be combined with an item capturing how angry shopping at the H&M makes a respondent feel? Then, what would the opposite of angry be? Clearly, using happy as the opposite of sad. Thus, a semantic differential may not be best for capturing anger unless some distinctive and unambiguous opposite exists.

Scoring Semantic Differentials

Like Likert scales, a numerical score can be assigned to each position on a semantic differential scale. For a seven-point semantic differential the scores could be 1, 2, 3, 4, 5, 6, 7 or -3, -2, -1, 0, +1, +2, +3. Marketing researchers generally assume that the semantic differential provides interval data. This assumption does have critics who argue that the data have only ordinal properties because the numerical scores are arbitrary and there is no way of knowing that the differences between choices are equal. Practically, the vast majority of social science researchers treat semantic differential scales as metric (at least interval). This is justified because the amount of error introduced by assuming the intervals between choices are equal (even though this is uncertain at best) is fairly small.

Constant-Sum Scale

A **constant-sum scale** demands that respondents divide points among several attributes to indicate their relative importance. Suppose Samsung wishes to determine the importance of smartphone attributes such as reliability, battery life, video/audio quality, camera quality, voice (call) quality, and an economical service plan. Respondents might divide a constant sum of 100 points to indicate the relative importance of those attributes as such:

constant-sum scale

A measure of attitudes in which respondents are asked to divide a constant sum to indicate the relative importance of attributes; respondents often sort cards, but the task may also be a rating task.

Divide 100 points among the following characteristics of a smartphone indicating how important each characteristic is when determining which phone will deliver the best overall experience.

Characteristic	Points
Reliability	20
Battery Life (length of time between charges)	20
Video Quality	5
Audio Quality	10
Camera Quality	10
Voice (Call) Quality	20
Economical Service	15
Total	100

The constant-sum scale requires respondents to understand that their responses should total to the total number of points. In the case above, that number is 100. As the number of stimuli increases, this technique becomes increasingly complex. Fortunately, electronic questionnaires eliminate math errors by having the software trigger an error notice whenever responses do not match the total. The respondent could adjust the responses until the sums do indeed match the total. If respondents follow the instructions correctly, the results will approximate interval measures.

This technique may be used for measuring brand preference. The approach, which is similar to the paired-comparison method, is as follows:

Divide 100 points among the following brands based on your degree of preference for each:

Brand	Points
Coca-Cola	30
Pepsi-Cola	25
Dr Pepper	45
Total	100

Although the constant sum scale is widely used, strictly speaking, the scale is flawed because the last response is completely determined by the way the respondent has scored the other choices. Although the flaw is probably somewhat complex to understand the problem relates to a lack of freedom for the respondent and the potential for error, particularly in the last choice. Despite the flaw, surveys sometimes employ constant-sum scales for practical reasons.

Graphic Rating Scales

A **graphic rating scale** presents respondents with a graphic continuum. The respondents are allowed to choose any point on the continuum to indicate their attitude. Typically a respondent's score is determined by measuring the length (in millimeters) from one end of the graphic continuum to the point marked by the respondent. Many researchers believe that scoring in this manner strengthens the assumption that graphic rating scales of this type are interval scales. Alternatively, the researcher may divide the line into predetermined scoring categories (lengths) and record respondents' marks accordingly. In other words, the graphic rating scale has the advantage of allowing the researcher to choose any interval desired for scoring purposes. Electronic questionnaires allow the use of a slider scale. The sliders function much the same as a graphics rating scale as shown in Exhibit 10.9.

graphic rating scale

A measure of attitude that allows respondents to rate an object by choosing any point along a graphic continuum. Electronic slider scales work much the same way.

EXHIBIT 10.9

With online surveys, a slider performs the function of the graphic ratings scale.

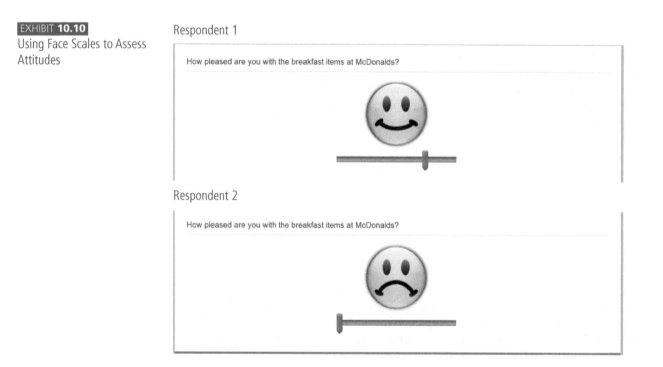

Use the sliding scales below to indicate how important each factor is to you when selecting classes to take at your university:

| Not Important At All | | | | | | | | Extremely Important | |
| 0 | 10 | 20 | 30 | 40 | 50 | 60 | 70 | 80 | 90 | 100 |

Convenience of time the class is offered

Research record of instructor

Whether the class is offered online

The class is scheduled for two days a week

Knowing that some of your friends will be in the class

EXHIBIT 10.10

Using Face Scales to Assess Attitudes

Respondent 1

How pleased are you with the breakfast items at McDonalds?

Respondent 2

How pleased are you with the breakfast items at McDonalds?

Research to investigate children's attitudes has used happy-sad face scales. Exhibit 10.10 illustrates one such approach. Here, the respondent chooses an attitude by sliding the scale up and down using the tab to the right of the face. As the respondent moves the left or right, the face smiles or frowns, correspondingly. The first respondent is fairly pleased with the idea of hot breakfast items at McDonald's. However, the second respondent has a very negative attitude toward the idea. Notice the position of the tab corresponding to each face.

Among the attitude rating approaches discussed in this chapter, Likert scales and semantic differentials account for the majority of applications. The Research Snapshot below suggests that attitudes can help make a story complete.

Liking the Look

What is beauty? Obviously, consumers like beautiful things. But, the idealized image of beauty changes over time. For example, attitudes about the ideal size of women change with time as can be seen by the depiction of women in media over decades and even centuries. Likewise, how much makeup is too much? Consumer attitudes toward wearing makeup or how much makeup is beautiful change over time and these changes have a huge impact on sales in the beauty and cosmetics industry. In 2017, American consumers' attitudes seem split on the question. Forty-three percent of Americans in a survey suggest that women tend to wear too much makeup. However, 35 percent of respondents suggest women tend to wear just the right amount of makeup. Perhaps reflecting American attitudes, fashion trends display extremes. The trends as depicted in the fashion industry are toward minimalists looks or toward extreme makeup applications. For example, fashion trends recommend "no-makeup"

aniarenard/Shutterstock.com

makeup, accented by bright red lipstick, or conversely, heavy applications of makeup with particular emphasis on eye blush. The cosmetics industry, like so many others, succeeds or fails as a consequence of consumer attitudes.

Sources: https://www.statista.com/statistics/752467/consumer-attitudes-makeup-worn-by-women/; http://www.harpersbazaar.com/beauty/makeup/g8357/makeup-trends-2017/, accessed December 21, 2017.

Ranking

A ranking is different than a rating scale in that respondents simply order alternatives on some characteristic. Consumers often *rank order* their preferences so, in this sense, ranking scales have considerable validity. An ordinal scale may be developed by asking respondents to rank order (from most preferred to least preferred) a set of objects or attributes. Respondents easily understand the task of rank ordering product attributes or arranging a set of brand names according to preference. Like the constant-sum scale, however, the ranking scale suffers from inflexibility in that if we know how someone ranked five out of six alternatives, we know the answer to the sixth. Thus, a respondent does not rate each category independently as in a typical ratings scale. Additionally, ordinal scaling only allows us to know that one option is preferred over another—not how much one option is preferred over another.

To the Point

" My tastes are very simple. I only want the best. "

—OSCAR WILDE

Paired Comparisons

Consider a situation in which a chain saw manufacturer learned that a competitor had introduced a new lightweight (6-pound) chain saw. The manufacturer's lightest chain saw weighed 9 pounds. Executives wondered if they needed to introduce a 6-pound chain saw into the product line. The research design employed a **paired comparison** approach. The company built a prototype of a 6-pound chain saw. Then, they painted both the 9- and 6-pound saws from their competitor the same color as their own 9- and 6-pound chain saws so color differences would not be responsible for any preferences. Respondents then saw two chain saws at a time and picked the one they preferred. Three pairs of comparisons allowed the researchers to determine the saw each respondent liked best.

paired comparison

A measurement technique that involves presenting the respondent with two objects and asking the respondent to pick the preferred object; more than two objects may be presented, but comparisons are made in pairs.

The following question illustrates the typical format for asking about paired comparison preferences.

I would like to know your overall opinion of two brands of adhesive bandages. They are Curad and Band-Aid. Overall, which of these two brands—Curad or Band-Aid—do you think is the better one? Or are both the same?

Curad is better. _____

Band-Aid is better. _____

They are the same. _____

If researchers wish to compare four brands of pens on the basis of attractiveness or writing quality, six comparisons $[(n)(n-1)/2]$ will be necessary. Paired comparisons sometimes require respondents to assess similarity instead of preference by asking which of the two choices is more similar to some third choice. With either similarity or preference, if the number of comparisons is too large, respondents become fatigued and do not carefully discriminate the choices.

Direct Assessment of Consumer Attitudes

Attitudes, as hypothetical constructs, cannot be observed directly. We can, however, infer one's attitude by the way he or she responds to multiple attitude indicators. The researcher can then sum the scores on the multiple indicators of attitude. Consider the following three semantic differential items capturing a consumer's attitude toward Microsoft Word:

very bad ___ ___ ___ ___ ___ ___ ___*very good*

very unfavorable ___ ___ ___ ___ ___ ___ ___*very favorable*

very negative ___ ___ ___ ___ ___ ___ ___ *very positive*

A summed score over these three items would represent a latent (unobservable) attitude construct. How do you feel about Netflix subscriptions? Use the scale to find your score.

The decision whether to use ranking, sorting, rating, or a choice technique is determined largely by the problem definition and especially by the type of statistical analysis desired. For example, ranking provides only ordinal data, limiting the statistical techniques that may be used.

How Many Scale Categories or Response Positions?

Should a category scale have four, five, or seven response positions or categories? Or should the researcher use a graphic scale with an infinite number of positions? The original developmental research on the semantic differential indicated that five to eight points is optimal. However, the researcher must determine the number of meaningful positions that is best for the specific project. This issue of identifying how many meaningful distinctions respondents can practically make is basically a matter of sensitivity. For example, how sensitively can students discriminate the difficulty of college courses? The answer to the question may help determine the number of response categories.

The number of response categories can influence research conclusions. Think about a service employee asked to respond to an item asking about job satisfaction using a two-point response scale of either "no" or "yes." Can the two-point scale adequately capture the range of responses that employees might actually feel? Would we really expect that all people who respond "yes" have the same amount of satisfaction? Typically, a yes or no satisfaction question will yield about 80 percent yes responses. In other words, the data are typically skewed with a small number of scale points. If the scale is expanded to the typical 5-point Likert format, the "yes" responses are likely to be spread across multiple categories. Similarly, a scale with too few points may suppress variance that truly exists. Thus, a scale should be adequately sensitive to capture a respondent's opinion or feelings.

What happens if the same question is asked with scales of varying numbers of response categories? Some research suggests that skewness is reduced by including more scale points, particularly for attitudinal and satisfaction type items. Additionally, including more scale points produces less extreme patterns of results with typical responses closer to the midpoint of the scale. Thus, as long as adding category responses does not become taxing to respondents, more categories are better than fewer. However, scales with 5 to 10 scale points typically display results suggesting they are appropriate for use in statistical procedures like regression.[17]

Others offer a few caveats to these findings. Research finds that less capable respondents sometimes provide more valid responses with fewer rather than more scale points.[18] In addition, the inclusion of labels over all scale points tends to produce slightly more acquiescence bias than a scale with labels only on the end point. As a result, the use of labels over all choices is preferable when scores will be compared directly across respondents. Scores with only the ends labeled are somewhat preferable for use with statistics like regression analysis.

Balanced or Unbalanced Rating Scale?

The fixed-alternative format may be balanced or unbalanced. For example, the following question, which asks about parent-child decisions relating to television program watching, is a **balanced rating scale**:

Who decides which movies your family will see?

Child decides all of the time.	*Child decides most of the time.*	*Child and parent decide together.*	*Parent decides most of the time.*	*Parent decides all of the time.*
____	____	____	____	____

This scale is balanced because a neutral point, or point of indifference, is at the center of the scale.

Unbalanced rating scales may be used when responses are expected to be distributed at one end of the scale, producing a skewed distribution. The skewed distribution may indicate error and can also interfere with the ability to draw meaningful statistical inferences. Marketing researchers often face situations where "end-piling" will occur. One reason for this is that researchers often ask questions for which respondents are fully expected to give more positive than negative responses. For instance, satisfaction scales (job or customer) generally show this pattern. After all, if an employee has stayed in one job for some years or a customer has already selected a place to do business, we should expect that they would provide a positive response. Unbalanced scales, such as the following one, may mitigate this type of "end piling:"

Dissatisfied	Somewhat Satisfied	Satisfied	Very Satisfied	Completely Satisfied
○	○	○	○	○

The scale contains three "satisfied" responses and only two "dissatisfied" responses above. Researchers choose between a balanced or unbalanced scale depending on the nature of the concept or knowledge about attitudes toward what is measured. When researchers expect respondents are predisposed toward one end of a concept or the other, unbalanced scales are appropriate. Satisfaction and importance scores usually skew toward positive responses, so unbalanced scales may better capture any true variance that exists.

Forced-Choice Scales?

In many situations, a respondent does not have a strong attitude or opinion toward an issue. A **forced-choice rating scale** compels the respondent to answer using some design or technical aspect. Design-wise, the scale can eliminate a neutral response. A balanced scale with an even number of scale choices accomplishes this task. Consider the Likert item shown below:

	Strongly Disagree	Disagree	Slightly Disagree	Slightly Agree	Agree	Strongly Agree
The U.S. Federal Tax Code is fair to all American taxpayers	1	2	3	4	5	6

balanced rating scale

A fixed-alternative rating scale with an equal number of positive and negative categories; a neutral point or point of indifference is at the center of the scale.

unbalanced rating scales

A fixed-alternative rating scale that has more response categories at one end than the other, resulting in an unequal number of positive and negative categories.

forced-choice rating scale

A fixed-alternative rating scale that requires respondents to choose one of the fixed alternatives.

Technically, software can require a respondent to fill in an answer before finishing the survey. Unanswered items are flagged with some indicator.

Some IRBs suggest that forcing a response by using survey technology borders on unethical. One way around this problem is to use a **non-forced-choice scale** including either a "prefer not to answer," "no opinion", or "don't know" category, as in the following example:

How does your attitude toward Community Bank compare with your attitude toward First National Bank?

○ *Community Bank is much better than First National Bank.*
○ *Community Bank is better than First National Bank.*
○ *Community Bank is worse than First National Bank.*
○ *Community Bank is much worse than First National Bank.*
○ *Don't know.*

Asking this type of question allows the investigator to separate respondents who cannot make an honest comparison. The argument for forced choice is that people really do have attitudes, even if they are only somewhat knowledgeable about alternatives and should be able to answer the question. Respondents are not provided with an easy out by simply selecting "neutral." The use of forced-choice questions is associated with higher incidences of "no answer." Perhaps when respondents really can't make up their mind, they will leave an item blank if they are given that choice.

Opponents of the forced-choice approach argue that error results when respondents are required to answer questions for which they lack a firm position, and they argue that response rates will be lower because respondents will quit when forced to answer questions. However, research indicates that forced-choice items do not tend to produce greater error, supporting the argument that people do have some opinion on practically all issues.[19] Further, the total survey response rate and item response rate (leaving items blank or choosing "don't know") is not affected by forced-choice approaches. Thus, researchers can apply forced-choice responses without significant risk of harming the survey process.

Single or Multiple Items?

Whether to use a single item or a measure made up from responses to several items depends on several characteristics of the phenomenon.

- The complexity of the phenomenon measured
- The number of dimensions of the phenomenon
- The level of abstraction of the phenomenon

Hopefully, the definition of the concept studied makes answers to these questions simple. A single item can assess some very simple or concrete concepts.

"*Did you watch Big Brother last night?*"
_____ yes _____ no
"*Do you like pistachio ice cream?*"
Don't Like at All _____ _____ _____ _____ _____ Like a Lot

Other indices such as social class require multiple items to form an index. Latent constructs like the personality trait of extraversion generally require multiple item scales for valid measures. Multiple item scales provide the researcher more flexibility and power in assessing validity.

Attitudes and Intentions

Behavioral researchers often model behavior as a function of intention, which in turn is considered a function of attitudes. Attitudes are considered a function of a person's beliefs about some activity weighted by their evaluations of those characteristics. This type of research is sometimes referred to as a **multi-attribute model** or reasoned action approach. A brand like Fendi may wish to measure

---

non-forced-choice scale

A fixed-alternative rating scale that provides a "don't know" or "no opinion" category or allowing respondents to indicate that they cannot say which alternative is their choice.

To the Point

"*Refusing to have an opinion is a way of having one, isn't it?*"

—LUIGI PIRANDELLO

multi-attribute model

A model that constructs an attitude score based on the multiplicative sum of beliefs about an option times the evaluation of those belief characteristics.

its Facebook followers' attitude toward Lucy Hale, or other social media influencers, before paying her to endorse Fendi products in Facebook postings.

Alex Segre/Alamy Stock Photo

Multi-attribute Attitude Score

Attitudes are modeled with a multi-attribute approach by taking belief scores assessed with some type of rating scale like those described and multiplying each belief score by an evaluation also supplied using some type of rating scale, and then summing each resulting product. For instance, a series of Likert statements might assess a respondent's beliefs about the reliability, price, service, and styling of a Honda Fit.

	Strongly Disagree	Disagree	Neutral	Agree	Strongly Agree
The Honda Fit is the most reliable car in its class.	SD	D	N	A	SA
The Honda Fit has a low price for a car of its type.	SD	D	N	A	SA
I know that my Honda dealer will provide great service if I buy a Honda Fit.	SD	D	N	A	SA
The Honda Fit is one of the most stylish cars you can buy.	SD	D	N	A	SA

Then, respondents may use a simple rating scale to assess how good or bad is each characteristic. For example, the scale may appear something like this with instructions for the respondent to indicate the relative evaluation of each characteristic.

All things considered ...						
Buying a car that is reliable is						
Very bad	○	○	○	○	○	○	Very good
Buying a car with a low price is						
Very bad	○	○	○	○	○	○	Very good
Buying a car from a dealer with excellent service is						
Very bad	○	○	○	○	○	○	Very good
Buying a car with the latest styling is						
Very bad	○	○	○	○	○	○	Very good

The respondent's attitude toward buying a Honda Fit would be found by multiplying beliefs by evaluations. If a respondent provided the following belief scores using Likert scales for each belief item

Honda Fit reliability	5
Honda Fit pricing	3
Honda Fit dealer service	2
Honda Fit styling	1

and the following evaluation scores using the rating scale shown in the preceding

Reliability	*6*
Low pricing	*3*
Dealer service	*4*
Styling	*2*

then her attitude score could be computed as

Beliefs	×	Evaluations	=	(B)(E)
5		6		30
3		3		9
2		4		8
1		2		2
	Total			49

The multi-attribute attitude score for this consumer would be 49. A researcher may also ask respondents to rate a competitor's product. In this case, the product might be a Chevy Sonic. Using the same four characteristics, a score for the competitor can be obtained. The scores can then be compared to see which brand has a competitive advantage in terms of consumer attitudes.

Marketing researchers employ this approach frequently. The key advantages lie in how diagnostic the results can be. Not only can a researcher provide management with feedback on the relative attitude scores, but he or she can also identify characteristics that are most in need of being improved. In particular, poor belief scores on characteristics that respondents rate very favorably (or as highly important) indicate the characteristics that managers should change to improve competitive positioning. In this case, the Fit does well on reliability, and the strong belief score on this characteristic is largely responsible for shaping this consumer's attitude. If the Chevy Sonic scored only a 2 on reliability, the result would diagnose a problem that managers should address. The Sonic has a relatively low score on a very meaningful characteristic.

Behavioral Intention

According to reasoned action theory, people form intentions consistent with the multi-attribute attitude score. Intentions represent the behavioral expectations of an individual toward an attitudinal object. Typically, the component of interest to marketers is a buying intention, a tendency to seek additional information, or plans to visit a showroom. Category scales for measuring the behavioral component of an attitude ask about a respondent's likelihood of purchase or intention to perform some future action, using questions such as the following:

How likely is it that you will purchase a Honda Fit within the next 6 months?

○ Very Unlikely

○ Unlikely

○ Somewhat Unlikely

○ Undecided

○ Somewhat Likely

○ Likely

○ Very Likely

TIPS OF THE TRADE

- Research questions and hypotheses reveal the concepts to measure during the research.
- When planning to use parametric statistical analysis (those involving means and standard deviations), scales with at least 5 response points provide the greatest flexibility.
- Coefficient α provides an estimate of scale reliability. It is only applicable to multiple item scales with three or more items to be formed into a composite. The following guide can be used in judging the results from estimating coefficient α.
  - Above 0.8, very good reliability
    - Scale can be used as is from a reliability standpoint.
  - From 0.70 to 0.79, good reliability
    - Scale can be used as is from a reliability standpoint.
  - From 0.60 to 0.69, fair reliability
    - Scale can be used as is with caution.

- Below 0.6, further refinement or modifications to the scale should be made before using.
- Whenever there is a question about the number of scale points to use, it is better to use more rather than fewer scale points.
- Forced-choice questions have their place in marketing research.
  - Researchers should strongly consider providing a "don't know" response option when using forced-choice mechanisms.
- Attitude scores have no absolute meaning, so results for more than one brand are needed to provide diagnostic recommendations.
- Although online survey platforms make constructing a questionnaire easy, the user needs to pay careful attention to the way the software fills in things like category labels automatically.

© George Doyle & Ciaran Griffin

:: SUMMARY

1. **Determine what things need to be measured to address a research question.** Researchers can always know what key concepts he or she must measure by examining the research questions. The researcher must measure these concepts to address the research questions. Every concept measured requires a conceptual and operational definition. Operational definitions tell how individual variables come together to represent a concept and measurement aims to represent those variables in a systematic and reliable way.

2. **Distinguish levels of scale measurement.** Four levels of scale measurement can be identified. Each level is associated with increasingly more complex properties. Nominal scales assign numbers or letters to objects for identification or classification. Ordinal scales arrange objects based on relative magnitude of a concept. Thus, ordinal scales represent rankings. Interval scales also represent an ordering based on relative amounts of a concept, but they also capture the differences between scale values. Thus, interval scales allow stimuli to be compared to each other based on the difference in their scale scores. Ratio scales are absolute scales, starting with absolute zeros at which there is a total absence of the attribute. Nominal and ordinal scales are discrete. The mode is the best way to represent central tendency for discrete measures. Ratio measures are continuous, and interval scales are generally treated as continuous. For continuous measures, the mean represents a valid representation of central tendency.

3. Create an index or composite measure. Indexes and composite measures are formed by combining scores mathematically from multiple items. For instance, a composite score can be formed by adding a respondent's scores to multiple scale items, each intended to represent the same concept. The end result of the addition is a summed scale. Index scores and composite measures scores are generally obtained in much the same way. However, they differ theoretically from composite measures of latent constructs in that index scores do not have to relate theoretically or statistically to one another.

4. Assess scale reliability and validity. Reliability, validity, and sensitivity are characteristics associated with good measurement. Internal consistency is necessary for good reliability and is assessed most often using coefficient α. Coefficient α should be at least above 0.70 to have good reliability. Validity is assessed in components. A construct measure that exhibits adequate construct validity is one that is likely well measured. Construct validity consists of face or content validity, convergent validity (internal consistency), discriminant validity, criterion validity, and fit validity. Multivariate statistical procedures like factor analysis can be helpful in providing evidence of construct validity.

5. Understand why the concept of attitude is so important in marketing research. Attitudes are a relatively enduring predisposition to respond consistently to various things including people, activities, events, and objects. Attitudes are predispositions toward behavior and, as such, represent rules that inform a person as to the appropriate reaction in a given situation. Attitudes consist of three components: (a) the affective, or the emotions or feelings involved; (b) the cognitive, or awareness or knowledge; and (c) and the behavioral, or the predisposition to action. Attitudes are so important to business because they tend to predict behavior. If we know one's attitude toward a brand, we can predict with some accuracy whether he or she may purchase and use that brand's products.

6. Design a scale that measures an attitudinal concept. Numerous scaling approaches exist for assessing an attitude. With a Likert scale, respondents indicate their attitudes by checking how strongly they agree or disagree with carefully constructed statements. An attitude can be represented with a series of Likert scale items. Typically, Likert scales contain between five and seven response points. A five-item Likert scale states a phrase with which a respondent expresses agreement. The response points would be "strongly disagree," "disagree," "neutral," "agree," and "strongly agree." A semantic differential uses a series of attitude scales anchored by bipolar adjectives and can be used to create a simple scale that directly measures one's attitude toward some object or activity. Constant-sum scales require the respondent to divide a constant sum into parts, indicating the weights to be given to various attributes of the item being studied. A forced-choice question uses an even number of response points and eliminates a neutral middle from the choice set.

7. Implement a multi-attribute model. A multi-attribute model represents a respondent's attitude about some activity, object, event, or idea by taking belief scores assessed with some type of rating scale and multiplying each belief score by an evaluation of the matching characteristic, also supplied using some type of rating scale, and then summing those products together. These attitude scores are expected to predict behavioral intentions with some degree of confidence. Multi-attribute models provide highly diagnostic information to competitive businesses and thus, they are widely applied.

∷ KEY TERMS AND CONCEPTS

:: QUESTIONS FOR REVIEW AND CRITICAL THINKING

1. Define *measurement*. How is your performance in a marketingc research class being measured?
2. What is the difference between a *concept* and a *construct*? In what ways is the definition of the term *variable* similar or different?
3. Consider the following research questions or hypotheses. What variables need to be measured in each?
   a. Are consumers who spend more time and are more committed to Facebook more likely to have an Amazon Prime account?
   b. Do demographic variables relate to a consumer's knowledge of social media influencers?
   c. The temperature inside the supermarket will determine how much time shoppers spend in the store such that when the store is cold they will spend less time shopping than when the store is warm.
   d. Product price is related positively to product quality.
   e. Consumer perceptions of value from a service provider are related negatively to the likelihood of switching service providers.
4. An official in the financial office is considering an applicant for financial aid. The officer uses the following process. If the student has a GPA in the 90th percentile among the admission group, 5 points are added. If the student has an ACT or SAT score in the 90th percentile among the admission group, 5 points are added. If the student comes from a family whose cumulative household income was less than $70,000/year for the last 3 years, 8 points are added. If the student is from out of state, 5 points are added. What variables are being used to determine eligibility for this financial aid? What would your approximate score be on this scale? Is it best described as an index or a composite scale? Explain your response.
5. What role does an operational concept definition play in planning a research project?
6. Describe the concept of measurement level and the four different levels of scale measurement.
7. Consider the different grading measuring scales described at the beginning of the chapter. Describe what level of measurement is represented by each. Which grading measurement scale do you think contains the least opportunity for error?
8. Look at the responses to the following survey items that describe how stressful consumers believed a Christmas shopping trip was using a 10-point scale ranging from 1 (no stress at all) to 10 (extremely stressful):
   a. How stressful was finding a place to park? <u>9</u>
   b. How stressful was the checkout procedure? <u>5</u>
   c. How stressful was trying to find exactly the right product? <u>4</u>
   d. How stressful was finding a store employee? <u>6</u>
      i. What would be the stress score for this respondent based on a summated scale score?
      ii. What would be the stress score for this respondent based on an average composite scale score?
      iii. Do any items need to be reverse-coded? Why or why not?
      iv. How could the concept of split-half reliability be applied using a sample of 100 respondents who gave answers to these four questions?
9. How is it that marketing researchers can justify treating a 7-point Likert scale as interval?
10. What are the components of construct validity? Describe each.
11. Why might a researcher wish to use more than one question to measure attitude toward obtaining an Amazon Prime account?
12. How can a researcher assess the reliability and validity of a multi-item composite scale?
13. Indicate whether the following measures represent a nominal, ordinal, interval, or ratio scale:
    a. Prices on the stock market
    b. Marital status, classified as "married" or "not married"
    c. Whether a respondent has ever been unemployed
    d. Course grades: A, B, C, D, or F
    e. Blood-alcohol content
    f. Number of Facebook friends
    g. The color of one's eyes
    h. The size of one's pupils
14. What is an *attitude*? Why do businesses place so much emphasis on measuring attitudinal concepts?
15. Attitudes are sometimes called tri-partite, meaning they have three components. What are the three components of an attitude?
16. Distinguish between rating and ranking. Which is a better attitude measurement technique? Why?
17. State the difference between a balanced and unbalanced scale. Consider the examples in Exhibit 10.7. Are any unbalanced?
18. What are key differences between a 5-item and a 6-item Likert scale?
19. Describe the way a semantic differential scale could be constructed to measure the behavioral component of attitudes.
20. What is a fundamental weakness of a constant sum or ranking scale?
21. What is a multi-attribute model of consumer attitudes?
22. Look at the table. The b columns represent belief scores for two competing products. The e column represents the evaluations of those characteristics. Compute the attitude score for each competitor and comment on the competitive positioning of each.

Characteristic	$b_{Brand A}$	$b_{Brand B}$	e
Price	5	3	6
Quality	6	2	3
Convenience	1	2	4
Ease of use	3	5	1
Looks	1	7	5

23. If a Likert summated scale has 10 scale items, do all 10 items have to be phrased as either positive or negative statements, or can the scale contain a mix of positive and negative statements? Explain.
24. What are the advantages of using a slider scale?
25. A researcher thinks many respondents will answer "don't know" or "can't say" if these options are printed on an attitude scale along with categories indicating level of agreement. The researcher does not print either "don't know" or "can't say" on the questionnaire because the resulting data would be more complicated to analyze and report. Is this proper?

:: RESEARCH ACTIVITIES

1. Define each of the following concepts, and then operationally define each one by providing correspondence rules between the definition and the scale:
   a. A good bowler
   b. Purchasing intention for a hair salon
   c. Consumer involvement with cars
   d. A workaholic
   e. Fast-food restaurant
   f. Online social networking addict
   g. Attitude toward leaving advice (reviews) on Tripadvisor.com

2. Use the ACSI scores found at http://www.theacsi.org to respond to this question. Using the most recent two years of data, test the following three hypotheses:

   a. American consumers are more satisfied with breweries than they are with wireless telephone services.
   b. American consumers are more satisfied with discount and department stores than they are with automobile companies.
   c. American consumers are most satisfied with Southwest Airlines relative to other airlines.

3. Go to http://www.queendom.com/tests. Click on the lists of personality tests. Take the hostility versus kindness test. Do you think this is a reliable and valid measure of how prone someone is to generally act in a hostile manner? Would it be ethical to assign prospective employees a hostility score to be used in a hiring index based on results from this or a similar test?

Satisfaction with Mass Marketing

Case 10.1

A retail consultant studies local Walmart stores to try to assess customer satisfaction with the shopping experience. She begins by examining the ACSI scores for retailers. In the late 2000s, Walmart instituted a policy of increasing the width of the aisles and decreasing the amount of floor space containing huge product displays. Management believes that this was a bad move because when consumers see less, they buy less. Managers argue that the best operating policy is "piling high and selling cheap!" Put as much product on the sales floor as possible and price them as low as possible. This policy is supported by keeping distribution costs low. In addition, management believes that labor costs must be kept low to maintain profitability. The local Walmart is worried about losing business to smaller local supermarkets and dollar stores. In response, Walmart is growing through Neighborhood Walmart stores that are smaller in size and located in densely populated areas rather than suburbs.

Questions

1. What type of attitude scale is used by the ACSI, if any?
2. What type of attitude study might you design if you were the consultant? What research questions might you pose for the study?
3. Design a survey that would measure beliefs and attitudes toward Walmart and a competing dollar store.
4. How would you use results from this approach to diagnose potential problems for Walmart?

Ryan McVay/Getty Images

Questionnaire Design

LEARNING OUTCOMES

After studying this chapter, you should be able to:

1. Know the key decisions in questionnaire design
2. Choose between open-ended and fixed-alternative questions
3. Avoid common mistakes in writing questionnaire items
4. Minimize problems with order bias
5. Understand principles of survey flow
6. Use latest survey technology to reduce respondent error
7. Appreciate the importance of pretesting survey instruments

iStock.com/Opidanus

Chapter Vignette:

Ask a Sensitive Question, Get a Sensitive Answer

Survey researchers believe that the responses people give to questionnaire items provide a valid representation of the interests, opinions, or behaviors studied. Researchers should always pay careful attention to how a question is asked, but particularly so when the subjects are sensitive and reveal potentially self-incriminating or embarrassing facts about a person. Consider how a typical respondent might react to the following questions:

- Are your Facebook friends annoying?
- How much time do you spend viewing pornographic websites or videos?
- When you are behind the wheel of a car, are you always a responsible driver?
- Are you very satisfied with your home life?
- Are you satisfied when you think about whether you have exceeded your career aspirations?

A large percentage of respondents would agree with the first question. In fact, growth in Facebook users in the United States has ceased and younger consumers, in particular, are turning to other platforms such as WhatsApp, Snapchat, Telegram, and Instagram as more convenient outlets for social networking. Despite the lack in growth, Facebook has more than 2,000,000,000 users. So, do Facebook users put up with annoying friends? Also, if the question was asked in a survey

initiated on a friend's Facebook site, would the answer be the same?

Nearly nine in ten respondents would say they would never visit a pornographic website or watch a pornographic video. Yet, pornographic websites are highly visited. Some estimates suggest that 30 percent of all bandwidth on the Internet is consumed by people viewing pornographic content. Pornographic sites have more viewers than Netflix, Amazon, and Twitter combined. A study also asked respondents anonymously whether or not their driving contributed to a recent automobile accident (the survey

Iakov Filimonov/Shutterstock.com

gave both parties in a recent accident a chance to respond). Maybe it's not so surprising, but the vast majority of people who have recently been in a car accident, when surveyed, say that the other driver was to blame for the incident. Thus, questions that involve self-incrimination may not yield truthful results.

Marketing researchers must take care in asking *relevant* questions in ways that produce the most *truthful* results. The question order can be important. Imagine how responses to the last two questions listed above might change if the order is reversed. The way a researcher words a question also can influence how much a respondent believes that the answer is truly anonymous and can't be linked to him or her personally. Thus, truthful results result from not only asking the right question, but from asking it the right way.[1]

Introduction

Survey researchers use a questionnaire like a carpenter uses a hammer. The questionnaire is the primary tool for building responses to research questions. Many people may believe asking a question is very simple. However, the quality of response cannot be good when the question is bad.

Questionnaire design is one of the most critical stages in the survey research process. Businesspeople and managers who are inexperienced at marketing research frequently believe that constructing a questionnaire is a simple task that they can do without the assistance of a professional researcher. Amateur researchers like these think they can write an effective questionnaire in minutes. Unfortunately, newcomers who naively believe asking questions is easy generally end up with useless results. Ask a bad question and you get bad results!

Basic Considerations in Questionnaire Design

People don't understand questions just because the wording is grammatically correct. Respondents may not know what the researcher is talking about. For instance, a question may ask about a product that the respondent doesn't know. Alternatively, a question may not mean the same thing to everyone interviewed. Finally, people may refuse to answer personally sensitive questions. A skilled survey researcher composes the questionnaire in a way that minimizes error due to potential issues like these.

Even though we discuss questionnaire items as questions, often they are not questions at all but simply words, statements, phrases, or images used to evoke a response. We saw examples of different approaches to question/item design in the previous chapter. The chapter uses the terms *question* and *item* interchangeably.

For a questionnaire to fulfill a researcher's purposes, the questions must meet the basic criteria of *relevance* and *accuracy*. To achieve these ends, a researcher who is systematically planning a questionnaire's design must make several decisions—typically, but not always, the decisions take place in the following sequence:

1. What should be asked?
2. How should questions be phrased?
3. In what sequence should the questions be arranged?
4. What questionnaire layout will best serve the research objectives?
5. How can the questionnaire encourage complete responses?
6. How should the questionnaire be pretested and then revised?

What Should Be Asked?

Certain decisions made during the early stages of the research process will influence the questionnaire design. The preceding chapters stressed good problem definition and clear research questions. This leads to specific research hypotheses that, in turn, clearly indicate what the researcher must

RESEARCH IN
ACTION!

As a consumer, you are well familiar with questionnaires based on the frequent requests for surveys from virtually every interactive source. As a researcher, you now should have already created some survey questions of your own based on the different types of questions introduced in the last chapter. The next step of your project involves compiling and organizing these questions into a well-designed questionnaire. The layout and design of your questionnaire is an essential contributing factor to the success of your overall project. Therefore, you will need to spend some time on eliminating any potential biases, leading questions, and structural design flaws discussed in this chapter by

carefully wording, rewording, and changing your questionnaire. Remember, the more time you spend on pretesting your survey now, the higher quality data you will have at the end!

measure. Different types of questions may be better at measuring certain things than are others. In addition, the communication medium used for data collection—that is, telephone interview, personal interview, snail mail, or Web-based questionnaire—must be determined. This decision is another forward linkage that influences the structure and content of the questionnaire. The specific questions asked will be a function of the previous decisions.

The latter stages of the research process will have an important impact on questionnaire wording. Researchers should consider the data analysis tools that he/she will use when designing questionnaires. Certain question types do not yield data appropriate for certain statistical tools.

Questionnaire Relevancy

A questionnaire is *relevant* to the extent that all information collected addresses a research question and helps a decision-maker address a current marketing problem. Asking a wrong question or an irrelevant question is a common pitfall. If the marketing task is to pinpoint store image problems, questions asking for political opinions may be irrelevant. The researcher should be specific about data needs and have a rationale for each questionnaire item. Irrelevant questions are more than a nuisance because they make the survey needlessly long. In a study where two samples representing the same types of businesspeople received either a one- or three-page printed questionnaire, the response rate was nearly twice as high for the one-page survey.[2]

Conversely, many researchers, after conducting surveys, find that they omitted some important questions. Therefore, when planning the questionnaire design, researchers must think about possible omissions. Is information on the relevant demographic and psychographic variables being collected? Would certain questions help clarify the answers to other questions? Will the results of the study provide the answer to the marketing manager's problem?

Questionnaire Accuracy

Once a researcher decides what to ask, accuracy becomes the primary concern. *Accuracy* means that the information is valid, meaning it faithfully represents reality. Although experienced researchers generally believe that questionnaires should use simple, understandable, unbiased, unambiguous, and nonirritating words, they cannot produce a systematic procedure for ensuring effective question writing across all types of projects. Obtaining accurate answers from respondents depends strongly on the researcher's ability to design a questionnaire that facilitates recall and motivates respondents to cooperate. Respondents tend to be more cooperative when the subject of the research interests them. In addition, when questions are not lengthy, difficult to answer, or ego threatening, respondents are more likely to respond and provide unbiased answers.

Question wording and sequence also substantially influence accuracy, which can be particularly challenging when designing a survey for diverse audiences. Wine industry executives rely on questionnaires to assess what U.S. markets know about wine. Expert wine drinkers might recognize what a researcher means by common wine terms such as *Champagne* and *Burgundy*. They understand the terminology and see items using such terms as *accurately worded*. However, respondents with less expertise may interpret the same questions differently. These respondents may inaccurately associate all sparkling wine with "champagne" and may think of a California "burgundy" when answering the question (Champagne and Burgundy are both names that refer specifically to wines from regions in France).[3] Thus, even relatively simple questions can produce inaccurate answers.

Question Phrasing: Open- or Closed-Ended Statements?

Questions can be phrased in many ways. The researcher may choose from many standard question formats developed over time in previous research studies. This section presents a classification of question types and provides some helpful guidelines for writing questions.

Open-Ended Response versus Fixed-Alternative Questions

We can separate questionnaire items into two basic types based on the amount of freedom respondents have in providing a response. The following sections define open-ended or closed question formats.

open-ended response questions

Questions that pose a problem and ask respondents to answer in their own words.

Open-ended response questions pose a problem or topic and ask respondents to answer in their own words. If the interviewer asks a question in a personal interview, the interviewer may probe for more information, as in the following examples:

- *What search engines can you think of other than* Google.com?
- *How do you feel about the political and economic situation today?*
- *What things do you like most about your iPad?*
- *Where do you usually buy your clothes?*
- *How much extra are you willing to pay for an electric car?*

fixed-alternative questions

Questions in which respondents are given specific, limited-alternative responses and asked to choose the one closest to their own viewpoint.

Open-ended response questions are free-answer questions. **Fixed-alternative questions**—sometimes called *closed-ended questions*—give respondents a limited number of specific alternative responses from which to choose. For example:

Do you use social media apps, such as Facebook, Instagram, or Snapchat?

        Yes   No

How much time daily do you spend on social media apps, such as Facebook, Instagram, or Snapchat?

more than 5 hours/day	3-5 hours/day	1-2 hours/day	less than 1 hour/day	I don't use social media.

Courtesy of Qualtrics.com

Using Open-Ended Response Questions

Open-ended response questions offer several advantages. They are particularly beneficial when the researcher implements an exploratory research design. At this point, researchers may not even know the relevant range of responses to some question. Consider an open-ended question concerning willingness to pay for an electric car. Are consumers willing to pay anything extra? What is the most that people might be willing to pay? Early on, the researcher may have no good idea of what to expect. The initial responses may be helpful in assessing ranges of responses that might be useful in developing structured responses used in a descriptive design. However, researchers can employ numeric open-ended responses with some confidence based on evidence suggesting that open-ended willingness to pay measures accurately forecast demand.[4]

Open-ended questions also identify which words and phrases people spontaneously give to the free-response question. Respondents are free to answer with whatever is at the top of their minds. By obtaining free and uninhibited responses, the researcher may find some unanticipated reaction toward the product. Such responses will reflect the flavor of the language that people use in talking about goods or services and thus may provide a source of new ideas for advertising copywriting or ways to word structured scale items.

Open-ended response questions also are valuable at the beginning of an interview. They are good first questions because they allow respondents to warm up to the questioning process and can stimulate memory for past events. The following question illustrates an open-ended question as an opener:

In the space below, tell us about an incident in which you felt a strong sense of nostalgia.

Courtesy of Qualtrics.com

This question may be followed up with structured questions about how the sense of nostalgia influences feelings about brands or retailers. Further, the open-ended response provides the potential for interpretive research approaches that potentially provide deep insights into the experience.

Open-ended responses also offer some disadvantages. The cost of administering open-ended response questions is on average higher than that of administering fixed-alternative questions. As each respondent's written answer offers a somewhat unique perspective, someone must manually summarize, categorize, or interpret the responses. Once a classification scheme is developed, a data editor can code responses within each data record.

Another potential disadvantage of open-ended responses is an increased possibility of interviewer bias. In an oral interview, interviewer instructions state that answers are to be recorded verbatim. Rarely does even the best interviewer record every word spoken by the respondent. Interviewers have a tendency to take shortcuts. When this occurs, the interviewer may well introduce error because the final answer may reflect a combination of the respondent's and interviewer's ideas.

Also, articulate individuals tend to give longer answers to open-ended response questions. Such respondents often are better educated and from higher-income groups, and therefore, they may not be representative of the entire population. Yet, these better-educated, wealthier respondents may give a disproportionately large share of the responses.

Fixed-Alternative Questions

In contrast, fixed-alternative questions require less interviewer skill, take less time, and are easier for the respondent to answer. This is because answers to closed questions are classified into standardized groupings prior to data collection. Standardizing alternative responses to a question provides comparability of answers, which facilitates coding, tabulating, and ultimately interpreting the data.

However, when a researcher is unaware of the potential responses to a question, he/she should not use fixed-alternative questions. If the researcher assumes what the responses will be but is in fact wrong, he or she will have no way of knowing the extent to which the assumption was incorrect. Sometimes, the researcher only becomes aware of this type of error after launching the survey. Consider, for instance, the fixed-alternative question about willingness to pay for an electric car. What if the researcher chose those particular price categories without careful consideration of the potential range of responses, and then, more than half of respondents select "more than $3,000"? Then, the question format has likely suppressed variation and should probably have included categories above $3,000.

Unanticipated alternatives emerge when respondents believe that closed answers do not adequately reflect their feelings. They may make comments to the interviewer or write additional answers on the questionnaire indicating that the exploratory research did not yield a complete array of responses. After the fact, researchers can't do very much to correct a closed question that does not provide a valid set of alternatives. Therefore, a researcher may find exploratory research with openended responses valuable before writing a descriptive questionnaire. The researcher should strive to ensure that there are sufficient response choices to include the relevant range of responses as well as an "other" choice for respondents who do not see their answer among the choice set.

> ### To the Point
> *"If you ask a stupid question, you may feel stupid; if you don't ask a stupid question, you remain stupid."*
> —TONY ROTHMAN

How much more are you willing to pay for an electric car as opposed to a diesel car with the same horsepower?

- ◎ $0
- ◎ $1 - $249
- ◎ $250 - $749
- ◎ $750 - $1,499
- ◎ $1,500 - $2,999
- ◎ More than $3,000
- ◎ Other _____

Courtesy of Qualtrics.com

Also, a fixed-alternative question may tempt respondents to check an answer that is more prestigious or socially acceptable than the true answer. Rather than stating that they do not know why they chose a given product, they may select an alternative among those presented, or as a matter of convenience, they may select a given alternative rather than think of the most correct response.

Most questionnaires mix open-ended and closed questions. As we have discussed, each form has unique benefits. In addition, a change of pace can eliminate respondent boredom and fatigue.

Types of Fixed-Alternative Questions

This section identifies and classifies different types of fixed-alternative questions.

The **simple-dichotomy (dichotomous-alternative) question** requires the respondent to choose one of two alternatives. The answer can be a simple "Yes" or "No" or a choice between "this" and "that." For example:

> **simple-dichotomy (dichotomous-alternative) question**
> A fixed-alternative question that requires the respondent to choose one of two alternatives.

Did you make any calls with a home (landline) phone during the last 7 days?

○ Yes   ○ No

Several types of questions provide the respondent with *multiple-choice alternatives.* The **multiple-choice question** requires the respondent to choose one—and only one—response from among several possible alternatives. For example:

multiple-choice question

A fixed-alternative question that requires the respondent to choose one response from among multiple alternatives.

What is your major?						
	Marketing	Management	Journalism	Engineering	Other business	Other
Indicate your major here:	○	○	○	○	○	○

The **frequency-determination question** is a multiple-choice question that asks for an answer about the general frequency of occurrence. For example:

frequency-determination question

A fixed-alternative question that asks for an answer about general frequency of occurrence.

How much time do you spend studying Marketing Research weekly?

more than 3 hours/week   between 2 and 3 hours/week   between 1 and 2 hours/week   less than 1 hour/week
○ ○ ○ ○

Attitude rating scales, such as the Likert scale, semantic differential, slider scale, and so on, are fixed-alternative questions, too. Chapter 10 discussed these scale types.

The **checklist question** allows the respondent to provide multiple answers to a single question. The respondent indicates past experience, preference, and the like merely by checking off items. In many cases the choices are adjectives that describe a particular object. A typical checklist question might ask the following:

checklist question

A fixed-alternative question that allows the respondent to provide multiple answers to a single question by checking off items.

Please select the sources below you use most frequently to obtain the latest financial news. (select all that apply)

☐ Wall Street Journal
☐ Bloomberg Business Week
☐ Financial Times
☐ USA Today
☐ CNN
☐ Local Newspaper
☐ Facebook
☐ Twitter
☐ Other _____

A major problem in developing dichotomous or multiple-choice alternatives is the framing of response alternatives. There should be no overlap among categories. Alternatives should be *mutually exclusive*, meaning only one dimension of an issue should be related to each alternative. The following listing of self-report, personal income groups illustrates a common error:

- Under $20,000
- $20,000–$40,000
- $40,000–$60,000
- $60,000–$80,000
- $80,000–$100,000
- $100,000 or more

How many respondents with incomes of $40,000 will be in the second group and how many will be in the third group? A respondent who actually had a $40,000 income could equally as likely choose either. Researchers have no way of knowing how a true $40,000- per-year respondent responded. Grouping alternatives without forethought about analysis is likely to diminish accuracy.

Also, few people relish being in the lowest category and some may not wish to report belonging to the highest income group either. To negate the potential bias caused by respondents' tendency to avoid an extreme category, researchers often include a category lower than the lowest expected answer and a category higher than the highest expected answer.

Phrasing Questions for Self-Administered, Telephone, and Personal Interview Surveys

The means of data collection—telephone interview, personal interview, self-administered Web-based questionnaire—will influence what is the best question format and phrasing. In general, questions for mail, Internet, and telephone surveys must be less complex than those used in personal interviews. Questionnaires for telephone and personal interviews should be written in a conversational style. Exhibit 11.1 illustrates how a question may be revised for a different medium.

EXHIBIT **11.1**
Best Question Formats Vary by the Interview Medium

Format for Internet or snail-mail self-administered survey:

How satisfied are you with your mobile phone service provider?

- ○ Very Dissatisfied
- ○ Somewhat dissatisfied
- ○ Slightly dissatisfied
- ○ Neither satisfied nor dissatisfied
- ○ Slightly satisfied
- ○ Somewhat satisfied
- ○ Very satisfied

Format for telephone or personal interview:

How satisfied are you with your mobile phone service provider? Would you say that you are very dissatisfied, dissatisfied, neither dissatisfied or satisfied, satisfied, or very satisfied?
_____ very dissatisfied
_____ dissatisfied
_____ neither
_____ satisfied
_____ very satisfied

In a telephone survey about attitudes toward police services, the questionnaire not only asks about general attitudes such as how much respondents trust their local police officers and whether the police are "approachable," "dedicated," and so on, but it also provides basic scenarios to help respondents put their expectations into words. For example, the interviewer tells respondents to imagine that someone had broken into their home and stolen items and that the respondent called the police to report the crime. The interviewer then asks how quickly or slowly the respondent expects the police to arrive.[5]

When a question is read aloud, remembering the alternative choices can be difficult. Consider the following question from a personal interview:

There has been a lot of discussion about the potential health risks to nonsmokers from secondhand tobacco smoke. How serious a health threat to you personally is the inhaling of this secondhand smoke, often called passive smoking: Is it a very serious health threat, somewhat serious, not too serious, or not serious at all?

1. Very serious
2. Somewhat serious
3. Not too serious
4. Not serious at all
5. (Don't know)

The last portion of the question was a listing of the four alternatives that serve as answers. The interviewer uses the listing at the end to remind respondents of the alternatives. The fifth alternative, "Don't know," is in parentheses because, although the interviewer knows it is an acceptable answer, it is not read. The researcher only uses this response when the respondent truly cannot provide an answer.

Avoiding Mistakes

No one size fits all rules determine how to develop a questionnaire. Fortunately, research experience has yielded some guidelines that help prevent the most common mistakes.

Simpler Is Better

Words used in questionnaires should be readily understandable to all respondents. The researcher usually has the difficult task of adopting the conversational language of people at lower education levels without talking down to better-educated respondents. Remember, not all people have the vocabulary of a college graduate. Many consumers, for instance, have never gone beyond a high school education.

Respondents can probably tell an interviewer whether they are married, single, divorced, separated, or widowed, but providing their *marital status* may present a problem. Researchers should avoid technical jargon commonly used by top corporate executives when surveying retail workers, industrial users, or consumers. "Brand image," "positioning," "marginal analysis," and other corporate language may not have the same meaning for or even be understood by a store owner-operator in a retail survey. The vocabulary used in the following question from an attitude survey on social problems probably would confuse many respondents:

When effluents from a paper mill can be drunk and exhaust from factory smokestacks can be breathed, then humankind will have done a good job in saving the environment.... Don't you agree that what we want is zero toxicity, meaning no effluents?

Besides being too long, complex, and confusing, this question is leading.

To the Point
❝I don't know the rules of grammar.... If you're trying to persuade people to do something, or buy something, it seems to me you should use their language, the language they use every day, the language in which they think. We try to write in the vernacular.❞

—DAVID OGILVY

Avoid Leading and Loaded Questions

leading question

A question that suggests or implies certain answers.

Leading and loaded questions are a major source of bias. A **leading question** suggests or implies certain answers. A media study of environmental consciousness asked consumers this question:

Many environmentally conscious individuals are washing their clothes less often because of concerns for the environment. How has the concern for the environment affected your washing behavior?

- ○ Wash much more
- ○ Wash more often
- ○ Wash about the same
- ○ Wash less often
- ○ Wash rarely

Courtesy of Qualtrics.com

The potential "bandwagon effect" implied in this question threatens the study's validity. After all, who would want to look bad for not being environmentally conscious? *Partial mention of alternatives* is a variation of this phenomenon:

What do you usually drink first thing in the morning?

- ○ Coke
- ○ Coffee
- ○ Milk

Courtesy of Qualtrics.com

This item may produce an artificially high percentage of Coke, coffee, and milk drinkers because other categories, such as water, tea, or juice, do not appear.

loaded question

A question that suggests a socially desirable answer or is emotionally charged.

A **loaded question** suggests a socially desirable answer or is emotionally charged. Consider the following question:

What most influences your opinion on controversial political issues?

- ○ Analysis based on knowledge
- ○ Media officials
- ○ Late night comedians
- ○ Coworker opinion

Courtesy of Qualtrics.com

Most respondents will choose the first response. Why? Even though the question is not that emotionally charged, the first response builds self-esteem more so than the other choices by making the choice seem logical and well thought out.

Certain answers to questions are more socially desirable than others. For example, a truthful answer to the following classification question might be painful:

Where did your rank academically in your high school graduation class?

- ○ 1st (top) quarter
- ○ 2nd quarter
- ○ 3rd quarter
- ○ 4th (bottom) quarter

Courtesy of Qualtrics.com

When taking personality or psychographic tests, respondents frequently can interpret which answers are most socially acceptable even if those answers do not portray their true feelings. For example, what are the socially desirable answers to the following questions on a self-confidence scale?

	Strongly Disagree	Disagree	Neither Agree nor Disagree	Agree	Strongly Agree
I am capable of handling myself in most social situations	⊙	⊙	⊙	⊙	⊙
I seldom fear that my actions will cause others to have low opinions of me	⊙	⊙	⊙	⊙	⊙

Courtesy of Qualtrics.com

An experiment conducted in the early days of polling illustrates the unpopularity of change.[6] Comparable samples of respondents were simultaneously asked two questions about the presidential succession. One sample was asked,

> *"Would you favor or oppose adding a law to the Constitution preventing a president from succeeding him/herself more than once?"*

The other sample was asked,

> *"Would you favor or oppose changing the Constitution in order to prevent a president from succeeding him/herself more than once?"*

Fifty percent of respondents answered negatively to the first question. For the second question, 65 percent of respondents answered negatively. Thus, the public would rather add to than change the Constitution even though an addition is a change.

Asking respondents "how often" they use a product or visit a store leads them to generalize about their habits, because there usually is some variance in their behavior. In generalizing, a person is likely to portray an *ideal* behavior rather than an *average* behavior. For instance, brushing your teeth after each meal may be ideal, but busy people may skip brushing occasionally. An introductory **counterbiasing statement** or preamble to a question that reassures respondents that their "embarrassing" behavior is not abnormal may yield truthful responses:

counterbiasing statement

An introductory statement or preamble to a potentially embarrassing question that reduces a respondent's reluctance to answer by suggesting that certain behavior is not unusual.

> *Some people have the time to brush three times daily but others do not. How often did you brush your teeth yesterday?*

If a question embarrasses the respondent, it may elicit no answer or a biased response. This is particularly true with respect to personal or classification data such as income or education. The problem may be mitigated by introducing the section of the questionnaire with a statement such as this:

> *To help classify your answers, we'd like to ask you a few questions. Again, your answers will be kept in strict confidence.*

A question statement may be leading because it is phrased to reflect either the negative or the positive aspects of an issue. To control for this bias, the wording of attitudinal questions may be reversed for 50 percent of the sample. This **split-ballot technique** is used with the expectation that two alternative phrasings of the same question will yield a more accurate total response than will a single phrasing. For example, in a study on economy car buying behavior, one-half of a sample of imported-car purchasers received a questionnaire in which they were asked to agree or disagree with the statement:

split-ballot technique

Using two alternative phrasings of the same question for respective halves of a sample to elicit a more accurate total response than would a single phrasing.

> *"Small domestic cars are cheaper to operate than small imported cars."*

The other half of the import-car owners received a questionnaire in which the statement read:

> *"Small imported cars are cheaper to operate than small domestic cars."*

The results to the two questions were averaged to get an opinion score for perceived economy of imports versus domestics.

Avoid Ambiguity: Be as Specific as Possible

Items on questionnaires often are ambiguous because they are too general. Consider such indefinite words as *often, occasionally, regularly, frequently, many, good,* and *poor.* Each of these words has many different meanings. For one consumer *frequent* reading of *Fortune* magazine may be reading six or seven issues a year. Another consumer may think reading two issues a year is frequent.

Questions such as the following one, used in a study measuring the reactions of consumers to a television boycott, should be interpreted with care:

Please indicate the statement that best described your family's television viewing during the boycott of the Exploration Network.

- ○ We watched a lot of programs on the Exploration Network.
- ○ We occasionally watched programs on the Exploration Network.
- ○ We watched hardly any programs on the Exploration Network.
- ○ We did not watch the Exploration Network.

Some marketing scholars suggest that the rate of diffusion of an innovation depends on the perception of product attributes such as *divisibility*, which refers to the extent to which the consumer may try an innovation on a limited scale.[7] An empirical attempt to test this theory using semantic differentials was a disaster. Pretesting found that the bipolar adjectives *divisible–not divisible* were impossible for consumers to understand because they did not have the theory in mind as a frame of reference. A revision of the scale used these bipolar adjectives to assess the extent to which a respondent felt he/she could try out a new product:

Testable ___ ___ ___ ___ ___ ___ ___ *Not testable*
(sample use possible)   *(sample use not possible)*

However, the question remained ambiguous because the meaning was still unclear sending the researchers back for more pretesting using more concrete wording such as "can you try before you buy?"

A brewing industry study on point-of-purchase advertising (store displays) asked:

What degree of durability do you prefer in your point-of-purchase advertising?

- ○ Permanent (lasting more than 6 months)
- ○ Semipermanent (lasting 1 to 6 months)
- ○ Temporary (lasting less than 1 month)

Here the researchers clarified the terms *permanent, semipermanent,* and *temporary* by defining them for the respondent. However, the question remained somewhat ambiguous. Beer marketers often use a variety of point-of-purchase devices to serve different purposes—in this case, what is the purpose? In addition, analysis was difficult because respondents were merely asked to indicate a preference rather than a *degree* of preference. Thus, the meaning of a question may not be clear because the frame of reference is inadequate for interpreting the context of the question. A student research group asked this question:

What media do you rely on most?

    ○ *Television*

    ○ *Radio*

    ○ *Web sources*

    ○ *Social networks*

    ○ *Newspapers*

This question is ambiguous because it does not ask about the content of the media. "Rely on most" for what—news, sports, finance, entertainment?

Avoid Double-Barreled Items

A question covering several issues at once is referred to as a **double-barreled question** and should always be avoided. Making the mistake of asking two questions rather than one is easy—for example,

Please indicate how much you agree with the following statement:
Labor unions and management are most responsible for the current economic crisis.

When a respondent agrees, so they mean both unions and management, unions or management are responsible? One cannot tell.

When multiple questions are asked in one question, the results may be exceedingly difficult to interpret. Consider the following question from a magazine survey titled "How Do You Feel about Being a Woman?"

Between you and your husband, who does the housework (cleaning, cooking, dishwashing, laundry) over and above that done by any hired help?

- ⊙ I do all of it
- ⊙ I do almost all of it
- ⊙ I do over half
- ⊙ We split the work fifty-fifty
- ⊙ My husband does over half

The answers to this question do not tell us if the wife cooks and the husband washes the dishes. The next Research Snapshot provides additional insight into this question.

A survey by a consumer-oriented librarian asked a sample of visitors,

Are you satisfied with the present system of searching for materials using a smart device or computer?

○ Yes   ○ No

A respondent may feel torn between a "Yes" to one part of the question and "No" to the other part. The answer to this question does not tell the researcher the source of any problem should someone answer "No". Further, a Likert statement from a study dealing with student perceptions of managerial ethics:

Top international sales managers sometimes buy liquor and prostitutes for important customers.

Strongly Disagree	Disagree	Nor Agree or Disagree	Agree	Strongly Agree
⊙	⊙	⊙	⊙	⊙

The item intends to discover students' attitudes about selling as a career.[8] However, perhaps this would be better as two separate questions rather than one to learn respondents' specific beliefs. Then no ambiguity would exist about beliefs concerning what sales managers might buy for customers. A sales manager who takes a customer out for dinner may buy drinks but might never think of buying prostitutes. So, as is, what would a strongly agree or strongly disagree response really mean?

Avoid Making Assumptions

Consider the following question:

Should Macy's continue its excellent gift-wrapping program?

- ⊙ Yes
- ⊙ No

double-barreled question
A question that may induce bias because it covers two or more issues at once.

Who Really Does Housework?

SolStock/E+/Getty Images

Who does housework? What seems like a simple question becomes not so simple when one needs a precise answer. one recent survey suggests that, on average, women spent approximately 42 hours a week doing housework compared to approximately 23 hours a week for men. According to these results, women do almost twice as much housework as men. This gap decreases by two hours if the husband is unemployed. On closer inspection, however, these results suggest that the average married couple spends 65 hours a week doing housework. Really? Do couples really put in nearly 10 hours a day on housework?

That result doesn't seem plausible on first glance, but a number of factors related to survey design may influence the result. First, what is housework? Does housework include driving the kids to school, driving to the grocery store, or driving to work? Does it include time going out to get the newspaper or time spent perusing yummly.com for recipe ideas? A broader definition of housework will yield higher numbers. Second, respondents who do very little housework are not that likely to report to such a survey. Thus, response bias may occur based on the type of person who does respond. Third, the question is prone to socially desirable responding. The socially desirable response for both men and women is to admit to doing a significant amount of housework.

Perhaps an interesting side note is that the more couples report doing housework, the higher the frequency of intimacy they report. Perhaps one factor behind the apparent relationship is that respondents who report a lot of housework exhibit a response pattern using the upper ends of scales more than the lower parts. If researchers want accurate answers to such questions, they should insure confidentiality, have a very good definition of the phenomena being studied, and be able to convey that definition in a survey instrument. Sometimes, behavioral evidence can validate (or invalidate) survey results. people who do more housework do not have more children than other couples. Does this behavioral result say anything about potential bias in the survey results?

Sources: Craig, L. and P. Simminski (2011), "If Men Do More Housework, Do Their Wives Have More Babies?" *Social Indicators Research*, 101 (2), 255–258. Shellenbarger, S. (2009), "Housework Pays Off Between the Sheets," *Wall Street Journal*, (october 21), D1–D3. Horne, R. M., Johnson, M. D., Galambos, N. L., and Krahn, H. J. (2017), "Time, Money, or Gender? Predictors of the Division of Household Labour Across Life Stages," *Sex Roles*, 1–13.

This question has a built-in assumption: that people believe the gift-wrapping program is excellent. By answering "Yes," the respondent implies that the program is, in fact, excellent and that things are fine just as they are. When a respondent answers "No," the opinion is to discontinue the program implying that it isn't excellent. But, perhaps the respondent thinks Macy's should wrap gifts but doesn't buy the built-in excellence assumption. What answer would that respondent mark?

Another frequent mistake is assuming that the respondent had previously thought about an issue. For example, the following question appeared in a survey concerning Jack-in-the-Box:

"Do you think Jack-in-the-Box restaurants should consider changing their name?"

Respondents have not likely thought about this question beforehand. Most respondents answered the question even though they had no prior opinion concerning the name change. Researchers that desire an informed opinion will end up with responses based on too low a level of involvement in a case like this.

Avoid Taxing Respondents' Memory

A simple fact is that sometimes, we can't remember everything. Researchers writing questions about past behavior or events should recognize that certain questions may make serious demands on the respondent's memory. Writing questions about prior events requires a conscientious attempt to minimize the problems associated with forgetting.

In many situations, respondents cannot recall details without some type of assistance. For example, a telephone survey conducted during the 24-hour period following the airing of a Super Bowl might establish whether the respondent watched the Super Bowl and then asked:

Do you recall any commercials on that program?

If the answer is positive, the interviewer might ask, "What brands were advertised?" These two questions measure **unaided recall**, because they give the respondent no clue as to the brand of interest.

If the researcher suspects that the respondent may have forgotten the answer to a question, he or she may rewrite the question in an **aided-recall** format—that is, in a format that provides a clue to help jog the respondent's memory. For instance, the question about an advertised beer in an aided-recall format might be "Do you recall whether there was a brand of beer advertised on that program?" or "I am going to read you a list of beer brand names. Can you pick out the name of the beer that was advertised on the program?" Aided recall is less taxing to the respondent's memory.

Telescoping and squishing are two additional consequences of respondents' forgetting the exact details of their behavior. *Telescoping* occurs when respondents believe that past events happened more recently than they actually did. The opposite effect, *squishing*, occurs when respondents think that recent events took place longer ago than they really did. A potential solution to this problem may be to refer to a specific event that is memorable—for example, "How often have you gone to a sporting event since the World Series?" Because forgetting tends to increase over time, the question may concern a recent period: "How often did you watch any Netflix programming last week?" In situations in which "I don't know" or "I can't recall" is a meaningful answer, simply including a "don't know" response category may solve the question writer's problem. Exhibit 11.2 summarizes some key wording mistakes and tips on minimizing them.

unaided recall

Asking respondents to remember something without providing any clue.

aided-recall

Asking the respondent to remember something and giving them a clue to help.

Order Bias

Question Sequence

The order of questions, or the question sequence, may serve several functions for the researcher. If the opening questions are interesting, simple to comprehend, and easy to answer, respondents' cooperation and involvement can be maintained throughout the questionnaire. Asking easy-to-answer questions teaches respondents their role and builds their confidence.

A mail survey among department store buyers drew an extremely poor return rate. A substantial improvement in response rate occurred, however, when researchers added some introductory questions seeking opinions on pending legislation of great importance to these buyers. Respondents completed all the questions, not only those in the opening section.

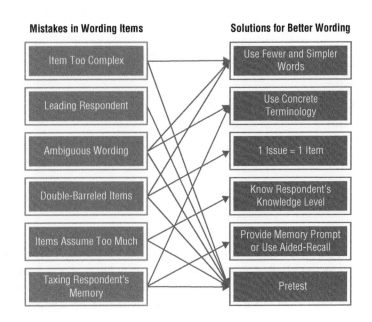

Mistakes in Wording Items

- Item Too Complex
- Leading Respondent
- Ambiguous Wording
- Double-Barreled Items
- Items Assume Too Much
- Taxing Respondent's Memory

Solutions for Better Wording

- Use Fewer and Simpler Words
- Use Concrete Terminology
- 1 Issue = 1 Item
- Know Respondent's Knowledge Level
- Provide Memory Prompt or Use Aided-Recall
- Pretest

EXHIBIT **11.2**
Avoiding Common Wording Mistakes in Questionnaire Design

In their attempt to "warm up" respondents toward the questionnaire, student researchers frequently ask demographic or classificatory questions at the beginning. This generally is not advisable, because asking for personal information such as income level or education may embarrass or threaten respondents. Asking potentially embarrassing questions or personal questions at the end of the questionnaire usually is better. At that point, the respondent may be comfortable with the questioning in general, but also, if the respondent breaks off at that point, the researcher still has a nearly complete questionnaire to work with.

Order bias results when a particular sequencing of questions affects the way a person responds or when the choices provided as answers favor one response over another. In political elections involving candidates lacking high visibility, such as elections for county commissioners and judges, the first name listed on a ballot often receives the most votes. For this reason, election boards should consider ballots that list candidates' names in different positions across voters as a way of equaling out any votes that just go to the first person on the list.

Asking specific questions before asking about broader issues is a common cause of order bias. For example, bias may arise if questions about happiness with life in general are asked before asking about happiness with specific aspects of one's life. Consider the following three questions (each rated out of 100 points):

1. Tell us how happy you are with your life in general? _____
2. Tell us how happy you are with your marriage? _____
3. Tell us how happy you are with your career achievements? _____

Responses to Question 1 are on average higher when asked in this order. Asking Questions 2 and/or 3 first significantly lowers average reported happiness with life. Respondents may overlook specific aspects when answering the general question but then overweight these aspects relative to other nonmentioned aspects.[9] Specific questions may thus influence the more general ones more than general questions will influence specific ones.

Because of this bias, ask general questions before specific questions to obtain the best idea of the true overall impression. This procedure, known as the **funnel technique**, allows the researcher to understand the respondent's overall frame of reference before asking questions that are more specific. The funnel technique reduces bias from one or two specific items.

Order bias

Results when a particular sequencing of questions affects the way a person responds or when the choices provided as answers favor one response over another.

funnel technique

Asking general questions before specific questions in order to obtain unbiased responses.

Randomized Presentations

Consider how later answers might be biased by previous questions in this questionnaire on environmental pollution:

Mark the response that best matches your feelings about the severity of each environmental issue.

	Not Severe	Somewhat Severe	Severe	Very Severe	Extremely Severe
Air pollution from automobiles	◎	◎	◎	◎	◎
Air pollution from open fires	◎	◎	◎	◎	◎
Air pollution from industrial smoke	◎	◎	◎	◎	◎
Air pollution from foul odors	◎	◎	◎	◎	◎
Noise pollution from airplanes	◎	◎	◎	◎	◎
Noise pollution from cars, trucks, scooters, motorcycles	◎	◎	◎	◎	◎
Noise pollution from industry	◎	◎	◎	◎	◎
Noise pollution from loud music	◎	◎	◎	◎	◎

Courtesy of Qualtrics.com

Not surprisingly, researchers found that the responses to the air pollution questions were highly correlated—in fact, almost identical. With attitude scales, an *anchoring effect* also may exist. The first concept measured tends to become a comparison point from which one makes subsequent evaluations. One way to avoid order bias is to randomize question order. Each respondent receives the questions in a different order depending upon the randomization routine. For instance, a set of twenty questions can be assigned positions using random numbers to assign the order. Internet surveys make randomizing question order convenient and easy. Randomization of items on a questionnaire susceptible to the anchoring effect reduces bias.[10] Even the different response categories can be randomized. These options practically eliminate order bias.

A related problem is bias caused by the order of alternatives on closed questions. To avoid this problem, researchers can employ electronic questionnaires making randomization of the choices easy. This makes sense for multiple-choice responses that do not have a logical order. For instance, a question asking respondents to choose their favorite brand of potato chip could randomize the alternatives to avoid the one on top getting more responses just out of convenience. Alternatively, the standard Likert scale format is logically ordered from 1 representing the strongest disagreement (lowest agreement) to 5, in the case of a 5-point scale, representing the highest agreement. Randomizing the response order in such a case could be confusing to the respondent. With complete randomization, question order is random and respondents see response alternatives in different random positions.

Not surprisingly, marketing researchers rarely print alternative questionnaires with either randomized questions or responses. If printed questionnaires are used, randomization would make data coding very difficult and create a high opportunity for coding error. Thus, printed survey instruments are disadvantageous when randomization is needed.

Randomized Response Techniques

Researchers who need to ask embarrassing or incriminating questions sometimes employ randomized response approaches that try to demonstrate to the respondent that even the researcher would not be able to know how the respondent answered the question. **Randomized response techniques** involve randomly assigning respondents to answer either the question of interest (embarrassing) or a mundane question free from the possibility of embarrassment. Researchers use an approach like this when studying sensitive issues including sexually transmitted diseases, sexual behaviors, pornography consumption, cigarette consumption, abortion, and voting behaviors, among other things.[11] The following illustration gives an idea of how this works.

Suppose a marketing researcher was studying relationships between manufacturing firms' sales personnel and a retail firms' buying agents. The researcher wants the answer to this question:

H) Have you ever lied about a product's shipping date in order to close a deal?

Rather than asking this question alone. The survey offers respondents an alternate question:

T) Choose a card from the deck provided. Is the card red?

Alternate questions H and T are followed by a single "Yes" or "No" response scale. The instructions then tell respondents to flip a coin. If the flip turns out heads, respondents should answer question H. If the flip turns out tails, respondents should answer question T. In this way, respondents get the idea (which is true) that the researcher can't tell what question the respondent answered.

However, in any group of respondents, the researcher can compute the percentage of people who lied based on the observed numbers of "Yes" responses and the known statistical probability of a coin flip. In other words, any difference from 50 percent "Yes" can be attributed to the presumably honest answers of respondents.[12] Thus, researchers can address hypotheses involving whether or not automobile industry personnel lie about delivery dates more often than computer industry personnel or whether one culture or sex differs from another. The use of randomized response techniques remains controversial based in part on the willingness and ability of respondents to follow procedures. For now, researchers should consider using the approach when studying relatively capable respondents.

Survey Flow

Survey flow refers to the ordering of questions through a survey. Previously, we discussed order bias as one aspect of survey flow. Other aspects of survey flow can affect response quality. This section discusses issues that facilitate good flow and thereby valid responses.

randomized response techniques

Involve randomly assigning respondents to answer either the question of interest (embarrassing) or a mundane and unembarrassing question.

survey flow

The ordering of questions through a survey.

breakoff

Term referring to a respondent who stops answering questions before reaching the end of the survey.

filter question

A question that screens out respondents who are not qualified to answer a second question.

branching

Directing respondents to alternative portions of the questionnaire based on their response to a filter question.

survey blocks

Sections of a questionnaire that feed the respondent a set of related items that often deal with one unique condition of an experiment.

Oftentimes certain sections of a questionnaire are irrelevant to a particular respondent. Asking a question that does not apply to the respondent or that the respondent is not qualified to answer may be irritating or cause a biased response or even a survey breakoff. A **breakoff** means the respondent stops answering questions resulting in an incomplete survey. We'll have more on breakoffs later in the chapter.

A **filter question** can serve as a **branching** mechanism directing respondents to an appropriate part of the questionnaire using skip logic. Asking:

"Where do you generally have check-cashing problems in Springfield?"

may elicit a response even though the respondent has had no check-cashing problems. He or she may wish to please the interviewer with an answer. The respondent could first encounter a filter question such as:

"Do you ever have a problem cashing a check in Springfield? _____ Yes _____ No"

The responses provided would branch respondents who say "Yes" to questions about the places where checks cannot be cashed while respondents who say "No" skip to the next block of questions.

One way of setting up branching is by establishing blocks in online surveys. These **survey blocks** allow the researcher to combine related questions into individual sections or sets within the survey to keep a pleasant and organized survey flow. Additional advantages of blocks include the possibility of randomizing blocks, skipping certain blocks based on filter questions, and even incorporating experimental designs. Here, each block represents a different experimental condition, which can be randomly assigned to respondents. As a result, researchers can collect all their data within one survey rather than having to create multiple versions of similar surveys as necessary with regular paper-pencil questionnaires. However, creating blocks can also present challenges for the researcher. For example, when downloading the data from a survey software program into a data analysis software, the different blocks need to be merged into one set of questions with an additional variable indicating the type of condition each respondent completed. This extra step during the data cleaning process can be rather time consuming and tedious. Furthermore, since every respondent only answers questions within a certain condition, more data need to be collected to ensure a sufficient sample size for each experimental condition i.e., block.

Exhibit 11.3 gives an example of a flowchart plan for a survey addressing a rental car company's sponsorship of a top racer in the Tour de France bicycle race. In this case, the company (Europcar) is evaluating the sponsorship's effectiveness across different markets and potential markets. The first question serves as a filter and qualifies respondents based on whether or not they are old enough to rent a car. Next, respondents provide unaided top of mind awareness and then rate attitudes toward rental car companies, including Europcar. Respondents then reveal whether they spent any significant time viewing the Tour de France. If the respondent viewed for more than one hour, questions assessing the respondent's awareness of sponsorships are provided and so forth. The survey allows research questions involving how much the awareness of Europcar is affected by the sponsorship and how attitudes toward the company might be changed relative to the sponsorship.

Good survey flow, sometimes called *layout*, and physical attractiveness are crucial in mail, Internet, and other self-administered questionnaires. For different reasons, a good layout in questionnaires designed for face-to-face and telephone interviewers is also important.

Traditional Questionnaires

A good layout is neat and attractive, and the instructions for the interviewer should be easy to follow. The responses "It Depends," "Refused," and "Don't Know" enclosed in a box to the side indicate that these answers are acceptable but responses from the 5-point scale are preferred.

Survey researchers can increase response rates by investing in an attractive and well-designed questionnaire. Self-response printed questionnaires should never be overcrowded. Margins should be of decent size, white space should be used to separate blocks of print, and the unavoidable columns of multiple boxes should be kept to a minimum. A question should not begin on one page and end on another page. Splitting questions may cause a respondent to read only part of a question, to pay less attention to answers on one of the pages, or to become confused. For Web-based

EXHIBIT **11.3**
Survey Flow for Tour de France Sponsorship

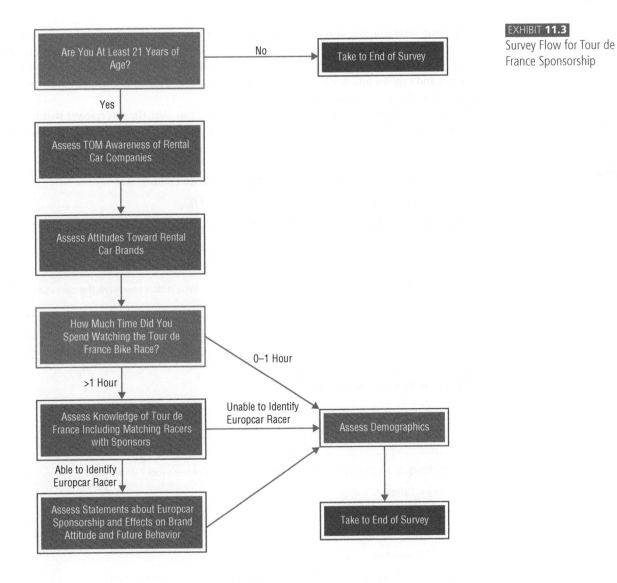

surveys, again do not crowd a page and try to minimize the amount of scrolling a respondent has to do to see all the items.

Researchers should strive to keep questionnaires as short as possible. A booklet form of questionnaire is preferable to stapling a large number of pages together. Also, do not try to put too many questions on a page—paper or electronic. In situations in which it is necessary to conserve space on the questionnaire or to facilitate data entry or tabulation of the data, a multiple-grid layout may be used. The **multiple-grid (matrix table) question** presents several similar questions and corresponding response alternatives arranged in a grid format. For example:

multiple-grid (matrix table) question

Several similar questions of the same format all arranged in a grid format.

On your recent visit to Starbucks,...

	Yes	No	Not sure
Did you order a beverage?	○	○	○
Did you order any food?	○	○	○
Did your receive your order reasonably quickly?	○	○	○
Did the barista make your order correctly?	○	○	○
Were the bathrooms clean?	○	○	○

Courtesy of Qualtrics.com

By using several forms, special instructions, and other tricks of the trade, the researcher can design the questionnaire to facilitate the interviewer's job of following interconnected questions. Exhibit 11.4 illustrates portions of an interview form used by a telephone interviewer. Note how the layout and easy-to-follow instructions for interviewers in Questions 1, 2, and 3 help the interviewer follow the question sequence.

Instructions often appear in capitalized or bold letters to alert the interviewer that it may be necessary to proceed in a certain way. For example, if a particular answer is given, the instructions

EXHIBIT 11.4

Illustrates Portions of an Interview Form Used by a Telephone Interviewer

1. Did you recently take your car to the Standard Auto Repair Center?

   −1 Yes   **(SKIP TO Q. 3)**   −2 No

2. **(IF NO, ASK:)** Did you have the repair work done?

   −1 Yes   −2 No
   ↓   ↓

   1. Where was the repair work done?_____   1. Why didn't you have the car repaired?
   _____   _____
                                                  _____
                                                  _____

   2. Why didn't you have the repair work done
      at the Standard Auto Repair Center?_____
   _____
   _____
   _____

3. **(IF YES TO Q. 1, ASK:)** How satisfied were you with the repair work? Were you . . .

   −1 Very satisfied

   −2 Somewhat satisfied

   −3 Somewhat dissatisfied

   −4 Very dissatisfied

   (IF SOMEWHAT OR VERY DISSATISFIED:) In what way were you dissatisfied?
   _____
   _____
   _____

4. **(ASK EVERYONE:)** Do you ever buy gas at the 95th Street Standard Center?

   −1 Yes   −2 No   **(SKIP TO Q. 6)**

5. **(IF YES, ASK:)** How often do you buy gas there?

   −1 Always

   −2 Almost always

   −3 Most of the time

   −4 Part of the time

   −5 Hardly ever

6. Have you ever had your car washed there?

   −1 Yes   −2 No

7. Have you ever had an oil change or lubrication done there?

   −1 Yes   −2 No

say to skip certain questions or go to a special sequence of questions. To facilitate coding, fixed alternative responses can be precoded when possible, as in Exhibit 11.4. Skip logic can easily be built into electronic questionnaires to perform this routing automatically.

Layout is extremely important when questionnaires are long or require the respondent to fill in a large amount of information. In many circumstances, using headings or subtitles to indicate groups of questions will help the respondent grasp the scope or nature of the questions to be asked. Thus, at a glance, the respondent can follow the logic of the questionnaire.

Survey Technology

Many guidelines for laying out paper questionnaires apply to Internet questionnaires too. Given the increasing reliance on Internet or Web-based surveys, we discuss many survey flow issues in this important context. Survey software programs like Qualtrics, SurveyMoney, and SurveyPlanet allow several special features that facilitate design and allow important data to be collected that may be difficult otherwise. Smartphones and tablet computers also provide another medium for administering surveys. These same software programs often provide formats amenable to these media as well. Earlier, we learned how electronic questionnaire designs facilitate randomization. Here, we learn about a few other features of self-administered Internet surveys.

Response Quality

Once a respondent agrees to participate, he or she has an ethical obligation to complete the task in a responsible fashion. However, this is not always the case. For instance, the researcher can build in questions that test whether or not the respondent is paying attention. Consider the following item:

Choose "disagree" to this item for administrative purposes.

⊙ Strongly Disagree

⊙ Disagree

⊙ Neutral

⊙ Agree

⊙ Strongly Agree

Courtesy of Qualtrics.com

Suppose a respondent chooses "strongly agree." Obviously, he or she is not responding responsibly. At this point, the researcher can build in branching or skip logic that breaks the survey off if a respondent selects anything other than "disagree." An alternative is to build in a popup that reminds the respondent to pay attention.

Timing

Survey software provides easy mechanisms for timing respondents as they move through a survey. The software routinely records the total time that someone spends responding to a survey. However, the survey also can record time spent on individual pages or even individual questions. The timers produce potentially useful behavioral data and also help identify types of respondent error such as speeding. The presumption is that **speeders**, those who move through a survey much faster than the average respondent, cannot be providing reliable responses.

Typically, "timing questions" record the amount of time a respondent took before clicking somewhere on a page, the amount of time until they made the last click on a page, and the total amount of time they spent on a page. The time a respondent spent on a page can be an important outcome in studies involving attitude change or information processing. For example, ad features may be built in precisely to encourage consumers to spend more time viewing the ad. Timing also

speeders

Respondents who take relatively little time to move through a survey—so little that the veracity of their responses is questionable.

can provide another check on response quality. For instance, if respondents spend less time on a page than it takes to read a question, then they are not likely paying very close attention and, as a result, the response quality is called into question.

Similarly, if the total time spent responding is too fast, indicating a speeder, then the respondent may be marking responses randomly or without paying attention.[13] Respondents who take one and one-half standard deviations less time than usual appear likely to be offering "satisficing" responses leading to substantially high response error. Thus, those taking a standard deviation and half less than the median response are flagged as speeders. In some instances though, particularly with short questionnaires, even less deviation may indicate speeding. Research suggests that mTurk workers are on average speeders relative to other types of respondents.[14] Some survey software programs let you control the amount of time a respondents has to spend on a certain question by setting a timer as to when the forward button appears. This technique can alleviate some of the issues of speeders since it prevents respondents from moving on to the next question too quickly.

Randomized Assignment

At times, the researcher needs to assign a certain set of items to specific respondents. In implementing experimental designs, the researcher assigns a certain set of conditions to each respondent. For instance, in a 2 X 2 between-subjects experiment examining the effect of price level (below or above market price) and quality (an extended warranty that lasts 2 years versus a basic warranty that last 60 days), the researcher needs to assign each subject to one of the four experimental conditions. Electronic survey software facilitates this assignment. One way to accomplish this is to place each of the four stimuli in a separate survey block and then to set up a survey flow that randomly assign subjects to one of those four blocks. Typically, the software will allow even assignment to help make sure that approximately the same number of subjects respond to each of the four conditions.

Physical Features

Several physical features of questionnaires can influence responses.

heat map question

A graphical question that tracks the parts of an image or advertisement that most capture a respondent's attention.

Tracking Interest

Electronic questionnaires sometimes allow us to come close to tracking behavior beyond timing using special question types such as a heat map. Exhibit 11.5 displays a **heat map question** tracking the way a respondent views an advertisement for a watch. The rectangles that together form a

EXHIBIT **11.5**

Tracking Points of Interest Using a Heat Map. Heat Maps Identify What Spots in a Graphic Attract a Respondent's Attention.

The Coca-Cola Company

grid would not be visible to the respondent. However, any cursor activity in each grid would be recorded, allowing the researcher to know what parts of the ad captured the respondent's attention the most. This type of question mimics behavioral pupil tracking and provides an indication of what parts of an advertisement or image capture the most attention.

Status Bar

With a paper questionnaire, a respondent can flip through a questionnaire and know about how many questions are in a survey. Multiple page Web-based surveys do not provide this opportunity. However, the researcher may provide a **status bar** as a visual indicator of questionnaire length. The status bar usually resembles a thermometer and the more the bar is filled the closer the respondent is to the finish. Exhibit 11.6 shows an online survey page including a status bar at the bottom of the page. In this case, the respondent appears to be nearly finished.

 Status bars are a matter of courtesy to the respondent. However, when a survey involves multiple branches, the status bar can sometimes be misleading. The survey in the exhibit initially asked a filter question, "Do you drive an automobile?" Respondents who indicated "No" were taken immediately to the end of the survey. Thus, the more branching a survey involves, the less useful the status bar becomes.

status bar

In an Internet questionnaire, a visual indicator that tells the respondent what portion of the survey he or she has completed.

Prompting

Web-based surveys allow limited interactivity. One useful piece of feedback comes in the form of a prompt message. Prompting, in this form, informs the respondent that he/she has skipped an item or provided implausible information. In Exhibit 11.6, the message tells the respondent that the question describing the car must be answered before moving forward with the survey. In this case, the researcher has set this question to be a forced response. In other instances, a prompt may indicate that implausible answers have been provided such as when a constant scale sum does not add up to the proper total.

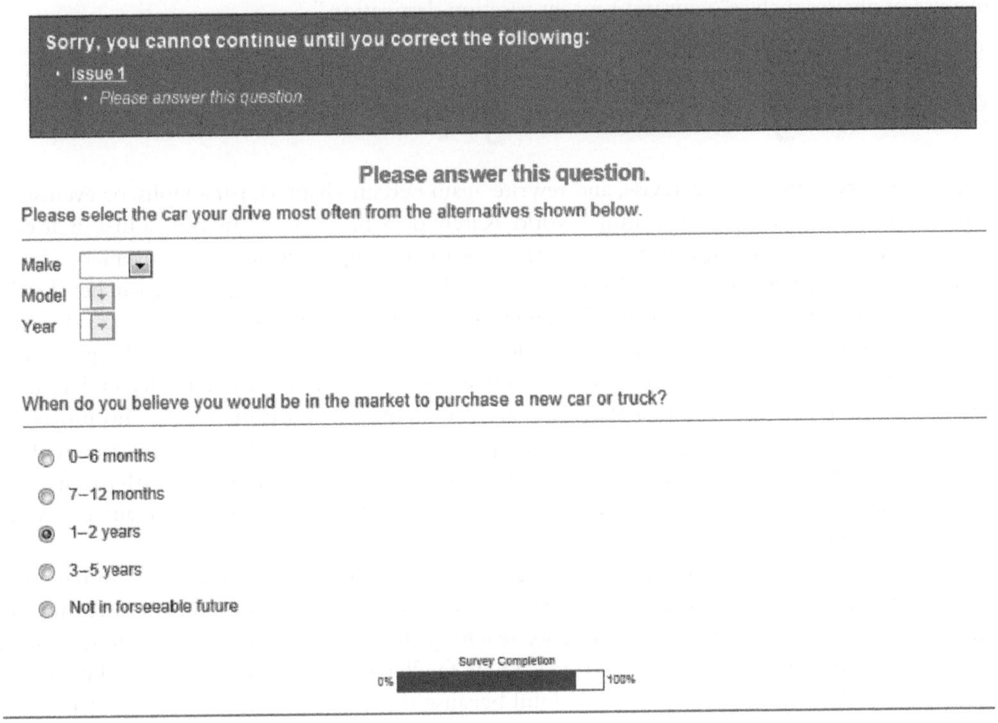

EXHIBIT **11.6**

Illustration of Status Bar and Prompts

Courtesy of Qualtrics.com

Prompting of this type reduces item nonresponse (fewer items are skipped) at the expense of increasing breakoffs.[15] Respondents may get frustrated with the demands to provide answers and simply quit answering all questions. This is particularly true if the prompt asks a respondent to fill in open-ended items or items a respondent views as sensitive or personal. Overall, prompts should be used for critical questions because blank answers to these are practically equivalent to a survey nonresponse anyway.

Piping

piping software

Software that allows question answers to be inserted into later questions.

Survey software can systematically or randomly manipulate the questions a respondent sees. **Piping software** allows responses to a previous question to be inserted into later questions. For instance, a researcher studying vacation destinations conducts an online survey about consumer perceptions of their most recent vacation spot. After initial screening to make sure the person has taken a vacation in the past year, the respondent encounters this question:

> In what place (resort area, city, or geographic region) did you spend the largest part of your most recent vacation?

Courtesy of Qualtrics.com

Whatever the respondent writes in this box will be inserted into future questions about the destination. If the respondent put Disney World, the future question would appear as:

> How many nights did you stay at Disney World?

Piping makes question wording much simpler because the respondent's answer replaces repetitive use of phrases such as "your most recent vacation destination."

Pretesting and Revising Questionnaires

Many novelists write, rewrite, revise, and rewrite again certain chapters, paragraphs, or even sentences. The researcher works in a similar world. Rarely does he or she write only a first draft of a questionnaire. Usually the questionnaire is tried out on a group, selected on a convenience basis, that is similar in makeup to the one that ultimately will be sampled. Although the researcher should not select a group too divergent from the target market—for example, selecting business students as surrogates for businesspeople—pretesting does not require a statistical sample. The pretesting process allows the researcher to determine whether respondents have any difficulty understanding the questionnaire and whether there are any ambiguous or biased questions. This process is exceedingly beneficial and may also involve not just the content of the questions but the method of asking as shown in the Research Snapshot on the next page. Making a mistake with twenty-five or fifty subjects can avoid the potential disaster of administering an invalid questionnaire to several hundred individuals.

For a questionnaire investigating teaching students' experience with Web-based instruction, the researcher had the questionnaire reviewed first by university faculty members to ensure the questions were valid, and then asked twenty teaching students to try answering the questions and indicate any ambiguities they noticed. Their feedback prompted changes in the format and wording. Pretesting was especially helpful because the English-language questionnaire was used in a school in the United Arab Emirates, where English is spoken but is not the primary language.[16]

Tabulating the results of a pretest helps determine whether the questionnaire will meet the objectives of the research. A **preliminary tabulation** often illustrates that, although respondents can easily comprehend and answer a given question, that question is inappropriate because it does not provide relevant information to help solve the marketing problem. Consider the following example from a survey among distributors of high-tech medical equipment such as MRI machines:

preliminary tabulation

A tabulation of the results of a pretest to help determine whether the questionnaire will meet the objectives of the research.

Please indicate the percentage of new client contacts that you have made in the last two years that originated from the following sources:

E-mail	0
Phone Call	0
Linked-In Message	0
Facebook Message	0
In-person Cold Call	0
Professional Meeting Attendance	0
Other	0
Other	0
Total	0

Courtesy of Qualtrics.com

Although this may seem like a simple question, pretesting may uncover potential problems. For instance, can respondents add up scores to total 100? If using an online format, the survey software can use a routine to prompt respondents should the scores not total to 100. But, if the task is too difficult, the researcher should revise the question. Also, is some other category frequent enough in occurrence to be listed as one of the options? If an open-ended "other" box reveals some category showing up a lot, the item should include it as an explicit choice. If, on the other hand, very few pretest respondents choose any response for "other," only one "other" response should be used to avoid confusion that may come from including two.

What administrative procedures should be implemented to maximize the value of a pretest? Administering a questionnaire exactly as planned in the actual study often is not possible. For example, mailing out a questionnaire might require several weeks that simply cannot be spared. Pretesting a questionnaire in this manner would provide important information on response rate but may not point out why questions were skipped or what questions are ambiguous or confusing. Personal interviewers can record requests for additional explanation or comments that indicate respondents' difficulty with question sequence or other factors. This is the primary reason why researchers employ interviewers often in pretest work. Self-administered questionnaires are not reworded as personal interviews, but interviewers are instructed to observe respondents and ask for their comments after they complete the questionnaire. When pretesting personal or telephone interviews, interviewers may test alternative wordings and question sequences to determine which format best suits the intended respondents.

No matter how the pretest is conducted, the researcher should remember that its purpose is to uncover any problems that the questionnaire may cause. Thus, pretests typically are conducted to answer questions about the questionnaire such as the following:

- Can the questionnaire format be followed by the interviewer [respondent for self-response]?
- Does the questionnaire flow naturally and conversationally?
- Are the questions clear and easy to understand?
- Can respondents answer the questions easily?
- Which alternative forms of questions work best?
- What overall and item response rates can be expected?

Pretests also provide means for testing the sampling procedure—to determine, for example, whether interviewers are following the sampling instructions properly and whether the procedure is efficient. Pretests also provide estimates of the response rates for mail surveys and the completion rates for telephone surveys.

I Give Up!

The questionnaire design not only aims to get valid data—but design features also assist in getting data at all. No matter what the interview mode, a large portion of respondents give up before finishing and abandon the survey. With snail-mail questionnaires, the number is impossible to determine. However, phone interviews and online surveys allow an assessment of not only how many breakoffs occur but also when they occur. When designing online surveys, keep the following guidelines in mind when attempting to minimize nonresponse problems due to breakoffs:

- Make sure the questionnaire is visually appealing and easy to read. Clutter causes respondents to give up.
- Don't put too many questions on a single page or the task looks burdensome and leads respondents to give up.
- Sensitive questions lead respondents to give up.
- Respondents give up in the face of long questions.
- Open-ended questions in a majority closed-ended survey lead respondents to give up.
- The more sophisticated the sample, the more items capturing greater variance (like sliders and high response rates)

and those not containing labels on all response categories can be used effectively.
- One important element in a pretest is estimating how many people give up without finishing.
- Follow these rules and you won't have to give up on Web-based surveys.

Sources: Peychev, A. (2009), "Survey Breakoff," *Public Opinion Quarterly*, 71 (Spring), 74–97. Weijters, B., E. Cabooter, and N. Schillewaert (2010), "The Effect of Rating Scale Format on Response Styles: The Number of Response Categories and Response Category labels," *International Journal of Research in Marketing*, 27, 236–247.

Usually a questionnaire goes through several revisions. The exact number of revisions depends on the researcher's and client's judgment. The revision process usually ends when both agree that the desired information is being collected in an unbiased manner.

Designing Questionnaires for Global Markets

Marketing research is now a global enterprise. Researchers must take cultural factors into account when designing questionnaires. The most common problem involves translating a questionnaire into other languages. A questionnaire developed in one country may be difficult to translate because equivalent language concepts do not exist or because of differences in phrasing and vernacular. Although Spanish is spoken in both Mexico and Venezuela, one researcher found out that the Spanish translation of the English term *retail outlet* works in Mexico but not in Venezuela. Venezuelans interpreted the translation to refer to an electrical outlet.

Counting on an international audience to speak a common language such as English does not necessarily bridge these gaps, even when the respondents actually do speak more than one language. Cultural differences incorporate many shades of meaning that may not be captured by a survey delivered in a language used primarily for, say, business transactions. In a test of this idea, undergraduate students in twenty-four countries completed questionnaires about attitudes toward school and career. Half received the questionnaire in English, and half in their native language. The results varied, with country-to-country differences smaller when students completed the questionnaire in English.[17]

Some survey software tools like Qualtrics provide a free translation service that will allow one to write a survey in one language and have it administered in another. This may be useful for very exploratory surveys and as a first effort in translation. Marketing researchers usually apply more rigor in making sure the meanings match across languages.

International marketing researchers often have questionnaires back translated. **Back translation** is the process of taking a questionnaire that has previously been translated from one language to

back translation

Taking a questionnaire that has previously been translated into another language and having a second, independent translator translate it back to the original language.

another and having it translated back again by a second, independent translator. The back translator is often a person whose native tongue is the language that will be used for the questionnaire. This process can reveal inconsistencies between the English version and the translation. For example, when a soft-drink company translated its slogan "Baby, it's cold inside" into Cantonese for research in Hong Kong, the result read "Small Mosquito, on the inside, it is very cold." In Hong Kong, *small mosquito* is a colloquial expression for a small child. Obviously the intended meaning of the advertising message had been lost in the translated questionnaire.[18]

TIPS OF THE TRADE

- Keep questionnaire wording simple:
  - Use shorter words that have concrete meaning.
  - Use shorter statements—one line is best—never more than two lines.
  - When questioning about frequency, try to use numbers instead of vague terms like *rarely*.
- Design questionnaire for the least capable respondent in the sampling frame.
- In general, funnel respondents from general to specific questions.
- Randomize question order when possible to avoid order bias.

- Once a questionnaire exceeds a dozen questions, build in automated response quality checks.
- Keep appearance of questionnaire neat and clean to avoid breakoffs.
- Pretests are invaluable in spotting things such as mistake-prone questions, projected overall response rates, and item response rates based on breakoffs.
  - A revised questionnaire is better than an initial questionnaire.
- Use random assignment to balance out presentation of experimental conditions.
- Be aware that speeding can kill response quality.

:: SUMMARY

1. Know the key decisions in questionnaire design. The data gathered via a questionnaire must be both relevant and accurate to be of value. A researcher systematically planning a survey faces several decisions that will shape the value of the questionnaire. What should be asked? How should questions be phrased? In what sequence should the questions be arranged? What questionnaire layout will best serve the research objectives? How can the questionnaire encourage complete responses? How should the questionnaire be pretested and revised if needed?

2. Choose between open-ended and fixed-alternative questions. Open-ended response questions pose some question and ask a respondent to answer in his or her own words. They provide the respondent with flexibility and may allow for meaningful, interpretive conclusions. Open-ended response questions are especially useful in exploratory research or at the beginning of a questionnaire. However, they make a questionnaire more expensive to analyze and interpret because an interviewer must review each response. As a result, interviewer bias can influence the responses to such questions. Alternatively, fixed-alternative questions require less interviewer skill, take less time, are easier to answer, and encourage breakoffs less. In fixed-alternative questions, the researcher provides respondents with specific limited alternative responses and asks them to choose the one closest to their own viewpoint. Care must be taken to formulate the responses so that they do not overlap and to make sure all plausible response categories are provided.

3. Avoid common mistakes in writing questionnaire items.   Survey language should be simple to allow for variations in vocabulary and knowledge. Researchers with strong opinions should seek assistance in making sure a questionnaire is free of leading or loaded questions, which subtly encourage one response over another. Two other common problems are item ambiguity and double-barreled questions, which asks two or more questions at the same time. By keeping each question short and stated with simple, concrete terminology, these problems can be reduced. Researchers who ask respondents about past specific behaviors should consider giving some sort of assistance to prime memory or employ aided-recall questions.

4. Minimize problems with order bias.   A person's response to a question can vary based on where in the sequence of items that question appears. Researchers often employ the funnel technique of survey design. This technique involves asking the most general questions about some subject first and the most specific questions about a subject last. Once all subjects have been covered, any remaining sensitive or demographic items are included. Randomization also plays a role in reducing order bias. Survey software makes the randomization of questions and the randomization of responses simple—both approaches reduce order bias. The randomized response technique also offers a way to make respondents comfortable answering even very embarrassing questions.

5. Understand principles of survey flow.   Survey flow refers to the ordering of questions through a survey. Some surveys involve branching that takes respondents to different parts of the questionnaire based on a response to a specific question. Branching is implemented by having respondents who do not qualify based on a filter question skip questions that a qualified respondent answers.

6. Use latest survey technology to reduce respondent error.   Internet surveys allow researchers effective tools to monitor respondents as they move through a survey. Response quality checks and timing questions monitor whether a respondent is paying attention. Respondents who are not fulfilling their responsibility can be branched out of the survey or given a prompt to notify them of a problem. Internet questionnaires also can include special questions that track behavior including timing and heat-map questions.

7. Appreciate the importance of pretesting survey instruments.   Pretesting helps reveal errors while they can still be corrected easily. A preliminary tabulation may show that, even if respondents understand questions, the responses are not relevant to the marketing problem. Often, the most efficient way to conduct a pretest is with interviewers to generate quick feedback. International marketing researchers must take cultural factors into account when designing questionnaires. The most widespread problem involves translation into another language. International questionnaires are often back translated.

:: KEY TERMS AND CONCEPTS

aided-recall, *313*
back translation, *324*
branching, *316*
breakoff, *316*
checklist question, *305*
counterbiasing statement, *309*
double-barreled question, *311*
filter question, *316*
fixed-alternative questions, *302*
frequency-determination question, *305*

funnel technique, *314*
heat map question, *320*
leading question, *308*
loaded question, *308*
multiple-choice question, *305*
multiple-grid (matrix table) question, *317*
open-ended response questions, *302*
order bias, *314*
piping software, *322*
preliminary tabulation, *323*

randomized response techniques, *315*
simple-dichotomy (dichotomous-alternative)
   question, *304*
speeders, *319*
split-ballot technique, *309*
status bar, *321*
survey blocks, *316*
survey flow, *315*
unaided recall, *313*

:: QUESTIONS FOR REVIEW AND CRITICAL THINKING

1. What are six critical questions for a researcher in designing a questionnaire?

2. Evaluate and comment on the following questions taken from several questionnaires:

    a. A university computer center survey on the university health center:

    Check the response that best reflects how often you use the university health center.

    _____*Infrequently*
    _____*Occasionally*
    _____*Frequently*
    _____*Never*

    b. A survey of advertising agencies:

    Do you understand and like the Federal Trade Commission's new corrective advertising policy?

    _____*Yes*   _____*No*

    c. A survey on a new, small electric car:

    Assuming 90 percent of your driving is in town, would you buy this type of car?

    _____*Yes*   _____*No*

    If this type of electric car had the same initial cost as a current General Motors full-size, fully equipped car, went from 0 to 60 mph in 16 seconds, and could go 175 miles between recharging, would you buy one?

    _____*Yes*   _____*No*

    d. A *student* survey:

    Since the beginning of this semester, approximately what percentage of the time do you get to campus using each of the forms of transportation available to you per week?

    *Walk*_____
    *Bicycle*_____
    *Public transportation*_____
    *Drive*_____

    e. A survey of DH motorcycle company's retail dealers:

    Should the DH company continue its generous cooperative advertising program?

    .f. A survey of media use by residents of a retirement community in Florida:

    Courtesy of Qualtrics.com

    g. A government survey of consumers who have sold a car during the year:

    When you sold your car recently, which of the following reflects your opinion of the deal?

    ○ I feel like it was a big financial loss to me
    ○ I feel like it was a big financial gain to me
    ○ The sale really added to my income for the year
    ○ I think I was paid about as much as the car was worth

    Courtesy of Qualtrics.com

    h. A pro-modern art society's face-to-face survey of the general public:

    Modern art adds greatly to the quality of life in our community. Do you believe that more tax dollars should go to support modern art?

    _____*Yes*   _____*No*

    i. A telephone survey of the U.S. general public:

    In the next year, after accounting for inflation, do you think your real personal income will go up or down?

    _____*Go up more than 15%*
    _____*Go up more than 5%*
    _____*Go up*
    _____*Stay the same*
    _____*Go down*
    _____*Go down 5%*
    _____*Go down more than 5%*
    _____*(Don't know)*

    j. On average, individuals should drink 12 cups of water a day to maintain a healthy lifestyle. How much water do you drink daily?

    *Cups =*_____

    k. A telephone survey of voters:

    Since agriculture is vital to our state's economy, how do you feel about the administration's farm policies?

    A) Strongly favor
    B) Somewhat favor
    C) Somewhat oppose
    D) Strongly oppose
    E) Unsure

3. The following question was asked of a sample of television viewers using a snail-mail survey approach:

    What type of fan do you consider yourself to be for different sports and sports programs?

    • *Diehard Fan: Watch games, follow up on scores and sports news multiple times a day*
    • *Avid Fan: Watch games, follow up on scores and sports news once a day*
    • *Casual Fan: Watch games, follow up on scores and sports news occasionally*
    • *Championship Fan: Watch games, follow up on scores and sports news only during championships or playoffs*
    • *Non-Fan: Never watch games or follow up on scores*
    • *Anti-Fan: Dislike, oppose, or object to a certain sport*

    Does this question do a good job of avoiding ambiguity? If this is exactly how it looked, what improvements would you suggest?

4. What is the difference between a *leading question* and a *loaded question*?

5. Design one or more open-ended response questions to measure reactions to public smartphone usage by others. What advantages and disadvantages does the open-ended format provide?

6. What are some general guidelines for avoiding common mistakes in writing questionnaire items?

7. Do you think the order of the questions below might affect responses? Explain.

What is your attitude toward Geico Insurance television commercials?

| Very Unfavorable | Unfavorable | Neutral | Favorable | Very Favorable |

What is your attitude toward television commercials?

| Very Unfavorable | Unfavorable | Neutral | Favorable | Very Favorable |

Survey Completion
0% 100%

Courtesy of Qualtrics.com

8. What is the funnel technique? What does it do?

9. When might a researcher wish to randomize both question order and the order of responses? Provide an example.

10. Define randomized response technique. Provide an example company that might benefit from using the technique in its marketing research?

11. Design a short telephone survey interview form that measures what types of programs residents of Peoria would like to see available through Netflix.

12. What advantages do Internet surveys offer in terms of order bias and survey flow?

13. Define the term *survey "breakoff."*

14. List at least three factors that increase nonresponse through breakoffs.

15. Provide an example where a filter-item is needed to implement branching in a survey.

16. What is a status bar? When might a status bar be inappropriate?

17. The Apple Assistance Center exists to solve problems for users of MacBook, iPhone, and iPad products. Design a text-message questionnaire that assesses users' satisfaction with the Apple Assistance Center.

18. Respondents have a duty to follow the survey instructions once they agree to participate. Are Internet or personal surveys better for making sure respondents maintain integrity in responding?

19. Visit pollseverywhere.com. What types of surveys may benefit from questions administered via pollseverywhere.com?

20. Define pretesting. Pretests cost time and money. How should a researcher decide if further pretesting is needed?

21. What is back translation?

∷ RESEARCH ACTIVITY

1. Search the Internet to find out a little about Nando's Chicken Restaurant. Design a Web-based survey with a five-item questionnaire assessing how consumers in your town would react to a Nando's location.

2. Design an eight-question Internet survey that assesses how effective the introductory Marketing course at your school has been. Include a filter question that first asks respondents whether they have completed the course and branch those that have not completed it out of the survey.

3. Try to find two friends that know the same foreign language. Write five Likert questions and five other fixed-alternative questions that measure how exciting a retail store environment is to shop in. Have one of your friends interpret the question into the foreign language. Have the other take the translation and state each question in English. How similar is the translated English to the original English? Comment.

4. Use the survey flow feature in a survey software program to set up an assignment of subjects to questions that ask each about their attitude toward either Instagram, Pinterest or Snapchat, which includes randomization so that only each subject answers about only one of the social media outlets.

Frontier Golf Simulators

Case 11.1

It's "Virtually" the Same Game?!

The business of sports is growing tremendously and it is fueled in part by athletes that take on celebrity status. None typifies this better than Tiger Woods. Tiger is a brand representing a multimillion dollar entity unto itself. Traditionally, golf had a stigma of being for wealthy, stodgy, old businessmen who hardly knew how to have a good time. That image is common in many countries outside of the United States to this day. Companies like Nike and Callaway have invested large sums of money and effort to draw a different and more diverse demographic to the game of golf.

With the changing demographic of the actual players comes a marketing challenge of just how to best meet the needs of these segments that are quite new to the game. For instance, indoor golf simulators have started to increase in popularity and offer a chance to play some golf even in an urban setting. These simulators have the distinct advantage of being able to accurately show the player's ball flight and ball spin, as well as the actual yardage the ball travels. A further advantage is that with these simulators, a foursome can finish an entire round of golf in just under an hour instead of four hours or more! Additionally, this round of golf can be played at St. Andrews or Pebble Beach without the expense and hassle of traveling to these mystical sites.

Brian Scheler is the director of marketing for Frontier Golf Simulators, a San Antonio, Texas-based company which operates five state-of-the-art golf simulators. The pricing structure is either $30 per hour for "walk-ins" or a player can take a membership much like he or she might at a real golf club. In addition to the simulators, the facility has a restaurant and bar so that patrons can eat and drink while they tee it up. Brian has the unique challenge of marketing and ultimately selling time on these simulators. Unfortunately, Mr. Scheler is unsure how to best spend his very limited marketing budget. Mr. Scheler understands that the traditional golfer has different wants and needs than does the entertainment-seeking golfer. Does virtual golf offer value in the same way as real golf? If not, the simulators may not appeal to real or traditional golfers at all.

Faced with not knowing exactly what people like most about the simulators, Brian decides to create a survey to determine what people like most about their simulator experience and how to most effectively market his product to maximize the customer's experience and ultimately create returning customers.

1. Conduct secondary research by searching golf options available to customer in the geographic area using the Internet. Be sure to include simulators and live golf. Identify a competitive set and the value proposition of each.
2. What types of issues can be addressed with open-ended questions and what type of issues can be addressed with fixed-alternative questions?
3. How would the structure of the survey change if Brian decides to administer the survey via the telephone versus an online survey?
4. Develop a survey that will address Brian's need to better understand his customers.
5. Assume Brian wants to use social media to reach a target audience. Identify key words he would use to describe his target audience in light of the competitive set you identified earlier.

Source: Prepared by Kevin James, University of Texas-Tyler

A Lengthy Affair

Case 11.2

Sandy Sultan has just received a job for one of the top accounting firms in her town. The firm is expanding into business consulting and she has been hired as the firm's marketing researcher. A cosmetic company client has hired the firm to help deal with its competitive situation. One of the partners comes in and tells Sandy that the project calls for developing a questionnaire that evaluates the importance of thirty different cosmetic brands, have respondents rate each of the thirty brands on five core values of the cosmetic company, and then have respondents assess each of the major competitors based on the availability of the thirty brands. In addition, the partner is certain that the best sampling approach is a mail survey to reach the Gen Z, Millennials, Gen Y, and Baby Boomers target population. After the meeting Sandy goes back to her office feeling depressed. Sandy believes that this questionnaire will induce respondent fatigue because it will be far too long. Furthermore, sending a mail survey to these four diverging age groups might lead to a very low response rate. Can she really go through with this project?

1. Should Sandy do exactly what the partner suggests or risk losing the business for the firm and perhaps her job by suggesting a different approach?
2. What might be an alternative approach?
3. How many questionnaire items would be needed if Sandy moved forward as suggested?
4. What different types of surveys could be created to target each different age group?

Sampling Designs and Sampling Procedures

LEARNING OUTCOMES

After studying this chapter, you should be able to:

1. Explain reasons for taking a sample rather than a complete census

2. Describe the process of identifying a target population and selecting a sampling frame to represent it with a sample

3. Compare random sampling and systematic (nonsampling) errors with an emphasis on how online access can reduce or increase error

4. Identify types of nonprobability sampling, including their advantages and disadvantages

5. Summarize various types of probability samples

6. Discuss how to choose an appropriate sample design

Chapter Vignette:

Harvest Time at Domaine Chandon

apa Valley's Domaine Chandon is the United States's largest producer of sparkling wine. The company, whose parent is the French company Moët & Chandon, among the largest Champagne producers in France and owners of the prestigious Dom Pérignon brand, produces millions of bottles of Napa Valley sparkling wine annually. More recently, Domaine Chandon also emphasizes still wines (non-sparkling) produced from the better vineyard parcels including noteworthy bottlings of Pinot Noir and Pinot Meunier.

Harvest time arrives in the Napa Valley every fall. October typically marks harvest-time, but depending on the weather, the best time to harvest grapes for wine production can vary from late August until about Thanksgiving. Pick grapes too early, and the wine becomes too acidic and "green." Pick grapes too late, and the wine becomes too alcoholic and "fat." Choosing the best time to harvest is crucial to making good wine and therefore to business success.

Sampling is an extremely relevant topic to the wine industry and takes place in many, many forms. Perhaps no sample is more critical, though, than the sample used to determine if the grapes are ready for harvest. Think of looking out over the thousands of acres of vineyard, each with thousands of vines, and each one of those with thousands of grapes. The winemaking team cannot possibly test every grape or even every vine.

Think of the different ways one might try to gather a sample of grapes and use those to judge the quality of all the other fruit. The winemaking team could:

1. Stop conveniently along the long drive onto their property toward their 5-star restaurant and taste a few dozen grapes while also taking brix readings (sugar level measure) with a mechanical device.

2. Send workers out to select a bunch of grapes from each vineyard and have them sent to the lab for tasting and analysis (including brix readings).

3. Go out to the highest point on the property and the lowest point on the property and gather fruit for tasting and analysis.
4. Have workers go out and taste one grape from every vine and record the results on a tablet computer.
5. Take a tractor and drive through the vineyards in a large circle to gather bunches of grapes for analysis back in the lab.
6. Use a computer routine to randomly select 200 GPS coordinates throughout the property and have a bunch of fruit selected from each of those coordinates for tasting and brix analysis.

Every day that harvest doesn't take place brings the possibility of disaster due to disease or bad weather. A prolonged rain during this time will likely dilute the flavor of the fruit and bring on rot. Thus, management is very interested in getting the harvest done. In much the same way, researchers sample populations of people to try to know when they are ready to make a purchase or to just know their feelings and opinions. Just as with Domaine Chandon, if the researcher makes a bad sampling decision, the result is likely to produce bad wine—or management whining!

Introduction

Sampling is a critical part of the marketing research process. However, sampling also is a part of everyday life. Most websites that sell books provide a way for potential customers to sample their products. Typically, they'll allow a customer to see the first chapter or the first few pages. A customer in a bookstore, on the other hand, picks up a book, looks at the cover, skims a few pages throughout the book, and gets a sense of the writing style and content before deciding whether the book is worth buying. Which sampling process provides a better indication of the entire book? This chapter tries to provide insight that allows an answer to questions like this one.

Sampling is defined in terms of the population being studied. A **population (universe)** is any complete group—for example, of people, sales territories, stores, products, or college students—whose members share some common set of characteristics. Each individual member is referred to as a **population element**. A relevant population for many durable goods might be all U.S. homeowners. They share the fact that they own a home in the United States. The researcher then faces many choices about how to sample this important consumer population.

Cautious researchers might like to study every element of a population to draw conclusions with the most certainty. A **census** is an investigation involving measurement of all the individual elements that make up the population—a total enumeration rather than a sample. Thus, if we wished to know whether more Texans drive pickup trucks than sedans or SUVs, we could contact every Texan driver and find out whether each drives a pickup truck, a sedan, or an SUV. We would then know the answer to this question definitively. In the same way, a customer who reads an entire book should have an accurate opinion of whether it is worth reading or not!

Like a bookstore customer thumbing through pages, marketing researchers use sampling because contacting the entire population is impossible, inconvenient, or far too expensive. For researchers, the process of sampling can be quite complex. Sampling is a central aspect of marketing research, requiring indepth examination. In the end, sampling does much to determine how realistic marketing results will be and to what extent they can predict outcomes of marketing decisions. However, like in everyday life, researchers often face resource limitations that encourage them to use less than the most rigorous sampling approach.

The sampling process involves drawing conclusions about an entire population by taking measurements from only a portion of all population elements. A **sample** is a subset of some larger population that researchers observe or measure in some way in an effort to estimate what the entire population is like. In statistical terms, sample observation allows the researcher to estimate population parameters.

population (universe)
Any complete group of entities that share some common set of characteristics.

population element
An individual member of a population.

census
An investigation involving measurement of all the individual elements that make up a population.

sample
A subset of some larger population that is measured or observed in some way to infer what the entire population is like.

Why Sample?

When a customer visits a tasting room in Napa Valley, he or she *samples* the producer's wine. The customer samples wine by having a small taste from multiple bottles of wine, each containing a different type of wine. From this, the consumer decides if he or she likes a particular wine. If each

If you are involved in a market research job consulting for a local, regional, or national company that involves opinions, attitudes, feelings, or behavior relating to something they currently offer or would like to offer, then you are likely going to be doing some survey research. If you want the survey results to have value in terms of representing a relevant set of consumers, consider the following questions:

1. Can the firm define to whom the marketing effort is targeted? The answer to this question reveals the target population.
2. Does a sampling frame exist that matches the target population, if not perfectly, closely.
3. Do the resources exist to use a representative, random sampling approach?
4. If not, what kind of sample can be obtained and what are its shortcomings in terms of representing the target population?
5. Does the client understand the sample limitations?

guest consumed the entire bottle before making a decision, he or she would be far too inebriated to have any idea about the other bottles. In addition, if the goal is to decide whether or not the wines taste good, giving each person a bottle of wine would soon get very expensive. Thus, the customer is left to make judgments based on a very small sample. Similarly, and for some of the same reasons (costs), scientific studies try to draw conclusions about populations by measuring a small sample rather than taking a census.

Pragmatic Reasons

Marketing research projects almost always have budget and time constraints. If Apple wished to take a census of all previous visitors to its Manhattan location to understand what motivates some to leave without purchasing anything or talking to a service rep, they would likely be unable to do so. Apple would not have any way of identifying every visitor. They may be able to use NFC to recognize some users by the iPhones, but not everyone who enters the store is an Apple customer or has location services at Apple's disposal. Thus, even with advanced technology, Apple could not possibly conduct such a census. Constraints usually prevent researchers concerned with large populations from using data derived from a census.

On the other hand, a researcher who wants to investigate a population with an extremely small number of population elements may elect to conduct a census rather than a sample because the cost, labor, and time drawbacks would be relatively insignificant. For a company that wants to assess salespersons' satisfaction with its computer networking system, circulating a questionnaire to all twenty-five of its employees is practical. In that case, no inferential statistics (we will cover these in a later chapter) are necessary, as any observed difference is a true difference. In most situations, however, many practical reasons favor sampling. Sampling cuts costs, reduces labor requirements, and gathers vital information quickly. These advantages may be sufficient in themselves for using a sample rather than a census, but there are other reasons. The Research Snapshot on page 338 describing the origins of the Gallup poll describes its very practical origins. Ultimately, sampling is a practical matter.

Accurate and Reliable Results

Another major reason for sampling is that most properly selected samples give results that are reasonably accurate. If the elements of a population are quite similar, only a small sample is necessary to accurately portray the characteristic of interest. Thus, a population consisting of 10,000 eleventh-grade students in all-boys Catholic high schools will require a smaller sample than a broader population consisting of 10,000 high school students from coeducational, public, secondary schools.

A visual example of how different-sized samples allow one to draw conclusions is provided in Exhibit 12.1. A sample is similar to a jigsaw puzzle that isn't solved yet. Even without looking at the box cover, the puzzler probably doesn't have to wait until every piece is in place to draw a conclusion of what the picture will be. However, as more pieces are put in place, which is analogous to more units being sampled, conclusions can be made with greater confidence. Thus, larger samples allow conclusions to be drawn with more confidence that they truly represent the population.

A sample may even on occasion be more accurate than a census. Interviewer mistakes, tabulation errors, and other nonsampling errors may increase during a census as workers suffer from burnout, fatigue, incompetence, or dishonesty. In a sample, increased accuracy may sometimes be possible because the fieldwork and tabulation of data can be more closely supervised. In a field survey, a small, well-trained, closely supervised group may do a more careful and accurate job of collecting information than a large group of nonprofessional interviewers who try to contact everyone. The U.S. Census Bureau conducts surveys on samples of populations as a way of checking the accuracy of the actual census of those populations. If the conclusions drawn from the sample disagree with the census results, the census is deemed inaccurate and becomes a candidate to be redone because an accurate census is required by law every ten years.

EXHIBIT **12.1**

A Puzzle Is a Sample Until It Is Done! The Sample Allows One to Guess at the Picture.

haveseen/Shutterstock.com

Destruction of Test Units

Many research projects, especially those in quality-control testing, require the destruction of the items being tested. Even if it was possible to test every grape prior to the harvest, this would mean there would be nothing left to make wine with! This is the exact situation in many marketing strategy experiments. For example, if an experimental sales presentation were presented to every potential customer, no prospects would remain to be contacted after the experiment. In these examples, the test units have been destroyed or ruined for the purpose of the research project. Obviously, the destruction of test units presents a major argument not to do research using a census rather than a sample.

Identifying a Relevant Population and Sampling Frame

Before taking a sample, researchers must make several decisions. Exhibit 12.2 presents these decisions as a series of sequential stages, but the order of the decisions does not always follow this sequence. These decisions are highly interrelated. The steps listed in this exhibit are discussed here and in the next two chapters.

Defining the Target Population

The first question in sampling is, "What population are we trying to project?" In other words, what larger group is intended to be represented by using a sample? This question is rarely as easy as it may seem and often the matter isn't given much thought. However, researchers should always address the question of generalization in any research report or article.

EXHIBIT **12.2**

Stages in the Selection of a Sample

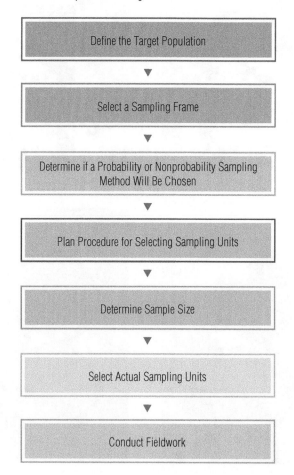

Define the Target Population

▼

Select a Sampling Frame

▼

Determine if a Probability or Nonprobability Sampling Method Will Be Chosen

▼

Plan Procedure for Selecting Sampling Units

▼

Determine Sample Size

▼

Select Actual Sampling Units

▼

Conduct Fieldwork

Polling agencies conduct research to predict election results. What is the relevant population? *Registered voters* seem to be a reasonable choice and fortunately, a list of registered voters is generally available in public records. However, the actual election results will be determined by who actually votes, not who is registered to vote. If a study is supposed to represent those who actually will vote, registered voters no longer form the most relevant population. Identifying a sample that represents likely voters is much more difficult because no such list exists.

The population must be defined accurately for the research to produce good results. One survey concerning organizational buyer behavior had purchasing agents whom sales representatives regularly contacted rate preferred product characteristics. After the research proved less than helpful, investigators discovered that industrial engineers were actually making the purchasing decisions. For consumer research, the appropriate population element frequently is the household rather than an individual member of the household. This presents some problems if household lists are not available or if input cannot be obtained from the entire household.

Consider how difficult identifying a relevant population is for a company like Anthropologie or Michael Kors. What is the population of "fashion consumers?" However, the entire population of fashion consumers is likely not relevant for either of these companies. Clearly, no precise list of population members exists in this case. Even if they are directing a study at "loyal customers," questions such as defining a loyal or a disloyal consumer remain. Companies that use loyalty programs can maintain a list, but the presumption is that only these consumers are truly loyal. In other words, no consumers who do not have a card are loyal. This assumption may be reasonable but is clearly not perfect. Thus, a sample drawn from this list is more precisely described as representing the population of customers who have a loyalty card than as representing truly loyal customers.

One approach for defining the **target population** is to ask and answer questions about crucial population characteristics. This list illustrates the process:

1. Is a list available that matches our population? If so, can we use it? Is valid contact information available and can they be reached with an appropriate communication method?
   - A mobile phone service provider like Verizon or AT&T would have a list of all of its customers. But, they would not have a list of potential customers.
2. Who are we not interested in?
   - Researchers studying the behavior of retail buyers (who make decisions for retailers about what will be sold in the store) are not interested in undergraduate college students.
   a. What are the relevant market segment characteristics?
      - Companies generally appeal only to specific market segments. For example, consider Abercrombie and Fitch's (A&F) brand image. Certainly, A&F shoppers belong to a specific market segment with specific characteristics.
   b. Are we only interested in a regional population? If so, how do we determine the borders?
      - For example, does the "U.K. market" include England, Scotland, and Wales (Great Britain)? Or does it include only England, or does it also include Northern Ireland, or maybe even the Republic of Ireland, which is not actually part of the United Kingdom?
      - What states comprise the southern United States or the western United States? Does either include Hawaii?
3. Should the study include multiple populations?
   - When launching a new product in multiple countries, each country may constitute a distinct population rather than the entire population. Each population may need to be contacted through a different medium with a different approach.

Answers to these questions help researchers and decision-makers focus on the right populations of potential respondents. The sample is implemented using the tangible, identifiable characteristics that also define the population. A baby food manufacturer might define the population as women of childbearing age. However, a more specific *operational definition* would be women between the ages of 18 and 50. Although this definition by age may exclude a few women who are capable of childbearing and include some who are not, it is still more explicit and provides a manageable basis for the sample design. Perhaps there are other reasons why this isn't a perfect population description. One important thing to remember is that if the population members cannot be reached by an appropriate communication method, they cannot be part of a sample.

target population

All of the units (consumers in the case of many marketing problems) collectively to whom a research question applies.

George Gallup's Nation of Numbers

Civil engineers conduct surveys using a transit that takes measures at specific points, and from that information, he or she generates a description of a piece of land. In somewhat the same way, George Gallup pioneered sampling theories that allow a sample survey to determine public opinion. You didn't have to talk to everybody, he said, as long as you randomly selected interviews according to a sampling plan.

Most of Gallup's work was based on the idea of random sampling. Today, truly random sampling has become increasingly difficult based on changes in the methods of communication. Although most polling agencies stick to telephone interviews to predict things like election outcomes, with varying success, major companies have turned to other means to identify and contact members of samples. The results are not perfect, but companies like Procter & Gamble, General Mills, and McDonald's are discovering ways that the shortcomings

of online samples can be corrected using many of the same techniques that phone interviewers have used for years. The Gallup Poll remains the best-known branded poll in the United States. Gallup's daily tracking poll relies on a sampling approach that blends about 30 percent landline phone contacts with 70 percent cell phone contacts. Gallup supplements phone calls with other methods across its other vehicles.

Sources: Excerpted from "George Gallup's Nation of Numbers," *Esquire*, (December 1983), pp. 91–92; http://www.gallup.com/178685/methodology-center.aspx, accessed December 24, 2017.

The Sampling Frame

sampling frame

A list of elements from which a sample may be drawn; also called working population.

In practice, the sample will be drawn from a list of population elements that often differ somewhat from the defined target population. A list of elements from which the sample may be drawn is called a **sampling frame**. The sampling frame is also called the *working population* because these units will eventually provide units involved in analysis. A simple example of a sampling frame would be a list of all members of the American Medical Association. Similarly, companies that maintain consumer panels can provide a list of individuals that comprise a sampling frame.

• • • • • • •

Ralph Lauren, like other lifestyle brands, caters to a market with specific lifestyle characteristics and aspirations. Defining the target population as clothing would miss the mark.

A **sampling frame error** occurs when certain sample elements are excluded or when the entire population is not accurately represented in the sampling frame. An election poll relying on a telephone directory as a sampling frame uses households with listed phone numbers, not households that are likely to vote. Phone directories are very limited as discussed earlier because of multiple reasons including the fact that they typically do not include cell phones. The Research Snapshot describes this issue in more detail.

In practice, almost every list excludes some members of the population. For example, would a university e-mail directory provide an accurate sampling frame for a given university's student population? Perhaps the sampling frame excludes students who registered late and includes students who have resigned from the university. The e-mail directory also will likely list only the student's official university e-mail address. However, many students may not ever use this address, opting to use a private e-mail account instead. Thus, the university e-mail directory could not be expected to perfectly represent the student population. However, a perfect representation isn't always possible or needed.

sampling frame error

An error that occurs when certain sample elements are not listed or are not accurately represented in a sampling frame.

Sampling Services

Some firms, called *sampling services* or *list brokers*, specialize in providing lists or databases that include the names, addresses, phone numbers, and e-mail addresses of specific populations. Lists offered by companies such as this are compiled from subscriptions to professional journals, credit card applications, warranty card registrations, and a variety of other sources. One sampling service obtained its listing of households with children from an ice cream retailer who gave away free ice cream cones on children's birthdays. The children filled out cards with their names, addresses, and birthdays, which the retailer then sold to the mailing list company.

A valuable source of names is Equifax's series of city directories. Equifax City Directory provides complete, comprehensive, and accurate business and residential information. The city directory records the name of each resident over eighteen years of age and lists pertinent information about each household. The reverse directory pages offer a unique benefit. A **reverse directory** provides, in a different format, the same information contained in a telephone directory. Listings may be by city and street address or by phone number, rather than alphabetical by last name. Such a directory is particularly useful when a retailer wishes to survey only a certain geographical area of a city or when census tracts are to be selected on the basis of income or another demographic criterion. Many such directories are easily accessible via the Internet.

reverse directory

A directory similar to a telephone directory except that listings are by city and street address, or by phone number rather than alphabetical by last name.

Online Panels

Online survey services routinely provide access to **online panels** for a modest fee. Researchers contract with the panel provider to get access to a relevant sampling frame. The typical panel comprises a list of e-mail addresses with each address identifying an individual who has agreed to participate in research surveys. Qualtrics, the best-known online survey platform, provides access to, but does not manage, such panel services. Other companies such as Research Now's SSI, Innovate MR, and Offerwise, actually manage panels and can connect a researcher to a panel. Professional panel managers can easily stratify the entire sampling frame on many characteristics of interest and provide a narrower sampling frame representing a specific occupation, users of particular online services, or recent purchasers of some durable goods. The more specific the profile requested, the more expensive the panel. Panel members typically receive some small incentive in return for their membership. The incentive could be a small cash payment, coupons, or contributions to charitable causes. Later, we discuss the advantages and disadvantages of using an online panel as a sampling frame. Like with any panel, users hiring online panel services need to stick to reputable firms that are willing to fully disclose their methodology. Survey researchers should be aware though that not all providers of panel access professionally manage panels and oftentimes a low price means low quality.

online panels

Lists of respondents who have agreed to participate in marketing research along with the e-mail and contact information of these individuals.

Sampling Frames for International Marketing Research

The availability of sampling frames varies dramatically around the world. Not every country's government conducts a census of population. In some countries no voter registration lists exist, and accurate maps of urban areas are unobtainable. However, in Taiwan, Japan, and other Asian countries, a researcher can build a sampling frame relatively easily because those governments release some census information. If a family changes households, updated census information must be reported to a centralized government agency before communal services (water, gas, electricity, education, and so on) are made available.[1] This information is then easily accessible in the local *Inhabitants' Register*. Fortunately, many of the online panels include members from nations around the world. Some firms, like Gazelle Global Research, specialize in maintaining panels globally. The panels can be stratified by country or by region within a country just as they can in the United States.

Sampling Units

sampling unit

A single element or group of elements subject to selection in the sample.

The elements of a population must be selected according to a specified procedure when sampling. The **sampling unit** is a single element or group of elements that is eligible for selection via the sampling process. For example, an airline may sample passengers by taking every twenty-fifth name on a complete list of passengers flying on a specified day. In this case the sampling unit would be the same as the element. Alternatively, the airline could first select certain flights as the sampling unit and then select certain passengers on each flight. In this case the sampling unit would contain many elements.

primary sampling unit (PSU)

A term used to designate a unit selected in the first stage of sampling.

secondary sampling unit

A term used to designate a unit selected in the second stage of sampling.

tertiary sampling unit

A term used to designate a unit selected in the third stage of sampling.

If the target population has first been divided into units, such as airline flights, additional terminology must be used. A unit selected in the first stage of sampling is called a **primary sampling unit (PSU)**. A unit selected in a successive stage of sampling is called a **secondary sampling unit** or (if three stages are necessary) **tertiary sampling unit**. When there is no list of population elements, the sampling unit generally is something other than the population element. In a random-digit dialing study, the sampling unit will be telephone numbers.

Random Sampling and Nonsampling Errors

An advertising agency sampled a small number of shoppers in grocery stores that used Shopper's Video, an in-store advertising network. The agency hoped to measure brand awareness and purchase intentions. Investigators expected this sample to be representative of the grocery-shopping population. However, if a difference exists between the value of a sample statistic of interest (for example, the sample group's average willingness to buy the advertised brand) and the value of the corresponding population parameter (the population's average willingness to buy), a *statistical error* has occurred. Earlier, we introduced two basic causes of differences between statistics and parameters:

1. random sampling errors
2. systematic (nonsampling) error

random sampling error

The difference between the sample result and the result of a census conducted using identical procedures.

An estimation made from a sample is not the same as a census count. **Random sampling error** is the difference between the sample result and the result of an accurate census. Of course, the result of a census is unknown unless someone actually takes one. Random sampling error occurs because of chance variation in the selection of sampling units. The sampling units, even if properly selected according to sampling theory, may not perfectly represent the population because of chance variation.

Picture 50 students in a typical undergraduate research class. If the class is the population and the instructor uses a random sample of 10 students to estimate the average height of a student in the class, a random selection process should make sure that the 10 tallest students are not selected for the sample. Although this is theoretically possible, the odds that this would occur are astronomical. The difference between the average of the randomly selected 10 students and the actual average of the population (50 students) represents random sampling error.

Random Sampling Error

Random sampling error will come back into play later when the issue of hypothesis testing surfaces. At this point, recognize that *random sampling error* is a technical term that refers *only* to statistical fluctuations that occur because of chance variations in the elements selected for the sample. Random sampling error is a function of sample size. As sample size increases, random sampling error decreases.

Let's return to the classroom of 50 students. If the researcher is very lazy, a sample of 1 can be used to estimate student height. The chance of randomly selecting the tallest student is 1 in 50, the same as the odds of selecting the student who matched the median. Either way, the confidence that the sample is matching the true population value should not be very high. A strong likelihood exists that by doubling the sample size to two observations, the estimated value could change a great deal. Conversely, if the researcher is very cautious, a sample of 49 might be taken. Now, even if the tallest person in the class is in the sample, there are 48 other observations that are also considered. The estimate of the average height now is much more confident. Also, the value should not change very much when one more observation is added to the calculation. When someone releases poll results and describes them with a margin of error of 3, 5, or 10 percent, that margin of error is determined by the sample size.

Systematic Sampling Error

Systematic (nonsampling) errors result from nonsampling factors, primarily the nature of a study's design and the correctness of execution. These errors are systematic in some way and *not* due to chance fluctuations. For example, in our classroom example, if a researcher chose a sampling frame consisting of all students sitting in the first two rows, a strong likelihood exists that systematic error would be introduced because shorter students tend to sit up front in an effort to see what is going on instead of the back of another student's head. Sample biases such as these account for a large portion of errors in marketing research. Errors due to sample selection problems are non-sampling errors and should not be classified as random sampling errors.

Systematic But Not obvious Sampling Error

We touched on some of these topics in earlier chapters. For example, telephone samples cannot represent the entire U.S. population because the now majority of consumers without a landline phone usually share something in common with each other. For instance, they tend to be younger than average. Likewise, a random sample of U.S. home-owners would not represent all U.S. consumers because home-owners tend to be relatively older and more likely to have children than apartment dwellers. If a researcher cannot obtain a random, representative sample of the target population, he or she should aim to gather a sample that matches the population demographically.

Facebook surveys allow researchers to reach a large sample rapidly—both an advantage and a disadvantage. Sample size requirements can be met overnight or in some cases almost instantaneously. A researcher can, for instance, release a survey during the morning in the Eastern Standard Time zone and have all sample size requirements met before anyone on the West Coast wakes up. If rapid response rates are expected, and a national sample is desired, steps must be taken to distribute the questionnaire evenly across all time zones. In addition, a survey released during the middle of the day, just like a phone sample conducted in the middle of the day, is likely to exclude people with full-time jobs in a systematic way because they are at work. Thus, the survey should probably remain active for a minimum of 12 hours or so.

The ease and low cost of an Internet survey also contributes to the flood of online questionnaires. As a result, frequent Internet users may be more selective about which surveys they bother answering. A polling agency that tracks U.S. Presidential approval may systematically select a random sample of people on the street in the five largest U.S. cities to assess approval of the U.S. President. Although the method of selection is systematic, error occurs to the extent that rural residents do not share the opinion of the President that urban dwellers do.

Website Visitors

Many Internet surveys use volunteer respondents who happen to visit an organization's website intentionally or by happenstance. These *unrestricted samples* are clearly not random samples. They may not even represent people with an interest in that particular website because of the haphazard manner by which many respondents arrived at a particular site. The term opt-in in survey research refers to conditions in which survey respondents choose to participate in a survey through self-selection rather than by being selected systematically through some sampling routine. Opt-in surveys result in convenience samples.

A better technique for sampling website visitors is to select sampling units randomly. Survey software can be used to trigger a pop-up survey to each one-hundredth (or whatever number) visitor. Or, the software can even adjust the triggering of the survey based on information gathered on the respondent's Web behavior. For example, the opportunity to become a respondent might be timed so that at least 30 seconds have to be spent on the home page before the respondent becomes part of the sampling frame. This may prevent random page visitors from becoming a large part of the sample. Respondents who are selected to participate are first prompted to see if they would like to participate. If the person clicks "Yes," the site presents the questionnaire as a pop-up or as a new browser window.

Randomly selecting website visitors can cause a problem by overrepresenting frequent visitors. Several programming techniques and technologies (using cookies, registration data, or prescreening) are available to help accomplish more representative sampling based on site traffic. Cookies contain information that reveals the frequency of visits.

Panel Samples

Professional consumer panels provide a practical sampling frame in many situations. A good panel provider knows basic characteristics of each member. Panels become particularly useful in screening out sampling units who do not fit the characteristics of a relevant population. If the relevant target population is men, the e-mail addresses belonging to female respondents are omitted from the frame. However, panels are not perfect.

Panel sampling frames may contain a high proportion of respondents who simply like to fill out questionnaires or give their opinion. Thus, a professionally managed panel takes every effort to control for potential variance in respondent characteristics that may affect responses.[2] Thus, as the concern for representativeness increases, the more steps the researcher must take to ensure that the sampling units do indeed represent the population.

Consider Harris Interactive Inc., an Internet survey research organization, which maintains a panel of more than 6 million individuals internationally. A database this large allows the company to draw simple random samples, stratified samples, and quota samples from its panel members.[3] Harris Interactive oversamples, meaning it sends disproportionately more invitations to demographic groups known to under-respond such as males 18 to 24 years old. Practically all groups can be reached through panel surveys with the possible exception of the elderly (over 75 years of age) and the impoverished.

To ensure that survey results are representative, Harris Interactive uses a *propensity-weighting* scheme. The research company does parallel studies—by phone as well as over the Internet—to test the accuracy of its Internet data-gathering capabilities. Researchers look at the results of the telephone surveys and match those against the Internet-only survey results. Next, they use propensity weighting to adjust the results, taking into account the motivational and behavioral differences between the online and offline populations. (How propensity weighting adjusts for the difference between the Internet population and the general population is beyond the scope of this discussion.)

In addition to these steps, panel members may be asked screening questions to make sure that the screening characteristics are accurately working. For example, a researcher interested in coffee shop drinkers in the Midwest may want respondents to compare other shops to Starbucks. Thus, the population may be limited to consumers who frequent Starbucks. Although the online panel may be screened to include only communities where Starbucks has coffee shops, the researcher would be well advised to include screening questions that check on the familiarity of respondents with Starbucks.

Opting In

opt in

In survey research, the term refers to situations in which a respondent chooses to participate in research rather than being selected for participation through some random process.

In many cases, researchers place survey links on websites or social network pages. Anyone who visits the page can potentially become part of the sample that responds to the particular survey. In this case, if a visitor clicks through and responds to the survey, he or she has not been selected from a sampling frame. Instead, the term **opt in** refers to this behavior as the respondent decided on his/her own accord to respond and provide data for the researcher. In other cases, the opt in may be more general and represent an agreement to participate in research in general. Such is the case when a panel solicits members.

By whatever technique the sampling frame is compiled, it is important *not* to send unauthorized e-mail to respondents. If individuals do not *opt in* to receive e-mail from a particular organization, they may consider unsolicited survey requests to be spam. A researcher cannot expect high response rates from individuals who have not agreed to be surveyed. Spamming is not tolerated by experienced Internet users and can easily backfire, creating a host of problems—the most extreme being complaints to the Internet service provider (ISP), which may shut down the survey site.

Low response rates also can be a problem for survey results. This can occur when after someone opts in, they opt out by not finishing the task. Presuming the goal is to generalize to some population, if the low response rates do not occur systematically, the researcher should conclude that some characteristic correlates with responding. If that's the case, then the sample's ability to generalize is damaged. Also, low response rates can increase expense as additional sampling units or even samples may be required. Survey completion rates can be enhanced by embedding highly interesting questions at key points in the survey at which point respondents may otherwise sense fatigue.[4] However, care needs to be taken to make sure the questions don't cause certain types of people to respond more than other types of people.

Sites like Amazon's Mechanical Turk provide another opportunity for respondents to opt in to surveys. However, these respondents do not participate as members of any panel but rather as an unscreened, paid respondent. Therefore, respondents who participate after coincidentally or intentionally finding a survey on a website of this type are not random and cannot be considered representative of the general consumer population.

Less Than Perfectly Representative Samples

Random sampling errors and systematic errors associated with the sampling process may combine to yield a sample that is less than perfectly representative of the population. Exhibit 12.3 illustrates two nonsampling errors (sampling frame error and nonresponse error) related to sample design. The total population is represented by the area of the largest rectangle. Sampling frame errors eliminate some potential respondents. Random sampling error (due exclusively to random, chance fluctuation) may cause an imbalance in the representativeness of the group. Additional errors will occur if individuals refuse to be interviewed or cannot be contacted. Such nonresponse error may also cause the sample to be less than perfectly representative. Notice that if the top half of the total population comes from one part of town and the bottom half comes from another part of town, by the time the planned sample is reached, the portion from the lower part of the exhibit is overrepresented and this continues to the actual sample where 25 percent more of the sample (represented by four people as opposed to three) comes from the lower portion of town. The actual sample overrepresents this portion of town.

EXHIBIT 12.3 Errors Associated with Sampling

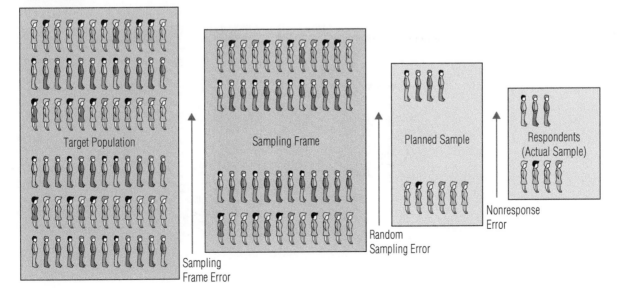

Probability versus Nonprobability Sampling

probability sampling

A sampling technique in which every member of the sampling frame has a known, nonzero probability of selection.

nonprobability sampling

A sampling technique in which units of the sample are selected on the basis of personal judgment or convenience; the probability of any particular member of the population being chosen is unknown.

Several alternative ways to take a sample are available. The main alternative sampling plans may be grouped into two categories: probability techniques and nonprobability techniques.

In **probability sampling**, every element in the sampling frame has a *known, nonzero probability* of selection. The simple random sample, in which each member of the population has an equal probability of being selected, is the best-known probability sample.

In **nonprobability sampling**, the probability of any particular member of the population or sampling frame being chosen is unknown. The selection of sampling units in nonprobability sampling is quite arbitrary, as researchers rely heavily on personal judgment. Technically, no appropriate statistical techniques exist for measuring random sampling error from a nonprobability sample. Therefore, projecting the data beyond the sample is, technically speaking, statistically inappropriate. Nevertheless, researchers sometimes find nonprobability samples best suited for a specific research purpose. As a result, nonprobability samples are pragmatic and are used in market research.

Data taken from Internet samples can be divided into probability and nonprobability samples. With probability samples, the likelihood of any panel member being selected as a potential respondent is fixed, nonzero, and known. Likewise, any relevant stratified portion of a panel being selected is fixed, nonzero, and known. Well-managed panels represent probability samples as the panel management procedures control invitations to participate in any survey. Thus, results derived from samples whose members are selected randomly from such panels can generalize to the sampling frame and perhaps even to broader populations like U.S consumer households presuming panel membership is maintained to provide such representation. On the other hand, crowdsourced data from any Web source, including Mechanical Turk, clearly represents nonprobability sampling. The researcher has no control over who clicks through to respond or who sees the work request.

Although probability sampling is more scientific and preferred, nonprobability sampling becomes a reality when expedience or thriftiness overrides precision. All too often, researchers pressed for time or budget, or for lack of understanding of the importance of knowing who constitutes the target population and sampling frame, treat nonprobability samples like probability samples.[5] A nonprobability sample always presents a limitation in terms of generalizability.

Exhibit 12.4 summarizes visually the goal of sampling. The left frame represents a valid, generalizable sample. If we think that there is a most typical representative of the target population at the center of that circle, a sampling frame, and then a probability sample free of bias, would produce a generalizable result. To the extent that any systematic process enters that changes exactly what type of observations are included in the sample, a lack of generalizability (error) results. The right frame illustrates such an occurrence where either a poor sampling frame is used or a convenience sample that opts-in, but may not share a lot in common with the target population, provides data. The following sections provide some terminology relevant to the use of various sampling approaches.

EXHIBIT 12.4

Summarizing Sampling Processes

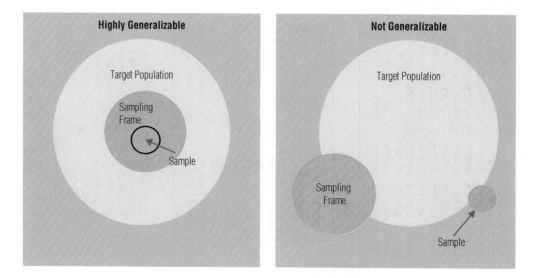

Convenience Sampling

As the name suggests, **convenience sampling** refers to sampling by obtaining people or units that are conveniently available. A researcher may ask his/her Facebook friends to respond to a survey about a new product offering he/she has been asked to study. News media often present person-on-the-street interviews that ask passersby to answer questions or offer opinion on matters of the day. The interviews offer a *survey* of opinion. Given the prevalence of media headquarters in New York City, the interviews often take place on the streets near Times Square. Often, the results are comical. Many passersby cannot answer questions like who is the vice president of the United States, where Israel is on a map, or what the names of two U.S. Supreme Court justices are. Do you think these survey results, although convenient, provide an accurate portrayal of typical Americans? Although it may not seem scientific, marketing researchers do sometimes choose respondents because they are convenient.

Researchers generally use convenience samples to obtain results quickly and economically. At times, a sample through other means may be impractical or impossible to obtain. For example, many Internet surveys are conducted with volunteer respondents who, either intentionally or by happenstance, come across a survey invitation on Facebook, Twitter, or some other website. Although this method produces a large number of responses quickly and at low cost, visitors to a website comprise a sample's relevance. Respondents, are likely not representative because of the haphazard manner by which many of them arrived at the website or because of self-selection bias.

Similarly, research looking at cross-cultural differences in organizational or consumer behavior typically uses convenience samples. Rather than selecting cultures with characteristics relevant to the hypothesis being tested, the researchers conducting these studies often choose cultures to which they have access (for example, because they speak the language or have contacts in that culture's organizations). Further adding to the convenience, cross-cultural research often defines "culture" in terms of nations, which are easier to identify and obtain statistics about. But, complications exist with this approach, including the fact that many nations include several cultures and some people in a given nation may be more involved with the international business or academic community than with a particular ethnic culture.[6] Here again, the use of convenience sampling limits how well the research represents the intended population.

The user of research based on a convenience sample should remember that projecting the results beyond the specific sample is inappropriate. Convenience samples are best used for exploratory research when additional research will subsequently be conducted with a probability sample. University professors conducting marketing research will frequently use a student sample out of convenience. This can be appropriate if the emphasis in the research design lies in internal validity. In other words, to see if the effect put forth in a hypothesis holds under circumstances allowing maximum control of outside effects, such as in a lab experiment. The use of student sampling is inappropriate when the researcher intends the results to generalize to a larger population.

Researchers studying employees often will study those from one company or even one unit of a company. These studies are convenience samples unless the sole intent is to generalize no further than the particular company or unit. Data derived from paid crowdsourcing like MTurk requests also clearly represent convenience samples with similar precautions about generalization.

Judgment Sampling

Judgment (purposive) sampling is a nonprobability sampling technique in which an experienced individual selects the sample based on his or her judgment about some appropriate characteristics required of the sample member. Researchers select samples that satisfy their specific purposes, even if they are not fully representative. The consumer price index (CPI) is based on a judgment sample of market-basket items, housing costs, and other selected goods and services expected to reflect a representative sample of items consumed by most Americans. Test-market cities often are selected because they are viewed as typical cities whose demographic profiles closely match the national profile. A fashion manufacturer regularly selects a sample of key accounts that it believes are capable of providing information needed to predict what may sell in the fall. Thus, the sample is selected to achieve this specific objective.

convenience sampling

The sampling procedure of obtaining those people or units that are most conveniently available.

To the Point

"A straw vote only shows which way the hot air blows."

— O. HENRY

judgment (purposive) sampling

A nonprobability sampling technique in which an experienced individual selects the sample based on personal judgment about some appropriate characteristics of the sample member.

Quota Sampling

Suppose your university administration wants to investigate the experiences of the undergraduate student body. Although 95 percent of the students are full-time, the administration may wish to ensure that both full-time and part-time students are included in the sample. In this case, the researcher may decide to have the sample of 200 students consist of 150 full-time and 50 part-time students. This quota would ensure that the part-time students are well represented, whereas strict probability sampling procedures might not include a sufficient number of those students (10).

quota sampling

A nonprobability sampling procedure that ensures that various subgroups of a population will be represented on pertinent characteristics to the exact extent that the investigator desires.

The purpose of **quota sampling** is to ensure that the various subgroups in a population are represented on pertinent sample characteristics to the exact extent that the investigators desire. Stratified sampling, a probability sampling procedure described in the next section, also has this objective, but it should not be confused with quota sampling. In quota sampling, the interviewer has a quota to achieve. For example, the interviewer may be assigned 100 interviews, 75 with full-time students, and 25 with part-time students. The interviewer is responsible for finding enough people to meet the quota. Aggregating the various interview quotas yields a sample that represents the desired proportion of each subgroup.

Possible Sources of Bias

The logic of classifying the population by pertinent subgroups is essentially sound. However, because respondents are selected according to a convenience sampling procedure rather than on a probability basis (as in stratified sampling), the haphazard selection of subjects may introduce bias. For example, a college professor hired some of his students to conduct a quota sample based on age. When analyzing the data, the professor discovered that almost all the people in the "under 25 years" category were college-educated. Interviewers, being human, tend to prefer to interview people who are similar to themselves.

Quota samples tend to include people who are easily found, willing to be interviewed, and middle class. Fieldworkers exercise considerable leeway in the selection of actual respondents. Interviewers often concentrate their interviewing in areas with heavy pedestrian traffic such as downtowns, shopping malls, and college campuses. Telephone interviewers are asked to screen based on demographic or other screening characteristics to fill quotas of certain types of respondents. Online surveys also can include screening questions that screen out potential respondents for which quotas already are met.

Advantages of Quota Sampling

The major advantages of quota sampling over probability sampling are speed of data collection, lower costs, and convenience. Although quota sampling has many problems, carefully supervised data collection may provide a representative sample of the various subgroups within a population. Quota sampling may be appropriate when the researcher knows that a certain demographic group is more likely to refuse to cooperate with a survey. For instance, if older men are more likely to refuse, a higher quota can be set for this group so that the proportion of each demographic category will be similar to the proportions in the population. A number of laboratory experiments also rely on quota sampling because it is difficult to find a sample of the general population willing to visit a laboratory to participate in an experiment.

Snowball Sampling

snowball sampling

A sampling procedure in which initial respondents are selected by probability methods and additional respondents are obtained from information provided by those initial respondents.

Snowball sampling involves using some process for selecting a few initial respondents and then uses those respondents to seek out additional respondents. The researcher may use a probability sampling approach to contact the initial respondents. However, a nonprobability approach also is used such as when students are asked to snowball initial respondents or when Facebook friends are asked to invite their own Facebook friends. The approach can be useful when the relevant target population is narrow and potentially difficult to reach otherwise.

For instance, a nonprofit organization may need data from homeless people in New York City and San Francisco to address research questions related to their services. Given the difficulty in reaching the homeless through traditional media, an alternative is to gain the cooperation of a small number of homeless people and ask them to recruit a few others each. In the movie, *The Help*, Skeeter employs snowball sampling to create a sample of former African-American housekeepers.[7]

Bias is likely to enter into the study because a person suggested by someone also in the sample has a higher probability of being similar to the first person. If there are major differences between those who are widely known by others and those who are not, this technique may present some serious problems. Snowball sampling presents serious problems for generalizability. When generalizability is not a concern, such as when recruiting participants for focus group interviews, snowball sampling can be useful.

Probability Sampling

All probability sampling techniques employ chance selection procedures. The random probability process eliminates bias inherent in nonprobability sampling procedures. Note that the term *random* refers to the procedure for selecting the sample members and not the data in the sample. *Randomness* characterizes a procedure whose outcome cannot be predicted because it depends on chance. Randomness should not be thought of as unplanned or unscientific—it is the basis of all probability sampling techniques. This section will examine the various probability sampling methods.

Simple Random Sampling

Simple random sampling is a sampling procedure ensuring that each element in a population has an equal chance of being included in a sample. Examples include drawing names from a hat and selecting the winning raffle ticket from a large drum. If the names or raffle tickets are thoroughly stirred, each person or ticket should have an equal chance of being selected. In contrast to other, more complex types of probability sampling, this process is simple in that only one stage of sample selection is required.

Suppose a researcher is interested in selecting a simple random sample of all Honda auto dealers in California, New Mexico, Arizona, and Nevada. Presume that 105 Honda dealers exist in these states and the researcher would like a sample of 25 dealerships. Each dealer's name is assigned a number from 1 to 105. The researcher can then use a random number generator, like those available online (see random.org, for example) or in Excel, to find 25 random numbers between 1 and 105. He or she can then contact the 25 dealerships corresponding to the 25 random numbers drawn. For example, if 60 is the random number generated, then the dealer assigned that number earlier is selected for the sample.

Random number generators greatly facilitate random sample selection. Here is how they work. A number is first assigned to each element of the population (i.e., alphabetical, chronological, digits from a student number, etc.). Assuming the population is 99,999 or fewer, five-digit numbers may be selected from the table of random numbers merely by reading the numbers in any column or row, moving up, down, left, or right. A random starting point should be selected at the outset. For convenience, we will assume that we have randomly selected as our starting point the first five digits in columns 1 through 5, row 1, of the table generated by random.org, mentioned previously. The first number in our sample would be 73265; moving down, the next numbers would be 34663, 62549, and so on.

The random-digit dialing (RDD) technique of sample selection requires that a telephone interviewer identify the exchange or exchanges of interest (the first three numbers in a phone number after the area code) and then use a table of numbers to select the next four numbers. In practice, however, the exchanges are not always selected randomly. Researchers who wanted to find out whether black Americans with African ancestry prefer being called "black" or "African-American" narrowed their sampling frame by selecting exchanges associated with geographic areas where the proportion of this population was at least 30 percent. The reasoning was that this made the survey procedure far more efficient, considering that the researchers were trying to contact a

simple random sampling

A sampling procedure that assures each element in the population has an equal chance of being included in the sample.

To the Point

"Make everything as simple as possible, but not simpler."

—ALBERT EINSTEIN

group representing less than 15 percent of U.S. households. This initial judgment sampling raises the same issues we discussed regarding nonprobability sampling. In this study, the researchers found that respondents were most likely to prefer the term *black* if they had attended schools that were about half black and half white.[8] If such experiences influence the answers to the question of interest to the researchers, the fact that blacks who live in predominantly white communities are underrepresented may introduce bias into the results. The result reduces the generalizability of the results.

Systematic Sampling

systematic sampling

A sampling procedure in which a starting point is selected by a random process and then every *n*th number on the list is selected.

Suppose a researcher wants to take a sample of 1,000 from a population of 2,000,000 names. With **systematic sampling**, he or she would draw every 2,000th name from a list of population members. This simple process illustrates how to find the interval between selected observations:

$$\text{Interval} = \frac{\text{Population Size}}{\text{Sample Size}} = \frac{2,000,000}{1,000} = 2,000$$

A starting point is selected randomly; then every *n*th number on the list is selected. In this case, the researcher selects every 2,000th name. Because the starting point may well not be at the beginning, this may actually yield only 999 names. A random number can be used to select one more if the sample needs to be exactly 1,000.

Stratified Sampling

stratified sampling

A probability sampling procedure in which simple random subsamples that are more or less equal on some characteristic are drawn from within each stratum of the population.

The usefulness of dividing the population into subgroups, or *strata*, whose members are more or less equal with respect to a characteristic, was illustrated in our discussion of quota sampling. The first step is the same for both stratified and quota sampling: choosing strata on the basis of existing information—for example, classifying retail outlets based on annual sales volume. However, the process of selecting sampling units within the strata differs substantially. In **stratified sampling**, a subsample is drawn using simple random sampling within each stratum. This is not true of quota sampling.

The reason for taking a stratified sample is to obtain a more efficient sample than would be possible with simple random sampling. Suppose, for example, that urban and rural groups have widely different attitudes toward energy conservation, but members within each group hold very similar attitudes. Random sampling error will be reduced with the use of stratified sampling because each group is internally homogeneous, but there are comparative differences between groups. More technically, a smaller standard error may result from this stratified sampling because the groups will be adequately represented when strata are combined.

Another reason for selecting a stratified sample is to ensure that the sample will accurately reflect the population on the basis of the criterion or criteria used for stratification. This is a concern because occasionally simple random sampling yields a disproportionate number of one group or another, and consequently, the sample ends up being less representative than it could be.

A researcher can select a stratified sample as follows. First, a variable (sometimes several variables) is identified as an efficient basis for stratification. A stratification variable must be a characteristic of the population elements known to be related to the dependent variable or other variables of interest. The variable chosen should increase homogeneity within each stratum and increase heterogeneity between strata. The stratification variable usually is a categorical variable or one easily converted into categories (i.e., subgroups). For example, a pharmaceutical company interested in measuring how physicians prescribe a certain drug might choose physicians' specialty as a basis for stratification. In this example the mutually exclusive strata are cardiologists versus pediatricians.

Next, for each separate subgroup or stratum, a list of population elements must be obtained. (If such lists are not available, they can be costly to prepare, and if a complete listing is not available, a true stratified probability sample cannot be selected.) Using a table of random numbers or some other device, a *separate* simple random sample is then taken within each stratum. Of course, the researcher must determine how large a sample to draw for each stratum. This issue is discussed in the following section.

Proportional versus Disproportional Sampling

If the number of sampling units drawn from each stratum is in proportion to the relative population size of the stratum, the sample is a **proportional stratified sample**. Sometimes, however, a researcher selects a disproportional stratified sample to try to obtain an adequate number of sampling units in each stratum. Sampling more heavily in a given stratum than its relative population size warrants is not a problem if the primary purpose of the research is to estimate some characteristic separately for each stratum and if researchers are concerned about assessing the differences among strata.

Suppose a research question concerned what was the average total bill of retail customers in Missouri based on the average total reported by retail stores. The percentage breakdown of Missouri retail outlets is presented in Exhibit 12.5. A proportional sample of retail stores would use the same percentages as in the population. However, the small percentage of warehouse club stores underrepresents the relative amount of money consumers spend in these large stores. To avoid underrepresenting the large warehouse clubs in the sample, the researcher can take a disproportional sample.

In a **disproportional stratified sample**, the sample size for each stratum is not allocated in proportion to the population size but is dictated by analytical considerations, such as variability in store sales volume. The logic behind this procedure relates to the general argument for sample size: As variability increases, sample size must increase to provide accurate estimates. Thus, the strata that exhibit the greatest variability are sampled more heavily to increase sample efficiency—that is, produce smaller random sampling error. Complex formulas (beyond the scope of an introductory course in marketing research) have been developed to determine sample size for each stratum. A simplified rule of thumb for understanding the concept of optimal allocation is that the stratum sample size increases for strata of larger sizes with the greatest relative variability. Other complexities arise in determining population estimates. For example, when disproportional stratified sampling is used, the estimated mean for each stratum has to be weighed according to the number of elements in each stratum in order to calculate the total population mean.

proportional stratified sample

A stratified sample in which the number of sampling units drawn from each stratum is in proportion to the population size of that stratum

disproportional stratified sample

A stratified sample in which the sample size for each stratum is allocated according to analytical considerations.

Cluster Sampling

Cluster sampling is an economical sampling approach that retains the characteristics of a probability sample. Consider a researcher who must conduct 500 personal interviews with physicians scattered throughout the United States. Travel costs are likely to be enormous because the amount of time spent traveling will be substantially greater than the time spent in the interviewing process. If a pharmaceutical marketer can assume the product will be equally successful in Phoenix and Baltimore, cluster sampling provides an alternative. The assumption is that respondents in a cluster that is sampled are the same as respondents in an unsampled cluster.

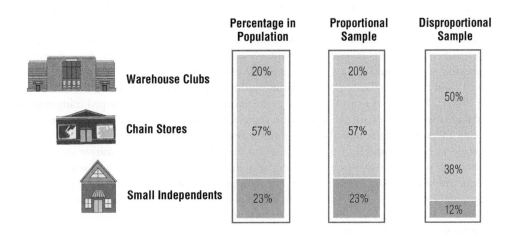

EXHIBIT 12.5

Disproportional Sampling: Hypothetical Example

A Natural Match

Slow food, biodynamic, no GMO, cage free, shopping small, organic, natural, etc. What do all of these terms mean? That's an important question. But, perhaps just as important a question to food sellers is whether or not their market cares about whatever these terms mean. Organic salads alone account for nearly $1 billion in sales in the U.S. each year. The detailed regulations that justify the various labels confuse even experts and are a matter of debate and controversy. Thus, the typical consumer likely will not know exactly what each means and may even distrust some labels. The market size is lucrative, but in studying consumers with an eye toward selling more natural or organic products, just who should be sampled?

Private and public sector researchers examine research questions related to the way consumers respond to such labels. Take a look at Exhibit 12.4. If a researcher is trying to understand the typical "organic salad" purchaser in terms of what they know and how they respond to various labels, questions like these may be important: What is the relevant target population? Are all consumers in the U.S. in the target population? Do demographic or geographic factors influence the relevance for the research question? Do households with children respond the same as individuals? Are urban and rural consumers equally concerned about consuming natural

foods? Does the research question concern expanding sales within the current organic market or creating sales among consumers not currently in the market? All of these questions and more are important in defining the target market, identifying a sampling frame, and extracting a sample. Conversely, if a convenience sample is taken from a downtown San Francisco Whole Foods store, what type of target population could it represent?

In the end, knowing better how to label natural products depends on a natural match with the desired market segment.

Sources: http://www.nielsen.com/us/en/insights/news/2017/tops-of-2017-fresh-organic.html, accessed December 28, 2017. Chait, J. (2017), "Who Buys Organic Food: Different Types of Consumers," *Sustainable Businesses*, https://www.thebalance.com/who-buys-organic-food-different-types-of-consumers-2538042, accessed December 29, 2017.

---

cluster sampling

An economically efficient sampling technique in which the primary sampling unit is not the individual element in the population but a large cluster of elements; clusters are selected randomly.

In **cluster sampling**, the primary sampling unit is no longer the individual element in the population (e.g., grocery stores) but a larger cluster of elements located in proximity to one another (e.g., cities). The *area sample* is the most popular type of cluster sample. A grocery store researcher, for example, may randomly choose several geographic areas as primary sampling units and then interview at a sample of grocery stores within the geographic clusters. Interviews are confined to these clusters only. No interviews occur in other clusters. Cluster sampling is classified as a probability sampling technique because of either the random selection of clusters or the random selection of elements within each cluster. Some examples of clusters appear in Exhibit 12.6.

Cluster samples become attractive when lists of a sample population are not available. For example, when researchers investigating employees and self-employed workers for a downtown revitalization project found that a comprehensive list of these people was not available, they decided to take a cluster sample, selecting organizations (business and government) involved in the project as the clusters. A sample of firms within the central business district was developed using stratified probability sampling to identify clusters. Next, individual workers within the firms (clusters) were randomly selected and interviewed concerning the revitalization project.

Ideally a cluster should be as heterogeneous as the population itself—a mirror image of the population. A problem may arise with cluster sampling if the characteristics and attitudes of the elements within the cluster are too similar. For example, geographic neighborhoods tend to have residents of the same socioeconomic status. Students at a university tend to share similar beliefs. This problem may be mitigated by constructing clusters composed of diverse elements and by selecting a large number of sampled clusters.

Population Element	Possible Clusters in the United States
U.S. adult population	States Counties Metropolitan Statistical Areas Census Tracts Blocks Households
College seniors	Colleges
Manufacturing firms	Counties Metropolitan Statistical Areas Localities Plants
Airline travelers	Airports Planes
Sports fans	Football Stadiums Basketball Arenas Baseball Parks

EXHIBIT 12.6
Examples of Clusters

Multistage Area Sampling

Multistage area sampling is a cluster sampling approach involving multiple steps that combine some of the probability techniques already described. Typically, geographic areas are randomly selected in progressively smaller (lower-population) units. For example, a political pollster investigating an election in Texas might first choose counties within the state to ensure that different areas are represented in the sample. In the second step, precincts within the selected counties may be chosen. As a final step, the pollster may select blocks (or households) within the precincts, then interview all the blocks (or households) within the geographic area. Researchers may take as many steps as necessary to achieve a representative sample.

The U.S. Census Bureau provides maps, population information, demographic characteristics for population statistics, and so on, by several small geographical areas; these may be useful in sampling. Census classifications of small geographic areas vary, depending on the extent of urbanization within Metropolitan Statistical Areas (MSAs) or counties.

multistage area sampling

Sampling that involves using a combination of two or more probability sampling techniques.

What Is the Appropriate Sample Design?

A researcher who must decide on the most appropriate sample design for a specific project will identify a number of sampling criteria and evaluate the relative importance of each criterion before selecting a sampling design. This section outlines and briefly discusses the most common criteria. The Research Snapshot on the previous page illustrates how important the sampling design would be to any survey about U.S. consumption habits.

Degree of Accuracy

Selecting a representative sample is crucial for a researcher desiring to make accurate inferences, predictions or forecasts. However, the degree of accuracy required or the researcher's tolerance for sampling and nonsampling error may vary from project to project, especially when cost savings or another benefit may be a trade-off for a reduction in accuracy. In particular, if accuracy represents the generalizability of results to a broad population, haphazard sampling is problematic. Generalizability may not always be a concern though.

For example, when the sample is part of an exploratory research project, accuracy may not be the highest priority. For other, more conclusive projects, the sample result must precisely represent a population's characteristics, and the researcher must be willing to spend the time and money needed to achieve that accuracy. When researchers use a convenience sample, they may sometimes even think backward and only describe what population the results might extend to based on the sample that can be obtained. Any results are qualified based on the deviation of that population from a relevant target population (see Exhbit 12.4). Typically, a market research report will qualify results based on sampling characteristics.

Resources

The cost associated with the different sampling techniques varies tremendously. If the researcher's financial and human resources are restricted, certain options will have to be eliminated. For a typical graduate student working on a thesis or dissertation, conducting a representative, national survey is often out of the question because of limited resources. Managers concerned with the cost of the research versus the value of the information often will opt to save money by using a nonprobability sampling design rather than make the decision to conduct no research at all.

Time

A researcher pressured to meet a deadline or complete a project quickly will be more likely to select a simple, less time-consuming sample design. A researcher may have questions about a convenience sample and how well it represents the relevant population of consumers in the United States. However, he or she can obtain the convenience sample very quickly and may be willing to trade-off speed for any increased accuracy that would come from drawing his or her own sampling frame. Such trade-offs need to be explicitly acknowledged as a potential limitation in the subsequent research report.

Advance Knowledge of the Population

Advance knowledge of population characteristics, such as the availability of lists of population members, is an important criterion. In many cases, however, no list of population elements exists. This is especially true when the population element is defined by ownership of a particular product or brand, by experience in performing a specific job task, or on a qualitative dimension. A lack of adequate lists may automatically rule out systematic sampling, stratified sampling, or other sampling designs, or it may dictate that a preliminary study, such as a short telephone survey using random digit dialing, be conducted to generate information to build a sampling frame for the primary study. Social media can be used to reach out to brand fans. Procter & Gamble could reach Tide fans by going to the detergent's Facebook page. However, because they would not find a list of all Tide users by doing so, nor could one be generated from this page, the resulting sample would be a convenience sample. Its usefulness would depend on the nature of the research question.

National versus Local Project

Geographic proximity of population elements will influence sample design. When population elements are unequally distributed geographically, a cluster sample may become much more attractive. A sample that represents all households in the United States and Canada becomes the goal for the few household products that show no regional, demographic, or lifestyle bias. Few products exhibit this characteristic. For instance, market researchers investigating opinions of North American consumers about the Fiat Mini should sample from large urban areas rather than rural areas based on the knowledge that rural residents do not often purchase a Fiat.

TIPS OF THE TRADE

- Online panels are a practical reality in marketing research. A sample can be obtained quickly and generally comes close to matching general population parameters if the results come from a professional organization maintaining a well-managed panel. Well-managed panels can provide a probability sample. Like many things though, the better-run panels are more expensive than more haphazardly managed panels. Professional panel companies are willing and able to disclose the methodology for maintaining representative panels.
- Crowdsourced panels (such as MTurk) involve unknown respondents who opt in without a personal invitation and provide little ability for generalization in the vast majority of marketing and consumer research settings.
- Convenience samples do have appropriate uses in marketing research. Convenience samples are particularly appropriate when:
  - Exploratory research is conducted.
  - The researcher is primarily interested in internal validity (testing a hypothesis under any condition) rather than external validity (understanding how much the sample results generalize to a target population).
- When cost and time constraints only allow a convenience sample:
  - Researchers can try to think backward and project on the population for whom the results apply based on the nature of the convenience sample. Of course, this depends on reliable data describing the demographic and other relevant population characteristics of individual respondents.
- The research report should address the adequacy of the sample. The report should qualify the generalizability of the results based on sample limitations.

:: SUMMARY

1. Explain reasons for taking a sample rather than a complete census. Sampling involves drawing conclusions about an entire population by taking measurements from only a portion of that population. The practical nature of research is clearly illustrated in sampling. Sampling is used because of the practical impossibility of measuring every population member. Seldom would a researcher have the time or budget to do so. Also, a researcher would rarely need to measure every unit, as a well-designed and executed sampling plan can yield results that may even be more accurate than an actual census. Samples also are needed in cases where measurement involves destruction of the measured unit.

2. Describe the process of identifying a target population and selecting a sampling frame to represent it with a sample. The first problem in sampling is to define the target population. Incorrect or vague definition of this population is likely to produce misleading results. The chapter contains an example list of questions that illustrate considerations needed in making a decision about the relevant population. A sampling frame is a list of elements, or individual members, of the overall population from which the sample is drawn. A sampling unit is a single element or group of elements subject to selection in the sample. Sometimes, a list of actual population members exists and can serve as a sampling frame. Professionally managed panels can assist in identifying a sampling frame from which to sample in survey research.

3. Compare random sampling and systematic (nonsampling) errors with an emphasis on online access can reduce or increase error. Two sources of discrepancy between the sample results and the population parameters exist. One, random sampling error, arises from chance variations of the sample from the population. Random sampling error is a function of sample size and may be estimated using the central-limit theorem (discussed in a later chapter). Systematic, or nonsampling, error comes from sources such as sampling frame error, responses from uninvited individuals, or systematic nonresponses from persons not contacted or who refuse to participate. Professional panels like those available from companies like Nielsen enable access to sampling frames representative of many relevant consumer populations. Online access to such panels can be purchased. Pure crowd-source options allow individuals to opt-in without an invitation or a verified identity in sampling frame. Caution needs to be used in generalizing results from pure opt-in approaches.

4. Identify the types of nonprobability sampling, including their advantages and disadvantages. The two major classes of sampling methods are probability and nonprobability techniques. Nonprobability techniques include convenience sampling, judgment sampling, quota sampling, and snowball sampling. They are convenient to use but more subject to systematic sampling error. Sorting out the systematic sampling error from the random sampling error also proves problematic.

5. Summarize various types of probability samples. Probability samples are based on chance selection procedures. These include simple random sampling, systematic sampling, stratified sampling, and cluster sampling. With these techniques, random sampling error can be accurately predicted. The process for selecting sample units from a population is described in the chapter. A true probability sample can be costly both in terms of money and time.

6. Discuss how to choose an appropriate sample design. A researcher who must determine the most appropriate sampling design for a specific project will identify a number of sampling criteria and evaluate the relative importance of each criterion before selecting a design. The most common criteria concern accuracy requirements, available resources, time constraints, knowledge availability, and analytical requirements. Internet sampling presents some unique issues. Convenience samples drawn from website visitors or crowdsourced options are problematic with respect to generalizability.

∷ KEY TERMS AND CONCEPTS

census, *333*

cluster sampling, *350*

convenience sampling, *345*

disproportional stratified sample, *349*

judgment (purposive) sampling, *345*

multistage area sampling, *351*

nonprobability sampling, *344*

online panels, *339*

opt in, *342*

population (universe), *333*

population element, *333*

primary sampling unit (PSU), *340*

probability sampling, *344*

proportional stratified sample, *349*

quota sampling, *346*

random sampling error, *340*

reverse directory, *339*

sample, *333*

sampling frame, *338*

sampling frame error, *339*

sampling unit, *340*

secondary sampling unit, *340*

simple random sampling, *347*

snowball sampling, *346*

stratified sampling, *348*

systematic sampling, *348*

target population, *337*

tertiary sampling unit, *340*

∷ QUESTIONS FOR REVIEW AND CRITICAL THINKING

1. If you decide whether you want to see an entire movie based on a 90-second trailer are you using a sampling technique? Could this be described as a scientific sampling technique? Explain your answer.

2. What is the difference between a census and a sample? What are the reasons why a sampling process is so often used in place of a census? Why is it that a sample can sometimes be as accurate as, or more accurate than, a census?

3. Define sample, sampling unit, sampling frame, and target population.

4. How might the target population differ for a researcher doing separate projects for two retailing companies—one for H&M and one for Nordstrom?

5. Name some possible sampling frames for research questions involving the following:
   a. Online travel agencies
   b. Frequent Instagram users
   c. Golf course greenskeepers (responsible for the condition of the golf course)
   d. Dog owners
   e. Harley-Davidson owners
   f. Tattoo wearers
   g. Minority-owned businesses
   h. Women over six feet tall
   i. Architects
   j. Fast-food consumers in California

6. Describe the difference between a random and systematic sampling error.

7. What is a nonprobability sample? Give some examples.

8. Is a convenience sample ever appropriate? Explain.

9. When would a researcher use a judgment, or purposive, sample?

10. What are pros and cons of using MTurk crowdsourcing to provide a sample for a marketing research study? Would you advise someone trying to explain which type of appeals for energy efficient technology for new automobiles will be effective on U.S. consumers to use a sample taken from MTurk?

11. Sally receives an online survey invitation to participate in research about "people and diet habits." After clicking through, the first question asks Sally to indicate her race by checking the corresponding box. After answering this question, she is thanked for his/her interest but told "we already have enough responses from people like you and you do not need to participate in the survey." How would you describe the sampling process likely involved? What type of sampling is likely being used?

12. What role can screening questions play in trying to understand and control systematic variance from sources such as Internet surveys, online panels, or other types of directories?

13. What are the benefits of stratified sampling?

14. What geographic units within a metropolitan area are useful for sampling?

15. Outline the step-by-step procedure you would use to select the following:
   a. A random sample of 275 students from your university
   b. A quota sample of 50 light users and 50 heavy users of beer from Facebook users
   c. A sample of regular Twitter users to explore social network relationships
   d. A random sample of Netflix users

16. Selection for jury duty is supposed to be a random process. Comment on the following computer selection procedures, and determine if they are indeed random:
   a. A sampling frame is derived from all local citizens who pay property taxes.
   b. Three-digit numbers are randomly generated to select jurors from a list of licensed drivers. If the weight information listed on the license matches the random number, the person is selected.
   c. A sampling frame is taken by identifying every adult in the jurisdiction's zip codes who has received an Amazon Prime delivery within the last week.
   d. A random number process is used to select adults exiting the local Walmart store.

17. Provide an example of marketing research in which a sample that is truly representative of all of North America is needed. If you cannot provide an actual example, try to contrive a situation that would require such a sample. How often would such a target population be needed?

18. To ensure a good session, a company selects focus group members from a list of articulate participants instead of conducting random sampling. The client did not inquire about sample selection when it accepted the proposal. Is this ethical?

:: RESEARCH ACTIVITY

1. Develop a sampling plan to study the lunch habits of undergraduate and graduate students of your university. Research questions involve who has the most market share and what the preferred food types and price points are for this particular school. Explain your choices.

2. Suppose Amazon hires you to conduct a study of U.S. household consumer attitudes toward their brand and potential new service offerings. To make things simple, you decide to sample people only from Louisiana. Using www.census.gov, how well would a representative sample of households in Louisiana match the U.S. household population in general? Write a statement of limitations for such research.

Who's Fishing?

Washington Times columnist Gene Mueller writes about fishing and other outdoor sporting activities. Mueller commented that although interest groups express concerns about the impact of saltwater fishers on the fish population, no one really knows how many people fish for recreation or how many fish they catch. This situation would challenge marketers interested in the population of anglers.

How could a marketer get an accurate sample? One idea would be to contact residents of coastal counties using random-digit dialing. This sampling frame would include many, if not all, of the people who fish in the ocean, but it would also include many people who do not fish—or who fish for business rather than recreation. A regional agency seeking to gather statistics on anglers, the Atlantic Coastal Cooperative Statistics Program, prefers to develop a sampling frame more related to people who fish.

Another idea would be to use state fishing license records. Privacy would be a drawback, however. Some people might not want their records shared, and they might withhold phone numbers or provide an inaccurate e-mail address. Further complicating this issue

for Atlantic fishing is that most states in the Northeast do not require a license for saltwater fishing. Also exempt in some states are people who fish from the shore and from piers.

A political action group called the Recreational Fishing Alliance suggests that charter fishing businesses collect data from its customers. One local angler suggests putting a HIT on MTurk to request responses from U.S. saltwater fishermen in return for a $1 payment.

Questions

1. Suppose you were consulted on the project investigating saltwater fishers and how many and what types of fish they catch. Do any of the approaches mentioned above have prospects as an accurate, relevant, and generalizable sample? What advice would you give about sampling? What method or combination of methods would generate the best results?

2. What other criteria besides accuracy would you expect to consider? What sampling methods could help you meet those criteria?

Big Data Basics: Describing Samples and Populations

LEARNING OUTCOMES

After studying this chapter, you should be able to:

1. Use basic descriptive statistics to analyze data and make basic inferences about population metrics
2. Distinguish among the concepts of population, sample, and sampling distributions
3. Explain the central-limit theorem
4. Use confidence intervals to express inferences about population characteristics
5. Understand major issues in specifying sample size
6. Know how to assess the potential for nonresponse bias

iStock.com/Opidanus

Chapter Vignette:

Prime-Time Customers

With all the talk of artificial intelligence, big data, and marketing analytics, business students may get the impression that data analysis is complicated and that businesses rely on sophisticated statistical analysis to make all types of decisions. Sometimes though, the most basic descriptive statistics tell the story.

Rawpixel.com/
Shutterstock.com

For millions of Amazon customers, buying time is now Prime-Time! Amazon's retail business strategy lies more in growth than in profitability. Amazon wants to sell everything to everybody! To do that, Amazon looks for ways to *buy customers*. For about $100 a year, Amazon allows a customer to enter its Amazon Prime "loyalty" program. In return, U.S. Amazon's Prime customers receive perks like free shipping, which could be next day in certain areas, free Amazon Prime Music and Video streaming, and Amazon Dash button availability for the customer's favorite items. Amazon, more than loyalty, wants to create inertia that makes them the only option that comes to mind for buying practically all everyday products. Amazon sees big numbers as success. Big numbers of customers and big numbers of sales. Like the entire Prime program equates to a marketing tactic referred to as a loss-leader (losing money on a particular item to hopefully make it up on additional purchases),

Amazon's low prices for Alexa and smart speakers indicates they too may be loss-leaders.

How is this strategy working out for Amazon? Researchers present the following descriptive statistics:

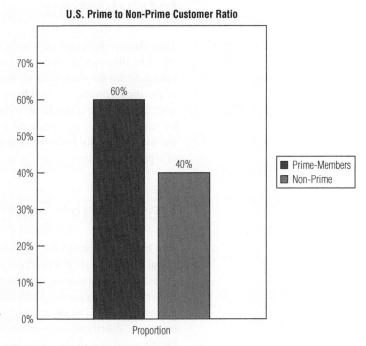

U.S. Prime to Non-Prime Customer Ratio

That means that nearly 100 million of Amazon's U.S. customers as of 2018 are Prime-Time. That number has doubled since 2015. Amazon may see more work ahead as they look to duplicate this success in the U.K. and other markets. The same statistics in the U.K. indicate:

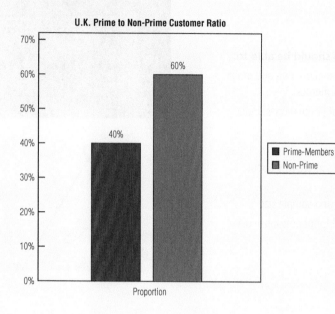

U.K. Prime to Non-Prime Customer Ratio

Interestingly, although Amazon guards details about its profitability closely, the non-Prime customers likely deliver higher margins. In fact, Amazon's Prime program likely is unprofitable. All of the free shipping creates cost pressures coupled with the

expenses of producing content for streaming services. However, Amazon's goals for Prime are likely not stated in profitability but in growth. In fact, all of Amazon's retail profitability is low with margins of 1–3 percent. In contrast, Amazon's Web services are highly profitable and help feed the overall growth strategy. And if revenue growth also is an issue, a simple comparison of Prime versus non-Prime average revenue is revealing:

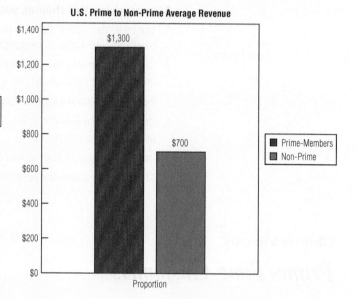

U.S. Prime to Non-Prime Average Revenue

Thus, the simple frequency statistics and means support growth strategies at Amazon. It's Prime-Time.[1]

Introduction

This chapter provides an entrée into the world of marketing analytics. As suggested in the vignette, although big data analysis sounds like a very complicated thing, we can learn a lot from summarizing the data with elementary, basic statistics. This chapter gives an overview of some of the most commonly used basic statistics. All of these statistics are univariate in the sense that only one variable is involved in the computation. This overview also provides good background for understanding equations related to sample size requirements. These equations complement the material in the previous chapter, providing us with a better understanding of the usefulness of a particular sample.

Descriptive Statistics and Basic Inferences

The boom in demand for marketing research analysts exists because raw data alone are seldom useful. Raw data are just numbers and words with little meaning. Analysts must somehow identify diagnostic data, meaning data useful in decision making, and then summarize the information. Otherwise, the decision-makers will be lost amidst the vast quantities of data available to even small businesses today. The most basic statistical tools for summarizing information from data include frequency distributions, proportions, and measures of central tendency and dispersion. Statistics like these often provide a summary number that allows analysts to compare the characteristics of a

Does your market research project involve estimates? They usually do. If so, some basic statistics of some type are likely necessary and may actually be able to address some research questions.

For instance, an entrepreneur wishing to start a business online may have some idea of the price needed to make the project viable. The resulting research question may lead one to compare consumers' willingness to pay (WTP) with that benchmark. In other words, does the central tendency for WTP meet or exceed the benchmark? Similarly, ongoing businesses may want to know whether they have more detractors than supporters based on NPS scores (discussed in an earlier chapter). Here, the frequency distribution of consumers in each group becomes an important value to compute. A surprisingly large number of research questions can be addressed with basic, univariate, statistics like those discussed in this chapter. Even better, they lend themselves to straightforward and easily understood reporting.

sample with some population benchmark, characteristics of another sample, or some other critical value. Analysts and decision-makers refer to such numbers as **metrics**. After providing summary metrics, the researcher then adds to that information about the sample validity. The combination of summary metrics from basic statistics *and* a valid sample proves vital in making effective marketing and business decisions.

Databases like those available through census.gov and the CIA *Factbook* provide a glimpse into the way analysts can represent volumes of data with summary statistics. At these sites, we can find table after table of figures associated with numbers of births, number of workers by industry, populations, and other data that represent *statistics*. Specifically, these tables provide descriptive statistics. Another type of statistics, **inferential statistics**, allows inferences about a whole population from a sample. For example, a firm test-markets a new product in Sacramento and Birmingham because it wishes to make an inference from these sample markets to predict what will happen throughout the United States. Therefore, two applications of statistics exist, each consistent with descriptive or inferential statistics, respectively:

1. to describe characteristics of the population or sample and
2. to generalize from a sample to a population.

metrics

A summary number that allows analysts to compare the characteristics of a sample with some population benchmark, characteristics of another sample, or some other critical value.

inferential statistics

A summary representation of data from a sample that allows us to understand (i.e., infer from sample to population) an entire population.

What Are Sample Statistics and Population Parameters?

Inferential statistics allow us to make a judgment about a population using data from a sample. Recall, a sample is a subset, usually a very small portion of the total number of elements in a given population. Data from a sample are always uncertain. Certainty in judging the population comes only from a census, meaning all population elements are measured.

Sample statistics are summary measures computed only from the sample data. **Population parameters** are summary characteristics of information describing a specific population. Sample statistics become inferential when we use them to make inferences (guesses) about population parameters. In our notation, we will generally represent population parameters with Greek lowercase letters—for example, μ or α— and sample statistics with English letters, such as X or S. We use parameter estimates derived from a sample (English letters) to guess what the population characteristics (Greek letters) might be. In most marketing research projects, the actual population parameters are unknown and we rely on the estimates in generalizing their values.

sample statistics

Summary measures about variables computed using only data taken from a sample.

population parameters

Summary characteristics of information describing the properties of a population.

Frequency Distributions

One of the most common ways to summarize sample data is to construct a *frequency table*, or **frequency distribution**. Frequency distributions can be depicted with a table or a chart and indicate the number of times (i.e., the frequency) a particular value of a variable occurs. If your instructor took a sample of student grade observations at the end of the term, the table would indicate how many students made A, and how many made B, C, D, and F. Exhibit 13.1

frequency distribution

A table or chart summarizing the number of times a particular value of a variable occurs.

illustrates a frequency distribution of sample of university credit union customers' responses to a question that asked:

■ How much money do you currently have (i.e., what is your current balance) in the local university credit union checking account?

Frequency distributions are particularly useful in summarizing nominal or ordinal variables. The table provides a quick summary of balances reported by these respondents.

percentage distribution

A frequency distribution organized into a table (or graph) that summarizes percentage values associated with particular values of a variable.

A frequency calculation also typically includes the distribution of relative frequency, or a **percentage distribution**. To develop a frequency distribution of percentages, divide the frequency of each value by the total number of observations, and multiply the result by 100. Based on the data in Exhibit 13.1, Exhibit 13.2 shows the percentage distribution of account balances; that is, the percentage of people holding deposits within each range of values.

probability

The long-run relative frequency with which an event will occur.

Probability is the long-run relative frequency with which an event will occur. Inferential statistics uses the concept of a probability distribution, which is conceptually the same as a percentage distribution, except that the data represent probabilities. Exhibit 13.3 shows the probability distribution of the credit union balances. In other words, the table shows how likely a sample respondent is to have a balance within each range listed.

Proportions

proportion

The percentage of elements that meet some criterion for membership in a category.

When a frequency distribution portrays only a single characteristic in terms of a percentage of the total, it defines the **proportion** of occurrence. A proportion, such as the proportion of freshman at a university, indicates the percentage of population elements that successfully meet a criterion for membership in a category. A proportion may be expressed as a percentage, a fraction, or a decimal value. In the example used here and illustrated in Exhibit 13.3, the probabilities are equal to the

EXHIBIT **13.1**
Frequency Distribution of Deposits

Amount	Frequency (Number of People Who Hold Deposits in Each Range)
Under $3,000	499
$3,000–$4,999	530
$5,000–$9,999	562
$10,000–$14,999	718
$15,000 or more	811
	3,120

EXHIBIT **13.2**
Percentage Distribution of Deposits

Amount	Percent (Percentage of People Who Hold Deposits in Each Range)
Under $3,000	16
$3,000–$4,999	17
$5,000–$9,999	18
$10,000–$14,999	23
$15,000 or more	26
	100

EXHIBIT **13.3**
Probability Distribution of Deposits

Amount	Probability
Under $3,000	.16
$3,000–$4,999	.17
$5,000–$9,999	.18
$10,000–$14,999	.23
$15,000 or more	.26
	1.00

proportion of consumers in each deposit category. For example, 23 percent have a bank balance between $10,000 and $14,999.

Top-Box/Bottom-Box Scores

Managers are often very interested in the proportion of consumers choosing extreme responses. A **top-box score** generally refers to the portion of respondents who choose the most favorable response toward an option usually related to customer opinion. The top-box metric can show, for instance, the portion of consumers who would most likely recommend a business to a friend or be most likely to make a purchase. The logic is that respondents who choose the extreme response are really unique compared to the others. Managers often ask about the top-box metric.[2] Healthcare service providers pay particular attention to the top-box numbers. One ICU unit assessed a sample of family members of patients receiving ICU care. The survey suggested a top-box score of 69 percent.[3] That value becomes useful in benchmarking improvements in ICU services.

Sometimes, however, the opposite perspective is more diagnostic. Thus, managers are well-served also to examine the **bottom-box score**, the portion of respondents who choose the least favorable response to some questions about customer opinion. The bottom-box metric is more diagnostic of customer problems and often signals a need for some managerial reaction. Using the NPS as an example, the percent of bottom-box responders would indicate how many people are actively seeking to harm a brand's reputation. Analysts often apply benchmark measures to consumers who already are brand customers. Thus, the top-box often contains the largest group of responses. In cases like these in particular, the bottom-box score is very useful. In any event, the frequency distribution of responses provides useful descriptive data.

top-box score

The portion of respondents who choose the most positive choice in a multiple-choice question usually dealing with customer opinion.

bottom-box score

The portion of respondents who choose the least favorable response to some question about customer opinion.

Central Tendency Metrics

Think about how many actions our phones provide data for. Number of texts, number of page views, app usage statistics, and so much more. The central tendency for those measures provides some indication of how we interact with media. On a typical day, a sales manager counts the number of sales calls each sales representative makes. He or she wishes to inspect the data to find the center, or middle area, of the frequency distribution. Put another way, what is the most typical number of sales calls? The analyst can represent central tendency with basic descriptive statistics like the mean, median, or mode.

The Mean

We all use regularly the notion of an average. The **mean** is just the mathematical average of a set of numbers and represents the most common representation of central tendency. As such, it is a widely-used metric. The Dow Jones Industrial *Average* is famous metric that provides a benchmark for corporate financial performance. Has the firm done at least as well as the Dow's mean? To express the mean mathematically, we use the summation symbol, the capital Greek letter *sigma* (Σ). A mathematical representation of summation looks like this:

mean

A basic statistic that quantifies central tendency computed as the arithmetic average.

$$\sum_{i=1}^{n} X_i$$

which is a shorthand way to write the sum of

$$X_1 + X_2 + X_3 + X_4 + X_5 + \cdots + X_n$$

Below the Σ is the initial value of an index, i in this case, and above it is the final value of i, which also equals n, the total number of observations.

Suppose a sales manager supervises the eight salespeople listed in Exhibit 13.4. To express the sum of the salespeople's calls in Σ notation, we just number the salespeople (this number becomes the index number) and associate subscripted variables with their numbers of calls:

We then write an appropriate Σ formula and evaluate it:

$$\sum_{i=1}^{8} X_i = X_1 + X_2 + X_3 + X_4 + X_5 + X_6 + X_7 + X_8$$

$$= 4 + 3 + 2 + 5 + 3 + 3 + 1 + 5$$

$$= 26$$

EXHIBIT **13.4**
Number of Sales Calls per
Day by Salesperson

Index		Salesperson	Variable		Number of Calls
1	=	Mike	X_1	=	4
2	=	Patty	X_2	=	3
3	=	Billie	X_3	=	2
4	=	Bob	X_4	=	5
5	=	John	X_5	=	3
6	=	Frank	X_6	=	3 .
7	=	Chuck	X_7	=	1
8	=	Samantha	X_8	=	5
		Total		=	26

This notation is the numerator in the formula for the arithmetic mean:

$$\text{Mean} = \frac{\sum_{i=1}^{n} X_i}{n} = \frac{26}{8} = 3.25$$

The notation $\sum_{i=1}^{n} X_i$ means add together all the Xs whose subscripts are between 1 and n inclusive, where n equals 8 in this case. The formula shows that the mean number of sales calls in this example is 3.25.

Researchers generally wish to know the population mean, μ (lowercase Greek letter *mu*), which is calculated as follows:

$$\mu = \frac{\sum_{i=1}^{N} X_i}{N}$$

where

N = number of members in the population

In the case of the sales manager, if the total population of salespeople under his or her supervision is 8 N would be 8. Often, though, we will not have complete data needed to calculate a population mean, μ, so we will calculate a sample mean, $\bar{X}$ (read "X bar"), with the following formula:

$$\bar{X} = \frac{\sum_{i=1}^{n} X_i}{n}$$

where

n = number of observations made in the sample

More likely than not, you already know how to calculate a mean. However, knowing how to distinguish among the symbols Σ, μ, and X is helpful to understand statistics.

In this introductory discussion of the summation sign (Σ), we have used detailed notation that includes the subscript for the initial index value (i) and the final index value (n). However, from this point on in the chapter, we'll omit the details for simplicity and the symbol Σ will mean summed overall observations in the sample or population, as the case may be.

Although widely relied upon, the mean can be misleading, particularly when extreme values or outliers are present. Thus, researchers should sometimes rely on other central tendency indicators.

The Median

median

A measure of central tendency that is the midpoint; the value below which half the values in a distribution fall.

The **median**, is the midpoint of a distribution, or the 50th percentile. In other words, the median is the value below which half the values in the sample fall. In the sales manager example, 3 is the median because half the observations are greater than 3 and half are less than 3. In cases like this, with an even number of observations, the median equals the average of the two middle observations, in this case both are 3.

The median is a better metric for central tendency in the presence of extreme values or outliers. For instance, a professor gives a marketing research test and one student makes a 99, another makes a 98, the next highest grade is 51, and the remaining 17 grades range from 30 to 50. If the professor considered that everyone who scores "above average" passes, the result could be only 5 or 6 students passing as the mean would be on the order of 46. Perhaps the students would prefer the professor based passing around the median. If so, half of the students would pass by definition.

The Mode

In the fashion industry, *mode* refers to a particular, popular, style. In statistics the **mode** is the measure of central tendency that identifies the value that occurs most often. In our example of sales calls, Patty, John, and Frank each made three sales calls. The value 3 occurs most often, so 3 is the mode. The mode is determined by listing each possible value and noting the number of times each value occurs. The mode is the best measure of central tendency for data that is less than interval and for data approaching a unimodal distribution with one large peak (many observations have the same response with relatively few other responses).

mode

A measure of central tendency; the value that occurs most often.

Dispersion Metrics

The mean, median, and mode summarize the central tendency of frequency distributions. Accurate analysis of data also requires knowing the tendency of observations to depart from the central tendency. Thus, another way to summarize the data is to calculate the dispersion of the data, or how the observations vary from the mean. Consider, for instance, the twelve-month sales patterns of the two products shown in Exhibit 13.5. Both have a mean monthly sales volume of 200 units, but the dispersion of observations for product B is much greater than that for product A. There are several measures of dispersion.

The Range

The simplest representation of dispersion is the range, the distance between the smallest and the largest values of a frequency distribution. In Exhibit 13.5, the range for product A is between 196 units and 202 units (6 units), whereas for product B the range is between 150 units and 261 units (111 units). The range does not take into account all the observations; it merely tells us about the extreme values of the distribution.

Just as people may be fat or skinny, distributions may be fat or skinny. Although we do not expect all observations to be exactly like the mean, in a skinny distribution they will lie a short distance from the mean. Product A is an example; the observations are close together and reasonably close to the mean. In a fat distribution, such as the one for product B, they will be spread out. Exhibit 13.6 illustrates this concept graphically with two frequency distributions that have identical modes, medians, and means but different degrees of dispersion.

	Units Product A	Units Product B
January	196	150
February	198	160
March	199	176
April	200	181
May	200	192
June	200	200
July	200	201
August	201	202
September	201	213
October	201	224
November	202	240
December	202	261
Average	**200**	**200**

EXHIBIT **13.5**
Sales Levels for Two Products with Identical Average Sales

EXHIBIT **13.6**
Low Dispersion versus High
Dispersion

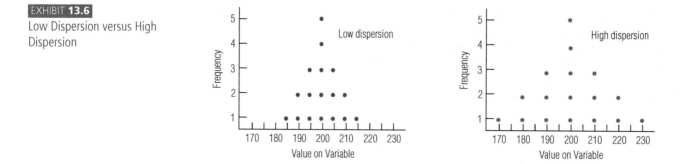

The interquartile range is the range that encompasses the middle 50 percent of the observations—in other words, the range between the bottom quartile (lowest 25 percent) and the top quartile (highest 25 percent).

Deviation Scores

A method of calculating how far any observation is from the mean is to calculate individual deviation scores. To calculate a deviation from the mean, use the following formula:

$$d_{i_i} = X_i - \bar{X}$$

For the value of 150 units for product B for the month of January, the deviation score is −150; that is, $150 - 200 = -50$. If the deviation scores are large, we will have a fat distribution because the distribution exhibits a broad spread.

Why Use the Standard Deviation?

Statisticians have derived several quantitative indexes to reflect a distribution's spread, or variability. The *standard deviation* is perhaps the most popular indicator of spread, or dispersion. Learning about the standard deviation will be easier if we first look at several other potential metrics indicating dispersion. Each is limited in a way that the standard deviation is not.

First is the average deviation. We compute the average deviation by calculating the deviation score of each observation value (i.e., its difference from the mean), summing these scores, and then dividing by the sample size (n):

$$\text{Average deviation} = \frac{\Sigma(X_i - \bar{X})}{n}$$

Although this measure of spread seems interesting, it is never used. Positive deviation scores cancel out negative deviation scores with this formula, leaving an average deviation value of zero no matter how wide the spread may be. Hence, the average deviation is a useless spread measure.

One might correct for the disadvantage of the average deviation by computing the absolute values of the deviations. In other words, we use only the absolute value of each deviation. The formula for the mean absolute deviation is

$$\text{Mean absolute deviation} = \frac{\Sigma|X_i - \bar{X}|}{n}$$

Because this procedure eliminates the problem of always having a zero score for the deviation measure, it becomes more useful to express deviations in terms of variance.

Variance

Another means of eliminating the sign problem caused by the negative deviations canceling out the positive deviations is to square the deviation scores. The following formula gives the mean squared deviation:

$$\text{Mean squared deviation} = \frac{\Sigma(X_i - \bar{X})^2}{n}$$

This result is useful for describing the overall variability. However, we typically wish to make an inference about a population from a sample, and so the divisor $n - 1$ is used rather than n in most practical marketing research problems.[4] The divisor changes from n to $n - 1$ to provide an unbiased estimator. This equation for spread, called sample **variance**, has the following formulation:

$$\text{Variance} = S^2 = \frac{\Sigma (X_i - \bar{X})^2}{n - 1}$$

variance

A metric of variability or dispersion. Its square root is the standard deviation.

Sample variance is a very good index of dispersion. The variance, S^2, will equal zero if and only if each and every observation in the distribution is the same as the mean. The variance will grow larger as the observations tend to differ increasingly from one another and from the mean.

Standard Deviation

Variance is an extremely important and useful analytical concept. That said, it has one drawback as a summary metric showing dispersion. The variance reflects a squared unit of measurement. For instance, if measures of sales in a territory are made in dollars, the mean number will be reflected in dollars, but the variance will be in squared dollars. Because of this, statisticians often take the square root of the variance. Using the square root of the variance for a distribution, called the **standard deviation**, eliminates the drawback of having the measure of dispersion in squared units rather than in the original measurement units. The formula for the standard deviation is

standard deviation

A quantitative index of a distribution's spread, or variability; the square root of the variance for a distribution.

$$S = \sqrt{S^2} = \sqrt{\frac{\Sigma (X_i - \bar{X})^2}{n - 1}}$$

Exhibit 13.7 illustrates that the calculation of a sample standard deviation requires the researcher to first calculate the sample mean. In the example with eight salespeople's sales calls (Exhibit 13.4), we calculated the sample mean as 3.25. Exhibit 13.7 illustrates how to calculate the standard deviation for these data.

Let's return to thinking about the original purpose for measures of dispersion. We want to summarize the data from survey research and other forms of marketing research. Indexes of central tendency, such as the mean, help us interpret the data. In addition, we wish to calculate a measure of variability that will give us a quantitative index of the dispersion of the distribution. We have looked at several measures of dispersion to arrive at two very adequate means of measuring dispersion: the variance and the standard deviation. The term given is for the sample standard deviation, S. The variance gives us a summary indicator of the reasonable ranges of variable observations. If

X	$(X - \bar{X})^1$	$(X - \bar{X})^2$
4	$(4 - 3.25) = \quad .75$	.5625
3	$(3 - 3.25) = \quad -.25$	0.0625
2	$(2 - 3.25) = -1.25$	1.5625
5	$(5 - 3.25) = \quad 1.75$	3.0625
3	$(3 - 3.25) = \quad -.25$	.0625
3	$(3 - 3.25) = \quad -.25$	.0625
1	$(1 - 3.25) = -2.25$	5.0625
5	$(5 - 3.25) = \quad 1.75$	3.0625
Σ^a	$0^{[a]}$	13.5000

$n = 8 \qquad \bar{X} = 3.25$

$$S = \sqrt{\frac{\Sigma (X - \bar{X})^2}{n - 1}} = \sqrt{\frac{13.5}{8 - 1}} = \sqrt{\frac{13.5}{7}} = \sqrt{1.929} = 1.39$$

[a]The summation of this column is not used in the calculation of the standard deviation.

EXHIBIT 13.7
Calculating a Standard Deviation: Number of Sales Calls per Day for Eight Salespeople

we are assessing the utilitarian value someone finds from their Amazon Prime membership, the mean would provide the central tendency and the standard deviation the dispersion. A small standard deviation (in the extreme 0) would mean that all respondents report about the same value. For instance, Amazon may wish to know not only how much consumers are willing to pay (WTP) for membership, but how much WTP varies. A large standard deviation reveals a lack of consensus about WTP Amazon Prime. Dispersion is in some ways more important than central tendency statistically. Explanatory and predictive statistical techniques require variance to work. Statistically, practically all meaning comes from some aspect of variance or covariance.

The term for the population standard deviation, σ is practically the same and in large samples produces nearly the same value (the divider would be n rather $n-1$). Nevertheless, you should understand that σ measures the dispersion in the population and S measures the dispersion in the sample. These concepts are crucial to understanding statistics.

Distinguish between Population, Sample, and Sample Distribution

Roulette is a common casino game and a casino may contain many roulette wheels. If someone wanted to know whether the roulette wheels were fair, they may make many observations of which number the ball lands on as the result of a spin. It might not be possible to record the results of all spins of the roulette wheel, but someone could probably record results over a several-hour period on one or more wheels. Does the resulting data reveal any type of pattern? What would a pattern suggest? This basic image provides the idea behind statistical distributions.

The Normal Distribution

normal distribution

A symmetrical, mean-centered, bell-shaped distribution that describes the expected probability distribution of observations.

One of the most common probability distributions in statistics is the **normal distribution**, commonly represented by the *normal curve*. This mathematical and theoretical distribution describes the expected distribution of sample observations or outcomes. Think of it as a tally of observed values. The normal curve is symmetrical, centered around the mean, bell shaped, and almost all (99.7 percent) of its values are within ±3 standard deviations from its mean. An example of a normal curve, the distribution of IQ scores, appears in Exhibit 13.8. The IQ score is normed to 100 meaning that 100 is an average IQ score. In this example, 1 standard deviation for IQ equals 15. Someone with an IQ score of 70 is 2 standard deviations below average and scores better than 2.28 (2.14 + 0.14) percent of others. That

● ● ● ● ● ● ●

By recording the results of spins of the roulette wheel, one could find the distribution of the results. If the wheel is fair, what should the distribution look like?

nvuk/Shutterstock.com

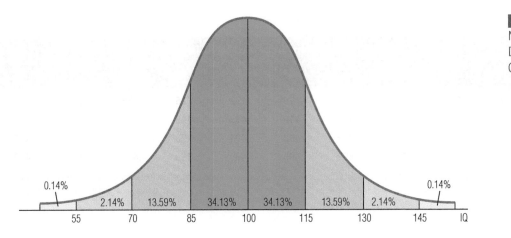

EXHIBIT **13.8**
Normal Distribution:
Distribution of Intelligence
Quotient (IQ) Scores

percentage is found by summing the percentages for the shaded areas below 70. A person scoring 145 is 3 standard deviations above average and better than 99.86 percent of others.

The **standardized normal distribution** is a specific normal curve that has several characteristics:

1. It is symmetrical about a mean of 0.
2. The mean coincides with the normal curve's highest point (the mode).
3. The normal curve has an infinite number of cases (it is a continuous distribution), and the area under the curve has a probability density equal to 1.
4. The curve has a standard deviation of 1. Exhibit 13.9 illustrates these properties. Exhibit 13.10 is a summary version of the typical standardized normal table found at the end of many statistics textbooks. A complete table of areas under the standardized normal distribution can be found on the Internet at **http://www.mathsisfun.com/data/standard-normal-distribution-table.html** or in the statistical appendix on www.cengagebrain.com.

The standardized normal distribution is a purely theoretical probability distribution, but it is a most useful distribution in inferential statistics. Statisticians have spent a great deal of time and effort making it convenient for researchers to find the probability of any portion of the area under the standardized normal distribution. All we have to do is transform, or convert, the data from other observed normal distributions to the standardized normal curve. In other words, the standardized normal distribution is extremely valuable because we can translate, or transform, any normal variable, X, into the standardized value, Z. Exhibit 13.11 illustrates how either a skinny distribution or a fat distribution can be converted into the standardized normal distribution. This ability to transform normal variables has many pragmatic implications for the marketing researcher.

standardized normal distribution

A purely theoretical probability distribution that reflects a specific normal curve for the standardized value, Z.

To the Point

"To study the abnormal is the best way of understanding the normal."

—WILLIAM JAMES

EXHIBIT **13.9**
Standardized Normal
Distribution

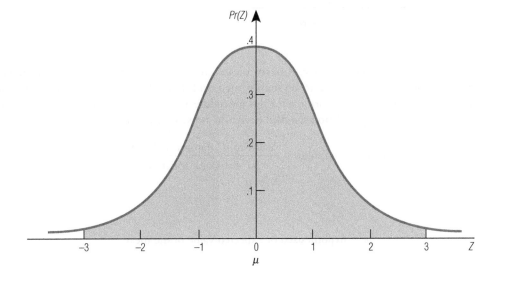

EXHIBIT 13.10 Standardized Normal Table: Area under Half of the Normal Curve[a]

Z Standard Deviations from the Mean (Units)	Z Standard Deviations from the Mean (Tenths of Units)[a]									
	.0	.1	.2	.3	.4	.5	.6	.7	.8	.9
0.0	.000	.040	.080	.118	.155	.192	.226	.258	.288	.315
1.0	.341	.364	.385	.403	.419	.433	.445	.455	.464	.471
2.0	.477	.482	.486	.489	.492	.494	.495	.496	.497	.498
3.0	.499	.499	.499	.499	.499	.499	.499	.499	.499	.499

[a] Area under the segment of the normal curve extending (in one direction) from the mean to the point indicated by each row-column combination. For example, about 68 percent of normally distributed events can be expected to fall within 1.0 standard deviation on either side of the mean (0.341 x 2). An interval of almost 2.0 standard deviations around the mean will include 95 percent of all cases (.477 + .477).

EXHIBIT 13.11

Standardized Values Can Be Computed from Flat or Peaked Distributions Resulting in a Standardized Normal Curve

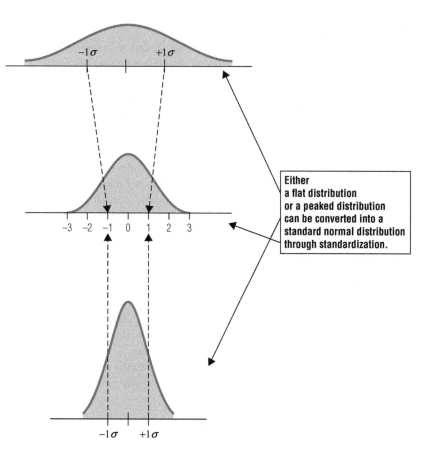

Either a flat distribution or a peaked distribution can be converted into a standard normal distribution through standardization.

Computing the standardized value, Z, of any measurement expressed in original units is simple: Subtract the mean from the value to be transformed, and divide by the standard deviation (all expressed in original units). The formula for this procedure and its verbal statement follow. In the formula, note that σ, the population standard deviation, is used for calculation.[5]

$$\text{Standardized value} = \frac{\text{Value to be transformed} - \text{Mean}}{\text{Standard deviation}}$$

$$Z = \frac{X - \mu}{\sigma}$$

where

μ = hypothesized or expected value of the mean

Suppose that in the past a toy manufacturer has experienced mean sales, μ, of 9,000 units and a standard deviation, σ, of 500 units during September. The production manager wishes to know whether wholesalers will demand between 7,500 and 9,625 units during September of the upcoming year. Because no tables are available showing the distribution for a mean of 9,000 and a standard deviation of 500, we must transform our distribution of toy sales, X, into the standardized form using our simple formula. The following computation shows that the probability (Pr) of obtaining sales in this range is equal to 0.893:

$$Z = \frac{X - \mu}{\sigma} = \frac{7{,}500 - 9{,}000}{500} = -3.00$$

$$Z = \frac{X - \mu}{\sigma} = \frac{9{,}625 - 9{,}000}{500} = 1.25$$

Using Exhibit 13.10, we find that

When $Z = |-3|$, the area under the curve (probability) equals 0.499.

When $Z = |1.25|$, the area under the curve (probability) equals 0.394.

Thus, the total area under the curve is $0.499 + 0.394 = 0.893$. (The area under the curve corresponding to this computation is the shaded areas in Exhibit 13.12.) The sales manager, therefore, knows there is a 0.893 probability that sales will be between 7,500 and 9,625.

Population Distribution and Sample Distribution

Before we outline the technique of statistical inference, three additional types of distributions must be defined: population distribution, sample distribution, and sampling distribution. When conducting a research project or survey, the researcher's purpose is not to describe the sample of respondents, but to make an inference about the population. As defined previously, a population, or universe, is the total set, or collection, of potential units for observation. The sample is a smaller subset of this population.

A frequency distribution of the population elements is called a **population distribution**. The mean and standard deviation of the population distribution are represented by the Greek letters μ and σ. A frequency distribution of a sample is called a **sample distribution**. The sample mean is designated $\overline{X}$, and the sample standard deviation is designated S.

population distribution
A frequency distribution of the elements of a population.

sample distribution
A frequency distribution of a sample.

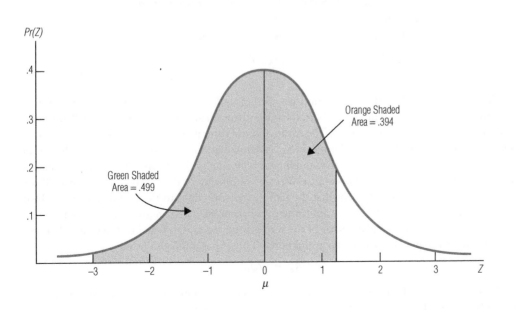

EXHIBIT **13.12**
Standardized Distribution Curve

Sampling Distribution

The concepts of population distribution and sample distribution are relatively simple. However, we must now introduce another distribution, which is the crux of understanding statistics: the *sampling distribution of the sample mean.* The sampling distribution is a theoretical probability distribution that in actual practice would never be calculated. Hence, practical, business-oriented students might wonder why the notion of the sampling distribution is important. Statisticians, with their mathematical curiosity, ask themselves, "What would happen if we were to draw a large number of samples, say 50,000, each having n elements, from a specified population?" Assuming that the 50,000 samples were selected randomly, the 50,000 sample means, $\bar{X}_s$, could themselves be arranged in a frequency distribution (rather than the individual observations). Because different sample units would be selected in each of the different samples, the sample means would not be exactly equal. The shape of the sampling distribution is of considerable importance to statisticians. If the sample size is sufficiently large and if the samples are randomly drawn, we know from the central-limit theorem that the sampling distribution of the mean will be approximately normally distributed.

A formal definition of the sampling distribution is as follows:

sampling distribution

A theoretical probability distribution of sample means for all possible samples of a certain size drawn from a particular population.

> *A **sampling distribution** is a theoretical probability distribution that shows the functional relation between the possible values of some summary characteristic of n cases drawn at random and the probability (density) associated with each value over all possible samples of size n from a particular population.*[6]

The term finite-sample distribution is sometimes used synonymously with sampling distribution. With some thought, one can see that this implies the sampling distribution as a portrayal of the means of all possible samples of a given size.

The sampling distribution's mean is called the *expected value* of the statistic. The expected value of the mean of the sampling distribution is equal to μ. The standard deviation of a sampling distribution of $\bar{X}$ is called **standard error of the mean** $(S_{\bar{X}})$ and is approximately equal to

standard error of the mean

The standard deviation of the sampling distribution.

$$S_{\bar{X}} = \frac{\sigma}{\sqrt{n}}$$

To review, for us to make an inference about a population from a sample, we must know about three important distributions: the population distribution, the sample distribution, and the sampling distribution. They have the following characteristics:

Amount	Mean	Standard Deviation
Population distribution	μ	σ
Sample distribution	X	S
Sampling distribution	$\mu_X = \mu$	$S_{\bar{X}}$

We now have much of the information we need to understand the concept of statistical inference. To clarify why the sampling distribution has the characteristic just described, we will elaborate on two concepts: the standard error of the mean and the central-limit theorem. You may be wondering why the standard error of the mean, $S_{\bar{X}}$, is defined as $S_{\bar{X}} = \sigma/\sqrt{n}$. The reason is based on the notion that the variance within the sampling distribution of the mean will be less if we have a larger sample size for independent samples. We can see intuitively that a larger sample size allows the researcher to be more confident that the sample mean is closer to the population mean. That is, the closer a sample becomes to a census the more accurately we can guess the mean. In actual practice, we estimate the standard error of the mean using the sample's standard deviation because again, the actual population parameter is unknown. Thus, $S_{\bar{X}}$ is estimated using

$$S_{\bar{X}} = S/\sqrt{n}$$

Note that as sample size increases, the spread of the sample means around μ decreases. Thus, with a larger sample size we will have a skinnier sampling distribution.

Central-Limit Theorem

The fact that the means of random samples of a sufficiently large size will be approximately normal in form and that the mean of the sampling distribution will approach the population mean is very valuable. Mathematically, this assertion represents the **central-limit theorem**, which states, as the sample size, n, increases, the distribution of the mean, $\overline{X}$, of a random sample taken from practically any population approaches a normal distribution (with a mean μ and a standard deviation $\sigma/\sqrt{n}$).[7] The central-limit theorem works regardless of the shape of the original population distribution. In other words, the distribution of averages quickly approaches normal as sample size increases. Exhibit 13.13 illustrates how the distribution of means of bimodal observations will increasingly approach normal.

A simple example will demonstrate the central-limit theorem. Assume that a consumer researcher is interested in the number of dollars children spend per week while using smartphone gaming apps. Assume further that the population the consumer researcher is investigating consists of all ten-year-old children in a certain school. In this elementary example, the population consists of only six individuals. Exhibit 13.14 shows the population distribution of app expenditures. Alice, a relatively deprived child, spends only $1 per week, whereas Freddy, the rich kid, spends $6 per week. The average weekly expenditure is $3.50, so the population mean, μ, equals 3.5 (see Exhibit 13.15).

central-limit theorem

The theory that, as the sample size increases, the distribution of sample means of size n, randomly selected, approaches a normal distribution.

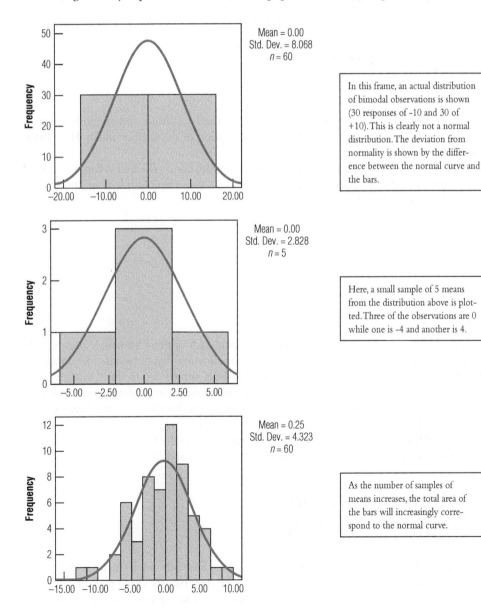

Mean = 0.00
Std. Dev. = 8.068
$n = 60$

In this frame, an actual distribution of bimodal observations is shown (30 responses of −10 and 30 of +10). This is clearly not a normal distribution. The deviation from normality is shown by the difference between the normal curve and the bars.

Mean = 0.00
Std. Dev. = 2.828
$n = 5$

Here, a small sample of 5 means from the distribution above is plotted. Three of the observations are 0 while one is −4 and another is 4.

Mean = 0.25
Std. Dev. = 4.323
$n = 60$

As the number of samples of means increases, the total area of the bars will increasingly correspond to the normal curve.

EXHIBIT 13.13

The Mean Distribution of Any Distribution Approaches Normal as n Increases

EXHIBIT **13.14**
Population Distribution:
Hypothetical Child App
Expenditures

Child	Child App Expenditures
Alice	$1.00
Becky	2.00
Noah	3.00
Tobin	4.00
George	5.00
Freddy	6.00

EXHIBIT **13.15**
Calculation of Population
Mean

X
$1.00
2.00
3.00
4.00
5.00
6.00
Σ $21.00

$$\text{Calculations}: \mu = \frac{\Sigma X}{n} = \frac{21}{6} = 3.5 = \mu_{\bar{x}}$$

Now assume that we do not know everything about the population, and we wish to take a sample size of two, to be drawn randomly from the population of the six individuals. How many possible samples are there?

The answer is 15, as follows (these are the possible combinations—the first column compares Alice to the other five kids, the second compares Becky to the remaining four having already been compared to Alice, and so forth):

1, 2

1, 3   2, 3

1, 4   2, 4   3, 4

1, 5   2, 5   3, 5   4, 5

1, 6   2, 6   3, 6   4, 6   5, 6

A skeptic about the central-limit theorem can compute each of these 15 sample means easily and then plot a frequency distribution of each of these means to see that indeed the distribution is approximately normal (1.5, 2, 2.5,..., 5.5). If we increased the sample size to three, four, or more, the distribution of sample means would more closely approximate a normal distribution. Although this simple example is not a proof of the central-limit theorem, it should give you a better understanding of the nature of the sampling distribution of the mean.

The theoretical knowledge about sampling distributions helps us solve two basic and very practical marketing analytics problems: (1) estimating population parameters and (2) determining sample size.

Estimation of Parameters and Confidence Intervals

Apple, Samsung, and other marketers that introduce new products with much fanfare could rely on sampling and statistical estimation to prepare for the new product launch. Using past data, they can form expectations about when sales should peak. For instance, a new phone's sales peak about 30 days after its release. They know from data that by the end of the first month, X percent of all sales of this new product are realized. With this information, the company can tell within 5 percent how many units of this new product will be sold in total. Making a proper inference about population parameters is highly practical for a marketer that must have the inventory appropriate for a short selling season.

Suppose you are a product manager for Con-Agra Foods and you recently invited Facebook friends of Swiss Miss to test a reformulated Swiss Miss Healthy Green Cocoa Mix. As a result, 800 households participated in the Green Cocoa trial. After the trial, 80 percent of sample respondents said they would buy the product when available on retailer shelves. Among that 80 percent, 76 percent reported that they never previously tried a diet or low-calorie cocoa mix. Fifty percent of sample respondents suggested they would purchase the new healthy product over the current Swiss Miss offering. How can you be sure there were no statistical errors in this estimate? How confident can you be that these figures approximate the actual population of cocoa mix consumers?

Point Estimates

Our goal in using statistics is to make an estimate about population parameters. A population mean, μ, and standard deviation, σ are constant and typically unknown. Such is the case if we are evaluating advertising options and would like to know how much time married men aged 21–29 years spend using Twitter each week. The real population values are unknown so we need to guess them using a sample. As we have discussed, $\bar{X}$ and S are random variables that will vary from sample to sample with a certain probability (sampling) distribution. The Research Snapshot on the next page illustrates making estimates of what is normal.

Consider a practical example of a 24-hour fitness company considering the addition of racquetball to their facilities. The company needs an estimate of the average number of days customers participate in this sport each week. When statistical inference is needed, the population mean, μ, is a constant but unknown parameter. To estimate the average number of playing days, we could take a sample of 300 racquetball players throughout the area where our entrepreneur is thinking of building club facilities. If the sample mean, $\bar{X}$ equals 2.6 days per week, we might use this figure as a **point estimate**. This single value, 2.6, would be the best estimate of the population mean. However, we would be extremely lucky if the sample estimate were exactly the same as the population value. A less risky alternative would be to calculate a confidence interval.

point estimate

An estimate of the population mean in the form of a single value, usually the sample mean.

● ● ● ● ● ● ●

Brand managers rely on samples to estimate probabilities of events like new product adoption and cannibalization in making brand management decisions.

Source: Conagra Brands, Inc

RESEARCH SNAPSHOT

Are You Facebook Normal?

Are you normal? A quiz at www.blogthings.com will give you an answer to that question (a site that offers many quizzes where one can compare themselves with others and find things out about themselves—like what is your number? Or color? Just search for "normal.") It consists of twenty questions covering things like whether or not you change towels every day, whether you have closer to $40 or $100 on hand, whether you are comfortable using the bathroom with another person in the room, and so forth. Once the user finishes the quiz, the site provides him or her with a normal score by comparing the responses to the overall distribution of responses. Similarly, Facebook users can test how "normal" they are and compare their normalness to their Facebook friends. This Facebook app asks questions about how much you like your body, how you really feel about the people you know, and

whether you think you are mentally ill. Millions have responded to these questions and one's normalness is determined against that distribution. The author of this book scored 55 percent normal on blogthings but only 19 percent normal according to Facebook. I suppose that brings us back to test reliability!

Confidence Intervals

confidence interval estimate

A specified range of numbers within which a population mean is expected to lie; an estimate of the population mean based on the knowledge that it will be equal to the sample mean plus or minus a small sampling error.

If we specify a range of numbers, or interval, within which the population mean should lie, we can be more confident that our inference is correct. A **confidence interval estimate** is based on the knowledge that $\mu = \bar{X} \pm$ an amount that matches sampling error. After calculating an interval estimate, we can determine how probable it is that the population mean will fall within this range of statistical values. In the racquetball project, the researcher, after setting up a confidence interval, would be able to make a statement such as, "With 95 percent confidence, I think that the average number of days played per week is between 2.3 and 2.9." This information can be used to estimate market demand because the researcher has a certain confidence that the interval contains the value of the true population mean.

The crux of the problem for a researcher is to determine how much random sampling error to tolerate. In other words, what should the confidence interval be? How much of a gamble should be taken that μ will be included in the range? Do we need to be 80 percent, 90 percent, or

confidence level

A percentage or decimal value that tells how confident a researcher can be about being correct; it states the long-run percentage of confidence intervals that will include the true population mean.

99 percent sure? The **confidence level** is a percentage or decimal value that indicates the probability that the results will be correct. Traditionally, scientific researchers use a 95 percent confidence level. Although there is nothing magical about a 95 percent confidence level, we select this confidence level in our examples based on convention. After providing abbreviations and equations, we illustrate step-by-step how to do the computation.

As mentioned, the point estimate gives no information about the possible magnitude of random sampling error. The confidence interval gives the estimated value of the population parameter, plus or minus an estimate of the error. We can express the idea of the confidence interval as follows:

$$\mu = \bar{X} \pm \text{a small sampling error}$$

More formally, assuming that the researchers select a large sample (more than thirty observations), the small sampling error is given by

$$\text{Small sampling error} = Z_{c.l.} S_{\bar{X}}$$

where

$Z_{c.l.}$ = value of Z, or standardized normal variable, at a specified confidence level ($c.l.$)

$S_{\bar{X}}$ = standard error of the mean

The precision of our estimate is indicated by the value of $Z_{c.l.}S_{\bar{X}}$. Let's start by finding the range of possible error, E, as follows:

$$E = Z_{c.l.}S_{\bar{X}}$$

Thus,

$$\mu = \bar{X} \pm E$$

where

$\bar{X}$ = sample mean (commonly pronounced X-bar)

E = range of sampling error

or

$$\mu = \bar{X} \pm Z_{c.l.}S_{\bar{X}}$$

The expression of "confidence" using $\pm E$ is stated as one-half of the total confidence interval. One-half of the interval is less than the mean and the other half is greater than the mean.

The following step-by-step procedure can be used to calculate confidence intervals:

1. Calculate $\bar{X}$ from the sample.
2. Assuming σ is unknown as is generally the case, estimate the population standard deviation by finding S, the sample standard deviation.
3. Estimate the standard error of the mean, using the following formula:

$$S_{\bar{X}} = \frac{S}{\sqrt{n}}$$

4. Determine the Z-value associated with the desired confidence level. Divide the confidence level by 2 to determine what percentage of the area under the curve to include on each side of the mean.
5. Calculate the confidence interval.

The following example shows how calculation of a confidence interval can be used in preparing a demographic profile, a useful tool for market segmentation. Suppose a client plans to open an indoor golf facility in downtown Houston to cater specifically to working women who play golf. In a survey of 100 women who work in downtown Houston, the research analyst hired by the client finds that the mean age $(\bar{X})$ in the sample is 37.5 years, with a standard deviation (S) of 12.0 years. Even though 37.5 years is the "expected value" and the best guess for the true mean age in the population (μ), the likelihood is that the mean is not exactly 37.5. Thus, a confidence interval around the sample mean provides useful intelligence to the client:

1. $\bar{X} = 37.5$ years
2. $S = 12.0$ years
3. Then, $S_{\bar{X}} = \dfrac{12.0}{\sqrt{100}} = 1.2$

4. Suppose you wish to be 95 percent confident—that is, assured that 95 times out of 100, the estimates from a sample of 100 would include the population parameter. Including 95 percent of the area requires that 47.5 percent (one-half of 95 percent) of the distribution on each side be included. From a Z-table (see Exhibit 13.10 or the full table available online, you find that 0.475 corresponds to the Z-value 1.96.
5. Substitute the values for $Z_{c.l.}$ and $S_{\bar{X}}$ into the confidence interval formula:

$$\mu = 37.5 \pm (1.96)(1.2)$$
$$= 37.5 \pm 2.35$$

You, the analyst, report back to the client that the μ is between the range from 35.2 to 39.9 years. Intervals constructed in this manner will contain the true value of μ 95 percent of the time.

Step 3 can be eliminated by entering S and n directly in the confidence interval formula:

$$\mu = \bar{X} \pm Z_{c.l.}\frac{S}{\sqrt{n}}$$

Remember that $S/\sqrt{n}$ represents the standard error of the mean, $S_{\bar{x}}$. Its use is based on the central-limit theorem.

If you wanted to increase the probability that the population mean will lie within the confidence interval, you could use the 99 percent confidence level, with a Z-value of 2.57. You may want to calculate the 99 percent confidence interval for the preceding example; you can expect that μ will be in the range between 34.4 and 40.6 years.

We have now examined the basic concepts of inferential statistics. You should understand that sample statistics such as the sample means, $\bar{X}$s, can provide good estimates of population parameters such as μ. You should also realize that there is a certain probability of being in error when you estimate a population parameter from sample statistics. In other words, there will be a random sampling error, which is the difference between the survey results and the results of surveying the entire population. If you have a firm understanding of these basic terms and ideas, which are the essence of statistics, the remaining statistics concepts will be relatively simple for you. The Research Snapshot shows how simple descriptive statistics can be used to contrast Walmart and Target shoppers.

Sample Size

When asked to evaluate a marketing research project, most people, even those with little marketing research training, begin by asking, "How big was the sample?" Intuitively we know that the larger the sample, the more accurate the research.

Random Error and Sample Size

Random sampling error varies with sample size. In statistical terms, increasing the sample size decreases the width of the confidence interval at a given confidence level. Our estimates become more precise. Following from above, we compute a confidence interval from sample statistics as

$$\text{Confidence interval} = \bar{X} \pm Z\frac{S}{\sqrt{n}}$$

One can easily see that the equation includes the sample size in the denominator that determines the error range (E):

$$E = Z\frac{S}{\sqrt{n}}$$

Thus, if n increases, E decreases.

Students familiar with the law of diminishing returns in economics will easily grasp the concept that increases in sample size reduce sampling error at a *decreasing rate*. For example, doubling a sample of 1,000 will reduce random sampling error by 1 percentage point, but doubling the sample from 2,000 to 4,000 will reduce random sampling error by only another half percentage point. More technically, random sampling error is inversely proportional to the square root of n. Thus, at some pointing, analysts find it inefficient to increase the sample further. Given the budget and the relative degree of imprecision that the decision-maker will tolerate, the marketing research analyst makes an informed decision on how big a sample will be used.

Factors in Determining Sample Size for Questions Involving Means

Three factors are required to specify sample size: (1) the variance, or heterogeneity, of the population; (2) the magnitude of acceptable error; and (3) the confidence level. Suppose one wishes to find out whether nine-year-old boys are taller than seven-year-old boys. Intuitively we know that even with a very small sample size, we can obtain the correct information. This is based on the fact that the determination of sample size depends on the research question and the variability within the sample.

The *variance*, or *heterogeneity*, of the population is the first necessary bit of information. As introduced earlier in the chapter, we often use the *standard deviation* of the population to represent

Promises, Promises

The opening vignette described Amazon Prime services. Customers pay for Prime services and in return, Amazon promises benefits. Nobody likes broken promises and when somebody pays extra so their purchased products arrive on-time, particularly at Christmastime, a broken promise is serious business. Amazon Prime faces charges of "false advertising" as some customers complain that Amazon Prime's delivery promises are lies. In particular, the Advertising Standards Authority in London is considering the merits of the accusation. Does Amazon promise Prime customers free next day delivery and *not deliver* on the perk?

Undoubtedly, sampling and statistics will be involved in addressing the question. In particular, when such accusations lead to legal hearings in court, research experts often get involved as both sides try to make their respective cases. Amazon Prime packages number in the hundreds of millions each holiday season. Surely, Amazon's promise cannot be absolute as certainly something will go haywire with some of these deliveries. Questions like these may be relevant and can be addressed with principles from this chapter:

1. What portion of Amazon Prime deliveries fail to show up on time?
2. Does that portion of failed deliveries vary with the season?
3. How large a sample is needed to reach a conclusion with sufficient confidence to draw a conclusion on the charges?
4. Does a confidence interval for the portion of packages with a failed delivery include 0?
5. What portion of Amazon Prime customers who complain renew their membership the next year?

False advertising? Well, that depends on the statistics.

Sources: Hodgson, C. (2017), "Amazon Prime May Be Investigated After Late-Delivery Complaints," *Business Insider*, (December 18), http://www.businessinsider.com/amazon-prime-advertising-standards-authority-complaints-2017-12, accessed December 31, 2017. Siddique, H. (2017), "Amazon Prime Could Face Investigation Over Delivery Complaints," *The Guardian*, (December 17), https://www.theguardian.com/technology/2017/dec/17/amazon-prime-investigation-delivery-complaints, accessed December 31, 2017.

response heterogeneity. Only a small sample is required if the population is homogeneous. For example, predicting the average age of graduate business students requires a smaller sample than predicting the average age of people who use Google. As *heterogeneity* increases, so must sample size. A pharmaceutical company testing the effectiveness of an acne medicine, for instance, should require a sample large enough to account for the varying range of skin types.

The *magnitude of error*, or the confidence interval, is the second necessary bit of information. Defined in statistical terms as E, the magnitude of error indicates how precise the estimate must be, or in other words, the *precision level*. From a managerial perspective, the importance of the decision to the well-being of the firm will probably influence the analyst's specifications of this range. If, for example, the acne medication tests favorably both in terms of user results and sales within a test-market sample, the firm may launch capital investments necessary to begin production of the medicine on a global scale. Given the resources involved should the firm commit to production, the tolerance in precision is likely very small and, as a result, so will the acceptable range of error. In other cases, the estimate need not be extremely precise. For example, knowing the household incomes of the acne medication users may not be so important a question particularly because the medication is available by prescription and will be covered by most insurance plans. Thus, the analysts may be happy with an error in estimated income of ±\$15,000 in total household income instead of $E = \pm\$500$. Seldom would a marketing researcher need more precision than ±\$5,000 in estimating a market segment's mean household income.

The third factor of concern is the *confidence level*. In our examples, we will typically use the 95 percent confidence level. This, however, is an arbitrary decision based on convention; there is nothing sacred about the 0.05 chance level (i.e., the probability of 0.05 of the true population parameter being incorrectly estimated). Exhibit 13.16 summarizes the information required to determine sample size. In fact, while basic researchers use 0.05 most often, applied marketing researchers more commonly are content with less precision.

Variable	Symbol	Typical Source of Information
Standard deviation	S	Pilot study or rule of thumb
Magnitude of error	E	Managerial judgment or calculation $(ZS_{\bar{x}})$
Confidence level	$Z_{c.l.}$	Managerial judgment

Estimating Sample Size for Questions Involving Means

Once the preceding concepts are understood, determining the actual size for a simple random sample is quite easy. The researcher must follow three steps:

1. Estimate the standard deviation of the population.
2. Make a judgment about the allowable magnitude of error.
3. Determine a confidence level.

The only problem is estimating the standard deviation of the population. Ideally, similar studies conducted in the past will give a basis for judging the standard deviation. In practice, researchers who lack prior information conduct a pilot study to estimate the population parameters so that another, larger sample of the appropriate sample size may be drawn. This procedure is called **sequential sampling** because researchers take an initial look at the pilot study results before deciding on a larger sample to provide more definitive results.

The first step involves estimating the standard deviation. A rule of thumb for estimating the value of the standard deviation is to expect it to be one-sixth of the range. If researchers conducting a study on smartwatch purchases expect the price paid to range from $100 to $700, a rule-of-thumb estimate for the standard deviation would be $100 ($600 × 1/6).

For the moment, assume that the standard deviation has been estimated in some preliminary work. If our concern is to estimate the mean of a particular population, the formula for sample size is

$$n = \left(\frac{ZS}{E}\right)^2$$

where

Z = standardized value that corresponds to the confidence level

S = sample standard deviation or estimate of the population standard deviation

E = acceptable error amount, plus or minus error factor (recall the range is one-half of the total confidence interval)[8]

Suppose a survey researcher studying annual expenditures on lipstick wishes to have a 95 percent confidence level ($Z = 1.96$) and a range of error (E) of less than $2. If the estimate of the standard deviation is $29 based on a pilot study, the required sample size is calculated as follows:

$$n = \left(\frac{ZS}{E}\right)^2 = \left(\frac{(1.96)(29)}{2}\right)^2 = \left(\frac{56.84}{2}\right)^2 = 28.42^2 = 808$$

On the other hand, if a range of error (E) of $4 is acceptable, the required sample size becomes much smaller:

$$n = \left(\frac{ZS}{E}\right)^2 = \left(\frac{(1.96)(29)}{4}\right)^2 = \left(\frac{56.84}{4}\right)^2 = 14.21^2 = 202$$

Thus, doubling the range of acceptable error reduces sample size requirements dramatically. Stated conversely in a general sense, doubling sample size will reduce error by only approximately one-quarter. Thus, the added precision from a larger sample may often not be worth the added costs.

Population Size and Required Sample Size

The Nielsen Company estimates television ratings. Throughout the years, is it possible to rate 100 million plus viewers with a sample of approximately 5,000 households? The answer to that question is that in most cases the size of the population does not have a major effect on the sample

---

sequential sampling

The application of results from one or more pilot studies prior to deciding on the sample size for a definitive study.

size. Even though the population is very large, a sample that comprises only a small portion of the population can be accurate. As suggested earlier, the variance of the population has a greater effect on sample size requirements than does the population size.

Sometimes, the population size may be small, such as Boeing or Airbus trying to make inferences about firms that might purchase a new airliner. When the population is relatively small, a finite correction factor is applied to adjust sample size requirements. Typically, an analyst applies this correction when the sample will represent more than 5 percent of a finite population. If the sample is large relative to the population, the foregoing procedures may overestimate the required sample size. The finite correction factor for small samples is

$$\sqrt{\frac{(N - n)}{(N - 1)}}$$

where

$N =$ population size

$n =$ sample size

Determining Sample Size for Proportions

Researchers frequently are concerned with determining sample size for problems that involve estimating population proportions or percentages. When the question involves the estimation of a proportion, the researcher requires some knowledge of the logic for determining a confidence interval around a sample proportion estimation (p) of the population proportion (π). For a confidence interval to be constructed around the sample proportion (p), an estimate of the standard error of the proportion (S_p) must be calculated and a confidence level specified.

The precision of the estimate is indicated by the value $Z_{c.l.} S_p$. Thus, the plus-or-minus estimate of the population proportion is

$$\text{Confidence interval} = p \pm Z_{c.l.} S_p$$

If the researcher selects a 95 percent probability for the confidence interval, $Z_{c.l.}$ will equal 1.96 (from Z-table). The formula for S_p is

$$S_p = \sqrt{\frac{pq}{n}} \text{ or } S_p = \sqrt{\frac{p(1 - p)}{n}}$$

where

$S_p =$ estimate of the standard error of the proportion

$p =$ proportion of successes

$q = 1 - p$, or proportion of failures

Suppose that 20 percent of a sample of 1,200 television viewers recall seeing an advertisement. The proportion of successes (p) equals 0.2, and the proportion of failures (q) equals 0.8. We estimate the 95 percent confidence interval as follows:

$$\text{Confidence Interval} = p \pm Z_{c.l.} S_p$$

$$= 0.2 \pm 1.96 S_p$$

$$= 0.2 \pm 1.96 \sqrt{\frac{p(1 - p)}{n}}$$

$$= 0.2 \pm 1.96 \sqrt{\frac{0.2(1 - 0.2)}{1.200}}$$

$$= 0.2 \pm 1.96 \sqrt{\frac{0.16}{1.200}}$$

$$= 0.2 \pm 1.96(0.0115)$$

$$= 0.2 \pm 0.023$$

Thus, the population proportion who see an advertisement is estimated to be included in the interval between 0.177 (0.2 − 0.023) and 0.223 (0.2 + 0.023), or roughly between 18 and 22 percent, with 95 percent confidence (95 out of 100 times).

Sample size for a proportion requires the researcher to make a judgment about confidence level and the maximum allowance for random sampling error. Furthermore, the size of the proportion influences random sampling error, so an estimate of the expected proportion of successes must be made, based on intuition or prior information. The formula is

$$n = \frac{Z_{c.l.}^2 \, pq}{E^2}$$

where

n = number of items in sample

$Z_{c.l.}^2$ = square of the confidence level in standard error units

p = estimated proportion of successes

$q = 1 - p$, or estimated proportion of failures

E^2 = square of the maximum allowance for error between the true proportion and the sample proportion, or $Z_{c.l.} S_p$ squared

Suppose a researcher believes that a simple random sample will show that 60 percent of the population (p) recognizes the name of an automobile dealership. The researcher wishes to estimate with 95 percent confidence $(Z_{c.l.} = 1.96)$ that the allowance for sampling error is not greater than 3.5 percentage points (E). Substituting these values into the formula gives

$$n = \frac{(1.96)^2 (0.6)(0.4)}{0.035^2}$$

$$= \frac{(3.8416)(0.24)}{0.001225}$$

$$= \frac{0.922}{0.001225}$$

$$= 753$$

Determining Sample Size on the Basis of Judgment

Just as sample units may be selected to suit the convenience or judgment of the researcher, sample size may also be determined on the basis of managerial judgments. Using a sample size similar to those used in previous studies provides the inexperienced researcher with a comparison with other researchers' judgments.

Another judgmental factor that affects the determination of sample size is the selection of the appropriate item, question, or characteristic to be used for the sample size calculations. Several different characteristics affect most studies, and the desired degree of precision may vary for these items. The researcher must exercise some judgment to determine which item will be used. Often the item that will produce the largest sample size will be used to determine the ultimate sample size. However, the cost of data collection becomes a major consideration, and judgment must be exercised regarding the importance of such information.

Another consideration stems from most researchers' need to analyze various subgroups within the sample. For example, suppose an analyst wishes to look at differences in retailers' attitudes by geographic region. The analyst will want to make sure to sample an adequate number of retailers in the New England, mid-Atlantic, and South Atlantic regions to ensure that subgroup comparisons are reliable. There is a judgmental rule of thumb for selecting minimum subgroup sample size. Each subgroup to be separately analyzed should have a minimum of 100 units in each category of the major breakdowns. The total sample size is computed by totaling the sample sizes necessary for these subgroups.

Assess the Potential for Nonresponse Bias

Researchers provide an assessment of generalizability in their reports. How much can we count on metrics derived analytically from a sample to truly represent the relevant population? As we see above, sample size and heterogeneity influence the generalizability assessment, as do the concepts of probability and nonprobability sampling from the previous chapter. Earlier, we introduced the notion of nonresponse bias. Nonresponse bias, in particular the bias caused when sample units provide no response, can significantly damage generalizability.

The reason that nonresponders must be considered routinely a threat to external validity is that there could be some systematic reason that members selected for inclusion from a sampling frame did not respond. People with very busy lives are less likely to respond to a survey request than people with a lot of time on their hands. People with very busy lives likely share other things in common. They likely work more hours, are more likely to be involved in family activities (be married and have children in the home), share commonalities in age and lifestyle, and so forth. Any systematic connection between sample unit characteristics and their likelihood to respond is a potential source for bias.

The concern for potential bias brings us back to the notion of response rates. Researchers worry particularly for the potential of bias when survey response rates are low. Given that response rates from randomly drawn probability samples are commonly less than 10 percent, the concern for bias exists practically all the time. In fact, though, a high response rate does not free the sample from nonresponse bias. Consider the case when a financial incentive encourages people to respond. In those cases, the respondents who most need, or who are most sensitive to, the incentive are more likely to respond. Again, a systematic influence creates the potential for bias.

A detailed treatment of the topic goes beyond the scope of this chapter. However, some basic procedures can be followed in an effort to increase confidence in the generalizability of the sample.[9] These pieces of advice complement the discussion of probability and nonprobability sampling from the previous chapter.

1. A well-managed sampling frame that contains accurate information on individual respondents provides the greatest potential for generalizability. A Nielsen panel provides an example of such a sampling frame.
2. **Auxiliary variables** provide a useful means of detecting potential systematic reasons for nonresponse (or conversely response). Auxiliary variables are those that the researcher should build into a survey that allow a comparison between sample units that do respond and those that do not respond. Auxiliary variables do not have to be involved in the research questions. For instance, a consumer panel manager should know basic demographic information and other factoids about every member of the panel. The best auxiliary variables are those known to correlate with survey participation or those that might influence dependent variables. For any project using a sample derived from the panel, the researcher can measure these same variables and then compare the known sampling frame values with the values of those who do respond as a way of indicating potential problems with generalizability. For instance, the following hypothetical values on auxiliary variables illustrate their use:

auxiliary variables

Auxiliary variables are those that the researcher should build into a survey that allow a comparison between sample units that do respond and those that do not respond.

Auxiliary Variable	Known Value in Sampling Frame	Values Observed among Respondents
Percent female	50.5%	60.1%
Average time online daily	3.9 hours	4.2 hours
Political identification	31% Democrat/27% Republican/40% independent	38% Democrat/30% Republican/25% independent
Percent owning home	64%	52%

In this case, the data are not supporting generalizability. The values observed among sample respondents differ significantly on all but one auxiliary variable (average time online daily is about the same). Thus, the researcher would have to caution management against making strong inferences about the population from this sample. However, even when the sample response rate is low, if a number of auxiliary variables show correspondence, the researcher can express confidence in generalizability as the chance of something systematic causing nonresponse is not evident. The use of auxiliary variables further illustrates the advantage of using a probability sample taken from a well-managed sampling frame with known characteristics.

3. A high response rate in and of itself does not guarantee freedom from bias.

4. Post hoc sampling procedures can be employed, which adjust the contact of individuals in a way that tries to over-contact types of people that were not likely to respond to the initial sampling plan.

Although researchers often avoid the question of generalizability, particularly when the research employs convenience samples, it remains a critical question because the answer determines if the data have value beyond the respondents.

TIPS OF THE TRADE

- Measures of central tendency tell how much some phenomenon typically exists among a sample or population. The appropriate central tendency statistic varies with the nature of the data.
  - The mean is the most commonly used measure of central tendency.
  - The median is more appropriate when the data display extreme values or outliers.
  - The mode is appropriate when the data are less than interval.
- Sample size estimates often require some estimate of the standard deviation that will exist in the sample.
  - Larger samples allow predictions with greater precision that can be expressed over a smaller range.
  - Increases in precision usually require disproportionately large increases in sample size and bring about inefficiencies.

- The amount of risk involved in a decision determines how much precision is needed.
  - Greater precision means more resources are required.
  - The balance between precision and resources generally answers the sample size question.
  - Only the riskiest of decisions require very large samples (i.e., 1,000 or more).
  - Representative samples of 300 to 500 respondents can provide adequate representation for most marketing decisions.
- Low response rates (under 10 percent) are common in marketing research.
  - Researchers should employ auxiliary variables to compare sample characteristics with the values known to exist in the relevant population.
  - A well-managed sampling frame provides the best tool to accomplish the check for nonresponse bias.

:: SUMMARY

1. **Use basic descriptive statistics to analyze data and make basic inferences about population metrics.**   Calculating a mean and a standard deviation to "describe" or profile a sample is a commonly applied descriptive statistical approach. The term *metrics* is used almost interchangeably with the noun, statistics, but emphasizes the fact that values will be compared. Inferential statistics investigate samples to draw conclusions about entire populations. A frequency distribution shows how frequently each response or classification occurs. A simple tally count illustrates a frequency distribution. A proportion indicates the percentage of group members that have a particular characteristic. Three commonly applied measures of central tendency are the mean, median, and mode. For most samples, the mean, median, and mode produce different values. Measures of dispersion further describe a distribution. The range is the difference between the largest and smallest values observed. The most useful measures of dispersion are the variance and standard deviation.

2. **Distinguish among the concepts of population, sample, and sampling distributions.**   The techniques of statistical inference are based on the relationship among the population distribution, the sample distribution, and the sampling distribution. The population distribution is a frequency distribution of the elements of a population. The sample distribution is a frequency distribution of a sample. A sampling distribution is a theoretical probability distribution of sample means for all possible samples of a certain size drawn from a particular population. The sampling distribution's mean is the expected value of the mean, which equals the population's mean. The standard deviation of the sampling distribution is the standard error of the mean, approximately equal to the standard deviation of the population, divided by the square root of the sample size.

3. **Explain the central-limit theorem.**   The central-limit theorem states that as the sample size increases, the distribution of sample means of size *n*, randomly selected, approaches a normal distribution. This means that even if a distribution has a nonnormal distribution, the distribution of averages taken from samples of these numbers is normally distributed. This allows inferential statistics to be used. This theoretical knowledge can be used to estimate parameters and determine sample size.

4. **Use confidence intervals to express inferences about population characteristics.**   Estimating a population mean with a single value gives a point estimate. The confidence interval estimate is a range of numbers within which the researcher is confident that the population mean will lie. The confidence level is a percentage that indicates the long-run probability that the confidence interval estimate will be correct. Many research problems involve the estimation of proportions. Statistical techniques may be used to determine a confidence interval around a sample proportion.

5. **Understand the major issues in specifying sample size.**   The statistical determination of sample size requires knowledge of (1) the variance of the population, (2) the magnitude of acceptable error, and (3) the confidence level. Several computational formulas are available for determining sample size. Furthermore, a number of easy-to-use tables have been compiled to help researchers calculate sample size. The main reason a large sample size is desirable is that sample size is related to random sampling error. A smaller sample makes a larger error in estimates more likely.

6. **Know how to assess the potential for nonresponse bias.**   Nonresponse bias causes problems because it means that the sampling units that participated are different from those that did not participate. Auxiliary variables are an important tool in assessing the potential for such bias. A well-managed sampling frame, which provides a probability sample, is a primary tool in dealing with nonresponse bias. The end goal is assessing the generalizability of the metrics observed in the sample.

:: KEY TERMS AND CONCEPTS

auxiliary variables, *381*

bottom-box score, *361*

central-limit theorem, *371*

confidence interval estimate, *374*

confidence level, *374*

frequency distribution, *359*

inferential statistics, *359*

mean, *361*

median, *362*

metrics, *359*

mode, *363*

normal distribution, *366*

percentage distribution, *360*

point estimate, *373*

population distribution, *369*

population parameters, *359*

probability, *360*

proportion, *360*

sample distribution, *369*

sample statistics, *359*

sampling distribution, *370*

sequential sampling, *378*

standard deviation, *365*

standard error of the mean, *370*

standardized normal distribution, *367*

top-box score, *361*

variance, *365*

:: QUESTIONS FOR REVIEW AND CRITICAL THINKING

1. What is the difference between descriptive and inferential statistics?

2. Define the analytical notion of metrics.

3. Suppose the speed limits in thirteen countries in miles per hour are as follows:

	Country	Highway Miles per Hour
1.	Italy	87
2.	France	82
3.	Hungary	75
4.	Belgium	75
5.	Portugal	75
6.	Great Britain	70
7.	Spain	62
8.	Denmark	62
9.	Netherlands	62
10.	Greece	62
11.	Japan	62
12.	Norway	56
13.	Turkey	56

What is the mean, median, and mode for these data? Feel free to use your computer (statistical software or spreadsheet) to get the answer. Which is the best measure of central tendency for these observations?

4. Prepare a frequency distribution for the data in Question 3.

5. Why is the standard deviation rather than the average deviation typically used?

6. Calculate the standard deviation for the data in Question 3.

7. Draw three distributions that have the same mean value but different standard deviation values. Draw three distributions that have the same standard deviation value but different mean values.

8. A smartphone manufacturer surveyed 100 retail phone outlets in each of the firm's sales regions. An analyst noticed that in the South Atlantic region the average retail price was $165 (mean) and the standard deviation was $30. However, in the Mid-Atlantic region the mean price was $170, with a standard deviation of $15. What do these statistics tell us about these two sales regions?

9. A marketing analytics professional stated that "all information in data comes from variability." Do you agree? Why or why not?

10. What is the sampling distribution? How does it differ from the sample distribution?

11. What would happen to the sampling distribution of the mean if we increased the sample size from 5 to 25?

12. Suppose a fast-food restaurant wishes to estimate average sales volume for a new menu item. The restaurant has analyzed the sales of the item at a similar outlet and observed the following results:

$\bar{X} = 500$ (mean daily sales)

$S = 100$ (standard deviation of sample)

$n = 25$ (sample size)

The restaurant manager wants to know into what range the mean daily sales should fall 95 percent of the time. Perform this calculation.

13. In the example on page 378 of research on lipstick, where $E = \$2$ and $S = \$29$, what sample size would we require if we desired a 99 percent confidence level?

14. Suppose you are planning to sample cat owners to determine the average number of cans of cat food they purchase monthly. The following standards have been set: a confidence level of 99 percent and an error of less than 5 units. Past research has indicated that the standard deviation should be 6 units. What is the required sample size?

15. What is a standardized normal curve?

16. Using the formula in this chapter, a researcher determines that at the 95 percent confidence level, a sample of 2,500 is required to satisfy a client's requirements. The researcher actually uses a sample of 1,200, however, because the client has specified a budget cap for the survey. What are the ethical considerations in this situation?

17. Draw the distribution that should result from an honest roulette wheel. Draw the distribution from a dishonest roulette wheel. Assuming samples of 500 spins were taken from each wheel, what would the distribution of sample means of 10 look like for each wheel?

18. A random number generator and other statistical information can be found at http://www.random.org. Flip some virtual coins. Perform twenty flips with an Aurelian coin. Perform twenty flips with a Constantius coin. Perform frequency tables for each result. What conclusion might you draw? Would the result change if you flipped the coins 200 times or 2,000 times?

19. What role do auxiliary variables play in inferential marketing statistics?

:: RESEARCH ACTIVITIES

1. Look up at least five academic journal articles (such as those appearing in the *Journal of Business Research, Journal of the Academy of Marketing Science, Journal of Marketing, Journal of Personal Selling and Sales Management, Journal of Consumer Research*) in an area of interest to you that involve survey research. Do they all discuss the sample and sample size? From any description about the sample provided, can the reader make a judgment about what population the statistics generalize to (presuming inferential statistics are involved)?

2. Use an online library service to find basic business research studies that report a survey "response rate" or number of respondents compared to number of contacts. You may wish to consult journals, such as the *Journal of Business Research, the Journal of Marketing, the Journal of the Academy of Marketing Science, or the Journal of Personal Selling and Sales Management*. Find at least ten such studies. What is the average response rate across all of these studies? Do the resulting sample sizes seem adequate? Do the researchers mention whether or not the results generalize to some population? Write a brief report on your findings.

3. This activity would make a good in-class assignment. Assign each student a random number. Then, randomly select eight students and ask each a small number of survey questions such as (feel free to add a few of your own):
   a. What is your political affiliation?
   b. What is your religious affiliation?
   c. Do you park a car on campus?
   d. What is your major?
   e. How old are you in years?

Now, assuming your instructor compiles results for the entire class, compare your results from your sample of eight to the class results. How well does your sample generalize to the entire class? Compare your sample of eight results and then that of the entire class to data available from your university website on these questions (some of this should be available from institutional research at your school). How well do your sample eight and the sample that is your entire class generalize to the entire university? This illustrates the use of auxiliary variables.

Coastal Star Sales Corporation

Case 13.1

Download the data sets for this case from
www.cengagebrain.com.

Coastal Star Sales Corporation is a West Coast wholesaler that markets leisure products from several manufacturers. Coastal Star has an eighty-person sales force that sells to wholesalers in a six-state area, which is divided into two sales regions. Case Exhibit 13.1-1 shows the names of a sample of eleven salespeople, some descriptive information about each person, and sales performance for each of the last two years.

Questions

1. Calculate a mean and a standard deviation for each variable.
2. Set a 95 percent confidence interval around the mean for each variable.
3. Calculate the median, mode, and range for each variable.
4. Organize the data for current sales into a frequency distribution with three classes: (a) under $500,000, (b) $500,000 to $999,999, and (c) $1,000,000 and over.
5. Organize the data for years of selling experience into a frequency distribution with two classes: (a) less than five years and (b) five or more years.
6. Convert the frequency distributions from Question 5 to percentage distributions.

CASE EXHIBIT 13.1-1 Salesperson Data: Coastal Star Sales Corporation

Region	Salesperson	Age	Years of Experience	Sales Previous Year	Sales Current Year
Northern	Jackson	40	7	$ 412,744	$ 411,007
Northern	Gentry	60	12	1,491,024	1,726,630
Northern	La Forge	26	2	301,421	700,112
Northern	Miller	39	1	401,241	471,001
Northern	Mowen	64	5	448,160	449,261
Southern	Young	51	2	518,897	519,412
Southern	Fisk	34	1	846,222	713,333
Southern	Kincaid	62	10	1,527,124	2,009,041
Southern	Krieger	42	3	921,174	1,030,000
Southern	Manzer	64	5	463,399	422,798
Southern	Weiner	27	2	548,011	422,001

::::::: **PART FIVE**
Basic Data Analytics

A670209

Nonstock/Jupiter Images

Basic Data Analysis

LEARNING OUTCOMES

After studying this chapter, you should be able to:

1. Prepare qualitative data for interpretation or data analysis
2. Know what descriptive statistics are and why they are used
3. Create and interpret tabulation and cross-tabulation tables
4. Perform basic data transformations
5. Understand the basics of testing hypotheses using inferential statistics
6. Be able to make statistical inferences with p-values and with confidence intervals
7. Conduct a univariate *t*-test

Chapter Vignette:

Don't Tell Me!

Most people think that the last thing businesses like to hear is a consumer complaint. However, a bigger problem may occur when consumers don't complain. Complaints often provide key data that allow businesses to improve the way they deal with customers. By improving service, the businesses keep more customers and become more profitable. Thus, when consumers truly have a problem, management should welcome complaints. From another perspective, a relatively large number of complaints indicates a potential problem with management. Thus, many businesses set specific targets for minimizing complaints. Realizing that some consumers are chronic complainers, most of these targets don't strive for perfection but settle on some reasonable number. For instance, a business may set a target of fewer than twenty-five complaints per week. Research is needed to help set the target and then assess firm performance against that standard.

Who complains the most? A recent study examined the demographics of the "complainer." Among 162 complainers in the sample (out of 237 consumers in total with 75 reporting no bad experiences in the last twelve months), the results reveal the percentage of people in each group make up the "complainer":

Age	< 25	26–39	40–53	54 or more
Percentage	43.6	35.3	66.7	65.9

Does this mean that older people are more likely to complain? Does this mean that older consumers are better sources of marketing information or just chronic complainers that the firm may be better off without? Other research looks at complaining and political orientation. Although we may think of older people as more conservative, the results suggest that a conservative poltical orientation leads to less complaining than a more liberal political orientation. Understanding may involve more than one variable. Perhaps part of the answer lies in drawing meaning from basic statistics like these. Delta Airlines, for example, changed policies concerning the use of guide pets on board Delta flights based on a high incidence of complaints mentioning pets. The new policies placed greater restrictions on what types and how pets can accompany passengers.[1]

Introduction

We now turn to research tools that allow researchers to make inferences beyond central tendency and dispersion. As researchers, we infer whether some condition exists in a population based on what we observe in a sample. Alternatively, the research could be more exploratory and the researcher could be using statistics simply to search for some pattern within the data. Basic marketing analytics like those discussed in this chapter, though elementary, can provide powerful insight into marketing decision making.

Coding Qualitative Responses

Researchers often summarize and bring meaning to qualitative data by developing some type of logical coding scheme. The researcher sometimes uses interpretive software to assist in coding observations into categories. A researcher will even combine an interpretive approach with basic quantitative analyses to address a research question. Either way, some coding is necessary. Any mistakes in coding can dramatically change the conclusions. **Coding** represents the way a specific meaning is assigned to a response within previously edited data. Codes represent the meaning in data by assigning some measurement symbol to different categories of responses. This may be a number, letter, or word. The proper form of coding relates back to the level of scale measurement. Researchers code nominal data by using a word, letter, or any identifying mark. On the other hand, numbers typically are most appropriate for ordinal, interval, and ratio measures.

Thus, **codes** often, but not always, are numerical symbols. However, codes, more broadly speaking, are rules for interpreting, classifying, and recording data. In qualitative research, the codes are usually words or phrases that represent themes. In purely interpretive research, numbers are seldom used for codes. For example, a qualitative researcher may apply a code to a hermeneutic unit describing in detail a respondent's reactions to several different glasses of wine. After reading through the text several times, and applying a word-counting routine, the researcher realizes that appearance, the nose (aroma), and guessing (trying to guess what the wine will be like or what type of wine is in the glass) are important themes. A code is assigned to these categories. After considerable thought and questioning of the experience, the researcher builds a network, or grounded theory, that suggests how a wine may come to be associated with feelings of romance.

coding

The process of assigning a numerical score or other character symbol to previously edited data.

codes

Rules for interpreting, classifying, and recording data in the coding process; also, the actual numerical or other character symbols assigned to raw data.

Structured Qualitative Responses and Dummy Variables

Qualitative responses to structured questions, such as "yes" or "no," can be stored in a data file literally ("yes" or "no") or with letters such as "Y" or "N." Alternatively, they can be represented with numbers, one each to represent the respective category. Since this represents a nominal numbering system, the actual numbers used are arbitrary.

Class coding is an approach that can be used if the data are not going to be directly used to perform computations. **Class coding** assigns numbers to categories in an arbitrary way merely as a means of identifying some characteristic. If packages come in three colors, the class codes may be 1 for blue, 2 for red, and 3 for green. Class coding works for representing treatment conditions in experimental variables or categorical blocking variables like ethnicity or highest degree obtained.

class coding

Coding that assigns numbers to categories in an arbitrary way merely as a means of identifying some characteristic.

dummy coding

Numeric "1" or "0" coding where each number represents an alternate response such as "female" or "male."

Even though the codes are numeric, the variable is classificatory. Any numbers assigned serve only to separate affirmative from negative responses. For statistical purposes the research may consider adopting **dummy coding** for dichotomous responses like "yes" or "no." Dummy coding assigns a 0 to one category and a 1 to the other. So, for yes/no responses, a 0 could be "no" and a 1 would be "yes." Similarly, a "1" could represent a female respondent and a "0" would be a male respondent. Dummy coding provides the researcher with more flexibility in how structured, qualitative responses are analyzed statistically. Dummy coding can be used when more than two categories exist, but because a dummy variable can only represent two categories, multiple dummy variables are needed to represent a single qualitative response that can take on more than two categories. In fact, if k is the number of categories for a qualitative variable, $k - 1$ dummy variables are needed to represent the variable.

effects coding

An alternative to dummy coding using the values of −1 and +1 to represent two categories of responses.

An alternative to dummy coding is **effects coding**. Effects coding is performed by assigning a +1 to one value of a dichotomous variable and a −1 to the other. Dummy coding is more widely used in general, although effects coding has some advantages in the way experimental results are presented. Either way is an acceptable technique for coding structured qualitative data. Both dummy and effects coding represent qualitative phenomena in a way that facilitates basic data analysis.

The Nature of Descriptive Analysis

descriptive analysis

The elementary transformation of raw data in a way that describes the basic characteristics such as central tendency, distribution, and variability.

Perhaps the most basic statistical analysis is descriptive analysis. **Descriptive analysis** is the elementary transformation of data in a way that describes the basic characteristics such as central tendency, distribution, and variability. A researcher takes responses from 1,000 American consumers and tabulates their favorite soft drink brand and the price they expect to pay for a six-pack of that product. The mode for favorite soft drink and the average price across all 1,000 consumers would be descriptive statistics that describe central tendency in two different ways. Averages, medians, modes, variance, range, and standard deviation typify widely applied descriptive statistics.

Descriptive statistics can summarize responses from large numbers of respondents in a few simple statistics. When a sample is used, the sample descriptive statistics are used to make inferences about characteristics of the entire population of interest. The researcher examining descriptive statistics for any one particular variable is using univariate statistics. Because they are so simple, descriptive statistics are used very widely.

In Chapter 10, we learned that the level of scale measurement can help the researcher choose the most appropriate statistical tool. Exhibit 14.1 shows the specific descriptive statistic appropriate for each level of measurement. Also, remember that all statistics appropriate for lower-order scales (nominal is the lowest) are suitable for higher-order scales (ratio is the highest). So, a frequency table could also be used for interval or ratio data. Frequencies can be represented graphically as shown and are a good way of visually depicting typical survey results.

Consider the following data. Sample consumers were asked where they most often purchased beer. The result is a nominal variable that can be described with a frequency distribution (see the bar chart in Exhibit 14.1). Ten percent indicated they most often purchased beer in a drug store, 45 percent indicated a convenience store, 35 percent indicated a grocery store, and 7 percent indicated a specialty store. Three percent listed "other" (not shown in the bar chart). The mode is

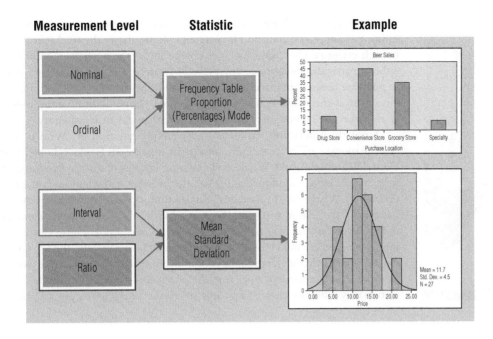

EXHIBIT **14.1**
Levels of Scale Measurement and Suggested Descriptive Statistics

convenience store since more respondents chose this than any other category. A similar distribution may have been obtained if the chart plotted the number of respondents ranking each store as their favorite type of place to purchase beer.

The bottom part of Exhibit 14.1 displays example descriptive statistics for interval and ratio variables. In this case, the chart displays results of a question asking respondents how much they typically spend on a bottle of wine purchased in a store. The mean and standard deviation are displayed beside the chart as 11.7 and 4.5, respectively. Additionally, the frequency distribution is shown with a histogram. A **histogram** is a graphical way of showing the frequency distribution in which the height of a bar corresponds to the frequency of a category. Histograms are useful for any type of data, but with continuous variables (interval or ratio) the histogram is useful for providing a quick assessment of the distribution of the data. A normal distribution line is superimposed over the histogram providing an easy comparison to see if the data are skewed or multimodal.

histogram

A graphical way of showing a frequency distribution in which the height of a bar corresponds to the observed frequency of the category.

Creating and Interpreting Tabulation

Tabulation refers to the orderly arrangement of data in a table or other summary format. When this tabulation process is done by hand the term *tallying* is used. Counting the different ways respondents answered a question and arranging them in a simple tabular form yields a **frequency table**. The actual number of responses to each category is a variable's frequency distribution. A simple tabulation of this type is sometimes called a *marginal tabulation*.

Tabulation tells the researcher how frequently each response occurs. This starting point for analysis requires the researcher to count responses or observations for each category or code assigned to a variable. A frequency table showing where consumers generally purchase beer can be computed easily. The tabular results that correspond to the chart would appear as follows:

tabulation

The orderly arrangement of data in a table or other summary format showing the number of responses to each response category; tallying.

frequency table

A table showing the different ways respondents answered a question.

Response	Frequency	Percent	Cumulative Percentage
Drug store	50	10	10
Convenience store	225	45	55
Grocery store	175	35	90
Specialty	35	7	97
Other	15	3	100

The frequency column shows the tally result or the number of respondents listing each store, respectively. The percent column shows the total percentage in each category. The cumulative percentage shows the percentage indicating either a particular category or any preceding category as their preferred place to purchase beer. From this chart, the mode indicates that the typical consumer buys beer at the convenience store since more people indicate convenience store as the place where they usually buy beer than any other category.

Similarly, Americans' responses to the simple question of "Who is your favorite movie star?" were recently tabulated. Overall, Tom Hanks, Johnny Depp, Denzel Washington, John Wayne, and Harrison Ford were the top five based on frequency of being mentioned as the favorite.[2] However, the response varied by generation. Where are the actresses? Sandra Bullock came in 6th and Jennifer Lawrence 7th, both just missing the top 5. Maybe the list is a little surprising in that several names may not seem so contemporary. Look a little closer, and John Wayne, who would be over 110 if he were still alive, remains the top movie star for the Matures generation. In contrast, Tom Hanks is number one among Boomers, but Jennifer Lawrence tops the list for Millennials. The idea that generation may influence choice of favorite movie star brings us to cross-tabulation.

• • • • • • •

Who is your favorite movie star? Does your choice agree with others of your generation?

Cross-Tabulation

A frequency distribution or tabulation can address many research questions. As long as a question deals with only one categorical variable, tabulation is the best approach to communicate the result. Although frequency counts, percentage distributions, and averages summarize considerable information, simple tabulation may not yield the full value of the research when multiple variables are involved. **Cross-tabulation** is a more appropriate technique for addressing research questions involving relationships among multiple less-than interval variables. A cross-tabulation is a combined frequency table. Cross-tabulation allows the inspection and comparison of differences among groups based on nominal or ordinal categories. One key to interpreting a cross-tabulation table is comparing the observed table values with hypothetical values that would result from pure chance.

Exhibit 14.2 summarizes cross-tabulations from consumers' responses to different ways of obtaining music in the United States.[3] The study contrasts a questionable method of obtaining music online (downloading from an illegal file sharing site) by a basic demographic variable—generation. A sample of 214 consumers of varying ages provides the data. When given a choice between obtaining a music file via the Internet, 166 of the 214 would choose to purchase it legally from a site like iTunes, while 48 would obtain it free even if the download were illegal. The cross-tabulation comes by looking at how generation membership (a less-than interval variable) influences choice of methods to obtain the music. Exhibit 14.2 breaks down the results and suggests that the Millennial generation suggests a preference toward obtaining the music illegally (35 of 53) while older generations tend toward purchasing the music rather than downloading illicitly.

cross-tabulation

The appropriate technique for addressing research questions involving relationships among multiple less-than interval variables; results in a combined frequency table displaying one variable in rows and another in columns.

Contingency Tables

Exhibit 14.3 shows an example of cross-tabulation results using contingency tables. A **contingency table** is a data matrix that displays the frequency of some combination of possible responses to multiple variables. Two-way contingency tables, meaning they involve two less-than interval

contingency table

A data matrix that displays the frequency of some combination of possible responses to multiple variables; cross-tabulation results.

EXHIBIT **14.2**

Cross-Tabulation from Consumer Ethics Survey

Generation	Purchase Download	Download Illegally	Total
Millennial	18	35	53
Gen X	41	12	53
Boomer	54	1	55
Mature	53	0	53
	166	48	214

(A) Cross-Tabulation of Question "Do you shop at Target?" by Sex of Respondent			
	Yes	**No**	**Total**
Men	150	75	225
Women	180	45	225
Total	330	120	450

(B) Percentage Cross-Tabulation of Question "Do you shop at Target?" by Sex of Respondent, Row Percentage			
	Yes	**No**	**Total (Base)**
Men	66.7%	33.3%	100% (225)
Women	80.0%	20.0%	100% (225)

(C) Percentage Cross-Tabulation of Question "Do you shop at Target?" by Sex of Respondent, Column Percentage		
	Yes	**No**
Men	45.5%	62.5%
Women	54.5%	37.5%
Total	100%	100%
(Base)	(330)	(120)

EXHIBIT 14.3

Different Ways of Depicting the Cross-Tabulation of Biological Sex and Target Patronage

variables, are used most often. A three-way contingency table involves three less-than interval variables. Beyond three variables, contingency tables become difficult to analyze and explain easily.

Two variables are depicted in the contingency table shown in panel A:

■ Row Variable: Biological Sex: ___Male ___Female
■ Column Variable: "Do you shop at Target? YES or NO"

Several conclusions can be drawn initially by examining the row and column totals:

1. 225 men and 225 women responded as can be seen in the Total column. This means that altogether 450 consumers responded.
2. Out of this 450 total consumers, 330 consumers indicated that "yes" they do shop at Target and 120 indicated "no," they do not shop at Target. This can be observed in the column totals at the bottom of the table. These row and column totals often are called **marginals** because they appear in the table's margins.

Researchers usually are more interested in the inner cells of a contingency table. The inner cells display conditional frequencies (combinations). Using these values, we can draw some more specific conclusions:

3. Out of 330 consumers who shop at Target, 150 are male and 180 are female.
4. Alternatively, out of the 120 respondents not shopping at Target, 75 are male and 45 are female.

This finding helps us know whether the two variables are related. If men and women equally patronize Target, we would expect that hypothetically, 165 of the 330 shoppers would be male and 165 would be female. Clearly, these hypothetical expectations (165 male/165 female) are not observed. What is the implication? A relationship exists between respondent sex and shopping choice. Specifically, Target shoppers are more likely to be female than male. Notice that the same meaning could be drawn by analyzing non-Target shoppers.

marginals

Row and column totals in a contingency table, which are shown in its margins.

A two-way contingency table like the one shown in part A is referred to as a *2 × 2 table* because it has two rows (Men and Women) and two columns (Yes and No). Each variable has two levels. A two-way contingency table displaying two variables, one (the row variable) with three levels and the other with four levels, would be referred to as a *3 × 4 table*. Any cross-tabulation table may be classified according to the number of rows by the number of columns (*R* by *C*).

Percentage Cross-Tabulations

When data from a survey are cross-tabulated, percentages help the researcher understand the nature of the relationship by making relative comparisons simpler. The total number of respondents or observations may be used as a **statistical base** for computing the percentage in each cell. When the objective of the research is to identify a relationship between answers to two questions (or two variables), one of the questions is commonly chosen to be the source of the base for determining percentages. For example, look at the data in parts A, B, and C of Exhibit 14.3. Compare part B with part C. Selecting either the row percentages or the column percentages will emphasize a particular comparison or distribution. The nature of the problem the researcher wishes to answer will determine which marginal total will serve as a base for computing percentages.

statistical base

The number of respondents or observations (in a row or column) used as a basis for computing percentages.

Elaboration and Refinement

The *Oxford Universal Dictionary* defines *analysis* as "the resolution of anything complex into its simplest elements." Once a researcher has examined the basic relationship between two variables, he or she may wish to investigate this relationship under a variety of different conditions. Typically, a third variable is introduced into the analysis to elaborate and refine the researcher's understanding by specifying the conditions under which the relationship between the first two variables is strongest and weakest. In other words, a more elaborate analysis asks, "Will interpretation of the relationship be modified if other variables are simultaneously considered?"

Elaboration analysis involves the basic cross-tabulation within various subgroups of the sample. The researcher breaks down the analysis for each level of another variable. If the researcher has cross-tabulated shopping preference by sex (see Exhibit 14.3) and wishes to investigate another variable (say, marital status), a more elaborate analysis may be conducted. Exhibit 14.4 breaks down the responses to the question "Do you shop at Target?" by sex and marital status. The data show women display the same preference whether married or single. However, married men are much more likely to shop at Target than are single men. The analysis suggests that the original conclusion about the relationship between sex and shopping behavior for women be retained. However, a relationship that was not discernible in the two-variable case is evident.

The cross-tabulation in Exhibit 14.4 is consistent with an interaction effect. The combination of the two variables, sex and marital status, is associated with differences in the dependent variable. Interactions between variables examine moderating variables. A **moderator variable** is a third variable that changes the nature of a relationship between the original independent and dependent variables. Marital status acts as a moderator variable in this case. The interaction effect suggests that marriage changes the relationship between sex and shopping preference.

In other situations, the addition of a third variable to the analysis may lead us to reject the original conclusion about the relationship. When this occurs, the elaboration analysis suggests the relationship between the original variables is spurious. Although it is not likely obvious at this stage, elaboration analysis provides the basis for much of the big data mining. When automated, elaboration analysis searches for interesting relationships as we see below.

elaboration analysis

An analysis of the basic cross-tabulation for each level of a variable not previously considered, such as subgroups of the sample.

moderator variable

A third variable that changes the nature of a relationship between the original independent and dependent variables.

EXHIBIT 14.4

Cross-Tabulation of Marital Status, Sex, and Responses to the Question "Do You Shop at Target?"

	Single		Married	
	Men	Women	Men	Women
"Do you shop at Target?"				
Yes	55%	80%	86%	80%
No	45%	20%	14%	20%

How Many Cross-Tabulations?

Surveys may ask dozens of questions, and hundreds of categorical variables can be stored in a data warehouse. Computer-assisted marketing researchers can "fish" for relationships by cross-tabulating every categorical variable with every other categorical variable. Thus, every possible response becomes a possible explanatory variable. A researcher addressing an exploratory research question may find some benefit in such a fishing expedition. Marketing analytics software exists that automatically searches through volumes of cross-tabulations looking for relationships. These results may provide some insight into the market segment structure for some product. Alternatively, the program may flag the cross-tabulations suggesting the strongest relationship. CHAID (chi-square automatic interaction detection) software exemplifies software that makes searches through large numbers of variables possible. Data-mining can be conducted with CHAID, or similar techniques, and may suggest useful relationships. Brand managers likely have at least a passing interest in what leads a Tweet to be re-Tweeted. Enter CHAID. Researchers analyzed political marketing activity on Twitter based on successive categorizations created by cross-classifying Tweet characteristics with sender characteristics.[4] The results suggest the highest re-Tweets for negative Tweets that originate from a Twitter account categorized as having a high number of followers. In contrast, the lowest re-Tweets come when the Tweet's message content reflects on a candidate's personal life. Although marketing analytics that mines data for information that may predict sales sounds complicated, cross-tabulation provides a basis for many of the search routines.

Outside of exploratory research, researchers should conduct cross-tabulations that address specific research questions or hypotheses. When hypotheses involve relationships among two categorical variables, cross-tabulations are the right tool for the job. However, as the number of categorical variables becomes greater, depicting the results in a table shown in a report or presentation becomes difficult and complicated to interpret. Therefore, as the number of variables moves beyond three, analysts may not depict them in a report.

Data Transformation

Simple Transformations

Data transformation (also called *data conversion*) is the process of changing the data format from the original form into a format more amenable to analytics appropriate for achieving the given research objectives. Researchers often recode the raw responses into modified or new variables. For example, many researchers believe that less response bias will result if interviewers ask respondents for their year of birth rather than their age. This presents no problem for the research analyst because a simple data transformation is possible. The raw data coded as birth year can easily be transformed to age by subtracting the birth year from the current year. In fact, some software automatically records dates in formats such as the amount of time since the arrival of January 1, 1900, or the arrival of January 1, 1980, considered the birth date of the PC age. The analyst may find it helpful to transform these into more user friendly formats.

In earlier chapters, we discussed recoding and creating summated scales. Reverse coding and the creation of composite scales represent common data transformations. Collapsing or combining adjacent categories of a variable is another common form of data transformation used to reduce the number of categories. A Likert scale may sometimes be collapsed into a smaller number of categories. For instance, consider the following Likert item administered to a sample of state university seniors:

data transformation

Process of changing the data from their original form to a format suitable for performing a data analysis addressing research objectives.

To the Point

"All that we do is done with an eye to something else."

—ARISTOTLE

	Strongly Disagree	Disagree	Neutral	Agree	Strongly Agree
I am satisfied with my college experience at this university	○	○	○	○	○

The following frequency table describes results for this survey item:

Strongly Disagree	Disagree	Neutral	Agree	Strongly Agree
110	30	15	35	210

The distribution is bimodal because two peaks exist in the distribution, one at either end of the scale. Since the vast majority of respondents (80 percent = (110 + 210)/400) indicate either strongly disagree or strongly agree, the variable responses act a lot like a categorical variable. Customers either strongly disagreed or strongly agreed with the statement. So, the researcher may wish to collapse the responses into two categories. While multiple ways exist to accomplish this, the researcher may assign the value 0 to all respondents who either strongly disagreed or disagreed and the value 1 to all respondents who either agreed or strongly agreed. Respondents marking neutral would be excluded from analysis.

Perhaps the 110 dissatisfied students differ in some important way from the 210. Perhaps their exam scores are also bimodal. Exhibit 14.5 shows an example of a bimodal distribution. Here, 125 students scored 45 and 125 scored 95. Only 100 students made some score between these values. Thus, the mean or mode would be a misleading indicator of expected values with a true bimodal distribution.

Problems with Data Transformations

median split

Dividing a data set into two categories by placing respondents below the median in one category and respondents above the median in another.

Researchers often perform a median split to collapse a scale with multiple response points into two categories. The **median split** means respondents below the observed median go into one category and respondents above the median go into another. Although this is common, the approach makes the most sense when the data do indeed exhibit bimodal characteristics. When the data are unimodal, such as would be the case with normally distributed data, a median split will lead to greater error.

Exhibit 14.6 illustrates this problem. Clearly, most respondents either slightly agree or slightly disagree with this statement. The central tendency could be represented by the median of 3.5, a mean of 3.5, or the mode of 3.5 (3 and 4 each have the same number of responses so the mode

EXHIBIT **14.5**
Bimodal Distributions Are Consistent with Transformations into Categorical Values

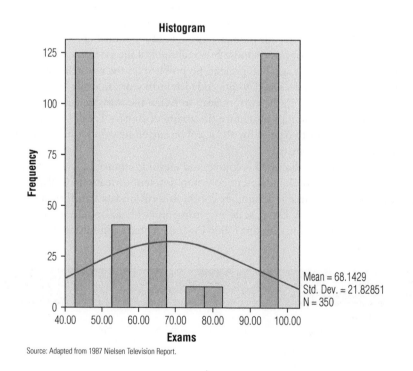

Source: Adapted from 1987 Nielsen Television Report.

EXHIBIT 14.6
The Problem with Median Splits with Unimodal Data

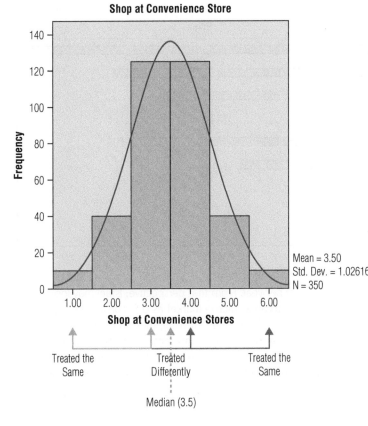

Shop at Convenience Store

Frequency Distribution: X1 = I Do Most of My Shopping at Convenience Stores.		
Response Category (Code)	**Counts**	**Cumulative Percentage**
Strongly Disagree (1)	10	2.86%
Disagree (2)	40	14.29%
Slightly Disagree (3)	125	50.00%
Slightly Agree (4)	125	85.71%
Agree (5)	40	97.14%
Strongly Agree (6)	10	100.00%

Median = 3.5

Recode to Complete Data Transformation:

Old Values	1	2	3	4	5	6
New Values	1	1	1	2	2	2

Mean = 3.50
Std. Dev. = 1.02616
N = 350

is set between the two). The "outliers," if any, appear to be those not indicating something other than slight agreement or slight disagreement. In all likelihood, the respondents indicating slight disagreement are more similar to those indicating slight agreement than they are to those respondents indicating strong disagreement. Yet, the recode places values 1 and 3 in the same new category, but places values 3 and 4 in a different category (see the recoding scheme in Exhibit 14.6). The distribution does not support a median split into two categories and so a transformation collapsing these values into agreement and disagreement is inappropriate.

When a sufficient number of responses exist and a variable is ratio, the researcher may choose to delete one-fourth to one-third of the responses around the median to effectively ensure a bimodal distribution. This helps to mitigate the logical inconsistency illustrated in Exhibit 14.6. Median splits should always be performed only with great care and with adequate justification, though, as the inappropriate collapsing of continuous variables into categorical variables ignores the information contained within the untransformed values. Justification for a median split commonly is found in the ability to apply a more parsimonious statistical approach than would be possible using the raw data values.

Index Numbers

The consumer price index and wholesale price index are secondary data sources that are frequently used by marketing researchers. Price indexes, like other **index numbers**, represent simple data transformations that allow researchers to track a variable's value over time and compare a variable(s) with other variables. Recalibration allows scores or observations to be related to a certain base period or base number.

For instance, if the data are time-related, a base year is chosen. The index numbers are then computed by dividing each year's activity by the base-year activity and multiplying by 100. Index

index numbers

Scores or observations recalibrated to indicate how they relate to a base number.

Wine Index Helps Marketers

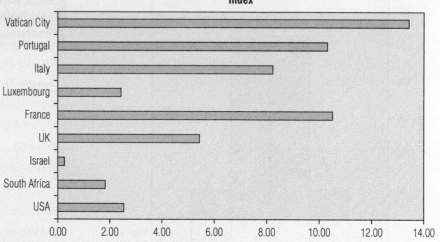

How much wine do consumers around the world drink? Some standard of comparison would be useful in giving this question perspective. Using 1968 U.S. wine consumption as a standard (1.07 gallons / person = 4.05 liters/person), per capita wine consumption can be depicted in this chart:

Consumers in the U.S. drink 2.5 times as much wine today as they did back in 1968. However, that still does not place the U.S. in the top countries per capita as they fall far behind Italy (8.2 times the wine U.S. consumers drank in 1968), Portugal (10.3), and France (10.5), all of whom trail per capital consumption in Vatican City, where the approximately 900 residents drink 13.4 times as much wine as 1968 U.S. consumers. In contrast, although Israel produces a considerable amount of wine, their wine index is only 0.25. Thus, the bulk of their wine production growth may be destined for foreign markets.

However, when looking for growth opportunities, marketing managers may wish to consider total consumption for the country per year. From that perspective, Israel may look to the U.S. as an attractive market as U.S. consumers together drink over 3 billion liters of wine, making the U.S. number 1 in terms of overall wine consumption. In contrast, the Vatican City total market is about 45,000 liters per year! Clearly, different indices of the same data tell quite different stories.

Sources: http://www.wineinstitute.org/files/World_Per_Capita_Wine_Consumption_Revised_Nov_2015.pdf, accessed January 17, 2018.

numbers require ratio measurement scales. Marketing managers may often chart consumption in some category over time. Grocers may wish to chart the U.S. wine consumption index. Using 1968 as a base year (4.05 liters per year), the current U.S. wine consumption index is about 2.5, meaning that the typical American consumer drinks 10.3 liters of wine per year (see the Research Snapshot).[5]

Tabular and Graphic Methods of Displaying Data

Tables, graphs, and charts may simplify and clarify data. Graphical representations of data may take a number of forms, ranging from a computer printout to an elaborate pictograph. Tables, graphs, and charts, however, all facilitate summarization and communication. For example, see how the simple frequency table and histogram shown in Exhibit 14.6 provide a summary that quickly and easily communicates meaning that would be more difficult to see if all 350 responses were viewed separately.

Today's researcher has many convenient tools to quickly produce charts, graphs, or tables. Even basic word processing programs include chart functions that can construct the chart within the text document. Bar charts (histograms), pie charts, curve/line diagrams, and scatter plots are among the most widely used tools. Some choices match well with certain types of data and analyses.

To the Point

The thing to do is to supply light.
—WOODROW WILSON

Hypothesis Testing Using Basic Statistics

Descriptive research and causal research designs often climax with hypotheses tests. Generally, hypotheses should be stated in concrete fashion so that the method of empirical testing seems almost obvious.

Empirical testing typically involves inferential statistics. This means that an inference can be made about some population based on observations of a sample representing that population. Statistical analysis can be divided into several groups based on how many variables are involved:

- **Univariate statistical analysis** tests hypotheses involving only one variable.
- **Bivariate statistical analysis** tests hypotheses involving two variables.
- **Multivariate statistical analysis** tests hypotheses and models involving multiple (three or more) variables or sets of variables and potentially involving multiple equations.

For now, the focus is on univariate statistics. Thus, we examine statistical tests appropriate for drawing inferences about a single variable.

Hypothesis Testing Procedure

Hypotheses are tested by comparing an educated guess with empirical reality. The process can be described as follows:

- First, the hypothesis is derived from the research objectives. The hypothesis should be stated as specifically as possible and should be theoretically sound.
- Next, a sample is obtained and the relevant variables are measured. In univariate tests, only one variable is of interest.
- The measured value obtained in the sample is compared to the value either stated explicitly or implied in the hypothesis. If the value is consistent with the hypothesis, the hypothesis is supported. If the value is not consistent with the hypothesis, the hypothesis is not supported.

An example univariate hypothesis is illustrated here:

H1: The average number of children per family in zip code 70360 is greater than 1.5.

If a sample is drawn from this zip code and the average number of children per family is 0.075, the hypothesis is not supported. If the average number of children is 3.3, the result supports the hypothesis. As the mean becomes smaller than 3.3 and approaches the theoretical expected value of 1.5, the chance becomes smaller that the data support the stated hypothesis. The exact point where the hypothesis changes from not being supported to being supported depends on how much risk the researcher is willing to accept and on the variability of the measure.

Typical univariate hypotheses set up a comparison of some observed sample mean against a benchmark value. The test addresses the question, "Is the sample mean truly different from the benchmark?" But, how different is really different? If the observed sample mean is 1.55 and the benchmark is 1.50, would the hypothesis still be supported? Probably not! When the observed mean is so close to the benchmark, we do not have sufficient confidence that a second set of data using a new sample taken from the same population might not produce a finding conflicting with the benchmark. In contrast, when the mean turns out well above 1.50, perhaps 3.3, then we could more easily trust that another sample would not produce a mean equal to or less than 1.50.

While the terminology of null and alternative hypotheses is common in statistical theory, it is also commonly confusing. Therefore, we'll avoid using the term *null hypothesis* when at all possible. Students usually understand hypothesis testing more easily by focusing on what the findings should look like if the proposed hypothesis is true. If the hypothesis mentioned earlier is true, an observed sample's mean should be noticeably greater than 1.50. We test to see if this idea can be supported by the empirical evidence. A statistical test's significance level becomes a key indicator of whether or not a hypothesis can be supported. Likewise, confidence intervals provide a useful alternative in making statistical inference.

Significance Levels and Statistical Inference

A **significance level** is a critical probability associated with a statistical hypothesis test that indicates how likely it is that an inference supporting a difference between an observed value and some statistical expectation is true. The term **p-value** stands for probability value and is essentially

univariate statistical analysis

Tests of hypotheses involving only one variable.

bivariate statistical analysis

Tests of hypotheses involving two variables.

multivariate statistical analysis

Statistical analysis involving three or more variables or sets of variables or even multiple equations.

significance level

A critical probability associated with a statistical hypothesis test that indicates how likely an inference supporting a difference between an observed value and some statistical expectation is true. The acceptable level of Type I error.

p-value

Probability value, or the observed or computed significance level; p-values are compared to significance levels to test hypotheses.

another name for an ***observed*** or ***computed*** significance level. Exhibit 14.7 discusses interpretations of p-values for different kinds of statistical tests. The probability in a p-value is that the statistical expectation (null) for a given test is true. So, low p-values mean there is little likelihood that the statistical expectation is true. This means the researcher's hypothesis positing (suggesting) a difference between an observed mean and a population mean, or between an observed frequency and a population frequency, or for a relationship between two variables, is likely supported.

Traditionally, researchers have specified an acceptable significance level for a test prior to the analysis. Later, we will discuss this as an acceptable amount of Type I error. Most typically, researchers set the acceptable amount of error, and therefore the acceptable significance level, at 0.1, 0.05, or 0.01. If the p-value resulting from a statistical test is less than the prespecified significance level, the results support a hypothesis implying differences. To illustrate, if an analyst is comparing sales in two districts and sets the acceptable Type I error at 0.1 and the p-value resulting from the test is 0.03, then the results support a hypothesis suggesting differences in sales in the two districts.

Type I and Type II Errors

Hypothesis testing using sample observations is based on probability theory. We make an observation of a sample and use it to infer the probability that some observation is true within the population the sample represents. Because we cannot make any statement about a sample with complete certainty, there is always a chance that an error will be made. When a researcher makes the observation using a census, meaning that every unit (person or object) in a population is measured, then conclusions are certain. Researchers very rarely use a census, though, and thus, statistical conclusions are susceptible to two types of inferential errors (see Research Snapshot on page 401).

EXHIBIT **14.7**

p-Values and Statistical Tests

Test Description	Test Statistic	
Compare an Observed Mean with Some Predetermined Value	Z or t-test—Low p-Values Indicate the Observed Mean Is Different Than Some Predetermined Value (Often 0)	$\alpha = .025$ $\alpha = .025$ $m = 3.0$ $\bar{X}$
Compare an Observed Frequency with a Predetermined Value	X^2—Low p-Values Indicate That Observed Frequency Is Different Than Predetermined Value	$df = 1$ 1
Compare an Observed Proportion with Some Predetermined Value	Z or t-test for Proportions—Low p-Values Indicate That the Observed Proportion Is Different Than the Predetermined Value	50%
Bivariate Tests:		
Compare Whether Two Observed Means Are Different from One Another	Z or t-test—Low p-Values Indicate the Means Are Different	$\mu = 0$
Compare Whether Two Less-Than Interval Variables Are Related Using Cross-Tabs	X^2—Low p-Values Indicate the Variables Are Related to One Another	$df = 3$ 3
Compare Whether Two Interval or Ratio Variables Are Correlated to One Another	t-test for Correlation—Low p-Values Indicate the Variables Are Related to One Another	$r = 0$

RESEARCH
SNAPSHOT

The Law and Type I and Type II Errors

Although most attorneys and judges do not concern themselves with the statistical terminology of Type I and Type II errors, they do follow this logic. For example, our legal system is based on the concept that a person is innocent until proven guilty. Assume that the null hypothesis is that the individual is innocent. If we make a Type I error, we will send an innocent person to prison. Our legal system takes many precautions to avoid Type I errors. A Type II error would occur if a guilty party were set free (the null hypothesis would have been accepted). Our society places such a high value on avoiding Type I errors that Type II errors are more likely to occur.

Type I Error

Suppose the observed sample mean described earlier leads to the conclusion that the mean is greater than 1.5 when in fact the true population mean is equal to 1.5. A Type I error has occurred. A **Type I error** occurs when a condition that is really true in the population is rejected based on statistical observations. When a researcher sets an acceptable significance level a priori (α), he or she is determining how much tolerance he or she has for a Type I error. Simply put, a Type I error occurs when the researcher concludes that there is a statistical difference based on a sample result when in reality one does not exist in the population. When testing for relationships, a Type I error occurs when the researcher concludes a relationship exists when in fact one does not exist.

type I error

Occurs when a condition that is true in the population is rejected based on statistical observations in a sample.

Type II Error

Conversely, if our null hypothesis is indeed false, but we conclude that we should not reject the null hypothesis, we make what is called a Type II error. In this example, our null hypothesis that the mean is equal to 1.5 is not true in the population. However, our sample data indicates the mean does not differ from 1.5. So, a Type II error is the probability of failing to reject a false hypothesis. This incorrect decision is called beta (β). In practical terms, a Type II error means that our sample does not show a difference between an observed mean and a benchmark when in fact the difference does exist in the population. Alternatively, for correlation type relationships, a **Type II error** is created when the sample data suggests that a relationship does not exist when in fact a relationship does exist. Such an occurrence is related to statistical power. A sample size is sometimes too small to provide the power needed to find a relationship.

type II error

Occurs when the sample data suggests that a relationship does not exist when in fact a relationship does exist.

Unfortunately, without increasing sample size, the researcher cannot simultaneously reduce Type I and Type II errors. They are inversely related. Thus, reducing the probability of a Type II error increases the probability of a Type I error. In marketing problems, Type I errors generally are considered more serious than Type II errors. Thus, more emphasis is placed on determining the significance level, α, than in determining β.[6]

Univariate Tests of Means

At times, a researcher may wish to compare some observation against a preset standard. A univariate *t*-test is appropriate for testing hypotheses involving some observed mean against some specified value such as a sales target. The *t*-distribution, like the standardized normal curve, is a symmetrical, bell-shaped distribution with a mean of 0 and a standard deviation of 1.0. When sample size (*n*) is larger than 30, the *t*-distribution and Z-distribution are almost identical. Therefore, while the *t*-test is strictly appropriate for tests involving small sample sizes with unknown standard deviations, researchers commonly apply the *t*-test for comparisons involving the mean of an interval or ratio measure. The precise height and shape of the *t*-distribution vary with sample size.

More specifically, the shape of the *t*-distribution is influenced by its degrees of freedom (*df*). The degrees of freedom are determined by the number of distinct calculations that are possible given a set of information. In the case of a univariate *t*-test, the degrees of freedom are equal to the sample size (*n*) minus one. If a sample size is 46 ($n = 46$) then the degrees of freedom for a univariate *t*-test is 45 $(df = 46-1 = 45)$.

Exhibit 14.8 illustrates *t*-distributions for 1, 2, 5, and an infinite number of degrees of freedom. Notice that the *t*-distribution approaches a normal distribution rapidly with increasing sample size. This is why, in practice, marketing researchers usually apply a *t*-test even with large samples. The practical effect is that the conclusion will be the same since the distributions are so similar with large samples and the correspondingly larger numbers of degrees of freedom.

Another way to look at degrees of freedom is to think of adding four numbers together when you know their sum—for example,

4

2

1

+X

12

The value of the fourth number has to be 5. The values of the first three digits could change to any value (freely vary), but the fourth value would have to be determined for the sum to still be equal to 12. In this example there are three degrees of freedom. Degrees of freedom can be a difficult concept to understand fully. For most basic statistical analyses, the user only needs to remember the rule for determining the number of degrees of freedom for a given test. Today, with computerized software packages, the number of degrees of freedom is provided automatically for most tests.

Univariate *t*-test

Ultra-luxury car makers may set a sales goal that involves selling more than 1,000 cars per year worldwide as a means of deciding whether to put that car into production. The research question of "Will sales exceed 1,000 cars?" involves a univariate analysis. More specifically, a univariate *t*-test may result from survey data of prospective customers.

To calculate a *t* statistic, one uses this formula:

$$t = \frac{\bar{X} - \mu}{S_{\bar{X}}}$$

EXHIBIT **14.8**

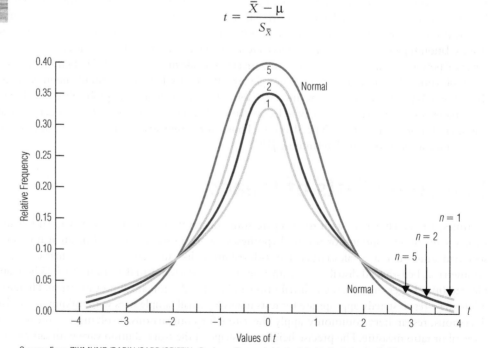

Source: From ZIKMUND/BABIN/CARR/GRIFFIN, *Business Research Methods* (with Qualtrics Card), 8E.

with $n - 1$ degrees of freedom. Suppose a luxury car retailer believes that the number of cars sold per week for a new prototype model is not going to be 20, which is the average for the current models of luxury cars. The manager records the number of sales for the first twenty-five weeks of a new prototype production run. Are the sales different from twenty per week? The substantive hypothesis is

H_1: Cars sold will be greater than (or less than) 20: $\mu \not= 20$

1. The researcher calculates a sample mean and standard deviation. In this case, suppose $\bar{X} = 22$ and S (sample standard deviation) = 5.
2. The standard error is computed ($S_{\bar{x}}$):

$$S_{\bar{x}} = \frac{S}{\sqrt{n}}$$
$$= \frac{5}{\sqrt{25}}$$
$$= 1$$

3. The researcher then finds the t-value associated with the desired confidence level or statistical significance. If a 95 percent confidence level is desired, the significance level is 0.05.
4. The critical values for the t-test are found by locating the upper and lower limits of the confidence interval. The result defines the regions of rejection. This requires determining the critical value of t. For 24 degrees of freedom ($n = 25, df = n - 1$), the critical t-value is 2.064.
5. The formula provides this result:

$$t_{abs} = \frac{\bar{X} - \mu}{S_{\bar{x}}}$$
$$t_{abs} = \frac{22 - 20}{1} = \frac{2}{1} = 2$$

The observed mean of 22 is inserted for the sample mean ($\bar{X}$) and the hypothesized value of 20 is inserted for the population mean (μ). We can see that the observed t-value of 2.00 is less than the critical t-value of 2.064 at the 0.05 level when there are $25 - 1 = 24$ degrees of freedom. As a result, the p-value is greater than 0.05 and the hypothesis is not supported. We cannot conclude with 95 percent confidence that the mean is not 20.

The Z-distribution and the t-distribution are very similar, and thus the Z-test and t-test will provide much the same result in most situations. However, when the population standard deviation (σ) is known, the Z-test is most appropriate. When σ is unknown (the situation in most business research studies), and the sample size greater than 30, the Z-test can also be used. When σ is unknown and the sample size is small, the t-test is most appropriate. In fact, marketing researchers rely heavily on the t-test whenever sigma, σ, is unknown.

Confidence Interval for Difference

A confidence interval around the mean difference proves useful in understanding the hypothesis test as well. In fact, the confidence interval provides a better idea of the true magnitude of a tested effect than does a p-value test of significance. The t-test above amounts to testing whether the observed differences are greater or less than 0. Using the values above, the confidence interval (CI) for the difference in means can be computed as follows:

$$CI_{1-\alpha} = t_{abs} \pm t_{\alpha(\text{critical})} \frac{S}{\sqrt{n}}$$

Substituting the values into the formula yields:

$$CI_{.95} = 2.00 \pm 2.06 \frac{5}{\sqrt{25}} = 2.00 \pm 2.06$$

Expressing the range relative to the observed difference of means of 2, the 95 percent confidence interval becomes:

$$(2 - 2.06):(2 + 2.06) = -0.06:4.06$$

With 95 percent confidence, the difference in the mean ranges from just below 0 to just above 4. Given that 0 is included in the *CI*, the hypothesis of a mean greater than 20 (or less than) is not supported. A *CI* that does not include 0 would support a difference between the observed values and the hypothesized mean (or test value). Confidence intervals provide the user with a clear idea of the expected size of effect, information not contained in a p-value.

TIPS OF THE TRADE

- A frequency table can be a very useful way to depict basic tabulations.
- Cross-tabulation and contingency tables are a simple and effective way to examine relationships among less-than interval variables.
  - When a distinction can be made between independent and dependent variables (that are nominal or ordinal), the convention is that rows are independent variables and columns are dependent variables.
- A continuous variable that displays a bimodal distribution is appropriate for a median split.

- Median splits should be performed on variables that display a normal distribution only with caution.
- Importantly, median splits on unimodal, continuous variables should be performed only after deleting one-fourth to one-third of the responses around the median to help prevent logically inconsistent classifications.
- P-values and confidence intervals facilitate hypothesis testing. Confidence intervals have the added advantage of demonstrating the size and potential range of an effect.

∷ SUMMARY

1. Prepare qualitative data for interpretation or data analysis. Qualitative data interpretation benefits from coding. Coding can help identify key themes. Coding involves assigning some representative value to units of data having similar meaning. One of the most basic forms of coding is dummy coding. Dummy coding involves representing dichotomies with values of 0 and 1.

2. Know what descriptive statistics are and why they are used. Descriptive analyses provide descriptive statistics. These include measures of central tendency and variation. Statistics such as the mean, mode, median, range, variance, and standard deviation are all descriptive statistics. These statistics provide a basic summary describing the basic properties of a variable.

3. Create and interpret tabulation and cross-tabulation tables. Statistical tabulation is another way of saying that we count the number of observations in each possible response category. In other words, tabulation is the same as tallying. Tabulation is an appropriate descriptive analysis for less-than interval variables. Frequency tables and histograms are used to display tabulation results. Cross-tabulation is the appropriate technique for assessing relationships among multiple less-than interval variables. The key to interpreting a cross-tabulation result is to compare actual observed values with hypothetical values that would result from pure chance. When observed results vary from these values, a relationship is indicated.

4. Perform basic data transformations. Data transformations are often needed to assist in data analysis and involve changing the mathematical form of data in some systematic way. Basic data transformations include reverse coding, summating scales, creating index numbers, and collapsing a variable based on a median split.

5. Understand the basics of testing hypotheses using inferential statistics. Hypothesis testing can involve univariate, bivariate, or multivariate statistics. Hypotheses are derived from research questions and should be stated in specific and testable terms. A sample is drawn. The sample represents a relevant population and then an inference about the population is made based on the descriptive statistics developed from the sample.

6. Be able to use a p-value to make statistical inferences. A p-value is the probability value associated with a statistical test. The probability in a p-value is the probability that the expected value for some test distribution is true. In other words, for a *t*-test, the expected value of the *t*-distribution is 0. If a researcher is testing whether or not a variable is significantly different from 0, then the p-value that results from the corresponding computed *t*-value represents the probability that the true population mean is actually 0. For most marketing research hypotheses, a low p-value supports the hypothesis. If a p-value is lower than the researcher's acceptable significance level (i.e., 0.05), then the hypothesis is usually supported.

7. Conduct a univariate *t*-test. A univariate *t*-test allows a researcher to test inferences comparing some sample observation against a predetermined standard. Often, the predetermined standard represents some benchmark such as a sales target or scrap rate. The *t*-test results allow an inference about a relevant population based on the mean derived from a sample. Confidence intervals are particularly useful in depicting results.

∷ KEY TERMS AND CONCEPTS

bivariate statistical analysis, *399*
class coding, *389*
codes, *389*
coding, *389*
contingency table, *392*
cross-tabulation, *392*
data transformation, *395*
descriptive analysis, *390*
dummy coding, *390*

effects coding, *390*
elaboration analysis, *394*
frequency table, *391*
histogram, *391*
index numbers, *397*
marginals, *393*
median split, *396*
moderator variable, *394*
multivariate statistical analysis, *399*

p-value, *399*
significance level, *399*
statistical base, *394*
tabulation, *391*
Type I error, *401*
Type II error, *401*
univariate statistical analysis, *399*

:: QUESTIONS FOR REVIEW AND CRITICAL THINKING

1. How does coding allow qualitative data to become useful to a researcher?
2. What are five descriptive statistics used to describe the basic properties of variables?

3. What is a *histogram*? What is the advantage of overlaying a normal distribution over a histogram?
4. A survey asks respondents to respond to the statement "My work is interesting." Interpret the frequency distribution shown here (taken from an SPSS output):

Category Label	Code	Abs. Freq.	Rel. Freq. (Pct.)	Adj. Freq. (Pct.)	Cum. Freq. (Pct.)
Very true	1	650	23.9	62.4	62.4
Somewhat true	2	303	11.2	29.1	91.5
Not very true	3	61	2.2	5.9	97.3
Not at all true	4	28	1.0	2.7	100.0
	•	1,673	61.6	Missing	
	Total	2,715	100.0	100.0	
Valid cases	1,042		Missing cases	1,673	

5. Use the data in the following table to
   a. prepare a frequency distribution of the respondents' ages;
   b. cross-tabulate the respondents' genders with cola preference; and
   c. identify any outliers.

Individual	Gender	Age	Cola Preference	Weekly Unit Purchases
John	M	19	Coke	2
Al	M	17	Pepsi	5
Bill	M	20	Pepsi	7
Mary	F	20	Coke	2
Jim	M	18	Coke	4
Karen	F	16	Coke	4
Tom	M	17	Pepsi	12
Sassi	F	22	Pepsi	6
Amie	F	20	Pepsi	2
Dawn	F	19	Pepsi	3

6. Data on the average size of a soda (in ounces) at all thirty major league baseball parks are as follows: 14, 18, 20, 16, 16, 12, 14, 16, 14, 16, 16, 16, 14, 32, 16, 20, 12, 16, 20, 12, 16, 16, 24, 16, 16, 14, 14, 12, 14, 20. Compute descriptive statistics for this variable. Comment on the results. Presuming the first fifteen are drink sizes in the American League and the last fifteen are drink sizes in the National League, test the hypotheses: Soft drink sizes are larger at American League Ball Parks than at National League Ball Parks. Do the data represent a sample or a census?

7. The following computer output shows a cross-tabulation of frequencies and provides frequency number (N) and row (R) percentages.
   a. Interpret this output including an impression about whether or not the row and column variables are related.
   b. Critique the way the analysis is presented.

Have You Read a Book in Past Three Months	Have High School Diploma?		
	Yes	No	Total
Yes	489	174	663
	73.8	26.2	
No	473	378	851
	55.6	44.4	
	. . . . . .	. . . . . .	. . . . . .
Total	962	552	1514

8. List and describe at least three basic data transformations.
9. What conditions suggest that a ratio variable should be transformed into a dichotomous (two group) variable represented with dummy coding?
10. A data processing analyst for a research supplier finds that preliminary computer runs of survey results show that consumers love a client's new product. The employee buys a large block of the client's stock. Is this ethical?

11. Make a list of the lowest prices for the following products at walmart.com and at amazon.com:
Gain Laundry Detergent (64 load min)
Evian Spring Water (1 Liter)
Science Diet Cat Food (15.5 lb. bag)
Titleist NXT Golf Balls (1 dozen new)
Coppertone Water Babies 50 SPF Sunscreen Spray
2 lb. Barilla Spaghetti
Luvs Diapers (size 2, 216 ct)
Otterbox iPhone Case (latest model)
Raid Roach Spray (17.5 oz can)
Jose Cuervo Original Margarita Mix (approx. 59 oz bottle)

What is the mean and median for each? Which is the better indicator of central tendency? Use Excel or other software to generate a frequency distribution for each retailer. Test the hypothesis that Amazon's prices will add up to less than $100.
12. Describe the basic hypothesis testing procedure.
13. What is a p-value and how is it used? Compare the use of p-values with the use of a confidence interval in testing hypotheses.
14. A researcher is asked to determine whether a productivity objective (in dollars) of better than $75,000 per employee is possible. A productivity test is done involving twenty employees. What conclusion would you reach? The sales results are as follows:

28,000	105,000	58,000	93,000	96,000
67,000	82,500	75,000	81,000	59,000
101,000	60,500	77,000	72,500	48,000
99,000	78,000	71,000	80,500	78,000

:: RESEARCH ACTIVITIES

1. Go the website for the Chicago Cubs baseball team (http://chicago.cubs.mlb.com). Use either the schedule listing or the statistical information to find their record in the most recently completed season. Create a data file with a variable indicating whether each game was won or lost and a variable indicating whether the game was played at home in Wrigley Field or away from home. Using a computer and software such as Excel, SPSS, JMP, or SAS,

a. Compute a frequency table and histogram for each variable.
b. Use cross-tabulations to examine whether a relationship exists between where the game is played (home or away) and winning.
c. Extra Analysis: Repeat the analyses for the Houston Astros baseball team (http://www.astros.com). What does this suggest for the relationship between playing at home and winning?

Premier Motorcars

Case 14.1

Case prepared by Mitch Griffin, Bradley University. Premier Motorcars is the new Fiat dealer in Delavan, Illinois. Premier Motorcars has been regularly advertising in its local market area that the new Fiat 500 averages 30 miles to a gallon of gas and mentions that this figure may vary with driving conditions. A local consumer group wishes to verify the advertising claim. To do so, it selects a sample of recent purchasers of the Fiat 500. It asks them to drive their cars until at least two tanks of gasoline have been used up and then calculate the mileage in miles per gallon. The researcher can then calculate descriptive statistics indicating what the actual mileage of the Fiat 500 is based on the observations from the sample. The data in Case Exhibit 14.2-1 portray the results of the tests.

Questions

1. Formulate a statistical hypothesis appropriate for the consumer group's purpose.
2. Calculate the mean average miles per gallon. Compute the sample variance and sample standard deviation.
3. Construct the appropriate statistical test for your hypothesis, using a 0.05 significance level.
4. Use at least two different software packages to conduct the statistical test. For instance, use Excel and a statistics package like SPSS or JMP. Are the results the same? Comment.

CASE EXHIBIT 14.2-1 Miles per Gallon Information

Purchaser	Miles per Gallon	Purchaser	Miles per Gallon
1	30.9	13	27.0
2	24.5	14	26.7
3	31.2	15	31.0
4	28.7	16	23.5
5	35.1	17	29.4
6	29.0	18	26.3
7	28.8	19	27.5
8	23.1	20	28.2
9	31.0	21	28.4
10	30.2	22	29.1
11	28.4	23	21.9
12	29.3	24	30.9

Source: Case prepared by Mitch Griffin, Bradley University.

MaxyM/Shutterstock.com

Testing for Differences between Groups and for Predictive Relationships

LEARNING OUTCOMES

After studying this chapter, you should be able to:

1. Choose an appropriate statistic based on data characteristics
2. Compute a χ^2 statistic for cross-tab results
3. Use a *t*-test to compare a difference between two means
4. Conduct a one-way analysis of variance test (ANOVA)
5. Appreciate the practicality of modern statistical software packages
6. Understand how the General Linear Model (GLM) can predict a key dependent variable

Chapter Vignette:

What Color Is Cheap?

*A*n entire field exists called sensory marketing. With sensory marketing, the focus rests on how things that can be sensed by any of the 5 human senses affects consumer choice and experience. While sensory elements include touch, taste, smell, and sound, one of the most basic elements is sight, and in particular, sensations related to color. A host of research exists that examines how the change in color of a shopping environment, a package color, a background, or a font changes consumer perceptions. Package color and font color account for a great deal of research. Questions related to color often lend themselves to statistics applied in simple comparisons of frequency of choice or perceptions of value.[1]

For instance, if the market research question deals with what color of price presentation leads consumers to perceive greater savings, some simple comparisons of consumer perceptions will prove useful. In fact, results suggest that displaying the price in a bold, red font enhances consumer perception of savings. Research examining differences between consumers exposed to a product description with the price in red versus black font reveal a savings advantage for the red font:

By comparing the way consumers react to prices in different colors, like **$39.99** versus **$39.99**, the color of cheap appears to be red. A basic *t*-test can examine whether the difference is statistically meaningful. However, breaking things down a little further reveals

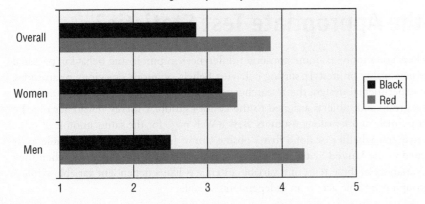

Savings Perceptions by Color

that the effect is just a little more complicated. The preference appears mostly due to men's perception of what is cheap. Thus, price color interacts with consumer gender, an effect that can be revealed with analysis of variance.

Does this mean that men are more likely to buy the product with the "red" price? When given the option to purchase the product promoted online with a red versus black price, men do not show a greater likelihood to purchase. A chi-square test can be used to compare the frequency with which men selected the product in red versus black.

Color affects other perceptions as well. Consumers tend to prefer environmentally conscious choices. When asked to choose the most environmentally conscious between products identical except for the package color, green tends to be chosen over others. The chart below shows how results from a choice experiment can be depicted.

The chart displays cross-tabulation results demonstrating a clear advantage for green packages. The experiment involves consumers making a selection between three alternative food products and then between three alternative detergents. A

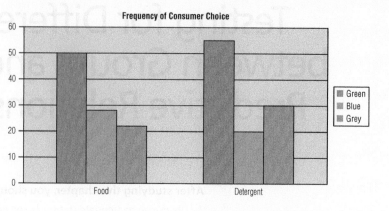

chi-square like those discussed in the chapter reveals that consumers tend to choose green when looking for environmentally conscious products. In fact, the ability for the sensed color to influence perceptions of environmental responsibility may be strong enough so that package color could lead to misperceptions. The likelihood of consumers making mistakes due to package color is a matter for more marketing research. In any event, basic statistics can address many research questions.

Introduction

The opening vignette illustrates very typical types of statistical comparisons conducted by marketing researchers. Earlier, we discussed scale measurement levels. Recall that only ratio level measures have absolute meaning. Thus, one shouldn't be surprised to find out that so much of meaning comes from comparing things. In other words, the saying "It's all relative" is not far off the mark. This chapter explains the mechanism underlying basic bivariate statistical analyses. **Bivariate statistics** means that two variables are involved. The chapter goes further toward its end and explains a more generalized format for building statistical models involving more than two variables.

bivariate statistics

Statistical analyses approaches that involve two variables.

What Is the Appropriate Test Statistic?

Marketing researchers commonly examine consumer differences in purchasing behavior, personal characteristics like personality or lifestyle, surfing behavior, beliefs, opinions, emotions, or attitudes. In the most basic experimental design, the researcher tests differences between subjects assigned to an experimental group and subjects assigned to the control group. A survey researcher may be interested in whether male and female consumers view a Web page for the same amount of time. A researcher also may test whether or not a firm's business units in Europe are as profitable as its business units located in the United States. Such tests are bivariate **tests of differences** when they involve only two variables. In these tests, one variable often acts like a dependent variable while a classification or grouping variable acts as an independent variable.

tests of differences

An investigation of a hypothesis stating that two (or more) groups differ with respect to measures of another variable.

Exhibit 15.1 on page 411 illustrates that the type of measurement, the nature of the research question or hypothesis, and the number of groups compared influence the statistical choice. Often researchers are interested in testing differences in mean scores between groups or in comparing the distribution showing how two groups' scores vary across response categories. We will focus our attention on these issues.[2] The rest of the chapter focuses on how to choose the right statistic for two-group comparisons and perform the corresponding test. Exhibit 15.1 below provides a frame of reference for the rest of the chapter by illustrating various possible comparisons involving observations of three golfers. In this case, samples of each's golf shots are analyzed statistically using an appropriate statistic.

More generally, choosing the right statistic boils down to what type and how many variables are involved in a particular research question or hypothesis. Commonly, hypotheses can be expressed either as tests of differences between groups or as relationships between variables. Research questions and hypotheses typically imply that variables are either dependent or independent. Dependent variables are those that respond to independent variables. In a causal research design, independent variables cause dependent variables.

EXHIBIT 15.1 Some Bivariate Hypotheses, Statistical Approach, and Results

Information	Golfer Dolly	Golfer Lori	Golfer Mel	Hypothesis or Research Question	Level of Measurement Involved	Statistic Used	Comment	Result
Average Driver Distance (meters)	135	150	185	Lori hits her drives further than Dolly	Golfer = Nominal; Drive Distance = Ratio	Independent Samples *t*-test to compare mean distance	Only data for Lori and Dolly are used	Supported (*t* = 2.27, p < .05; CI₉₅: 2.1–27.9)
s	30	25	30					
Average 7-Wood Distance (meters)	140	145	150	Mel hits her driver further than her 7-wood	Club = Nominal (7-wood or driver); 7-Wood Distance = Ratio	Paired-Samples *t*-test to compare mean distances for Mel	Only the data for Mel are used (std of diff = 30)	Supported (*t* = 6.39, df = 29, p < .05)
s	30	30	30					
Sample size (number of balls hit with each club)	35 drives 28 7-woods	35 drives 28 7-woods	30 drives 30 7-woods	A relationship exists between golfers and 7-wood distance	Golfer = Nominal; Distance = Ratio	One-Way ANOVA to compare means for the three groups	All data for 7-wood distance are used (MSE = 30)	Not supported (*F* = 0.83, ns)
Number of Drives in Fairway	6	25	11	Mel drives the ball more accurately than Dolly	Golfer = Nominal; Accuracy = Nominal (Right, Fairway, Left)	Cross-Tabulation with χ² Statistic	Resulting cross-tabulation table is 2 rows × 3 columns (rows = golfer and columns = accuracy (fairway, right, left)	Supported (χ² = 5.1, df = 2, p < .05), Mel is more likely to hit fairway, Mel hit 5 more fairways than Dolly.
Drives missing right of fairway	21	8	10	A relationship exists between golfers and accuracy	Golfer = Nominal; Accuracy = Nominal (Right, Fairway, Left)	Cross-Tabulation with χ² Statistic	Cross-tabulation is now 3 rows × 3 columns	Supported (χ² = 24.5, df = 4, p < 0.05), Lori is more likely to hit fairways than Mel, who is more likely to hit fairways than Dolly
Drives missing left of fairway	8	2	9					

The answers to two questions make finding an appropriate analytical approach easy:

1. How many independent variables (IV) and dependent variables (DV) are involved in the analysis?
2. What is the scale level of the independent and dependent variables involved in the analysis?

Exhibit 15.2 provides a useful guide in choosing a test. For instance, with one nominal IV and one nominal DV, the analyst employs cross-tabulation with a χ^2 test. When a single IV represents a nominal classification variable and the DV is interval, the analyst employs one-way ANOVA (an independent samples *t*-test can provide the same result if the classification variable contains only two categories). Notice that in several other cases the appropriate statistic would be a statistic that is beyond the scope of this chapter. Fortunately, the tests described in this chapter represent those commonly used in marketing research and account for a large bulk of analytics and inferential tests. Users may find it useful to refer back to this particular exhibit when trying to decide which statistical tool fits a given research question or hypothesis.

Market research reports very often involve cross-tabulation tables. For instance, consider an analyst asked to examine the following research question addressing the effectiveness of city taxi company marketing strategy aimed at *steering* riders away from ride-share back toward cabs:

When arriving to Miami International Airport, is a domestic vacationer more likely to choose a taxi than a ride-share (Uber, Lyft, Juno, etc.) relative to a vacationer from an international destination?

Jonathan Weiss/Shutterstock.com

EXHIBIT 15.2

How to Choose a Statistic?

What Best Describes Your Independent Variable(s)?	Which Category Best Fits Your Dependent Variable(s)?		
	A) 1 Nominal or Ordinal DV	B) 1 Interval or Ratio DV	C) More than 1 Related DV
1) 1 Nominal or Ordinal IV	Cross-Tabulation with χ^2	*t*-test (2 groups) or one-way ANOVA	Multivariate GLM
2) 2 or More Nominal or Ordinal Ivs	Cross-Tabulation with χ^2	n-way ANOVA	Multivariate GLM-ANOVA
3) 1 Interval or Ratio IV	*t*-test	Simple Regression or Correlation	Correlation or Multivariate Regression
4) More than 1 Interval or Ratio IV	Logistic Regression	Multiple Regression	Multivariate Regression Approaches
5) Mix of Less and More than Interval Ivs	Logistic Regression	Multiple Regression or GLM-ANCOVA	Multivariate GLM-MANCOVA

Color Guide:

Bivariate Statistic Discussed in Chapter

Statistical Tool Beyond Scope of this Chapter

Form of GLM Discussed later in this Chapter

Note: For illustration of statistical tools beyond scope of this Chapter, see *Chapters 17–23 in* Exploring Marketing Research: Cengage. Chart not intended to be exhaustive of all possibilities.

Most data-driven market research projects involve some type of statistical comparison. Even big data analysis depends on basic comparisons like those illustrated in the chapter. Chances are, you find yourself facing a project that involves some basic statistical analysis. Exhibits 15.1 and 15.2 should provide a useful guide to steer you toward an appropriate analysis for your data. Exhibit 15.1 provides some illustrations that may be analogous to your data in some way, and Exhibit 15.2 serves as a decision tool. Using 15.2, find the cell that best fits your situation. If for example, you need to analyze a nominal dependent variable, like selected extended warranty or not, by another nominal variable, such as whether the respondent lives in or outside of the city limits, you would locate cell A1 by answering the questions about your variables. Similarly, with an interval dependent variable and several interval independent variables, you would locate cell B4. A chart like this is useful to students working on a project, taking an exam, or to market researchers looking for a useful guide.

The research question involves a categorical (nominal) independent variable, a consumer's country in two categories (USA or International), and a categorical (nominal) dependent variable, type of ride hired (taxi or ride-share). Thus, the test would involve a single less-than interval dependent variable and a single less-than interval independent variable. The appropriate analytical tool for a statistical inference is a χ^2 test computed from the corresponding 2 (USA/International) × 2 (Taxi/Ride-share) cross-tabulation table. If the test involved choosing between three brands (Taxi/Uber/Lyft), the appropriate analytical tool remains cross-tabulation with a χ^2 test.

Cross-Tabulation Tables: The χ^2 Test for Goodness-of-Fit

Cross-tabulation was introduced in the previous chapter as a way of representing relationships between variables. Cross-tabulations are intuitive and easily understood. They also lend themselves well to graphical analysis using tools like bar charts. Cross-tabulation also can be very useful in big data analytics.

Two-variable cross-tabulations communicate analytical results easily and clearly. Thus, analysts use them very much. Cross-tabulations are much like tallying. When two variables exist, each with two categories, four cells result. Each cell contains the count of observations matching a particular combination of characteristics. The χ^2 distribution provides a means for testing the statistical significance of a contingency table. In other words, the bivariate χ^2 test examines the statistical significance of relationships between two less-than interval variables.

The χ^2 test for a contingency table involves comparing the observed frequencies (O_i) with the expected frequencies (E_i) in each cell of the table. The goodness- (or closeness-) of-fit of the observed distribution with the expected distribution is captured by this statistic. Remember that the convention is that the row variable is the independent variable and the column variable is the dependent variable. Although cross-tabulation is appropriate when both variables are nominal or ordinal, interval variables are used in a cross-tabulation if the response range is very small. Such is the case if a variable only takes on values of 1, 2, or 3, for example. Once a variable has more than four categories, a cross-tabulation table loses its advantage of simplicity in communicating the result.

To the Point

"You got to be careful if you don't know where you're going, because you might not get there."

—YOGI BERRA

We could use a χ^2 test to examine a research question asking whether or not Papa John's restaurants were more likely to be located in a stand-alone location or in a shopping center. The univariate (one-dimensional chi-square is 3.6, with 1 df) analysis suggests that the majority of the locations (60 percent) are stand-alone units:

Location	One-Way Frequency Table
Stand-alone	60 stores
Shopping Center	40 stores
Total	100 stores

The analyst, however, is presented with a more interesting question. Is there any effect of location on Papa John's restaurants' performance? Suppose the researcher analyzes the situation further by examining the following bivariate hypothesis:

Stand-alone locations are more likely to be profitable than are shopping center locations.

While the researcher is unable to obtain the dollar figures for the profitability of each unit, a press release indicates which Papa John's units were profitable and which were not. Cross-tabulation using a χ^2 test is appropriate (see Exhibit 15.2) because

- the independent variable (location) is less-than interval; and
- the dependent variable (profitable/not profitable) is less-than interval.

The data can be recorded in the following 2×2 contingency table:

Location	Profitable	Not Profitable	Total
Stand-alone	50	10	60
Shopping Center	15	25	40
Totals	65	35	100

Several conclusions appear evident. One, it seems that more stores are profitable than not profitable (65 versus 35, respectively). Secondly, more of the profitable restaurants seem to be in stand-alone locations (50 out of 65). However, is the difference strong enough to be statistically significant?

Is the observed difference between stand-alone and shopping center locations the result of chance variation due to random sampling? Is the discrepancy more than sampling variation? The χ^2 test allows us to conduct tests for significance in the analysis of the R × C contingency table (where R = row and C = column). The formula for the χ^2 statistic is the same as that for one-way frequency tables:

$$\chi^2 = \sum \frac{(O_i - E_i)^2}{E_i}$$

where

χ^2 = chi-square statistic

O_i = observed frequency in the ith cell

E_i = expected frequency in the ith cell

Again, as in a univariate χ^2 test, a frequency count of data that nominally identify or categorically rank groups is acceptable.

If the researcher's hypothesis is true, the frequencies shown in the contingency table should not resemble a random distribution. In other words, if location has no effect on profitability, the profitable and unprofitable stores would be spread evenly across the two location categories. This is really the logic of the test in that it compares the observed frequencies with the theoretical expected values for each cell.

After obtaining the observations for each cell, the expected values for each cell must be obtained. The expected values for each cell can be computed easily using this formula:

$$E_{ij} = \frac{R_i C_j}{n}$$

where

R_i = total observed frequency count in the ith row

C_j = total observed frequency count in the jth column

n = sample size

Only the total column and total row values are needed for this calculation. Thus, the calculation could be performed before the data are even tabulated. The following values represent the expected values for each cell:

Location	Profitable	Not Profitable	Total
Stand-alone	(60 × 65)/100 = 39	(60 × 35)/100 = 21	60
Shopping Center	(40 × 65)/100 = 26	(40 × 35)/100 = 14	40
Totals	65	35	100

Notice that the row and column totals are the same for both the observed and expected contingency matrices. These values also become useful in providing the substantive interpretation of the relationship. Variance from the expected value indicates a relationship.

The actual bivariate χ^2 test value is calculated in the same manner as for a univariate test. The one difference is that one finds the degrees of freedom by multiplying the number of rows minus one $(R - 1)$ times the number of columns minus one $(C - 1)$ rather than simply the number of cells minus one:

$$\chi^2 = \Sigma \frac{(O_i - E_i)^2}{E_i}$$

with $(R - 1)(C - 1)$ degrees of freedom. One can plug in the observed and expected values into the formula as follows:

$$\chi^2 = \frac{(50 - 39)^2}{39} + \frac{(10 - 21)^2}{21} + \frac{(15 - 26)^2}{26} + \frac{(25 - 14)^2}{14}$$
$$= 3.102 + 5.762 + 4.654 + 8.643$$
$$= 22.16$$

The number of degrees of freedom equals 1:

$$(R - 1)(C - 1) = (2 - 1)(2 - 1) = 1$$

From an Internet chi-square calculator (such as https://www.danielsoper.com/statcalc/calculator .aspx?id=11) or the chi-square distribution table on the companion website (www.cengagebrain.com), we see that the critical value at the 0.05 probability level with 1 *df* is 3.84. Thus, we are 95 percent confident that the observed values do not equal the expected values when the $\chi^2 = 3.84$ and we have 1 *df* as in a 2 × 2 contingency table. As the χ^2 becomes greater, we would have more confidence that the row variables are associated with systematic differences in the column variables. Before the analyst concludes support for the hypothesis, he or she must check and see that the deviations from the expected values are in the hypothesized direction. Since the difference between the stand-alone locations' observed profitability and the expected values for that cell are positive, the hypothesis is supported. Location is associated with profitability. Thus, testing the hypothesis involves two key steps:

1. Examine the statistical significance of the χ^2 resulting from the observed contingency table.
2. Examine whether the differences between the observed and expected values are consistent with the hypothesized prediction.

Proper use of the χ^2 test requires that each expected cell frequency (*E*) have a value of at least 5. If this sample size requirement is not met, the researcher should take a larger sample as a way of increasing the frequency.

JMP is a point-and-click statistics software package from SAS, one of the pioneers in statistical software. JMP makes a trial version available at **jmp.com**. The JMP screenshot on at the left shows a cross-tabulation result depicting whether the living arrangement of a university student influences the type of transportation the student uses to get to class. The mosaic frame at the top of the output depicts in colors the proportion of profitable locations (colored blue) for both the stand-alone and shopping center categories. The red areas indicate not profitable locations. The contingency table shows the cross-tabulation results. The top number in each cell shows the observed cell frequency count and the bottom numbers show the percentage of the column and row totals that this cell comprises. The numbers in the bottom of the output show the chi-square statistic result.

A separate graphic (p. 417) displays contingency results generated by the SPSS software. In this case, the results depict a tally of customers who received a promise to be paid $20 for visiting their carrier's phone store to see the newest Samsung smartphone. The column variable indicates that overall, 83 customers switched and 49 kept their old phones. Among the 83 who switched, 59 visited the AT&T store and 24 visited the Verizon store. In contrast, 41 of 65 customers who visited the Verizon store kept their old phone. The χ^2 of 36.96 (37.0) with 1 *df* ($p < 0.0001$) suggests the relationship between the brand of phone store visited and switching phones is significant.

● ● ● ● ● ● ●

Here is the cross-tabulation (contingency analysis) as computed by SAS JMP. The output includes a Mosaic Plot of the results in addition to the tabled values. Notice, the chi-square at the bottom is 22.16 with a *p*-value less than 0.001. The tabled values support the hypothesis that stand-alone locations are more profitable.

▼ Contingency Analysis of Performance By Location

▼ Mosaic Plot

▼ ▼ Contingency Table

	Performance		
Count Total % Col % Row %	NOT	PROFIT	Total
ALONE	10 10.00 28.57 16.67	50 50.00 76.92 83.33	60 60.00
SC	25 25.00 71.43 62.50	15 15.00 23.08 37.50	40 40.00
Total	35 35.00	65 65.00	100

Test	ChiSquare	Prob>ChiSq
Pearson	22.161	<.0001*

Test	Prob	Alternative Hypothesis
Left	<.0001*	Prob(Performance=PROFIT) is greater for Location=ALONE than SC
Right	1.0000	Prob(Performance=PROFIT) is greater for Location=SC than ALONE
2-Tail	<.0001*	Prob(Performance=PROFIT) is different across Location

The *t*-Test for Comparing Two Means

When a researcher needs to compare means for a variable grouped into two categories based on some less-than interval variable, a *t*-test is appropriate. One way to think about this is as testing the way a dichotomous (two-level) independent variable is associated with changes in a continuous dependent variable. Several variations of the *t*-test exist.

Doing a Cross-tab

Contingency analysis is simplified with statistical software. In this case, SAS JMP and SPSS provide very easy ways to perform the tests. In SAS JMP:

1. Click on Analyze.
2. Choose Fit Y by X.
3. Enter a nominal or ordinal independent variable as an X factor and a nominal or ordinal dependent variable as a Y factor. Click OK.
4. The results will appear in an output box. Contingency analysis can also be accessed through the consumer analysis function.

In SPSS:

1. Click on Analyze.
2. Choose Descriptive Statistics.
3. From the choices, select Cross-Tabs.
4. Enter a nominal or ordinal independent variable as in the Row box and a nominal or ordinal variable in the Column box.

5. Click on Statistics and choose Chi-Square. Then click Continue to close the Statistics box and then OK.
6. The results will appear in the output.

Courtesy of spss statistics 17.0

Example Contingency results from SPSS. These results point to significantly greater switching among AT&T store customers relative to Verizon store customers.

Carrier * Choice Crosstabulation

| | | | Choice | | |
			Switch	Keep	Total
Carrier	Verizon	Count	24	41	65
		% within Carrier	36.9%	63.1%	100.0%
		% within Choice	28.9%	83.7%	49.2%
		% of Total	18.2%	31.1%	49.2%
	ATT	Count	59	8	67
		% within Carrier	88.1%	11.9%	100.0%
		% within Choice	71.1%	16.3%	50.8%
		% of Total	44.7%	6.1%	50.8%
Total		Count	83	49	132
		% within Carrier	62.9%	37.1%	100.0%
		% within Choice	100.0%	100.0%	100.0%
		% of Total	62.9%	37.1%	100.0%

Chi-Square Tests

	Value	df	Asymp. Sig. (2-sided)	Exact Sig. (2-sided)	Exact Sig. (1-sided)
Pearson Chi-Square	36.962[a]	1	.000		
Continuity Correction[b]	34.803	1	.000		
Likelihood Ratio	39.515	1	.000		
Fisher's Exact Test				.000	.000
Linear-by-Linear Association	36.682	1	.000		
N of Valid Cases	132				

a. 0 cells (0.0%) have expected count less than 5. The minimum expected count is 24.13.

b. Computed only for a 2x2 table

Independent Samples *t*-Test

**independent samples
t-test**

A test for hypotheses stating
a difference in means of an
at-least interval dependent
variable divided into two
groups formed based on some
less-than interval classificatory
variable.

Most typically, the research analyst will apply the **independent samples *t*-test** to test for differences between means taken from two independent samples or groups. For example, if we measure the price for some designer jeans at 30 different retail stores, of which 15 are Internet-only stores (pure clicks) and 15 are bricks-and-clicks stores, we can test whether the prices are different based on store type with an independent samples *t*-test. The *t*-test for difference of means assumes the two samples are drawn from normal distributions and that the variances of the two populations are approximately equal (homoscedasticity). Another way to look at the test is that it uses a nominal or ordinal independent variable (that classifies things into two groups) to predict an interval or ratio dependent variable.

Independent Samples *t*-Test Calculation

The *t*-test actually tests whether the differences between two group means is zero. Not surprisingly, this idea can be expressed as the difference between two population means:

$$\mu_1 = \mu_2, \text{which is equivalent to,} \ \mu_1 - \mu_2 = 0$$

However, since this is inferential statistics, we test the idea by comparing two sample means:

$$\left(\bar{X}_1 - \bar{X}_2 = 0 \right)$$

A verbal expression of the formula for *t* is

$$t = \frac{\text{Sample mean 1} - \text{sample mean 2}}{\text{Variability of random means differences}}$$

Thus, the *t*-value is a ratio with information about the difference between means (provided by the sample) in the numerator and the standard error in the denominator. The question is whether the observed differences have occurred by chance alone. To calculate *t*, we use the following formula:

$$t = \frac{\bar{X}_1 - \bar{X}_2}{S_{\bar{X}_1 - \bar{X}_2}}$$

where

$\bar{X}_1$ = mean for group 1

$\bar{X}_2$ = mean for group 2

$S_{\bar{X}_1 - \bar{X}_2}$ = pooled or combined standard error of difference between means

**pooled estimate of the
standard error**

An estimate of the standard
error for a *t*-test of independent means that assumes the
variances of both groups are
equal.

A **pooled estimate of the standard error** is a better estimate of the standard error than one based on the variance from either sample. The pooled standard error of the difference between means of independent samples can be calculated using the following formula:

$$S_{\bar{X}_1 - \bar{X}_2} = \sqrt{ \left(\frac{(n_1 - 1)S_1^2 + (n_2 - 1)S_2^2}{n_1 + n_2 - 2} \right) \left(\frac{1}{n_1} + \frac{1}{n_2} \right) }$$

where

S_1^2 = variance of group 1

S_2^2 = variance of group 2

n_1 = sample size of group 1

n_2 = sample size of group 2

Take a look back at Exhibit 15.1. The hypothesis in the top row suggests that Lori hits her drives further than does Dolly. Here, the grouping or independent variable is golfer. The data involved in the calculation is summarized here:

Dolly	Lori
$\bar{X}_1 = 135$	$\bar{X}_2 = 150$
$S_1 = 30$	$S_2 = 25$
$n_1 = 35$	$n_2 = 35$

This particular *t*-test tests whether the difference in distance between Lori's and Dolly's drives is different than 0. A higher *t*-value is associated with a lower p-value. As the *t* gets higher and the p-value gets lower, the researcher has more confidence that the means are truly different. The relevant data computation is

$$S_{\bar{X}_1 - \bar{X}_2} = \sqrt{\left(\frac{(n_1 - 1)S_1^2 + (n_2 - 1)S_2^2}{n_1 + n_2 - 2}\right)\left(\frac{1}{n_1} + \frac{1}{n_2}\right)}$$

$$= \sqrt{\left(\frac{(35 - 1)(30)^2 + (35 - 1)(25)^2}{35 + 35 - 2}\right)\left(\frac{1}{35} + \frac{1}{35}\right)}$$

$$= 6.60$$

The calculation of the *t*-statistic is

$$t = \frac{\bar{X}_1 - \bar{X}_2}{S_{\bar{X}_1 - \bar{X}_2}}$$

$$t = \frac{135 - 150}{6.60}$$

$$= \frac{-15}{6.60}$$

$$= -2.27$$

This graphic shows an independent *t*-test conducted with SAS. Click on Analyze, choose ANOVA, select a classification variable and an analysis variable, and click Run.

Source: SAS Institute

Here, the *t*-value is negative only because Dolly's score, which is the lower of the two, is put into the first place. Reversing the order would create a *t*-value of $+2.27$. In a test of means between groups, degrees of freedom are calculated as follows:

$$df = n - k$$

where

$$n = n_1 + n_2$$
$$k = \text{number of groups}$$

In our example *df* equals 68 (35 + 35 − 2). If the 0.01 level of significance is selected, reference to the tabled values of the *t*-distribution (see www.cengagebrain.com or a Web-based p-value calculator) yields the critical *t*-value. The critical *t*-value of 2.75 must be surpassed by the observed *t*-value if the hypothesis test is to be statistically significant at the 0.01 level. The calculated value of *t*, 5.39, exceeds the critical value of *t* for statistical significance, so it is significant at $\alpha = 0.01$. The p-value is less than 0.01. In other words, this research shows that business students have significantly more positive attitudes toward business than do sociology students. The Research Snapshot on page 422 provides an overview of situations calling for an independent samples *t*-test.

The discussion above, strictly speaking, applies to comparisons where the population variances (and therefore standard deviations) are the same in each group. In most survey research, that assumption is safe. However, a slightly different formula exists for situations when the assumption of equal variances is not supported. That formula is expressed as:

$$t = \frac{\bar{X}_1 - \bar{X}_2}{\sqrt{\dfrac{S_1^2}{n_1} + \dfrac{S_2^2}{n_1}}}$$

Although this formula is simpler than the one for unequal variances, the computation of *df* for this test is complicated and not presented here. As you will see below, the value is provided by software routines that compute independent samples *t*-tests.

Practically Speaking

In practice, computer software is used to compute the *t*-test results. Exhibit 15.3 displays a typical *t*-test printout. These particular results examine the following research question:

> *RQ: Does religion relate to price sensitivity in restaurants?*

This question was addressed by asking a sample of 100 consumers to report how much they would be willing to pay per person for a nice dinner at one of the better restaurants in town. A research assistant showed each respondent a menu from the restaurant and then asked the respondent what amount per person he or she would pay (including tip) if dining there. The sample included 57 Catholics and 43 Protestants. Because no direction of the relationship is stated (no hypothesis is offered), a two-tailed test is appropriate. Although instructors still find some value in having students learn to perform the *t*-test calculations, practitioners almost always generate and interpret computer generated results today.

The interpretation of the *t*-test is made simple by focusing on either the p-value or the confidence interval and the group means. Here are the basic steps:

1. Examine the difference in means to find the "direction" of any difference. In this case, Catholics are willing to pay over $10 more than Protestants.
2. Compute or locate the computed *t*-test value. In this case, $t = 0.998$.
3. Find the p-value associated with this *t* and the corresponding degrees of freedom. Here, the p-value (two-tailed significance level) is 0.321. This suggests a 32 percent chance that the means are actually equal given the observed sample means. Assuming a 0.05 acceptable Type I error rate (α), the appropriate conclusion is that the means are not significantly different.

EXHIBIT 15.3 Independent Samples *t*-test Results

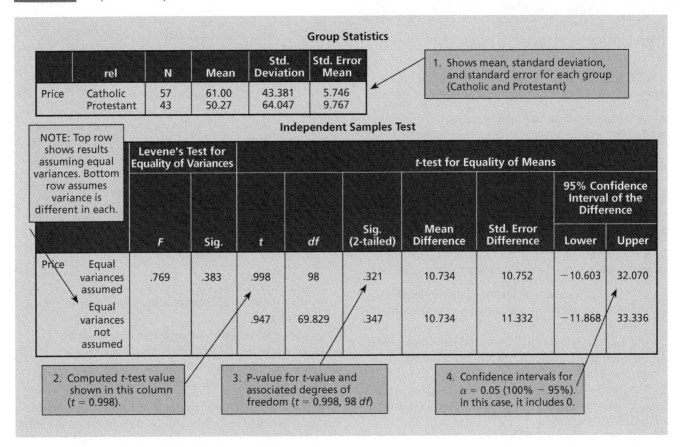

4. The difference can also be examined using the 95 percent confidence interval $(-10.603 < \bar{X}_1 - \bar{X}_2 < 32.070)$. Since the confidence interval includes 0, we lack sufficient confidence that the true difference between the population means is not really 0. The result suggests that the difference may well be 0.

Notice here that the results for the *t*-test are practically the same (.998 versus .947) whether equal or unequal variances are assumed even though the standard deviations appear different in each group. Consequently, the conclusions are the same using either assumption. In marketing research, we often deal with values that have variances close enough to assume equal variance. This isn't always the case in the physical sciences where variables may take on values of drastically different magnitude. Thus, the rule of thumb in survey research, particularly survey-based research, is to use the equal variance assumption.

Second, notice that even though the means appear to be not so close to each other, the statistical conclusion is that they are the same. The substantive conclusion is that Catholics and Protestants would not be expected to be willing to pay different prices. Why is it that the means do not appear to be similar, yet that is the conclusion? The answer lies in the variance. Respondents tended to provide very wide ranges of acceptable prices. Notice how large the standard deviations are compared to the mean for each group. Since the *t*-statistic is a function of the standard error, which is a function of the standard deviation, a lot of variance means a smaller *t*-value for any given observed difference. When this occurs, the researcher may wish to double-check for outliers. A small number of wild price estimates could be inflating the variance for one or both groups. An additional consideration would be to increase the sample size and test again.

Third, a *t*-test is used even though the sample size is greater than 30. Strictly speaking, a *Z*-test can test this difference. Researchers often employ a *t*-test even with large samples. As samples get larger, the *t*-test and *Z*-test tend to yield the same results. Although a *t*-test can be used with large samples, a *Z*-test should not be used with small samples. Also, a *Z*-test can be used in instances where the population variance is known ahead of time.

Marketing Expert "T-eeze"

When is an independent samples *t*-test appropriate? Once again, we can find out by answering some simple questions:

- Is the dependent variable interval or ratio?
- Can the dependent variable scores be grouped based upon some meaningful categorical variable?
- Does the grouping result in scores drawn from independent samples (hint: this means that one respondent's score on the DV does not influence another respondent's score on the DV)?
- Are two groups involved in the research question?

When the answer to all questions is yes, an independent samples *t*-test is appropriate. To conduct the test in SPSS:

1. Click on Analyze and then choose Compare Means.
2. From the options shown, choose independent samples *t*-test.
3. Move the dependent variable into the Test Variables box.
4. Place the independent variable into the Grouping Variable box.
5. Click on Define Groups and enter the two values of the independent variable to be compared (0 and 1 if dummy coded). Click Continue.
6. Then click OK and the results will appear in the output window.

In JMP:

1. Click on Analyze and then choose Fit Y by X.
2. Place the interval or ratio dependent variable in the Y Response box.

3. Place the less-than interval independent variable in the X Factor box.
4. Click on OK. Results will appear in an output box.
5. Click on the small red upside down triangle next to "Oneway Analysis…"
6. The *t*-test results will appear.

In Excel, *t*-test results can be obtained by going to formulas, then selecting "t.test" from the statistical functions and entering the location of the values for each group, respectively. The variables must be sorted by the values of the independent variable before the function can compute the values. A *t*-test also can be accessed from the Data Analysis add-in for Excel. After clicking on Data Analysis, choose *t*-test: Two Samples Assume Equal (or Unequal as may be appropriate) Variances and enter the data in the same manner.

Courtesy of spss statistics 17.0

Paired-Samples *t*-Test

What happens when a researcher needs to compare two means that are not from independent samples? Such might be the case when the same respondent provides two comparable scores; for instance, when a respondent rates both how much he or she is satisfied with Uber and how much he or she is satisfied with Lyft. Since the same person provided satisfaction scores for both brands, the assumption that the scores are independent is not realistic. Additionally, if one compares the prices that retailers charge online versus in stores using data from 50 bricks-and-clicks retailers (those with both online and in-store retail options), the samples cannot be considered independent because each pair of observations is from the same sampling unit.

A **paired-samples *t*-test** is appropriate in this situation. The idea behind the paired–samples and another *t*-test can be seen in the following computation:

paired-samples *t*-test

An appropriate test for comparing the scores of two interval variables drawn from related populations.

$$t = \frac{\bar{d}}{s_d / \sqrt{n}}$$

where $\bar{d}$ is the average difference between means, s_d is the standard deviation of the observed differences between means, and n is the number of observed differences between means. The test has degrees of freedom equal to one minus the total number of paired differences. Researchers also can compute the paired-samples t-test using statistical software. For example, using SPSS, the click-through sequence would be:

Analyze → Compare Means → Paired-Samples t-test

A dialog box then appears in which the "paired variables" should be entered. When a pairedsamples t-test is appropriate, the two numbers being compared are usually scored as separate variables.

Exhibit 15.4 displays a paired-samples t-test result. A sample of 208 amusement park consumers was asked to rate how satisfied they felt both before and after visiting a new water rapids ride. The research question is, "How does the new water attraction affect customer satisfaction?" Each respondent provided two satisfaction scores much as in a within-subjects experimental design. The bar chart depicts the means for each variable (satisfied1 is the score before and satisfied2 is the score after riding the new attraction). The t-test results suggest that average difference of -0.40 (rounded to 2 decimals) is associated with a t-value of -4.8. As can be seen using either the p-value ($p < 0.0001$) or the confidence interval ($-0.24 < \bar{d} < -0.56$), which does not include 0, the difference is significantly different from 0. Therefore, the results suggest that the new attraction may not have been such a good idea!

Management researchers have used paired-samples t-tests to examine the effect of downsizing on employee morale. For instance, job satisfaction for a sample of employees can be measured immediately after the downsizing. Some months later, employee satisfaction can be measured again. The difference between the satisfaction scores can be compared using a paired-samples t-test. Results suggest that the employee satisfaction scores increase within a few months of the downsizing as evidenced by statistically significant paired-samples t-values.[3]

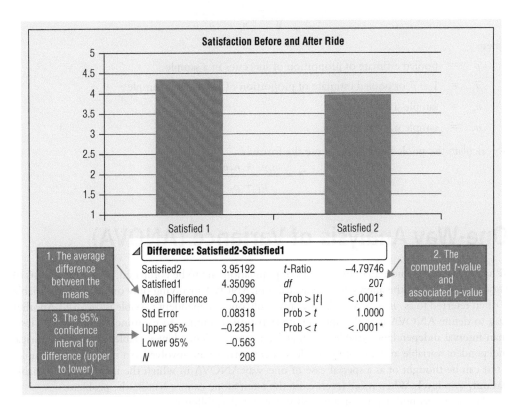

EXHIBIT **15.4**
Illustration of Paired-Samples
t-test Results

The Z-Test for Comparing Two Proportions

Z-test for differences of proportions

A technique used to test the hypothesis that proportions are significantly different for two independent samples or groups.

What type of statistical comparison can be made when the observed statistics are proportions? Suppose a researcher wishes to test the hypothesis that wholesalers in the northern and southern United States differ in the proportion of sales they make to discount retailers. Testing whether the population proportion for group 1 (p_1) equals the population proportion for group 2 (p_2) is conceptually the same as the t-test of two means. This section briefly describes **Z-test for differences of proportions**, which requires a sample size greater than 30.

The test is appropriate for a hypothesis of this form:

$$H_0 : \pi_1 = \pi_2$$

which may be restated as

$$H_0 : \pi_1 - \pi_2 = 0$$

Comparison of the observed sample proportions p_1 and p_2 allows the researcher to ask whether the difference between two *large* random samples occurred due to chance alone. The Z-test statistic can be computed using the following formula:

$$Z = \frac{(p_1 - p_2)(\pi_1 - \pi_2)}{S_{p_1 - p_2}}$$

where

p_1 = sample proportion of successes in group 1

p_2 = sample proportion of successes in group 2

$\pi_1 - \pi_2$ = hypothesized population proportion 1 minus hypothesized population proportion 2

$S_{p_1} - p_2$ = pooled estimate of the standard error of differences in proportions

To calculate the standard error of the differences in proportions, use the formula

$$S_{p_1 - p_2} = \sqrt{\overline{p}\,\overline{q}\left(\frac{1}{n_1} + \frac{1}{n_2}\right)}$$

where

$\overline{p}$ = pooled estimate of proportion of successes in a sample

$\overline{q}$ = $1 - \overline{p}$, or pooled estimate of proportion of failures in a sample

n_1 = sample size for group 1

n_2 = sample size for group 2

To calculate the pooled estimator, $\overline{p}$, use the formula

$$\overline{p} = \frac{n_1 p_1 + n_2 p_2}{n_1 + p_2}$$

One-Way Analysis of Variance (ANOVA)

analysis of variance (ANOVA)

Analysis involving the investigation of the effects of a treatment variable on an interval-scaled dependent variable—a hypothesis-testing technique to determine whether statistically significant differences in means occur between two or more groups.

When the means of more than two groups or populations are to be compared, one-way **analysis of variance (ANOVA)** is the appropriate statistical tool. ANOVA involving only one grouping variable is often referred to as *one-way* ANOVA because only one independent variable is involved. Another way to define ANOVA is as the appropriate statistical technique to examine the effect of a less-than interval independent variable on an at-least interval dependent variable. Thus, a categorical independent variable and a continuous dependent variable are involved. An independent samples t-test can be thought of as a special case of one-way ANOVA in which the independent variable has only two levels. When more levels exist, the t-test alone cannot handle the problem.

The statistical null hypothesis for ANOVA is stated as follows:

$$\mu_1 = \mu_2 = \mu_3 = \cdots = \mu_k$$

The symbol k is the number of groups or categories for an independent variable. In other words, all group means are equal. The substantive hypothesis tested in ANOVA is

At least one group mean is not equal to another group mean.

As the term *analysis of variance* suggests, the problem requires comparing variances to make inferences about the means.

Consider how a sample of prices for a notebook computer could be explained by the source of the price. Specifically, the independent variable could be thought of as "source," meaning the advertised price was for a website purchase or for an instore purchase. The dependent variable is price. Since only two groups exist for the independent variable, either an independent samples t-test or one-way ANOVA could be used. The results would be identical.

However, assume that source involved three group levels. Prices would now be compared based on whether the retailer was a bricks-and-clicks retailer (multichannel, meaning real and virtual stores), a bricks-only store (only physical stores) or a clicks-only retailer (virtual or Internet stores only). One-way ANOVA would be the choice for this analysis.

Simple Illustration of ANOVA

ANOVA's logic is fairly simple. Look at the following data table describing how much coffee respondents report drinking each day based on which shift they work (GY stands for Graveyard shift, which is typically from about 5:00 p.m. until about 1:00 a.m.).

Day	1
Day	3
Day	4
Day	0
Day	2
GY	7
GY	2
GY	1
GY	6
Night	6
Night	8
Night	3
Night	7
Night	6

The following table displays the means for each group and the overall mean:

Shift	Mean	Std. Deviation	N
Day	2.00	1.58	5
GY	4.00	2.94	4
Night	6.00	1.87	5
Total	4.00	2.63	14

Exhibit 15.5 plots each observation with a bar. The long blue vertical line illustrates the total range of observations. The lowest is 0 cups and the highest is 8 cups of coffee for a range of 8. The overall mean is 4 cups. Each group mean is shown with a different colored line that matches the bars corresponding to the group. The day shift averages 2 cups of coffee a day, the graveyard shift 4 cups, and the night shift 6 cups of coffee per day.

Here is the basic idea of ANOVA. Look at the dark double-headed arrow in Exhibit 15.5. This line represents the range of the differences between group means. In this case, the lowest mean is 2 cups and the highest mean is 6 cups. Thus, the blue vertical line corresponds to the total variation (range) in the data and the thick double-headed black vertical line corresponds to the variance

EXHIBIT 15.5 Illustration of ANOVA Logic

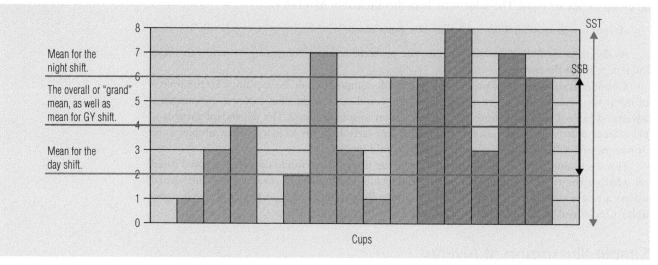

accounted for by the group differences. As the thick black line accounts for more of the total variance, then the ANOVA model suggests that the group means are not all the same, and in particular, not all the same as the overall mean. This also means that the independent variable, in this case work shift, explains the dependent variable. Here, the results suggest that knowing when someone works explains how much coffee they drink. Night-shift workers drink the most coffee.

Partitioning Variance in ANOVA

The responses to any continuous variable contain a certain amount of variance. We have been discussing variable comparisons created by separating observations into groups. ANOVA works by breaking the total variance in a response down into components that are either due to some grouping variable or due to variance within groups.

Total Variability

An implicit question with the use of ANOVA is, "How can the dependent variable best be predicted?" Without any additional information, the error in predicting an observation is minimized by choosing the central tendency, or mean for an interval variable. For the coffee example, if no information was available about the work shift of each respondent, the best guess for coffee drinking consumption would be four cups. The total error (or variability) that would result from using the **grand mean**, meaning the mean over all observations, to predict all values can be thought of as:

grand mean

The mean of a variable over all observations.

$$\text{SST} = \text{Total of (observed value} - \text{grand mean)}^2 = \sum_{t=1}^{n}(x_i - \overline{\overline{x}})$$

Although the term *error* is used, this really represents how much total variation exists among the measures.

Using the first observation, the error of observation would be

$$(1 \text{ cup} - 4 \text{ cups})^2 = 9$$

The same squared error could be computed for each observation and these squared errors totaled to give SST.

Between-Groups Variance

ANOVA tests whether "grouping" observations explains variance in the dependent variable. In Exhibit 15.5, the three colors reflect three levels of the independent variable, work shift. Given this additional information about which shift a respondent works, the prediction changes. Now, instead of guessing the grand mean, the group mean would be used. So, once we know that someone works the day shift, the prediction would be that he or she consumes 2 cups of coffee per day. Similarly, the graveyard and night-shift predictions would be 4 and 6 cups, respectively. Thus, the **between-groups variance** can be found by taking the total sum of the weighted difference (weighted by the sample size of each group or n_g) between group means and the overall mean as shown:

between-groups variance

The sum of differences between the group means and the grand mean summed over all groups for a given set of observations.

$$SSB = \text{Total of } n_{group}(\text{group mean} - \text{grand mean})^2$$

The weighting factor (n_{group}) is the specific group sample size. Let's consider the first observation once again. Since this observation is in the day shift, we predict 2 cups of coffee will be consumed. Looking at the day shift group observations in Exhibit 15.5, the new error in prediction would be

$$(2 \text{ cups} - 4 \text{ cups})^2 = (-2)^2 = 4$$

The error in prediction has been reduced from 3 using the grand mean to 2 using the group mean. This squared difference would be weighted by the group sample size of 5, to yield a contribution to SSB of 20.

Next, the same process could be followed for the other groups yielding two more contributions to SSB. Because the graveyard shift group mean is the same as the grand mean, that group's contribution to SSB is 0. Notice that the night-shift group mean is also 2 different than the grand mean, like the day shift, so this group's contribution to SSB is likewise 20. The total SSB then represents the variation explained by the experimental or independent variable. In this case, total SSB is 40. The reader may look at the statistical results shown in Exhibit 15.6 to find this value in the Sum of Squares column.

EXHIBIT 15.6 Interpreting ANOVA

Tests of Between-Subjects Effects   (Dependent Variable: Coffee)

Source	Type III Sum of Squares	df	Mean Square	F	Sig.
Corrected Model	40.000[a]	2	20.000	4.400	.039
Intercept	221.538	1	221.538	48.738	.000
Shift	40.000	2	20.000	4.400	.039
Error	50.000	11	4.545		
Total	314.000	14			

[a]R Squared = .444 (Adjusted R Squared = .343)

1. This row shows overall F-value testing whether all group means are equal. The sums of squares column calculates the SST, SSE, and SSB (shift row).

Shift	Mean	Std. Error	95% Confidence Interval	
			Lower Bound	Upper Bound
Day	2.000	.953	2.099	4.099
GY	4.000	1.066	1.654	6.346
Night	6.000	.953	3.901	8.099

2. This column shows the group means for each level of the independent variable.

Within-Group Error

within-group error or variance

The sum of the differences between observed values and the group mean for a given set of observations; also known as total error variance.

Finally, error within each group would remain. Whereas the group means explain the variation between the total mean and the group mean, the distance from the group mean and each individual observation remains unexplained. This distance is called **within-group error or variance**. The values for each observation can be found by

$$SSE = \text{Total of (Observed Mean} - \text{Group Mean)}^2 = \sum_{i=1}^{n}(x_i - \overline{x}_g)^2$$

Again, looking at the first observation, the SSE component would be

$$SSE = (1\,\text{cup} - 2\,\text{cups})^2 = 1\,\text{cup}$$

This process could be computed for all observations and then totaled. The result would be the total error variance—a name sometimes used to refer to SSE since it is variability not accounted for by the group means. These three components are used in determining how well an ANOVA model explains a dependent variable.

The *F*-Test

F-test

A procedure used to determine whether there is more variability in the scores of one sample than in the scores of another sample.

The **F-test** is the key statistical test for an ANOVA model. The *F*-test determines whether there is more variability in the scores of one sample than in the scores of another sample. The key question is whether the two sample variances are different from each other or whether they are from the same population. Thus, the test breaks down the variance in a total sample and illustrates why ANOVA is *analysis of variance*.

The *F*-statistic (or *F*-ratio) can be obtained by taking the larger sample variance and dividing by the smaller sample variance. Using tabled values of the *F*-distribution (see www.cengagebrain .com) is much like using the tables of the *Z*- and *t*-distributions that we have previously examined. These tables portray the *F*-distribution, which is a probability distribution of the ratios of sample variances. These tables indicate that the distribution of *F* is actually a family of distributions that changes quite drastically with changes in sample sizes. Thus, degrees of freedom must be specified. Inspection of an *F*-table allows the researcher to determine the probability of finding an *F* as large as a calculated *F*.

Using Variance Components to Compute *F*-Ratios

In ANOVA, the basic consideration for the *F*-test is identifying the relative size of variance components. The three forms of variation described briefly earlier are:

1. SSE—variation of scores due to random error or within-group variance due to individual differences from the group mean. This is the error of prediction.
2. SSB—systematic variation of scores between groups due to manipulation of an experimental variable or group classifications of a measured independent variable or between-group variance.
3. SST—the total observed variation across all groups and individual observations.

The Research Snapshot on page 430 provides additional insight into the mechanics of ANOVA. In addition, the Web resources provided with the text provide some illustrations of how to perform an analysis like this using SPSS, JMP, SAS, or EXCEL.

Thus, we can partition total variability into *within-group variance* and *between-group variance*. The *F*-distribution is a function of the ratio of these two sources of variances:

$$F = f\left(\frac{SSB}{SSE}\right)$$

A larger ratio of variance between groups to variance within groups implies a greater value of *F*. If the *F*-value is large, the results are likely to be statistically significant.

A Different but Equivalent Representation

F also can be thought of as a function of the between-group variance and total variance.

$$F = f\left(\frac{SSB}{SST - SSB}\right)$$

In this sense, the ratio of the thick black line to the blue line representing the total range of data presents the basic idea of the F-value.

Practically Speaking

Exhibit 15.6 displays the ANOVA result for the coffee-drinking example. Again, today, an analyst will use software to get answers even for a small problem like this. The days of hand calculations are gone. Even though this example presents a small problem, one-way ANOVA models with more observations or levels are interpreted in the same way.

In interpreting results, the first thing to check is whether the overall model F is significant (see Exhibit 15.6). In this case, the computed $F = 4.40$ with 2 and 11 degrees of freedom. The p-value associated with this value is 0.039. Tables of F-values also can be found online (http://www.socr.ucla.edu/Applets.dir/F_Table.html, for example or at cengagebrain.com). Thus, we have high confidence

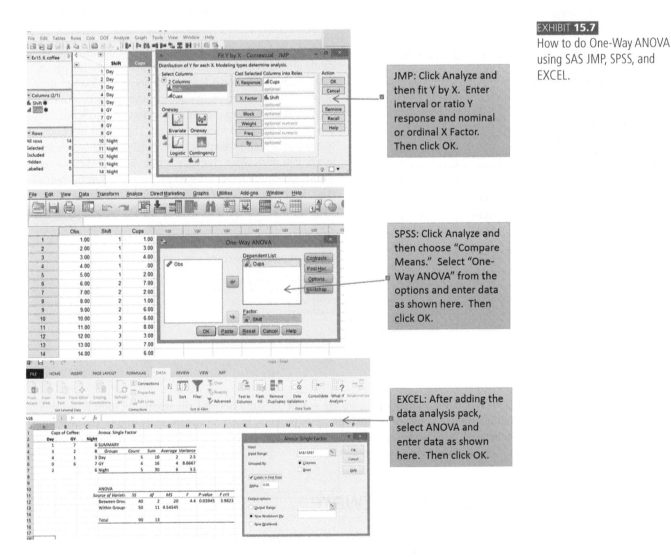

EXHIBIT 15.7
How to do One-Way ANOVA using SAS JMP, SPSS, and EXCEL.

JMP: Click Analyze and then fit Y by X. Enter interval or ratio Y response and nominal or ordinal X Factor. Then click OK.

SPSS: Click Analyze and then choose "Compare Means." Select "One-Way ANOVA" from the options and enter data as shown here. Then click OK.

EXCEL: After adding the data analysis pack, select ANOVA and enter data as shown here. Then click OK.

Is the Price Right?

Marketing researchers often find themselves in situations where they would like to test relationships between a combination of nominal and continuous variables with some continuous dependent variable.

Some marketing researchers recently sought to explore combinations of wine label characteristics and the way they influence how much a consumer is willing to pay. The research questions involved whether customers are willing to pay (WTP) a higher price when (a) the label describes the wine with a technical versus casual description (EXP1), (b) the wine is from France or Oregon (EXP2), and (c) when the consumer's wine knowledge varies ($Q5_2$). Consumers tasted a wine (actually in all cases they tasted the same wine) and were shown the bottle. The label contained the two experimental variables: the description of the wine (either technical or casual) and the origin of the wine (France/Oregon). Wine knowledge was assessed based on the results of a 100-point test assessing how knowledgeable each respondent was about wine. The model can be expressed as:

$$WTP = \bar{\bar{Y}}_{WTP} + \Delta EXP1 + \Delta EXP2 + \Delta EXP1 \times \Delta EXP2 + BQ5_2$$

Univariate Analysis of Variance

Tests of Between-Subjects Effects

Dependent Variable: WTP

Source	Type III Sum of Squares	df	Mean Square	F	Sig.
Corrected Model	2714.807[a]	4	678.702	4.239	.003
Intercept	27818.172	1	27818.172	173.762	.000
$Q5_2$	558.065	1	558.065	3.486	.065
Exp1	39.563	1	39.563	.247	.620
Exp2	1233.614	1	1233.614	7.706	.007
Exp1 × Exp2	766.289	1	766.289	4.786	.031
Error	16009.383	100	160.094		
Total	96353.000	105			
Corrected Total	18724.190	104			

a. R Squared =.145 (Adjusted R Squared = .111)

Means by Condition

		Description		
		Casual	Technical	Overall
Place of Origin	Oregon	22.04	24.69	23.37
	France	33.59	26.89	30.24
	Overall	27.82	25.8	26.8

The researchers examine the research question using a GLM approach within SPSS. They agree that a 0.1 Type I error rate is acceptable in this analysis. After opening the data file, the researcher chooses Analyze, General Linear Model, then Univariate. After entering the correct variables the program produces the results:

$$WTP = \bar{\bar{Y}}_{WTP} + \Delta EXP1 + \Delta EXP2 + \Delta EXP1 \times \Delta EXP2 + BQ5_2$$

The ANOVA table suggests that the model explains a significant amount of variance in WTP. The wine's origin significantly affects WTP. Subjects are willing to pay an average of $30.50 when the wine is French but only $23.53 when they believe it is from Oregon. In addition, the interaction between origin and the presentation of information is significant as seen by the F of 4.86 for Exp1× Exp2. The means by condition suggests that presenting a technical description results in a higher price when the wine is from Oregon ($25.74 versus $21.32) but a lower price when the wine is from France ($33.94 versus $27.06). Finally, the parameter estimate (not shown here) for wine knowledge is −0.09 suggesting that for every point higher in wine knowledge, the subjects are willing to pay 9 cents less for the wine. As a decision maker for a wine company, how could you use this information?

Source: See Moulard, J. G., B. J.Babin, and M. Griffin (2015), "How Aspects of a Place Affect a Wine's Authenticity and Value Perception: The Role Country of Origin and Technical Terroir," *International Journal of Wine Business Research*, forthcoming.

in concluding that the group means are not all the same. Second, the researcher must remember to examine the actual means for each group to properly interpret the result. Doing so, the conclusion reached is that the night-shift people drink the most coffee, followed by the graveyard-shift workers, and then lastly, the day-shift workers.

Statistical Software

Businesses increasingly rely on data-driven marketing analytics. The marketing research analyst has access to statistical software that facilitates statistical analysis by quickly and easily providing results for *t*-tests, cross-tabulations, ANOVA, GLM, and more. Some data mining routines even automate some of this analysis. Some of the most common statistical software packages are SPSS, owned by IBM, SAS, and its user - friendly product called JMP (a free trial is available at jmp.com). Excel includes basic data analysis functions and an add-in data analysis function that contains procedures like ANOVA. Basic JMP components also become available on the Excel toolbar if both packages are installed on a computer. Most universities provide students with access to one or more of these software packages. Aside from trial versions available for students, SAS makes its basic statistics package available for free to university students and faculty. SAS can be accessed through Amazon's Web Services. A host of other options are available on the Web including freeware like R (r-project. org). R is not new at all but is now gaining in popularity because it is available for free, and because of its open-source nature, niche users may find a program specific to their needs. However, few would describe R as a user-friendly alternative, particularly for beginning researchers. Marketing researchers continue to widely use packages like SPSS, SAS, EXCEL, and JMP, because they offer an easy-to-use interface and a standardized approach to statistics.

General Linear Model

Multivariate dependence techniques are variants of the **general linear model (GLM)**. Simply, the GLM is a way of modeling some process based on how different variables cause fluctuations from the average dependent variable. Fluctuations can come in the form of group means that differ from the overall mean as is in ANOVA or in the form of a significant slope coefficient as in regression.

general linear model (GLM)

A way of explaining and predicting a dependent variable based on fluctuations (variation) from its mean. The fluctuations are due to changes in independent variables.

GLM Equation

The basic idea can be thought of as follows:

$$\hat{Y}_i = \bar{\bar{Y}} + \Delta X + \Delta F + \Delta XF$$

Here, $\bar{\bar{Y}}$ represents a constant, which can be thought of as the overall mean of the dependent variable, ΔX and ΔF represent changes due to main effect independent variables (such as experimental variables) and blocking independent variables (such as covariates or grouping variables), respectively, and ΔXF represents the change due to the combination (interaction effect) of those variables. Realize that Y_i in this case could represent multiple dependent variables, just as X and F could represent multiple independent variables. This form is an ANOVA representation. An Analysis of Covariance (ANCOVA) representation would add a continuous covariate (X_c):

$$\hat{Y}_i = \bar{\bar{Y}} + \Delta X + \Delta F + \Delta XF + BXc$$

B is a regression coefficient as described later.

Regression analysis and n-way ANOVA represent common forms that the GLM can take. SAS and SPSS both contain programs specifically referred to by GLM. They are particularly useful in analyzing data from experiments but GLM can also be used to produce regression results.

Regression Analysis

Simple regression investigates a *straight-line relationship* of the type

$$Y = \alpha + \beta X$$

where Y is a continuous dependent variable and X is an independent variable that is usually continuous, although a dichotomous nominal or ordinal variable can be included in the form of a dummy variable. Alpha (α) and beta (β) are two parameters that must be estimated so that the equation best represents a given set of data. These two parameters determine the height of the regression line and the angle of the line relative to horizontal. When these parameters change, the line changes. Together, they represent the changes from the overall mean of the dependent variable for a regression form of the GLM. Regression techniques have the job of estimating values for these parameters that make the line *fit* the observations the best.

The result is simply a linear equation, or the equation for a line, just as in basic algebra! Parameter α represents the Y intercept (where the line crosses the γ-axis) and β is the slope coefficient. The slope is the change in Y associated with a change of one unit in X. Slope may also be thought of as rise over run. That is, how much Y rises (or falls, if negative) for every one unit change in the x-axis. A mathematical estimation of the line completes the regression progress by providing estimates for the intercept (b_0) and slope coefficient (b_1):

$$Y_i = b_0 + b_1 X_1 + e_i$$

Interpreting Multiple Regression Analysis

Multiple regression analysis

An analysis of association in which the effects of two or more independent variables on a single, interval-scaled dependent variable are investigated simultaneously.

Multiple regression analysis is an extension of simple regression analysis allowing a metric dependent variable to be predicted by multiple independent variables. Thus, one dependent variable is explained by more than one independent variable. When trying to explain sales, plausible independent variables include prices, economic factors, advertising intensity, and consumers' incomes in the area. A simple regression equation can be expanded to represent multiple regression analysis where each X is a different independent variable and each b is the slope coefficient corresponding to the respective variable:

$$Y_i = b_0 + b_1 X_1 + b_2 X_2 + b_3 X_3 + \cdots + b_n X_n + e_i$$

Parameter Estimate Choices

The estimates for α and β are the key to regression analysis. In most business research, the estimate of β is most important. The explanatory power of regression rests with β because this is where the direction and strength of the relationship between the independent and dependent variable is explained. A Y-intercept term is sometimes referred to as a constant because α represents a fixed point. An estimated slope coefficient is sometimes referred to as a regression weight, regression coefficient, parameter estimate, or sometimes even as a *path* estimate. The term *path* estimate is a descriptive term adapted because of the way hypothesized causal relationships are often represented in diagrams:

For all practical purposes, these terms are used interchangeably. Parameter estimates can be presented in either raw or standardized form. One potential problem with raw parameter estimates is due to the fact that, like covariance values, they reflect the measurement scale range. So, if a simple regression involved distance measured with miles, very small parameter estimates may indicate a strong relationship. In contrast, if the very same distance is measured with centimeters, a very large parameter estimate would be needed to indicate a strong relationship. Generally, the raw slope coefficient is abbreviated with a small letter b.

standardized regression coefficient (β)

The estimated coefficient indicating the strength of relationship between an independent variable and dependent variable expressed on a standardized scale where higher absolute values indicate stronger relationships (range is from -1 to $+1$).

Researchers often explain regression results by referring to a **standardized regression coefficient (β)**. A standardized regression coefficient, like a correlation coefficient, provides a common metric allowing regression coefficients for different variables to be compared to one another no matter what the original scale range may have been. Due to the mathematics involved in standardization, the standardized Y-intercept term is always 0.

Researchers use shorthand to label regression coefficients as either "raw" or "standardized." The most common shorthand is as follows:

- $\mathbf{B}_0$ or $\boldsymbol{b}_0$—raw (unstandardized) Y-intercept term; an estimate of what was referred to as α earlier.
- $\mathbf{B}_1$ or $\boldsymbol{b}_1$—raw regression coefficient or estimate.
- $\boldsymbol{\beta}_1$—standardized regression coefficients.

The bottom line is that when the actual units of measurement are the focus of analysis, such as might be the case in trying to forecast sales during some period, raw (unstandardized) coefficients are most appropriate. When the goal is explanation of some outcome by examining a series of relationships, standardized regression coefficients are more appropriate because they allow for the size of the relationship for each independent variable to be compared directly. A β of 0.6 is a stronger relationship than a β of 0.2. With unstandardized coefficients, this comparison cannot be made directly.

Steps in Interpreting a Multiple Regression Model

Multiple regression models often are used to test some proposed theoretical model. For instance, a researcher may be asked to develop and test a model explaining business unit performance. Why do some business units outperform others? Multiple regression models can be interpreted using these steps:

1. Examine the model F-test. If the test result is not significant, the model should be dismissed and there is no need to proceed to further steps.
2. Examine the individual statistical tests for each parameter estimate. Independent variables with significant results can be considered a significant explanatory variable.
3. Examine the model R^2. No cutoff values exist that can distinguish an acceptable R^2 across all regression models. However, the absolute value of R^2 is more of interest when the researcher is more interested in prediction than explanation. In other words, the regression is run for pure forecasting purposes. When the model is more oriented toward explaining which variables are most important in determining (or not determining) the dependent variable, cutoff values for the model R^2 are inappropriate.
4. A next step would be to diagnose multicollinearity. Simply put, this is the extent to which the independent variables are redundant. A detailed discussion of this topic is beyond the scope of this particular chapter. However, a simple check for problems can be obtained by taking a look at the Variance Inflation Factors (VIF). Most statistical packages allow these to be computed. VIFs of between 1 and 2 are generally not indicative of serious problems with multicollinearity. As they become larger, the results become more susceptible to interpretation problems because of overlap in the independent variables.

Exhibit 15.8 illustrates this step-by-step process using regression results from an SPSS output an SPSS. The regression model explains marketing employees' bonuses for a Fortune 500 company. The independent variables are Tools (a dummy variable representing whether the employee uses a new social network mining tool coded 1 if the employee installed the software and 0 if not), Hours (number of hours working in field per week), and Exp (experience in the industry in years). In this case, the researcher is using a maximum acceptable Type I error rate of 0.05. The conclusion reached from this analysis is that hours spent in the field pays off in increased bonus amounts ($\beta = 0.69, \text{p} < 0.05$). Multiple regression represents a generalized form of the GLM. The steps for interpreting different variations of the GLM generally follow the same sequence. The versatility of the GLM makes it an essential tool for marketing research.[4]

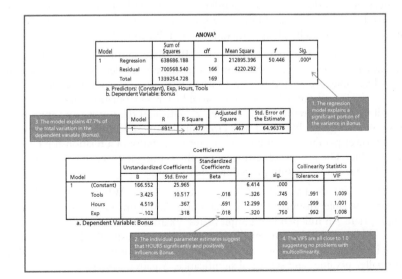

EXHIBIT 15.8

Illustration of Steps for Interpreting a Multiple Regression Model

TIPS OF THE TRADE

- Cross-tabulations are widely applied in market research reports and presentations.
  - Cross-tabs can be very useful in big data analysis exploring data for useful relationships.
  - Cross-tabulations are appropriate for research questions involving predictions of categorical dependent variables using categorical independent variables.
  - A chi-squared test helps establish the extent of relationship between variables but the cross-tab table shows the nature of any relationship. Both must be interpreted.
  - When more than four categories exist, cross-tabulation tables can become difficult to present clearly.
  - Independent variables are placed in rows and dependent variables are placed in columns.
- A *t*-test can be used to compare means.

- An independent samples *t*-test predicts a continuous (interval or ratio) dependent variable with a categorical (nominal or ordinal) independent (grouping) variable.
- A paired-samples *t*-test compares means from two different responses from the same sampling unit. Therefore, the sampling is dependent.
- A one-way ANOVA extends the concept of an independent samples *t*-test to more than two groups.
- Simple hand calculations can be useful in learning what statistical procedures actually do. However, in conducting actual tests, take advantage of computer software whenever permissible.
- The GLM represents a versatile model useful in examining a wide range of marketing issues. In particular, the ANOVA and regression forms are used widely.

© George Doyle & Ciaran Griffin

:: SUMMARY

1. Choose an appropriate statistic based on data characteristics. A skilled researcher can quickly determine the appropriate statistic for a given research question. In this chapter, we learned that if the researcher can distinguish independent from dependent variables, know how many of each are involved in the analysis, and know the level of scale measurement for each, choosing the right statistic becomes easy. The chapter includes an exhibit to make statistic selection easy.

2. Compute a χ^2 statistic for cross-tab results. Bivariate statistical techniques analyze scores on two variables at a time. A cross-tabulation is a useful way of depicting and analyzing the way two categorical variables are related to one another. For instance, a nominal independent variable may be used to predict a nominal dependent variable. Cross-tabulations are very useful and lend themselves well to depicting results in charts. The χ^2 statistic is the test statistic appropriate for testing relationships among variables used in a cross-tabulation table. Higher χ^2 values are generally associated with lower p-values and therefore greater probability of a relationship between the row and column variables. The process of testing a hypothesis using a χ^2 statistic is similar in concept to practically all the hypotheses testing procedures that follow.

3. Use a *t*-test to compare a difference between two means. When a researcher needs to compare means for a variable grouped into two categories based on some less-than interval variable, a *t*-test is appropriate. An independent samples *t*-test examines whether a dependent variable like price differs based on a grouping variable like biological sex. Statistically, the test examines whether the difference between the mean for men and women is different from 0. Larger *t*-values are associated with smaller p-values and statistical significance. A paired-samples *t*-test examines whether the means from two variables that are not independent are different. A common situation calling for this test is when the two observations are from the same respondent or sampling unit. A simple before-and-after test calls for a paired-samples t-test so long as the dependent variable is continuous.

4. Conduct a one-way analysis of variance test (ANOVA). ANOVA is the appropriate statistical technique to examine the effect of a less-than interval independent variable on an at-least interval dependent variable. Conceptually, ANOVA partitions the total variability into three types: total variation, between-group variation, and within-group variation. As the explained variance represented by SSB becomes larger relative to SSE or SST, the ANOVA model is more likely to be significant, indicating that at least one group mean is different from another group mean.

5. Appreciate the practicality of modern statistical software packages. Hand calculations using a simple calculator can sometimes be a good way for getting the feel of exactly what some statistic is doing; however, even small applications are usually better performed with the help of some statistical software whether it be Excel, SPSS, SAS, JMP, or some other package. This saves time and helps reduce mathematical errors. Almost all commercial statistical software provide point and click convenience.

6. Understand how the General Linear Model (GLM) can predict a key dependent variable. The General Linear Model is a widely used way of representing statistical effects as systematic deviations from the population mean. ANOVA and Linear Regression are among the most common forms of the GLM. The results should be analyzed based on how well they account for variation in the dependent variable and based on what specific independent variables relate significantly to the dependent variable.

:: KEY TERMS AND CONCEPTS

bivariate statistics, *410*
analysis of variance (ANOVA), *424*
between-groups variance, *427*
F-test, *428*
general linear model (GLM), *431*
grand mean, *426*
independent samples *t*-test, *418*

multiple regression analysis, *432*
paired-samples *t*-test, *422*
pooled estimate of the standard error, *418*
standardized regression coefficient (β), *432*
tests of differences, *410*
within-group error or variance, *428*
Z-test for differences of proportions, *424*

:: QUESTIONS FOR REVIEW AND CRITICAL THINKING

1. What bivariate statistical test of differences is appropriate in the following situations?
   a. Comparison of average campaign contributions (in \$) of Democrats, Republicans, and Independents.
   b. Advertising managers and brand managers have responded "Yes," "No," or "Not sure" to an attitude question. The advertising and brand managers' responses are to be compared.
   c. One-half of a sample received an incentive in a mail survey while the other half did not. A comparison of response rates is desired.
   d. A researcher believes coupon links pushed through Facebook.com will generate more sales than coupon links pushed through Twitter.com.
   e. A manager wishes to compare the job performance of a salesperson before ethics training with the performance of that same salesperson after ethics training.

2. Perform a χ^2 test on the following data (hint: set up a spreadsheet to perform the calculations as a good way of learning what the test really does):
   a. Do managers and line employees differ in their response to the statement, "Increased regulation is the best way to ensure safe products"?

	Agree	Disagree	No Opinion
Managers	58	66	8
Line Employees	34	24	10
Totals	92	90	18

   b. Test the following hypothesis with the following data: Women are more likely to have a pinterest.com account.

	Yes	No
Male	25	75
Female	80	20

3. Interpret the following computer cross-tab output including a χ^2 test. Variable EDUCATION is a response to "What is your highest level of educational achievement?" HS means a high school diploma, SC means some college, BS means a bachelor's degree, and MBA means a master of business administration. Variable WIN is how well the respondent did on a set of casino games of chance. A 1 means they would have lost more than \$100, a 2 means they approximately broke even, and a 3 means they won more than \$100. What is the result of exploring a research question that education influences performance on

casino gambling? Comment on your conclusion and any issues in interpreting the result.

The SAS System
The FREQ Procedure
Table of Education by WIN

Education Frequency Percent Row Pct Col Pct	Win			Total
	1	2	3	
MBA	3	10	4	17
	1.12	3.72	1.49	6.32
	17.65	58.82	23.53	
	3.19	10.31	5.13	
BS	11	19	12	42
	4.09	7.06	4.46	15.61
	26.19	45.24	28.57	
	11.70	19.59	15.38	
SC	33	30	27	90
	12.27	11.15	10.04	33.45
	35.67	33.33	30.00	
	35.11	30.93	34.62	
HS	47	38	35	120
	17.47	14.13	13.01	44.61
	29.17	31.67	29.17	
	50.00	39.18	44.57	
Total	94	97	78	269
	34.94	36.06	29.00	100.00

Statistics for Table of Education by WIN

Statistic	df	Value	Prob
Chi-Square	6	7.5275	0.2748

Sample Size = 269

4. What statistic is appropriate to analyze the potential relationship between a nominal independent variable and a ratio dependent variable?

5. Test the following hypothesis using the data summarized in the following table. Interpret your result:

H1: Internet retailers offer lower prices for tablet computers than do traditional in-store retailers.

Retail Type	Average Tablet Price	Standard Deviation	n
E-tailers	$371.95	$50.00	25
In-store retailers	$360.30	$45.00	25

6. Selected territories in a company's eastern and western regions were rated for sales potential based on the company's evaluation system. A sales manager wishes to conduct a *t*-test of means to determine whether there is a difference between the two regions.

Conduct this test, preferably using a statistical software package, and draw the appropriate conclusion:

Region	Territory	Rating	Region	Territory	Rating
West	1	74	East	8	81
West	2	88	East	9	63
West	3	78	East	10	56
West	4	85	East	11	68
West	5	100	East	12	80
West	6	114	East	13	79
West	7	98	East	14	69

How would this result change if the company only had seven territories in the West and seven in the East?

7. How does an independent samples *t*-test differ from the following?
   a. one-way ANOVA
   b. paired-samples *t*-test
   c. a χ^2 test

8. Are *t*-tests or Z-tests used more often in marketing research? Why?

9. A sales force received some management-by-objectives training. Are the before/after mean scores for salespeople's job performance statistically significant at the 0.05 level? The results from a sample of employees are as follows (use your computer and statistical software to solve this problem):

Salesperson	Before	After	Salesperson	Before	After
Carlos	4.84	5.43	Tommy	4.00	5.00
Sammy	5.24	5.51	Laurie	4.67	4.50
Melanie	5.37	5.42	Ronald	4.95	4.40
Philippe	3.69	4.50	Amanda	4.00	5.95
Cargill	5.95	5.90	Brittany	3.75	3.50
Dwight	4.75	5.25	Mathew	3.85	4.00
Amy	3.90	4.50	Alice	5.00	4.10
Kallua	3.20	3.75	Jake	4.00	5.15

10. Using the "CAR" data that accompanies the text (see website), consider the following problem. The data describe attitudes of car owners from Germany and the United States toward their automobiles. The variable "ATT" is how much respondents like their current car (attitude), "ATTNEW" is their attitude toward a new car called the Cycle. The "COUNTRY" variable is self-explanatory. The "SPEND" variable is how much the respondents spend on average on products to keep their cars clean (in Euros). Using SPSS or other statistical software, test the following hypotheses:

H1: The owners' attitudes toward the Cycle are more favorable than attitudes toward their current cars.
H2: Germans like their cars more than Americans.

11. Interpret the following output examining group differences for purchase intentions. The three groups refer to consumers from three states: Florida, Minnesota, and Hawaii.

Tests of Between-Subjects Effects
Dependent Variable: int2

Source	Type III Sum of Squares	df	Mean Square	F	Sig.
Corrected Model	681.746[a]	2	3340.873	3.227	0.043
Intercept	308897.012	1	308897.012	298.323	0.000
State	6681.746	2	3340.873	3.227	0.043
Error	148068.543	143	1035.444		
Total	459697.250	146			
Corrected Total	154750.289	145			

Law
Dependent Variable: int2

State	Mean	Std. Error	95% Confidence Interval Lower Bound	95% Confidence Interval Upper Bound
F	37.018	4.339	28.441	45.595
M	50.357	4.965	40.542	60.172
H	51.459	4.597	42.373	60.546

12. The following table gives a football team's season-ticket sales, percentage of games won, and number of active alumni for the years 2001–2018.

Year	Season-Ticket Sales	Percentage of Games Won	Number of Active Alumni
2001	4,995	40	NA
2002	8,599	54	3,450
2003	8,479	55	3,801
2004	8,419	58	4,000
2005	10,253	63	4,098
2006	12,457	75	6,315
2007	13,285	36	6,860
2008	14,177	27	8,423
2009	15,730	63	9,000
2010	15,805	70	9,500
2011	15,575	72	9,530
2012	15,900	75	9,550
2013	14,010	80	9,560
2014	12,500	82	9,575
2015	10,900	30	9,540
2016	9,998	25	9,580
2017	12,750	78	9,705
2018	14,050	78	10,000

a. Enter the data into an electronic file.
b. Estimate a regression model for sales = Percentage of games won using EXCEL, JMP, SPSS, or some other statistical software.
c. Estimate a regression model for sales = Number of active alumni.
d. Estimate a multiple regression model predicting sales using year, percentage of winning, and number of active alumni as independent variables.
e. If *sales* is the dependent variable, which independent variable do you think explains sales better? Explain.

13. Interpret the following regression results. Performance is the dependent variable, dummy is a variable coded 1 if the employee has a marketing degree and 0 otherwise, sales is the typical sales level for the employee's region, and experience is the years the employee has been on the job. These results are produced with a regression program instead of the GLM-univariate ANOVA program.
   a. List the independent variables in order from greatest to least in terms of how strong the relationship is with performance.
   b. When might one prefer to use an ANOVA program instead of a multiple regression program?

```
                    The SAS System
                   The REG Procedure
                    Model: MODEL 1
            Dependent Variable: performance

           Number of Observations Read 40
           Number of Observations Used 40


                  Analysis of Variance

                           Sum of    Mean of
        Source         DF  Squares   Squares   F Value  Pr > F

        Model           3  173.63814  57.87938   13.87   <.0001
        Error          36  150.23410   4.17317
        Corrected Total 39 323.87225


           Root MSE           2.04283   R-Square   0.5361
           Dependent Mean    81.23468   Adj R-Sq   0.4975
           Coeff Var          2.51473
```

Parameter Estimates

Variable	Label	DF	Parameter Estimate	Standard error	t-Value	Pr >|t|	Standardized Estimate
Intercept	Intercept	1	72.68459	2.88092	25.23	<.0001	0
Dummy	Dummy	1	3.80621	0.66442	5.73	<.0001	0.66546
Sales	Sales	1	0.00038324	0.00016507	2.32	0.0260	0.26578
Experience	Experience	1	0.02829	0.03866	0.73	0.4689	0.08475

::RESEARCH ACTIVITIES

1. How ethical is it to do business in different countries around the world? An international organization, Transparency International, keeps track of the perception of ethical practices in different countries. Visit the website and search for the latest corruption indices (**https://www.transparency.org/news/feature/corruption_perceptions_index_2016**). Using the data found here for 2016, test the following research questions.

   a. Are nations from Europe and North America perceived to be more ethical than nations from Asia, Africa, and South America? Include Australia and New Zealand with Europe.

   b. Are there differences among the corruption indices between 2012 and 2016?

2. Using the retail data available in the resources for this chapter, examine the following research questions: (1) Verizon consumers have a more favorable attitude than do AT&T consumers. (2) Are consumers with a coupon willing to pay the same amount as are consumers without a coupon? (3) Does the combination of store/phone brand and coupon influence willingness to pay (WTP_ACC)? The following table contains a guide to the file.

X1	X2	X3	INT1	INT2	INT3	Traditional	ATT1	ATT2	ATT3	ATT4	Q31	Q32	Q135	AGE	WTP_ACC	TotTime
Retail Phone Store. 0=Verizon, 1=ATT	Where promotion was delivered, 0=BNM (physical store) and 1=Online	Was$s Off Coupon Provided, 0=no, 1=yes	Intention Likert Scale Item 1	Intention Likert Scale Item 2	Intention Likert Scale Item 3	Did respondent view phone as traditional	Attitude Semantic Differential 1	Attitude Semantic Differential 2	Attitude Semantic Differential 3	Attitude Semantic Differential 4	Switch or keep old phone? 0 =switch, 1 =keep	Time of day store visited. 1= day, 2=night	Gender, 1=male, 2=female	in years	Willingness to pay for phone plus add-ons and accessories	Total times shopping

Old School versus New School Sports Fans

Case 15.1

Download the data sets for this case from **www.cengagebrain.com** *or request them from your instructor.*

Three academic researchers investigated the idea that, in American sports and society, there are segments with conflicting views about the goal of competition in society (i.e., winning versus self-actualization) and the acceptable/desirable way of achieving this goal. Persons who believe in "winning at any cost" in sports can be labeled new school individuals according to the researchers. The new school is founded on notions of the individual before the team, loyalty to the highest bidder, and high-tech production and consumption of professional sports. On the other hand, people may value the traditions and process of sports more highly. They believe that "how you play the game matters." The researchers label these individuals as old school individuals. The old school emerges from old-fashioned American notions of the team before the player, sportsmanship, and competition simply for "love of the game."

The researchers tried to measure New School/Old School orientation by asking agreement with several attitude statements (the survey contained over 15 items in total but only 10 were used here after some initial analyses). The scores on these ten statements allowed the researchers to form a composite measure representing Old School orientations. Based on their composite scores, respondents were grouped into low, middle, and high Old School groups. A low Old School orientation conversely could be thought of as a high New School orientation. One research question of interest is whether men and women differ in their orientation toward competition in sports. Case Exhibit 15.1-1 shows the computer output of a cross-tabulation to relate the gender of the respondent (GENDER) with the New School/Old School grouping (OLDSKOOL). In the results, the Pearson Chi-Square can be used to interpret statistical significance.

Questions

1. Is this form of analysis appropriate for the research question?
2. Interpret the computer output and critique the analysis.
3. Explore the GLM (General Linear Model) procedure in SAS, SPSS, or JMP (access using "fit model") by testing a model using show_off as the dependent variable and gender as the independent variable.

a. Interpret the result.

b. Add age as a covariate and repeat the analysis. Interpret the result.

CASE EXHIBIT **15.1-1**   SPSS Output

| | | Contingency Table | | |
| | | OLDSKOOL | | |
Count Total % Col % Row % Expected	Low	Middle	High	Row Totals
Woman	37	40	8	85
	13.70	14.81	2.96	31.48
	45.68	27.03	19.51	
	43.53	47.06	9.41	
	25.5	46.5926	12.9074	
Men	44	108	33	185
	16.30	40.00	12.22	68.52
	54.32	72.97	80.49	
	23.78	58.38	17.84	
	55.5	101.407	28.0926	
Column Totals	81	148	41	270
	30.00	54.81	15.19	

(gender — row grouping label on left)

| Tests | | | |
N	DF	-LogLike	RSquare (U)
270	2	5.7424309	0.0218
Test	ChiSquare		Prob>ChiSq
Likelihood Ratio	11.485		0.0032*
Pearson	11.654		0.0029*

International Operations at Carcare Inc.

Case 15.2

CarCare is considering expanding its operations beyond the United States. The company wants to know whether it should target countries with consumers who tend to have a positive attitude toward their current cars. It has gathered data on U.S. and German car owners. The data are included in the "car" data set that can be viewed on the website at www.cengagebrain.com (car.sav or car.xls) or available from your instructor. Using the data, conduct a correlation and simple regression analysis using spending as the dependent variable and attitude toward the current car as the independent variable.

1. Test the hypothesis: Attitude toward one's car is related positively to spending for car-care products.
2. Would you recommend they do more research to identify nations with relatively favorable attitudes toward the cars they own?

Ryan McVay/Getty Images

:::::: Communicating Research Results

LEARNING OUTCOMES

After studying this chapter, you should be able to:

1. Create an outline for a research project using the basic parts of a final report

2. Explain how to use tables for presenting numerical information

3. Summarize how to select and use the types of research charts

4. Know how to give an effective oral presentation

5. Discuss the importance of Internet reporting and research follow-up

iStock.com/Opidanus

Chapter Vignette:

Effective Research Is a Stone's Throw Away

Alex Hammond/Alamy Stock Photo

The Rosetta Stone represents one of the greatest findings in the history of communication. The stone dates back to several centuries before Christ but was discovered near the ancient city of Rosetta, Egypt, at the end of the eighteenth century. What made this discovery so special? The etchings on the stone represented a decree to the peoples of that time, which was written not only in hieroglyphics but also in ancient Greek. French and British researchers worked for decades and eventually produced a translation between the ancient Greek and the hieroglyphic script. They learned that hieroglyphics were not just pictures but that over time, hieroglyphics had developed into a language with symbols that took on phonetic characteristics including sound. This breakthrough meant that scores of ancient etchings could now communicate effectively because of the translation code made possible by the Rosetta Stone.[1]

Fortunately, marketing researchers don't have to write research reports on stones, but effective communication can still be pretty hard! The research report is the tool that translates what most people could not possibly understand into a useful report that communicates important information for business managers, marketing executives, policy makers, or other marketing researchers. Marketing practitioners lack working knowledge of multivariate data analysis, ethnography, phenomenology, or most other technical aspects of marketing research. So even if researchers conduct the marketing research properly, the research can still be a complete failure if the researcher is unable to produce a user-friendly, concise, and actionable research report. In fact, science itself is of little use unless one can effectively communicate its meaning.[2]

Employers often view excellent writing skills as a necessary requisite when evaluating marketing research candidates. Unfortunately, these same employers are often disappointed with technical employees' communication skills. These employees are expected not only to write formal research reports but also to make effective oral presentations and, increasingly, to deliver effective and accurate communication via Internet media, including online meetings, blogs, and even tweets. Imagine the task of translating results of a months-long research project into a 140-character tweet![3] Sounds like a job for another Rosetta Stone!

Introduction

Researchers can easily be tempted into rushing through the research report. By the time the data is collected, the researchers may well feel exhausted or burned out and ready to move on to something new. With all the *real* work done, the results just need to be documented. This feeling can be disastrous, however. If people who depend on the findings of the research have to wade through a disorganized presentation, find themselves confused by technical jargon, or detect sloppiness of language or thought, they will probably discount the entire report and make decisions without considering the research findings. So the research report is a crucial means for showcasing the importance of your research findings and communicating the benefits of the whole project. This chapter explains the communication of research results using written reports, presentations, and follow-up conversations.[4]

The Project and the Report

A **research report** is a formal presentation and/or written document that communicates research results and draws appropriate conclusions following from a research project. The report provides the *answers* and documents procedures to the interested audience. For an applied market research project, the report presents the results that fulfill the proposal's deliverables, including specific managerial recommendations. In fact, deliverables should be a logical conclusion of the report contents. A basic marketing researcher writes a similar report that often takes the form of a white paper or scholarly research paper targeted for publication in a research journal such as the *Journal of Marketing*, the *Journal of the Academy of Marketing Science*, or the *Journal of Business Research*. A written research report often coincides with a formal presentation delivered in person and/or via the Internet.

research report

An oral presentation or written document of research results, strategic recommendations, and/or other conclusions to a specific audience.

To the Point

"It is a luxury to be understood."

—RALPH WALDO EMERSON

Report Format

Every significant research project produces a report of some kind. While report contents might be specific to each report, research reports in general document the entire process of the research project. Market and marketing researchers tend to follow some conventions with respect to the **report format**. This research report format follows consensus about what ordered parts and contents comprise a professional research document. Following a conventional format makes these documents more user friendly and easier to read.

Although we think of the research report as the culmination of a research project, the report outline that describes the standard format serves as a useful guide for the entire research project. If students are asked to complete a research project for this class, the report outline can be utilized as a step-by-step guide in completing the project. Thus, the student resources for the text contain a file with the outline that can be used as a guide. The student needs to complete the relevant parts

report format

A standard outline that marketing research reports use as a guide to make sure that the key elements are presented in a logical and usable order.

RESEARCH IN ACTION!

You have nearly reached the end of the research project. By now you have developed an idea, supported it with background information, stated research objectives, created a suitable research design, collected data, analyzed your results, and interpreted your findings to reach some final recommendations. Your final step includes preparing a written research report and a presentation to share your project with an interested audience. This chapter will provide you with formatting guidelines and tips on how to create a concise, well-written report that will effectively communicate the benefits of your research. Remember, it is important to keep your audience in mind when finalizing your report and to adapt format, terminology, and formality accordingly. In addition, visuals can be an excellent tool to highlight important information and key findings in the report as well as in the presentation.

andresr/E+/Getty Images

noted in the research outline to finish the project. Not all parts are included in all reports. However, parts that are common to all reports are noted in the outline.

Large research companies also use standard templates that allow the researcher to fill in the custom information derived from the specific research project. These large companies may sometimes employ a technical writing staff to assist in the production of reports. Not every report fits the exact template, and occasionally some reports may omit a section or include other sections that are not part of the basic template. But most research projects will follow an outline that includes the following major elements:

1. Title page
2. Letter of transmittal
3. Letter of authorization
4. Table of contents (and lists of figures and tables)
5. Executive summary
   a. Objectives
   b. Results
   c. Conclusions
   d. Recommendations
6. Body
   a. Introduction
      1. Background
      2. Objectives
   a. Methodology
   b. Results
   c. Limitations
   d. Conclusions and recommendations
3. Appendix
   a. Data collection forms
   b. Detailed calculations
   c. General tables
   d. Bibliography
   e. Other support material

Exhibit 16.1 illustrates this format graphically.

Statistics Show 20 Percent of Report Statistics Are Misleading. Oh Yeah??!!

Pressmaster/Shutterstock.com

People may not like math, but when it comes to making judgments, people like numbers. Just consider how many news stories in the paper or news report some poll results, trends, or other statistics. Similarly, many ads make claims backed up by statistics. Consider these *facts* taken from newspaper reports:

"Visa announced that its new credit card will carry an adjustable rate set monthly at four percent above the prime rate, in line with other variable-rate cards."

This is a common mistake: confusing *percentage* and *percentage points*. A rate set so slightly above the prime rate would be an unusually good bargain. For example, at the time of this writing, the U.S. federal prime rate is 3.25 percent; prime plus 4 percent would be just 3.38 percent, far below the rates charged by most credit cards. The writer probably meant Visa would charge prime rate plus four percentage points, which in this example would be 7.25 percent.

"Battling Hunger, a food pantry, said it delivered 110,000 tons of food to Detroit last Thanksgiving. The food was delivered to help residents there overcome the effects of a severe economic slump, particularly in the automobile industry."

Can you spot any problems with such statements? Looking carefully, each of these examples is potentially misleading. Misleading reports may not have to do with the numbers themselves, but with other details such as the units

of measure or standards of comparison. In this case, 110,000 tons equals 220 million pounds of food. Can that be reasonable? Even if the food pantry served a million people—all of Detroit plus some suburbanites—it would have distributed 220 pounds of food to each individual. Not likely. When numbers are this unrealistic, the writer should check the calculations, including the decimal point's location, and the units. perhaps this writer meant 110,000 pounds or 110 tons.

"More Americans tell pollsters they are currently more often happy than worried."

This seems simple enough. However, what the story does not point out is that the poll results contain only results taken on the weekend. People who are polled on weekdays give the opposite picture—they are more worried than happy. So pay attention to the details before jumping to conclusions.

Sources: Based on Bialik, C. (2009), "In Ads, 1 out of 5 Stats Is Bogus," *Wall Street Journal*, (March 11), 12. Bialik, C. (2011), "U.S. news— The Numbers Guy: happy? Statisticians Aren't Buying It," *Wall Street Journal*, (March 26), 2.

EXHIBIT 16.1 Report Format

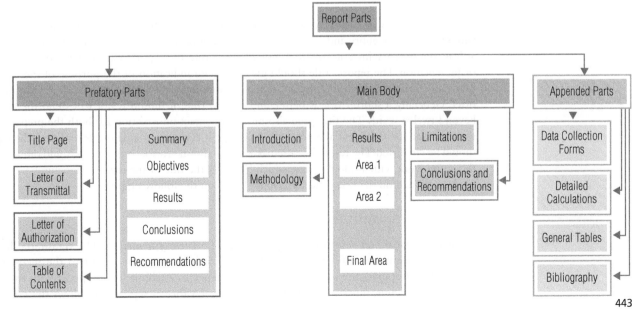

Tailoring the Format to the Project

The format of a research report may need to be adjusted for two reasons: (1) to obtain the proper level of formality and (2) to decrease the complexity of the report. The format given here is for the most formal type of report, such as one for a large project done within an organization or one done by a research agency for a client company. A formal report typically arrives to the client bound in a permanent cover and may be hundreds of pages long. Electronic versions usually are made available and are typically in a pdf format to maximize compatibility. If the report contains potentially sensitive information, the electronic files are password protected.

In less-formal reports, parts are shorter or sometimes omitted. Just as we choose our clothing to match the formality of an occasion, not every report comes dressed, so to speak, in a tuxedo or long evening gown. A formal report includes all prefatory parts in detail—title page, copies of letters of transmittal and authorization, and table of contents. Like changing into an everyday business suit from a tuxedo, dropping down to the next lower level of formality involves eliminating parts of the prefatory material that are inessential in such a situation and reducing the complexity of the report body as well. In general, as the report moves down through the sport coat and slacks and then blue jeans stages, more prefatory parts are dropped, and the complexity and length of the report body are reduced.

How does the researcher decide on the appropriate level of formality? The general rule is to include all the parts needed for effective communication in the particular circumstances—and no more. This depends on how far up in management the report is expected to go and how routine the matter is. A researcher's immediate supervisor does not need a 100-page, *black-tie* report on a routine project. However, the board of directors does not want a one-page *blue jeans* report on a big project that backs a major expansion program. The researcher may take a formal report presented to top management and strip it of some prefatory parts (and thus reduced in formality) for wider circulation within the company. The condensing of the report in this fashion would take place only with top management approval. And remember, no matter if the final research report is formal and complex or simple and straightforward, it should always be well-written. Clear, concise writing is the key to a successful completion of a research project.

The Parts of the Report

To the Point
"The covers of this book are too far apart."
—AMBROSE BIERCE

As previously mentioned, research reports follow the same general outline. Research reports are a form of technical writing, and as such, readers may well expect the paper to follow this format. Here, the old adage "If it ain't broke, don't fix it" truly applies.

Title Page

The *title page* provides a name for the report, states for whom the report was prepared (when prepared for a specific entity and not for public consumption), tells who performed the research (lists at least the primary investigators responsible) and wrote the report, and gives the date of release or presentation. The report's title should give a concise indication of the purpose of the research project. Researchers often find it challenging to come up with a title that is both descriptive and brief. Generally, a shorter title is better, and a good rule of thumb is not to extend the title far beyond twelve words. The title page also provides contact information for both the preparer and the recipient. On confidential reports, the title page lists names of individuals to whom the report should be circulated. The research team makes sure to bound formal reports neatly and often covers the entire work with a title fly-page, which lists only the title of the report. Page numbers should not be included on the title page, but should begin on the following pages.

Letter of Transmittal

Relatively formal and very formal reports include a *letter of transmittal*. The transmittal letter's purpose is to announce formally the release of or delivery of the report to the recipient. A transmittal letter gives the research personnel a chance to establish some rapport with the users of the report. Thus, this is typically the only part of a formal report that allows the writer to strike a personal or even slightly informal tone. The transmittal should not dive into the report findings, although providing a broad overview of the research objectives accomplished by the research is permissible.

A transmittal letter's opening paragraph releases the report and briefly identifies the factors of authorization. The letter comments generally on findings and matters of interest regarding the research. The closing section expresses the writer's personal interest in the project just completed and in doing additional, related work. Overall, the letter explains how the report represents a key deliverable and invites further discussion on the matter.

Letter of Authorization

The *letter of authorization* is a letter to the researcher that approves the project, details who has responsibility for it, and describes the resources available to support it. The researcher receives and does not write this letter; however, he or she may include it in the report to signify client approval of the work. In many situations, simply referring to the authorization in the letter of transmittal suffices. If so, the letter of authorization need not be included in the report. In some cases, though, the reader may be unfamiliar with the authorization or may need detailed information about it. In such cases, the report should include this letter, preferably an exact copy of the original. Nowadays, the letter of authorization might be provided in form of an e-mail communication between the research company and the client. In these cases, a copy of the e-mail correspondence can be included to represent a letter of authorization.

The Table of Contents

A *table of contents* is essential to any report more than a few pages long. It should list the divisions and subdivisions of the report with page references. The table of contents and the final outline of the report coincide with one another, but the table of contents usually shows only the first-level subheadings and at most only up to the second-level subheadings. For short reports, it is sufficient to include only the first-level headings. If the report includes many figures and/or tables, a list of these should immediately follow the table of contents. Theses and dissertations, which are often a research report of sorts, nearly always include a list of exhibits.

The Executive Summary

The summary, or *executive summary* as it is called more often, briefly explains why the research project was conducted, what aspects of the problem were considered, what the outcome was, and what should be done. The executive summary is a vital part of the report. Studies have indicated that nearly all managers read a report's summary, while only a minority read the body of the report. Thus, the writer's only chance to produce an impact may be in the executive summary.

While the executive summary is located at the beginning of the research report, researchers should write the summary after completing the rest of the report. The executive summary represents the essence of the report. Executive summaries should be one page long (or, at most, two pages), so the writer must carefully sort out what is important enough to be included in it. Several pages of the full report may have to be condensed into one summarizing sentence. Some parts of the report may be condensed more than others; the number of words in the summary need not be in proportion to the length of the report section being discussed. The summary should be self-sufficient. In fact, the summary is often detached from the report and circulated by itself.

The summary contains four elements. First, it states the objectives of the report, including the most important background information and the specific purposes of the project. Second, it presents the methodology and results, third the conclusions and fourth, any recommendations. These are opinions based on the results and constitute an interpretation of the results. Finally come recommendations, or suggestions for action, based on the conclusions. In many cases, managers prefer not to have recommendations included in the report or summary. Whether or not recommendations are to be included should be clear from the particular context of the report.

The Body

introduction section

The part of the body of a research report that discusses background information and the specific objectives of the research.

The *body* constitutes the bulk of the report. The first part, the **introduction section**, provides an overview of the background factors and the main objectives of the research project. It continues with discussions of the methodology, results, and limitations of the study and finishes with conclusions and recommendations based on the results.

The introduction explains why the researcher conducted the project and what the research procedures aimed to discover. Introductions should include the basic authorization and submittal data. The relevant background comes next. Enough background should be included to explain why the project was worth doing, but the background need not include unessential historical factors. The question of how much background is enough depends on the needs of the audience. A government report that will be widely circulated requires more background than a company's internal report on customer satisfaction. The last part of the introduction explains exactly what the project tried to discover. It discusses the statement of the problem and research questions as outlined in the research proposal. Each purpose presented here should have a corresponding entry in the results section later in the report.

research methodology section

The part of the report body that describes the research process, which often includes explanations of potentially complex, technical procedures.

The second part of the body is the **research methodology section**. This part is a challenge to write because it must describe the research process, which often includes potentially complex, technical procedures, and do so in a manner appropriate for the audience. Complex technical details can be included in a technical appendix. Sometimes, the report includes a glossary of technical terms. Four points should be included in the research methodology section:

1. *Research design.* Was the study exploratory, descriptive, or causal? Did the data come from primary or secondary sources? Were results collected by survey, observation, or experiment? A copy of the survey questionnaire or observation form should be included in the appendix. Why was this particular design suited to the study?

2. *Sample design.* What was the target population? What is the sampling frame? What sample units are selected? How were they selected? How large was the sample? What was the response rate? The researcher should save detailed computations to support these explanations for the appendix.

3. *Data collection and fieldwork.* How many and what types of fieldworkers were used? What training and supervision did they receive? Was the work verified? How were the data collected? Across what time frame were data collected? This section is important for establishing the degree of accuracy of the results.

4. *Analysis.* This section should outline the general statistical methods used in the study, but the information presented here should not overlap with what is presented in the results section.

results section

The part of the body of a report that presents the findings of the project. It includes tables, charts, and an organized narrative.

The **results section** should make up the bulk of the report and should present, in some logical order, those findings of the project that bear on the research objectives. The report organizes results as a continuous narrative, designed to be convincing but not to oversell the project. Summary tables and charts aid the interpretation portrayed in the discussion. These tables and charts may serve as points of reference to the data and free the prose from excessive regurgitation of detailed facts. Comprehensive or detailed charts, however, should be included in an appendix. Sometimes research projects might incorporate more than one type of research design or utilize secondary research to drive primary survey research. Even for these alternative formats, the guidelines for the research methodology and results section still apply. The final report would simply reflect individual methodology and results sections for each corresponding research design and component of the project.

Because no research is perfect, a professional report includes a discussion of limitations. The researcher should report problems arising with nonresponse error or other sampling procedures. However, the discussion of limitations should avoid overemphasizing the weaknesses; its aim should be to provide a realistic basis for assessing the results. For example, the use of a student sample to represent consumers could be a potential limitation that could be discussed in this section of the report.

conclusions and recommendations section

The part of the body of a report that provides opinions based on the results and suggestions for action.

The last part of the body is the **conclusions and recommendations section**. As mentioned earlier, conclusions are based on the results, and recommendations are suggestions for action. The conclusions and recommendations are presented in this section in more detail than in the summary, and the text should include justification as needed.

The Appendix

The *appendix* presents the "too . . ." material. Any material that is too technical or too detailed to go in the body should appear in the appendix. This includes materials of interest only to some readers or subsidiary materials not directly related to the objectives. Some examples of appendix materials are data collection forms, detailed calculations, discussions of highly technical questions, detailed or comprehensive tables of results, and a bibliography (if appropriate). Much appendix material gets posted securely online for access on an as-needed basis.

Basic Marketing Research Report

The outline described applies especially to applied market research projects. When basic research reports are written, such as might be submitted and potentially published in an academic business journal, the outline changes slightly since some components become irrelevant. A common outline used in basic marketing research proceeds as follows:

1. Abstract
2. Introduction
3. Background
   a. Literature review
   b. Hypotheses
4. Research Methods
5. Results
6. Discussion
   a. Implications
   b. Limitations
   c. Future research
7. Conclusions
8. References
9. Appendixes

Using Tables Effectively

Used properly, **graphic aids** can clarify complex points or emphasize a message. Used improperly or sloppily, they can distract or even mislead a reader. Graphic aids work best when they are an integral part of the text. The graphics should always be referenced and interpreted in the text. This does not mean that the writer should exhaustively explain an obvious chart or table, but it *does* mean that the text should point out the key elements of any graphic aid and relate them to the discussion in progress.

Several types of graphic aids may be useful in research reports, including tables, charts, maps, and diagrams. The following discussion briefly covers the most common ones, tables and charts. The reader interested in other types of graphic material should consult more specialized sources.

graphic aids
Pictures or diagrams used to clarify complex points or emphasize a message.

Creating Tables

Tables are most useful for presenting numerical information, especially when several pieces of information have been gathered about each item discussed. For example, consider how hard following the information in Exhibit 16.2 might be with only narrative text and no graphical aids. Using tables allows a writer to point out significant features without getting bogged down in detail. The body of the report should include only relatively short summary tables, with comprehensive tables reserved for an appendix.

EXHIBIT **16.2** Basic Data Illustration

| Number of Graphic | Table 162E. Per Capita Bottled Water Consumption 2014–2016 (liters/person) | Title |

Country	2014	2015	2016
Brazil	59.6	62.8	61.5
France	116.2	121.4	125
Germany	170.1	175.2	174.5
Mexico	241.3	240.8	240.8
Spain	50.9	54.9	58.5
U.K.	29.9	32.6	35.8
USA	129.1	138.2	148.8

Note: Consumption is reported in liters per person by country.
Source: Statista Database

Column Headings / Row Headings / Notes including sources

Each table should include the following elements:

- *Number.* The number is indexed to the List of Exhibits/Tables/Figures/Charts provided along with the table of contents. For an electronic report, this list may be hyperlinked to the graphics list for easy navigation. Some authors prefer to use the term *exhibit* to refer to all tables, charts, and figures—all graphics in general. Others prefer to number tables, charts, and figures separately. The numbering of Exhibits/Tables/Figures/Charts should occur in ascending order throughout the text.
- *Title.* The title should indicate the contents of the table and be complete enough to be intelligible without referring to the text.
- *Stubheads and bannerheads.* The stubheads contain the captions for the rows of the table, and the bannerheads (or boxheads) contain those for the columns.
- *Notes.* Any explanations or qualifications for particular table entries or sections should be given in notes placed at the bottom of the table or footnotes appearing at the bottom of the page.
- *Source notes.* If a table is based on material from one or more secondary sources rather than on new data generated by the project, the sources should be acknowledged, usually below the table.

Using Charts Effectively

Charts translate numerical information into visual form to summarize and communicate meaning. Often, the researcher sacrifices numerical precision in return for easy communication in transferring data to graphical form. Each chart should include the following elements:

- *Figure number.* Reports number charts (and other illustrative material) consecutively and usually do so separately from tables. The numbers allow for easy reference from the text. If there are many charts, a list of them should be included after the table of contents.
- *Title.* The title should describe the contents of the chart with just a few words. Numbers sometimes go at the top and sometimes at the bottom of a graphic. However, the placement should remain consistent across all charts in a document.

■ *Explanatory legends.* A good graphic includes keys to aid in the explanation and to help the reader interpret the chart without the necessity of reading the report in detail. Explanatory legends of this sort include color codes to match to chart components, labels for axes, scale numbers, and a way to understand any abbreviations.

■ *Source and footnotes.* Any secondary sources for the data should be acknowledged. Footnotes may be used to explain items, although they are less common for charts than for tables.

Charts are subject to distortion, whether unintentional or deliberate. Researchers must use special care to represent true scale values faithfully in all graphical aids. In fact, presenters can intentionally alter scale values in an effort to skew the interpretation of the data. Intentionally altering scales for this purpose is clearly unethical and unintentionally doing so is sloppy.

A particularly severe kind of distortion comes from treating unequal intervals as if they were equal. Typically, someone does this when trying to distort the interpretation of some meaning intentionally. Exhibit 16.3 shows this type of distortion. Here, both charts show the rate of change in U.S. gross domestic product over a period from 2014 to 2018. Does one chart appear to show more steady growth than the other does? The top chart shows greater fluctuation including two periods of declining growth. The bottom chart shows only steady growth. On close inspection, however, the two charts are not using the same intervals. The top chart shows every quarter from 2014 to 2018 in addition to annualized data. The bottom omits the first quarter of each year. Perhaps not coincidentally, the periods of lowest growth tended to happen in the first quarter over this period.

Researchers sometimes are tempted to choose the scale values for axes on charts in a way that may make a small finding seem much larger than it really is. Consider Exhibit 16.4. It displays results

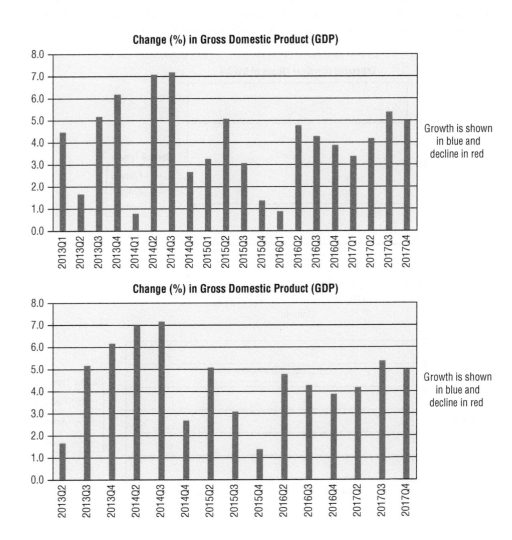

EXHIBIT 16.3
Two Differing Depictions of the Same Data

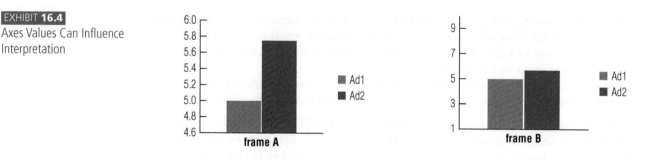

EXHIBIT **16.4**
Axes Values Can Influence
Interpretation

of an experiment testing the difference between two alternative advertising designs on purchase intention. Subjects recorded their purchase intentions after viewing one of the ads using a 10-point scale scored from 1 (Extremely Unlikely to Buy) to 10 (Very Likely to Buy). Both frames in the exhibit display exactly the same data. However, would a reader draw the same conclusion from either frame? Frame A makes ad 2 seem much more advantageous relative to ad 1. In contrast, frame B leads to the conclusion that there is very little difference between the two. In this case, frame A is misleading because notice that the y-axis uses a minimum value of 4.6 and a maximum value of 6.0, while frame B uses the actual scale minimum and maximum values of 1 and 10. Researchers sometimes feel the need to exaggerate the size of an effect by choosing a misleading scale range to make some effect seem relatively important. Often, the researcher gets confused about the difference between statistical significance and practical significance and tries to turn one into the other by making the graphic exaggerate an effect.

Distortions can also occur by accident as statistical tools that generate such graphs may automatically insert inappropriate minimum and maximum values. Interaction effects can be particularly prone to distortions. Consider Exhibit 16.5, which shows the very same effect as depicted

EXHIBIT 16.5

A Small-Scale Range for the
Y-Axis Can Mislead the User

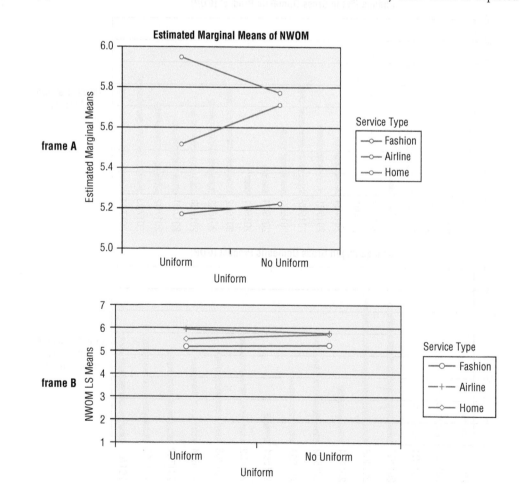

automatically by two separate software packages. The exhibits depict an interaction effect between two nominal, experimental variables (service type depicts the type of service a subject is describing, and uniform depicts whether the service employee involved in a situation wore a uniform). The dependent variable is how likely the subject would be to spread negative word of mouth (NWOM). Frame A shows the results in a chart automatically generated by SPSS. Frame B shows the results in a chart automatically generated by JMP. Unless the reader looks closely, frame A points to a conclusion that subjects react quite differently across the three service types. Notice the difference in slopes of the lines that can signify an interaction. Frame B, however, shows that all three lines are similar and leads to the conclusion that the combination of service type and uniform does not make much of a difference. Now, look closely at the y-axes. Frame A compresses the response range of NWOM to 5.2 to 5.9, only 0.7 out of a total scale range of 7 points. Frame B, on the other hand, depicts the full scale range. In this case, frame B gives the more accurate picture. The actual statistical result for the interaction produces an $F_{(df=2,203)}$ or 0.42, which yields a *p*-value of 0.7 (not statistically significant).

Researchers sometimes get so emotionally involved in conducting and presenting research that they may not realize their graphics are misleading. Often, a misleading graphic results from zeal or carelessness rather than intentional deception. Unfortunately, misleading graphics are all too common. Again, however, the researcher should always use great caution in making sure that graphics do nothing to encourage an inappropriate conclusion. Otherwise, the chart may contribute to the old adage "Statistics don't lie, but liars use statistics."

Marketing researchers should always try to present results as faithfully as possible. In this case, using the entire scale range would lead to a more accurate conclusion. In other instances where a larger range of values may be in play, perhaps in plotting the price someone actually paid for their last car, the minimum axes value need not be 0, but it should reflect the minimum plausible price that someone would pay. For example, one may set the scale range in this instance by the actual minimum and maximum prices reported across all respondents. One way to avoid misleading graphics is by not relying on automatically generated visuals of software programs, but instead recreating graphics. Taking the time to design exhibits allows one to personalize the content as well as the look of the graphics that can elevate the final research report. Various tools are available to the researcher to assist in this step of the report writing process, which are discussed next.

Pie Charts

One of the most useful kinds of charts is the pie chart, which shows the composition of some total quantity at a particular time. As shown in the example in Exhibit 16.6, each angle, or *slice*, is proportional to its percentage of the whole. Companies often use pie charts to show sources of sales revenues or to depict the relative size of market segments. Each slice in a pie chart should contain a label or legend identifying the slice and giving the percentage of the total comprised by that segment. Pie charts are also often used to summarize demographic characteristics of the sample, such as gender, or age. However, the writer should try to avoid including too many small

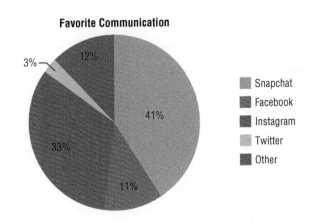

Favorite Communication

Snapchat
Facebook
Instagram
Twitter
Other

41%
33%
11%
3%
12%

EXHIBIT **16.6**
A Pie Chart Depicting a Sample of Tenth Graders' Choice to a Question Asking Their Favorite Means of Communication

slices; about six slices is a typical maximum. In this case, the pie chart shows results from a sample of several hundred tenth graders depicting their favorite means of communicating with friends. A company is interested in how to get students to spread advice on help with school assignments. The pie chart quickly depicts the results and points to Snapchat and Instagram as attractive communication vehicles.

Line Graphs

Line graphs are useful for showing the relationship of one variable to another. The dependent variable generally is shown on the vertical axis and the independent variable on the horizontal axis. The most common independent variable for such charts is time, but it is by no means the only one. Exhibit 16.7 shows a *simple line graph* depicting the proportion of worldwide Internet users over time. The increasing slope visually suggests steady growth.

Bar Charts

A bar chart shows changes in the value of a dependent variable (plotted on the vertical axis) at discrete intervals of the independent variable (on the horizontal axis). A simple bar chart is shown in Exhibit 16.8 on page 453.

The *multiple-bar chart* shows how multiple variables relate to the primary variable. In each of these cases, each bar or segment of the bar needs to be clearly identified with a different color or pattern. However, too many variables or too much detail should be avoided since it negates the benefit of charts to make relationships easy to grasp.

Infographics

infographic

Visual graphics that communicate report information.

An **infographic** is another tool that can be used to visually depict key components of a research project. It is a graphical format that communicates complicated data or complex content in an easy to understand manner by being visually engaging. Rather than focusing on one or two variables as common in previously discussed charts and graphs, infographics can summarize elements

EXHIBIT **16.7**

A Line Graph Depicting Percentage of Internet Users Worldwide by Year

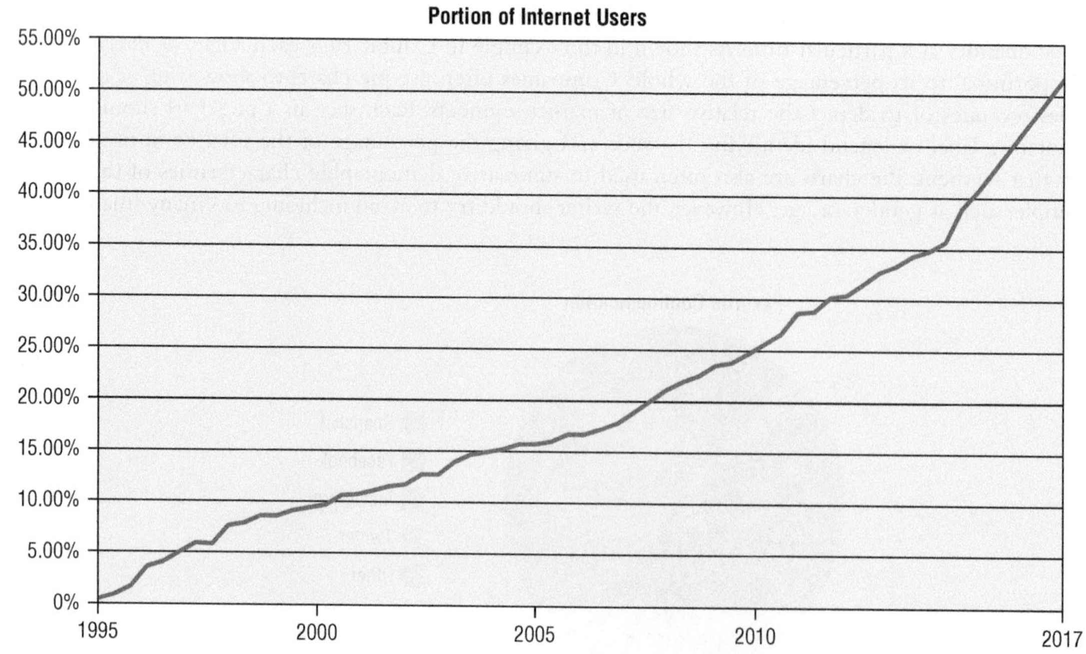

Portion of Internet Users

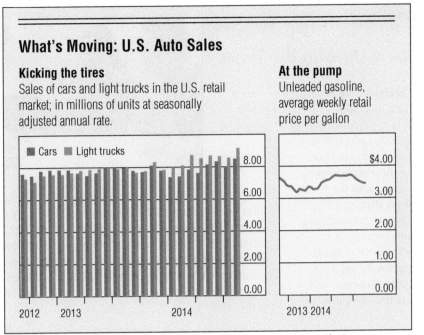

Source: http://online.wsj.com/mdc/public/page/2_3022-autosales.html#autosalesA, accessed June 17, 2018.

EXHIBIT 16.8
Graphic Combining a Multiple-Bar Chart and a Line Chart to Depict Trends in Car versus Truck Sales in the United States.

oral presentation

A spoken summary of the major findings, conclusions, and recommendations, given to clients or line managers to provide them with the opportunity to clarify any ambiguous issues by asking questions.

of multiple research findings and can even incorporate some background details. However, traditional charts, histograms, diagrams, and so forth can still be integrated in this graphical format while pictures and words are added to convey the overall data driven message.

The flow of an infographic follows a top-down reading pattern and various boxes can be used to break up the graphic into individual sections. As with any visual aid, long sentences should be avoided and instead keywords should guide the reader through the information. There are many software programs and tools available to help with the creation of infographics, such as free infographic templates from PowerPoint.[5] Some additional tools are Piktochart, BeFunky, or Visme that offer templates, designs, and graphical elements for easy infographic creation.[6]

Oral Presentation

The conclusions and recommendations of most research reports are presented orally as well as in writing. The purpose of an **oral presentation** is to highlight the most important findings of a research project and provide clients or line managers with an opportunity to ask questions. The oral presentation may be as simple as a short video conference with a manager at the client organization's location or as formal as a report to the company board of directors. One rule stands above all when preparing a presentation—be as straightforward as possible.

The female fashion consumer's eight paths to e-purchase

The eight paths shown in the infographic below represent the different ways a customer can purchase a fashion item online. Canny merchants should devise strategies thereby maximizing sales along each path.

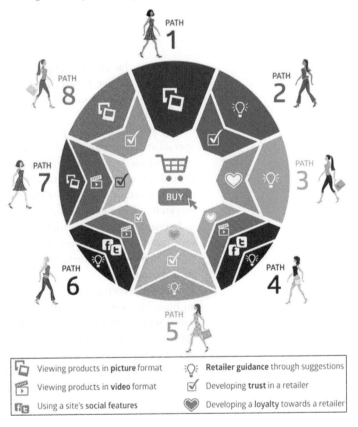

What Is a Flip Chart? Keeping Up with the Times

Tools used to deliver marketing research presentations have progressed immensely since using flip charts and magic markers. While first technological advances in the form of LCD projectors gained momentum in the 1970s and 1980s, the common presentation software we know today did not gain popularity until the late 1990s. Since these early beginnings, presentation standards have progressed with the introduction of the Internet and being physically present is no longer a necessity for the presenter. Remote presentations can now be hosted by Skypetype software programs and 360-degree handheld cameras can project a sense of being in the actual meeting room. Even taking notes during a presentation can be instantaneously shared with audience members via a digital whiteboard that connects to a computer that mirrors your screen.

Modern marketing research presentations also go beyond utilizing PowerPoint slides. Instead, alternative presentation software and tools are becoming more common. For example, Prezi and Haiku Deck incorporate high-quality, visually appealing backdrops in their templates, which offer a welcoming change to the ubiquitous PowerPoint presentations. Another tool that is suitable for presenting complex data is infographic, which can summarize part of or the entire research project in one graphical format. By creating a simple and visually appealing graphic, researchers can present their findings in an engaging yet sophisticated way. All these technological advancements are continuously pushing the boundaries of presentations in marketing research today. Let's see what the next few years will bring to the table.

Sources: Angeles, S. (2017), "Beyond PowerPoint: Presentation Tools for Small Businesses," *Business News Daily*, (June, 26), https://www.businessnewsdaily.com/6525-business-presentation-tools.html, accessed January 24, 2018. Modicum (2017), "4 Cool Gadgets to Enhance Your Presentations," *Forbes*, (April, 23), https://www.forbes.com/sites/propointgraphics/2017/04/23/4-cool-gadgets-to-enhance-your-presentations/#365292828abf, accessed January 24, *2018*. Dessart, L. (2016), "Capturing Consumer Engagement," Journal of *Marketing Management News*, (March, 21) http://www.jmmnews.com/capturing-consumer-engagement/, accessed January 25, 2018. (from original article Dessart, L., Veloutsou, C., & Morgan-Thomas, A. (2016). Capturing consumer engagement: duality, dimensionality and measurement. *Journal of Marketing Management*, 32. http://dx.doi.org/10.1080/0267257X.2015.1130738)

Realize this rule also applies in nontraditional presentation formats. Today's researcher has to be prepared to give personalized presentations to busy executives and to use Internet-based tools to prepare presentations that can be viewed at the user's leisure. The Research Snapshot discusses these trends briefly.

In a traditional oral presentation, preparation is the key to effectiveness. Communication specialists often suggest that a person preparing an oral presentation begin at the end.[7] In other words, while preparing a presentation, a researcher should think about what the client should know after completing the presentation. The researcher should select the three or four most important findings for emphasis and rely on the written report for a full summary. The researcher also needs to be ready to defend the results of the research. This is not the same as being defensive; instead, the researcher should be prepared to deal in a confident, competent manner with the questions that arise. Remember that even the most reliable and valid research project is worthless if the managers who must act on its results are not convinced of its importance.

As with written reports, researchers need to adapt the presentation to the audience. Delivering an hour-long formal speech when a 10-minute discussion is what management asked for (or vice versa) will reflect poorly on both the presenter and the report. The terminology also needs to be appropriate for the audience. A group of marketing researchers can tolerate more jargon than a group of managers.

Lecturing or reading to the audience is sure to impede communication at any level of formality. The presenter should refrain from reading prepared text word for word. By relying on brief notes, familiarity with the subject, and as much rehearsal as the occasion calls for, the presenter will foster better communication. He or she should avoid research jargon when appropriate and use short, familiar words. The presenter should maintain eye contact with the audience and repeat the main points. Because the audience cannot go back and replay what the speaker has said, an oral presentation often is organized around a standard format: *Tell them what you are going to tell them, tell them, and tell them what you just told them.*

Graphic and other visual aids can be as useful in an oral presentation as in a written report. Presenters can choose from a variety of media. Slides, videos, and on-screen computer-generated graphics are useful for larger audiences. For smaller audiences, the researcher may put visual aids on posters or flip charts. Another possibility is to make copies of the charts for each participant, possibly as a supplement to one of the other forms of presentation. Still another is to use a small personal computer or a tablet computer to flip through a presentation. This latter option is best if the audience is only one person. The most important factor to consider is to match the presentation method to the audience and the formality of the overall research project.

Whatever medium is chosen, each visual aid should be designed to convey a simple, attention-getting message that supports a point on which the audience should focus its thinking. As they do in written presentations, presenters should interpret graphics for the audience. The best slides are easy to read and interpret. Large typeface, multiple colors, bullets that highlight, and other artistic devices can enhance the readability of charts. What should be avoided are complete, long sentences on slides or other visual aids that distract the audience from listening to the presenter and instead, shifts their attention to reading the text.

Using gestures during presentations can also help convey the message and make presentations more interesting. Also, invite participation from the audience. Here are some tips on actually making the presentation:[8]

- Generally, introduce yourself while displaying the title of the presentation. Acknowledge any others who materially assisted in the project.
- Open up your arms to embrace your audience. Keep your arm actions at the height between your waist and shoulders.
- Drop your arms to your sides when not using them.

● ● ● ● ● ● ●

Subtle Gestures Can Improve a Presentation.

Some gestures are used to draw attention to points illustrated by visual aids. For these, gesturing with an open hand can seem more friendly and can even release tension related to nervousness. In contrast, a nervous speaker who uses a laser pointer may distract the audience as the pointer jumps around in the speaker's shaky hand.[9]

Reports on the Internet and Follow-Up

Many clients want numerous employees to have access to research findings. One easy way to share data is to make executive summaries and reports available on a company intranet or in an appropriate place on the Internet. In addition, a company can use information technology on the Internet to design questionnaires, administer surveys, analyze data, and share the results in a presentation- ready format. Real-time data capture allows for beginning-to-end reporting. A number of companies offer fully Web-based research management systems—for example, many companies also provide online research reports on key topics of interest.

Self-Contained Presentations

The researcher should keep some key points in mind when preparing a stand-alone presentation that can be viewed at the convenience of the user:

1. Make sure the title page indicates who did the research and for whom it was done.
2. Keep in mind that viewers may use all sorts of media devices to view the presentation. As a result, simpler is better. Keep any videos, audio, or photos in as small a file as possible and in a file that would work on almost any device.
3. Limit the number of words on a slide just as in an oral presentation.
4. Annotate any potentially complex material with text call-outs or simple audio or video recordings.
5. Use self-advancing slides but always include an easy way for the user to move forward, stop, or repeat the presentation.
6. Include links to any technical appendices that support the work.
7. On the last slide, provide clear and unambiguous contact information for easy follow-up.

As previously discussed, an infographic can also be used as a self-contained presentation. In addition to static visuals, scrolling effects or clickable icons can be incorporated to increase reader engagement.[10] This type of interactivity not only enhances user participation, but also creates lasting impressions that can lead to potential future business.

Follow-Up Reports

research follow-up
Recontacting decision-makers and/or clients after they have had a chance to read over a research report in order to determine whether additional information or clarification is necessary.

Research reports and oral presentations should communicate research findings so that managers can make business decisions. In many cases, the manager who receives the research report is unable to interpret the information and draw conclusions relevant to managerial decisions. For this reason, effective researchers do not treat the report as the end of the research process. They conduct a **research follow-up,** in which they recontact decision-makers and/or clients after the latter have had a chance to read over the report. The purpose is to determine whether the researchers need to provide additional information or clarify issues of concern to management. Just as marketing research may help an organization learn about its customers' satisfaction, the research follow-up can help marketing research staffers ensure the satisfaction of their customers marketing managers.

TIPS OF THE TRADE

- Research reports, like all communications, are interpreted by the receiver. Try to be clear and unambiguous in preparing the research report.
- Research reports should generally follow the principles of good technical writing.
- Whenever possible, have someone else proof the report and slides before submitting them to the client or editor.
- Whenever possible, stick to the standard outline for the paper.
- The executive summary is critically important because on occasion it is the only part read in detail by the client.
  - Keep it short—about 400 words maximum except for the longest reports.
  - Highlight the key findings with bullet points.
  - Write it last—after finishing the rest of the report and presentation.
- Consider the audience in preparing the report and presentation.

- Make the communication understandable.
  - Avoid jargon and put any complex statistical output in a technical appendix.
  - Use charts and tables to illustrate findings. When suitable, utilize tools such as policymap and infogaphics throughout the report and/or the presentation.
- Good ethical practices dictate that charts, graphics, and tables be presented in a way that minimizes the likelihood of misinterpreting meaning.
- Presentation slides should be clear and legible.
  - Err toward larger font, not smaller.
  - Err toward fewer words, not more.
  - When slides are posted to be viewed via the Internet, annotate complex issues with pop-ups or balloon inserts.

:: SUMMARY

1. **Create an outline for a research project using the basic parts of a final report.** A research report is an oral or written presentation of research findings directed to a specific audience to accomplish a particular purpose. Report preparation is the final stage of the research project. The consensus is that the format for a research report should include certain prefatory parts, the body of the report, and appended parts. The report format should be varied to suit the level of formality of the particular situation. The prefatory parts of a formal report include a title page, letters of transmittal and authorization, a table of contents, and a summary.

2. **Explain how to use tables for presenting numerical information.** Tables present large amounts of numerical information in a concise manner. They are especially useful for presenting several pieces of information about each item discussed. Short tables are helpful in the body of the report; long tables are better suited for an appendix. Each table should include a number, title, stubheads and bannerheads, footnotes for any explanations or qualifications of entries, and source notes for data from secondary sources.

3. **Summarize how to select and use the types of research charts.** Charts present numerical data in a way that highlights their relationships. Each chart should include a figure number, title, explanatory legends, and a source note for secondary sources. Pie charts show the composition

of a total (the parts that make up a whole). Line graphs show the relationship of a dependent variable (on the vertical axis) to an independent variable (horizontal axis). Most commonly, the independent variable is time. Bar charts show changes in a dependent variable at discrete intervals of the independent variable—for example, comparing one year with another or one subset of the population with another. Researchers need to pay careful attention to avoid distorted interpretations of graphics based on manipulations of the scale values used on axes or some other intentional or careless inaccuracy.

4. **Know how to give an effective oral presentation.** Most research projects are reported orally as well as in writing, so the researcher needs to prepare an oral presentation. The presentation should defend the results without being defensive. The presentation must be tailored to the situation and the audience. The presenter should practice delivering the presentation in a natural way, without reading to the audience. Graphic aids are useful supplements when they are simple and easy to read. Gestures also add interest and emphasis.

5. **Discuss the importance of Internet reporting and research follow-up.** Posting a summary of results online gives clients ready access to that information. Some online survey software processes the data and displays results in a presentation-ready format. Keep in mind that users often access online materials using many different types of media devices. Self-contained presentations should stay simple. In the follow-up stage of a research project, the researchers recontact decision-makers after submitting the report. This helps the researchers determine whether they need to provide further information or clarify any issues of concern to management.

:: KEY TERMS AND CONCEPTS

conclusions and recommendations section, *446*
graphic aids, *447*
infographics, *452*
introduction section, *446*
oral presentation, *453*

report format, *441*
research follow-up, *456*
research methodology section, *446*
research report, *441*
results section, *446*

:: QUESTIONS FOR REVIEW AND CRITICAL THINKING

1. List the different sections of the market research report and explain the main points to be included in each part.
2. What types of tables might be used to describe some of the various statistical tests discussed in previous chapters?
3. What is the difference between a *basic marketing research paper and an applied market research report*?
4. What is a *pie chart*? What is a *bar chart*? When might one be preferable over the other?
5. Why might a researcher create a graphic that leads a user to overestimate the size of some effect? Describe with an example.
6. How might a marketing researcher unintentionally distort results of an independent *t*-test examining brand A's customer satisfaction

against brand B's customer satisfaction where customer satisfaction is measured on a 0 to 100 point satisfaction scale (0 = no satisfaction to 100 = complete satisfaction)? How might the researcher intentionally distort the interpretation of these results?
7. What are some basic business research journals? Find some published research reports in these journals. How do they meet the standards set forth in this chapter?
8. What rules should be followed when preparing slides for self-contained presentations like those posted online?
9. What ethical concerns arise when you prepare (or read) a report?

10. The following stacked column chart shows per capita package water consumption from 2014 to 2016. The same data is summarized in Exhibit 16.2 in a table. Compare and contrast both visuals based on how different aspects of the data is highlighted in each.

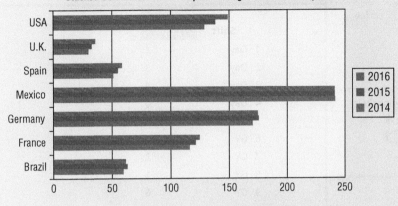

:: RESEARCH ACTIVITY

1. This activity can be used for the term-long project. In the resources that accompany this book, you will find a PowerPoint file that contains a detailed outline for a research project. This file contains a skeleton or template of a final research presentation. The outline also serves as the framework for a research report. Using instructions from your instructor regarding the topic and nature of a research report, fill in the information needed to turn the outline into an actual research report. In some cases, you will need to insert slides to fill in a section. For example, the results will likely take multiple slides to communicate effectively. Your instructor will provide guidance as to other details in terms of turning this into an oral presentation, a formal written report, a slidenet.com presentation or other Internet presentation, and so forth. This activity gives you the opportunity to gain real-world research expertise.

2. Input "Amazon.com" or "Apple" in an Internet search engine along with other key words that may lead you to research reports that describe some aspect of these mammoth companies' marketing efforts. Try limiting results with the word *report* should you be overwhelmed with information. Find one of the articles that actually presents some research reports, such as consumer reactions to innovations. Prepare PowerPoint slides that contain appropriate charts to present the results.

3. Using data from Exhibit 15.6, which described coffee drinking habits by the shift that workers work (shown again here), prepare a pie chart(s) and at least one other type of chart that depicts some meaning from the data. For instance, show the proportion of workers in each shift (a pie chart works well for this) and show the means of coffee drinking by shift. Use a statistical package like SAS JMP or SPSS to create the charts. Also, create the charts using Excel or PowerPoint. Next, try using infographics to depict the same information. What software seems to be the most easy and most flexible in creating charts? Which chart looks the most appealing?

	Shift	Cups
1	Day	1
2	Day	3
3	Day	4
4	Day	0
5	Day	2
6	GY	7
7	GY	2
8	GY	1
9	GY	6
10	Night	6
11	Night	8
12	Night	3
13	Night	7
14	Night	6

Ex15_6_coffee - JMP

File Edit Tables Rows Cols DOE Analyze Graph Tools View Window Help

Ex15_6_coffee

Columns (2/1)
Shift **
Cups **

Rows
All rows   14
Selected   0
Excluded   0
Hidden   0
Labelled   0

Source: SAS Institute

Consumer Price Knowledge

Case 16.1

A recent study investigated one major area of marketing decisions: pricing practices.[11] Specifically, the study addressed consumer knowledge and attitudes about the practice of online retailers adjusting their prices according to customer characteristics, such as how frequently they buy from the retailer. Price discrimination has long been commonplace in many industries, but the Internet provides a way of implementing large-scale price discrimination. Realize that price discrimination isn't always a bad thing for individual consumers as sometimes he or she is the beneficiary of a low price.

For example, a rental car company may offer a consumer a low rate on a rental car if the person's recent Web history has shown a search for hotels. Someone who goes straight to the rental car site may not get such a discount. Another website selling cameras charged different prices for the same model depending on whether the visitor to the site had previously visited sites that supply price comparisons. In general, price discrimination is legal unless it discriminates by race or sex or involves antitrust or price-fixing laws (such as two competitors agreeing to charge certain prices).

Ryan McVay/Getty Images

The study consisted of telephone interviews conducted with a sample of 1,500 adults, screened to find persons who had used the Internet in the preceding thirty days. The questionnaire gathered demographic data and data about Internet usage. In addition, the interviewer read seventeen statements about basic laws and practices related to price discrimination and the targeting of consumers according to their shopping behaviors. Respondents were asked whether each of these statements was true or false. Case Exhibits 16.1-1, 16.1-2, 16.1-3, and 16.1-4 summarize some of the results from this study.

Questions

1. The information provided here is not detailed enough for a formal report, but assume that you are making an informal report in a preliminary stage of the reporting process. Which of these findings do you want to emphasize as your main points? Why?

2. Prepare a written summary of the findings, using at least two tables or charts.

3. Prepare two tables or charts that would be suitable to accompany an oral presentation of these results. Are they different from the visual aids you prepared for question 2? Why or why not?

4. How could you use tools like infographics to create graphics for a presentation? Go to one of the websites introduced in this chapter and create a suitable infographic for this case.

EXHIBIT **16.1-1**

Selected Information about the Sample

Sex	
Male	48%
Female	52%
Online Connection at Home	
Dial-up connection only	31%
Cable modem (with/without dial-up)	18%
DSL (with/without dial-up)	25%
Cable or DSL with another method	13%
Don't know	4%
No connection at home	9%
Self-Ranked Expertise Navigating the Internet	
Beginner	14%
Intermediate	40%
Advanced	34%
Expert	12%

Source: Joseph Turow, Lauren Feldman, and Kimberly Meltzer, "Open to Exploitation: American Shoppers Online and Offline, " APPC Report. June 2005, p. 15, downloaded at http://www.annenbergpublicpolicycenter.org.

EXHIBIT **16.1-2**

Responses to Selected Knowledge Questions

Statement	Response*		
	True	False	Don't Know
Companies today have the ability to follow my activity across many sites on the Web.	80%	8%	12%
It is legal for an *online* store to charge different people different prices at the same time of day.	38%	29%	33%
By law, a site such as Expedia or Orbitz that compares prices on different airlines must include the lowest airline prices.	37%	32%	31%
It is legal for an *offline* store to charge different people different prices at the same time of day.	29%	42%	29%
When a website has a privacy policy, it means the site will not share my information with other websites or companies.	59%	25%	16%

*When the numbers do not add up to 100%, it is because of a rounding error. **Boldface** type indicates the correct answer.

Source: Joseph Turow, Lauren Feldman, and Kimberly Meltzer, "Open to Exploitation: American Shoppers Online and Offline, " APPC Report. June 2005, p. 20, downloaded at http://www.annenbergpublicpolicycenter.org.

EXHIBIT **16.1-3**

Responses to Selected Attitude Questions

Statement	Response*			
	Agree	Disagree	Neutral	Don't Know
It's okay if a store charges me a price based on what it knows about me.	8%	91%	—	1%
It's okay if an *online* store I use charges different people different prices for the same products during the same hour.	11%	87%	1%	1%
It would bother me to learn that other people pay less than I do for the same products.	76%	22%	1%	1%
It would bother me if websites I shop at keep detailed records of my buying behavior.	57%	41%	2%	1%
It's okay if a store I shop at frequently uses information it has about me to create a picture of me that improves the services it provides for me.	50%	41%	2%	1%

*When the numbers do not add up to 100%, it is because of a rounding error.

Source: Joseph Turow, Lauren Feldman, and Kimberly Meltzer, "Open to Exploitation: American Shoppers Online and Offline," APPC Report. June 2005, p. 22, downloaded at http://www.annenbergpublicpolicycenter.org.

EXHIBIT **16.1-4**

Predicting Knowledge Score from Selected Demographics

	Unstandardized Regression Coefficient (*B*)	Standardized Regression Coefficient (β)
Education	0.630*	0.200
Income	0.383*	0.150
Self-perceived ability to navigate Internet	0.616*	0.149
Constant	2.687	
R^2	0.148	

*Significance <0.001 level.

Source: Joseph Turow, Lauren Feldman, and Kimberly Meltzer, "Open to Exploitation: American Shoppers Online and Offline," APPC Report. June 2005, p. 29, downloaded at http://www.annenbergpublicpolicy center.org.

A Final Note on Marketing Research

Hopefully, after reading and studying the material in this book, you can now understand and apply basic processes that help identify key research questions and turn raw data into intelligence. Thus, after sifting through a vast sea of information, this intelligence helps someone make a better decision, which, in turn, helps make someone's life better. The consumer who gets something of greater value is better off and the people who produced and marketed the product also are better off. Marketing research is a very important and useful area of knowledge that can lead to meaningful skills. Never before has marketing research played a more important role in business success. The set of cases that follows provides the reader with one last chance to gain experience through real-world applications of marketing research. If you are still hungry for more about marketing research, there are many more advanced topics that can increase your skills in one of the specialized areas of research!

Comprehensive Cases with Computerized Databases

::::::: COMPREHENSIVE CASES

Case 1 You Can Look It Up!

Not only is the amount of data collected ever growing, but more and more of it can be accessed easily through the Internet. Web crawlers can even be used to scrape (search and store) data from the Web. Marketers benefit from the ready availability of consumption data online. For instance, consider how many marketers have a stake in the way that American consumers spend money on food. For instance, do Americans spend more money on food in the home or away from home? Does the answer to the question vary based on American consumers' incomes or generation?.

The U.S. Census Department and U.S. Bureau of Labor Statistics maintain a huge amount of data relevant to the way U.S. citizens earn and spend money. Spending is tracked based on quarterly surveys that typically involve responses from approximately 7,000 U.S. households. If one searches for the Bureau of Labor Statistics (BLS) consumer expenditure survey, he/she likely will find a listing of tables available that break down consumer spending per household across dozens and dozens of categories by a myriad of characteristics. Table 1101, for instance, breaks down household consumer spending by household income showing proportionate spending in many categories (i.e., % of all income or spending). Suppose a restaurant group like Darden, Inc., faced decision statements related to what types of restaurants should be developed based on opportunities in different income market segments. Prior to gathering primary data, the researchers charged with the task come across the data in Table 1101. With it, they can investigate questions such as:

1.   Do upper-middle and lower-middle consumers spend the same amount of money proportionately on food at home?

2.   Do upper-middle and lower-middle consumers spend the same amount of money on food away from home?

3.   Do all household income levels spend proportionately equal amounts on alcoholic beverages?

4.   Do U.S. consumers in each income category spend more on alcoholic beverages than nonalcoholic beverages?

Considering the research questions above, address the following items:

1.   Search the Internet and try to find the latest Consumer Expenditure Survey results by income quintile (meaning each progressive 20 percent of income – lowest 20 percent, second lowest 20 percent, third 20 percent, fourth 20 percent, and highest 20 percent). Prepare a bar chart displaying expenditures on food as a portion of all expenditures. Also, prepare a bar chart displaying the "share" of total income spent on food by income category.

2.   Typically, Table 1101 will report total food expenditures and "food at home" expenditures. Compute "food away from home" for each income group by subtracting the "food at home" from the "food" expenditures.

3.   Perform statistical tests that examine each of the first two research questions above. Report your results.

4.   Perform statistical tests that address the last two research questions above (numbers 3 and 4). Report your results.

5.   What might the data in the table suggest about restaurant opportunities in each "income group" market?

Case 2 Good Times at GoodBuy?

This case uses the GoodBuy Retail data set.[1] The data are available in the online student resources.

GoodBuy is a large big box retailer that has a track record of success offering popular brands of electronics such as Samsung, Sony, LG, and HP. Although the bulk of their sales revenue comes from big-ticket items like computers, big-screen HD televisions, and smartphones (for which they receive supplementary revenue for selling contracts to data suppliers), the margin is higher for smallticket items (under $100) that include accessories for the other electronics. Many of these accessories are unplanned purchases that customers discover in the store. They sell a disproportionate portion of accessories in-store as opposed to online as customers are able to actually try a lot of them out in the store or have the product demonstrated by a service associate. Management believes one strategy for increasing sales of these items is through more purchases from loyal customers. Thus, the overall decision statement expressed to the research team is:

■ In what ways can we allocate resources to consistently encourage our current customers to spend more time in a GoodBuy store and increase purchases of valuable accessories?

In particular, they have approximately $500K allocated per store that can be directed toward enhancing the atmosphere by creating more spacious and luxurious shopping space. This would include leasing out space to Samsung and Apple to operate their own stores within each store. In addition, "living rooms" would allow shoppers to experience all the store's major products in a home-like environment. Alternatively, they could direct this investment toward more multimedia promotion about the low prices at GoodBuy.

After some discussion between the research team and GoodBuy management, the researchers mention that they recently conducted a survey of shoppers (the GoodBuy data from Exhibit 20.3) that contains relevant data. They translate the decision statement into research questions related to:

■ How does the store atmosphere affect customer loyalty?
■ Do customers bond with other customers in the store and does this lead to positive reactions among consumers?

In the prospectus for the research, the lead researcher describes the situation background as follows:

The other shoppers are a prominent part of the shopping atmosphere. As shoppers see others who share curiosity about the same sorts of products, they interact and enhance the shopping atmosphere. We know from previous research across other retail types that consumers enjoy shopping with others that they view as similar to themselves. Thus, as a consumer's attitude toward the other shoppers improves, so does their attitude of the shopping atmosphere. Both of these are factors known to increase customer satisfaction, which is a conduit to increased customer loyalty. One of the slides prepared for the presentation summed this theory up as shown in Case Exhibit 2.1.

The lead researcher comes to you and asks you to serve as the analyst for this project. Using the data available, she encourages you to use the scales available to measure the impression of other GoodBuy shoppers (ATS1–ATS4) and the favorableness of the GoodBuy atmosphere (ATM1–ATM4), along with the customer satisfaction (CSD1–CSD5) and loyalty scales (LOY1–LOY4), to test the theory above using multivariate data analysis. Your job is to supply a brief report to her that can be used as a key part of the presentation that will go to GoodBuy management.

Use the following questions to help shape your report:

1. Are the data appropriate for multiple regression analysis? If so, explain your choice. If not, suggest an alternative.
2. The researcher suggests that you first use only half of the data to do an initial analysis (split the entire sample randomly into two halves of 200 respondents each). Do you think that is a good idea? Explain.
3. Do the multiple scale items seem to represent any multiple item scales that could represent constructs? If so, choose one and compute a coefficient alpha reliability estimate using statistical software.

CASE EXHIBIT **2.1** The Proposed Theory of Customer Loyalty

[1]GoodBuy is fictional although elements of the story are based on actual trends in the retail industry.

Case 3 Attiring Situation

(Download the data sets for this case from www .cengagebrain.com or request them from your instructor.) RESERV is a national level placement firm specializing in putting retailers and service providers together with potential employees who fill positions at all levels of the organization. This includes entry-level positions and senior management positions. One international specialty clothing store chain has approached them with

issues involving key characteristics of retail employees. The two key characteristics of primary interest involve the appearance of potential employees and problems with customer integrity.

Over the last five years, store management has adopted a very flexible dress code that allowed employees some flexibility in the way they dressed for work. Casual attire was permitted with the idea that younger customers could better identify with store employees, most of whom are younger than average. However, senior management had just become aware of how some very successful companies tightly control the appearance of their sales force. The Walt Disney Company, for example, has strict grooming policies for all employees, provides uniforms (or costumes) for most *cast members*, and does not permit any employee to work if they have a visible tattoo. Disney executives discuss many positive benefits from this policy and one is that customers are more responsive to the employees. Thus, it just may be that the appearance of employees can influence the behavior of customers. This influence can be from the greater identity that employees display—meaning, they stand out better and may encourage acquiescence through friendliness.

Senior research associate, Michael Neil, decides to conduct an experiment to examine relevant research questions including:

RQ1: How does employee appearance affect customer purchasing behavior?

RQ2: How does employee appearance affect customer ethics?

Mr. Neil decides the problem can best be attacked by conducting a laboratory experiment. In the experiment, two variables are manipulated in a between-subjects design. The experiment includes two experimental variables which are controlled by the researcher and subjects' biological sex, which was recorded and included as a blocking variable. The experimental variables (and blocking variable) are:

Name	Description	Values
X_1	A manipulation of the attire of the service-providing employee	0 = Professional Attire (Neatly groomed w/business attire) 1 = Unprofessional Attire (Unkempt hair w/jeans and t-shirt)
X_2	The manner with which the service-providing employee tries to gain extra sales—or simply, the close approach	0 = Soft Close 1 = Hard Close
Gender	Subject's biological sex	0 = Male 1 = Female

Three dependent variables are included:

Name	Description	Range
Time	How much time the subject spent with the employee beyond what was necessary to choose the slacks and shirt.	0–10 minutes
Spend	How much of the $25 the subject spent on extra products offered for sale by the retail service provider	$0–$25
Keep	How much of the $25 the subject kept rather than returning to the researcher	$0–$25

Additionally, several variables were collected following the experiment that tried to capture how the subject felt during the exercise. All of these items were gathered using a 7-item semantic differential scale.

Name	Description
SD1	Low Quality–High Quality
SD2	Dislike–Like
SD3	Unfavorable–Favorable
SD4	Negative–Positive
SD5	Easy–Difficult
SD6	Restful–Tiring
SD7	Comfortable–Uncomfortable
SD8	Calm–Tense

The experiment was conducted in a university union. Subjects were recruited from the food court area. RESERV employees approached potential subjects and requested their participation in a study that examined how customers really bought things. Subjects would each receive vouchers that could be exchanged for merchandise in return for their participation. Each potential subject was informed that the participation could take between 20 and 40 minutes to complete. Upon agreeing to participate, subjects were escorted to a waiting area where they were provided with further instructions and mingled with other participants before entering a small room that was set up to resemble an actual retail clothing counter.

Each subject was told to play the role of a customer who had just purchased some dress slacks and a shirt. The employee was to complete the transaction. Once the subject entered the mock retail environment, a research assistant who was playing the role of the retail employee entered the room. As a retail sales associate, one important role was to suggest add-on sales. Several dozen accessory items ranging from socks and handkerchiefs to small jewelry items were displayed at the counter.

As a result of this experimental procedure, each subject was randomly assigned to one of four conditions, each corresponding to a unique combination of the experimental variables described above. In other words, the employee was either:

1. Dressed professionally and used a soft close (i.e., "Perhaps you would like to see some additional accessories") in trying to sell merchandise beyond the slacks and shirt.
2. Dressed unprofessionally and used a soft close.
3. Dressed professionally and used a hard close (i.e., "You really need to match this up with some coordinated accessories which happen to be on sale today only") in trying to sell merchandise beyond the slacks and shirt.
4. Dressed unprofessionally and used a hard close.

Thus, RESERV wishes to use this information to explain how employee appearance encourages shoppers to continue shopping (TIME) and spend money (SPEND). Rather than simply asking purchase intentions, each subject was given $25 (in one-dollar bills) which they were allowed to *spend* on accessories. This allowed each subject to participate in an actual transaction.

In addition, the experiment did not provide explicit instructions on what was to be done with the money that was left over. Once the simulated shopping trip was complete, subjects were taken to another small room where they completed a questionnaire containing the semantic differential scales and demographic information alone and at their own pace. Because the instructions did not specifically tell subjects what to do with the money they possessed following the experiment, this allowed the researchers to operationalize a behavioral dependent variable (KEEP) that simulated questionable consumer behavior based on the implied assumption that the money was to be either handed to the research assistant when complete or turned in along with the questionnaire. In other words, subjects who kept money were considered as behaving less ethically than those who left the money behind or turned it in to a member of the research team.

1. Develop at least three hypotheses that correspond to the research questions.
2. Test the hypotheses using an appropriate statistical approach.
3. Suppose the researcher is curious about how the feelings captured with the semantic differentials influence the dependent variables SPEND and KEEP. Conduct an analysis to explore this possibility. Are any problems present in testing this?
4. Critique the experiment from an internal and external validity viewpoint.
5. What conclusions would be justified by management regarding their employee appearance policy?

Case 4 Values and the Automobile Market

(Download the data sets for this case from www .cengagebrain.com or request them from your instructor.)
In the last decade, the luxury car segment became one of the most competitive in the automobile market. Many American consumers who purchase luxury cars prefer imports from Germany and Japan.

A marketing vice president with General Motors once commented, "Import-committed buyers have been frustrating to us." This type of thinking has led industry analysts to argue that to successfully compete in the luxury car segment, U.S. carmakers need to develop a better understanding of the consumers so that they can better segment the market and better position their products via more effective advertising. Insight into the foreign-domestic luxury car choice may result from examining owners' personal values in addition to their evaluations of car attributes, because luxury cars, like many other conspicuously consumed luxury products, may be purchased mainly for value-expressive reasons.

Industry analysts believe it would be important to assess whether personal values of consumers could be used to explain ownership of American, German, and Japanese luxury cars. Further, they believe they should also assess whether knowledge of owners' personal values provides any additional information useful in explaining ownership of American, German, and Japanese luxury cars beyond that obtained from their evaluations of the cars' attributes.

Personal values are likely to provide insights into reasons for ownership of luxury cars for at least two reasons. First, Americans have always had a very personal relationship with their cars and have used them as symbols of their self-concept. For instance, people who value a *sense of accomplishment* are quite likely to desire a luxury car that they feel is an appropriate symbol of their achievement, whereas people who value *fun, enjoyment, and excitement* are likely to desire a luxury car that they perceive as fun and exciting to drive. An advertiser trying to persuade the former segment to purchase a luxury car should position the car as a status symbol that will help its owners demonstrate their accomplishments to others. Similarly, an advertiser trying to persuade the latter segment to purchase a luxury car should position the car as a fun and exciting car to drive. In other words, effective advertising shows consumers how purchasing a given product will help them achieve their valued state, because brands tied to values will be perceived more favorably than brands that deliver more mundane benefits.

Second, when a market is overcrowded with competing brands offering very similar options—as is the case with the luxury car market—consumers are quite likely to choose between brands on the basis of value-expressive considerations.

METHOD

Data were collected via a mail survey sent to 498 consumers chosen at random from a list obtained from a syndicated research company located in an affluent county in a southern state. The list contained names of people who had purchased either a luxury American car (Cadillac or Lincoln Mercury), a luxury German car (Mercedes or BMW), or a luxury Japanese car (Infiniti or Lexus) within the last year. A cover letter explained that the survey was part of an academic research project. People were asked to return the questionnaires anonymously to a university address (a postage-paid envelope was provided with each survey). Beyond an appeal to help the researchers, respondents were not offered any other incentive to complete the surveys. Of the 498 questionnaires originally sent, 17 were returned by the post office as undeliverable. One hundred fifty-five completed surveys were received, for a response rate of 32.2 percent.

The Survey Instrument

The survey included questions on (1) various issues that people consider when purchasing new cars, (2) importance of car attributes, (3) importance of different values, and (4) demographics (sex, age, education, and family income). Questions relating to the issues that people consider when purchasing new cars were developed through initial interviews with consumers and were measured with a 7-point Likert scale with end anchors of "strongly agree" and "strongly disagree" (See Case Exhibit 4.1). A list of 12 car attributes was developed from the initial interviews with consumers and by consulting *Consumer Reports*. (See Case Exhibit 4.2.) The importance of each attribute was measured with a 7-point numerical scale with end points labeled "very important" and "very unimportant." The

List of Values (LOV) scale in Case Exhibit 4.3 was used to measure the importance of values. Respondents were asked to rate each of the eight values (we combined fun, enjoyment, and excitement into one value) on a 7-point numerical scale with end points labeled "very important" and "very unimportant."

CASE EXHIBIT 4.1 Issues That Consumers Consider When Buying Luxury Automobiles

Having a luxury car is a major part of my fun and excitement.[a] (Issue 1)

Owning a luxury car is a part of "being good to myself." (Issue 2)

When I was able to buy my first luxury car, I felt a sense of accomplishment. (Issue 3)

I enjoy giving my friends advice about luxury cars. (Issue 4)

Getting a good deal when I buy a luxury car makes me feel better about myself. (Issue 5)

I seek novelty and I am willing to try new innovations in cars. (Issue 6)

I tend to buy the same brand of the car several times in a row. (Issue 7)

I tend to buy from the same dealer several times in a row. (Issue 8)

I usually use sources of information such as *Consumer Reports* in deciding on a car. (Issue 9)

I usually visit three or more dealerships before I buy a car. (Issue 10)

I would read a brochure or watch a video about defensive driving. (Issue 11)

When buying a new luxury car, my family's opinion is very important to me. (Issue 12)

My family usually accompanies me when I am shopping for a new luxury car. (Issue 13)

I usually rely upon ads and salespersons for information on cars. (Issue 14)

I usually rely upon friends and acquaintances for information on cars. (Issue 15)

When shopping for a car, it is important that the car dealer make me feel at ease. (Issue 16)

Most of my friends drive luxury import cars. (Issue 17)

Most of my friends drive luxury domestic cars. (Issue 18)

I think celebrity endorsers in ads influence people's choices of luxury cars. (Issue 19)

I would not buy a luxury car if I felt that my debt level is higher than usual. (Issue 20)

[a]Note: Subjects' responses were measured with 1 as "strongly agree" and 7 as "strongly disagree."

CASE EXHIBIT 4.2 Car Attributes

Attribute	Code	Attribute	Code
Comfort	Comfort	Low maintenance cost	Lomc
Safety	Safety	Reliability	Rely
Power	Power	Warranty	Warrant
Speed	Speed	Nonpolluting	Nonpol
Styling	Styling	High gas mileage	Gasmle
Durability	Durabil	Speed of repairs	Repairs

CASE EXHIBIT 4.3 List of Values

Value	Code	Value	Code
Fun-Enjoyment-Excitement	Fun	Sense of accomplishment	Accomp
Sense of belonging	Belong	Warm relationship	Warm
Being well respected	Respect	Security	Security
Self-fulfillment	Selfful	Self-respect	Selfres

The Sample

Of the 155 respondents in the sample, 58 (37.4 percent) owned an American luxury car, 38 (24.5 percent) owned a European luxury car, and 59 (38.1 percent) owned a Japanese luxury car. The majority of the sample consisted of older (85 percent were 35 years of age or above), more educated (64 percent were college graduates), and economically well-off (87.2 percent earned $65,000 or more) consumers.

THE CODE BOOK

Case Exhibit 4.4 lists the SPSS variable names and identifies codes for these variables. (Note that this data set is also available in Microsoft Excel.)

CASE EXHIBIT 4.4 List of Variables and Computer Codes

ID—Identification number

AGE (categories are 2 = 35 years and under, 3 = 36 − 45 yrs, 4 = 46 − 55 yrs, 5 = 56 − 65 yrs, 6 = 65+ yrs)

SEX (1 = male, 0 = female)

EDUC—Education (1 = less than high school, 2 = high school grad, 3 = some college, 4 = college grad, 5 = graduate degree)

INCOME (1 = less than $35,000, 2 = $35,001 − $50,000, 3 = $50,001 − $65,000, 4 = $65,001, or greater)

CAR—Type of luxury car (American car, European car, Japanese car)

ISSUES—The sequence of issues listed in Case Exhibit 4.1. (Strongly agree = 1; strongly disagree = 7)

ATTRIBUTES—The sequence of car attributes listed in Case Exhibit 4.2. (Very important to you = 1; very unimportant to you = 7)

VALUES—The sequence of values listed in Case Exhibit 4.3. (Very important = 1; very unimportant = 7)

ADDITIONAL INFORMATION

Several of the questions will require the use of a computerized database. Your instructor will provide information about obtaining the VALUES data set if the material is part of the case assignment.

Questions

1. Is the sampling method adequate? Is the attitude-measuring scale sound? Explain.

2. Using the computerized database with a statistical software package, calculate the means of the three automotive groups for the values variables. Do any of the values variables show significant differences between American, Japanese, and European car owners?

3. Are there any significant differences on importance of attributes?

4. Write a short statement interpreting the results of this research.

Case materials based on research by Ajay Sukhdial and Goutam Chakraborty, Oklahoma State University.

Case 5 Say It Ain't So! Is This the Real Thing?

INTRODUCTION

David Ortega is the lead researcher for an upscale restaurant group hoping to add another chain that would compete directly with the upscale Smith and Wollensky restaurants (http://www.smithandwollensky.com). Smith and Wollensky is part of the Patina Restaurant Group. The average dinner check for a customer at Smith and Wollensky is typically $80 to $100.[1] Whenever a new venture of this type is planned, one has to wonder whether there are enough customers willing to pay premium prices given the large number of lesser priced alternatives. In fact, Smith and Wollensky is considering opening a lesser priced "Grill" that would be positioned so that the average customer check would be about half that of the original. What is it that people are willing to pay for and what sacrifices can be made to deliver a satisfying, if not luxurious, experience? How can he create a unique experience at a lower price? These are the questions facing David Ortega.

RESEARCH APPROACH

After considering how to study the issue, David decides a qualitative research approach will be useful. He hopes to develop a deep understanding of how the fine dining experience offers value and perhaps some insights into what intangibles create value for consumers in general. After considering the different options, he decides on a phenomenological approach. The primary tool of investigation is conversational interviewing. David plans to enter into casual conversations with businesspeople in the lounge of the downtown Ritz Carlton. He begins the conversation by commenting on the wine he is sipping—something like, "It isn't bad, but it's hard to believe they get $19 for a glass of this stuff."

[1]MacNealy, Jeremy (2006), "Smith and Wollensky on the Grill," The Motley Fool, http://www.fool.com/News/mft/2006/mft06040425.htm, accessed November 6, 2008.

RESULTS

Two weeks later, David has completed "conversations" with five consumers. He found them very willing and free to talk about the things they indulge in. He develops a field log of notes from the consumers' comments. The notes are recorded verbatim.[2] The following field notes are highlighted:

Respondent	Date/Time	Text
Joe, wm, 55, attorney	12/5/17 – 10:15 PM	Well, wine doesn't have to be expensive to be good. Beyond some basic price point . . . maybe $14 a bottle . . . I find a lot of good wines. But, the wine has to fit the situation. It has to add something. A fake Rolex will tell time; but a real Rolex tells you about you. I don't mind paying for something that's unique—even though it might not be my cup of tea. Chateau Masur is like that. It's from Lebanon! It isn't always elegant or delicious, but it is always real. You always know it comes from some place very unique and is made under the most trying circumstances.
Sally, hf, 45, medical sales	12/7/17 – 5:45 PM	We pay too much for a lot of stuff though. I like things to be genuine. When you ask for crab you get crab—not Krab with a "K." It's made of fish you know!
		. . .
		I love old neighborhood Italian restaurants. They aren't always expensive. But, they have character. I think that it is very easy to spoil. I might not want a checkered red and white table cloth at home, but the Italian restaurant has to have one. I have to smell the garlic from the parking lot. And, that cheap Chianti, the kind with the basket cradle—it had better be from Italy—it tastes sooo good there. You know, you could pay more, but a nice dinner there with a couple of friends is worth a lot.
		You know, the people who make great wine or who have great restaurants kind of luck into it. I don't think they really ever sent out a survey asking what the restaurant or the wine should be like. I think they said "I am going to make this the way that I want it to be . . ." and it just happens to be right! They are so committed to the product that it works—no matter the price. But commitment like that costs a little more usually—although they aren't in it for the money.
Hebert, wm, 40, oil executive	12/8/17 – 11:00 PM	How old is it? The older it is, the more it is worth—yeah! I like this French wine that has "depuis 1574," maybe its name is Hugel (trying to recall). Imagine the same family running that company for hundreds of years. I like to think about the family in the vineyards—the old man on a tractor with his sons running around the sides. Their kids are hanging around the barn.
		. . .
		You know, you can buy cheap things and get cheated too. We are free to be cheated at any price point! (laughter) I remember bringing home a bottle of "Louisiana Hot Sauce." Man, that stuff didn't have any heat to it at all. When I looked at the bottle, do you know where it was from? . . . Man, it was from Tennessee . . . can you believe that, Louisiana Hot Sauce from Tennessee!! What a scam.
		. . . .
		When I buy something nice, I want it to be real. Burgundy should be from Burgundy. Bordeaux should be from Bordeaux. Champagne should be from Champagne—not Texas or California! (laughter) Because I know in Champagne, they know how to make Champagne—sparkling wine. They have perfected the methods over hundreds of years. A good glass of Champagne is worth what you pay!
Angela, bf, 60, insurance executive	12/9/17 – 6:45 PM	Look at this hotel . . . when you just look at the price you think "this is crazy!" But, look at the attention to detail. Cleaning the floor is a production. Have you noticed the way they turn down your bed? Taking care of the plants is serious business to these people. I've stayed at a place like this in Florida—I loved it. At first, I couldn't put my finger on it. Then, it hit me. The place smelled like Florida. They have a way of giving everything the smell of sweet grass and citrus. It's terrific. Another one in California smelled of sandalwood and cypress. You have to be willing to pay more for people that care so much about what they do. Maybe that's your wine? Those smells make me think of those special places. When I drink a wine, I think about where it comes from too.
Burt, wm, 35, sales	12/9/17 – 9:30 PM	It's okay for something to be cheap . . . even fake! As long as I know it's fake. I've got three fake Rolexes. This one looks pretty good . . . looks genuine . . . but look at the way the second hand moves . . . it's jumping. A real one wouldn't do that!!
		I ate with this guy the other night who sent back a bottle of wine after ordering it. When the waiter pulled the cork, it didn't have Domaine Mas Blanc written on it—that's the name of the wine. He said, "How do I know it is real?" At first I thought he was crazy but after I looked at my fake Rolex . . . you know, I think he was right. When you spend $100 for a bottle, you want real stuff. But, if you spend $10 for a bottle of wine in a restaurant, who the hell cares? You didn't pay for it to be real . . . one day, when I pony up ten grand for a real Rolex, I'll send back the fakes!

Note: w = white; h = Hispanic, f = female, m = male, etc.

[2]For more comments along this same line, see Beverland, M., "The Real Thing: Branding Authenticity in the Luxury Wine Trade," *Journal of Business Research* 59 (February 2006), 251–258; Beverland, M., "Crafting Brand Authenticity: The Case of Luxury Wines," *Journal of Management Studies* 42 (July 2005), 103–129; and Wolff, C., "Blending High Style and Authenticity," *Lodging Hospitality* 61 (November 1, 2005), 72–76.

RESULTS

David decides to use a word count to try to identify the main themes. Hopefully, these themes can help clarify the business problem. Perhaps if the information can't answer the questions above, it will point him in the right direction. Whatever the case, David feels the project has helped him better understand the total value proposition offered by restaurants, wines, hotels, and other products.

Questions:

1. Comment on the research approach. Do you feel it was an appropriate choice?

2. David did not inform these respondents that he was doing marketing research during these conversations. Why do you think he withheld this information and was it appropriate to do so?

3. Using the Internet, try to identify at least three restaurants that Smith and Wollensky competes with and three with whom the new S&W Grill may compete.

4. Try to interpret the discussions above. You may use one of the approaches discussed in the text. What themes should be coded? What themes occur most frequently? Can the different themes be linked together to form a unit of meaning?

5. What is the result of this research? What should David report back to the restaurant group?

Case 6 TABH, INC., Automotive Consulting

(Download the data sets for this case from www .cengagebrain.com or request them from your instructor.) TABH consulting specializes in research for automobile dealers in the United States, Canada, Mexico, and Europe. Although much of their work is done on a pay-for fee basis with customers such as dealerships and dealership networks selling all major makes of automobiles, they also produce a monthly "white paper" that is sold via their website. This off-the-shelf research is purchased by other research firms and by companies within the auto industry itself. This month, they would like to produce a white paper analyzing the viability of college students attending schools located in small college towns as a potentially underserved market segment.

TABH management assigns a junior analyst named Michel Gonzalez to the project. Lacking time for a more comprehensive study, Michel decides to contact the traffic department at Cal Poly University in Pomona, California, and at Central Missouri State University in Warrensburg, Missouri. Michel wishes to obtain data from the students' automobile parking registration records. Although both schools are willing to provide anonymous data records for a limited number of students, Cal Poly offers Michel a chance to visit during the registration period, which just happens to be next week. As a result, not only can Michel get data from students' registration forms, but a small amount of primary data can be obtained by intercepting students near the registration window. In return, Michel is asked to purchase a booth at the Cal Poly career fair.

As a result, Michel obtains some basic information from students. The information results in a small data set consisting of the follow observations for 100 undergraduate college students in Pomona, California:

Variable	Description
Sex	Student's sex dummy coded with 1 = female and 0 = male
Color	Color of a student's car as listed on his or her registration form
Major	Student's major field of study (Business, Liberal Arts (LA), or Engineering (ENG))
Grade	Student's grade record reported as the mode (A, B, or C)
Finance	Whether the student financed the car he or she is driving or paid for it with cash, coded 0 = cash payment and 1 = financed
Residence	Whether the student lives on campus or commutes to school, coded 0 = commute and 1 = on campus
Animal	Michel asks each student to quickly draw a cartoon about the type of car they would like to purchase. Students are told to depict the car as an animal in the cartoon. Although Michel expects to interpret these cartoons more deeply when time allows, the initial coding specifies what type of animal was drawn by each respondent. When Michel was unsure of what animal was drawn, a second researcher was conferred with to determine what animal was depicted. Some students depicted the car as a dog, some as a cat, and some as a mule.

The purpose of the white paper is to offer car dealers considering new locations a comparison of the profile of a small town university with the primary market segments for their particular automobile. For instance, a company specializing in small pickup trucks appeals to a different market segment than does a company specializing in two-door economy sedans. Many small towns currently do not have dealerships, particularly beyond the "Big 3." Although TABH cannot predict with certainty who may purchase the white paper, it particularly wants to appeal to companies with high sales growth in the United States, such as Kia (http://www.kia .com), Hyundai (http://www.hyundai-motor.com), and potentially European auto dealerships currently without significant U.S. distribution, such as Smart (http://www.smart.com), among others. TABH also hopes the white paper may eventually lead to a customized project for one of these companies. Thus, the general research question is:

What are the automobile market segment characteristics of students attending U.S. universities in small towns?

This question can be broken down into a series of more specific questions:

- What segments can be identified based on identifiable characteristics of students?
- How do different segments view a car?
- What types of automobiles would be most in demand?

Questions:
1. What types of tests can be performed using the data that may at least indirectly address the primary research question?
2. What do you think the primary conclusions of the white paper will be based on the data provided?

3. Assuming a small college town lacked an auto dealership (beyond Ford, GM, and Chrysler), what two companies should be most interested in this type of location? Use the Internet if necessary to perform some cursory research on different car companies.
4. What are the weaknesses in basing decisions on this type of research?
5. Are there key issues that may diminish the usefulness of this research?
6. What kinds of themes might emerge from the cartoon drawings?
7. Are there any ethical dilemmas presented in this case?

Case 7 Knowing the Way

The Swamp Palace Museum (SPM) is an interactive museum that teaches visitors the ways of life on the swamps of the southern United States. Visitors can visit over 100 exhibits demonstrating the ecology of the swamp and the habits of the animals and insects that call the swamp home. Additionally, the museum includes several fast-food and full-service restaurants and opportunity for swimming and several thrill rides. The park covers over forty acres and includes miles and miles of pathways.

The park was originally supported with one-time government funding but now it has to become self-supporting. After five years of operation, the park has not lacked for visitors but has struggled just to break even. The Swamp Palace has sought help from the Marketivity Group to help them address the long-term viability of the park.

Initially, the Swamp Palace conducts exploratory research employing a participant-observer technique in which trained interviewers pretend to be park guests and engage in dialog with museum patrons. After employing interpretive techniques to the data gathered in these interviews, the Marketivity Group reports the exploratory results to management. The report emphasizes these key findings:

1. Patrons who complain tend to base their complaints over deficiencies in quality. Happy patrons voice nothing indicating a low quality theme.
2. Patrons also express a theme around value. Unhappy patrons believe the value offered by the park is low based in part on what is perceived as a high admission price.
3. Patrons express the difficulty in getting around in the park as a key theme. Even happy patrons joke about how difficult it is to find their way around.
4. As groups get larger, at least one member of the group was unhappy about having to accompany the others to the park.

After further subsequent discussions, Marketivity is hired to undertake a further study aimed at helping in addressing these decision statements:

- In what ways can Swamp Palace use technology to improve a customer's ability to effectively navigate around the museum?
- In what ways can Swamp Palace increase return visits by customers?
- Is participation in online coupon programs an effective way of increasing patronage and value?

Several technologies are considered as ways of enhancing value. One is a mobile phone app that will provide oral and visual navigation aids around the park. For instance, if someone says "take me to the Blind Bayou Bar," the phone will give directions using prominent museum landmarks. Second, Swamp Palace is considering subscribing to an Internet coupon program that would provide patrons with discounts. Marketivity translates these statements into several research questions including the following:

1. Do patrons who use a mobile phone navigation app report higher service quality and have an improved experience relative to those who do not?
2. Do patrons who use the mobile phone app have a greater likelihood of upgrading to a season pass?
3. Do patrons who use a coupon report more positive price perceptions?
4. Do patrons who use the mobile phone app have a greater likelihood of upgrading to a season pass?
5. What factors contribute to improved value perceptions?

Marketivity implements a quasi-experimental design over a one-week period in August. A sample of 200 visitors are randomly intercepted before entering the park. Approximately half are given the opportunity to download a free navigation app for their cell phone. Similarly, about half are invited to go to a kiosk and download a coupon from the Internet. The park provides Marketivity with employees to intercept the patrons and explain the research procedures. Upon exiting the park, the patrons are taken to a desk where they fill out a short questionnaire. The employee then keys the data into the computer. The variables in the data set are described in the following table.

Name	Description*	Values
Wayf	A variable indicating whether the patron was provided the mobile phone app on entering the park	Yes or No
Groupn	A variable indicating whether the patron used a Groupon discount to enter the park	1 = Yes / 2 = No
SQ1	Employees at SPM offer high-quality service	5-point Likert (SD to SA)
SQ2	The attractions at SPM are high in quality	5-point Likert (SD to SA)
SQ3	The food quality at SPM is very good	5-point Likert (SD to SA)
SQ4	The service at SPM is excellent overall	5-point Likert (SD to SA)
SQ5	The quality of SPM is very good	5-point Likert (SD to SA)
VAL1	The time I spent at SPM was truly a joy	5-point Likert (SD to SA)
VAL2	I enjoyed being engaged in exciting activities during my visit to SPM	5-point Likert (SD to SA)
VAL3	While at SPM, I was able to forget my problems	5-point Likert (SD to SA)
VAL4	I think SPM offers guests a lot of value	5-point Likert (SD to SA)
PriceP	The admission price is very fair	5-point Likert (SD to SA)
	Use the terms below to describe your feelings about your overall experience at the museum:	
FEEL1	Favorable —— Unfavorable	7-point Semantic Differential
FEEL2	Exciting —— Boring	7-point Semantic Differential
FEEL3	Happy —— Sad	7-point Semantic Differential
FEEL4	Delighted —— Terrible	7-point Semantic Differential
UPGRADE	Whether respondent agreed to upgrade their ticket to a season pass	1 = No / 2 = Yes / 3 = Undecided
Gender	Sex of respondent	1 = Female / 2 = Male
Age	Age group	1 = less than 18 / 2 = 19 − 24 / 3 = 25 − 35 / 4 = 36 − 45 / 5 = 46 or more
Others	How many others were with the patron	0 = None / 1 = 1 / 2 = 2 / 3 = 3 / 4 = more than 3

* Notes: Missing values in the data set are indicated by either an empty cell (sometimes with a . in the cell) or by the numeral 9. SPM stands for Swamp Place Museum, SD = Strongly Disagree (1) and SA = Strongly Agree (5).

Questions

1. Create frequency tables for Gender, Others, and Age. Are any problems evident with coding? Take any necessary corrective actions.
2. Compute a composite scale for the five SQ items and the four VAL items. Compute a coefficient alpha for each of the resulting service quality and value scales.
3. Perform an appropriate test of each research question RQ1, RQ2, RQ3, RQ4, and RQ5.
4. List an additional research question that can be addressed with a one-way ANOVA. Conduct the test.
5. List an additional research question that can be addressed with a GLM model. Conduct the test.
6. Summarize the implications for the decision statements that arise from the tests above. Make sure you cover whether the park should invest in the navigation system and coupon technologies.

ENDNOTES

Chapter 1

1 Martyn, D., A. Lau, P. Richardson, and A. Roberts (2018), "Temporal Patterns of Caffeine Intake in the United States," *Food and Chemical Toxicology*, 111, 71–83.

2 www.starbucks.com/about-us/, accessed January 6, 2018.

3 Fung, E. (2017), "Starbucks Asked to Keep Teavana Stores Open at Some Malls," *Wall Street Journal*, (December 5), https://www.wsj.com/articles/starbucks-asked-to-keep-teavana-stores-open-at-some-malls-1512494849, accessed January 6, 2018.

4 Chaudhuri, S. (2017), "Tea Turns Up the Temperature in the Fight Against Coffee," *Wall Street Journal*, (November 13), https://www.wsj.com/articles/can-hot-tea-be-as-cool-as-a-cup-of-joe-1510587330.

5 Burton, S., L. A. Cook, E. Howlett, and C. L. Newman (2014). "Broken Halos and Shattered Horns: Overcoming the Biasing Effects of Prior Expectations through Objective Information Disclosure," *Journal of the Academy of Marketing Science*, 1–17.

6 Kannan, P. K. and H. A. Li (2017), "Digital Marketing: A Framework, Review, and Research Agenda," *International Journal of Research in Marketing*, 34, 22–45. Exhibit 1.1 also draws on Kannan and Li (2017).

7 Tomsak, T., S. Reinecke, and A. Kuss (2018), "Marketing Implementation and Management Control," *Strategic Marketing*, https://doi.org/10.1007/978-3-658-18417-9_6. Ferrell, O. C., T. L. Gonzalez-Padron, T. Hult, and I. Maignan (2010), "From Market Orientation to Stakeholder Orientation," *Journal of Public Policy and Marketing*, 29 (Spring), 93–96; Sin, L. Y. M., A. C. B. Tse, O. H. M. Yau, R. P. M. Chow, J. S. Y. Lee, and L. B. Y. Lau, (2005), "Relationship Marketing Orientation: Scale Development and Cross-Cultural Validation," *Journal of Business Research*, 58 (February), 185–194.

8 http://www.italtrade.com/countries/americas/usa/spotlight/7661.htm, accessed January 7, 2018.

9 https://techbear.com/top-10-marketing-trends-2018/, accessed January 7, 2018.

10 http://wearedevelopment.net/2012/07/11/legos-approach-to-customerorientation/, accessed January 7, 2018.

11 Sebald, A. K. and F. Jacob (2018), "Help Welcome or Not: Understanding Consumer Shopping Motivation in Curated Fashion Retailing," *Journal of Retailing and Consumer Services*, 40, 188–203. Arnett, D. and M. Wittmann (2014), "Improving Marketing Success: The Role of Tacit Knowledge Exchange between Sales and Marketing," *Journal of Business Research*, 67 (March), 324–331. Lee, Ruby P., Gillian Naylor, and Qimei Chen (2011), "Linking Customer Resources to Firm Success: The Role of Marketing Program Implementation," *Journal of Business Research*, 64 (April), 394–400.

12 https://www.businesswire.com/news/home/20171030005405/en/Nespresso-Improves-User-Experience-Boutiques-Worldwide-Guest, accessed January 7, 2018.

13 http://opendorse.com/blog/2016-highest-paid-athlete-endorsers/, accessed January 8, 2018.

14 Bojanic, D. C. (2011), "The Impact of Age and Family Life Experiences on Mexican Visitor Shopping Expenditures," *Tourism Management*, 32 (April), 405–414.

15 Maldarelli, C. (2017), "E-cigarettes Might Actually Be a Safe Alternative for Quitting Smoking," *Popular Science*, (Feb. 7), https://www.popsci.com/e-cigarettes-safer-than-traditional-cigarettes-quitting-smoking, accessed January 7, 2018.

16 Mace, S. (2012), "The Impact and Determinants of Nine-Ending Pricing in Grocery Retailing," *Journal of Retailing*, 88 (March), 115–130.

17 https://www.statisticbrain.com/attention-span-statistics/, accessed February 18, 2017.

18 Meyners, J., C. Barrot, J. U. Becker and A. V. Bodapati (2017), "Reward-Scrounging in Customer Referral Programs," *International Journal of Research in Marketing*, 34, 382–398.

19 Ogden, S., S. Minahan, and D. Bednall (2017), "Promotional Competitions: A Taxonomy of Campaign Framing Choices Integrating Economic, Informational, and Affective Outcomes," *Journal of Promotion Management*, 23, https://doi.org/10.1080/10496491.2017.1297971.

20 Li, L. Y. (2011), "Marketing Metrics' Usage: Its Predictors and Implications of Customer Relationship Management," *Industrial Marketing Management*, 40 (January), 139–148.

21 Nielsen Inc. (2018), "Understanding Today's Food Shoppers," in *Insights*, (Jan. 8), The Nielsen Company: NY, NY. https://www.statista.com/statistics/765921/share-of-food-of-the-total-consumption-expenditure-by-food-type-in-france/, accessed January 11, 2018.

Chapter 2

1 Sources: Dwoskin, E. (2014), "What Secrets Your Phone Is Sharing about You," *Wall Street Journal*, (January 13), B1–B7. Walker, J. (2013), "Data Mining to Recruit Sick People," *Wall Street Journal*, (December 16), B1–B2.

2 http://royal.pingdom.com/2008/04/08/the-history-of-computer-data-storage-in-pictures/, accessed March 18, 2014.

3 Belicove, M. (2013), "Discovering Buried Treasure," *Entrepreneur*, 41 (5), 40.

4 Weinberg, B. D., L. Davis, and P. D. Berger (2013), "Perspectives on Big Data," *Journal of Marketing Analytics*, 1 (4), 187–201.

5 Columbus, L. (2017), "IBM Predicts Demand For Data Scientists Will Soar 28% By 2020," *Forbes*, (May 13), https://www.forbes.com/sites/louiscolumbus/2017/05/13/ibm-predicts-demand-for-data-scientists-will-soar-28-by-2020/#27fc6b217e3b, accessed November 26, 2017.

6 Martinez, M. G. and B. Walton (2014), "The Wisdom of Crowds: The Potential of Online Communities as a Tool for Data Analysis," *Technovation*, 34, 203–214.

7 http://www.fastcodesign.com/1669551/how-companies-like-amazon-use-big-data-to-make-you-love-them, accessed March 18, 2014.

8 Smith, D. G. and D. Strutton (2010), "Has e-Marketing Come of Age? Modeling Historical Influences on Post-Adoption Era Consumer Internet Behaviors, *Journal of Business Research*, 63 (October), 950–956.

9 Evan, A., G. Shankaranarayanan, and P. B. Berger (2010), "Managing the Quality of Marketing Data: Cost/Benefit

Tradeoffs and Optimal Configuration," *Journal of Interactive Marketing*, 24 (August), 209–221.

10 Zhou, K. Z. and C. B. Li (2010), "How Strategic Orientations Influence the Building of Dynamic Capability in Emerging Markets," *Journal of Business Research*, 63 (March), 224–231.

11 See Salesforce.com for more about their products and technology.

12 Primack, D. (2014), "Oracle Pays $400 Million for Buekai," *Fortune*, (2/25), 1.

13 Rigby, D. and C. Zook (2002), "Open-Market Innovation," *Harvard Business Review*, (October), 80–89.

14 http://internetworldstats.com, accessed November 29, 2017.

15 Ward, J. and A. Ostrom (2003), "The Internet as Information Minefield: An Analysis of the Source and Content of Brand Information Yielded by Net Searches," *Journal of Business Research*, 56 (November), 907–914.

16 Penna, M. D. (2014), "Mobile Marketing: Why Push Technology Notifications are the Marketer's New Power Tool, New School Marketing Blog, http://www.responsys.com/blogs/nsm/mobile-marketing/push-notifications-marketers-new-power-tool/, accessed March 21, 2014.

17 Ferguson, R. B., "Marines Deploy RFID," *e-Week*, 21 (November 15, 2004), 37. "Benefits of RFID Becoming More Visible" *DSN Retailing Today*, (August 8, 2005), 22.

18 Stevens-Huffman, L. (2013), "Profit from Big Data," *Smart Business Chicago*, (November), 14–17.

19 PR, N. (2014), "Big Data Applications in the Contact Center: Opportunities and Challenges. *PR Newswire US*.

20 Fielding, M. (2010), "C'est Délicieux," *Marketing News*, 44 (September 5), 6.

21 Stevens-Huffman (2013).

22 Hui, S. K., J. Inman, H. Yanliu, and J. Suher (2013). "The Effect of In-Store Travel Distance on Unplanned Spending: Applications to Mobile Promotion Strategies," *Journal of Marketing*, 77 (2), 1–16.

23 Strom, R., M. Vendel, and J. Bredican (2014), "Mobile Marketing: A Literature Review on Its Value for Consumers and Retailers, *Journal of Retailing and Consumer Services*, in press, http://dx.doi.org/10.1016/j.jretconser.2013.12.003/; Gao, T., A. J. Rohm, F. Sultan, and M. Pagani (2013), "Consumers Un-tethered: A Three-Market Empirical Study of Consumers' Mobile Marketing Acceptance," *Journal of Business Research*, 66, 2536–2544.

24 Caya, P., J. Nielsen, K. Pernice, and A. Schade (2018), "10 Best Intranets of 2018" http://www.nngroup.com/articles/intranet-design/, accessed June 4, 2018.

25 Gabriel, A. R. (2010), "Building Relationships," *Wall Street & Technology*, 28 (December), 16–17.

26 StrongView. (1). StrongView Publishes "A Practical Guide to Modern Marketing Analytics," *Business Wire* (English).

27 Dwoskin, E. (2014), "What Secrets Your Phone Is Sharing about You," *Wall Street Journal*, (January 13), B1–B4.

28 Soat, M. (2014), "En Plein Air," *Marketing News*, (February), 29–35.

29 See http://www.turn.com/news/open-data-partnership-announced, accessed June 4, 2018.

30 Hill, K. (2011), "Whac-A-Mole," *Forbes*, 187 (1/17), 36. Vascellaro, J. E. (2010), "Suit to Snuff Out "History Sniffing" Takes Aim at Tracking Web Users," *Wall Street Journal*, (December 6), B1–B2.

Chapter 3

1 Haytko, D. (2008), "Message from the Guest Editor," *Marketing Education Review*, 18 (Spring), 1.

2 *Economist* (2013), "Change Management," 409 (10/12), 80–81.

3 Blumenstyk, G. (2012), "One Business School Is Itself a Case Study in the Economics of Online Education," *Chronicle of Higher Education*, 59 (10/5), B14.

4 Cohen, P. and C. Bray (2016), "University of Phoenix Owner, Apollo Education Group, Will Be Taken Private," *New York Times* (Feb. 8), accessed October 31, 2017. World Atlas (2017), "Largest Universities in the U.S. by Enrollment," http://www.worldatlas.com/articles/largest-universities-in-the-united-states.html, accessed November 17, 2017.

5 Cited in Conant, J. (2008), *The Irregulars*, New York: Simon & Schuster.

6 Ruiz, D., D. Jain, and K. Grayson (2012), "Subproblem Decomposition: An Exploratory Research Method for Effective Incremental New Product Development," *Journal of Product Innovation Management*, 29, 385–404. Jaworski, B. and A. J. Kohli (2017), "Conducting Field-Based, Discovery-Oriented Research: Lessons from Our Market Orientation Research Experience," *AMS Review*, 4, 4–12. Zahay, D., A. Griffin, and E. Fredericks (2004), "Sources, Uses, and Forms of Data in the New Product Development Process," *Industrial Marketing Management*, 33 (October), 658–666.

7 Yoon, E., S. Carlotti, and D. Moore (2014), "Make Your Best Customers Even Better," *Harvard Business Review*, 92 (March), 23–25.

8 Organic Industry Survey (2017), https://ota.com/resources/organic-industry-survey, accessed November 15, 2017.

9 Salzman, A. (2016), "Is Whole Foods on the Brink of a Renaissance in 2017?" *Barrons*, (December 26), https://www.barrons.com/articles/is-whole-foods-on-the-brink-of-a-renaissance-in-2017-1483047179, accessed November 12, 2017. Wholefoodsmarket.com, accessed November 12, 2017. Petro, G. (2017), "Amazon's Acquisition of Whole Foods Is About Two Things: Data And Product," *Forbes*, (August 2), https://www.forbes.com/sites/gregpetro/2017/08/02/amazons-acquisition-of-whole-foods-is-about-two-things-data-and-product/#5e78d729a808, accessed November 17, 2017.

10 Hamilton, R. and A. Chernov (2010), "The Impact of Product Line Extensions and Consumer Goals on the Formation of Price Image," *Journal of Marketing Research*, 47 (February), 51–62.

11 Small Business BC (2017), "Market Research Mistakes to Avoid," *Small Business BC*, (January 18, 2017), http://smallbusinessbc.ca/article/market-research-mistakes-to-avoid/, accessed November 11, 2017.

12 Semans, D. S. (2014), "Nonprofit Marketing Research Is Vital," Georgia Nonprofit Now, https://www.gcn.org/blog/Resources/Nonprofit-marketing-research-is-vitaland-affordable, accessed November 11, 2017.

13 Einstein, A. and L. Infeld (1942), *The Evolution of Physics*, New York: Simon and Schuster, p. 95.

14 For example, see https://bea.gov/scb/, accessed November 4, 2017.

15 See Bhardwaj, S., I. Palaparthy, and A. Agrawal (2008), "Exploration of Environmental Dimensions of Servicescapes: A Literature Review," *The ICFAI Journal of Marketing Management*, 7(1), 37–48 for a relevant literature review.

16 Perdue, B. C. and J. O. Summers (1986), "Checking the Success of Manipulations in Marketing Experiments," *Journal of Marketing Research*, 23 (November), 317–326.

17 Babin, B. J., D. M. Hardesty, and T. A. Suter (2003), "Color and Shopping Intentions: The Effect of Price Fairness and Perceived Affect," *Journal of Business Research*, 56 (July), 541–551.

18 Oh, H. and C.H.C. Hsu (2014), "Assessing Equivalence of Hotel Brand Equity Measures in Cross-Cultural Contexts," *International Journal of Hospitality Management*, 36, 156–166.

19 Highberger, J. (2017), "Minneapolis Security Fails 95% of Security Tests, Sources Say," fox9.com, (July 19), http://www.fox9.com/news/msp-fails-95-percent-of-security-tests-sources-say, accessed November 17, 2017.

Chapter 4

1 Sources: Matthes, J., et al. (2013), "Consumers' Green Involvement and the Persuasive Effects of Emotional versus Functional Ads," *Journal of Business Research*, http://dx.doi.org/10.1016/j.jbusres.2013.11.054. Aldhous, P. and P. McKenna (2010), "Hey Green Spender, Spend a Buck on Me," *New Scientist*, 205 (February 20), 6–9. Veal, G. J. and S. Mouzas (2011), "Changes the Rules of the Game: Business Responses to New Regulation," *Industrial Marketing Management*, 40 (February), 290–300.

2 MRS Evidence Matters (2017), *The Researchlive Industry Report 2017*, Market Research Society: London.

3 https://www.getvero.com/resources/guides/the-amazon-experience/, accessed November 23, 2017.

4 http://ir.nielsen.com/investor-relations/shareholder-information/press-releases/Press-Release-Details/2017/Nielsen-Reports-4th-Quarter-and-Full-Year-2016-Results/default.aspx, accessed November 23, 2017.

5 Bowers, D. and M. Brereton (2017), "The AMA Gold Report 2017 Top 50 MR Firms," *Marketing News*, https://www.ama.org/publications/MarketingNews/Pages/the-ama-gold-report-2017-top-50-market-research-firms.aspx?sq=honomichl, accessed November 24, 2017.

6 http://www.jdpower.com/cars/articles/jd-power-studies/infographic-key-stats-and-findings-2017-us-vehicle-dependability, accessed November 24, 2017.

7 Bowers and Brereton (2017) ibid.

8 Reisinger, D. (2016), "Samsung Wins Appeal in $120M Patent Fight with Apple," *Fortune*, (Feb. 26), http://fortune.com/2016/02/26/apple-samsung-patent-appeal/, accessed January 25, 2018.

9 See Armstrong, J. S. (1989), "Why Do We Know? Predicting the Interests and Opinions of the American Consumer," *Journal of Forecasting*, 5 (September), 464.

10 Terdleman, D. (2014), "Esurance Twitter Contest Goes Viral but Ties Company to Offensive Tweets," cnet, (February 3), http://www.cnet.com/news/esurance-twitter-contest-goesviral-but-ties-company-to-offensivetweets/, accessed April 20, 2014. O'Reilly, L. (2016), "The Most-mentioned Brand on Twitter During the Super Bowl Didn't even Advertise on TV During the Game, *Business Insider*, (Feb. 8), http://www.businessinsider.com/esurance-most-mentioned-brand-super-bowl-2016-2, accessed November 24, 2017.

11 Goolsby, J. R. and S. D. Hunt (1992). "Cognitive Moral Development and Marketing," *Journal of Marketing*, 56(1). Cicala, J. E., A. J. Bush, D. L. Sherrell, and G. D. Deitz (2014). "Does

Transparency Influence the Ethical Behavior of Salespeople?" *Journal of Business Research*, 67 (September), 1787–1795.

12 Vitell, S., E. Ramos, and C. Nishihara (2010), "The Role of Ethics and Social Responsibility in Organizational Success: A Spanish Perspective," *Journal of Business Ethics*, 91 (February), 467–483. Singhapakdi, A., S. J. Vitell, D. J. Lee, A. M. Nisius, and B.Y. Grace. (2013). "The Influence of Love of Money and Religiosity on Ethical Decision-Making in Marketing." *Journal of Business Ethics*, 114 (1), 183–191. Kadic-Maglajlic, M. Mcevski, N. Lee, N. Boso, and I. Vida (2017), "Three Levels of Ethical Influences on Selling Behavior and Performance: Synergies and Tensions," *Journal of Business Ethics*, https://doi.org/10.1007/s10551-017-3588-1.

13 Robin, D. P., R. E. Reidenbach, and B. J. Babin (1997), "The Nature, Measurement and Stability of Ethical Judgments in the Workplace," *Psychological Reports*, 80, 563–580.

14 Miller, D. and B. Merrilees (2013). "Rebuilding Community Corporate Brands: A Total Stakeholder Involvement Approach," *Journal of Business Research*, 66 (2), 172–179.

15 Robin, D. P. 1970. "Toward a Normative Science in Marketing." *Journal of Marketing*, 32 (October) 1970, 73–76.

16 A firm that conducts surveys and is not involved in selling or telemarketing is generally considered exempt from federal do-not-call legislation. For more on the do-not call legislation, see https://www.ftc.gov/enforcement/statutes/do-not-call-registry-legislation, accessed November 24, 2017.

17 MMR Strategy Group (2012), "Should You Worry About Survey Response Rates?" http://mmrstrategy.com, accessed January 28, 2018.

18 ncsi.org (2017), http://www.ncsl.org/research/telecommunications-and-information-technology/state-laws-prohibiting-access-to-social-media-usernames-and-passwords.aspx, retrieved November 24, 2017.

19 Ante, S. E. and L. Weber (2013), "Memo to Employees: The Boss Is Watching," *Wall Street Journal*, (October 23), B1–B4. Silverman, R. E. (2013), "Tracking Sensors Invade the Workplace," *Wall Street Journal*, (March 7), B1–B2.

20 Soat, M. (2014), "En Plein Air," *Marketing News*, (February), 29–35.

21 http://coppa.org, retrieved November 24, 2017. http://www.coppanow.com/averagecoppa/, retrieved November 24, 2017.

22 http://www.kidsafeseal.com/aboutourprogram.html, accessed November 24, 2017.

23 Ahuja, R. D., M. Walker, and R. Tadepalli (2001), "Paternalism, Limited Paternalism and the Pontius Pilate Plight When Researching Children," *Journal of Business Ethics*, 32 (July), 81–92. Noguta, V. and C. A. Russell (2014), "Normative Influences on Product Placement Effects: Alcohol Brands in Television Series and the Influence of Presumed Influence," *Journal of Advertising*, 46–62.

24 Spangenberg, E., B. Grohmann, and D. E. Sprott (2005), "It's Beginning to Smell (and Sound) a Lot Like Christmas: The Interactive Effects of Ambient Scent and Music in a Retail Setting," *The Journal of Business Research*, 58 (November), 582–589. Michon, Richard, Jean- Charles Chebat, and L. W. Turley (2005), "Mall Atmospherics: The Interaction Effects of the Mall Environment on Shopping Behavior," *Journal of Business Research*, 58 (May), 576–583.

25 See, for example, Patterson, M. and J. Schroeder (2010), "Borderlines: Skin, Tattoos and Consumer Culture Theory," *Marketing Theory*, 10 (September), 253–267.

26 Akaah, I. P. and E.A. Riordan (1990), "The Incidence of Unethical Practice in Marketing Research: An Empirical Investigation," *Journal of the Academy of Marketing Sciences*, 90 (Spring), 143–152.

27 Sterling, T. (2011), "Committee: Dutch Professor Faked Data for Years," *AP Newswire*, (November 3). *Science* (2011), "Around the World," 333 (September 16), 1556.

28 Robinson, K. (2009), "Wal-Mart Push Polls Chicago, Claims 74% Support for New Store," *Chicago Sun Times*, (July 29), http://chicagoist.com/2009/07/29/is_wal-mart_push_polling_chicago.php, accessed April 21, 2014.

29 Brennan, M., S. Benson, and Z. Kearns (2005), "The Effect of Introductions on Telephone Survey Participation Rates," *International Journal of Market Research*, 47 (1), 65–74.

30 *Marketing News* (1995), "Marketers Value Honesty in Marketing Researchers," 29 (June 5), 27.

Chapter 5

1 Sources: Evans, J. (2017), "How Vans Became the Shoes Everyone's Wearing Again," *Esquire*, (Nov. 16), http://www.esquire.com/style/mens-fashion/a13446025/vans-shoes/; https://www.vfc.com/one-vf, accessed January 11, 2018. Pisani, J. (2018), "Service Makes Good Business Sense," *Huffington Post*, (January 12), https://www.huffingtonpost.com/entry/service-makes-good-business-sense_us_5a58e785e4b003efadb6ad10?utm_medium=organicsocial&utm_source=twitter&utm_campaign=values&utm_content=HuffPost_JimP_011817, accessed January 13, 2018.

2 Morse, J. M. and L. Richards (2013), *Readme First for a User's Guide to Qualitative Methods*, Thousand Oaks, CA: Sage.

3 See, for example, Edgerly, S. (2017), "Seeking Out and Avoiding the News Media: Young Adults' Proposed Strategies for Obtaining Current Events Information," *Mass Communication and Society*, 20, 358–377. Davis, D. F., S. L. Golicic, C. N. Boerstler, S. Choi, and H. Oh (2014), "Does Marketing Research Suffer from Methods Myopia?" *Journal of Business Research*, 66 (September), 1245–1250.

4 Herz, M. and K. H. Brunk (2017), "Conceptual Advances in Consumers' Semantic and Episodic Brand Memories: A Mixed Methods Exploration," *Psychology & Marketing*, 34, 70–91. Harrison III, R. L. (2013). "Using Mixed Methods Designs in the *Journal of Business Research* 1990-2010," *Journal of Business Research*, 66 (November), 2153–2162.

5 Babin, Barry J., William R. Darden, and Mitch Griffin (1994), "Work and/or Fun: Measuring Hedonic and Utilitarian Shopping Value," *Journal of Consumer Research*, 20 (March), 644–656.

6 Semon, Thomas T. (2002), "You Get What You Pay For: It May Be Bad MR," *Marketing News*, 36 (April 15), 7.

7 https://www.riteaid.com/about-us/wellness-stores, accessed January 18, 2018.

8 Thompson, C. J. (1997), "Interpreting Consumers: A Hermeneutical Framework for Deriving Marketing Insights from the Tests of Consumers' Consumption Stories," *Journal of Marketing Research*, 34 (November), 438–455 (see pp. 443–444 for quotation).

9 Thompson (1997).

10 While we refer to a hermeneutic unit as being text-based here for simplicity, they can actually also be developed using pictures, videotapes, or artifacts as well. Software such as ATLAS.ti allow files containing pictures, videos, and text to be combined into a hermeneutic unit.

11 Cruz, A.G.G., Y. Seo, and M. Buchanan-Oliver (2018), "Religion as a Field of Transcultural Practices in Multicultural Marketplaces," *Journal of Business Research*, https://doi.org/10.1016/j.jbusres.2017.07.022.

12 Del Fresno, M. (2011), Netnografia: Investigacion, Analisis e Intervencion. Social Online. Elsevier: London.

13 Komum, N., R. Gyrd-Jones, N. Al Zagir, and K.A. Brandis (2017), "Interplay between Intended Brand Identity and Identities in a Nike-Related Brand Community: Co-existing Synergies and Tensions in a Nested System," *Journal of Business Research*, 70, 432–440.

14 Reid, D. M. (1999), "Changes in Japan's Post-Bubble Business Environment: Implications for Foreign-Affiliated Companies," *Journal of International Marketing*, 7 (3), 38–63.

15 Silber, I., A. Israeli, A. Bustin, and O. B. Zyi (2009), "Recover Strategies for Service Failures: The Case of Restaurants," *Journal of Hospitality Marketing & Management*, 18 (July), 730–741.

16 Strauss, A. L. and J. Corbin (1990), Basics of Qualitative Research Techniques Procedures for Developing Grounded Theory. Publications: Newbury Park, CA.

17 Geiger, S. and D. Turley (2005), "Personal Selling as a Knowledge-Based Activity: Communities of Practice in the Sales Force," *Irish Journal of Management*, 26, 61–70.

18 Gummesson, E. (2014). Commentary on "The Role of Innovation in Driving the Economy: Lessons from the Global Financial Crisis," *Journal of Business Research*, 67 (January), 2743–2750.

19 Beverland, M. (2006), "The Components of Prestige Brands," *Journal of Business Research*, 59 (February), 251–258. Beverland, M. and F. J. Farrelly (2010), "The Quest for Authenticity in Consumption: Consumers' Purposive Choices of Authentic Cues to Shape Experienced Outcomes," *Journal of Consumer Research*, 36 (February), 838–856.

20 Businesswire (2014), "Research and Markets: UK E-Cigarette Market 2014–2018: British American Tobacco Plc, Lorrilard Inc., NIcocigs Ltd & Vivid Vapors Ltd Dominate the New Lucrative Market," *Business Wire*. May 14. Newswires, Ebschost (accessed June 11, 2014). Warren J. R. (2013), "Community-Based Preferences for e-Smoking Cessation," *Qualitative Research Reports in Communication*, 14, 10–18.

21 Woodyard, C. (2010), "Buick Wants to Know How They Really Feel," *USA Today*, (July 20), 3B.

22 Daunt, K. L. and L. C. Harris (2014), "Customers Acting Badly: Evidence from the Hospitality Industry," *Journal of Business Research*, 64, 1034–1042.

23 https://sproutsocial.com/insights/market-research-using-social-media/, accessed January 13, 2018. http://pizzaturnaround.com, accessed January 13, 2018.

24 Babin, B. J., W. R. Darden, and J. S. Boles (1995), "Salesperson Stereotypes, Consumer Emotions, and Their Impact on Information Processing," *Journal of the Academy of Marketing Science*, 23 (Spring), 94–105.

25 https://www.harley-davidson.com/us/en/index.html, accessed January 13, 2018.

26 Morton A., and S. J. Greenland (2018), "Tobacco CSR and the Ethics Game Paradox: A Qualitative

Approach for Evaluating Tobacco Brand Name Strategy Following Plain Packaging." In: D. Crowther, S. Seifi, A. Moyeen (eds), *The Goals of Sustainable Development. Approaches to Global Sustainability, Markets, and Governance*, Singapore: Springer.

27 http://www.innovationgames.com/why-and-how/, accessed January 13, 2018.

28 Arnold, M. (2010), "Sermo Offers On-Demand Physician Focus Groups," *Medical Marketing & Media*, 44 (November), 28.

29 Godes, David and Dina Mayzlin (2004), "Using On-Line Conversations to Study Word-of-Mouth Communications," *Marketing Science*, 23, 545–560.

30 F. Berge and I. Gaede (2017), Consumer Engagement in Social Media: A Netnographic Study of the Company-Owned Facebook Pages. Master Thesis: Uppsala University.

31 Wooliscroft, B., R. D. Tamilia, and S. J. Shapiro (2006), *A Twenty-First Century Guide to Aldersonian Marketing Thought*, NY: Springer.

32 Klahr, S. (2000), "Getting' Buggy with It," *Advertising Age's Creativity*, 8 (May), 9.

Chapter 6

1 Sources: https://www.medicare.gov/hospitalcompare/Data/HCAHPS-Star-Ratings.html, accessed December 3, 2017. http://whynotthebest.org, accessed December 3, 2017. https://www.healthgrades.com/quality/hospital-ratings-awards, accessed December 3, 2017. https://www.webmd.com/health-insurance/how-use-online-ratings-hospital#1, accessed December 3, 2017. https://health.usnews.com/health-care/best-hospitals/articles/best-hospitals-honor-roll-and-overview, accessed December 3, 2017.

2 Taves, M. (2014), "If I Could Have More Data…," *Wall Street Journal*, (March 24), R5.

3 See http://www.usinflationcalculator.com to find values to transform dollar values over time to a constant year values. Exchange rates can be found at http://markets.wsj.com/?mod=Home_MDW_MDC.

4 Queenan, J. (2013), "Lies, Damn Lies and Revised Numbers," *Wall Street Journal*, (June 9), C11.

5 Handley, L. (2017), "Business Could Lose $16.4 Billion to Online Advertising Fraud in 2017," CNBC (March 15), https://www.cnbc.com/2017/03/15/businesses-could-lose-164-billion-to-online-advert-fraud-in-2017.html, accessed December 7, 2017.

6 Ferdman, R. A. (2015), "The Slow Death of the Home-Cooked Meal," *The Washington Post*, https://www.washingtonpost.com/news/wonk/wp/2015/03/05/the-slow-death-of-the-home-cooked-meal/?utm_term=.b2260393ed07, accessed December 7, 2017.

7 Grow, B. (2005), "Yes, Ma'am, That Part Is in Stock," *Business Week*, (August 1), p. 32. https://www.bloomberg.com/news/articles/2005-07-31/yes-maam-that-part-is-in-stock, accessed December 7, 2017.

8 http://theaposition.com/larrygolfstheworld/golf/courses-and-travel/76/the-worlds-largest-golf-resort, accessed December 7, 2017.

9 https://www.instapaper.com.

10 https://www.cia.gov/library/publications/the-world-factbook/geos/ez.html, accessed December 7, 2017.

11 https://www.barrystickets.com/blog/mlb-ticket-prices/, www.teammarketing.com, http://www.espn.com/mlb/attendance/, accessed December 10, 2017.

12 Brown, M. (2017), "MLB Sets Record Revenues in 2017, Increasing More Than $500 Million Since 2015," *Forbes*, (November 22), https://www.forbes.com/sites/maurybrown/2017/11/22/mlb-sets-record-for-revenues-in-2017-increasing-more-than-500-million-since-2015/#42abade47880, accessed December 10, 2017.

13 Ozanian, M. (2017), "Baseball Ticket Prices for Every Team: Cubs Top MLG at 151," *Forbes*, (March 22), https://www.forbes.com/sites/mikeozanian/2017/03/22/baseball-ticket-prices-for-every-team-cubs-top-mlb-at-151-graphic/#29ad7dfa294a, accessed December 10, 2017.

14 This section is based on Levy, M. and B, Weitz (1992), *Retail Management* (Homewood, IL: Richard D. Irwin), pp. 357–358.

15 ATKearney (2017), *The 2017 Global Retail Development Index™: The Age of Focus*, ATKearney: Chicago.

16 For illustrations see Mesak, H., A. Bari, B. J. Babin, L. Birou, and A. Jurkus (2011), "Optimum Advertising Policy over Time for Subscriber Service Innovations in the Presence of Service Cost Learning and Customers' Disadoption," *European Journal of Operations Research*, 211 (June), 642–649. Puneet, M., J. P. Dube', K.Y. Goh, and P. K. Chintagunta (2006), "The Effect of Banner Advertising on Internet Purchasing," *Journal of Marketing Research*, 43 (February), 98–108.

17 Rosenberg, E. (2017), "The Business of Google," *Investopedia*, (November 13), https://www.investopedia.com/articles/investing/020515/business-google.asp, accessed December 11, 2017.

18 Hayashi, Y.Y., M. H. Hsieh, and R. R. Setiono (2009). "Predicting Consumer Preference for Fast-Food Franchises: A Data Mining Approach." *Journal of the Operational Research Society*, 60 (9), 1221–1229.

19 https://www.salesforce.com/products/einstein/overview/, accessed December 11, 2017.

20 Aril, D., C. Bauer, and R. W. Palmetier (2017), "Relational Selling: Past, Present, and Future," *Industrial Marketing Management*, https://doi.org/10.1016/j.indmarman.2017.07.018.

21 Mehta, N. (2007), "Investigating Consumers' Purchase Incidence and Brand Choice Decisions across Multiple Product Categories: A Theoretical and Empirical Analysis," *Marketing Science*, 26 (Mar/Apr), 457–479.

22 Tirunillai, S., and G. Tellis (2014). "Mining Marketing Meaning from Chatter: Strategic Brand Analysis of Big Data Using Latent Dirichlet Allocation," *Journal of Marketing Research*, 51 (August), 463–479.

23 Ekinci, Y., N. Uray, and F. Ulengin (2014). A Customer Lifetime Value Model for the Banking Industry: A Guide to Marketing Actions. *European Journal of Marketing*, 48 (3/4), 17.

24 Shipley, L. (2014), "How Open-Source Software Drives Innovation," http://mitsloanexperts.mit.edu/how-open-source-software-drives-innovation/, accessed December 11, 2017.

25 http://www.jdpower.com/ratings/study/North-America-Airline-Satisfaction-Study/2090ENG/Traditional-Carrier/1269, accessed December 11, 2017.

26 Weiss, A. M., N. H. Lurie, and D. J. MacInnis (2008), "Listening to Strangers: Whose Responses Are Valuable, How Valuable Are They, and Why?" *Journal of Marketing Research*, 45 (August), 425–436.

27 http://fortune.com/rankings/, accessed December 17, 2017.

28 http://www.theharrispoll.com/business/Top-Social-Responsibility-Scores.html, accessed December 11, 2017.

29 Salvemini, D. (2017), "Consumer Attitudes Toward Technology-Enabled Health Care," *Fox Business*, (March 7), http://www.foxbusiness.com/features/2017/03/07/consumer-attitudes-towards-technology-enabled-health-care.html, accessed December 11, 2017.

Chapter 7

1 Mcknight, J. and J. C. Coronel (2017), "Evaluating Scientists as Sources of Science in Evidence from Eye Movements, *Journal of Communication*, 67, 565–585. Kahneman, D. (2013), "Behavioral Economics and Investor Protection: Keynote Address," *Loyola University Chicago Law Journal*, 44, 1333.

2 Guerin, F. and C. Ballard (2017), "Do We Still Need to Ask Questions?" *Ipsos Connect*, (August), 1–4.

3 Vascellaro, J. E. (2005), "Who'll Give Me $50 for This Purse from Nana?" *Wall Street Journal*, (December 28), D1–D2. https://www.prnewswire.com/news-releases/coinstar-holiday-survey-results-reveal-the-majority-of-holiday-gift-givers-set-a-budget-yet-hidden-expenses-put-many-in-the-red-300533218.html, accessed November 25, 2017.

4 Adams, G. S., F. J. Flynn, and M. I. Norton (2012), "The Gifts We Keep on Giving: Documenting and Destigmatizing the Regifting Taboo," *Psychological Science*, 23, 1145–1150.

5 Brown, M. R., R. K. Bhadury, and N. K. Pope (2010), "The Impact of Comedic Violence on Viral Advertising Effectiveness," *Journal of Advertising*, 39 (Spring), 49–65.

6 Exhibit revised with assistance of Christo Boshoff, Stellenbosh University.

7 Groves, R. and L. Lyberg (2010), "Total Survey Error: Past, Present, and Future," *Public Opinion Quarterly*, 74, 849–879.

8 Cull, William L., Karen G. O'Connor, Sanford Sharp, and Suk-fong S. Tang (2005), "Response Rates and Response Bias for 50 Surveys of Pediatricians," *Health Services Research*, 40 (February), 213.

9 Douglas Aircraft (undated), *Consumer Research*, p. 13.

10 Raven, G. (2008), "Major Holocaust Polls Show Built-In Bias," *Journal of Historical Review*, http://www.vho.org/GB/Journals/JHR/15/1/Raven25.html, accessed January 1, 2018.

11 *Network World* (2009), "Goodbadugly," 26 (December 21), 5.

12 Wasserman, T., G. Khermouch, and J. Green (2000), "Mining Everyone's Business," *BrandWeek*, (February 28), 34.

13 Ward, C. D., B. Welch, A. Conley, et al. (2017), "It's About Time: Examining the Effect of Interviewer-Quoted Survey Time Estimates on Survey Efficiency," *Survey Practice*, 10 (2), 1–11.

14 Hof, R. D. (2005), "The Power of Us," *Businessweek*, (June 20), 74–82.

15 Cerrada, C. J., J. Weinberg, K. J. Sherman, and R. B. Saper (2014). "Inter-Method Reliability of Paper Surveys and Computer Assisted Telephone Interviews in a Randomized Controlled Trial of Yoga for Low Back Pain," *BMC Research Notes*, 7 (1), 1–10.

16 Kane, J. C., C. Rapaport, A. K. Zalta, D. Canetti, S. E. Hobfoll, and B. J. Hall (2014). "Regular Drinking May Strengthen the Beneficial Influence of Social Support on Depression: Findings from a Representative Israeli Sample during a Period of War and Terrorism," *Drug & Alcohol Dependence*, 140, 175–182.

17 Sources for MMS Story: Rosen, J. and A. Patel (2014), "Telemarketer

Agrees to $3.4 Million FTC Penalty over Unwanted Calls," *Today*, (May 29), http://www.today.com/news/telemarketer-agrees-3-4-million-ftc-penalty-over-unwanted-calls-2D79710375, accessed July 5, 2014. http://simplisafe.com/blog/revolution-will-not-be-robocalled, accessed July 5, 2014.

18 https://www.statista.com/chart/2072/landline-phones-in-the-united-states/, accessed November 28, 2017. https://www.digitaltrends.com/home/you-can-still-call-about-40-percent-of-u-s-households-on-a-landline/, accessed November 28, 2017.

19 https://www.wirelessweek.com/news/2015/12/nearly-half-us-homes-use-cellphones-only-shun-landlines, accessed November 28, 2017.

20 *Business Middle East* (2010), Database: Telecommunications, (September), 12.

21 Linshi, J. (2015), "1 in 3 People Worldwide Don't Have Proper Toilets, Report Says," *Time*, (July 1), http://time.com/3942630/toilets-who-unicef-report/, accessed November 28, 2017. https://www.statista.com/statistics/274774/forecast-of-mobile-phone-users-worldwide/, accessed November 28, 2017.

22 Brick, J. M., P. D. Brick, S. Dipko, S. Presser, C. Tucker, and Y. Yuan (2007), "Cell Phone Survey Feasibility in the U.S.: Sampling and Calling Cell Numbers versus Landline Numbers," *Public Opinion Quarterly*, 71 (Spring), 23–39.

23 Vicente and Reis (2010); Vicente, P. E. Reis and M. Santos (2009), "Using Mobile Phones for Survey Research," *International Journal of Marketing Research*, 51 (5), 613–633.

24 Curtin, R., S. Presser, and E. Singer (2005), "Changes in Telephone Survey Nonresponse over the Past Quarter Century," *Public Opinion Quarterly*, (Spring), 69 (1), 87–95.

25 Cuneo, A. Z. (2004), "Researchers Flail as Public Cuts the Cord," *Advertising Age*, (November 15), 3–52.

26 Keeter, S. (2017), "What Low Response Rates Mean for Telephone Surveys," Pew Research, (May 15), http://www.pewresearch.org/2017/05/15/what-low-response-rates-mean-for-telephone-surveys/, accessed November 28, 2017.

27 Callegaro, M., H. L. McCutheon, and J. Ludwig (2010), "Who's Calling? The Impact of Caller ID on Telephone Survey Response," *Field Methods*, 22 (May 12), 175–191.

28 Hembroff, L. A., D. Rusz, A. Rafferty, H. McGee, and N. Ehrlich (2005), "The Cost-Effectiveness of Alternative Advance Mailings in a Telephone Survey," *Public Opinion Quarterly*, 69 (Summer), 232–245.

29 Brennan, M., S. Benson, and Z. Kearns (2005), "The Effect of Introductions on Telephone Survey Endnotes 481 Participation Rates," *International Journal of Market Research*, 47 (1), 65–74.

30 http://www.marketingresearch.org/calling-cell-phones, accessed November 28, 2017.

31 In a client-based research project using a much higher financial incentive, response rates for courier service reached 55 percent as opposed to 8 percent for snail mail.

32 McLean, S. A., S. J. Paxton, R. Massey, J. M. Mond, B. Rodgers, and P. J. Hay (2014), "Prenotification but not Envelope Teaser Increased Response Rates in a Bulimia Nervosa Mental Health Literacy Survey: A Randomized Controlled Trial," *Journal of Clinical Epidemiology*, 67 (August), 870–876.

33 Smith, S. M., C. A. Roster, L. L. Golden, and G. S. Albaum (2016), "A Multi-group Analysis of Online Survey Respondent Data Quality: Comparing a Regular USA Consumer Panel to MTurk Samples," *Journal of Business Research*, 69, 3139–3148. Wessling, K. S., J. Huber, and O. Netzer (2017), "MTurk Character Misrepresentation: Assessment and Solutions," *Journal of Consumer Research*, 44, 211–230.

34 Shih, T. H. and S. Fan (2009), "Comparing Response Rates in E-mail and Paper Surveys: A Meta-Analysis," *Educational Research Review*, 4, 26–40.

35 Fricker, S., M. Galesic, R. Tourangeau, and T. Yan (2005), "An Experimental Comparison of Web and Telephone Surveys," *Public Opinion Quarterly*, 69 (Fall), 370–392.

36 Moskowitz, H. R. and B. Martin (2008). "Optimising the Language of E-Mail Survey Invitations," *International Journal of Market Research*, 50 (4), 491–510.

37 Porter, P. R. and M. E. Whitcomb (2007), "Mixed-Mode Contacts in Internet Surveys: Paper Is Not Necessarily Better," *Public Opinion Quarterly*, 71 (Winter), 635–648.

38 Gruen, T., T. Osmonbekov, and A. J. Czaplewski (2006), "eWOM: The Impact of Customer-to-Customer Online Know-How Exchange on Customer Value and Loyalty," *Journal of Business Research*, 59 (April), 449–456.

39 Singer, E. and C. Ye (2013), "The Use and Effects of Incentives in Surveys," *Annals of the American Academy of Political and Social Science*, 645 (January), 112–138.

40 Braunsberger, K., H. Wybenga, and R. Gates (2007), "A Comparison of Reliability between Telephone and Web-Based Surveys," *Journal of Business Research*, 60 (July), 758–764.

41 Sinclair, M., J. O'Toole, M. Malawaraarachci, and K. Leder (2012), "Comparison of Response Rates and Cost-Effectiveness for a Community-Based Survey: Postal, Internet and Telephone Modes with Generic or Personalised Recruitment Approaches," *BMC Medical Research Methodology*, 12 (August 31), 132.

Chapter 8

1 Colbin, K. (2017), "Of Course Google Is Spying on You," *MediaInsider*, (October 13), https://www.mediapost.com/publications/article/308708/, accessed December 13, 2017. Atherton, K. D. (2017), "Amazon Echo and the Internet of Things that Spy on You," *Popular Science*, (March 3), https://www.popsci.com/amazon-echo-privacy, December 13, 2017. Dunn, M. (2016), "Experts Warn You that Your Smart Kitchen Appliances Are Watching You," http://www.news.com.au/technology/online/security/experts-warn-your-smart-kitchen-appliances-are-watching-you/news-story/2edd5668551a4ecc8254bfec4df31b14, accessed December 13, 2017.

2 Dumas, A. (2007), "The Limits of Market Research Methods," *Advertising Age*, 78 (October 18), 27.

3 Naik, G. (2012), "Analytical Trend Troubles Scientists," *Wall Street Journal*, (May 3), A1–A12.

4 Redmond, E. C. and C. J. Griffith (2003), "A Comparison and Evaluation of Research Methods Used in Consumer Food Safety Studies," *International Journal of Consumer Studies*, 27 (January), 17–33.

5 Abrams, B. (2000), *The Observational Research Handbook* (Chicago: NTC Business Books), pp. 2, 105.

6 Phillips, A. (2011), "Researchers, Snoopers and Spies—The Legal and Ethical Challenges Facing Observational Research," *International Journal of Marketing Research*, 52 (2), 275–278.

7 Frizell, S. (2014), "There's a Right to Be Forgotten Industry – and It's Booming," *Time*, (July 18), http://time.com/3002240/right-to-beforgotten-2/, accessed December 14, 2017. Roberts, J. J. (2015), "The Right to Be Forgotten from Google? Forget it Says U.S. Audience," *Fortune*, (March 12), http://fortune.com/2015/03/12/the-right-to-be-forgotten-from-google-forget-it-says-u-s-crowd/, accessed December 14, 2017.

8 Phillips (2011).

9 Judah, G., R. Aunger, W. P. Schmidt, S. Michie, S. Granger, and V. Curtis (2011), "Experimental Pretesting of Hand-Washing," *American Journal of Public Health*, 99 (September 2), S405–411.

10 Ivana Mamic, L., and I. Arroyo Almaraz (2013), "How the Larger Corporations Engage with Stakeholders through Twitter," *International Journal of Market Research*, 55 (6), 851–872.

11 Parker, J. (2013), "A Typology of Retail Video Advertising," Doctoral Dissertation, Louisiana Tech University.

12 "Audience Measurement," Nielsen Media Research, http://www.nielsen.com/us/en/solutions/measurement/television.html, accessed December 14, 2017.

13 http://www.nielsen.com/us/en/solutions/capabilities/audio.html, accessed December 14, 2017.

14 Chaffey, D. (2017), "Facebook Ad Clickthrough Rates by Industry 2017," *Smart Insights*, (March 9), https://www.smartinsights.com/social-media-marketing/facebook-marketing/facebook-ad-clickthrough-rates-industry/, accessed December 14, 2017.

15 http://blog.infegy.com/marketing-disneys-new-star-wars-for-may-the-fourth, accessed January 30, 2018.

16 Hardekopf, B. (2017), "This Week In Credit Card News: Sending Cash Through An iPhone Text Message; Why The Buzz About Bitcoin?" *Forbes*, (Dec. 8), https://www.forbes.com/sites/billhardekopf/2017/12/08/this-week-in-credit-card-news-sending-cash-thru-an-iphone-text-message-why-the-buzz-about-bitcoin/#2f4cb2793d38, accessed December 13, 2017.

17 https://adwords.google.com/home/resources/success-stories/trivago-sees-more-clicks-lower-cpas-in-50-markets.html, accessed December 14, 2017.

18 Neff, J. (2005), "Aging Population Brushes Off Coloring," *Advertising Age*, 76 (July 25), 3–49.

19 Hardesty, D. M., R. C. Goodstein, D. Grewal, A. D. Miyazaki, and P. Kopalle (2014), "The Accuracy of Scanned Prices," *Journal of Retailing*, 90 (June), 291–300,

20 Barbanel, J. (2014), "Outside Public Housing, Cameras Abound," *Wall Street Journal*, (June 5), http://online.wsj.com/articles/police-identify-suspectin-prince-joshua-avittos-fatal-stabbingin-brooklyn-by-matching-dna-on-theknife-1401906762, accessed December 14, 2017.

21 Horovitz, B. (2007), "Marketers Take a Close Look at Your Daily Routines," *USA Today*, www.usatoday.com/money/advertising/2007-04-29-watching-marketing_N.htm, accessed December 14, 2017.

22 http://business.panasonic.co.uk/security-solutions/face-detection-software, accessed December 14, 2017.

23 Hotz, R. L. (2011), "The Really Smart Phone," *Wall Street Journal*, C1.

24 https://www.tobiipro.com/fields-of-use/marketing-consumer-research/, accessed December 14, 2017.

25 Lee, N. and A. J. Broderick (2007), "The Past, Present and Future of Observational Research in Marketing," *Qualitative Market*

Research: An International Journal, 10, No. 2, 121–129.

26 Yoon, C., R. Gonzalez, and J. R. Bettman (2009), "Using fMRI to Inform Marketing Research: Challenges and Opportunities," *Journal of Marketing Research*, 46, 17–19; Reimann, M., O. Schilke, B. Weber, C. Neuhaus, and J. Zaichkowski (2011), "Functional Magnetic Resonance Imaging in Consumer Research: A Review and Application," *Psychology & Marketing*, 28 (June), 608–637.

27 Krugman, H. B. (1981), statement as quoted in "Live, Simultaneous Study of Stimulus, Response Is Physiological Measurement's Great Virtue," *Marketing News*, (May 15), pp. 1, 20.

28 *New Media Age* (2005), "Mazda Turns to Eye-Tracing to Assist Revamp of European Site," (November 3), 8.

29 Koh, Y. (2014), "Twitter Shakes Up Strategy on Metrics," *Wall Street Journal*, (July 18), B1–B2. http://ssl. marketplace.org/topics/business/ twitter-may-change-metrics- reflectwider-audience, accessed December 15, 2017. https://www. statisticbrain.com/twitter-statistics/, accessed December 15, 2017.

Chapter 9

1 Ausick, P. (2017), "People Can Still Sue Tobacco Companies Over Health," *24/7 Wall St.*, (January 17), http://247wallst.com/ consumer-products/2017/01/17/ people-can-still-sue-tobacco- companies-over-health/, accessed December 17, 2017.

2 Seenan, G. (2005), "Smoker's Widow Loses Legal Fight," *The Observer* (June 1). http://www.guardian. co.uk/society/2005/jun/01/smoking. publichealth1, accessed December 17, 2017. Bolton, L. E., J. B. Cohen, and P. N. Bloom (2006), "Does Marketing Products as Remedies Create 'Get Out of Jail Free Cards'?" *Journal of Consumer Research*, 33, (June), 71–84; Smith, K. H. and M. A. Stutts, "The Influence of Individual Factors on the Effectiveness of Message Content in Antismoking Advertisements Aimed at Adolescents," *The Journal of Consumer Affairs*, 40 (2006), 261–293; Zhao, G. and C. Pechmann, "The Impact of Regulatory Focus on Adolescents' Response to Antismoking Advertising Campaigns," *Journal of Marketing Research*, 44 (November 2007), 671–687.

3 Babin, B. J., D. M. Hardesty, and T. A. Suter (2003), "Color and Shopping Intentions: The Intervening Effect of Price Fairness and Perceived Affect," *Journal of Business Research*, 56 (July), 541–551.

4 Christie, J., D. Fisher, J. Kozup, S. Smith, S. Burton, and E. Creyer, "The Effects of Bar-Sponsored Alcohol Beverage Promotions across Binge and Nonbinge Drinkers," *Journal of Public Policy and Marketing*, 20 (Fall 2001), 240–253.

5 Like Dragnet, the story is true but the brand names are fictitious.

6 Reitter, R. N. (2003), "Comment: American Media and the Smoking- Related Behaviors of Asian Adolescents," *Journal of Advertising Research*, 43 (March), 12–13.

7 https://www.hhs.gov/ash/oah/ adolescent-development/substance- use/drugs/tobacco/trends/index. html, accessed December 17, 2017. https://www.cdc.gov/tobacco/ campaign/tips/resources/data/ cigarette-smoking-in-united-states. html, accessed December 17, 2017.

8 Mitchell, V.-W., and S. Haggett (1997), "Sun-Sign Astrology in Market Segmentation: An Empirical Investigation," *Journal of Consumer Marketing*, 14, No. 2, 113–131.

9 Shiv, B., Z. Carmon, and D. Aneley (2005), "Placebo Effects of Marketing Actions: Consumers May Get What They Pay For," *Journal of Marketing Research*, 42 (November), 383–393.

10 Marcus, A. D. (2014), "Researchers Fret as Social Media Lift Veil on Drug Trials," *Wall Street Journal*, (July 30), A1–A10.

11 Smith, S. M., C. A. Roster, L. L. Golden, and G. S. Albaum (2016), "A Multi-Group Analysis of Online Survey Response Data Quality: Comparing a Regular USA Consumer Panel to mTurk Samples," *Journal of Business Research*, 69, (August), 3139–3148. Wessling, K. S., J. Huber, O. Netzer (2017), "MTurk Character Misrepresentation: Assessment and Solution," *Journal of Consumer Research*, 44, 211–230. Babin, B. J., M. Griffin, and J. F. Hair, Jr. (2016), "Heresies and Sacred Cows in Scholarly Marketing Publications," *Journal of Business Research*, 69, (August), 3133–3138.

12 Albergotti, R. (2014), "Facebook Lab Had Few Limits: Data Science Group Conducted Experiments on Users with Little Oversight," *Wall Street Journal*, (July 3), A1–A2.

13 Gneezy, A. (2017), "Field Experimentation in Marketing Research," *Journal of Marketing Research*, 54, 140–143.

14 White, J. B. (2010), "Why Toyota Rolled Over for Its SUVs," *Wall Street Journal*, (April 21), D1–D2.

15 Espinosa, J. A. and D. J. Ortinau (2016), "Debunking Legendary Beliefs about Student Samples in Marketing Research," *Journal of Business Research*, 69, (August), 3149–3158.

16 Wessling et al. (2017).

17 Paolacci, G., J. Chandler, and P. G. Iperirotis (2010), "Running Experiments on Mechanical Turk," *Judgment and Decision-Making*, 5 (August), 411–419.

18 Dagger, T. S. and P. J. Danaher (2014), "Comparing the Effect of Store Remodeling on New and Existing Customers," *Journal of Marketing*, 78 (May), 62–80.

19 See http://time.com/money/3764166/ money-back-guarantee-heineken- light/, accessed December 17, 2017.

20 Elliot, N. (2014), "Instagram Is the King of Social Media," *Forrester Research*, (April 29), http://blogs. forrester.com/nate_elliott/14-04- 29-instagram_is_the_king_of_social_ engagement, accessed December 17, 2017. http://heinekenusa.com/press- releases/heineken-debuts-new-8-5-oz- slim-can/, accessed December 17, 2017.

21 Ramage, N. (July 2005), "Testing, Testing 1, 2, 3," *Marketing Magazine*, 110, 1196; CNW_ Telbec, "Imperial Tobacco Canada Lives Up to Its Corporate Social Responsibility Promise," Groupe CNW (2007), http://www.newswire.ca/fr/ releases/archive/September2007/12/ c7976.html, accessed June 1, 2018.

22 Tybout, A. M. and G. Zaltman (1974), "Ethics in Marketing Research: Their Practical Relevance," *Journal of Marketing Research*, 21 (November), 357–368.

23 Albergotti (2014).

24 Reprinted with permission from Lee Martin, Geoffrey "Drinkers Get Court Call," *Advertising Age* (May 20, 1991). Copyright © 1991 Crain Communications, Inc.

Chapter 10

1 Hyken, S. (2016), "How Effective Is Net Promoter Score," *Forbes*, December 3, https://www.forbes .com/sites/shephyken/2016/12/03/ how-effective-is-net-promoter- score-nps/#e47bc6623e4c, accessed December 19, 2017. Raassens, N. and H. Haans (2017), "NPS and Online WOM: Investigating the Relationship Between Customers' Promoter Scores and eWOM Behavior," *Journal of Services Research*, 20, 322–334. Reichheld, F. F. (2003), "The One Number You Need to Grow," *Harvard Business Review*, 81, 46–54; Grisaffe, D. B. (2007), "Questions about the Ultimate Question: Conceptual Considerations in Evaluating Reichheld's Net Promoter Score (NPS)," *Journal of Consumer Satisfaction, Dissatisfaction and Complaining Behavior* 20, 36–53;

2 See Mollen, A., and H. Wilson (2010). "Engagement, Telepresence and Interactivity in Online Consumer Experience: Reconciling Scholastic and Managerial Perspectives," *Journal of Business Research*, 63, 919–925.

3 Periatt, J. A., S. A. LeMay, and S. Chakrabarty, "The Selling Orientation-Customer Orientation (SOCO) Scale: Cross-Validation of the Revised Version," *Journal of Personal Selling and Sales Management*, 24 (Winter 2004), 49–54.

4 Cohen, J. (December 1990), "Things I Have Learned (So Far)," *American Psychologist*, 45, 1304–1312.

5 Theacsi.org, accessed June 1, 2018.

6 In more advanced applications such as those involving structural equations analysis, a distinction can be made between reflective composites and formative indexes. See Hair, J. F., W. C. Black, B. J. Babin, and R. Anderson (2019), Multivariate Data Analysis, 8th ed. (London: Cengage International).

7 Bart, Y., V. Shankar, F. Sultan, and G. L. Urban, "Are the Drivers and Role of Online Trust the Same for All Web Sites and Consumers? A Large-Scale Exploratory Study," *Journal of Marketing*, 69 (October 2005), 133–152.

8 Cronbach, L. J. (2004), "My Current Thoughts on Coefficient Alpha an Successor Procedures," Center for the Study of Evaluation Report, 64, no. 3, http://epm.sagepub.com/cgi/ content/short/64/3/391, accessed December 21, 2017.

9 Hair et al. (2019). Hair, J.F., B.J. Babin, N. Krey (2017), "Covariance-Based SEM in the Journal of Advertising: Review and Recommendations," *Journal of Advertising*, 46, 163–177.

10 Burke Marketing Research, "Rough Commercial Recall Testing," Cincinnati, OH (undated).

11 Cox, K. K. and B. M. Enis(1972), The Marketing Research Process (Pacific Palisades, CA: Goodyear); Kerlinger, F. N. (1986), *Foundations of Behavioral Research*, 3rd ed. (Ft. Worth: Holt, Rinehart and Winston).

12 Bedard, P. (2017), "Shock Poll: NFL Now Least Liked Sport, Core Fans Down 31%," *Washington Examiner*, http://www.washingtonexaminer. com/shock-poll-nfl-now-least- liked-sport-core-fans-down-31/ article/2636837, accessed December 21, 2017. Rovel, D. (2017), "Falcons to Offer Lowest Concession Prices in Major Team Sports in 2017," *ESPNnews*, http://www.espn .com/nfl/story/_/id/15560867/ atlanta-falcons-offer-lowest-conces- sion-prices-major-team-sports-new- mercedes-benz-stadium, accessed December 21, 2017. O'Reilly, L. (2018), "CMO Today: Fans Lose Interest in NFL," (December 2), https://www.wsj.com/articles/ cmo-today-fans-lose-interest-in- nfl-unilever-trumpets-marketing- savings-google-tac-increases- 1517576717?mod=searchresults&p age=1&pos=6, accessed February 4, 2018.

13 Pappas, S. (2017), "Why Do Songs Get Stuck in Your Head?" *Livescience*, (March 5), https://www.livescience.

com/58120-why-songs-get-stuck-in-head.html, accessed December 21, 2017.

14 Romaniuk, J. (2013). "How Healthy is Your Brand-Health Tracker?: A Five-Point Checklist to Build Returns on a Critical Research Investment," *Journal of Advertising Research*, 53(1), 11–13.

15 Mochon, D., K. Johnson, J. Schwartz, and D. Ariely (2017), "What Are Likes Worth? A Facebook Page Field Experiment," *Journal of Marketing Research*, 54 (April), 306–317.

16 Osgood, C., G. Suci, and P. Tannenbaum (1957), *The Measurement of Meaning* (Urbana: University of Illinois Press). Seven-point scales were used in the original work; however, subsequent researchers have modified the scale to have five points, nine points, and so on.

17 Peterson, R. A. and W. Wilson (Spring 1992), "Measuring Customer Satisfaction: Fact and Artifact," *Journal of the Academy of Marketing Science* 20, 61–71; Dawes, J., "Do Data Characteristics Change According to the Number of Scale Points Used? An Experiment Using 5-Point, 7-Point and 10-Point Scales," *International Journal of Market Research* 50 (1), (2008), 61–77.

18 Weigters, B., E. Cabooter, and N. Schillewaert (2010), "The Effect of Rating Scale Format on Response Styles: The Number of Response Categories and Response Category Labels," *International Journal of Research in Marketing*, 27 (September), 236–247.

19 Roster, C. A., R. D. Rogers, and G. Albaum (2007), "A Comparison of Response Characteristics from Web and Telephone Surveys," *International Journal of Marketing Research*, 46 (Fall), 359–373. Albaum, G., C. A. Roster, J. Wiley, J. Rossiter, and S. M. Smith (2010), "Designing Web Surveys in Marketing Research: Does Use of Forced Answering Affect Completion Rates?" *Journal of Marketing Theory and Practice*, 18 (Summer), 285–293.

Chapter 11

1 Sources: De Jong, M. G., R. Pieters, and J. P. Fox (2010), "Reducing Social Desirability Bias through Item Randomized Response: An Application to Measure Underreported Desires," *Journal of Marketing Research*, 47 (February), 14–27. http://www.huffingtonpost.com/2013/05/03/internet-porn-stats_n_3187682.html, accessed August 18, 2014. http://www.businessinsider.com/decline-of-facebook-user-numbers-2014-4, accessed August 18, 2014. Moreau, E. (2017), "Hottest Social App Trends for Teens," Lifewire (October 11), https://www.

lifewire.com/hottest-social-app-trends-for-teens-3485940 accessed December 13, 2017.

2 Smith, R., D. Olah, B. Hansen, and D. Cumbo (November–December 2003), "The Effect of Questionnaire Length on Participant Response Rate: A Case Study in the U.S. Cabinet Industry," *Forest Products Journal*, 53, 31.

3 Giraud, G., C. Tebby, and C. Amblard (2011), "Measurement of Consumers' Wine-Related Knowledge," *Enometrica*, 4 (1), 33–42.

4 Miller, K. M., R. Hofstetter, H. Krohmer, and Z. J. Zhang (2011), "How Should Consumers' Willingness to Pay Be Measured? An Empirical Comparison of State-of-the-Art Approaches?" *Journal of Marketing Research*, 48 (February), 172–184.

5 Donahue, A. K. and J. M. Miller (2005), "Citizen Preferences and Paying for Police," *Journal of Urban Affairs*, 27 (4), 419–435.

6 Roll, C.W., Jr. and A. H. Cantril (1972), *Polls: Their Use and Misuse in Politics* (New York: Basic Books), pp. 106–107.

7 Other product attributes are relative advantage, compatibility, complexity, and uncommunicability.

8 Dawson, L. (Winter 1992), "Will Feminization Change the Image of the Sales Profession?" *Journal of Personal Selling and Sales Management*, 12. 21–32.

9 Lietz, P. (2010), "Research into Questionnaire Design: A Summary of the Literature," *International Journal of Market Research*, 52 (2), 249–272.

10 Malhotra, N. (2008), "Completion Time and Response Order Effects in Web Surveys," *Public Opinion Quarterly*, 22 (5), 914–934.

11 Holbrook, A. L. and J. A. Krosnick (2010), "Measuring Voter Turnout by Using Randomized Response Technique: Evidence Calling into Question the Method's Validity," *Public Opinion Quarterly*, 74, 328–343. De Jong, M. G., R. Pieters, and J. P. Fox (2010), "Reducing Social Desirability Bias through Item Randomized Response: An Application to Measure Underreported Desires," *Journal of Marketing Research*, 47 (February), 14–27.

12 See Holbrook and Krosniek (2010) for more details on computation.

13 Malhotra (2008).

14 Smith, S., C. A. Roster, L.L. Golden, and G. Albaum (2016), "A Multi-Group Analysis of Online Survey Respondent Data Quality: Comparing a Regular USA Consumer Panel to MTurk Samples," *Journal of Business Research*, 69, 3139–3148.

15 Peychev, A. (2009), "Survey Breakoff," *Public Opinion Quarterly*, 71 (Spring), 74–97.

16 Harzing, A.-W. (2005), "Does the Use of English-Language Questionnaires in Cross-National Research Obscure

National Differences?" *International Journal of Cross Cultural Management*, 5 (2), 213–224.

17 Harzing (2005).

18 Cateora, P. R. (1990), *International Marketing* (Homewood, IL: Richard D. Irwin), pp. 387–389.

Chapter 12

1 Brock, Sabra E. (1989), "Marketing Research in Asia: Problems, Opportunities, and Lessons," *Marketing Research*, (September), 47.

2 Langer, G. (2018), "Probability Versus Non-Probability Methods," in D. Vannette, J. Krosnick, eds., *The Palgrave Handbook of Survey Research*. Palgrave Macmillan. Cham.

3 http://theharrispoll.com, accessed December 25, 2017.

4 Hansen, J. M., and S. M. Smith (2012). "The Impact of Two-Stage Highly Interesting Questions on Completion Rates and Data Quality in Online Marketing Research," *International Journal of Market Research*, 54 (2), 241–260.

5 Babin, B. J., M. Griffin, and Joseph F. Hair, Jr. (2016), "Heresies and Sacred Cows in Scholarly Marketing Publications," *Journal of Business Research*, 69 (August), 3133–3138. Hulland, J., H. Baumgartner, and K. M. Smith (2017), "Marketing Survey Research Best Practices and Recommendations from a Review," *Journal of the Academy of Marketing Science*, DOI 10.1007/s11747-017-0532-y.

6 Craig, C. S. and S. P. Douglas (2011), "Assessing Cross-Cultural Theory and Research: A Commentary Issue," *Journal of Business Research*, 64 (June), 625–627.

7 Crossman, A. (2017), "What Is a Snowball Sampling in Sociology?" ThoughtCo., https://www.thoughtco.com/snowball-sampling-3026730, accessed February 4, 2018.

8 Sigenman, Lee., S. A. Tuch, and J. K. Martin, (2005), "What's in a Name? Preference for 'Black' versus 'African-American' among Americans of African Descent," *Public Opinion Quarterly*, 69 (Fall), 429–438.

Chapter 13

1 Moscaritolo, A. (2017), "How Much Did You Spend on Prime Last Year?" *PC World*, (April 25), https://www.pcmag.com/news/353302/how-much-did-you-spend-on-amazon-prime-last-year, accessed December 29, 2017. https://www.emarketer.com/Chart/Share-of-UK-Amazon-Buyers-Who-Have-Made-Prime-vs-Non-Prime-Purchases-Jan-March-2017-of-respondents/206676, accessed December 29, 2017. Tenebruso, J. (2017), "How Much the Average Amazon Prime Member Spends

Each Year," *The Motley Fool*, (April 29), https://www.fool.com/investing/2017/04/29/heres-how-much-the-average-amazon-prime-and-non-pr.aspx, accessed December 29, 2017. Greene, J. and L. Stevens (2017), "Amazon Wants Alexa to Enter Workforce," *Wall Street Journal*, (November 30), D1.

2 See Jurik, R., M. Moody, and J. Seal, "The Mean vs. the Top Box(es) Scores," *Marketing Research*, 20 (Summer 2008), 41–42.

3 Seman, J., G. Stoudt, R. Burke, et al. (2018), "835: High-Impact Variables that Influence Family Perception of ICU Care," *Critical Care Medicine*, 46 (January), 402.

4 The reasons for this are related to the concept of degrees of freedom, which is explained in a further discussion of analytics. At this point, just remember that anytime a sample is involved rather than a population, we divide by $n - 1$ as a correction for statistical bias that would occur otherwise.

5 In practice, most survey researchers will not use this exact formula. A modification of the formula, $Z = (X - \mu)/S$, using the sample standard deviation, is used frequently.

6 Hayes, W. L. (1963), *Statistics* (New York: Holt, Rinehart and Winston), p. 193.

7 Wonnacott, T. H. and R. J. Wonnacott (1972), *Introductory Statistics*, 2nd ed. (New York: Wiley), p. 125.

8 Note that the derivation of this formula is (1) $E = ZS_{\bar{X}}$; (2) $E = ZS/\sqrt{n}$ (3) $\sqrt{n} = ZS/E$; (4) $n = (ZS/E)^2$.

9 Groves, R. M. (2006), "Nonresponse Rates and Nonresponse Bias in Household Surveys," *Public Opinion Quarterly*, 70, 646–675.

Chapter 14

1 Sources: Prang, A. and D. Cameron (2018), "Delta to Require Advance Documentation for Service, Support Animals to Fly," *Wall Street Journal*, (Jan. 19), https://www.wsj.com/articles/delta-to-require-advance-proof-of-need-for-service-support-animals-to-fly-1516372227?mod=searchresults&page=1&pos=2, accessed January 20, 2018. Jung, K., E. Garbarino, D. A. Briley, and J. Wynhausen (2017), "Blue and Red Voices: Effects of Political Ideology on Consumers' Complaining and Disputing Behavior," *Journal of Consumer Research*, 44, 477–499. Phau, I. and M. Baird (2008), "Complainers versus Non-Complainers Retaliatory Responses towards Service Dissatisfactions," *Marketing Intelligence & Planning*, 26, 567–604. Ramsey, R. D. (2010), "How to Handle Customer Complaints," *The American Salesman*, 55 (June), 25–30.

2 http://www.businessinsider.com/americans-name-favorite-movie-stars-in-new-poll-2016-1, accessed

January 17, 2018. https://variety
.com/2016/film/news/tom-hanks-
favorite-movie-star-1201691227/,
accessed January 17, 2018.

3 Dilmperi, A., T. King, and C. Dennis
(2011), "Pirates of the Web: The
Curse of Illegal Downloading,"
*Journal of Retailing and Consumer
Services*, 18 (March), 132–140.

4 Walker, L., P. R. Baines, R. Dimitriu,
and E. K. Macdonald (2017),
"Antecedents of Retweeting in
a (Political) Marketing Context,"
Psychology & Marketing, 275–293.

5 http://www.wineinstitute.org/files/
World_Wine_Consumption_by_
Country_2015.pdf, accessed January
17, 2018.

6 See a comprehensive statistics text
such as Hair et al. (Multivariate Data
Analysis, London: Cengage, 2019) for a
more detailed explanation including a
discussion of power analysis associated
with Type II error.

Chapter 15

1 Sources: Puccinelli, N. M.,
R. Chandrashekaran, D. Grewal,
and R. Suri (2013), "Are Men
Seduced by Red? The Effect of
Red Versus Black Prices on Price
Perceptions," *Journal of Retailing*,
89, 115–125. Seo, J. Y. and D. L.
Scammon (2017), "Do Green
Packages Lead to Misperceptions:
The Influence of Package Colors
on Consumers' Perceptions of
Brands with Environmental Claims,"
Marketing Letters, 28, 357–369. Van
Droogenbroeck, E., L. Van Hove, and
S. Cordemans (2018), "Do Red
Prices Also Work Online? An
Extension of Puccinelli et al.,
(2013)," *Color Research & Application*,
43, 110–113.

2 Three nonparametric tests—the
Wilcoxon matched-pairs signed ranks
test, the Kruskal-Wallis test, and the
Mann-Whitney U test—can also be
used but are not described here.

3 See, for example, Armstrong-
Stassen, M. (2002), "Designated
Redundant but Escaping Lay-Off:
A Special Group of Lay-Off
Survivors," *Journal of Occupational
and Organizational Psychology*, 75
(March), 1–13.

4 For more description of multivariate
statistical tools, see Babin, B. J. (2016),
Exploring Marketing Research, (Mason,
OH: Cengage).

Chapter 16

1 Dowling, M., "Mr. Dowling's
Rosetta Stone Page," http://www.
mrdowling.com/604-rosettastone.
html, accessed August 21, 2011. Singh, S.
(2011), "The Decipherment of
Hieroglyphics," *BBC History*, http://
bbc.co.uk/history/ancient/egyptians/
decipherment_01.shtml, accessed
August 21, 2011.

2 Yore, L. D., M. K. Florence, T. W.
Pearson, and A. J. Weaver (2006),
"Written Discourse in Scientific
Communities: A Conversation
with Two Scientists about
Their Views of Science, Use of
Language, Role of Writing in
Doing Science, and Compatibility
between Their Epistemic Views
and Language," *International Journal
of Science Education*, 28 (February),
109–141.

3 Sullivan, E. A. (October 15, 2008),
"Twitterpated: Marketers Enamored
of Online Communication System,"
Marketing News, 8.

4 An earlier version of this chapter was
written by John Bush, Oklahoma
State University, and appeared in
Zikmund,, W. G. (1984), *Business
Research Methods* (Hinsdale, IL:
Dryden Press).

5 Elliott, A. (2014), "How to Turn a
Research Project into Infographics,"
Edudemic, (November 20) http://
www.edudemic.com/how-
classroom-project-infographic/,
accessed January 24, 2018.

6 Creative Bloq Staff (2017), "13
Incredible Tools for Creating
Infographics," *Creative Bloq*,
(November, 14), https://www.
creativebloq.com/infographic/tools-
2131971, accessed January 24, 2018.

7 "A Speech Tip," *Communication
Briefings*, 14, No. 2 (1995), p. 3.

8 These guidelines, adapted with
permission from Marjorie Brody
(President, Brody Communications,
1200 Melrose Ave., Melrose Park, PA
19126), appeared in "How to Gesture
When Speaking," *Communication
Briefings*, 14, No. 11 (1995), p. 4.

9 "Tips of the Month," *Communication
Briefings*, 24, No. 7 (May 2005), p. 1.

10 Clum, L. (2017), "Pro Tips for
Creating Interactive Infographics,"
Creative Bloq, (April 06), https://
www.creativebloq.com/
infographic/8-pro-tips-creating-
interactive-infographics-11133560,
accessed January 24, 2018.

11 Based on Bridis, T. (June 1, 2005),
"Study: Shoppers Naïve about
Online Pricing," *Information Week*,
downloaded from InfoTrac at
http://web2.infotrac.galegroup.
com; Annenberg Public Policy
Center (APPC), "Annenberg Study
Shows Americans Vulnerable to
Exploitation in the Online and
Offline Marketplace," *News Release*
(June 1, 2005), http://www.
annenbergpublicpolicycenter.
org; and Turow, J., L. Feldman, and
K. Meltzer (June 2005), "Open to
Exploitation: American Shoppers
Online and Offline," *APPC Report*,
downloaded at http://www.
annenbergpublicpolicycenter.org.

INDEX